A Citizen's BLUEPRINT

THE PDC MANIFESTO

EMGEE

authorHOUSE®

AuthorHouse™ UK Ltd.
1663 Liberty Drive
Bloomington, IN 47403 USA
www.authorhouse.co.uk
Phone: 0800.197.4150

Published by AuthorHouse 07/23/2014

ISBN: 978-1-4969-8284-1 (sc)
ISBN: 978-1-4969-8283-4 (hc)
ISBN: 978-1-4969-8285-8 (e)

A Citizen's
BLUEPRINT

A Citizen's Blueprint;

THE PDC MANIFESTO

Inspired by Thomas Paine (an English / American)
and his work 'Common Sense' published in 1776
which also inspired
the American Declaration of Independence

Dedication

To my parents
for all their love and unwavering support

and to my wonderful sister Judith
for all her tireless and unshakeable sibling loyalty

Index of Chapters

Introduction

A PATH BACK TO THE FUTURE

———

WANTED

Britain needs a new leader, a real leader – somebody prepared to take the country by the scruff of the neck and redress it after more than thirty years of stagnation if not deterioration in a political vacuum of self-interest and liberal compromise.

So, if you believe that you are that person; if you believe that you have the necessary qualities to fulfil the position – i.e. -

Strength of character, both moral and physical

Integrity

and a natural thirst for the truth and fairness in all things

...please let the country know because the British public is crying out for you.

———

That said; there are a few criteria that those
wishing to put themselves forward for consideration
should be aware of –

1) We do not want anyone who would just like to use the position for personal gain

2) We do not want anyone who might see the position as a way of simply writing their name in the history books. (legacy)...and

3) We certainly do not want anyone with a political agenda who would just like to wrap us up in more spin and false promises.

———

Anybody who can identify with any of the categories above is requested to abstain - *we have already had our fill of you* – but if the following symbols of our culture and heritage mean anything to you and you are prepared to stand up and defend them – then please put up your hand.

———

A mug of tea
A pint of Real ale in the pub
Cream tea and scones
Fish and chips
Roast beef and Yorkshire pudding - Sunday lunch
Steak & kidney pie
Strawberries and cream at Wimbledon

Cricket at Lords, the Oval or on the Village
green with cucumber sandwiches
Football - as it used to be played with fair-play as the standard
Henley regatta
Horse racing at Ascot
Hunting (without real foxes)
Pub games such as skittles, dominoes, darts and snooker
Rugby (both codes)
The Grand National at Aintree

Bentley cars (before they were sold off)
Jaguar (E-type)
Rolls Royce
The Mini

Concorde
The Red Arrows
The Spitfire

Steam Trains

Bobbies on the Beat
Bowler hats, striped trousers and umbrellas
Brass bands
Driving on the left
Good Manners
Monty Python's Flying Circus
Oxford English Dictionary
Pantomime
Regional accents
The BBC (when we could trust it)

Castles
Green countryside
Seaside beach huts and deck-chairs
Thatched cottages with entwined roses around the door
The White Cliffs of Dover
The Beauty of the Lake District

Guy Fawkes Night
Horatio Nelson & HMS Victory
Robin Hood
Sherlock Holmes
The Duke of Wellington
William Shakespeare
Winston Churchill

Big Ben
Black Taxi Cabs
Hyde Park
London Bridge
Nelson's Column & Trafalgar Square
Red Pillar Boxes and Red Telephone Boxes

Red Route-master double-decker buses
St Paul's Cathedral (for its architecture)
The London Eye
The Tower of London
The Union Jack – (Union flag)

The Pound Sterling and our coins proudly displaying Britannia

_ _ _ _ _ (your suggestion)

_ _ _ _ _ (your suggestion)

_ _ _ _ _ (your suggestion)

————

This list is by no means complete and I would gladly welcome any further suggestions that like-minded people would wish to add, that epitomise the texture of the society that I would like to re-invent.

————

We are all individuals but our culture and our history create the collective conscience out of which nationalism and pride are born; these are our roots and we should be proud of them.

By the way; who are these people who are continually berating and belittling our heritage? What is their agenda?

Could somebody please tell me what is wrong with having a strong national identity?

Ask the French, the Germans or the Australians if they have a problem with their national identity. They are proud of who they are.

Why shouldn't we be?

What is wrong with being British – standing up and celebrating, being proud of our flag, our heritage and of who we are? We are not perfect but we are who we are.

I am not talking about the Empire and Colonialism here, just about our cultural roots, our traditions and what makes us British today.

So;

- If you are still a proud citizen of this country – despite the hammering it has taken over the last thirty years or so...on all fronts
- If you are part of that generation which still has respectable morals and family values
- If you can relate to the above list in any way and would like to defend the culture that this country has represented with such pride on the world stage for centuries - and which was fashioned and fought for by the generations that went before us
- ...then maybe the contents of this missive could provide us all with a 'path back to the future' – before it's too late.

Let's put the pride back into Britain

———

This might sound a little nostalgic and to an extent it probably is, but my goal here and my burning desire is not to live in the past; I simply believe that we have reached a crucial point in our nation's history and that now is the time to retire the tired old political parties with their lumbering political machines which devote more time to spin, sleaze and criticising each other than actually fulfilling their role; it is time to introduce a more modern, forward thinking organization, in touch with the real needs and the real concerns of the citizens of this country.

———

A recent Internet Poll on Sky News asked this question;

Question	-	Do you trust your MP?	
Answers	-	Absolutely	- 3%
	-	MP's are only human	- 19%
	-	**NO WAY**	**– 78%**

This, I believe proves my point.

———————

So, what I would like to do is this;

I would like to use the past as a foundation for the future and to do this I would like to create a new political movement which would defend this cause.

It would be called the **People's Democratic Congress** and would regroup all the like-minded people who hold these values dear and who would like to safe-guard this nation and draw it back from the brink of the out-of-control, suicidal, downward spiral into oblivion that successive governments have misguidedly led us into over the last thirty years.

George Orwell once wrote; 'In a time of universal deceit, telling the truth is a revolutionary act'.

I believe it is time for the silent majority to act and to stop the rot. It is time for the ordinary citizens of this country to stand up and be counted; to stand up and say; enough is enough.

I also believe that this needs to be done while the generation that defended this country through the conflict of World War is still part of the voting electorate, because unfortunately the spoon-fed generations that have come since do not have any sense of duty or responsibility towards the safe-guarding of the future of this country which is being stealthily and inexorably infiltrated by those with more sinister agendas while our politicians sit back and let it happen in the name of political correctness, fearing the backlash of this or that pressure-group if they dare to act and offend an ethnic or social minority however small.

Could somebody please explain to our politicians - before it is too late - that it is not racist or anti-democratic to defend the country that you have been elected to represent?

It's a terrible reality but it is clear for all to see that the current crop of spine-less, clueless politicians is incapable of running this country correctly. They are afraid to stand up and defend this country. They have no real political ethos or vision and the only real agenda they do seem to care about is that of filling their own pockets with as much of the taxpayers' money as possible while inventing new tax after new tax in order to cover their incompetence and their ineptitude at financial management.

Citizens of Britain, please compare the last thirty years with those that went before, and then project into the future what the next thirty will have in store for us. You will realise that it is time to act; NOW.

———

Since the Second World War ended we have been obsessed in this country with civil liberties and human rights etc – but all on an individualistic level.

We now need a period where we put the collective needs of the country first – a period of unity during which we can redress the visibly and steadily crumbling society in which we now live.

We need to reinstate respect – not the respect that the rappers who blur our TV screens and twist our children's minds with – but the respect we should have for the values and morals which are the founding stones of a decent, civilised society.

———

The UK has been transformed into a feminist state over the last thirty years by the constant bombardment of our establishment for equal opportunities and female friendly laws, all of which have contributed to the softening of attitudes and a relaxation of the law to such an extent that nobody seems to take any notice of it anymore.

There is no longer any clear deterrent in this country; there is no steel and no resolve in our institutions and as a result people are prepared to chance it with a blatant disregard for what they see as woolly consequences.

———

This feminization of society has led to the mess we now find ourselves in, but this is not a criticism of the feminist movement itself. The feminist movement began with the most honourable of intentions both in its original conception and during its second wave in the 1960's but the systematic rounding off of all the edges that respecting its demands has provoked in every walk of life – whether it be sub-consciously or deliberately - has had catastrophic consequences for society as we know it.

Discipline and structure are masculine traits and the Women's Liberation Movement, with their 'We want it all, and we want it now' slogan have succeeded - in many areas - in transforming this country into the dustbin of Europe.

It has allowed the political correctness brigade and any number of minority pressure groups to ride its coat-tails and challenge the established authority on each and every issue at each and every level of our society - to a point where nobody dare do anything these days for fear of offending an ethnic or social minority however small.

That - together with the rise of the Health and Safety zealots - has made a mockery of everything this country used to stand for, and unfortunately, instead of being strong and facing these challenges head-on with logical, common-sense and reasoned policies, successive governments filled with spineless politicians have bent to the wishes of these naïve liberal lobbyists to the point that the country has tied itself up in knots.

———

NB; The women's movement believe that women could do a better job running the country than men, but here is a list of recent female politicians who have all failed to succeed in government – performing just as badly as their male counter-parts.

They have all tried, but through a catalogue of errors, bad judgement and typical political spin – (i.e. lying and cheating the public) they have all shown just as much blundering incompetence as their male peers and have presided over some of the most embarrassing moments that recent governments have had to face thanks to that inherent ineptitude.

Baroness Uddin *(Lab) fiddled her expenses as did* **Baroness Warsi** *(Con)*

Caroline Spelman *(Con) caught in the expenses scandal - paid her nanny £18K a year from the parliamentary allowance for 'helping with constituency admin' but paid her nothing for her work as a nanny*

Estelle Morris *(Lab) – education secretary under Tony Blair – admitted in her resignation letter to being ineffective*

Harriet Harman *(Lab) – anti-white-male feminist – this woman is a menace with her ultra-feminist, scatter-brain ideas about prostitution and her proposal that women should be accused of manslaughter rather than murder when they kill because of some convoluted sociological reasoning.*

Hazel Blears *(Lab) – staunch defender of the Labour party who regularly told untruths in her political rhetoric in order to defend the often indefensible party line, and was caught up in the expenses scandal dishonestly flipping properties to avoid capital gains tax*

Jacqui Smith *(Lab) – it is absolutely outrageous that somebody like Jacqui Smith, who was Home Secretary at the time, could pretend that her first home was the room she rented off her sister - and not the home where her husband and children lived – just so that that she could claim £116K in extra expenses. As Home Secretary her morality and her integrity should have been beyond reproach but this blatant deception showed a complete lack of respect for the position she held. Home Secretary is not just a job but a position of trust, representing the people of this country - She should not have* been ripping off the taxpayer by claiming these expenses even if it was within the rules - She also betrayed the Police by offering them only 1.9%, when the pay-rise suggested by an independent tribunal was 2.4%...and had a Home Office civil servant - and a Tory frontbench spokesman - arrested on trumped up charges because they exposed New Labour's systematic lies over illegal immigration; all behaviour unbecoming of a Home Secretary

Margaret Beckett (Lab) – housing minister – refused to pay back expenses when caught out

Nadine Dorries (Con) - another woman caught fiddling her expenses, who hypocritically criticised **Esther Rantzen** for her ideas on transparency while at the same time paying her neighbour Lynn Elson 34K and her 22yr old daughter 28K to work for her in a blatant show of nepotism, despite the rules

Patricia Hewitt (Lab) – another one caught out by the expenses scandal

Ruth Kelly (Lab) – woefully inept; admitted by consensus

Tessa Jowell (Lab) – caught up in a financial scandal involving her husband

Yvette Cooper (Lab) - devised and organised an underhand research scheme to covertly trick and trap employers in their employment procedures

———

Now I have nothing against women or the velvet revolution - which clearly needed to take place - and this list has in no way been compiled for any sexist or anti-feminist argument but by analysing the different statistics and data available it is clear that – despite what they might say - women are not necessarily any better at politics than men...though I do believe that women should be encouraged to play a greater part in the political process; a situation that I will address later.

———

So, feminism and equality - which brought about a series of broader cultural changes because their rise coincided with the weakening and decline of the UK judicial system - are now an integral part of our society but unfortunately, the raft of new anti-discrimination laws - that we have had to introduce, in order to implement those changes - have opened up a can of worms that all sorts of minority pressure groups have seized upon and exploited, twisting them to fit their own agendas – with the catastrophic results we are all now living with.

The steel, the backbone of our society - as represented by people like Winston Churchill - has been chipped away, piece by piece, leaving us all open and exposed and while I understand their fundamental argument, in denouncing the autocratic male world for their own gain, the militant feminists of the last thirty years - and those who have followed in their footsteps - have in fact unwittingly succeeded in destroying the very fabric of this country, bringing it to its knees with greater effect than two World Wars combined ever could.

This country is now in a state of complete and utter turmoil where equal opportunities are legally enforced whether the candidates are apt or not, where political correctness is observed to the point of self-destruction and where the Law itself is called into question on a daily basis by a multitude of opportunist minority groups each one defending its own agenda on the back of the anti-discrimination laws.

In fact every minority group with a grievance can now hold our society to ransom over the potential for discrimination and **The European Human Rights Charter -** which inverts centuries of law based on common sense, decency and morality – is being widely exploited by criminals and fundamentally misguided do-gooders alike – aided and abetted might I say by an army of unscrupulous lawyers just looking for their five minutes of notoriety and an easy pay-check - to bring the most outrageous cases to court.

I'm sure that the people who dreamed up The **EHRC** (European Human Rights Charter) were well meaning, but they didn't take into consideration the deviousness of human nature when drafting it and every possible loophole has since been exploited with devastating effect.

––––––

Needless to say, I am appalled and disillusioned at the way our country is being run, at the way our traditional values are being eroded one after the other, at the way our culture, our way of life, our history, our heritage and our national identity – which we went through two World Wars to protect - are all being systematically dismantled, given up so easily, without a fight by complacent and apathetic politicians who have failed to take up the mantle being slowly relinquished by religion; that of protecting and upholding our heritage and our way of life.

It is their job to show the way forward with strong guide-lines on what is acceptable and what is not in our society but it is clear that the current crop of politicians are not up to the job.

I am not against progress – we should always be going forward, looking to the future – but in order to do so intelligently – we need to know where we have come from – our roots, our heritage, our culture and our traditions all need to be protected.

It would also help though, if our politicians weren't persistently hindered and badgered by the multitude of so-called 'do-good' lobbyists who are slowly eating away at our society's foundations, like dry rot dilapidating it more and more each day with their constant demands for greater political correctness and campaigns to defend the human rights of those who don't respect or abide by them themselves.

I do not believe that pandering to the wishes of all these;

- social libertarians and lobbyists
- to the self-righteous defenders of moral standards
- to the hypocritical, conservatively-minded
- to the do-gooders and the hand-wringers
- to the pseudo-activists
- to the killjoys

- or to the zealots who hide behind lavishly funded, vociferous minority pressure groups (which in turn shelter behind the banner of charitable status)

...and who all use emotional blackmail and lies to influence a society becoming increasingly more obsessed with political correctness to a point where they are holding the Government to ransom...is the way forward.

Indeed, I have nothing but contempt for all those attention-seeking, conscientious objectors and bleeding heart, moral crusaders with their woolly liberal values who are simply trying to exist in a parallel world of hypothetical idealism.

This country is in a political straightjacket thanks to them and a nucleus of naïve, well-meaning but ultimately gullible and misguided lobbyists... and it's time that changed.

Initial Conclusion;

Over the last thirty years successive governments and their representatives, fearful more of losing their seats on the gravy train than protecting or leading this country, have demonstrated mass incompetence and wholesale inefficiency at every level and in every department of Westminster, creating a liberal inertia and political torpor in this country that will never again be equalled, mainly because most of those involved have since been caught out, moved on or retired.

These people consistently failed this country by abolishing - one by one - the freedoms that we have taken a thousand years of patient, heroic struggle to put in place and defend – thereby playing right into the hands of those who would like to see us change our way of life.

It is a fact that more people get killed on the road every year than through terrorist attacks but the draconian measures that have been put in place in this country to counter those potential attacks are having a real impact on the way the British people live their lives, modifying their behaviour whether they like it or not.

We, as a nation, have to stand firm and accept that unfortunately and to our great regret, once and a while, until we weed them all out, the price of our freedom and our right to live the way we want to live, might have to be paid in the occasional outrage.

I understand the need for caution in these matters but I believe that it is time for a new start, a new beginning...and instead of simply accepting the fact that we're going to live through a generation of terror;

-   where we face mounting threats from international terrorism,
-   where we cannot walk our streets in safety for fear of being shot or knifed by children as young as ten
-   or mugged by drug addicts looking for their next fix
-   or assaulted by binge-drinking yobs
-   or homeless illegal immigrants

...it is time to do something about it.

———

There is no greater threat to the people of this country than the retreat from reason and common sense that we are currently witnessing all around us, so...

-   Let's ignore all the mendacious spin and hyperbole of our self-serving politicians
-   Let's look beyond all the pointless clichéd rhetoric
-   Let's disregard all the empty and meaningless posturing

    ...and most importantly...

-   Let's put an end to all the sleaze and scandal

———

Endemic and systemic incompetence has riddled British politics for the last thirty years – especially during the New Labour period - but the alternative of a coalition between the Conservatives and the Liberal Democrats has proved just as unsuccessful and ineffective...because compromise politics which simply goes around in circles – due to ambivalent leadership and u-turn after u-turn - is not the solution;

We need change...real change.

We do not need a revolution, at least not yet; we just need a new impetus; we need a return to some kind of order through strong leadership so that we might counter the escalating crime and unrest; something that the current generation of incompetent, complacent and gutless politicians has failed to provide.

It is time to draw up a new road-map for the future with clear, well-defined guide-lines to give structure and direction back to a society that has been lacking and sadly neglected over recent years by politicians incapable of providing any strong leadership or definite direction.

It will take time and I believe that a period of strict-control of 10-15 years will be necessary, in order for us to re-group and consolidate after thirty years of woolly liberal policies that have driven us to the brink, and exposed us to international terrorism.

———

Britain is now a multi-cultural society, thanks to New Labour's much maligned 'open-door policy' on immigration but while this diversity has been mostly beneficial, it has nevertheless created ghetto communities within our towns and cities where vast numbers of immigrants live here in the UK as if they were still living in their own country, instead of integrating and embracing British culture and institutions.

This has caused tension and misunderstanding between the indigenous population and those from different ethnic faiths unwilling to integrate but I would like to defuse that tension by drawing up a set of clear and definite guidelines as to how British society could be run that should be respected by all.

This is the PDC Manifesto which I believe would take us forward into the 21st century on a positive footing.

———

The State and Religion

**The State should have priority on all matters –
even over and above any religious considerations**

The argument for separation between the State and the Church has been going on for centuries but as time has gone by, the tolerance that has set in on both sides has led to contradiction and confusion on so many levels; let there be no more contradiction or confusion.

We all, as citizens of this country need a common building block on which to found our society and that building block has to be the State.

So, with that in mind, we need a clear template on which to build the future; one single system of values that everyone from whatever background, adheres to...and until we experience Divine Intervention from whatever source or Deity that might be, which puts into place an alternative way of financing society and running an economy other than by raising taxes, we need to do it ourselves, and that means structuring our society in order to sustain itself, to provide for now and offer prosperity for future generations.

In this respect, the buck should stop with the State and in order for the State to assume that responsibility, it has to be recognised as being the only legal representative of the people and the enforcer of the laws it creates, above and beyond all other 'officialdom'.

We also need to put The State first because it is the State that protects every citizen of the country, by enforcing the laws which have been drawn up and democratically agreed upon by the electorate.

That is why the State has to take precedence over all other allegiances and that includes religion, because while it might sound like a cliché, it seems to me that a lot of what is wrong in the world can actually be laid at the door of Religion which I see as more of a force for evil than one for good.

So now it is time to create a new, modern 21ˢᵗ century secular society – not bound by the archaic, medieval rules of centuries past, or the woolly meandering of cowardly politicians who have tried for decades to pander to the demands of each and every ethnic minority just to keep their seats.

Some people in the UK have suggested a joint or amalgamated system of State Law and Sharia Law because of the growing prevalence of Islam in our country but I believe that where the Law of the land is concerned, it would be impractical to have such a duplicitous situation.

It would be confusing more than dangerous - and such a situation would undoubtedly be exploited by lawyers who would constantly point out the different interpretations of the law in order to make their cases, thereby creating new precedents on a daily basis and dragging out the legal process.

The reality is that our country is now inhabited by people from all over the world, who all contribute to the fabric of our society.

People from the Caribbean, India and Pakistan – which were part of the commonwealth at the time - were invited here after the Second World War to fill the huge holes in the labour-force and to help re-construct the country after the conflict.

A second wave of Indian immigrants – supplied with British passports thanks to the 1948 British Nationality Act brought in by Clement Attlee (Labour) which gave everybody in the commonwealth British citizenship – arrived in the 1950's and in the 1960's - after they were expelled from Kenya, Uganda and Zanzibar – yet another wave of immigrants arrived.

The 2010 census tells us that there are now 1.5 million Indians, 1.2 million Pakistanis and around one million people from the Caribbean living in this country today.

These people are second, third and fourth generation 'immigrants' who have been born in this country and have just as much right to be here as any other ethnicities who themselves are the result of previous migrations.

We have got to learn to live together but in order to do that we ALL have to live by the same rules; what we need is a common thread – common as in community, one identity – and common as in one law for all.

We need one single system of values that everyone adheres to; we cannot have the Indians living by their law, while the Pakistanis live by theirs and the Muslims live by theirs; without a common code, it will not work; resentment will fester and conflict will inevitably ensue.

So **NO,** no shared system – the lines governing the law need to be clearly drawn, noticeably defined and the same for everyone in the land.

———

The PDC and Religion

The PDC (Peoples Democratic Congress) would be open to all British nationals of all races but it would not be promoting the ideology of religion.

The colour of our skin is not of our choosing; we are all born with the genes of our parents; there is no choice involved in the matter, so there would be no discrimination on that basis and anybody from any culture would be welcome to join us.

However, those who have made the conscious decision to follow the teachings of some mystical supreme-being or prophet invented in medieval times to scare, control and manipulate the masses will have made **a choice** – whether that choice was forced upon them during childhood by the indoctrination of misguided parents...or arrived at on reaching an age of cognisant reasoning, it is **a choice** and one that would have no resonance in this party model for the following reasons.

Religion is the most divisive issue that Man has ever invented;

- it divides people's minds and it divides their hearts
- it divides families
- it divides communities
- it divides towns
- it divides cities...and
- it divides nations

It has been the single, most prominent and glaringly obvious reason for so many wars and conflicts over the centuries - and it is the No 1 killer of men because of that; way ahead of any plague, epidemic or medical illness.

The above is a statement of fact, and sadly, having studied the subject at great length, I predict that one day, without any shadow of a doubt, the cancer that is religion - with its short-sighted, narrow-minded, 'lets exclude / kill everyone who doesn't believe what we believe' approach - will inevitably play an integral part in the demise, the downfall and the eventual self-destruction of the human race.

Yes, one day Religion and blind faith will destroy us all. All that the human race has achieved over the centuries, all the knowledge we have assembled and all the technical expertise we have developed will all be wiped from the face of the earth...and not because of some intergalactic invasion...but because of something that doesn't exist anywhere but in our own minds.

It will be the ultimate irony / paradox; we will all die, and humanity – the most intellectually advanced species inhabiting this planet - will be wiped from the universe all because of its own stupidity.

———

Nonetheless, in the meantime, and for however long it lasts, the PDC would be promoting a secular society going forward that would allow EVERYONE to be equal without the prejudices of any religion.

———

The author's personal view of religion

I personally have issues with the question of religion having made my decision about it at a very early age; I must have been about 10 yrs old.

I was watching a TV programme after a hard day at school; I believe the programme was called 'The Tomorrow People' (not too sure about that) but the storyline (directed at children) was about an evil organisation trying to turn the pupils of a school against each other by mysteriously attributing different coloured badges to them...and as I recall, it became an ongoing battle between the 'blues' and the 'greens' as to who should 'rule their particular world'.

That was my first real exposure to **sectarianism** and to this day I still remember feeling uneasy about it; I thought it was wrong and divisive then, and I still believe it is wrong and divisive today.

As an individual, I do not believe in **hereditary indoctrination** either; in fact I abhor the indoctrination of children before they are of age to have an opinion, in order to perpetuate the dogma and the misguided beliefs of their parents. Religion should not be imposed on children - it should be every child's right to choose what they want to believe when they reach a cognisant age and in an ideal world that would be the case.

However, radical parents and the elders of every religious organisation are well aware that if they wait until the children have developed their own minds (*in adolescence*); it will be too late to indoctrinate them into their parochial way of thinking, so regrettably the indoctrination of small children will not be stopping any time soon.

Consequently, **Religion** is never going to go away but it is not only because of its perpetuation through the indoctrination of the next generation, it is also because, there are too many people living off it, using it as a meal-ticket, attaching as many ideals as they can think of to it, in order to exploit those without hope, the ignorant and the naive.

Religion provides jobs for many thousands of people, giving them a purpose, a way of life, an existence, but as stated previously I sincerely believe that with the invention of religion, man has created the weapon of his own misery and destruction, and the sectarian prejudices it engenders will ultimately be the undoing of the human race. The recent fight between rival groups of monks in front of the Holy Sepulchre in Jerusalem shows just how divisive and extremist it is.

In fact, ever since its invention religion has bred conflict between men...and examples are numerous throughout the ages – from the early Crusades when Christians fought against Muslims in battles sanctioned by the then Pope, all the way through to present-day Afghanistan where the Taliban (Sunni Muslims) with their Sharia Law are still fighting the West's forces, desperate to oppose change.

Over the years, religious conflicts have regularly broken out but here are some more recent examples;

- The Muslims, Sikhs and Hindus fought each other when Britain pulled out of India
- The Protestants and Catholics fought for years in Northern Ireland...and although an uneasy peace currently reigns, the issue has not really been resolved
- In Israel / Palestine, the Arabs (Hamas / Fatah) and the Jews are still squabbling seeing Jihad as the only solution.
- ...and in Lebanon, Iran and Iraq different factions of Islam are continually squabbling for power.

Human beings will always fight because we are biologically wired to do so. It has always been the case – *ever since man first evolved to set foot on this earth* - of the survival of the fittest and in that struggle to survive we do whatever we can to continue to exist; religion just gives us an excuse for conflict, an excuse to show our prowess, to beat our breasts and roar that we are better, stronger and more deserving to survive than our adversary.

It is a primal reflex that inhabits us all and will continue to do so as long as we exist but fortunately, over time, we have continued to evolve and our physical strength is no longer the only attribute that defines us these days.

Our intelligence and cognitive processing has evolved too, but the sad thing is that instead of using the enlightenment we have gained over the centuries through shared knowledge, through technological advance and through progress in so many other areas – all of which could be used to take all of humanity forward together in peace and harmony - certain civilised western countries are being held hostage and pegged back by those countries still anchored in those antiquated beliefs and religions of a bygone age.

I might be an idealist, but why can't we just believe in the capacity of mankind to do the right thing, rather than go around inventing hypothetical supreme beings and spirits that we hope will somehow save us one day and magically solve all our problems?

...especially as these imaginary deities – whose number seems to be increasing on a daily basis thanks to;

- the invention of new sects,
- the creativity of self-promoting evangelists
- and the publicity-machines of the 1800 'give-me-your-money' preachers

...do not seem to be doing a very good job of it.

Surely, if any of this was real, these omnipotent and compassionate divinities would be doing something to save their numerous devotees from the tsunamis, the hurricanes, the earthquakes, the plagues and the general dying all around us?

———

Religion in schools and in Society

That said; I have nothing against people wanting to believe in religion; it is their absolute right and they are free to believe whatever they want to believe as long as they do not try to impose it unilaterally on others.

After all, there are people in this world who believe –

- in angels
- in astrology
- in extra-terrestrials
- in Father Christmas
- in ghosts

- in homeopathy
- in luck
- in psychics and fortune-tellers
- in superstition
- in the bogey-man
- in the power of crystals
- in the tooth fairy
- in UFO's
- and in voodoo

Whatever gets you through the day, I say.

So let us be clear on this; if the PDC was to become a fully-functioning political party - while it would not promote religion - it would not discriminate against any section of the community either for their religious views and no judgement would be made.

However, I do believe that a person's faith should be kept a private matter and not displayed openly on the streets to any great degree where it can lead to sectarianism.

We need to promote integration at all levels, so if elected the PDC would remove Religion from the classroom - and the school environment - in order to prevent that sectarianism gaining a foot-hold in the playground.

Unfortunately, parents would still be able to indoctrinate their children in the privacy of their own homes or in designated religious buildings such as churches and mosques, but it would no longer be taught as a matter of fact in public schools.

I would say at this point however that I am against the corporal mutilation of children for religious reasons – circumcision and excision / female genital mutilation which are no less than minor medical surgeries performed by unqualified elders are an abuse of parental and religious power.

NB - Germany recently banned circumcision

Of course, faith schools fall into the category of 'designated buildings' as an exception to this rule, but in order to continue their existence these schools would need to be self-funding. There would be no more government subsidies and grants allocated to them as the PDC would be against education segregated on the basis of faith, ethnicity or social class – it is just socially divisive.

In the rest of the schools we would be teaching the more logical and reasoned evolutionary theory of the planet, though of course - in order to present a balanced picture - the creationist theory and other religious dogmas would also be explained to the children so that they were aware of them and could converse, connect and relate to those from a religious back-ground.

This is not a crusade against any one culture – it is a way of putting aside the one element of conflict and destruction that has dogged humanity for centuries while still allowing people the right and the freedom to continue practising what they believe in, within their communities and in the privacy of their own homes.

I repeat; I am not anti-Muslim or anti-Jew or anti any other culture. I am pro-British and I would like to create a new, modern, multi-cultural, 21st century society which is not divided either by the colour of one's skin, or by the clothes that one wears.

I want a society where all those who believe in the British culture and our way-of-life reunite, under one banner irrespective of their ethnicity or beliefs.

The ostentatious wearing of Religious or Ethnic Symbols

As for the ostentatious wearing of Religious or Ethnic Symbols, I believe a degree of discretion and tolerance should be applied.

- A small Roman Catholic cross worn on a chain is not the end of the world.
- The kippah or yarmulke (small cap) worn on the Jewish man's head should not cause offence either, although I do believe that the full orthodox hat, beard and ringlets (peyots) of the Hasidic / Chassidic Jews do present a less than welcoming characteristic; a deterrent to open exchange.
- Sikhs wear the turban as the Guru's gift but it is not obligatory / mandatory; there are Sikhs that don't wear them, so a more discreet model could be worn on an everyday basis – while the larger, more-elaborate ceremonial turbans could be kept for special occasions within the community.
- Muslim men wear beards - but some don't - so maybe a compromise could be found there too.
- Muslim women wear the veil but the Qur'an has no specific requirement for women to cover their faces or their bodies with the burka or chador. The Prophet Muhammad's wives did not wear them initially; it was only when he began adopting Persian / Byzantine customs that they were introduced in the 'Verses of the Curtain'. All the Qur'an really asks is that both men and women dress modestly; the veil - whether it is viewed as a symbol of oppression or as a rejection of Western values - is not imposed by the Qur'an. There is no obligation for women to wear them.

And herein lies the problem; just like terrorists, bank-robbers and other criminals who wear balaclavas to protect their identity – women who wear the veil show a lack of respect for the other person while demanding respect for themselves. Anybody who covers their face to mask their identity – be it for cultural, religious or terrorist reasons – shows they have something to hide, creating a barrier to open exchange.

Of course, I understand the modesty argument that surrounds the burka and a Muslim woman's desire to repel the unwanted attention of strange men but the burka as a symbol creates not only a physical barrier, it creates a social barrier too.

It is a barrier to open exchange and while the burka might only be a perceived threat because of its all-enveloping form – integration, which is our only goal, is not possible if these people refuse to abide by our laws.

The PDC would want integration for all, and part of that integration and citizenship would also mean playing a part in our way of life. However, as a recent court case clearly highlighted, a problem does exist - a Muslim woman who had been selected as a jury member refused to remove her veil and reveal her identity...and while I can understand her position, we simply cannot allow Muslim women whose face we cannot see and whose identity we cannot verify to sit on jury-service... it's simply not reasonable...and yet as British citizens they should be able to.

Surely it is common sense to anybody, in the current climate, that there is a perfectly reasonable argument for controlling the wearing of identity-concealing veils where there is a perceived security risk?

Going forward, I suggest that a light scarf to cover the hair could suffice.

This is an extreme example but it proves a point; if a KKK style operation wanted to walk around the streets of the UK in their robes with their conical hats and their faces covered, revealing just their eyes, would we stand for it?

No, we would not – and yet they might claim that that is their 'religion' too.

So, because there is no real obligation and because of the ongoing terrorist threat in this country, but not only that, the PDC would not accept this dissimulation of a person's identity.

The Law of the land has to be clear and dogmatic on this issue; no exception should be made and anybody who feels that they are unable to respect that law, for whatever reason would have to find another country which did allow ostentatious religious symbolism.

I stress; this is not an anti-Muslim measure; this is a pro-democracy measure which liberates women and would allow us all to feel a little safer.

NB; The French banned the burka in April 2011, (three women were recently stopped at Paris airport and refused entry into France) and Holland and Belgium have since followed suit.

———

Additional arguments against the burka;

A member of Abu Qatada's entourage recently tried to smuggle a mobile phone into him in prison under her burka

A gang of thieves recently attacked Selfridges in London using burkas to conceal the hammers that they were going to use to break open the jewellery showcases

...while, at least two known criminals have managed to escape justice in this country by donning the burka to avoid security staff and CCTV recognising them at the airport.

———

Comments on Islamic / Muslim Ideology –

———

There are six main religions in the world;

- The **Christians** (named after Jesus Christ) who believe in the God concept; and while they do have their issues about guilt, shame, sin and paedophilia; they preach mainly about forgiveness and social integration.
- The **Buddhists** preach about escaping from suffering and gaining personal enlightenment (nirvana); though Buddha is not a God.

- The **Hindus** believe in the eternal cycle much like the Buddhists but rather than calling it birth, life, death and rebirth, they call it reincarnation.
- The **Jews (Judaism)** believe in a God that pre-dates Jesus Christ by 2000 years but the teachings are along the same lines.
- The **Sikhs** believe in a God, equality and sharing
- And then we have **Islam /** the **Muslims** who believe the purpose of existence is to love and serve God

---

Reflection –

All six of these religions appear to be promoting peace and love - of one kind or another - which is a glaring paradox in itself considering the number of people that religion has killed over the centuries, but why does Islam - and the Muslim faith in particular - get such a bad press?

Maybe this is why;

There are two main denominations of Islam; the Sunni who represent between 75 and 90% of Muslims and the Shia who represent 10 to 20% of the Muslim population.

The vast majority of these people are peace-loving human beings but unfortunately among them there is a minority of hard-line fundamentalists who have twisted the message of the Qur'an and Jihad to wage a Holy War on the infidels, the kafir or the apostates (i.e. everyone who is not a Muslim) believing that once we are all dead, we will all be resurrected to be judged again by their God on Judgement Day.

The Jihad forms part of Shia Islam (though it is often considered as the 6th pillar of Islam itself) but those who interpret it as a holy war against anyone who does not believe as they do, should read and re-read this passage from the Qur'an;

"And fight in the cause of Allah with those who fight with you, but do not exceed the limits, for Allah does not love those who exceed the limits. And kill them wherever you find them, and drive them out from where they drove you out as persecution is worse than slaughter, but do not fight with them at the Sacred Mosque (in Makkah) unless they fight with you there, but if they do fight you, then slay them; such is the reward of the unbelievers. But if they desist, then Allah is Forgiving, Merciful. And fight with them until there is no persecution, and religion should be only for Allah, but if they desist, then there is no hostility except against the oppressors." (Qur'an, 2:190-192)

This is proof that the Qur'an has no issue with other faiths; self-defence by all means but why so much conflict...why the slaughter of so many innocents?

The reason is that those that want to 'kill the infidels / unbelievers' are just extremists who want to fight, who want to follow their primal, testosterone-fuelled instinct of survival and wreak havoc, death and destruction on everyone else; it gives them a purpose in life and sadly they use a misguided interpretation of the Qur'an to justify their actions.

———

However, the Jihad or Holy War that we call Terrorism is not the only reason that Islam and the Muslim faith is considered in such bad light; there are other reasons;

For example;

It is only the Muslims – granted they are extremists - who issue decrees or fatwas - which are basically orders to kill - against anybody they don't like, be it political opponents, writers (Salman Rushdie) or cartoonists (Kurt Westergaard and Molly Norris) – though I fail to see how they justify offering a financial reward for the murder of these people when the Qur'an does not condone the taking of life.

———

Dutch film director Theo van Gogh was sadly shot eight times and stabbed to death in Amsterdam in 2004 by radical Islamist Mohammed Bouyeri because he had produced a film that highlighted the plight of women in Islam and criticised their treatment.

———

It is only the Muslims – granted they are extremists – who stand in our streets and use our laws on the freedom of speech to spit bile and hatred towards others and threaten to behead all the infidels, i.e. us.

It is only the Muslims who still stone women to death – *lapidation* - on the streets, and treat them as submissive slaves forcing them to dress in a certain way, to be chaperoned constantly, to walk two steps behind their men and not allowing them to drive etc.

It is only the Muslims – granted they are extremists - who hijack airplanes and fly them into buildings (9/11) or set bombs to go off on buses (7/7) or during crowded marathons (Boston) in an attempt to kill as many innocent people as possible,

...and it is only the Muslims who seem to want to drag us all back to the Middle Ages; just look at how the fundamentalists are reversing progress in countries like Indonesia and Turkey.

NO OTHER RELIGION DOES THESE THINGS

———

Three recent court-cases in the UK have not helped either;

1) An Islamic teacher was jailed recently for kicking and hitting children during religious lessons in a mosque
2) A woman was jailed for beating a 12yr old girl with a ladle because she didn't read enough of the Qur'an; the girl was found to have 57 different injuries

3) ...and finally a mother was jailed for beating her 7yr old son to death with a stick 'like a dog' (her words) for not reciting the scriptures correctly

Granted, these might be isolated incidents but no other religion does this; no other religion incites this kind of cruel, sadistic punishment. Many religions control their disciples with fear and threats but none seem to have the propensity for malicious barbarism that we see in Islam.

This is of course only my opinion but as an outside observer I do think that there is an underlying but inherent malevolence to these medieval teachings that translates as chastisement through violence and I find it more than a little unsettling.

———

Now, every religion has its ideas on Armageddon; it is one of those scare tactics that they all use as a controlling mechanism to frighten people into blindly following their doctrines, but if they are really looking to be accepted in society then the Muslims need to weed out the radical tendencies among them to prove to the rest of the world that they are not hell-bent on taking over the planet, one community at a time, one suicide bomb at a time, killing innocents and anyone who doesn't agree with them, because that is the perception of many people around the world today; that Muslims are not to be trusted because they have an agenda which ultimately entails world domination; world domination through the spread of ideology I hasten to add, not through military force.

That is what many people are afraid of; that is what many people don't understand and that is possibly why many people don't trust them.

That is also why the leaders of the Muslim faith should be doing a lot more to change our perception of them.

...and once again, therein lies the dichotomy...because I also believe that even if the Muslim authorities were to come out and announce that there were no more fanatics and no more radicals - because of all the terror and all the bloodshed and all the violence that has already gone on - the world still wouldn't believe them.

This is because while we are busy teaching tolerance and acceptance, the Muslims would still be quietly colonising whole communities in anticipation of world dominance (the day of judgement) because that is simply a cornerstone of their faith.

They believe that there is only one God; that eventually He will prevail over all others and that is what they are all working towards...

Islam in the UK

Here in the UK, while our mealy-mouthed politicians are busy looking after themselves and creating a generation of badly educated, amoral, risk-averse, work-shy narcissists - who would rather binge-drink with not a care in the world or a thought for the future - others with a more long-term agenda have been hard at work infiltrating our society at every possible level.

In fact, this country has been and continues to be surreptitiously invaded a little more every day by an ideology with which we have no natural affinity and yet nobody has so far had the gumption to point it out; least of all our spineless 'political leaders' who dare not comment on it for fear of being called a racist and losing their seat on the gravy-train, but the facts are there...and the evidence is clear.

Of course, this is not a military invasion and it is not being orchestrated as such by any one person in particular but the strategy is infallible; plant a seed and over time its roots will spread until one day it is the only tree in the garden.

Now, ideological and cultural change is a very very slow process, much like erosion or evolution itself but as citizens of this country I believe that we should be aware of what is happening all around us.

Followers of the Muslim faith see their ascendancy to the dominant position in our country as inevitable, as a matter of course, as their destiny. It is one of the dominant themes of the Qur'an...and by taking advantage of the immense but ultimately naïve tolerance of the British people, Islam and the Muslim faith is slowly but inexorably spreading its message and extending its influence around this country a little more every day, infiltrating every sector of our society; our councils, our suburbs and even our grass-roots in many areas, creating a network of devotees whether the British people like it or not.

It's all very tactical; just as footballers abuse the sportsmanship of other teams to gain an advantage; the Muslims are enjoying the same kind of benefits.

These people are very clever and while they are not always 'victims', they play the part well, by appealing constantly to the British sense of compassion and tolerance...

...and then, when the gullible and indulgent British public – unaided by any strong leadership from above – ties itself in knots trying to bend over backwards in order to accommodate them...and to accept the idea of multi-cultural diversity, these same people exploit that gullibility and that indulgence for their own self-serving agendas, believing firmly in the inevitability that one day; through the sheer weight of their numbers and the strategic positioning of a number of key adherents they will have a good enough stranglehold over British society to become the dominant culture here.

This passive invasion, this subtle geographical progression will take the time it takes - however long that might be - but the Muslims believe it is inevitable and proof of their growing influence in Britain is already easy to perceive.

For example, some Muslims are already calling for special Bank Holidays for themselves...and the introduction of certain elements of Sharia Law into British Law concerning family matters; laws which quite possibly already exist within the confines of their own closed communities.

Norwegian killer (Anders Behring Breivik) said that Islam is like a Trojan horse that has been introduced into our midst and is about to overpower and destroy our unsuspecting western societies; that is a worst case scenario of course because not all Muslims are evil and malevolent but I do believe that our vigilance needs to be stepped-up as any weakening of our resolve **to maintain who we are and what we stand for** will quickly be exploited by those more radical elements seeking to destabilise and change our society.

I would point out however, that while it is true that the radicals have been abusing our tolerance and exploiting our leniency to try to impose their own culture, the vast majority of Muslims hold more moderate views and are in fact peaceful human beings who simply believe that Islam is the only way...and that one day through the sheer weight of their numbers, they will inevitably be the dominant force in this country – and in due course the rest of the world.

They are in no rush; they are playing the long game because they see the Day of Judgement as an inevitability; that is simply their belief.

———

25% of the world's population is already Muslim so they are already well on their way.

———

So, taking all this into account, I believe that it is time for this country to act, to define clear-cut, unambiguous boundaries about what is acceptable and what is not for all religions - not only Islam - before another religious conflict erupts.

We might not be able to stem the tide of this theological osmosis. If it is inevitable that this country is to become a Muslim nation, then so be it; it will not be in my lifetime and I would never presume to predict the future, but as long as;

- **we are aware** of the fact that the ultimate goal of Islam is to be the dominant creed on this planet whenever their Judgement day comes - however far in the future that might be and however peacefully they might have achieved that goal...and
- we do our best in the meantime to withstand the threat of that 'inevitability' for as long as possible, then our children will be safe for a couple of generations at least; after that, it would be up to them to carry on the fight if they felt our democracy was still worth fighting for.

I re-iterate here once again for anybody who might still be unaware. I am not against multi-cultural societies – but I am against those who are dedicated to undermining the peaceful, democratic society in which we have chosen to live our lives, with religious doctrines and dogma.

Again, I stress; we, the British people are not bigots, we are not intolerant; we have proved it time and time again...but through our repeated attempts to integrate ethnic minorities into our society, we have left ourselves vulnerable and wide open to abuse from those with destructive agendas who wish to infiltrate our country in order to impose their own radical ideals.

That said; let me be clear – As much as I disagree with Islam's crusade for world domination, I also have no time for the doctrine of misery, the empty promises of salvation, the self-flagellation, the repentance and guilt advocated by the Catholic Church.

The complex and ongoing question of paedophilia aside – which I believe is a self-imposed scourge brought about by the *contra nature* vow of celibacy which itself is no more than a medieval control mechanism – I abhor the hypocrisy of a church;

- which visits guilt upon innocent children and burdens them with that guilt (for 'sins' that they did not commit) for the rest of their lives, and
- which forces its clergy to live a Spartan and often inhumane existence, based on poverty and self-deprivation
- while at the same time, its hierarchy lives a life of decadent luxury and comfort; the Vatican PLC is one of the richest companies in the world and has a multi-million pound property portfolio including some of the world's most sumptuous palaces, all of which are furnished with some of the world's most priceless art.

...and lets not forget all the false prophets and the fraudulent, self-glorifying TV evangelists with their 1800 numbers...and those sadly misguided Christians of the American Mid-West who brainwash and indoctrinate their children in Jesus camps.

The way these people frighten their children with the guilt of sin and horrific images of the devil and death (red poster dripping with blood) is outrageously cruel and those involved, be it the preachers themselves or the ill-advised parents should really be held to account – and shamed.

Whether this is through the naiveté and ignorance of blind-belief, the refusal to recognise that we now live in the 21st century or on the contrary a well-orchestrated scam simply to extract money from gullible parents, this kind of thing should not be happening.

———

Benjamin Franklin once wrote;

'To follow by faith alone is to follow blindly'

...we should always remember that phrase.

———

So, in the words of **Albert Einstein,** 'I am a deeply religious non-believer' and that is why - for all the reasons already mentioned – plus the wars and the crusades - there would be no religious component to the PDC. It is just too often, a cause of conflict.

The **Dalai Lama** once said; 'This is my simple religion; there is no need for temples, no need for complicated philosophy. Our own brain, our own heart is our temple, the philosophy is kindness'.

Let that be our creed; **kindness and respect**.

————

NB - I hate hypocrisy in all things, so what about the hypocrisy of these mainly Muslim women who are having virginity repairs on the NHS?

Surely these women are entering into marriage on the back of a lie. If they have had sex and not respected the faith they profess to follow then they should stand up and say so – and if their future spouses find that fact intolerable then they should not be getting married in the first place.

As I said, I hate hypocrisy in all its forms, and this particular hypocrisy from these people who are constantly trying to impose the purity of their religion on us, is ethically reprehensible.

The British tax-payer should not be paying the bill for...or condoning this medieval hokum?

————

FOR INFORMATION

NOTES ON SHARIA LAW

Not all Muslims are Taliban. The Taliban are fundamentalist Islamists who follow the strict Sunni Islamist teachings but here – for your information – are some of the decrees imposed by the Taliban in Afghanistan according to **Sharia Law** before the international forces stepped in; taken from the book 'My Forbidden Face' written by Latifa in 2002

- A young woman must not engage in conversation with a young man – if they do, then they will be married immediately after the breach
- Alcohol is forbidden
- All babies must have Muslim names
- All Muslims must say their prayers at the specified times, wherever they might find themselves
- All offenders will be punished on the public square
- Anyone possessing a firearm must deposit it at the nearest mosque
- Displaying photographs of animals or humans is forbidden
- Engaged women are forbidden from going to a beauty parlour even during preparations for the wedding
- Families are forbidden from taking photographs or making videos even at weddings
- Men must grow beards and shave moustaches
- Men must wear a turban or beret
- Men must wear traditional dress only – suits and ties are forbidden
- Muslim families must not listen to music, even during wedding ceremonies
- No male doctor is allowed to touch the body of a woman under the pretext of a consultation
- Nail polish, lipstick and make-up are forbidden for women

- No merchant can sell women's undergarments
- Non-Muslims must wear yellow clothes and fly yellow flags over their houses
- Public transport will be segregated – separate buses for men and women
- When Police are punishing an offender, no one has the right to criticise, intervene or question their actions
- Women and girls are forbidden to wear brightly coloured clothes, even beneath the burka
- Women and girls are not allowed to work outside the home
- Women and girls must wear the burka
- Women are not allowed to go to a man's tailor
- Women are not allowed to take taxis unless accompanied by a male
- Women who have to leave their homes must be accompanied at all times by a male member of the family

---

Other details of life under Sharia Law –

A widow with no family was beaten on the streets for being unaccompanied – but she didn't have anybody – she was just trying to get some food

A woman had her fingers cut off for wearing nail-polish

Another woman was whipped for wearing white shoes – the colour of the Taliban flag

By preventing women from working – and working as doctors in particular – the Taliban basically condemned women to illness and disease, notwithstanding the usual complications of the female condition concerning all aspects of childbirth – as male doctors are precluded from touching the female body; and yet the Qur'an states that there are only two occasions when a woman may show her private areas – to her husband and to her doctor

Ethnic cleansing through assassination and rape was rife in Afghanistan

In one town, a school-teacher and her pupils were beaten – the Taliban then threatened to stone the teacher's whole family to death in public if she failed to comply with their strict rules not to educate girls

The image that the author of this work paints, of row after row of children swaying backward and forward as they are mindlessly brain-washed into reciting the Qur'an word for word – terror in their poor innocent eyes - is sickening

Journalists were assassinated

One man was beaten, pummelled to death on the street with rifle-butts for watching videos

One woman, who was holding the Qur'an while being whipped, let it fall to the ground accidentally; but those whipping her did not pick it up. This shows an inconsistency and a hypocrisy as every Muslim knows that the Qur'an must never be placed directly on the ground.

The football stadium in Kabul was used for public executions – hangings, bullets in head – notably, two women accused of adultery were executed in the football stadium, yet nowhere in the Qur'an does it say that one should take life; indeed Mohammed prohibits the killing of women, children and civilians

The Taliban consider women as impure and untouchable – and yet at least three young virgins were gang-raped by fifteen of their followers – and often, raped women who are then considered un-clean through no fault of their own, are forced to marry their rapist

The Taliban have been known to kidnap children to use their organs to feed the internal-organ black-market

The Taliban killed 7 and 8 year old girls whose only crime was to try and get an education in a clandestine school in Taimani – they were all kidnapped, raped and strangled

Women are completely isolated by the system

Women were left without a voice or any human rights

Young women were press-ganged into marrying the Taliban

And of course, homosexuality is considered a crime in Islam – punishable by death

———

This book was written in 2002; we are now in 2014, twelve years have passed but just recently, the Taliban boarded a school-bus in Pakistan and shot Malala Yousafzai, a 14yr old girl in the head because she wanted to write about living through the same terror.

This all appears so barbarically medieval and archaically repressive.

Is that what Islam is all about, preventing young girls from getting an education, hiding their women away and treating them like second-class citizens?

Is that really why we are here; to shoot unarmed children for wanting a better future?

Is that the future that Islam wants to impose on the rest of the world; a return to the middle-ages?

———

Stop press - the Taliban recently descended on a village and beheaded 17 people for dancing. Is that justified or justifiable in anybody's eyes?

These people seem to lack the basic empathy that any human being should have for another human being and it makes me more than a little uncomfortable to know that these people exist.

These brutal acts of medieval barbarism have no place in a civilised world.

———

The Justice System

Over the last thirty years, the great majority of decent, law-abiding citizens in this country feel that they have been alienated and let down by both the **Police** and the **Justice** system.

In fact, both have become a laughing stock as the former concentrate more on meeting their targets and quotas while the latter, bending in every direction so as not to offend anybody, has lost its way with its lenient liberalism.

This decline in the justice system and by extension the rest of society coincided with the rebirth of feminism in the 1980's which itself went hand in hand with the rise of the PC (political correctness) movement, and the change of attitudes and the softening of ideas that both of these movements have provoked - in all walks of life - has left this country wide open to attack and abuse from all corners, leaving it in a state of total disarray.

Now, whether there is a real synchronicity between the two is up for discussion but the reality of the situation is that thirty years down the line – ever since the velvet revolution re-established itself and the PC movement came to the fore - the UK and its legal system has become one big mess, lacking structure, resolve and direction.

The PDC motto would be very simple;

those who abide by the law should be protected by it;
those that don't should feel its full force.

A glance at the newspaper headlines on any given day in 21ˢᵗ century Britain shows that the current justice system is not fit for purpose, and becoming steadily worse in its compassion for criminals, handing down softer and softer sentences and totally disregarding the needs and the grievances of the victims...

...and just like the politicians, the citizens of this country no longer trust it anymore to deliver the society in which they want to live.

I too, have had enough of the spectacle, of the procession of distraught families ushered into police interview-rooms and press calls or standing outside court-houses – mourning their murdered love-ones and feeling frustrated that the law is not doing its job either in catching the perpetrators or condemning them sufficiently harshly when they are caught and convicted;

This must change

Now, much to everyone's regret, this country will never be a crime-free utopia but I believe that it is time to tighten up the woolly justice system that government minister after government minister has allowed to develop by not standing up to the various pressure groups and bleeding heart liberals.

People of Britain; look back thirty years and then project yourself thirty years into the future; what will that future look like if we continue with the naive liberal values of rehabilitation for all. The reality is that some people are inherently evil and they simply cannot be reformed. They cannot be re-programmed; they are who they are and once they are broken they cannot be fixed.

There are those who say that punishment is only effective if there exists an opportunity for rehabilitation; I say that people only learn their lesson if they are made to pay for it.

Recent figures show that 20000 people spared a jail sentence reoffended while doing their 'community service' and ankle bracelets and ASBO's have proved just as ineffective.

This shows that the softly-softly approach of the liberal humanitarians doesn't work and consequently I have no time for those people who want to save everyone and who believe rather naively that everybody is inherently good and that evil people are just misunderstood...and deserve a second, a third and a fourth chance...No they do not.

I do not believe in the forgiveness and the rehabilitation of hardened criminals but I do believe in justice and the right for law-abiding citizens;

- to feel safe in their own homes,
- to be able to walk in the streets without the fear of attack
- and to have confidence that those that they have chosen to represent them will do so with honesty, integrity and efficiency.

Look how violence has spiralled out of control on our streets; knife crime went up 62% during the eleven years that New Labour was in charge. We have gangs aged 15 in Birmingham using automatic weapons to kill people (2 young girls were gunned down coming out of a club); one teenager was stabbed in the corridor of his school;

...look at how the lack of boundaries or the threat of prosecution as a deterrent has spawned a generation of internet trolls who spit out their bile on a daily basis

...look at how fire-fighters are abused when they respond to calls,

...look at how nurses and paramedics are abused in A&E

———

Now, look forward thirty years and what do you see; what kind of society will we be living in then if we carry on like this?

There is already little or no respect for the law, for our fellow man or for the property of others; our society is rife with mindless, callous, cold-blooded criminals and I believe that it is time to do something about it before it is too late.

We need to process these violent people out of our society; we need to purify the human gene-pool, rid it of all its psychopaths, its murderers and its paedophiles.

Bleeding heart politics can no longer be allowed to trump justice because criminals thrive on society's lily-livered tolerance and pseudo-understanding.

Let's stop it now.

———

To do this, we need to revise the penal system and to begin the process I would like to propose mandatory and undiluted sentences for certain crimes while re-introducing capital punishment for others; sometimes permanent removal from society is the only deterrent for certain crimes and certain individuals.

Man's inhumanity towards his fellow man is on permanent display these days thanks to 24/7 rolling news, so those who exude menace and evil need to be dealt with; we cannot be soft and diplomatic with criminals.

The PDC would be all about structure and clear direction, two elements that have been sorely lacking of late both in our institutions and in our society as a whole; however, we cannot have a structured society without the ultimate deterrent for wrongdoing because we are all human and the human being needs a code, needs boundaries in which to evolve and needs laws to respect, because without them he has no morality... and anarchy often ensues.

This means having a strong judicial system which is;

- perfectly clear (to understand),
- transparent (to avoid manipulation),

- airtight (to avoid dispute)
- and leaves no room for complacency

It must also be categorical and incontestable so that lawyers looking for loop-holes to exploit would come up empty-handed.

We need a deterrent that sends a message to both hardened criminals and potential criminals alike that if they do the crime they will be caught and they **WILL** pay the price **in full.**

The PDC Simplified Sentencing System

Category One A offences   -   Capital Punishment

Life should mean life for those who commit heinous crimes on the condition that they are convicted of those crimes by a unanimous decision without a shadow of a doubt that they are the perpetrator.

However; this would not mean 'life' in a cosy prison cell at the tax-payers expense; this life-sentence would mean **THEIR LIFE**

Category One B offences   -   15 years; this sentence would apply when the condition of absolute guilt had not been proven in court without a shadow of doubt. It would however include a clause allowing for the sentence to be extended if necessary depending on the results of a series of psychological evaluations undertaken during the last five years of the detention period to ascertain whether or not the individual was still a danger to the general public

Category Two offences   -   10-12 or 15 years

Category Three offences   -   1-3 or 5 years

Category Four offences   -   up to 1 year

Category Five offences   -   re-education followed by community service

––––––––

Category One offences - Capital punishment –

We, as human beings are capable of anything and everything; we see it every day on the TV and read about it every day in the newspapers - and while we have learned to be civilised in most cases these days, we are nevertheless still capable of responding to our basest instincts which were instilled in us originally for our survival.

That is why we will always need a legal deterrent as part of our democracy in order to keep these most basic instincts under control, because when unleashed they can be ruthless, they can be barbaric and they can know no bounds.

Nobody needs to be reminded of the numerous wars that we have fought with each other over the centuries; we, humans have a warrior instinct; it has helped us survive this far but the violence that these instincts generate has no place in a civilised society.

This is the 21st century but we still have wars in the world; we are still killing each other; look at Iraq and Afghanistan, look at the Rwanda genocide where thousands were brutally killed with machetes; look at the other African countries where war is a constant threat; Israel and Palestine, Russia and Chechnya are still at war and if not there, then somewhere else will flare up.

What I am trying to say is this; those instincts will always be a part of us and there will always be someone in our society who - if he thinks he can get away with it - will succumb to those basest instincts and try to impose them on others, probably linked with some form of criminal activity.

We need a deterrent against that behaviour, against that and the growing trend of incivility which now reigns on our streets; a trend which has been allowed to develop in this country by a generation of cowardly politicians and exacerbated over the past thirty years thanks to the unchecked numbers of refugees and immigrants flowing into our country who do not share our culture.

The gangs with their shallow and selfish ideals of monetary gain and power, together with the drug culture which has taken root here, led by Russian mobsters and Eastern European thugs need to be stamped out before it all gets out of hand - as it has in the USA, in Brazil and in Mexico where the drug cartels murder people on a daily basis with guns and knives, dismembering their bodies and leaving them on the streets as warnings to others not to cross them.

I have seen summary justice handed out in Syria and the bodies of those killed thrown indiscriminately off a bridge.

In Pakistan and in Afghanistan extra-judicial and summary killings are an everyday occurrence, and because so many of these people are coming to Britain to live, thanks to our lax border controls and our EU obligations, they are bringing their medieval cultures with them...and soon they will begin imposing these customs on us just as the Islamists are trying to impose the Sharia on us.

We cannot allow this kind of behaviour to take hold, because if we do, we will start to see the crime rates explode and ordinary citizens will be too frightened to leave their homes.

The people of Britain have already witnessed an increase in knife crime and gun crime - despite what the government and the police statistics might say; we have seen violence explode on our streets and we have seen family after family paraded outside a courthouse after the murder of a loved-one to be told that 'WE will learn our lessons and that it will never happen again'.

Meanwhile the perpetrators get handed ridiculously soft sentences if not early release – and then it does happen again...and again...and again.

Well I say no more soft sentences; we need a deterrent for these people and we need to apply it rigorously to make sure that the message sinks in before Britain and its culture is changed irrevocably. It is time to cream-off the evil.

Now of course we all know that crime will always exist – it's in our nature as human-beings – but we need to let the drug bosses, the gang leaders and the potential murderers know that if we catch them, there is a penalty waiting for them which befits their crime and will be imposed upon them without any compassion or clemency.

Remorse would be no excuse for pardon or leniency either; nor should the lobbyists or Human Rights protestors be allowed to interfere with appeals once the sentence has been pronounced and confirmed.

I understand that this is a difficult subject to address but it has to be done and we have to stand firm.

When **capital punishment** was abolished in 1965 the politicians went against public opinion in order to do so.

Well, I for one, am sick and tired of politicians getting elected and then not representing the views of those who elected them once they get to Parliament.

Politicians need to realise that they are in Parliament to represent the views of the people who elected them, not their own, and if they cannot do that objectively then they should find a new career.

I propose three categories for the death penalty;

- 1A) **Horror crimes** - Terrorists and Murderers who use guns, knives or bombs
- 1B) **Sexual Crimes** - Rapists and Paedophiles where the victim dies as a consequence

- 1C) **Crimes against Society / Humanity** (Organised crime, drug dealers, human-trafficking, illegal organ-harvesting, sex-gangs, honour-killing)

The gravity of the crime should be taken into consideration and given preference over the age of the offender; therefore, under the PDC proposals there would be no quarter given for the age or gender of the guilty party if the victim is killed; this might mean making some difficult decisions, swallowing some bitter pills in sacrificing some younger lives – but it is the price we will have to pay in order to redress the balance of good and bad in our culture which is now so inherently bad after years of not being dealt with.

Indeed, it has taken hold like gangrene and needs to be cut out...and the means will justify the end for future generations. It might be a hard pill to swallow in the short term but ultimately I believe that it would be worthwhile for the hundreds or thousands of potential victims it would save in the long run.

Of course we would hope that we would never have to make that call but the deterrent has to be there; it has to be on the table because society and the world at large would ultimately be a better place without these individuals.

We are all born with the potential to carry out crimes and commit evil deeds but it is up to our parents and society – through our teachers and role models – to show us right from wrong.

I believe that parents would do more to keep their offspring on the straight and narrow if they knew that they risked facing a real deterrent – i.e. the full wrath of the law

---

Survey on Sky News concerning the Death Penalty - 22/02/08

Question - Should the Death Penalty be re-instated?

Yes – 74%

No – 26%

Even in the Bible – Genesis – 9 / 6 – it is noted that a man who kills another man should perish by the hand of another.

———

Adage; when making soup, you must skim off the scum (actual culinary term) to improve its overall flavour and quality; a fitting analogy I believe.

———

Application method –

The Death Penalty would be administered through the Hypoxia method – which uses an inert gas – hydrogen – to painlessly starve the brain of oxygen – rendering the subject unconscious in 15 seconds – death ensuing 1 minute thereafter.

The alternative; it costs the British taxpayer £40K a year to keep an inmate in prison; over a 30year period that's £1.2 million for each person; surely there are any number of more deserving beneficiaries of that money that we could be financing (Nurses, teachers etc)

———

Reflection –

The concept of humanity and humanitarianism through socialisation is no more than a thin and very fragile veneer; a pseudo shield that we have created for ourselves in order to protect us from who we really are.

After all, we are just another species on this planet, another race of animals with the same instincts to hunt (in order to feed) and to protect our young as any other.

Those primal instincts are part of who we are; they are part of our DNA and for some among us no amount of social scaffolding can conceal or temper those hunting / killing impulses; we see it every day on the news.

In fact, it happens on a daily basis somewhere around the world so it clearly doesn't take much for us to revert back to type, to our primitive nature; just look at the wars we wage with one another.

Look at how we traffic other human beings for money, how we abduct and torture children and young women, chaining them in cellars for years on end.

Just look at how we kill other human beings through greed and revenge, for sexual gratification or in the name of any number of misguided ideologies, be it political or religious.

Just look at the recent riots here in the UK and the regular violence on our streets and it's getting worse and more frequent.

We all have a violent component to our nature; in some it is buried deeper than others, but when backed into a corner we all – as human beings - revert back to our animalistic instincts of self-preservation.

Indeed, we can all strike out, whether in anger or in self defence but if we want to live in a just society, then we have to legislate against the premeditated and excessive use of violence and the inevitable criminal activity that accompanies it.

That is why we need a deterrent that is up to the challenge.

Human beings are not all innately good; some are cruel, brutal and violent...and they need rules and boundaries in order to regulate that behaviour. Criminals in particular, especially those who fall into the categories mentioned above need to know what awaits them when they get caught.

There has to be a line '**not to cross**', that criminals are aware of, because, as it stands, the innocent are getting slaughtered on a daily basis and the law in its current form is not strong enough to defend them or punish those who commit these atrocities against them.

Here is a list of some of the most recent high-profile cases in the UK which would have qualified for consideration of the death penalty under the PDC;

Cases involving children;

- The case of 17 month old Peter Connelly, aka 'Baby P' who was killed by his mother Tracey Connelly and her partner – Baby Peter was found dead with more than 50 separate injuries on his body
- The case of 2yr old Keanu Williams whose mother Rebecca Shuttleworth beat him to death; Keanu was found with 37 separate injuries to his body including bite-marks, a fractured skull and a fist-sized tear in his stomach
- The case of 4yr old Daniel Pelka who died after a sustained campaign of unimaginable cruelty by his mother Magdalena Luczak and her partner Mariusz Krezolek (a wanted criminal in his homeland of Poland); Daniel was locked in a box-room, starved of food and force-fed salt, his arm was broken, his eyes were blackened and he was regularly held under water until he fell unconscious
- The case of 6 yr old April Jones who was abducted and killed by Mark Bridger
- The case of 6 yr old Toni-Ann Byfield who was shot in the back by drug-dealer Joel Smith who had already killed her 'father'
- The case of 8 yr old Victoria Climbie who was murdered by her aunt Marie-Therese Kouao and her partner Carl Manning in the most horrendous of circumstances

- The case of 10 yr old Holly Wells and her 10 yr old friend Jessica Chapman who were killed by Ian Huntley in Soham
- The case of 12 yr old Tia Sharp who was killed and hidden in the attic by her grandmother's boyfriend Stuart Hazell

Cases involving teenagers;

- The case of 13 yr old Amanda Jane Dowler aka 'Millie' who was killed by Levi Bellfield on her way home from school. Bellfield was also convicted of the murder of two other young women
- The case of 16 yr old Ben Kinsella who was killed in the street after a night out by Jade Braithwaite / Juress Kika and Michael Leroy Alleyne
- The case of 16 yr old Jimmy Mizen who was killed by Jake Fahri in a bakery-shop for trying to protect his brother
- The case of 18 yr old Robert Knox – an aspiring young actor who had appeared in one of the Harry Potter films - who was stabbed to death by Karl Bishop for trying to protect *his* younger brother

Cases involving adult murder;

- The case of a man who was forced to drink petrol and was then set ablaze by his tormentors (names withheld by the court)
- The case of Joanna Yeates who was killed by her neighbour Vincent Tabak in Bristol
- The case of Rachel Nickell who was murdered by Robert Napper on Wimbledon Common in front of her young son
- The case of Sally Anne Bowman who was killed by necrophiliac Mark Dixie only yards from her home
- The case of the two French students living in London who were stabbed 243 times by Dano Sonnex and Nigel Farmer
- The case of Charlotte Smith who was bludgeoned to death by her husband Devendra Singh which resulted in the most horrendous injuries.
- The mindless murder of young lawyer Tom ap Rhys Pryce in London

- The murder of the two female police officers; Fiona Bone and Nicola Hughes by Dale Cregan
- The recent case of Carl Mills who callously set fire to a house killing his partner Kayleigh Buckley, their daughter Kimberley and Miss Buckley's mother Kim

Cases involving serial rapists;

- The case of a man from Sheffield – identity not released - who repeatedly raped his two daughters over a 25 year period, (leading to 19 pregnancies) – reminiscent of the Josef Fritzl case in Austria and of the more recent case of the three women held prisoner in Cleveland, Ohio.
- The case of Delroy Grant aka 'The Night Stalker' who preyed on elderly and vulnerable women living alone
- The case of John Worboys aka 'the Black Cab Rapist' who drugged young women in his taxi before raping them. He was convicted on 12 charges but police believe there could easily have been over a 100 cases making Worboys the UK's most prolific rapist

Cases involving serial murderers;

- The case of Dennis Nilsen who killed up to 15 people in London but was only convicted on six counts
- The case of Dr Harold Shipman who was convicted of 15 murders but later admitted that it could potentially have been as many as 457
- The case of Fred and Rosemary West; convicted of 10 murders
- The case of Peter Sutcliffe; 'the Yorkshire Ripper' who killed 13 women
- The case of Steve Wright - aka 'the Suffolk Strangler' or 'the Ipswich Ripper' who killed five women in a six week period around the Ipswich area.

The list goes on and on but we cannot carry on preaching rehabilitation to psychopaths and people with no moral conscience.

Why should these people remain a burden on the British taxpayer for the duration of their sentence – which could be up to thirty years or more - after they have committed such heinous crimes?

The victims' families don't receive any help from the taxpayer; they are just left to grieve their loved-ones while the killers of those loved-ones have their every need taken care of. That is not right; that is not just.

We need to redress this balance. The victims and their families should get justice and a clean slate to help heal the wounds inflicted on them by these monstrous criminals.

Category Two offences – 10 – 12 or 15 years

In these cases the Judges would be allowed a certain amount of discretion depending on the seriousness of crime; however, once the sentence was pronounced there would be no reprieves, no reductions for pleading guilty and no half-sentences for good behaviour.

Example of a Category Two offence;

The case of two young boys who almost beat two other young boys to death; under the PDC, these two juveniles would receive an automatic Category Two sentence, their parents would receive a mandatory Category 3 sentence for their poor parenting and any remaining children from those parents would be fostered out to a responsible, caring home.

Paedophiles and those convicted of grooming children would get an automatic 15 year sentence and be subjected to surgical or chemical castration to prevent re-offending; **we must protect the young, the naive and the innocent.**

We cannot go back to branding these people with a Red P in the middle of their fore-heads but castration or sterilisation would be an option to avoid them polluting the gene pool for future generations.

Rapists and Groomers; (in cases involving older victims who weren't killed) would receive a Category Two sentence and on release would also face the possibility of chemical castration depending on a 'pre-release' psychological evaluation.

NB - If violence or firearms were used in committing any crime then a mandatory 15 year sentence would apply and as a consequence of <u>any</u> conviction we would also issue a seizure order for the assets, the bank accounts, the cars and the houses of anybody else having enjoyed the proceeds of that crime.

Category Three offences – 1 / 3 / 5 years –

White-collar crime and street violence.

These cases would also be subject to a 'coward's clause'; an automatic doubling of the sentence for those convicted of gang or group violence against any unarmed individual.

Category Four offences – up to 1 year – Shop-lifting etc

To save on preventative incarceration time – which can last several months because of the slow-moving legal system and costs the hard-pressed tax-payer a fortune - those people caught red-handed committing certain petty crimes would be offered a summary judgement.

This would take place in front of a judge and in the presence of legal representation – but would only be offered for crimes where the normal sentence would be a minimum of six months and up to a year.

The offender would have to serve a mandatory six-month period but the judge would use his / her discretion on what percentage of the sentence would have to be served thereafter depending on the seriousness of the crime.

We need to speed up the justice system and jailing people before they are tried while the police and the lawyers crystallise their cases often means people are incarcerated for a longer period than the sentence they are actually given, which currently entitles them to compensation. We need to eradicate this anomaly.

Of course, it would be imperative that the body of proof be undeniable and irrefutable and as stated earlier, this process would be limited solely to those caught in the act for crimes with a one year maximum sentence.

This system would also be applied to criminals of a younger age through a special children's court.

Category Five offences – Social disturbance etc

The reduction in our military capacity would open the way to Army Camps being transformed into Boot Camps where the thuggish element of our society currently running riot in our streets could be 're-trained' in the ways of the law;

People convicted of these minor crimes would be dealt with by age;

Centre A – (18+)

This would be a correctional centre for anybody 18 years and older where people would be taught the rules of society in a strict, disciplined environment. They would be taught trades in an apprentice-style work-programme and would practice those trades by constantly upgrading the camp's environment – electricians, plumbers, builders etc

Towards the end of their stay, they would be mandated to participate in Social or Community Service Work for local Councils – under supervision - clearing beaches and rivers to help the environment.

Long-term incarcerated prisoners could also spend their last six months in one of these camps learning how to get back into society.

Centre B – (6 to 17)

The current system of supervision orders, ASBO's and community service orders is not working for the current generation of mindless, aggressive, intellectually-challenged young thugs involved in much of the criminal activity we see happening on our streets today. These people are in desperate need of a complete re-programming.

Therefore, the PDC would propose a return to reform centres for these youngsters in the form of a military / army-style boot camp where they would be taught;

- discipline
- right from wrong
- morality
- boundaries
- a trade
- and a work ethic

…all the things that their 'modern-day' parents are not doing.

This would be a radical approach to today's unchecked youth behaviour but it would be for their own good and for the good of the country as a whole going forward; the British public has had enough of this lax justice.

NB - we would be very vigilant not to allow any internal network of bullying - culture and practices - to spring up and take hold in these centres...and any hint of such activity would be instantly sanctioned.

To summarise; every crime would be judged on it's 'seriousness' but it would inevitably fall into one of the above categories and guidelines would be put in place in order to eradicate the confusing variations in punishment which are currently being handed down in different regions around the country. We need consistency in Justice.

NB – the PDC would introduce exemplary sentences for those in public office who abuse the system – whether they be dishonest MP's or council officials, corrupt police-officers or crooked lawyers...and any dithering, limp or indecisive judges would be relieved of the responsibility of adjudicating.

The time for leniency is over.

This proposal is based on the 'Broken Window' theory...which states that if petty vandalism goes unpunished then worse crimes will follow; however, if petty crimes – such as smashing a window - are dealt with rigorously and immediately...and the criminal justice system demonstrates its robustness, the overall crime rates start to fall as a consequence.

The PDC would also name and shame offenders in their local newspapers, together with a confirmation of the sentence that had been handed down in order to warn future offenders of the consequences.

Finally; once they have served their time all convicted foreigners would be immediately deported without further ado directly from the prison to the airport. The Human Rights charter would have to be amended in order to do this but under the PDC the human rights of the vast majority of decent, law-abiding citizens of this country would take precedence over the individual rights of a criminal.

———

Major Legal Issues; particular crimes

Rape;

Rape is a terrible, heinous crime and it is only right that our society punishes it severely in order to protect the population.

However, while men are rightly condemned for this crime I find it a little disconcerting that - in keeping with the general trend of baulking responsibility - women are regularly exploiting the very society giving them that right to be safe and not violated.

Time after time we now hear of women;

- crying rape when no rape has occurred
- or crying rape when they were too drunk to know what they were doing
- or reporting a 'rape' the next day simply to assuage their own guilt for having a one-night-stand
- or more criminally crying rape in order to get revenge on a man or to extort money from him

It is outrageous that men are now;

- constantly under the spotlight just for being men
- constantly under suspicion as potential rapists when walking alone on the street
- constantly under suspicion as potential paedophiles when walking through a park
- or constantly under suspicion as potential thieves. What man has never seen a woman clutch her handbag to her side in the street while throwing a scornful glance in his direction? As a man, it is both embarrassing and humiliating.

This might seem like a sweeping generalisation but we have to stop demonising men.

The feminists have forced public opinion too far in their direction; women need to be more honest and more responsible for their actions.

Of course, if they are a victim of rape then they should have the full force and support of the law behind them – that goes without saying; but by the same token, they should not hide behind that law to remedy their personal failings.

Men are having their reputations ruined by false accusations and if equality is really a two-way street they too should be protected.

It is not right that alleged rape victims have their identities protected, while the men accused of perpetrating those crimes have their names splashed all over the papers, guilty or not.

———

Rape and the abuse of human dignity is an emotional subject and needs to be treated with extreme care by the legislature...and that is why the PDC would introduce a specific set of rules that apply solely to these crimes; we do not want to go down the road of secret courts or justice behind closed doors but in the case of rape;

- where emotions run high,
- where it is often one person's word against another's and
- where the stigma attached to both parties – if their identities are revealed - can often remain with them for the rest of their lives,

...I believe that we should make an exception in this one case in order to protect both parties' reputations...and to avoid media-driven hysteria and frenzy until a case is settled.

The PDC would propose a system where these morally sensitive and often emotional cases could be brought before a panel of three professional magistrates.

There would be legal representation of course for both parties together with their respective support-groups, but there would be no jury - because the emotional component often troubles peoples' judgement - and there would be no press present either.

The magistrates would hear the case and only when their deliberation had been concluded and justice had been served would the details of the case be transferred to the local press for publication - if deemed of interest to the wider public - by a clerk of the court.

This would however only apply to cases where a guilty verdict had been reached.

The innocent party's identity would be protected at all times unless they chose to disclose it themselves but those convicted...and any women who waste the magistrates' time with false accusations motivated by revenge, greed or denial of personal responsibility would be named and shamed in their local newspapers. This would hopefully prevent any money-driven opportunists inventing attacks for monetary gain.

These women would also be charged with contempt of court, lying to the court and wasting its time.

———

However, the process would not end there;

Once a rapist had been convicted and held in custody where he could no longer re-offend, provision would be made - possibly limited in time – for any other victims of the same perpetrator to come forward, safe in the knowledge that their assailant could no longer harm them...and those charges would be processed and added to the original sentence at a later date if found to be true.

———

NB – Murderers and paedophiles would also have their identities protected, but only until they were formally charged...to allow other victims or witnesses to come forward and finally, anybody found leaking peoples' identities before a trial (police, lawyers, court officials or journalists) would receive an automatic Category Three penalty themselves.

One last thing; as a deterrent to potential rapists, maybe we could look into introducing the anti-rape sheaths invented by South African doctor (Sonnet Ehlers) which contain a number of tiny hooks that pierce the skin of the rapist's penis and can only be removed through surgical intervention.

Gangs;

Amanda Platell (DM journalist) once commented – the breakdown of the family and the inexorable rise of single mothers has resulted in widespread teenage criminality, gang warfare and whole neighbourhoods being held to ransom by a feral underclass.

I believe this is true in some areas where a sub-culture has emerged of feral youths who roam our streets terrorising neighbourhoods, trashing bus-shelters, stealing cars and selling drugs outside clubs; in fact, there are approximately 200 gangs in London alone but I do not believe that it is as widespread throughout the country as it might become if we don't address the problem and nip it in the bud.

Criminal gangs are nothing new in this country. We have always had a problem with them but the gang-culture imported from America over the last twenty years or so - inspired by the rap-music-community which glamorises violence and crime – is one that needs to be eradicated before it takes too great a hold of our disaffected youth and our communities.

These delinquent louts or WIMPS as I call them – **W**anted **I**mprisoned by the **M**ajority of the **P**opulation - are dangerously disconnected from our mainstream society and its values, but what is most disconcerting is their willingness – mimicking the idols - to use violence to get what they want.

50 Cent and his 'get rich or die trying' ethos has already poisoned a lot of young minds in this country, to the point where it is almost impossible to go out on the streets in some parts of Britain these days and not encounter that thuggish element of people hanging out in clusters on street corners hurling abuse.

This kind of behaviour cannot be allowed to prevail.

We in this country have always welcomed and embraced new musical influences from around the world but the gangster culture that rap-music has brought with it is totally alien to our way of life.

Nevertheless we have put up with it - with our usual stoic reserve - as we have always accepted all-comers and all influences to these shores thereby confirming our legendary tolerance but as a citizen of this country I certainly don't want to see 'no-go areas' springing up in our inner-cities where the police dare not set foot for fear of violence and I don't believe that the British people would want that either.

Therefore, before this poison can develop its network of criminal activity or ingrain itself too deeply in our culture, I believe that we should cut out the gangrene that is gang-culture and purge our society of its undesirable elements.

This generation of arrogant thugs, these ignorant, intellectually challenged cavemen with no respect for the society they live in, who somehow believe they are significant because they carry weapons and threaten violence on the innocent, the defenceless and the vulnerable... need to be steadily and progressively removed from our society and to that end, the PDC would introduce a law outlawing gangs and belonging to a gang.

We would also ban gangster behaviour; hooded tops, happy-slapping and any other anti-social behaviour that prevents ordinary citizens from going about their lives as they see fit without the constant threat of violence and to enforce these measures we would create a special task-force with specific orders to target and dismantle these gangs one after the other and process their criminal leaders out of the system.

———

Not so long ago, celebrated musician Gary Numan, Gemma, his wife, and their two young daughters were confronted by a gang of boys between 12 and 14 who surrounded them and began shouting obscenities at Gemma about what they wanted to do to her, in front of her children; that is not acceptable and that is the kind of insidious behaviour we need to put a stop to before it establishes itself.

...but worse still, in a recent case two fourteen year olds and a sixteen year old were convicted for kicking a homeless person to death...for what...?, for a 'dare'. That is the level of intelligence we are going to have to deal with.

———

David Cameron, in a feeble attempt to snare young votes, cynically announced that youngsters who wear hoodies were just being defensive.

Of course they were being defensive; the reason they wear their hoodies in the first place is because they are cowards and want to hide their identities while they commit all sorts of crime. We cannot turn a blind eye to this obvious threat. These hoods are a menace; they cover a multitude of sins and that is why the PDC would look into banning them.

David Cameron also made an election pledge to jail any under-18 who carried a knife but this was overturned by Ken Clarke who said it was 'un-British'.

Knife crime subsequently went up another 10%

Ken Clarke needs to be retired, the sooner the better. His betrayal of Margaret Thatcher aside, the man is a dinosaur hopelessly out of touch and out of step with the country on every issue he tackles. EU, Justice etc

---

Addendum; the most recent development of gangs gang-raping young girls as young as 12 years old, to initiate them or punish them for whatever reason should not and would not be tolerated by the PDC. In fact, we would target this abusive behaviour as a priority and the perpetrators would be held to account **NO MATTER THEIR AGE**.

Guns;

The PDC would introduce a blanket ban on all guns and firearms apart from those destined for the Military and specialised Government Agencies who would still have to combat elements of organised crime.

We would also ban the production, the sale and the import of weapons – even replicas and toys; who wants a society with any un-necessary guns in it?, and as a reminder, those who contravene these rules would be liable to a Category Two criminal charge.

This rule would of course exclude our Military contracts.

Petty theft and violence;

The young engage in robbery, burglary, car theft, joyriding and violence because they know they will not be punished if they get caught. However, I believe that if parents knew that their offspring risked facing a real deterrent if they were caught, they would do more to stop them.

The PDC would introduce three stages of prosecution to counteract this behaviour –

1) a stern letter delivered in person to the parents personally (with signature) warning of the consequences of any repeat behaviour
2) community service, shaming the youths in fluorescent jackets in front of their peers and finally
3) boot-camp (see previous chapter)

———

We should not accept that the Emergency Services;

- Ambulances,
- the Fire Service and
- Hospital ER Services

...are abused either, by violent or drunken morons; from hoax calls to stone throwing to actual physical violence and aiming lasers at planes (these tend to be adolescents but not always)

———

Other theft;

We need to crack down on all the petty thieving that goes on, and the PDC would do that through a tougher justice system but there are several categories that we would prioritise; we would start by seeking out

- the immoral metal thieves who jammy memorial plaques off of monuments and war memorials to sell for scrap
- those who steal the lead off of church roofs etc... and
- those who steal the cables and metal from train tracks

The above would all be done in conjunction with a tightening of the rules concerning scrap-metal dealers.

Solutions –

- plaques could be made of a composite material that mimics metal

- roofs could be electrified with a low voltage to prevent petty criminals from stealing the lead...and
- the copper cables on train lines could be replaced with fibre-optic cables to discourage the metal thieves (The French have opted for this solution)

The PDC would also target the thieves who drill through the petrol tanks of decent people's cars to drain their petrol and address the problem of rip-off builders who prey on the vulnerable and the elderly. The decent, honest people of this country have had enough.

———

Home;

Burglary / Defence of the home –

These days, the dice seem to be loaded against honest law-abiding citizens who should have the right to legally defend themselves and their property from the abuse of mindless and thieving thugs.

The PDC would attempt to reverse this trend and rid this country of all those who are making the lives of decent, honest, law-abiding citizens a misery.

Of course, citizens should not take the law into their own hands when an intruder enters their home but clarification is needed as to what their rights are.

We need a law that clarifies the fact that you, as a home-owner should be able to defend your home from intruders and while exempting you from prosecution – up to the gate of your home.

I would not support people having guns but maybe we could introduce a reduced-voltage tazer-style system for home-use as a deterrent.

Have-a-go heroes in the street should also be exempt from prosecution after investigation of the incident to avoid abuse...and companies and public officials - including bullying energy providers – who have policies in place that include the threat to break into peoples' homes to read meters would have to rethink these policies as only legally authorised entry - with a Police escort - would be allowed.

The PDC would also look into setting up capture-homes rigged with undetectable smart water to snare burglars – like bait cars...and one final note; any burglaries that occur in December - which targeted the theft of people's festive preparations and children's presents - would be subject to an additional sanction on top of the mandatory sentence.

Arrest in the home –

An Englishman's home should be his castle except when the police have proof that a criminal is being harboured there – or the social services have proof that a child is being abused within its walls.

If the authorities only have an allegation about a person with no obvious or tangible proof, that person should not be woken up in the middle of the night and arrested in front of his/her family, thereby creating an instantaneous tabloid story.

Instead, the person should be quietly called into the police station at a reasonable hour to make a statement in response to the allegation, during which time his/her anonymity and his/her human rights should be respected.

Thereafter, if any proof of wrong-doing is uncovered and an arrest is made, then and only then should the story break in the news...

- too many innocent people are having their lives ruined over false accusations and the subsequent dragging of their names through the mud in the tabloids so that the papers can increase their distribution –

...and even that is too soon in some cases, as people who are ultimately not convicted of the crime have their lives turned upside down nevertheless, by the adverse publicity which of course in turn fuels the compensation claims that have to be paid out subsequently for wrongful arrest.

Hopefully the Leveson inquiry into the culture, practices and ethics of the British press will go some way towards addressing these delicate and complex matters, by introducing guidelines and setting some boundaries in this regard but as that report has yet to be published I cannot comment.

Alcohol abuse / Booze culture;

On the one hand, we need to be able to trust and respect the Police – this needs work - and on the other we need less 'attitude' and more understanding from the current generation of young people who have grown up

- without any real parenting
- with no discipline
- with no morals
- with no boundaries
- and no respect for society or their elders

These youngsters need to understand that the police are just doing their job – to protect and serve – and that they are human beings just like the rest of us.

Now, a lot of the time it is not the fault of these youngsters. It is the fault of their parents or at least of the society we live in which has allowed parental responsibility to ebb away in favour of the **Nanny State**, but because of

- the rise of feminism (women / mothers leaving the home to work),
- the health and safety rules
- the political correctness rules (restricting discipline)
- and the fact that many of them are no more than children themselves

...today's parents have simply abdicated their responsibility leaving the Nanny-State to take over. They simply rely on the teachers to do this for them when their children are in school (educate them, teach them respect, about morality and give them boundaries) and the police and social workers to do the same when they are out on the street.

Why do the young dislike the Police so much? – Because (without going into the criminal aspect of the matter) the Police try to impose discipline and boundaries on them that their parents have failed to do, in the home.

———

Booze drinking procedure / penalties under the PDC –

Teenagers

- arrested (hand-cuffed and zip-locked at the ankles)
- taken to special facility 'known as the tank' where medical staff and guards would take care of them
- parents or guardians would then be called
- after an overnight stay, the parents would come and pick them up and would have to sign them out

First time offender - parents or guardian would receive a warning

Second time offender – the parents would receive a fine or a percentage of their benefits would be withheld

Third time offender - the teenager would be kept in custody and sent to a 'brat-farm' for a period of 're-training'.

Over eighteen

- arrested (hand-cuffed and zip-locked at the ankles)
- taken to special facility 'known as the tank' where medical staff and guards would take care of them
- a family member or friend would be called

- after an overnight stay, a family member or friend would come and pick them up – signing them out

First time – warning

Second time – fine or a percentage of their benefits withheld

Third time – handed over to the judicial system

Cautions and fines;

We also need to review the concept of fines. I have never understood why people, who have been arrested for stealing because they have no money, are fined MORE money.

Surely, if they had money to pay fines they wouldn't have had to steal in the first place?

Cultural issues;

We need to find out why men, particularly Asian men – in the Rochdale and Oxford areas - are grooming young girls as young as twelve to be used as sex objects. There must be a fundamental integration problem here, because these people have brought their archaic traditions of arranged marriage to our country - and all that that entails concerning the rituals of imposed virginity and respect etc – and yet they treat the indigenous young women of this country with absolutely no respect whatsoever.

Eight Asian men were recently convicted of grooming 47 young women for sex, the youngest of those girls being 13yrs old but the spineless justice system, fearful of upsetting this particular ethnic minority, found that there was no link between the crimes and the ethnicity of the perpetrators.

How short-sighted is that? If there was no ethnic element to these horrible crimes, why did these men not choose girls from their own community or girls from another ethnic origin?

Of course there is an ethnic element but because the British establishment – the politicians and the judges - lack any moral fibre they have once again brushed it under the carpet to avoid any potential conflict, reprisal or racial tension.

This is another example of the political correctness paranoia that reigns in this country where nobody dare tell the truth for fear of being labelled a racist or whatever.

Imagine for one moment, if the situation was reversed and these criminals were gangs of young white men preying on vulnerable young Muslim girls. The bleeding-heart clubs would be lining up to demand justice...so why is it any different this way around?

It is time we removed the blinkers imposed on us by this political correctness gone mad, because it has reached a point where we – as a nation – are too afraid to condemn criminal activity because we don't want to be seen as bigots.

This might be culturally sensitive but justice has no colour, no creed and no culture.

It applies to everyone equally without exception...otherwise there is no point to it.

The truth is, that this group of criminals (who treat their own wives and daughters like second-class citizens through the perpetuation of the patriarchal rules handed down to them by their ancestors) consider that ordinary British women and young girls are immoral harlots, no matter their age (13 is not too young in their culture) and therefore they feel justified in abusing them in this way.

Some have argued that there is no correlation between these crimes and the ethnic background of the perpetrators; I disagree; these men do not attack or groom Asian girls because their families all know each other in the close-knit Asian communities and they would not want word to get back to their parents...

...and to confirm the theory, here are the names of those criminals prosecuted in the most recent high-profile grooming cases; their ages range from 19 to 55yrs old;

Burnley case -
Amjad Hussain
Shahid Hussain
Tanveer Butt

Carlisle case -
Azad Miah

Derby case -
Abid Saddique
Mohammed Llaqat

Oxford case -
Akhtar Dogar
Anjum Dogar
Assad Hussain
Kamar Jamil
Zeeshan Ahmed

Bassam Karrar from Eritrea
Mohammed Karrar from Eritrea

Rochdale case -
Abdul Aziz
Abdul Qayyum
Abdul Rauf
Adil Khan
Hamid Safi

Kabeer Hassan
Llaquat Shah
Mohammed Amin
Mohammed Sajid
Shabir Ahmed

Telford case one;
(...during which the defendants described their victims
aged between 13 and 17 as 'worthless whores, slags and sluts')

Abdul Rouf
Ahdel Ali
Mahroof Khan
Mohammed Ali Sultan
Mohammed Islam Choudhrey
Mohammed Younis
Noshad Hussain
Tanveer Ahmed
Mubarak Ali

Telford case two -
Adil Saleem
Amar Hussain
Amer Islam Choudhrey
Jahbar Rafiq
Shamrez Rachid

Now nobody is suggesting that this kind of reprobate behaviour is exclusive to the Pakistani community – the human gene-pool is full of sadistic degenerates of all nationalities - but there is clearly a deep-rooted psychological or cultural issue within the Pakistani community which pre-disposes these men to act in this disgusting and heinous way.

———

The PDC would address the eradication of these twisted cultural values by helping community elders / leaders to weed out the wayward minority among their older citizens, some even second-generation Britons.

We would also encourage parents of the younger generation to educate their sons more convincingly in areas such as respect and morality and request that they inform their young men of the consequences of their actions should they engage in such despicable activity, under the new, tighter PDC Justice system (Category Two + castration)

The role of a government is to protect the young, the vulnerable and the innocent who rely on it to provide a safe, stable environment in which to evolve.

Ref: Documentary about 'Britain's Sex Gangs' on Channel 4

That said; we should not lose sight of the Russian and the other Eastern European mobsters who are trafficking east-European women into this country to be used as prostitutes as part of their criminal operations either. (Drugs, guns etc)

We also need to tackle the gangs of Romanian gypsy mafia scamming the cash-machines on our High-streets. Recent Police figures estimate that over 90% of these crimes are carried out by Romanian gangs.

Foreign criminals;

The PDC would contact every country and clarify the existing Extradition / Deportation agreements with each of them (taking into account civil rights, human rights, voodoo, honour killing and forced marriage) while enforcing and extending the EU Prisoner Transfer Agreement already in place.

We would then look into setting up a system where a foreign national who commits a crime in this country would be charged and prosecuted in this country.

However, if an agreement could be reached with his or her native country which allowed him/her to serve their punishment in that country with a guarantee that it would indeed be carried out properly - together with an agreement that the UK government would be informed if that person's situation changed - we would be prepared to send him/her home to carry out his/her sentence.

If no such agreement was in place or if no agreement could be reached, the person would serve his/her time in a British prison and be deported immediately upon his/her release directly from the prison gate to the airport..

NB - Deportation proceedings would be started as soon as the sentence had been pronounced and not upon the prisoner's release to avoid them disappearing during a long drawn out appeals process.

———

The world is a violent and dangerous place and because we have relinquished control over our borders as part of the EU Treaty - which is expanding inexorably - we have naively opened our doors to most of Europe and almost all of its criminal population.

This is a dream situation for criminals; being able to pass from one country to the next - without any kind of control or any possibility of the host country refusing access - and the forthcoming arrival to our shores - in 2014 - of thousands more Romanians and Bulgarians on top of the heavy influx of Polish immigrants that we are still trying to absorb and assimilate has to be addressed.

That is why I believe Britain needs to strengthen its justice system to include a deterrent that is universally recognised by criminals from every country – one that everyone understands without the need for explanation or translators.

Therefore, under the PDC, every foreigner arriving at our borders by plane or by boat would be handed a leaflet with pictograms explaining our laws (as set out previously) in easily understandable terms and underlined with the consequences awaiting those who transgressed them.

Why should we do this? I hear the bleeding-heart liberals and the annoying civil liberties organisations crying out.

Well, the answer is simple; in the last five years, (since I began researching this manifesto) the UK has arrested almost 28000 Romanians amongst others, for various offences and has also had to prosecute;

- a Romanian gypsy who scammed £10 million in benefits,
- gangs from Iran and Nigeria smuggling illegal immigrants,
- paedophiles from Somalia
- rapists from Hungary, Jamaica, Romania and Lithuania,
- Romanian and Polish gangs (for stealing from cash-points and thieving metal),
- thousands of foreign shoplifters
- three Polish people for murdering a young woman (Catherine Wells-Burr) and leaving her body in a flaming car

...and murders committed by various people from the following countries;

Albania – Bangladesh - Czech Republic – Eritrea – India – Iran – Iraqi – Kosovo – Latvia – Lithuania – Moldova – Poland – Rwanda - Slovakia...and Zimbabwe

...not forgetting all the illegal immigrants and the growing number of those who contract into sham-marriages.

Indeed, recent figures show that we are convicting up to 50 foreigners a week, so surely we have to have the measures in place to counteract, to combat or to punish those who threaten the lives and the choices of the indigenous peace-loving majority.

———

...and finally, one last point; during the riots of 2010 there were over forty different nationalities involved; too many to mention them all; so surely this

indicates that there is an argument for foreigners of all nationalities to be better acquainted with our laws.

———

Late note; thanks to the EU, we now have a wave of Romanian street beggars and cash-point muggers roaming around the streets of London; children organised by their mothers to beg and steal. We need to take a good hard look at this problem both from the child labour standpoint (exploitation of children) and parental responsibility perspective.

I suggest an initiative similar to the one adopted by the Italians – where, after it was found that Romanians were the cause of much of the crime being committed, they were rounded up and automatically deported.

———

Courts, Lawyers and legal costs -

Lawyers;

What makes me uncomfortable about lawyers – is that they learn about the law, not to respect it or enforce it, but to manipulate it and find ways around it.

Now that is a paradox if ever there was one.

The people who know most about the law, the people who should know better, having studied it for years and taken the Hippocratic Oath now spend all their time chasing compensation payouts.

Whatever happened to honour and integrity and morality and upholding the law...rather than constantly undermining it?

We need to do something about the proliferation of ambulance-chasing legal-practices and the constantly increasing litigious culture introduced by the New Labour party.

Lawyers are supposed to uphold the letter of the law and as a citizen of this country, we would all like to believe that those who work in the legal system are the most honest and upstanding amongst us, but as we see on a daily basis, they too are forever finding ways of getting around it.

This is another example of why the British people have lost confidence in its institutions; to them, the whole judicial process appears to be riddled with corruption, lies and deception and the recent case of a lawyer involved in a £600K VAT fraud does nothing to dispel those suspicions.

...and if more proof was needed...in Scotland; they actually have an official political party called the 'Scotland against crooked lawyers' party.

What does that tell you?

Now, in William Shakespeare's Richard 3rd, the king suggested 'the first thing we do is kill all the lawyers'.

Of course, that would be a little too dramatic in 21st century Britain but if the PDC was elected into office we would immediately appoint an independent jurist to look into the loopholes and address some of the legal trickery currently being exploited by all these unscrupulous lawyers.

Costs –

Reflection;

There are four distinct areas of British life where people are still clinging onto the past and the privileges that come with it;

- **The hereditary grandees** *and the entitled gentry of the House of Lords who have haunted its walls for generation after generation feeding insatiably off the public purse*

- **The diplomatic corps;** *whose status and reputation depend largely on such shallow, ego-flattering criteria as the size of the ambassador's residence and the number of outrageously expensive parties they can host to impress their pompous, sycophantic peers; all of which, of course, are organised at great expense to the British tax-payer.*
- **The Military**; *where the top-brass still enjoy any number of grace and favour privileges, many of which pre-date the colonial wars... and finally*
- *Those at the very top of the* **legal profession** *who have been exploiting their position of privilege for centuries.*

Now I know that British people are reluctant to change - and especially those people who are accustomed to a life of privilege - but the simple fact is, that the British economy can no longer afford to support the quirks or the perceived privileges of times gone by.

The elitist mentality of entitlement tied to the class system – which incidentally, is a British idiosyncrasy that doesn't exist anywhere else in the world - no longer has tenure in the 21ˢᵗ century; the landowners, the aristocrats and the military families have had the run of this country for far too long and unless we shatter that particular glass ceiling, British society will never change or evolve.

Only by putting the class-system behind us will we be able to move forward because as long as we have a minority of 'haves' (as represented by the four categories above, though not exclusively) creaming off the cash and ruling over a majority of 'have-nots' (the rest of the British population) who have no choice but to shut up and pay up through their ever-increasing tax bills the potential for conflict will always exist.

It is time to get real; it is time to share the wealth more evenly; it is time to move into the 21ˢᵗ century.

The PDC would want to modernise and reform all areas of British life and one area that would need immediate attention is the legal system which is one of the most expensive legal systems in the whole world.

Now needless to say, I have already addressed the justice system itself in an earlier chapter so here I would like to concentrate on the financial issues that surround 'obtaining justice' in this country.

The British legal system – although respected around the world - is an archaic institution with an anachronistic mentality of aristocratic privilege and entitlement.

It is one of the last bastions of a bygone age which is held together by an out-dated hierarchy of wealthy scholars who retain a deluded concept of pseudo-superiority over the rest of us, all of which is anchored in a world that no longer exists.

Now I can understand tradition and legitimacy through the passage of time but I find it a little disconcerting – in the 21st century - to see those in the legal system still clinging on so desperately to the past - and the privileges / advantages that it represented.

In fact, it is almost comical to see them today, still wearing their powdered wigs and their school-teacher robes, doing whatever they can to retain their authority and hold onto the last vestiges of a time when British justice really stood for something.

Sadly, that was another time as we all know, and in the interceding years, the reputation of our legal system has been regularly tarnished, battered and bruised by any number of cases where the search for justice seems to have been usurped by the lure of monetary gain.

Now this is not a suggestion that members of the legal profession are doing anything wrong on a criminal level; it is a suggestion that the priority, the focus of our lawyers has shifted from upholding the law for everyone - as it should be - to making a conscious decision on whether or not to take on cases depending on how lucrative they might be... in order to make as much money as possible for the partners of their particular practice.

The justice-system has simply become a business; one of legalised extortion where clever legal-experts have - by taking advantage of their unregulated position - been able to elaborate a complex financial framework so opaque and so complicated - that it is beyond the comprehension of most ordinary citizens, making it impossible for those citizens to question its legality or its authenticity when they are presented with a bill for services rendered.

Solicitors, barristers and lawyers regularly charge hundreds of pounds for a phone call and then charge hundreds more to put that same phone-call down in writing, clearly abusing their clients' trust and their lack of expertise in the matter. One client in a recent case was presented with a bill for £200K before his case had even gotten to court.

I simply cannot see how a barrister or QC could possibly justify charging upwards of £1000 an hour for his services.

That is simply outrageous...and who <u>hasn't</u> heard a story of a divorcing couple left penniless by their respective legal representation whose fees were so exorbitant that they bordered on extortion, which is quite ironic really considering the circumstances and the people involved.

———

Greed is a modern-day plague that affects us all every day as we go about our lives; we are all human and that is why I believe it is time for the politicians to step in and call a halt to these abusive practices by regulating the financial side of this, the last remaining unregulated profession. We need transparency in this sector just like we do in many others because in any context where position and money are part of the equation, the potential for human failing is omnipresent.

Naturally, this would not infringe on the independence of the justice system but hopefully it would protect the citizens of this country from the financial cosh that they have been subjected to for decades by unscrupulous lawyers and barristers.

———

I believe that any sector that relies on the ignorance of others to thrive – especially a sector like the legal system where a measure of trust has to apply because of the very nature of the work - should not be allowed to continue unregulated, and that is why the PDC would order a comprehensive review of legal costs including a breakdown of every fee with a justification for its application; the people of this country should not have to bankrupt themselves and sell their homes in order to get justice, as is currently the case.

The PDC would also look into imposing an upper limit or a fixed fee for each category of misdemeanour (civil and criminal) in order to encourage competition between practices; divorce, death (wills) and house-buying should not be so expensive; it's not that complicated.

We would also look into bringing the cost of running a legal practice and chambers into line with reality. Those costs too are outrageous…

…and finally, we would look to develop and encourage the internet services which allow ordinary people to by-pass all the costly legal protocols that they currently have to pay for…with just a few clicks.

———

That said; this is not a witch-hunt against the legal profession; several other sectors including the banking sector, local councils, Westminster and the medical profession where doctors salaries are currently racing ahead, would all need to be addressed and reviewed.

———

Secondly…we cannot allow a two-tiered justice system to develop in this country where the rich and famous – and it is only the rich and famous who can afford it - pay out huge sums of money for super-injunctions to prevent the details of their sordid behaviour from being exposed to the public – just so that they can protect their brand, their marketing potential and commercial interests.

If these people were worried about their reputations or wanted to protect their families' feelings from the glare of public scrutiny then they should have thought about that before engaging in any inappropriate behaviour.

The justice system cannot be seen to be condoning deceit (partners and public), lies (partners) and manipulation of the truth (partners, public and third parties).

And finally; any case brought before the court over an amount of money which is less than the cost of holding the court session would be fast-tracked and dealt with by a magistrate.

Legal aid –

We spend £2billion a year on Legal Aid, much of it being exploited by imaginative and unscrupulous lawyers.

In fact, we now spend as much on legal-aid as we do on prisons – this has to be reviewed.

The PDC would look into the possibility of introducing a fixed-fee index for legal aid cases in order to avoid the current tendency to abuse the system by drawing out cases for longer than is necessary.

Compensation culture –

Firstly, I have to say that I find the compensation culture most distasteful. This 'screw the system any way you can' culture - imported from the USA - is all about sponging and victimhood and making a fast buck and it is bleeding our schools, our hospitals, our businesses and our local councils dry.

But that is not all; because of the compensation culture everyday insurance policies are being driven up and up making life more expensive for everyone, making it harder for the honest, working-class families up and down the country to make ends meet every month and for what...?

Greed, *the one word, the one common denominator, the one recurring theme that keeps coming up time and again, the more I research this book.*

Whatever happened to taking personal responsibility for one's actions?

Whatever happened to 'accidents happen'?

Why is everything that happens these days somebody else's fault?

Has the Nanny State invaded our lives and our psyche so completely and so deeply that we are now dependent on its handout-mentality for our every need?

This is all so depressing and the saddest part has to be that our Police and Armed Forces have now jumped on the gravy train too, tarnishing their reputation and abandoning their morality - and their legendary integrity - to the cult of greed along with the rest of the country.

The PDC would get rid of this compensation culture which is eating away at society like a cancer, and in doing so it would free up the courts for the real trials, so as to prosecute those who really deserve to have their actions scrutinised and sanctioned.

That would be the role of the Law Courts under the PDC; it would not be to reward careless employees or opportunist lawyers out to make a fast-buck.

Of course, in cases of gross negligence, compensation would still be considered but the culture of claiming compensation for an everyday accident that could have easily been avoided with a little more care and attention would no longer be a 'priority' under a PDC administration... and as part of the crack-down, we would also remove the possibility for people to bring stupid or frivolous cases to court, funded by the tax-payer (legal-aid) ...though if they so wished, these people could still bring a private case to court, as long as they paid for it themselves.

———

Comment;

Isn't it about time that we stopped sketching criminals in court?

This is the 21ˢᵗ century; we have high-definition cameras, we can stream live events from one side of the planet and back again in seconds and yet the British legal system still insists that we have artists' impressions of court proceedings drawn with crayons!

Surely we can improve on this while still respecting the law or is this just another example of a system that refuses to modernise?

———

Insurance fraud -

The compensation culture that has swept over here from the USA - which taps into the abandonment of responsibility ethos currently plaguing our society - has unfortunately exacerbated the natural greed of our adult population.

We have all become potential frauds now, as our first reflex whenever anything happens is 'who can I blame, who can I sue and how much compensation can I get?'

And what is worse; everybody is in on the deal.

Garages, break-down firms, the police and even the insurance companies themselves receive 'referral' fees for giving the details of accident victims to lawyers who then bombard those people with calls offering to represent them - while frequently encouraging them to exaggerate their injuries in order to increase their claim.

The idea is that everyone wins, because everyone gets a piece of the pie... but in fact, not everyone wins; the poor motorist, who always seems to be the loser, has seen his premium jump 30% in the past two years alone in order to pay for all these claims.

———

The astonishing boom in compensation claims for injuries allegedly sustained in road accidents is nothing less than a racket cooked up to enrich unscrupulous lawyers and their dishonest clients.

Figures show that the UK is now the 'whip-lash' capital of Europe with personal injury claims for whiplash being recorded in 78% of accidents costing £2.2 billion a year and adding up to £118 to everybody's annual insurance policy.

———

It is outrageous, the greed that now pervades our society but it is not only car-accident fraud that has fuelled the compensation culture.

It might have started the ball rolling but it has now engendered a whole raft of new fraudulent activity - from fraudulent house-insurance claims and false-burglaries to work-place accidents and often banal life-accidents, all of which the ambulance-chasing lawyers deliberately exploit in order to make a fortune for themselves (they wouldn't do it otherwise).

Combine that with the fact that fraudulent benefit scams are on the rise and you see that our society has become one big fraudulent mess.

Why is it that every aspect of life has become a racket?

The patient UK is ill and in dire need of a transfusion of good, of better education, of better parenting but most importantly of a better, stronger and more effective and efficient justice system.

We need stronger penalties for insurance fraud to reduce the temptation which would then reduce the premiums and we need good, honest lawyers who uphold the law rather than looking for ways of getting around it.

The PDC would clamp down on the 'cloning-of-car-number-plates' fraud and the countless 'crash-for-cash' rear-ending scams...and we would come down hard with a Category Two penalty for anyone involved in extreme cases of insurance fraud.

We would also overhaul the small-print in insurance policies and demand it be written in decent sized characters. Insurance companies seem to be trying any way they can not to pay up, even when claims are made in good faith. That is wrong and bordering on fraud.

Those insurance companies who deliberately make it hard to claim and do all they can not to pay out on genuine policies by using every trick in the book – and are proved to be doing so deliberately and on a regular basis – would have their directors prosecuted and their trading licences revoked.

I am sick of these companies cold-calling members of the public and pestering them for their business but then refusing to pay out on policies when they are genuine claims, citing obscure clauses in the small print of their contracts; transparency is the only way; opacity and underhand practices would not be tolerated.

Identity –

A criminal's identity should not be hidden behind unnecessary legal jargon – irrespective of age or position other than those involved in sensitive rape and paedophilia cases as mentioned previously.

Victims would always be protected but their aggressors and everybody else convicted of crime would be named and shamed.

It is a delicate issue but in this changing world where criminals are getting younger and younger the PDC would lift the ban on revealing the identity of children who commit serious offences; if they can do the crime, they must do the time and take the shame like any other criminal.

TV Licences –

More than 3000 people a week are prosecuted for not having a TV licence – that is 1 in 10 cases that currently clutter up our justice system. The PDC would ease that load by cancelling the TV license in favour of a screen tax on every home which would be added to the council tax and used in a transparent fashion in the investment in local cultural and sporting activity.

This measure would be introduced in conjunction with the dismantling of the BBC (see Media chapter)

Sentencing –

Another anomaly to be rectified is the right for a convicted criminal not to appear at his or her sentencing procedure. Under the PDC, he or she would be made to appear, to receive his or her sentence in person; enough of this bleeding-heart liberalism.

The PDC would also step up the enforcement of fine payments as the outstanding balance of fines-unpaid is unacceptable. If we have a system of monetary penalty then it has to be enforced or an alternative solution has to be made clear at the time of sentencing to encourage prompt payment.

Early release / probation –

Recent figures have shown that the Probation Service has consistently failed to reform hardened criminals and that over 200000 crimes were committed in 2012 by people under their supervision. This included 69000 violent crimes, 4300 robberies, 20000 burglaries, 10000 sex crimes and at least 45000 thefts.

Therefore, under the PDC, there would be no early-release and no probation.

Criminals would have to carry out their full sentence spending the last six months of that sentence following a social re-integration programme within the penal sphere.

Re-offending is an on-going problem - and will probably always exist - but maybe these people would think twice about re-offending having completed their full sentence, knowing what they would be going back to if caught again.

———

Cars –

Under the PDC there would be a Zero tolerance policy for drivers; no alcohol whatsoever.

Drivers who did drink and proceeded to cause a non-fatal accident would have their licenses revoked permanently and receive a Category Three conviction. (upper scale)

In a fatal accident, a manslaughter charge would be enforced. Category Two.

Those who kill by accident - while sober - would receive a Category Three conviction. (lower scale)

Young drivers – under 25 - who have no licence, no insurance and no respect for anybody or anything...and who kill innocent people – whether drunk or not - would face an automatic Category Two conviction.

The PDC would also impose <u>and enforce</u> a complete ban on phones and texting behind the wheel; anybody involved in an accident through speaking on a phone or texting would receive an automatic 6 months ban...plus an automatic manslaughter charge resulting in a Category Two conviction if the accident involved a person's death.

For those caught throwing rubbish out of a car, an immediate on-the-spot fine would be imposed and a point would be deducted from their license.

Each police force would be allowed to use bait cars to catch car-thieves just as they might use bait houses to catch burglars.

Additional penalties would be introduced for those who drive without a licence, insurance or tax.

Psychologists say that the male brain matures at 25 – so to save their hearing, we would suggest blocking music systems at a reasonable level. Hugely dissuasive fines would be imposed on those who modified or customised the volume levels of their sound-systems, similar to those imposed for fiddling with the mileage-counter.

Travellers -

The whole traveller lifestyle is based on marginalising themselves from mainstream society and cheating the system.

These people don't give birth in hospital, their children (when they can avoid it) don't go to school...and as adults they squat land to which they have no rights. They appropriate other people's property, they scavenge what they want for free and they do everything in their power to avoid paying taxes.

Indeed, they freely admit that they are thieves and marginals but travellers are outcasts by choice...because they simply refuse to recognise the law and they don't respect or care for anybody who is not one of their own; that is why they are constantly on their guard, constantly suspicious.

Sadly, much like religion, this is yet another case of people with an archaic mentality that has its roots and its traditions anchored firmly in the past refusing to live in the 21ˢᵗ century but - because of this closed mindset and the fact that travellers live in secretive, insular communities - the mainstream population mistrusts them just as much as they mistrust the rest of the population which inevitably leads to conflict.

This is because, while the public respects the rights of these people to live as they see fit, they see it as wrong and unfair that the rights of those who camp illegally on ground that does not belong to them should trump those of the land-owner and the innocent, law-abiding villagers who live nearby; there cannot be one rule for one and another rule for another.

The travellers have chosen a nomadic existence; they have chosen not to integrate and more importantly, they have chosen not to participate in the local community in any way or form...so why should the tax-payer and local communities create purpose-built sites for them to live on, when they themselves refuse to pay anything towards it?

Life is all about give and take and for peace and harmony to prevail between the general public and these travelling communities, it is only right and fair that they pay both their taxes and the costs of the services they feel entitled to, just like everybody else.

Therefore, in the interests of fairness, I believe that we should impose legality on the travelling community to make them abide by the law... and to do this the PDC would create a dedicated tax-squad mandated to recover any outstanding tax from the travellers who, up until now have used every trick in the book to avoid paying.

It is also worth mentioning here, that while these people don't often pay tax, they have absolutely no problem in claiming any benefits they feel entitled to.

...and as for the established camp-sites - set up and paid for by local tax-payers - maybe we could organise a system of pre-paid credit for the water and electricity supply to avoid any further bad-debt from people who just want to take from society without giving anything back.

NB - Legalising their situation would also mean making these people aware that knocking their women about is not acceptable – and that if they continue to do so then they would have to face the consequences of the new justice system just like everybody else.

The PDC would also look into new laws targeting bare-knuckle fighting and dog fighting.

Animal rights –

The PDC would have no problem with people who wanted to air their views. It is and would be their right as law-abiding citizens in a democracy.

However, as with the radical religious groups, there has to be a line.

The PDC would not tolerate;

- threats of physical violence or
- threats against a person's life
- or the threat to dig up a person's deceased loved-ones from their graves

Those who threaten and hound people to this extent, to within an inch of their lives should be met with the full force of the law.

Thugs and extremists would have no place in our society whether they be religious radicals or Animal Rights activists.

———

Divorce –

Pre-nuptial agreements should be rolled-out as standard practice.

If there is no pre-nuptial agreement in place, divorce settlements should be judged pro-rata to earnings made <u>during the marriage</u> and <u>not</u> on what was made before.

How I hate to see rapacious legal teams egging on vulnerable spouses to tear chunks out of each other as they fight for a greater share of their communal assets.

It's unethical and sullies the noble status of one of the pillars of our society.

We also need to look into the dirty tricks used by women to prevent fathers getting access to their children; often encouraged by their divorce lawyers –

- they claim that they have been abused,
- they claim poverty when they are actually financially secure,
- or they quit their jobs deliberately so as to screw every pound out of the departing spouse

That is all unacceptable.

Guilty until proven innocent seems to be the dictum for fathers in the British Family Law Courts.

That will have to change; the balance needs to be redressed.

Maybe we should also add a grand-parent clause to divorce settlements to allow grandparent's access to their grandchildren; as long as they have been vetted and have not been involved - in any negative way - in the child's life.

NB – the PDC would outlaw any immoral practices like 'honey-trapping' which is no more than 'entrapment'.

Streets –

The PDC would ban begging, spitting, urinating and littering in the street...and enforce it.

This would also include opportunist windscreen-cleaners at traffic lights.

We would also introduce a ban on hoodies and other similar clothes that allow people to hide their identity in public...and by the same token, we would also ban the hire and sale of official uniforms as fancy-dress costumes which has led to criminals posing as policemen, stopping cars and threatening people, or entering people's houses dressed as firemen / electricity meter readers in order to rob them.

We would also review the laws concerning stalkers and paparazzi.

...and finally, we would make squatting a criminal matter and not a civil one – so that police could intervene and evict undesirable elements.

London –

We need more integrity, both moral and financial...

London should no longer be considered a haven for the world's rich oligarchs; a place when they can come and stay with impunity while investing their ill-gotten gains buying up the major part of our capital's prime real-estate.

We need to stop the double standards.

...and finally;

In order to get the PDC message across – we would commission a series of ad-campaigns to be screened on a regular basis **before the watershed** – teaching young people about respect; respect for the elderly, respect for the police and respect for the emergency services, and informing them - and warning them - of the sanctions that will have been put in place in the new justice system.

And **after the watershed** – we would commission another series of informative advertisements warning drink-drivers, paedophiles, people traffickers, drug pushers, burglars and rapists of all ages of the new laws and the consequences they would face if they were caught committing these crimes.

Then once a week – as proof that we meant business - we would name and shame those caught with a photo (mug-shot) – e.g. –

This is John Smith from Solihull in Birmingham;
He was grooming young girls on the street
He raped 27 of them using his flash car
and offering them drugs and money

He has now been convicted,
along with his accomplices AB and CD
under the government's strict new law enforcement policy

All three have been castrated to avoid any repeat offending
and are now serving out their mandatory Group Two sentences
in various Hard Labour Facilities

We might also commission another series for cowboy tradesmen, street thugs, muggers, rioters and looters who have no respect for the law or people's private property.

...and then another for insurance fraudsters, especially those who drive without insurance or tax.

A running total of those caught would then
appear for each category.

———

These measures might appear harsh and even morally unacceptable to the lily-livered but citizens of Britain, keep in mind at all times – the 30 years that have just gone...and the 30 years to come.

New Labour introduced 3600 new offences during their time in office, many of which penalise honest, law-abiding citizens. The PDC would have a legal expert go through each one and get rid of any considered inappropriate, invasive or anti-constitutional.

We would also appoint an **anti-exploitation minister** to work in tandem with the justice minister – to deal exclusively with human traffickers, black-market employment and immoral landlords.

———

Looking forward to the 22nd century (if the death penalty is not an option)

As we have yet to set up **convict banishment sites** in a far-flung asteroid colony where we could transport all our unmanageable criminals - as they do in the science-fiction world - why not look into creating an island compound here on earth where all the murderers, the dictators, the drug dealers and the paedophiles from every country could be regrouped.

There would be no internet connection on the island, no computers or contact with the outside world…and no women of course, to avoid these people reproducing…but they could all live together in the freedom of their own island with no chains, no bars and no prison-warders.

They would have to survive through their own toil, crop-growing, farming etc and as people around the world began to respect the law more, for fear of being exiled there; their numbers would inevitably diminish through natural wastage.

There would only be one rule; don't ever try to leave…

…and to enforce that rule, armed guards - provided by every participating nation on a rota system – would be stationed on ships moored a mile off-shore in each direction.

This solution might appear harsh to some but it is nothing new - pirates used to maroon their undesirable companions - and it would instantly reduce the incarceration budgets of every participating country rather significantly.

Possible locations;

- Bouvet Island which is a Norwegian territory in the South Atlantic Ocean known as the most remote and isolated piece of land on the planet. It is currently uninhabited and is 1400 miles from the nearest land mass – Yes, it is covered in glacial ice to some extent for most of the year but it is nevertheless, the ideal place to send all our murderers, despots, drug dealers and paedophiles
- Saint Helena Island (where Napoleon was exiled) is another alternative…
- or Ascension Island

Or maybe we could reach some kind of agreement with Russia to send our worst criminals to Siberia to work there for free, clearing snow.

Or better still, we could develop anti-aggression drugs that could be administered to young thugs and gang-members to address their violent tendencies...or looking even further into the future perhaps we might perfect the science of selective lobotomisation.

Conclusion - There will always be people – in all walks of life – trying to beat the system – it's a facet of human nature but we must make sure that they are few and far between and that those who transgress are punished for their misdeeds.

Here is a sample list of some recent cases that clogged up the justice system and which should never be allowed to happen again

---

- A 10 year old boy was prosecuted for a racist comment in the schoolyard
- A Downs syndrome boy with a mental age of five was prosecuted as a racist
- A judge waived a man's curfew for attacking and injuring people so that he could go on a golfing holiday
- A man was stabbed in the middle of Oxford Street – one of London's busiest streets – at 4.45 PM – he had been charged with gang-raping a young girl but not yet convicted and in an unprovoked, unconnected attack he was stabbed in broad daylight
- A teenage girl was prosecuted for pinging a rival's bra-strap
- Another judge freed a child molester arguing that an eleven year old girl welcomed his advances
- Drug-addicts were offered free tickets to premier league football matches as part of their treatment

- Drugs – it was outrageous that two society-billionaires were let off with a caution for having 2Kg of drugs in their house; when anybody else would have been thrown in prison
- Power / energy companies need to be called to rights – regarding a recent case where they broke into a person's home to install a meter while the person was out – the person came back and didn't know how to use it, leaving him thus without heating, hot water and hot food – it was despicable – and furthermore, he didn't even owe them anything
- The CPS should not be used to deliberate on whether or not a boy threw a snowball at a girl which was one case recently looked at

Meanwhile - the judge who decided that six footballers were not guilty of raping two 12yr olds because the girls 'wanted sex' should be struck off – whether the girls wanted sex or not is not the issue; the legal age for sex is 16 and these men – all much older - should have known better.

———

Terrorism

'Disturbances in society are never more fearful than when those who are stirring up the trouble can use the pretext of religion to mask their true designs'; **Denis Diderot**

We cannot legislate for irrational extremism, fundamentalism and fanaticism but that does not mean that we should live our lives in fear.

We are not bigots in this country, we are not intolerant; in fact, we have done our utmost and more to welcome all cultures to our shores.

However, our patience is now being stretched too far – and if the Islamic community feels it is being targeted in any way then they should do more themselves to weed out the people who are creating this movement of mistrust between our two cultures.

I do understand and sympathise with the frustration of the peaceful elements of our society who feel that they are being victimised by the police and authorities; it is unfortunate for them and for the Muslim community as a whole – but the truth is – the atrocities that have been perpetrated against our citizens have been carried out mainly by young men who have a profile similar to and consistent with a Muslim faith follower.

It is a cliché and again I can understand why the Muslims feel aggrieved about the way that they are targeted and victimised by the rest of society, but unfortunately, the vast majority of terrorists arrested around the world have also been found to be Muslims.

Of course, it is wrong to generalise and the amalgam is too easy to make, but the fact remains that Muslims seem to be the only ones going around the world, threatening death and destruction on anybody who does not believe as they do. (infidels)

Fact – not all Muslims are terrorists –
but all the terrorists currently being sought are Muslims

However, Muslims are not being targeted indiscriminately on any racial witch-hunt – they are just the potential threat at the moment – and if the action being undertaken to protect the citizens of this country and prevent atrocities on the scale of 9/11 and 7/7 creates anger and resentment among the leaders of their community, then they should show us that they are peace-lovers, by preaching peace and harmony, instead of standing on our streets and delivering their anti-British, hate-filled rants full of venomous jibes and threats to kill us all.

All we ever hear about these days – in the media – is 'outraged Muslim leaders' complaining about a variety of so-called blights on their faith.

Well what about outraged British citizens who no longer feel safe in their own country, on their own streets, in their own homes and beds, who are unable to live their lives as they see fit because of the constant threat of terrorism, in airports and train stations etc – and what about the recent incident where – and I quote – 'a Muslim hate-mob hounded four British soldiers out of a house in Windsor, England'.

Then there was the case of Muslim extremists wanting to kidnap a British Muslim soldier and behead him like a pig.

This is intimidation not integration – this is a hardening of attitudes – compromise should be – by definition – two ways.

If British people went to a Muslim country and disobeyed their rules in the way that they do ours, we would be vilified at least…or murdered at worst.

Why should compromise be one way?

Freedom of speech is a fundamental democratic right - of course it is, but there has to be a limit to the poisonous narrative, a line that should not be crossed.

We cannot accept protestors on the streets of our capital city inciting racial hatred; banners and placards scrawled with the words 'Behead the Infidels' or 'Behead those who criticise Islam or Muslims' and threatening to slit the throats of those same infidels - i.e. all of us - as they did after 7 / 7; that was an outrageous abuse of our tolerance and it crosses the line of what is acceptable.

Some will say that it is only a minority and it probably is, but free speech has to have a limit and this militant behaviour cannot be tolerated in a civilised society.

If the Koran can be interpreted by these people in this way then it needs to be revised and clarified by the Muslim leadership so that we can all live in peace because until that happens, all non-Muslims will remain suspicious.

In other walks of life, we are making parents responsible for the errors of their children – why not make religious leaders and patriarchs responsible for the actions of their followers?

———

Islam is an authoritative political system which involves dominance and subjugation for its followers and the death and destruction of anybody non-Muslim.

- They strap bombs to their children and send them out to wreak havoc
- They hijack planes and fly them into buildings (USA)
- They blow-up trains and buses (Spain, UK)
- They blow-up innocent bystanders at a marathon (Boston)

Their only response to any situation where they feel their faith is under attack is more violence and more destruction – just look at what has happened over a stupid amateur video – the Muslims immediately riposted by destroying embassies, burning flags and killing people. It's barbaric and medieval.

The problem with terrorism is that we have people with medieval ideologies armed with 21st century weapons and they see the inalterable Jihadist mentality of self-sacrifice of themselves and anybody in close proximity to them when they commit these horrendous actions as an acceptable consequence of them following their religious beliefs; the innocent have no say in the matter.

No other religion advocates that

By the way; could somebody please explain to me why we use British taxpayers' money – to fund visits to this country by radical, hate-filled clerics who come here with the sole intention of delivering speeches full of vile venom on how Muslims are going to kill us all and take over the world?

Freedom of expression should have some limits when both our dignity and our National Security is at stake.

These people should show some moral rectitude towards humanity.

———

Under a PDC government, there would be no moratorium; terrorists or terrorist agencies would have six months to leave the country and once that time had elapsed any organisation still found here;

- collecting funds for terrorist activity
- scouting for recruits
- training recruits
- buying explosive materials or components
- in possession of explosive materials or components
- buying firearms and ammunition
- or in possession of firearms and ammunition

...would be immediately deactivated and its members prosecuted with the full force of the law.

––––––

By the same token, these people cannot be allowed to infiltrate sensitive areas or services vital to the community such as hospitals, water, gas, electricity etc where they could cause widespread havoc and inflict far-reaching devastation if given access.

We should err on the side of caution at all times and not help them in their crusade to eradicate us all, so in order to avoid a repeat of London 7/7 or of the Glasgow airport incident orchestrated by Medical Terrorists we need to remove potential terrorists from sensitive areas of society where they might be in a position to harm the country and its citizens in great numbers.

––––––

As stated previously, the PDC would not be against multi-cultural societies but the threat of radical individuals needs to be met with sterner resistance than is currently the case as these people have no limits and do not suffer from the British people's self-inflicted fear of not wanting to upset or annoy any marginal or ethnic group because of the need to respect EU imposed Human Rights charters etc.

These people, stuck in a medieval vacuum with archaic mentalities, will continue trying to impose their outdated religious beliefs and values on enlightened 21st century populations – but the problem we face is that they are defending these medieval values with the aid of modern-day weapons.

Those who use religion as their excuse to wreak havoc - should be dealt with; as the Bible would say – an eye for an eye. Those that – by their actions – do not respect the rights of others to live in peace and harmony should be made to forfeit the right to be protected by those same 'human rights' laws when they are prosecuted, just as they have ignored the rights of others when perpetrating their heinous acts.

The Death Penalty should apply to anybody connected with terrorists for whatever reason - **It should be an eye for an eye** – and there should be no age limit – no weakening of the rule which would allow bleeding-heart liberal lobbyists to plead for leniency for convicted killers.

Remember **Edmund Burke's** famous quote; 'All that's required for evil to triumph is for good men to do nothing'. The PDC would not stand by and do nothing.

———

NB – under a PDC administration; the cost of repairing any damage caused during a parade or demonstration would be billed back to the organisers to incite greater responsibility and awareness among those participating.

———

Author's comment;

The purpose of terrorism is to strike fear into the hearts of opponents in order to win political concessions, but in fact - despite the carnage and the killing that it engenders – it (terrorism) has the opposite effect, strengthening the resolve and the determination of those being targeted while isolating the terrorists in their narrow viewpoint.

Population

Immigration & Border Control

Population –

The UK is already the most densely populated country in Europe but it is predicted that the population will grow by another five million in the next eight years; this means that if immigration is maintained at the current rate, it could drive the population up to 77 million by 2035 and 85 million by 2081.

Net migration for the UK is currently running at between 252000 and 500000 a year depending on which study you read, but the truth of the matter is that more immigrants are settling in Britain than almost anywhere else in the world, giving the UK - at 11% - the highest proportion of immigrants of any country in the world; the number world-wide is only 3%.

Now, it is wonderful that people from all over the world want to come and live in our country; it means that they recognise our values and appreciate the way we do things, but unfortunately we simply cannot allow immigration to continue at its current rate because it is just unsustainable.

The British people are too kind, too generous and too trusting. They hate to refuse anybody anything but unfortunately they are very gullible and do not seem to realise the consequences of such uncontrolled immigration.

If they did, would they really want a three or four-fold increase in all their taxes in order to pay for all these extra people? I doubt it.

Of course, it would be great if we could accommodate everyone; the whole world living together as one, in harmony, all of us getting along, nobody ever fighting or even raising a voice...but sadly that is not reality and while I understand the concept of wanting to help everyone, wanting everyone to live as we do, in a democracy, it is simply naive to believe that we can just keep inviting everyone who wants to come here to do so.

Compassion and charity is one thing – reality is another.

That is why we have to curtail population growth; because we simply do not have the capacity to keep absorbing these ever-increasing numbers, either

-   in jobs,
-   in houses for them to live in,
-   in schools for their children to be taught in,
-   or beds in our hospitals to take care of them; our maternity units are already inundated.

...and other areas of our society are already under stress;

Social services and the Police Force, for example...both of which are being swamped by the extra burden put on them by this inordinate flood of people. Our transport system too - which was already creaking and overcrowded both on the road and the railway – is nearing implosion and our water and sewage systems are all struggling to cope.

———

Now, the population of the EU is 500 million people and under the EU rules, if they wanted to, all 500 million people living in the EU have the right to come and live here in the UK.

This is of course ridiculous but what the grey-suits in Brussels seem to have forgotten when they were deciding these rules, is that we are an island and that we can only physically support so many people. Quotas should have been put in place to take account of our island status.

I doubt that the question of rising tides or the constant erosion of our coastline and the subsequent loss of land - either for farming or for house-building - was ever mentioned either during these discussions; these Eurocrats just go along issuing diktat after diktat from their insular little world in Brussels without a thought for the consequences or of any future planning.

However, in the next century or so, because of the natural evolution of our island in a changing climatic world, these matters will become big issues.

Population levels will have to be re-defined because of reduced land-surface area.

We already have 2.33million people from the EU living here, but to give everybody in the EU community the right to come and settle here without taking these natural and social limitations into consideration during their deliberations - or at least imposing some kind of quota - is both negligent and short-sighted.

That said; increased population and reduced land-mass are not the biggest problems we face.

Self-sufficiency in food is already down to between 56 and 60% and if the UK's population continues to increase exponentially, then a day will come when there is not enough food to sustain everyone.

Currently we only produce 56-60% of our needs but that figure will continue to decrease if the population continues to increase; because more people means more houses, more houses means less land for farming and less land for farming means less food produced. People will start squabbling over food; it is human nature.

Another worry is that year on year the traditional crops that currently make up the 56-60% are yielding smaller and smaller harvests because of the irregular / warming weather patterns so even the 56-60% figure will soon be obsolete, whether we stay as we are or not.

So; we have a situation of ever-increasing demand against ever-diminishing supply; this is not rocket science; it is basic economics. We cannot keep increasing the population inexorably when the food supply is diminishing and the land-mass is shrinking – it is just not sustainable.

That is why we need to think about controlling the population of this country better, but not in any racist fashion; we need to control the population on the basis of how many people we can actually feed, using the food production levels of our country as a guideline.

Now, some will say; just increase imports...that is a solution, but the price of food on the world market is on a constant upward curve and it will only get more and more expensive due to increased demand from China and India. Surely, it would be better for everyone, the environment and the treasury included, if we simply reduced our food import levels through a better management of our population.

Furthermore, we need to take into account the looming energy crisis that is about to hit us as our nuclear power stations come to the inevitable end of their pre-programmed lifespan...because none of our lily-livered politicians has yet dared to put his cushy Westminster seat on the line and defy the dangerously naive and gullible environmentalists who believe a couple of windmills are going to generate enough energy to keep all our lights on for the next fifty years...and that's without adding to the current population.

And finally, we need to start working on a post-oil future and that too begins with reducing the population to a more sustainable level.

––––––

This problem, between decreasing self-sufficiency in food production and ongoing increases in population is going to be a major issue in the decade to come, but it will be compounded even more by the ridiculous and unnecessary, self-imposed targets set by recent governments of reducing greenhouse gases by 60% of 1990 levels by 2050.

That is just an impossible catch-22 situation.

Simple economic-maths tells us that we cannot keep increasing immigration numbers while trying to drastically reduce our green-house gas levels, nor can we continue to receive wave after wave of immigrants while slashing budgets for all the services needed to integrate them properly.

We have to do something to ward off the inevitable economic collapse that these 'out-of-control' policies will engender if we continue in this way.

Conclusion; We need to address the population issue and not for any bigoted reason. This is not about race, culture, ethnicity or any other of the inflammatory concerns that usually cloud this issue – this is just about facts and figures.

It is simply that to continue as it is, is unsustainable on every level.

We must set a limit now to avoid destroying the environment or putting our national security at risk.

Limiting immigration is sensible, not racist.

———

The word immigration is not a dirty word – it is simply the action of coming to live permanently in a foreign country as defined in the OED (Oxford English Dictionary) and we should not be afraid of discussing it, because while we in the UK are being politically-correct and typically British, sticking our heads in the sand and not wanting to offend anybody, it is happening every day, under our very noses whether we like it or not.

The problem has to be addressed and indeed, in a recent poll 71% of those asked believed that the UK is already too crowded - 81% of those asked wanted a cap on immigration and 1000 people an hour signed up to an e-petition that wants to limit immigration.

So while the politicians shy away and avoid the issue, it would appear that the British public do have their concerns and given a platform they are prepared to voice them.

The secret, open-door immigration policy which Tony Blair and New Labour used during their time in office to bolster their support under the guise of creating a multi-cultural society - and which documents recently revealed under the Freedom of Information Act informed us was a deliberate attempt on their part to make the country more multi-cultural and therefore more likely to vote Labour - saw an unprecedented 3.2 million extra migrants settle in the UK in just over ten years, which clearly accelerated and exacerbated the immigration problem.

In fact, during that period passport approvals rocketed by 500% and New Labour even put productivity targets on foreign embassy staff to send as many people here as possible...those staff, pressured to meet those targets, often cutting corners in the application process and rushing visas through - without the proper checks in place – allowing criminals and potential terrorists to be waved through unopposed.

By the way; how cynical was that...that Tony Blair, Gordon Brown and New Labour would even go to the point of deliberately transforming the whole cultural makeup of British society just to stay in power?

Was there really no limit to their folly?

Tony Blair and New Labour changed this country forever through that policy and while the huge influx of foreigners is clearly having a significant impact on our towns - as was his goal - the British people were never consulted; they were never asked if they wanted their culture and their way of life to be transformed in this way but unfortunately, that was par for the course for Tony Blair and New Labour; most of what they did was done behind the backs of the electorate.

Nevertheless, what is done is done. They did transform our population and the British taxpayers will be paying the price of Tony Blair and New Labour's cynical ploy for forever more.

Moreover, the consequences of this reckless, unfettered immigration which has flooded this country with masses of unskilled, poor quality citizens has impoverished this country beyond all recognition putting an intolerable pressure on public services.

Indeed far from promoting a multicultural society it has turned many urban areas / neighbourhoods into virtual ghettos – peppered with small immigrant minorities who refuse to integrate and who actively seek to undermine or destroy our society through acts of incivility and terrorism.

Of course a sensible number of talented immigrants helps to drive the economy but those coming here are people with nothing, who have lost everything for whatever reason, who are low-skilled and have nothing to offer our economy by way of talent other than to be a burden on our welfare state...and yet whenever the ordinary British person raises the issue or airs a grievance on the matter they are immediately labelled a bigot or a racist.

It is sad to hear phrases like; it's not our country any more; and I don't feel I belong in the place where I grew up; people now feel insecure in their own home-land.

Angele Merkele, the German Chancellor announced that multi-culturalism hadn't worked in Germany and David Cameron has since followed suit...but while he promised to cap immigration and get on top of the problem he hasn't followed through on his pledge; in fact he has done a U-turn on immigration like he has with so many other policies.

In truth, the Conservatives are no better at addressing the immigration problem than the cynical Labour Party as John **Major's** government relaxed border controls in 1994 and last year **Theresa May** deliberately relaxed those controls again, watering down passport checks without telling Parliament and thereby letting in countless potential criminals and terrorists.

Border control –

Because of

- our history of tolerance,
- our compassion,
- our natural indulgence
- our political-correctness culture
- and our collective national dislike for confrontation for fear of being branded racist or bigoted

...and because we are led by a variety of naive, bleeding-heart liberals and mealy-mouthed politicians, this country has become known worldwide by asylum seekers and traffickers alike as a soft touch...and because of that label, everybody and anybody is making a bee-line to get in here.

The UK has become a magnet for the misery of the world.

It has even become a refuge for terrorists who hide behind the EU Human Rights laws in order to stay here.

How ironic that is, that people who want to strip us of our most basic human right; i.e., that of living and breathing, are coming here and hiding behind their right to a life in this country while they plot to kill us all.

It is a travesty that in this country the right to a family life for a terrorist somehow trumps the rights of everyone else in the country not to have extremists or terrorists living among them (especially when quite often these people are illegal entrants in the first place).

This country is also a target for organised crime (former Soviet citizens, among others, abound in London having imported and set up their own networks since the break-up of the Soviet Union).

Then, of course, the UK is also seen as an Eldorado for asylum seekers looking to come here and exploit the benefits system from all over the world; look at our borders, look at Calais in France; they are queuing up to get over here and disappear into our system which is at the very least, inefficient.

All of these people are playing on our trusting nature and our lack of authoritative government to exploit our innate kindness and take advantage of us.

None of them gives a damn about respecting us; all they want is what they can get from us.

However, this situation cannot be allowed to go on indefinitely; we need to stem the tide of human misery arriving on our shores.

Asylum seekers

These people are drawn to our shores for many reasons; some of them genuine, some of them not so genuine.

However, groups like Migration-watch UK who monitor these matters, inform us that while the EU does not have a standard procedure for dealing with these people, under EU rules asylum seekers should declare themselves and their situation in the **first country they land in**, but this is not happening because the traffickers are cannily telling their charges not to say anything - or get their fingerprints taken - until they arrive in the UK...and sadly other EU countries are simply allowing this to happen so as to wash their hands of the problem and avoid any financial implication in dealing with these people themselves.

That is why so many people are coming here, not only for the benefits and the lifestyle but because other EU countries are simply funnelling them our way.

We also have to contend with further restrictions imposed by the UN.

Meanwhile, on the other side of the argument, pro-asylum groups like the Refugee Council reject any idea that asylum seekers have a plan to end up here.

How naïve are these people?

Of course asylum seekers have a plan; they don't leave their homes without a reason or a plan.

———

So it is clear that everyone in the world sees us as a soft-touch.

This cannot continue; it is time to tighten up the rules and change that mindset.

It cannot be right that 24-30% of asylum seekers win their case to stay here in the UK while in Greece; only 1% of asylum-seekers are allowed to stay, and that was before the current problems.

Furthermore, and to underline my point about our lax system, even those who lose their cases stay here anyway - according to the UK Border agency - melting into our society and working on the black market.

Cost –

The cost to the British taxpayer for dealing with asylum-seekers last year was £478 million.

We also spend over £73 million a year keeping failed asylum seekers housed and fed while repatriation and resettlement packages cost between £7,900 and £25,600 per person.

We have also spent over £80m in 4years on flights to deport illegal-immigrants.

Worth noting; an asylum seeker can claim £150 a week in benefits while a jobless British person can only claim £71 in jobseekers allowance; that cannot be right, we should be putting British citizens first.

These costs are unacceptable and need to be addressed.

The PDC would have a financial advisor breakdown these costs in order to streamline them and we would also look into the exploitative Legal Aid costs claimed by unscrupulous lawyers who deliberately prolong asylum-cases in order to fill their pockets.

Calais –

We need to do more to break the constant stream of people entering this country illegally via the port of Calais in France – the number has doubled in a year (2000 a month according to official French figures)

In fact, it has tripled in the last five years.

Ideally, as our EU partners the French should be working with us to resolve this situation but they don't feel responsible for it and see it as our problem, blaming it on the very generous benefits that are available in this country.

So, rather than help us to police it, the French have set up a series of waiting stations instead, all along the north coast of France for immigrants to use while they try to enter the UK illegally.

This action allows them to wash their hands of the problem and turn a blind eye.

More importantly, it means that they don't have to deal with or financially support these people themselves - despite the fact that under the 1951 Geneva Convention and EU rules governing these situations, refugees are supposed to claim asylum in the first safe country they land in.

Clearly they land in France before they land here but typically the French are treating us in the same selfish and hypocritical way they always treat their 'partners'.

Gallingly, however, this disregard of the Geneva Convention seems pretty widespread across Europe as the French are not alone in this. It has been reported that the Spanish and the Italians do exactly the same thing, telling any asylum seekers they come across to head for Calais where virtuous do-gooders and naive French humanitarians - easily exploited and manipulated by organised criminal gangs - provide food, showers and support for them until they can make their way across the channel illegally.

This has become a multi-million pound operation earning fortunes for the ruthless traffickers, the passers and the middle men who have no morals or compassion for the asylum-seekers but who clearly know how to use the naiveté of the French charity-workers to their advantage.

Our good heart and our gullibility is being abused and exploited by these people and it has to stop.

———

Actions –

Firstly, despite my reservations about the French character, I tend to agree with their position; our benefits are too generous and the allure of huge state handouts **is** what attracts many of these people to our shores; so, those benefits need to be scaled back and that information needs to be relayed back to these countries that the 'Eldorado' is closed.

We also have to ask the French to stop servicing these camps; they are unofficially facilitating this clandestine and illegal activity. However, we cannot expect them to pour money into helping us without some kind of return; that is just not the French way; it is not in their interest to help other than to uphold the EU rules, but as they clearly disregard those rules despite having drawn them up - we need to work out some kind of bi-lateral agreement with them.

Gordon Brown gave them £15m towards policing the problem but that didn't change anything, so another solution has to be found.

I believe that we need a temporary 'embassy-style' operation in Calais that can screen the genuine, bona-fide asylum seekers from the economic migrants under stricter new rules, until the stream of immigrants slows down due to the reduced attraction of our benefit-system – this would be manned by members of our new Border Police Force.

This bi-lateral agreement would have to include some kind of repatriation scheme but we would not be participating in any voluntary repatriation schemes which give people in Calais money to return home – these schemes are just being exploited by criminals.

NB - History suggests that relations between the French and the British are always going to be somewhat tenuous so in the long term we would have to have a more permanent solution in place to protect ourselves.

———

Secondly; we need to close the loop-hole that allows people to get on the Eurostar train legally - from Brussels to Lille - and then stay on board illegally through the channel tunnel.

———

We also need to change the transport arrangements for the Border Control personnel as the current operation of a coach to ferry them back and forth is being used by illegal-immigrants who hide under it.

Why not make the panels along the lower portion of the coach transparent – not very aesthetic I know, but very practical.

———

The lorry parks around Calais need to be better protected too – truckers are being threatened and assaulted – checks should be put in place to make sure that the truck-doors are sealed properly - here we also need to try to reach some kind of agreement with the French.

———

And finally, migrants desperate for money - some of whom are armed with guns and knives - are robbing British people coming out of or going into the ferry terminals, forming human chains across roads to make them stop their cars before demanding money and food – this is criminal activity and the French police should be doing more to stop this. Again, more cooperation is needed here too.

Of course, the ideal solution would be to help all these people in their countries of origin, to stop them from leaving in the first place...but that would need a concerted international effort as failed foreign policy and hopelessness is what is forcing them to look elsewhere.

The New Border Police Force

It is not right, in a democracy like ours that people over in Brussels - who were not elected by the citizens of this country - should be dictating our border policy.

The EU and its ECHR is what is preventing us from running our country properly and this has to change if we want to preserve our identity our and cultural heritage.

The EU's idea of everybody having the right to free-movement within the EU boundaries is a wonderful concept, but it is wholly impractical in the real world, much like the Peace and Love concept of the Hippie Movement in the Sixties which yearned for a place where we could all live in peace and harmony like in some vast land of Milk and Honey.

It is a fantasy - as many of the idealistic concepts dreamed up by the grey-suits in their ivory tower in Brussels tend to be - because it doesn't have any in-built controls; everyone can go anywhere without any control or question.

In fact the EU has surreptitiously become one big de-facto state without it ever having obtained its mandate or laid out its constitution, creating a nightmare situation for many and the UK in particular.

If they wanted to create one single state – and it is clear that the idealists in Brussels have every intention of doing just that – then they should have harmonised political, fiscal and monetary policies first, before raising all the border barriers and allowing this anarchic osmosis of populations, because, as it stands, all they have succeeded in doing is creating a hotchpotch of chaos and soon they will be adding to that bedlam by allowing the Romanians and Bulgarians to join in.

Meanwhile, to complicate things even further, people from outside the EU are claiming citizenship in other EU countries where the controls are practically non-existent and then using that right of movement in the EU to settle in the UK; this is abusive and cannot be allowed to continue.

We need to break free from all this and take back control but if we don't want identity cards, and a recent poll suggests that we don't, then we need to have stronger border control.

We need to restructure and strengthen the Border and Immigration Agency and as part of this process the PDC would introduce a new unified Border Police Force, a detachment of which would work in tandem with the French within the confines of the Customs area in Calais.

This new specially trained force would be stationed at Dover and would be responsible for securing our borders and our coastline in collaboration with the traditional Police Force and the Navy replacing the current UK Border Agency which has shown itself to be hopelessly incompetent and inefficient; indeed, it 'lost' between 124000 and 159000 people in the system due to New Labour's shambolic mismanagement of the immigration issue.

As part of this new structure, a data-base would also be set up in Dover – where all immigrants would be recorded, both legal and illegal.

Recent attempts at border-control have been a catastrophe of historic proportions.

'The Border Control Agency has a backlog of 276,000 cases; among them...

- 150,000 foreign workers who have outstayed their visas
- 101,000 untraced asylum seekers who have been lost in the system...and
- 3,900 foreign offenders who have been released back into the community by the courts in order to protect their Human Rights

The Home office has also lost track of 40000 illegal immigrants which means that there are in total over a million illegal immigrants currently living in the UK.

Now, a recent amnesty allowed 250000 of these people to stay and the virtuous do-gooders and bleeding-hearts would probably suggest we let the other million stay too, but it has been proved before that amnesties just encourage more people to come – look at what happened in Italy and in Spain.

We need to have a coherent policy going forward but in the meantime we need to stop immigration temporarily while we deal with the backlog of cases that have built up – 276000 - and process those that shouldn't be here, out of the system.

Our priority would be to sort out this mess and during that time immigration would be suspended or at least held to a minimum.

In-and-out checks would be re-introduced as part of this policy.

The PDC would put the necessary resources into this problem now, in order to avoid further problems long term.

I also like the idea of developing spy-in-the-sky drones to patrol our coastlines against illegal immigrants, terrorists / smugglers and incoming military threats.

NB; we would also incorporate into the budget an annual grant to the RNLI – without any political interference – so that they might continue their sterling work saving lives off our coasts.

Border Police duties
at all Ports, Airports and International train stations –

Firstly, the PDC would tighten the immigration rules and apply them correctly and efficiently.

All future visitors would be thoroughly checked and limited to a 90 day stay unless given special dispensation to stay longer.

No-one from a terrorist nation would be allowed in; if they do not like what is happening in their country, then they should change it; they would not be allowed to hide in our country.

Those entering this country would have to provide;

- a DNA sample,
- a thumb-print or
- retina scan
- and sign an agreement in which they agreed to respect the law.

...at the same time they would be made aware of the rules on accessing the NHS and the consequences and penalties of any transgressions, warned that they would be deported immediately in minor cases and informed that their DNA could be traced back to a particular country or ethnic origin if they had chosen to burn off their fingerprints.

People arriving at international ports and airports without legal identity documents and visas would be put straight back on the next plane – the responsibility would lie with the carrier for not checking that their papers were in order in the first place.

Suspicious passengers would be stopped because they look suspicious not because of the colour of their skin because a random selection of whites just to even the balance of racial mix is time-consuming and pointless.

———

At the border – immigrants would be issued with a two-sided form – the first side would be filled in at the border-control to prove legitimacy and the second side would have to be filled in by the town hall or civic centre where they took up residency.

They would then be made to read or explained a charter on British life which they would have to agree to conform to and abide by – if not – access to our country would be denied

If we went to their country – they would expect nothing less

Maybe we could even impose a limited stay on people; if they did not find a job that supported them within the first year of residency for example, they would have to leave again. 'Of course, we would have to build in some conditions to this protocol, such as;

- No getting married during the trial period
- No claiming residency through a relationship or through a child born during that time…and
- No claiming residency under the pretext of having purchased a pet cat or dog…

…but that should not be an issue.

Those that were allowed to stay would be monitored for the first three years of residency, by their local council – and anybody found abusing the system, not showing willing to integrate or not respecting our way of life would be immediately deported. There would be no legal process, no questions, and no human-rights lobbyists to complain as it would be inscribed as part of the immigration process.

———

Signs to be posted in all ports and airports;

Welcome to the **UK**
Please be aware before entering our country
that we impose Capital Punishment
for the following offences

Murder,
Terrorism,
Drug-running,
Aggravated Rape
Child molestation and paedophilia (in some cases),
Human-trafficking
Honour killing

If you believe yourself to be an innocent victim
please make yourself known and we will protect you

————

Welcome to the **UK**

Those visitors wishing to speed up the immigration formalities
are requested to proceed to the arrivals hall,
answer any questions asked of them politely and courteously
and enjoy their stay.

Those who do not wish to comply with our rules,
who are obnoxious, arrogant,
have an attitude or are unhelpful in any way
will not enjoy their experience,
so please be warned

————

New arrivals –

On arriving in this country immigrants would have to make their way to the nearest town hall or civic centre to their chosen place of residence - within a set period - in order to present the paperwork that had been handed to them at the border to get it validated.

The clerk would then fill in the second half of the paperwork and confirm the details on the data base to confirm the person's whereabouts. The completed paperwork would then allow for the application of a work permit.

The person would then be offered English lessons and informed once again of our laws.

They would then be made to read or explained a charter on British life for a second time, which they would have to agree to conform to and abide by, with a written signature.

If we went to their country – they would expect nothing less

Cultural Rules –
(to be read at point of arrival and again at civic registration)

(1) Archaic practices such as Forced Marriage and Honour Killing (e.g.; cases of Tulay Goren and Shafilea Ahmed) are illegal in the UK and will be prosecuted with the full force of the law.
If people want to continue these medieval activities they will have to find a new home where these archaic practices are still considered acceptable behaviour.

(2) We recognise that people believe in any number of things and therefore no judgement will be made on a religious belief. However, practices such as witchcraft and voodoo that actually put their participants in real physical danger or at least, at serious risk of harm will not be tolerated.

These people need to integrate 21ˢᵗ century Britain or move to a country which does tolerate such primitive and often barbaric behaviour

(3) Funeral Pyres are not acceptable in this country and if an immigrant cannot accept this and abide by the law of this land – then they should leave.

(4) Immigrants will need to produce a valid visa to gain employment and those that employ them illegally will be sanctioned – this will also apply to students whose visas have expired

(5) Immigrants will not be allowed to jump the housing queue
We have British citizens waiting on lists for years; again this is not bigotry, it is fair-play – nobody likes a queue-jumper, especially in Britain

(6) Polygamy is illegal in this country; our benefits system will be adjusted to reflect that so that it cannot be exploited, thereby encouraging this practice

(7) The practice of Muslims marrying their cousins is unacceptable
These people are producing children with terrible disabilities due to the genetic in-breeding

(8) Those with anti-western ideologies who do not feel at home in our country or in our society would be invited to leave

(9) Those already living here who help others to gain entry illegally will be informed that they would be liable for prosecution themselves and their visas revoked

NB - We should not be spending millions of pounds on translators and translating documents - Immigrants must learn our language in order to integrate, because without that communication skill they are unemployable, cannot integrate and are destined to a life limited to the margins of their ethnic group.

———

As well as dealing with immigration at the border itself, teams from the new Border Police would also be sent into immigrant communities to spread the word about integration and sham marriages...and to hammer home the message to obstinate or recalcitrant parents that behaviour such as forced / arranged marriage, honour killing and grooming would not be tolerated in this country. This message would be reinforced with a strong warning about the consequences for those who transgress and disrespect our laws.

The Border Police would also liaise with the government and the civic-centres of towns with a large concentration of immigrants to set up a service where vulnerable young women who had been abused or forced into cultural situations without their consent, could be welcomed and kept safe before being transferred to a women's refuge centre / boarding school, to protect them from any family recrimination.

...and as a final point, any family member found to be involved in any kind of abuse, in organising a forced marriage or engaging in any of those archaic traditions such as honour killing would be immediately prosecuted and / or deported depending on their situation.

Author's comment;

Shared identity is the foundation on which trust, co-operation and generosity are built. It is the very fabric of a successful, modern society; however, too much diversity in a too short a period of time - that does not allow for proper integration - threatens that social cohesion and leads to the ghetto-isation of society we are now seeing in our towns...where different ethnic groups are remaining within their own kind and culture rather than becoming a part of the greater community.

Indian culture;

Forced / arranged marriage

In India children as young as twelve - especially girls - are forced into arranged marriages by their parents for two reasons.

- Firstly, these girls are a burden on the meagre family food budget...and
- Second, the older they get the higher the dowry the girl's parents have to pay.

These medieval customs might well be part of India's culture but they have no place in 21st century Britain.

Again it comes down to questions of tradition and ignorance; tradition is very hard to change as it has been handed down from generation to generation and these poor people are ignorant in the sense that they are uneducated; most are illiterate and so, not knowing any better, they simply follow blindly what their parents did and their parents did before them.

However, this is not acceptable under British law and will not be tolerated.

Pakistani culture

Honour killing and the grooming of young girls will not be tolerated

As stated in a previous chapter, people have the right to believe whatever they want to believe; however if those people want to defend a tradition whereby they kill their daughters for refusing an arranged marriage – all for the defence of some hypothetical family honour - they should know that that behaviour is not acceptable and will not be tolerated under British law.

This brutal and barbaric culture - imported from rural Pakistan and based on misguided notions of family honour and perceived shame in the community - is not tolerable in the UK and anyone, any family wanting to perpetuate such traditions, who believe that it is right in any way, under any circumstance to kill their daughters on the grounds of perceived shame within the community will need to go and find a new home, in a new country which accepts such ignorant practice and condones such murder.

If it is perpetrated in this country strict punishment awaits as the parents of Shafilea Ahmed and Banaz Mahmod recently found out.

A conservative estimate suggests that one honour killing occurs every four weeks in this country; that is not acceptable.

Sham marriages –

Incredulously, as it stands today, 40% of marriages celebrated in register-offices around the UK are a sham. Four out of every ten marriages are set-up with the sole intention of defrauding the country.

That figure is outrageous; wholly unacceptable and as one of our first priorities, the PDC would mandate the new Border Police to reduce its prevalence significantly with a view to eradicating it completely in due course.

Furthermore, anybody involved in this wicked deception - which is no less than fraud and makes a mockery of the institution - including the fixers who arrange them, the clergy who perform them and the 'spouses' themselves who participate in them would face uncompromising prosecution. (Category Three)

Reflection;

It is an absolute disgrace that the New Labour governments of Tony Blair and Gordon Brown had such contempt for the people of this country when dealing with issues of immigration.

The cynical open-door policy aside, which allowed over three million immigrants to flood into the country almost unhindered, the New

Labour Party also removed the Primary Purpose Rule during their time in office which tripled the number of work-permits they granted and doubled spousal immigration.

The Primary Purpose Rule required foreign nationals to prove that the 'primary purpose' of their marriage was not simply to obtain British residency

This is more than cynical social-engineering, it is betrayal, betrayal of the trust that the voters of this country put in their politicians when electing them. People expect the politicians that they elect to have theirs and the country's best interests at heart while they are holding the reins of power; they certainly don't expect them to sell them and the country out for the promise of political gain further down the line; that is simply shameful.

So; we had the open-door policy, the removal of the Primary Purpose Rule...and then to compound the overall cynicism of the New Labour policy on immigration we had a complete and utter refusal from them and their ministers to address the problem of sham marriages.

Where was the executive morality; where was the integrity that should be innate in every leader and where were the men of principle during this time?

———

I believe that this conduct was on a par with a dereliction of duty and I find it incompatible with the role of an elected government, even if it was part of their deliberate attempt to change the make-up of our society.

Consequently, the PDC would attempt to redress this situation by setting up a 'department of verification' that would go back to 1997 when New Labour was first elected and we would ratify every single marriage licence issued during their time in office and since.

After that, every marriage that was found to be illegal or a sham would be instantly dissolved and the participating parties would all be prosecuted and / or deported.

Then, the rules that had been abused in order to organise these sham-marriages would be reviewed and tightened...and the Human Rights law that facilitates this kind of subterfuge would also be revised in order to close the loop-holes and prevent any more illegal immigrants marrying EU women (Polish etc) just to obtain residency.

A fixed penalty would be introduced for those involved in the organisation of these sham marriages of five years in prison. (Category Three)

This would quickly slow down and eventually stop the number of sham ceremonies taking place.

The PDC would also introduce a five-year delay-period before spouses – who have been brought into the country legally - could claim benefits. This would be after their husbands had fulfilled the financial requirements and proved their ability to support them (currently £18600)

Student visas –

The New Border Police would also look into questionable student visas by visiting each university in turn and interviewing foreign students on a one to one basis.

Recent figures show that up to 25% of students are bogus; they are not genuine students but come here to work illegally.

Any universities found to be flouting the law would be prosecuted and have their international student policy amended.

The PDC would also question the idea of mature students - over 21 years of age - who might be potential radicals.

———

Illegal immigrants -

Under a PDC administration, those people who are in this country illegally – whether they entered illegally or overstayed their visas - would be sent home.

This measure would also include those people sleeping rough and especially those poor souls camping out in Park Lane or living under the M4 at Heston. That is no life for them and the humanitarian option for them all is to send them home.

Immediacy laws would be passed by the PDC to avoid any long drawn out legal processes and the Human Rights Rule Eight would be suspended for six months taking a back seat to that of the legality of these people to be in this country in the first place.

All illegal immigrants would be allowed 90 days to get their affairs in order and as a gesture of good-will the PDC would provide basic transport at specific exit-points.

Then, after that 90 day period, those illegal immigrants who had not left willingly would be apprehended and offered a one way ticket to their home country.

Those that still refused to leave at that point on a voluntary basis or who refused to reveal their identity / nationality in an effort to stay in this country, would be detained on 'uncomfortable' prison-ships until their situation was 'resolved'.

And finally; the loophole that allows illegal immigrants the right to apply for citizenship here - after five years if they have managed to avoid detection - would be revoked.

———

I stress at this point that these are all ILLEGAL IMMIGRANTS who have no right to be in this country; these measures have no bearing on the millions of immigrants living here in all LEGALITY.

———

NB;

A legal immigrant found to be colluding with illegal-immigrants in order to get them into the country would have his/her paperwork cancelled

- Hauliers who were found to be bringing in illegal-immigrants in or on their trucks would face prosecution...and finally
- People found employing illegal-immigrants would also face prosecution

———

Radical immigrants -

There are people holding this country to ransom; their weapon

- political correctness (which they are exploiting)
- freedom of speech (which they are abusing)
- human rights (which they are manipulating)...and
- the social benefits and legal-aid systems that they are bleeding for all they are worth.

I am not racist; the colour of people's skin has no bearing whatsoever on how I think but when I see Muslim fanatics coming to this country illegally and twisting the laws of the land in order to gain residency, before setting out - like any other parasite - to destroy the host (in this case the country that has welcomed them in and given them food and shelter) I consider it the height of ingratitude and I don't see why it should be tolerated.

I am not paranoid either, but the history of mankind is full of warnings, about how once-advanced societies have declined within the space of a few generations, into squalid, self-indulgent chaos, ending in subjugation and enslavement at the hands of an invader who had not been so tolerant.

Needless to say; if people come to these shores with a pledge to respect our laws and our way of life, wanting to live in peace and harmony in our multi-cultural society, that's fine by me but if they have no real intention of integrating – and instead intend to work towards overpowering our democracy, replacing our institutions and steadily colonising our country I do not see a place for them in my vision of 21st century Britain.

I am sick of seeing these people spouting hate and violence, trying to indoctrinate the youth of today and warp their minds with ideas of centuries past...while hiding behind the Freedom of Speech Laws.

We need to get rid of these blood-thirsty extremists bent on destroying our culture.

...and finally; could somebody please answer me this - If these people harbour so much anger and resentment towards us, if they despise our country, our culture and our values so much; if they hate everything that Britain and the British people stand for, then why do they come to our shores to live amongst us? Surely, these people would be better off living somewhere else, somewhere where they could feel at home and somewhere where they wouldn't be milking the British taxpayers' generosity while they spouted their messages of hate.

Those that abuse the system

I believe that those who abuse our Immigration laws and hide behind Human Rights Charters (Geneva Convention etc) in order to stay in this country and screw our legal and social services for all they can get should be shown the door, in the same way as those who come here with no real intention of integrating – but only to create chaos within our communities.

Settled immigrants

Immigrant children who perpetrate crime and are convicted of that crime should be sent back to their country – with their family.

This would make parents more responsible and stimulate them to discipline their offspring in the respect of the law.

It would also act as a deterrent for the criminally-minded parents who deliberately use their children to commit crime, hiding behind their youth to avoid implication.

These measures should all go towards creating a safer and more relaxed environment for good honest, law-abiding citizens to live their lives.

However, I am not naive; I know that customs officers, policemen, lawyers and magistrates are all susceptible to gentle persuasion and getting their palms greased by criminals, because of the work they do; all we can do is ensure that they have all been made aware of the penalties that will be imposed on anybody getting caught in corrupt activities.

Customs -

The new Border Police would also take over the Customs Duties in ports, airports, in international train stations and around the country.

Customs Priorities – coming in;

- guns and weapons,
- drugs,
- illegal immigration and human trafficking

Customs priorities – going out;

- slick international syndicates are stealing cars to order in this country and shipping them abroad in containers to Africa and Pakistan via Durban in South Africa; teams of underworld criminals, expert in car theft are roaming our towns looking to steal Range Rovers, 4x4's; this needs to be stamped out.

One of their other missions would also be to collaborate with the regular Police in tackling criminal activity by international gangs involved in violence, drugs and people trafficking.

This would be done through the setting-up of specialist units within the Force to target and eradicate each of the scourges below;

Violence - Polish, Ukrainian and Russian mobsters are all operating in this country and since we have thrown open our borders many other Eastern European criminals have imported their activities too, not to mention Pakistan which always seems to be cited whenever international crime is discussed.

Drugs – the Border Police would also target the drug imports;

- from Colombian Cocaine gangs,
- from Pakistani / Bangladeshi and Indian Heroin gangs and
- from Vietnamese Cannabis gangs, their mules and their freight / cargo shipments

Reflection; The UK is top of the Euro league for drug abuse / trade with an estimated turnover of £5.3 billion a year. We have 332000 Class

'A' drug addicts in this country. Could somebody please explain to me how cocaine which is a banned substance in this country is available on every street corner and why there is such a tolerance around the celebrity lifestyle; everybody seems to be aware that celebrities are offered cocaine by the handful wherever they go, so why is nobody doing anything about it?

People trafficking / smuggling – the Border Police would also address the problem of gang masters who smuggle people in from Eastern Europe to work as prostitutes, or from China to work as cockle-pickers or drug cultivators / gardeners (re; Rageh Omar's Crime Invasion Series on Virgin TV about the new Underworld)

These are Category One or Two offences depending on the circumstances

The PDC would also provide additional funding to those officials who root out the unscrupulous bosses – already living here - who manage these illegal activities and operate these despicable dealings in human misery.

––––

Border Police Personnel

Under the PDC, there would be no more rewards for failure.

There would be no pay-offs or bonuses or gold-plated pensions for people found to be ineffective. Incompetence would not be rewarded as was the case recently when the person at the heart of the relaxed airport-terror-checks scandal was rewarded with a £250K pay-off; meanwhile, a known hijacker was found working at Heathrow.

Any staff not considered conscientious or productive enough in their efforts would be stood down and re-trained or guided into a more suitable profession.

––––

Human Rights

(European Charter for Human Rights)

We have already sacrificed so many of our freedoms in this country in the name of integration, multi-culturalism, political correctness and the meddling European human rights law that I believe it is now time to call a halt and take stock.

Of course, the basic Human Rights of every individual should be defended tenaciously but nowadays, for too many people in this country, 'human rights' have come to mean the defence of the rights of criminals, terror suspects and illegal immigrants at the expense of everyone else.

In fact, 72% of the British public believe that the ECHR is simply a charter for criminals to exploit (YouGov poll) and they are sick to the back teeth of the human rights of criminals being put before their own.

It cannot be right for example that the human rights of a 'harmless autistic computer geek' are being ignored...while killers accused of genocide, terrorists, hijackers and child-molesters are all protected and offered a safe haven in this country.

Even the head of the Equalities and Human Rights Commission – Trevor Phillips – admitted that 'the Human Rights laws have fallen into disrepute and are seen by the British public as protecting criminals, terror suspects and illegal immigrants at the expense of everyone else'.

Indeed, anyone with a logical, fair-minded approach to life can see that Article Eight of the European Convention on Human Rights is being abused on a regular basis and that our slavish observance of its undemocratic dogma at the expense of the majority of law-abiding citizens is sabotaging if not demolishing every aspect of Britain's immigration policies...

...and while we in Britain bend over backwards trying constantly to conform with every detail of every little ruling – typical of us Brits, playing by the rules – a country like France, which is a founder-member of the EU and prides itself as the 'land of human-rights' had no such qualms recently when deporting two known Islamist extremists. There was no consultation with the ECHR, no self-inflicted shame, no embarrassment and no public outcry from any liberal-minded activist. In fact, no sooner had President Sarkozy signed the expulsion order than the pair was put on flights out of the country.

President Sarkozy stated simply that 'those who make remarks contrary to the values of the Republic will be removed from the Republic; there will be no exceptions'.

We should be equally dogmatic and forthright in this country because in comparison, it took eight years and cost the British taxpayer over £3m to deport the radical cleric Abu Hamza to the USA. (His lawyers incidentally receiving over £1m to represent him in tax-payer funded legal aid).

Italy too, another EU member state, has also summarily deported people they regarded as undesirable, thereby ignoring the EU rules.

...and Australia - although not part of the EU - recently deported a British citizen convicted of rape (*who had been living there since 1967*) back to the UK even though he no longer had any ties here. Why can't we be more like that, more expeditious?

———

The more sceptical among us might see the European Convention on Human Rights as the EU's way of subtlety but deliberately erasing any sense of national identity, thereby creating a melting pot of nationalities so intermingled with each other that the only thing they have in common is their European identity.

That would be cynical, right...

...and yet it would appear that the EU directive 2004/38 suggests that this is indeed one of their fundamental objectives.

The Human Rights law is a good thing; nobody is contesting that but we need to stop defending the civil liberties of criminals, terror suspects and illegal immigrants at the expense of the peaceful, decent, law-abiding majority of this country.

Current figures show that 100 convicted foreigners are released onto our streets every month claiming that it is their human right to stay in this country and enjoy a family life here...while a recent estimate put the number of foreign offenders (murderers, rapists etc) released by the courts in order to protect their human rights at 3980. (This number has increased five-fold since the introduction of Article 8).

These criminals - who have no respect for our laws because they come from fractured cultures that do not impose the same civilised values on them that we do - are all walking our streets with impunity so as to uphold their human rights despite the fact that they have committed the most horrendous crimes and destroyed the lives of hundreds of ordinary British families by their actions.

Meanwhile, the people who were born and bred in this country and who respect the law have lost **their human rights** to live in peace and not be murdered or raped in their beds.

Every year 3200 foreign criminals, failed asylum seekers and EU benefit tourists (people who come with no intention of working; just claiming benefits) use the Human Rights laws to avoid deportation from this country while at the same time 1200 paedophiles and rapists are also using the ECHR to get their names removed from the Sex Register every year.

In the UK, we hand out almost £500,000 a week to prisoners to help them make human rights claims against the State for softer treatment in jail... while at the same time convicted drug addicts are using the Human Rights Charter to make frivolous claims to get compensation payments for them being forced to go without their drugs while locked-up.

This country is getting worse and worse every day in its compassion for criminals and its total disregard for their victims / the innocent.

How dangerous do these people have to be before the government sees fit to keep them away from the general public?

What about **OUR** rights? We should all have the right not to have our homes and our premises burgled, the right to walk on our streets without the fear of being mugged and the right not be raped or murdered.

It cannot be right in a just society that irrespective of their heinous crimes or the danger they represent to the British public that these people cannot be expelled.

If foreign nationals come here and prey on our society, they should be prosecuted and immediately sent back to where they came from - once they have served their sentence – no ifs, no buts; and they should most certainly not be allowed to use the Human Rights card to avoid that punishment.

When the Human Rights of the individual clash with or infringe upon the human rights and the safety of the majority, i.e. the general public, the rights of the majority must take precedence when it comes down to protecting them...and any undesirables who pose a threat to that state of affairs should be expelled post-haste.

The Home Office states 'protecting the public is our number one priority'; well why don't they show it? For too long the rights of foreign criminals have been placed above those of the British public; it's time that changed.

———

Conclusion –

In the UK a vast industry has sprung up around The Human Rights Act which enshrined the European Convention on Human Rights into British law...and of course those milking these laws - *it has enriched hundreds of lawyers such as Cherie Blair* - together with the usual collection of civil liberties organisations will defend them tooth and nail...but I believe that it is time for a re-think.

The ethics of the Human Rights Charter, the Lawyers' Charter and the rules that give naïve, misguided do-gooders the right to defend un-constitutional issues need a good overhaul.

We need to put an end to the rampant abuse of the ECHR law and to do so the PDC would introduce a new British Bill of Rights which would be an abrogated version of the ECHR adapted to the specific needs of this island nation and would include a modification to Article 8 which would no longer allow foreigners to claim the right to a family life in the UK in order to avoid deportation.

To do this we would have to withdraw from the jurisdiction of the European Court of Human Rights but we would have to do that anyway as part of the bigger picture in order to regain our sovereignty and set our own immigration laws. (see chapter on EU)

———

We cannot have judges in the EU over-riding our judiciary; it simply undermines our whole system and makes us look weak.

The Abu Qatada fiasco was a prime example of why we need to opt out of the ECHR and install our own version of it, adapted to our particular circumstances.

This man, who had been convicted in his own country in his absence, entered our country illegally on a false-passport and had been living here ever since on taxpayer-funded benefits, using legal aid (more taxpayer money) and the human rights law to defend himself in a desperate attempt to avoid being held responsible for his actions.

His affiliation to terrorism and his anti-Semitic rants had been captured on film and yet his Human Rights to stay in this country were given preference over those of the sixty million citizens who live here. This is absolutely outrageous and unacceptable, and that is why a British Bill of Human Rights would carry a clause stating that in cases of National Security - and only in cases of National Security - the government would have the right to over-rule a judge.

It is time for the politicians in Westminster to listen to what the people of this country want and not what the bureaucrats in Brussels want.

———

Now it is clear that some countries deliberately obstruct repatriation because they don't want their criminals back, which is understandable, but the truth is that we don't want them either so if Brussels doesn't want us to send them back to their countries of origin, maybe we should send them to Brussels or to the International Court in The Hague, and let the all-knowing bureaucrats there deal with them.

———

NB1 - While the basic human rights of all prisoners convicted of serious crimes in this country would be protected, some of those rights would nevertheless be suspended and held over for foreign nationals after release - until they were deported - to prevent them organising sham marriages or deliberately procreating in order to use the family tie argument as a reason / excuse to stay.

NB2 - The courts constantly fail to uphold our immigration rules so under the PDC any judges who found it too difficult to rule on these issues would be relieved of the responsibility and guided towards a less contentious function.

Here are a few of the cases where the Human Rights Law has been invoked

---

- 200 criminals from Somalia including drug-dealers and serial burglars cannot be deported from the UK having used Article 3 as their defence which prohibits torture or inhuman treatment
- A burglar argued that being in prison breached his human rights to be with his five children; he was subsequently released...but when he re-offended a few weeks later it didn't work a second time
- A Congolese man already convicted once for raping a 16yr old, struck twice more subjecting two young girls aged 4 and 7 to horrendous abuse – he used article 8 - the right to a family life - to stay here
- Another convicted criminal, fearful of returning home to persecution because he had western-style tattoos on his body was allowed to stay after he invoked Article 3 (as an aside; the PDC would offer anybody fearing this kind of persecution the chance of having the tattoos instantly lasered off)
- In another case, a dangerous sex-offender from Togo who should have been deported on his release from prison is still here, costing the taxpayer hundreds of thousands of pounds in benefit payments and legal costs
- A former policeman and a woman of 88 from Zimbabwe who had both fled Robert Mugabe's thugs were threatened with deportation back to Zimbabwe...while one of Robert Mugabe's former henchmen - who was known to have tortured opponents of the regime - was granted asylum here thanks to article 8
- In one absurd case, a judge was prevented from confiscating a convicted criminal's passport as the man argued that it was against his human rights to do so

- In another case, a convicted killer claimed it was his human right to have a birth-mark removed on the NHS so that he wouldn't be recognised or discriminated against in prison
- Another case saw a man from Pakistan allowed to stay here despite the fact that he ran a red light and ploughed into an Oxford graduate, killing her
- A man from Serbia, accused of genocide in the Balkan war used article 8 to stay here
- And in another ludicrous case, a man - who took photographs of a group of thugs who were trashing his property - was arrested for breaching **THEIR** human rights
- A Moroccan man who is in the UK illegally and who has claimed £400K in benefits because he was 'allegedly paralysed' from the neck down was filmed dancing at his wedding. We cannot deport him; Article 8
- One prisoner claimed it was his human right to have an artificial insemination procedure carried out on his wife at the NHS's expense. His wish was granted
- Another prisoner who battered and stabbed his partner to death argued that it was his human right to be allowed to write a paper on domestic violence and killing
- A serial criminal from Somalia with at least seventeen convictions to his name – who is in this country illegally - claimed that it is his human right to stay here because his country is not safe; **OUR** country is not safe while he and his ilk are here
- In another case, a shopkeeper was prevented from banning thugs, yobs and hooligans from the front of his shop – as it was against their human rights to be moved on
- A Conservative politician invoked his Human Rights to take his dog to work in the House of Commons
- An Albanian man who blasted another man to death in Tirana (Albania) with a sub-machine gun and who arrived in the UK on a false passport claimed asylum here as a war refugee. He has so far cost this country £500K in legal costs trying to send him back to Albania
- Another failed asylum-seeker - an Iraqi-Kurd - who had already been banned from driving, for driving without insurance and without a licence still got behind the wheel and ran over a 12yr

old girl. He then fled the scene, leaving her trapped beneath the car. She died. He was allowed to stay because he has two children; Article 8

- Another illegal immigrant due to be deported cited being a cat-owner as his reason for being allowed to stay here
- Convicted serial killer Dennis Nilson was allowed to have hard-core porn delivered to his cell claiming it was his human right
- Strangely, employers cannot hold important meetings on October 31st as pagans celebrate the Festival of Samhain on that day and claim it is their human right to do so
- In another case, a hate-preacher already banned in this country still managed to get in and is now using the human rights charter to demand his right to stay and preach his virulent anti-Semitism...and while his case is being considered he is staying in a five-bedroom detached house in London at the taxpayers' expense
- Two Portuguese brothers who clubbed and stabbed a man leaving him to die with a black bag taped over his head claimed article 8 in order to stay here.
- And finally, most recently, a Kenyan man - who arrived here as an illegal immigrant – has been allowed to stay despite admitting that he has killed up to 400 people in his homeland. He too, used the Human Rights argument; Article 3, to plead his case, living here on benefits while his request is considered.

Each of these cases shows how the Human Rights Law is clearly being exploited and I believe that it is now time to put an end to this abuse.

It is time for us to stop being a soft-touch; it is time for us to stop leaving ourselves open and vulnerable to exploitation by these criminals; it is time for a new generation of politicians to act and to defend OUR RIGHTS, the rights of the people...the citizens of this country...

...and more importantly it is time for us as a nation to regain

- our self-respect,
- our dignity,

- our integrity and
- the credibility

...that the previous (and in some cases current) generation of witless politicians signed over to Brussels with such casual alacrity and gay abandon without once having the decency or the courtesy to consult us, despite their numerous promises.

I am sick of seeing the British justice system constantly undermined and over-ruled by the unelected bureaucrats in Brussels. I am sick of people who know nothing about this country imposing their will on us without us having the possibility of veto.

It's time we re-took control of our own destiny so that we can tighten up (and toughen up) the rules so as to protect the decent, law-abiding people of this country.

There is still time but we have to act fast because we are fast becoming the world's dust-bin thanks to our EU affiliation.

The PDC would propose a British Bill of Human Rights designed specifically to work in harmony with our rule of law and adapted to our unique circumstances as an island nation; that is the way forward.

Hot off the press –

A recent ruling has decided that Human Rights Law should also apply to the field of battle which shows how ridiculous this obsession has become. The very nature of military conflict - in its most brutal form - doesn't respect the right to life.

That said, while I agree that our troops should always be correctly equipped when sent off to fight in our name - which was the crux of this ruling - I believe that the families of our service personnel need to understand that the inherent dangers involved in conflict mean that

Human Rights Law and Health & Safety procedures cannot always be adhered to in the heat of battle.

That said, if this new ruling has been devised as a way for bereaved families to obtain some financial compensation for their loss, then I suggest that they make their case against the political party responsible for sending their family-member to war in the first place and not the MOD or the government which might have changed in the intervening years.

Tony Blair and New Labour took us to war in Iraq and Afghanistan; maybe if they had thought more about the consequences and the compensation that they would have to pay out - as a party - as a result of their poor decision making, then perhaps they would not have been so gung-ho in sending our troops into these conflicts.

———

Prisons

During the thirteen years that **New Labour** was in office, successive Home Secretaries from Jack Straw to Alan Johnson completely ignored the fact that there was a problem with prison places, despite records showing that over 91000 people convicted of serious crimes in this country were not jailed during that time because of lack of places.

That is not just an illustration of complacency; it is a clear example of how the politicians of this country are so out of touch with reality, and unfortunately - as is so often the case when talking about politicians - the words incompetent and irresponsible immediately spring to mind.

Kenneth Clarke meanwhile – in his role as Minister without Portfolio in the Conservative/LibDem coalition – came up with a brilliant idea. He wanted to reduce prison numbers by reducing sentences and letting people out early, thereby reducing the need for more places.

His motto must have been; it's better to have hundreds of criminals out walking the street than behind bars...if it saves the government money in these times of austerity.

How short-sighted is that? Didn't the danger that he would be foisting on the British public ever figure into his reflection?

This strangely naive and fluffy liberal attitude revealed a complete disconnect with the rigours of today's 21st century Britain and showed a complete lack of understanding of the complexities of the human-race, its dark psychology and its pathological urges.

Any policy - that does not foresee or take into account the consequences of its implementation - is highly irresponsible and unbecoming of a politician, whose role - as an elected official – is to look after the interests and the safety of the British public.

So I say; enough of this limp-wristed, lily-livered liberalism!

Every government in recent years has pushed this problem into the long grass because of its controversial nature and its cost...but all they have done is store up problems for their successors, for that person with a back-bone who will hopefully come along one day, ready to stand up, take responsibility and tackle the problem.

I believe that deep-rooted reform is needed in the penal system of this country and in stark contrast to the gutless, pseudo-amnesty offered up by today's out-of-touch, has-been politicians the PDC would – as part of its new justice policy - reduce prison numbers by making sentences tougher, making thugs and criminals so reluctant to go to prison that they would think twice about doing the crime in the first place.

The PDC policy –

Firstly, as set–out in the Justice chapter earlier, the PDC would re-introduce Capital Punishment which would mean designing and constructing the CP Implementation Unit to carry out those sentences.

The location of this unit has yet to be sourced, but ideally - because of its function - it would be an Alcatraz or a Rikers Island-style facility situated in an isolated location, away from the general public so as to avoid any security issues.

As for the construction of the facility itself, it would more than likely be based on the North Branch Correctional Institution in Maryland USA which is considered the most secure facility currently operating around the world.

This construction would be the PDC's first priority and once the wheels had been set in motion on that project we would then look to toughen up the security procedures at our existing high-security facilities, putting an end to the softly, softly approach that has been so abused by all over the last thirty years..

At the moment, criminals and drug dealers are actually <u>breaking into</u> our jails to supply inmates with drug needs and even prostitutes; it is estimated that £100M of drugs circulate in our prisons every year. That cannot be allowed to continue.

The PDC would then put into place a plan to overhaul and renovate the existing network of lower-level prisons that have been allowed to fall into a state of disrepair by distracted or blinkered politicians. This work would eliminate the need for any other new construction – apart from the CP Implementation Unit - as I believe that the need for places would slowly decrease thanks to the introduction of the new justice system.

And finally, the PDC would re-examine the structure of our working prisons. The current system of open-prisons is clearly not working as they are leaking escaped prisoners at an alarming rate. I have nothing against the concept of prisoners working to earn credit for their keep and early release but we need better supervision and tighter control of these arrangements.

———

Now, it is worth noting that 70% of the prisoners currently residing in our jails are being held there for non-violent offences and that many of those 70% are in desperate need of some kind of help.

Illiteracy (numeric and language) is a huge problem amongst prisoners and while they are paying their dues to society, I believe that we should use that time to do all we can – within the limits of reasonable expectation – to help them improve their situation and subsequently their chances of a decent life once they are released.

It is in all our interests as a functioning society to help these people so that when they get out, they are not tempted to fall back into the same lifestyle that got them locked up in the first place.

Therefore, the PDC would set-up an intensive education and literary initiative for prisoners; we would provide physical training activities and we would organise apprenticeship-style work-shop programmes for those more intellectually-challenged where they might learn the skills and the work ethic necessary to improve their prospect of employment upon release...

...and finally, as part of their re-introduction to society all prisoners would be encouraged to partake in supervised work-programmes in the Community.

These people are not all bad and I believe that many of them deserve a second chance.

However, let me be clear. I do not agree with the ultra-liberal ideas of some...or the naive and gullible attitudes of others, notably the bleeding-heart humanitarians who believe erroneously that...everybody is inherently good and that evil people are just misunderstood...and therefore deserving of a second, a third and a fourth chance...

These people will be offered ONE chance; repeat offenders would not be signed-up again.

———

This leaves the other 30% of prisoners; these are the hard-liners, the incorrigibles.

Sadly, the human breeding process does not produce a perfect specimen every time.

Indeed, every day we see babies born with defects or illnesses that they have to carry with them their whole life...and every day our TV screens remind us that others amongst us have grown up to become murderers, rapists and paedophiles.

Now, I do not wish to go into the reasons why these people do what they do (genetics, background, up-bringing or social conditioning) but the fact is; they do it...and in an effort to make their detention as trouble-free as possible, the PDC would introduce a number of special protocols adapted specifically to the particular pathologies of each of these prisoners.

The basic human rights of these prisoners would of course be respected at all times but the PDC would not waste any resources on hopeless cases or lost causes. There is simply no point...because the sad truth is; some people simply cannot be helped.

———

NB; During construction of the CP Implementation Unit and the renovation of the other facilities, the PDC would commandeer and transform a couple of decommissioned warships to take on the extra capacity and house the overflow of non-violent prisoners until they were slowly re-absorbed into the system.

———

The PDC would also transform a number of disaffected Army camps into boot-camps for both adult and adolescent offenders convicted of Category 5 offences - *see chapter on justice* - and I would like to see the demobilised military personnel coming back from Afghanistan and Germany with their discipline and their structure take on the lead role of running these centres.

———

The PDC and the softly softly approach;

During detention, while a person's basic Human Rights would be upheld and respected at all times – all civil rights would be suspended on crossing the threshold of the prison; i.e.,

- the right to vote,
- the right to claim benefits and tax credits
- and the right to IVF treatment

In fact, no non-essential NHS funded cosmetic surgery or NHS funded artificial insemination would be offered to prisoners.

This might seem harsh to the bleeding-heart liberals but maybe losing the possibility of becoming a father would make some criminals think twice before committing the crime in the first place; besides it is often argued that children who are born to a parent absent for a long period suffer all kinds of trauma – Human Rights or not.

This measure would also remove the temptation for those who would just like to become fathers while inside...in order to demand 'a family life.

The whole point of being in prison is that you forfeit your liberties.

Now, I understand that there will always be a group of liberals trying to champion this cause, defending the criminals' right to a family – but the PDC would always be on the side of those who have suffered at the hands of these criminals; the victims and their families **whose rights were abused by the criminals in the first place.**

It is time to put an end to all this trite, liberal minded dogma which makes us and our prison service look weak and open to exploitation.

The PDC would review every policy and notably the new initiative of offering prison-officer houses to convicts.

The PDC would also make sure that nobody convicted of a crime could ever benefit from it financially – books, films, newspaper articles etc; that grey area would be clarified and loop-holes exploited by unscrupulous lawyers would be closed.

The PDC would also put a stop to prisoners claiming student grants and loans while in prison; the new rules on prisoner education would make this redundant.

The PDC would also review the fact that convicted prisoners are allowed a day off in prison to celebrate Pagan festivities such as Halloween. Rastafarians are given four days off prison-work to celebrate Rastafarian festivals – what hokum.

New Labour spent £221K on Play-station consoles for prisoners – that kind of profligate expenditure and liberal experiment would not be renewed.

And finally...anybody found in possession of drugs while inside, would have a year added automatically to their sentence for every time it happened.

Reflection –

It is a sad day for Britain when drug addicts convicted of crimes are offered compensation by the government for losing the right to take their drugs while in prison. That measure - probably defended by the over-indulgent Human rights activists would be revoked under the PDC

Upon release –

Under the PDC, micro-chips would be implanted under the skin of convicted prisoners considered susceptible to re-offend...and tampering with the chip would activate not only an alarm but an automatic period of re-incarceration.

The PDC would also look into tightening up the current probation service before slowly phasing it out; there are too many loop-holes currently being exploited by lawyers eager for an easy pay-day.

...and finally...going forward, the PDC would look into the concept of bounty-hunters - for bail-jumpers or those who didn't respect their probation conditions - to work alongside the official Law enforcement agencies.

———

Foreign prisoners -

We currently have 12000 foreign prisoners in our jails; let's deport them all back to their own countries with a life-long exclusion order banning them from ever returning to these shores.

This would immediately free up capacity in our prisons and reduce costs.

The PDC would draw up an agreement with every country – as part of a new extradition policy – that criminals convicted here could be sent back to their own countries to serve out their sentences and vice-versa.

This would not only save us money, it would allow prisoners to be closer to their friends and family networks.

———

The Police Force

Much like with the politicians, the people of this country have lost faith in their Police Force...but unlike the politicians it is not <u>all</u> the Police's fault.

Yes the Police have made some unfortunate alliances of late;

- signed some questionable pacts with the media
- and the politicians,
- and inevitably – as police officers are human beings, just like the rest of us – been involved in some suspicious, reprehensible and even corrupt behaviour

...but I believe that much of this turmoil is simply down to the fact that over the last decade or so, the Police Force in this country has been asked to fight an ever-increasing spiral of crime with an ever-decreasing budget...and in order to do that, they have been forced to cut corners.

It has become increasingly difficult to define the role of the Police in today's society, but everybody knows that it is very hard to fight with one hand tied behind your back...and the way that the Police have been hampered / hindered over the last decade by a succession of irresponsible and gutless politicians, trying to avoid the blame themselves while simultaneously trying to balance their Westminster books through budget cut after budget cut, is outrageous.

Of course, the pursuit of waste is an ongoing problem in any administration, and I'm sure that some areas needed to be addressed and economies needed to be made, but as far as the Police Force as a whole is concerned, I believe that the cuts have gone too far and have been too widespread.

This mayhem has led to fewer and fewer officers on the street and a growing trend for police-work to be carried out by proxy (at a distance) through a network of CCTV cameras, whether in speed-trap scenarios on the roads or in city-centres.

British Police-officers now spend more time watching screens, ticking boxes, meeting diversity quotas and assuring the politicians that targets are being met...than walking the beat; all to satisfy the galloping bureaucracy introduced by successive governments and their spineless ministers.

This is unacceptable. It is not what the British public wants.

The British public wants its Police-officers out patrolling the streets and arresting the thugs, the petty criminals and anyone else who doesn't respect the law; they want them fighting crime and keeping the peace, not sitting at their desks filling out forms.

After all, Sir Robert Peel didn't create the Metropolitan Police as a bureaucracy to showcase political correctness; he created it as a deterrent to urban crime and disorder.

Let's get back to that... and always keep in mind the PDC maxim;

> **Remember how things were thirty years ago...**
> **Look at how things are now...**
> **and think about how things might be in thirty years**
> **time if we don't do something to change things.**

In Britain, we police by consent, which means that we have the support and the backing of the British public to do so, but if we want to be proud of our police, if we want them to uphold our laws with rigour, integrity, respect and a devotion to duty, then it is imperative that we provide them with the tools and a budget that is sufficient enough and flexible enough to cover any and every eventuality.

The Police should never be put in a position where they are forced to mortgage their reputation or their authority trying to implement the misguided policies of irresponsible politicians who - cosseted away in their plush Westminster offices - have no idea what it is like to be on the front line and whose only pre-occupation is the bottom line.

Just as a soldier should not be sent to war – under-prepared and ill-equipped – a police-officer should not be sent out into the street without the right training, protection and back-up.

Otherwise, as in any situation, chaos will ensue.

It is a simple ethos; if you do not have the right tools, you cannot do the job properly.

The self-regarding politicians in Westminster need to realise this; that you simply cannot police a country properly by cutting corners, just as you cannot go to war on a fixed budget. These budgets have to be flexible and extendible in order to cater for the unexpected.

The Police Force is an essential service and should not be seen simply as a cost on the country's spreadsheet, because just like the military, it plays an integral part in maintaining our security and our democracy.

This makes the police indispensable; a cornerstone of our society and as such the Police Force should be recognised as a priority area - just like the military - and afforded a measure of protection from any budgetary restrictions.

Politicians must realise that some costs just have to be met if we wish to maintain our security at a reasonable level, both here at home and further afield, in the wider world.

Furthermore, I would add that our police should not have their reputations tarnished or their authority undermined by the very same politicians who slashed their budgets and imposed these impossible restraints on them. That is hypocrisy.

Especially, as those same politicians shamelessly helped themselves to the public purse during the expenses scandal while cynically betraying the police; offering them only a 1.9% pay-rise when an independent tribunal had already suggested that a rise of 2.4% would be more appropriate.

———

Secondly, let's stop serving up lies on crime figures which are so patently disconnected with the reality of what the public knows is happening on their streets.

Politicians will immediately dismiss this comment as untrue and spout more statistics to the contrary because it is in their nature to mislead us, but everyone knows that statistics can be massaged to reflect whatever the politician wants them to say...

...and as an aside I would suggest that we stop humiliating police officers by parading them in front of the cameras to downplay these problems, with scripted announcements that crime-rates are down when it is clearly not the case.

Police-officers are plainly uncomfortable, participating in this charade but we all know that they are only pawns, pushed onto the front-line to do the dirty-work and take the flack for cowardly politicians who dare not do it themselves.

The reality is that crime is going up; just ask anybody in the street and they will tell you; it is only the deluded, out of touch politicians in Westminster who cannot see it because it suits their cost-cutting agendas.

How they can stand up in the House of Commons and say that crime is on the decline when it clearly isn't, is ludicrous; that is a bare-faced lie which anybody could disprove on any given day by simply opening a newspaper.

—————

At the same time, I would also suggest that we stop irresponsible chief-constables putting forward idiotic solutions to social problems, such as the idea;

- to provide free drugs to users to stop them stealing to pay for their habit or
- to de-criminalise certain crimes with the proviso that saying 'sorry' will do or
- to reduce the age of consent to 13 so that paedophiles are protected.

—————

Corruption / corrupt activity –

The reputation of our police force has taken a hammering in recent years with a number of cases relating to corruption, cover-ups and inappropriate cosiness with the media all taking centre stage; the case of the Hillsborough debacle in which statements were altered and wholesale lies were told being the most high-profile.

That was a shameful episode in the police's history and it must serve as a marker, never to be repeated.

However, that was far from an isolated case and just recently in Cardiff we had a case where thirteen policemen were charged with framing three young men for murder; again, that is a complete betrayal of the police's vocation and the procedural failures that allowed it to happen must be addressed.

—————

The Hillsborough case and others like it led the BBC to conduct a survey last year entitled 'Can we trust the Police'? and sadly its findings - when they were screened as a documentary on BBC3 - were more than a little disheartening.

- 1 person in 3 thought that the Police were corrupt while
- 1 person in 5 thought that they were dishonest.

Now if that is the public perception of the Police, it needs changing and excuses like systemic failure and over-work as reasons for these problems should not be accepted.

We need to stamp out illegal practices in all walks of life; in the media, in politics and in the police-force, but while nobody believes a word that is written in the newspapers – that's just a given - we the British public cannot have a situation where we have no confidence in those that govern us or those who have the authority to police our streets.

All corrupt activity is morally wrong and the police should never;

- be involved with exchanging money for information,
- nor should they be alerting the press and phoning ahead before going to make an arrest – usually of a high-profile suspect - so that photographers can be on-site ready to witness it and take photographs. That smacks of perverting the course of justice and infringing on the rights of an individual to be considered innocent until proven guilty; trial by media is wholly unacceptable
- nor should they be selling on people's information and details to garages and insurance companies after traffic accidents, either for their own gain or to make up the shortfall in the police budget.

This behaviour is intolerable and the PDC would crack-down on all these practices.

———

Reflection –

Of course it is wrong for the police to supplement their income by revealing classified or confidential information to the media but I just wonder if...

- *after years of watching grasping **politicians** and **MEPs** with their snouts in the trough on so many different levels*
- *of seeing **the bankers** help themselves to multi-million pound salaries and bonuses,*
- *of witnessing **the lawyers** abusing the legal aid process to the tune of £2 billion a year,*
- *of observing **the doctors** double their salaries for doing half the work while opting out of evening and week-end surgeries...and*
- *...registering that **local public officials** were being awarded outrageous salaries and excessive pay-offs while their own meagre police salaries – fixed by the same kind of bureaucracy – had barely kept up with inflation despite the demands on their time almost doubling......they just felt a little left out.*

There is no excuse of course, but we tend to forget that police officers are human beings just like the rest of us with the same family obligations and the same human character flaws.

We expect them to be exemplary in all things, ethical, principled, honest, respectful and upstanding but police officers are not machines devoid of a moral compass; they see what is going on; they are not blind but without strong moral leadership from above, some have clearly allowed their heads to be turned by the underlying trend of moral corruption that seems to run right through the upper echelons of our 21st century society.

Everybody else seems to be on their own personal gravy train so I can understand the police thinking; hey; why not us; why should we be the only ones missing out?

Human behaviour - instincts aside - is learned behaviour, it is copied behaviour. We learn from our parents by copying them and following their example and we learn new things every day throughout our lives from those who surround us by copying them. Maybe the police were just following the example set by their 'pay-masters'?

Maybe they were just succumbing to the same temptation, the same human character flaw – covetousness – that all those in a position of trust or responsibility are faced with. It happens in all professions; some get corrupted, others don't. It's a choice we have to make in life.

That said; of course I cannot condone police corruption; clearly it shouldn't happen – and thankfully, in the vast majority of cases it doesn't - but the constant undermining of their authority from all quarters combined with regular and swingeing cuts to their budgets together with a lack of strong, consistent moral leadership from both their own hierarchy and the politicians in Westminster has allowed a number of demoralising cracks to appear in one of our most iconic institutions which in turn have led to a few cases of fraudulent activity.

This is dangerous territory but all hope is not lost; this latent corruption is not yet as endemic in the police-force as it might be elsewhere and therefore, before it takes hold and spreads like a cancer or gangrene it could easily be eradicated with a little 'corrective surgery'.

Weapons –

As stated previously, we police by consent in this country and to avoid the idea of a Police State imposing the law through the gun, police officers on the beat in this country would not carry firearms.

However, they would be equipped with a variety of other low-level defence options.

On the other hand, because of the escalating nature of crime in this country the PDC would increase the number of special weapons units to work in collaboration with the New Border Police, each of which would target a specific crime-category and they would indeed be equipped with the latest in technological innovation and the most accurate of firearms available.

––––––

Compensation culture –

How sad and twisted our society has become when our police officers are suing members of the public for compensation for tripping themselves up on a kerb while out on patrol or stubbing a big-toe during a H&S course.

This is a betrayal of the institution of policing.

Under the PDC, any member of the police force who thought they deserved compensation for such trivial, everyday mishaps would be re-assigned or guided towards a more suitable career.

––––––

Prosecution –

We do not live in a perfect world; we are all guilty of making mistakes and errors of judgement. However, when problems do occur and prosecutions do take place involving a member of the police-force, it is not right that they seem to be systematically whitewashed and cleared of any responsibility.

Sure, I understand the idea of closing ranks and standing up for each other, but in the eyes of the public this otherwise-commendable solidarity sends out the wrong message and gives them (the public) the impression of a two-speed justice; one for them and one for the police – much like with the politicians - thereby confirming the public's preconceptions and their suspicions that they (the police) and the law - are corrupt and dishonest.

This perception must be changed; accidents happen; mistakes are made; that's life; we are all human but we cannot build trust without honesty and transparency.

––––––

Streets –

The role of the Police and their mission needs to be;

- rolled flat,
- re-evaluated,
- and re-prioritised to catch the real criminals plaguing our inner cities

Recent governments have abandoned the streets but I believe it is now time to tackle the big issues and restore faith in the system; it's time to flush out and cleanse our society of all the parasites currently feeding off the misery of others or preying off those more fortunate than themselves.

So, rather than going after the soft targets and those that bring in revenue, the badly parked cars or the speed cameras, I believe that the police should be fighting the crime on our streets which are becoming more and more dangerous by the day.

At the moment, people feel that they cannot walk along the street without the risk of being attacked; that has to change and to remedy the problem we need a greater Police presence.

This would both reassure the public and help reduce the thuggish behaviour of those who see no boundaries to their vicious acts.

It would also eliminate the sickening happy slapping culture and reduce the growing tendency to carry arms (knives and even guns).

However, while they should be consistent and firm the Police should not be arrogant or superior in their dealings with the public.

One last thing; Stop and Search powers which force innocent people to prove their identity are a back-door into imposing ID cards in this country. They need to be rolled back and restricted to use on specific targets only, in order to avoid any Police-state psychosis.

Soft targets -

It is outrageous that pensioners have been arrested for confronting groups of foul-mouthed youths in order for the police to meet targets – while the thugs themselves are let off Scot-free.

In one case, a 60 year old woman who confronted a gang of youths was thrown to the ground and her arm was broken. When the Police finally turned up, it was the 60 year old woman who was arrested – the group of thugs was left unpunished.

In the same way, I don't think it is right that the police should target parents who are picking up their children from school.

It is outrageous that you don't see a police-officer all day and then between 3h20 and 3h30 they all appear outside the schools, not for the security of the children but to write tickets for parents who are badly or illegally parked.

I suggest a little common sense is in order here, a little consideration, a little tolerance and maybe an understanding that while rules must be adhered to, it is not necessary to fine people in that situation; the new community police that the PDC would set up could take over the security aspect of this role.

In the mean time, burglars, car thieves, muggers, rapists and murderers are free to go – or worse – arrested and then let out prematurely to re-offend.

We must get our priorities in the right order.

Fines –

Of course, badly parked cars and speeding motorists need to be sanctioned but fining people; ordinary citizens for dropping papers or sweets in parks should not be a police priority.

Naturally, it should be discouraged and the re-introduction of wardens in public parks would go a long way to doing that, but the primary role of the Police should not be distributing and collecting fines – acting like a subsidiary tax-collection service for the Government.

Catching those who stalk, mug and rob those same people of their hard-earned possessions should take precedence instead.

The police have alienated the population with their policies of targets and quotas in recent years and now I hear that they are threatening and frightening 5 year old children who play football on the street with £50 fines – what next?

———

Other issues –

Big brother / CCTV –

It is impossible to police by CCTV alone and while cameras can be a substitute for active policing in some cases the majority of the public would still rather see a patrol on their street.

We are currently the most watched population on the planet and yet one Chief Constable recently admitted that it was a fiasco – because despite the huge number of CCTV cameras now littering our streets, only 3% have actually helped in solving a crime.

The PDC would re-focus the Police away from Big Brother systems and get them back on the street in sufficient numbers to deal with real crime.

———

DNA Data-base –

We do not need a national DNA database to help the police to solve more crimes.

We need more Police on the street stopping those crimes from being committed in the first place.

In fact, if a data-base was created, the criminals would probably turn it to greater advantage than the Police - as they always seem to be one step ahead of the justice system and are prepared to invest in the best technology to abuse the system, transforming DNA data, planting innocent data at crime-scenes etc – one example, cigarette butts with people's DNA have been collected and planted at crime-scenes.

Identity cards would suffer the same abuse.

———

Cars (road-side speed cameras) -

Speed cameras were introduced in this country on the premise of improving security.

However, it seems apparent to everyone that these cameras have been positioned mostly where they would bring in the most cash.

Clearly the politicians told the police that they were cutting their budgets, and that therefore they would have to make up the shortfall by generating their own revenue via speed-cameras and on the spot fines.

No government ever reveals how much it earns from parking fines or speed cameras but a conservative estimate recently put the figure collected by New Labour during their time in office at £200 a minute – that is £100 million a year which proves that the explosion in the number of speed-cameras was all about revenue...and confirms once again that New Labour's priority - as always - was the money. It was never about people's safety.

I am not against the judicious use of speed cameras but I do believe that they should be used in the interest of the public in black-spots and for accident prevention, not placed arbitrarily just to catch people out in order to fill the chancellor's coffers.

The police and local councils should work together on this.

Meanwhile, we need to stop privileged people from finding ways of not paying these fines at all.

Under the PDC, while British drivers would be afforded time to pay any fine they might incur upon proof of address, official, diplomatic and foreign car drivers would be fined on the spot. Either the occupant or the chauffeur would have to pay...to avoid the paperwork getting 'lost' in the system. Equally, if the car was illegally parked, it would be towed to a secure pound, thereby forcing people to have a more responsible attitude.

New Labour was working on introducing road tolls in order to beat traffic jams but of course the real reason was to raise billions more for their bankrupt administration. It was just another pseudo measure using the environment issue to sting the motorist yet again. If we want fewer cars on the road, all we have to do is make speeding a six point penalty. Then, after two faults, having used up their 12 point capital, drivers would be banned for three / six months. No fines need be imposed but in tandem with a crackdown on people driving without a licence, this measure would encourage more responsible driving.

The PDC would also ban road-side memorials and random 'party signs' which distract drivers and take away their concentration.

NB – Just as the police should not be selling on accident details to insurance companies, the DVLA should not be selling information to clampers; BTW; in Scotland, clamping is banned; a Scottish judge ruled that it was no less than extortion and theft.

———

Cars – drivers

The cars on our roads have been improved considerably over recent years in terms of their reliability and their security. They are a lot safer and a lot more robust than they used to be, and so I believe that it is time to re-evaluate and revise the speed limits on our roads.

We currently have roads where speed limits were imposed in the fifties and have never been revised since; we have dual carriageways limited to 40mph; let's give some responsibility back to the people.

That said, under new guidelines, the PDC would also introduce a sliding scale which takes into account the age of drivers and the engine-size of the cars they drive.

I do not want to see the very young or the very old in charge of powerful engines so we would impose a 30yr age limit for example for a Ferrari in conjunction with the new car policy outlined in the 'industry' section.

Every car would be given a category in the showroom which would follow it throughout its life-cycle excluding young drivers or old drivers depending on its engine size.

———

Riots (demonstrations) -

The politicians in Westminster led the way into moral poverty in this country with their sexual infidelities and their expenses scandals...

...the bankers followed gaily in their footsteps taking irresponsible risks with the country's economy and greedily paying themselves bonus after bonus…

...and the youth – who already felt that they were being left behind with no prospects and no future - saw these so-called role-models doing it and thought 'what's good for the goose is good for the gander'; if the people up the top, the people running the country act like criminals, then why shouldn't we?

However, that was no excuse and as much as I sympathise with the vast majority of young people who have all been tarred with the same brush, I was nevertheless outraged to see these amoral, illiterate thugs motivated purely by consumer greed, intent on doing as much gratuitous damage and destruction as possible,

- wrecking our streets,
- wilfully damaging property
- setting it alight,
- looting
- and stealing indiscriminately

I say illiterate because during the riots, these young thugs deliberately targeted sports shops with designer logos (Footlocker and JD Sports) and shops selling mobile phones...while book-shops such as Waterstones etc were left completely untouched.

The PDC Solution -

Firstly; I believe that it is time to put a deterrent in place before these gangs of feral / lawless youths start ruling our streets as they pretend to do, in their apocalyptic video-games and to help with the identification of future criminals, the PDC would, as a first initiative, ban the sale and the wearing of hoodies.

Now, this idea might seem a little draconian and repressive at first, but the thinking behind it is straightforward and logical; nobody goes to a protest march wearing a hoodie, a scarf or a helmet if their intentions are peaceful.

If they do, then I believe it is safe to assume that their intentions are not peaceful, that their reasons for concealing their identity - more often than not - are to avoid detection when they engage in criminal activity or provoke arbitrary violence with law enforcement and therefore, under a PDC government, anybody participating in a march or demonstration found wearing a hoodie, whether the march was peaceful or not, would be arrested and held in custody until their identity had been established and their motivation had been elucidated.

This order would apply to any piece of clothing that was worn with the deliberate intent of hiding or obfuscating a person's identity (masks, scarves, helmets etc)

Reflection –

If you believe in a cause to the point of demonstrating your views on the street, you should stand up, be proud and have the courage of your convictions. Hiding your identity behind a mask, a hoodie or a scarf while making your point or presenting your argument simply takes away your credibility, your integrity and your legitimacy...and it makes you look like a criminal, potential or real.

Secondly; to counter-act the growing threat of violence on our streets the PDC would provide the police with a number of alternative operational tools so that they might maintain the peace, in any given situation, depending on the level of threat encountered; these would include...

For mass demonstrations;

- Water-cannons loaded with dye (like that which is used to stain bank-notes during robberies); this would mark skin and clothes temporarily to allow for violent perpetrators to be picked up later, after identification.

Or for smaller interventions;

Paint-ball style guns with the same index-marker dye pellets for targeting individuals

- and stun grenades

... which would either stop violent protestors in their tracks on the street or allow follow-up investigators to find later.

We would also add goggles to the police-officers' kit to protect them from potential acid attacks.

NB; a reverse-effect agent would be provided to local councils to disperse the dye in the aftermath.

We would also look into finding a way of blocking social-networking sites during emergency situations (riots) in order to prevent thugs and criminals communicating between themselves to agree targets or rendezvous points.

Then, looking ahead we would review the use of tazers (probably reducing the voltage currently being used which I believe is too high) and possibly develop tranquilising darts that could be used on hooded hooligans and violent front-line demonstrators - in extreme circumstances – to immobilize them until the security services could move in and arrest them.

And finally, all those arrested would be photographed and those **found guilty of offence** would have their mug-shots published in the crime pages of their local newspapers and plastered on bill-boards in their local communities along with the details of their crimes and their convictions. The naming and shaming of people might not stop everybody but it would make others think twice.

Now, several Councils have mooted the idea that people who have been convicted of criminal offences - who clearly do not respect the law (rioters) - should be evicted from council properties and their rights to all benefits removed.

I am not in complete agreement with that idea. I cannot see how making people homeless would be a sensible solution though I would support a cap on their benefits just to remind them, as a wake-up call, that they should not be biting the hand that feeds.

Other crime –

So, having taken back our streets with an increased police presence, the PDC would then tackle the other big issues facing our society, by creating a number of Specialised Task Forces – SAS style / SWAT teams recruited from the armed forces (which are slowly being scaled back) to work in collaboration with the New Border Police.

Their role would be to strategically target, weed out and eradicate the traffickers; among them...

- The Colombian cocaine gangs
- The Pakistani / Bangladeshi / Indian heroin gangs
- The Yardies from Jamaica who peddle crack, heroin and prostitution
- The Vietnamese 'Snake-head' gangs who are running cannabis factories in suburban houses around Britain and producing enough to supply Europe as well as our own addicts.
- The Chinese Triads who smuggle people into the country and exploit them in all kinds of ways (cockle-picking, drug mules and drug farm attendants)...and
- The East European / Russians who – thanks to the open borders - have exported their gun-running activities.

These specialised Task Forces would also target the car-gangs who steal, strip and sell cars for spare parts or doctor their factory registration – either from the street or by violent threats and carjacking...and then export them.

NB – forensic operations should not be outsourced to private companies – to maintain the integrity of evidence this delicate and time-sensitive work needs to be carried out in-house. The PDC would create a centralised Forensic Hub to deal with this.

Community Police –

...and finally, local constabularies have been merged into sprawling remote democracies over the last decade; we need to reverse that trend and in collaboration with local councils the PDC would create a network of community police stations integrated into the Magnet scheme (see industry chapter) whose job would be to survey local thugs and keep an eye on isolated, elderly people in the community thereby circumventing the need for vigilante or neighbourhood watch schemes which could be infiltrated by a thuggish element.

These ethnically sensitive teams funded jointly by central government and the local council would comprise six officers; two full-time morning shifts / two full-time evening shifts – and two weekend shifts covering the daylight hours.

They would patrol the streets on distinctive, energy-efficient Vespa-style transporters and liaise with the national police when a situation warranted such an intervention.

Bail –

The PDC would also review Bail Conditions;

The Law Society which represents the solicitors of this country is calling for a 28 day limit on police bail after which time; the police would have to go before a magistrate to justify an extension.

I believe that 28 days is too short a time to guarantee a thorough police investigation... so the PDC would introduce a three month limit; that seems more reasonable.

Then, after the three month period an application could be made for an extension of the bail conditions if the necessary conditions were met.

However, to avoid cases dragging on indefinitely as is currently the case, this request for an extension could only be **granted once**, guaranteeing that a suspect was either charged or released after six months.

In recent times - because there has been no real requirement for the police to act within a certain time - a culture of procrastination has been allowed to develop in these matters and as the PDC would be looking to speed up the justice system in all areas, this aimless meandering would be curtailed dramatically.

Conclusion –

The police are human beings and have their flaws and their failings just like the rest of us.

They don't always get it right and the cases of Jean-Charles de Menezes and Ian Tomlinson are proof of that...but while those two cases clearly exposed those human failings and should never have happened, they put the spotlight on the police, highlighting their mistakes, without ever mentioning the hundreds of thousands of positive interventions that the police carry out every day, up to and including paying the ultimate price (as the recent case of Fiona Bone and Nicola Hughes demonstrated) ...and which far outweigh those two unfortunate but thankfully isolated incidents.

The Police are there to enforce the law. It is what the British people want and therefore they should be given the tools to do it.

They should not have to look at protecting this country and its inhabitants as a business with a balance sheet and targets to reach.

I would much rather the police do an effective, efficient job of protecting the population and catching criminals – albeit at a loss – than see millions of taxpayer money being spent;

- overpaying politicians with perks and expenses

- or setting up hundreds of quangos populated by thousands of civil servants who bring nothing to the table

The Police should be a non-profit organisation and not another way of filling the government coffers through fines as the New Labour Party saw it.

———

Retirement –

The PDC would aim for equality in all areas and therefore, due to the fact that everyone is living a lot longer these days, the official retirement age of fifty-five for police officers would have to be phased out.

We would still maintain fifty-five as the age at which officers were withdrawn from active-service on the front-line - because of the physical demands of that position - but rather than lose all their knowledge and experience, the PDC would retain these officers and guide them towards a new role in the administration team or liaising with the new Border Police.

Some officers with good communication skills would be mandated to go around schools giving lectures and educating children about the law while others would be put forward for advisory roles in the security industry providing businesses with security management advice.

Nobody who had devoted his life and his career to protecting the public would be discarded without consideration.

———

However, we would need to weed out the over-zealous and excessively officious members of the police force...and here is a sample list of some recent cases which would never be allowed to happen again;

- A 12 year old girl was interrogated by a security officer and three uniformed policemen over trying out a nail varnish on <u>one thumb</u> in a Boots store

- A man was accused of kidnap when he made a citizen's arrest and detained a youth who was attacking him
- One man was arrested at home by five uniformed police officers – for allegedly dropping an apple core
- A man was arrested for 'harassing' a tree
- Another man was arrested for attempting to kick a flower
- Yet another was arrested for holding a door open on the Tube as his pregnant wife struggled to get on.
- A man was arrested for placing a foot in a lift door
- Another was arrested, his photo and DNA taken, for canoeing on a river
- A pensioner was given a criminal record for cutting down a tree in his own garden
- Children were arrested for playing rugby in the street
- Children were threatened with arrest for throwing snowballs
- Four police cars full of riot police were sent to a bowling green in Bristol to arrest pensioners for bowling without permission
- In one case police officers ignored yobs and drug-pushers standing outside a block of flats to swoop on a 71yr old woman accused of playing her music too loud
- Litter police dished out fines to children for dropping a piece of sausage from a sausage roll
- Two young girls were arrested for chalking a Hop-scotch grill on the pavement

It is preposterous that petty crimes such as sitting on a curb, driving a car 'too smart for the area' and dropping a banana skin, have been taken through the British justice system; we need to forget the target culture and concentrate on the real issues.

Warning –

The new Police and Crime Commissioners are a scandal waiting to happen; not only do they seem to believe that they are above the law;

- they are hugely overpaid,

- they are naming friends and family in posts of responsibility, (nepotism again)
- they are having whistleblowers who expose their indiscretions and wrongdoing arrested and
- they are already wasting hard-earned taxpayer money on spin-doctors to minimise the fallout of their mistakes...and one has already spent £17,000 of taxpayers money to decorate his office.

People this is a scandal waiting to happen; mark my words

———

Oh..oh..I spoke too soon...

Police and Crime Commissioners / Tsars

The Conservatives invented these new roles to save money and improve efficiency in the Police Force but as far as I can see these people seem to spend most of their time dreaming up gimmicky policies and being involved in scandal…after scandal;

For example…

- Kent's independent crime tsar Ann Barnes appointed Paris Brown as the first 'youth commissioner' without carrying out basic checks that would have revealed that the teenager had made offensive comments online…and then Ms Barnes spent almost £200,000 of taxpayers money on new offices
- Cumbria's Tory PCC Richard Rhodes took two chauffeur-driven trips to meetings costing the taxpayer £700…and when the news was leaked the whistleblower was arrested.
- At least a dozen PCC's have handed out well-paid deputy roles to friends and allies without advertising them or going through the proper recruitment process.
- Four PCC's have already been investigated by the Independent Police Complaints Commission for alleged criminal misconduct. Lancashire's Clive Grunshaw is facing charges while Durham's Ron Hogg is still under investigation
- Several other PCC's have caused controversy over expenses. Norfolk's Stephen Bett declared his home as his place of work in order to claim mileage for driving to and from the force's HQ

More information on the abuse of taxpayer's money;

The 41 PCCs and their deputies – elected under the Conservatives flagship criminal justice policy – have each cost an average of almost £3,000 in expenses; all this when police forces around the country have had to make 20% cuts.

In fact, the PCC's have...in their very first year... already claimed £120,000 in expenses, billing the taxpayer for flights, luxury hotels, chauffeur-driven limos and even a steak pasty.

However, the biggest claims were filed by £70,000-a-year Norfolk PCC Stephen Bett and his £56,000-a-year deputy Jenny McKibben. Together they racked up £6,914.01 in expenses, including £14.40 for driving to a 'colleague's funeral' and £81.20 for a two-day visit to the Royal Norfolk Show. Mr Bett also claimed £3,000 for his commute to work but has since said that he would pay it back.

Avon and Somerset PCC Sue Mountstevens, who eans £85,000 a year, claimed 267 hours of chauffeur-driven trips, totalling £3,761.70.

Gwent PCC Ian Johnston put in bills for a £200-a-night hotel and a £105.56 flight. His deputy Paul Harris billed the taxpayer for a car wash.

Durham PCC Ron Hogg, who recently warned in a speech that more police cuts were 'inevitable', submitted a £4.90 receipt for a pasty.

Kent PCC Ann Barnes also billed £17 for a taxi journey, writing: 'Taxi taken due to carrying confidential papers and being a heavy load.'

Northamptonshire PCC Adam Simmonds claimed £1,100.15 for a four-day trip to Stockholm and Cheshire PCC John Dwyer even claimed 30p for parking.

People of Britain...what do you think about this...?

Crime UK; the Balance of Power

On the one hand we have;

- The established local gangs who deal in gratuitous violence, theft and drugs
- Then we have the new criminal gangs moving in from Eastern Europe (Russia, Albania etc) who deal in gratuitous violence, drugs, prostitution and human trafficking...plus an ever-growing number of **individual** EU criminals flooding in here thanks to the EU's open border policy
- And finally we have the International crime syndicates who also deal in gratuitous violence, extortion, drugs, fraud, money laundering and people trafficking

These are all dangerous criminals but on top of these we also have our share of radical terrorists and an increasing number of psychopaths & sociopaths committing murders and rapes on our streets...together with the usual array of petty criminals committing more and more everyday crime (burglaries, robberies, street violence and social unrest)

We also have the 'gangsta' culture to deal with and the growing feral underclass of younger, small-time thugs, degenerates and reprobates who are not only disrespecting the law, they are ignoring it...

And last but not least, we have the universal abuse of the law based on selfish greed - that everyone seems to be participating in - modelled on the immoral actions of our leaders, the politicians and the bankers.

And on the other hand we have;

...fewer and fewer police with more and more paperwork having to cope with increasing crime rates and decreasing budgets leading to frustration and low morale among many forces.

Burn-out is already an issue in some areas as officers are constantly asked to do more to cover the shortfall in numbers, often stepping up to the detriment of their health and their families.

The conditions and the hours of police-work mean that recruitment is becoming a problem too...and as the numbers dwindle and the realisation sets in that they are fighting a losing battle the temptation for corruption is increasing and will continue to increase through the sheer weight of opportunity.

Cracks are already beginning to appear as the Hillsborough case and the Leveson inquiry have both revealed.

We tend to forget that while we expect our police to be model citizens, upstanding and law-abiding; they are no less human than the rest of us, with the same hopes, the same fears and the same human failings.

Conclusion –

The balance is clearly with the criminals at the moment so in 15 or 20 years time, if nothing is done to redress this imbalance – the criminals will have more or less taken over - outnumbering the police by a substantial number - and the ordinary British citizen will no longer dare to leave his / her house for fear of attack.

This situation reminds me of the film Mad Max where the 'police' were a dwindling minority of law-enforcers up against an ever-growing and uncontrolled lawlessness.

This is a kind of reverse evolution; its regression, a race to the bottom, the abandonment of morality and rules where only the criminals win... and this is the misery that awaits our children's children if we do not act now; right now to arrest this decline.

Global Warming and Climate Change

'Nature never deceives us; it is we who deceive ourselves'...Jean-Jacques Rousseau.

Apocalyptic stories of doomsday and Armageddon have littered our collective memory since time immemorial but this current episode in the history of the world will probably turn out to be the greatest, most colossal scare story that mankind will ever have imagined; it is the ultimate hoax, a scam at the very summit of human ingenuity on the same scale – as far as the potential generation of revenue is concerned - as those other great human follies, religion and war.

I am convinced that future generation will look back on this period and be absolutely astounded by the collective folly of our politicians while abhorring the single-minded ruthlessness of our multi-national corporations in exploiting that folly.

Now, it is a fact that politicians around the world have been duped into believing the hype on climate change, but sadly UK politicians - *career politicians who lack any kind of life-experience or moral fortitude who are just desperate to be seen as having a green agenda in order to appease the environmentalists and gain their votes* - have been manipulated by the Climate Change purveyors to a far greater extent than most, having put their faith in a whole lot of data engineered, or at least produced in part, by the same hugely unreliable computers which previously forecast that;

1) The Millennium bug would make the world's computers crash in 2000

2) We would have warm, dry summers in 2007 and 2008 in the UK and that

3) We would have a barbecue summer in 2009 in the UK.

None of these predictions came to pass; none of these theories stand up to scientific scrutiny and yet our politicians have literally decimated our economy, bringing poverty to many, on the back of these flawed findings.

––––––

Global Warming and Climate Change has been happening as part of the evolutionary cycle of this planet for over 400 million years, but the hysteria and the incredible over-reaction to the theory that it is actually a man-made phenomenon was first brought to the forefront of the world's consciousness - in recent times at least - by the ex-vice president of America, Al Gore in his dubious film 'An Inconvenient Truth' …and ever since that film was released the idea of Global Warming and Climate Change has spiralled out of all proportion, taking on an almost religious status among the fanatics to the point where anybody who now dares to question what has become the establishment's official viewpoint is immediately demonised and branded a 'denier' or a 'flat-earther'.

Indeed, these days, because of its potentially massive implications for each and every one of us, if we are not seen to be doing our bit for the planet, we are made to feel like pariahs and heretics.

…and yet, as most people would agree, even the scientists themselves;

- **nothing in science is ever <u>that</u> dogmatic, <u>that</u> absolute,**
- **nothing is ever <u>that</u> black and white…**

…there are always margins for error, two sides to an argument and two ways of interpreting scientific fact.

––––––

Meanwhile, Al Gore – whose film spawned all the hysteria - has gone on to become the world's first carbon billionaire thanks to his activities and his investments in this field.

What a stroke of genius that was on his part, to create a problem and then – surprise, surprise - be the person best placed to solve it, with all the lucrative spin-off benefits that that has brought to him and his corporate friends; Bravo Mr Gore!

Of course, he is not the only one; following his lead, politicians and companies the world over have now jumped on the environmental band-wagon, and are growing immensely rich by exploiting the government subsidies and carbon-reduction opportunities that have now been created thanks to his and others' global scare-mongering tactics.

Unfortunately for him though, Al Gore's reckless film with its bogus claims and its apocalyptic conclusions has since been discredited by any number of people and notably a judge in the US who considered it;

'*...fundamentally-flawed and riddled with blatant inaccuracies*' when he was asked to comment on it, even calling it '*distinctly alarmist*', when referring to one of the nine major flaws in the film which he himself found particularly cynical – the hockey-stick shaped graph which Mr Gore used to demonstrate his theory.

This was a graph that had been produced by a computer programme designed specifically to produce a hockey-shaped graph, no matter what data was fed into it; how unscrupulous, conceited and blatantly misleading is that?

––––––

At this point, I have to say that I completely lost faith in the Nobel Prize committee when it became politically correct and contrived to attribute the Peace Prize to Al Gore for this blatantly misleading film.

It is alarmist, deliberately one-sided, fatally flawed and serves only to fuel the hysteria around the debate on global warming which politicians are cleverly using to scare the masses and impose extra taxes on them.

Even the founder of the weather channel John Coleman – who should know a thing or two about climates – said '… that self-righteous hypocrite Al Gore should be sued for fraud over this scare-mongering film'.

———

That said; while the veracity of this particular film has been proved to be… lacking…the Climate Change issue itself has become a great story for the fiction writers.

Hollywood has been using the *'end of the world is nigh'* concept to scare people for decades, and never one to miss the opportunity of another potential windfall, it has jumped on the bandwagon again, exploiting the 'time is running out' psychosis and the apocalyptic imagery of destruction associated with it, to bring out a whole new raft of disaster movies.

Now this might just be a money-spinning exercise for the film studios but unfortunately – be it deliberate or not - it is also helping to drive home the scary establishment message and perpetuate the anxiety of millions of people who like frightened lambs are blindly following what their leaders want them to believe.

———

Sadly, US actor Leonardo DiCaprio also got involved in this misguided crusade and while I applaud his desire to raise awareness about the ecological crisis facing this planet - due to its natural evolution - in his film 'the Eleventh Hour', the bleak forecast and the pessimistic conclusions of his team of experts, do no more than heighten the hysteria already being hyped-up around the issue by the politicians.

———

Today, because of the mass hysteria stirred up by Al Gore's film, the Climate Change issue has become a major preoccupation for all the world's political classes, and yet since the film has been in the public domain, 650 international scientists and even Nobel Prize winners have come out and voiced their concerns over its findings and the issue of man-made global warning.

In fact, 300 eminent scientists have signed a declaration confirming that Climate Change is a myth, pointing to the fact that, as temperatures have not increased for over ten years, the theory that global-warming is man-made has absolutely no tenure.

Meanwhile, their theories, based on fact-based research going back many, many years suggest that the sun and the clouds create cyclical changes over centuries and that any human input to the problem is minute; in fact, if anything, their findings show that it was warmer back in the Middle-Ages than it is now.

These people are eminent scientists who know about these things – much more so than the gullible, un-qualified, lily-livered politicians, but because they have spoken out against the official political viewpoint, thereby threatening to take away the unexpected tax windfall which had so conveniently fallen into the laps of the politicians, many of them have been vilified, ostracised and had their research grants cancelled in retaliation.

Indeed, several have even been prevented from publishing their work and their conclusions in leading scientific journals because their findings contradict the official doctrine...which smacks of authoritarianism not democracy.

This is because, having gotten its hands on an unexpected goldmine, the political establishment is reluctant to listen to any argument which might jeopardise the potential of their newly-invented seam of wealth – and anything that counters or undermines their argument, **however misguided their own argument might be**, is summarily dismissed.

Naturally, the politicians believe that they know best; they want us to believe that they are right and that anybody who thinks otherwise is wrong…even though a study published in the December 2007 issue of the International Journal of Climatology, supported by the US sponsored Climate Change Science Program, concluded that Climate Change is a natural phenomenon and shows no human influence.

This is on top of all the scientists previously mentioned.

––––––

Update;

A more recent study by the UK Met Office produced a graph which shows in incontrovertible detail how the speed of Global Warming has been massively over-estimated.

Indeed, the study reported that Global Warming had stalled since 1998, conceding that previous forecasts were all inaccurate and misleading, adding that a number of leading climate scientists had also begun to admit that their worst fears would probably never be realised, acknowledging the miscalculations in their previous work.

This is all very well, but those forecasts have had a ruinous effect on energy bills in the UK and throughout the world. At least £100 has been added to every household energy bill in the UK in order to subsidise the green policies put in place as a result of these 'miscalculations'.

––––––

The fact is that thanks to the politicians clever manipulation of the issue, the Climate Change lobby has now monopolised the public consciousness so deeply that it excludes any counter argument; but let me ask you this; how much should we really trust these politicians – what degree of faith and credibility should we really put into their judgement, their wisdom and their moral compass?

After all, these are the same self-indulgent and self-serving individuals who presided over the worst banking crisis in decades, one which almost bankrupt every economy in the western world.

They are also the same people who displayed such a shameless lack of moral integrity during the recent expenses scandal here in the UK – where they raided the public purse for all they could get their hand on...

...and they are also the same neurotic group of people who created the hysteria around the potential bird and swine flu epidemics which also never materialised, but which allowed pharmaceutical companies to stockpile huge mountains of vaccination shots at the taxpayers expense making millions if not billions for those same pharmaceutical companies who might I add as an aside, regularly offer directorships to retiring politicians as part of their 'pension plans'.

I find it somewhat worrying that the people we have elected to lead us, the people we should be able to trust with our lives, have been so easily swayed into taking us down such obviously erroneous and expensive paths...unless of course they did it with a vested interest or a hidden agenda.

This is only speculation of course but let's hypothesise here that our politicians are really that naïve and only have our best interests at heart – just for argument's sake.

Should we really follow them blindly on their Climate Change crusade given their previous track record?

They will, of course, point to the scientific evidence to defend their position, but that evidence has been shown to be flawed, inconsistent and inconclusive even though they are still desperately trying to force-feed it to us.

So, again I ask; why should we submit and follow the politicians lead without question?

I draw a parallel here with another new-age concept; the shiny new satellite-navigation systems, which when installed in our cars, are supposed to lead us directly to our destination without fail.

These devices are supposedly infallible too – just like the politicians argument on Climate Change – and yet how many people have blindly followed their instructions only to find themselves lost down a country lane with no exit or heading over a cliff.

I repeat; should we really be letting the politicians lead us off a cliff without questioning their reasoning and their logic for doing so?

I would suggest then, that the simple fact that politicians are deliberately suppressing the counter-argument, shows that their own alarmist argument about Climate Change being man-made is so shaky that the only way that they can continue to promote their misguided agenda is to gag the counter-argument in any way possible, thus preventing debate – a political weapon used time and time again - and to great effect - down the ages by any number of totalitarian / authoritarian regimes, because as anyone knows; if you hammer at the collective consciousness for long enough - with wave after wave of manipulative propaganda, while suppressing the counter-argument, *especially if that propaganda contains the threat of catastrophic ramifications for those targeted if they do not convert immediately to the suggested way of thinking, however unfounded and outrageous those threats might be* - eventually the brow-beaten collective will be swayed and begin to believe the propaganda because unfortunately it is inherent in our nature to fear the unknown and what tomorrow might bring.

This kind of mind-conditioning, preying on people's fears and ignorance has worked very well down the ages for things like the voodoo culture and even for religion, both of which flourished among the uneducated masses through the peddling of intangible concepts like the afterlife, God's wrath, Judgement day, Heaven and Hell etc, and these same tactics are now being used by the Climate Change lobby to impose their political agenda.

Isn't that just so typically cynical of the political classes; using our natural, inherent fears and our insecurities against us, to exploit us and take advantage of us, by promoting only the scary side of their argument - just so that they can manipulate us and impose more control on us?

That in itself is as morally objectionable and ethically reprehensible as the concept of selling life after death which voodoo and religion did before them.

The reality is that the Climate Change psychosis really all comes down to political and corporate greed – and only two types of people benefit from it – **politicians** because they exploit the scare-mongering opportunities to impose more taxes on their citizens…and **private enterprise** because they are making a fortune through government subsidies and – ultimately pointless in many cases - renewable energy contracts etc.

Now, Al Gore's film with its glaringly-inaccurate 'revelations' was released in 2006 and ever since, we have been bombarded from all quarters with the Climate Change issue and threats of catastrophic, cataclysmic consequences if we don't pull back from the brink.

However, it would now appear – if the leaked e-mails from the East Anglia Climate Research Unit are to be believed – that a chink has appeared in the politicians infallible argument that Climate Change is man-made, which would suggest that once again they have in fact been conspiring to deceitfully manipulate the public opinion on this issue, just as they did for the war in Iraq previously.

Indeed, some of those who have worked for the IPCC (Intergovernmental Panel on Climate Change) even attested to the errors, the manipulation and the downright fraud at the heart of its research.

...and this is where it gets complicated because Climate Change is no longer just a scientific issue; it has become a political issue as well... because of its scale.

Politicians around the world have cleverly hijacked the Climate Change issue as a way of covering up their ineptitude and incompetence, using it as a very convenient way of raising money to top up their reserves and cover their budgetary mismanagement, playing on the naiveté of their citizens to fraudulently impose extra stealth taxes on them, believing that by simply attaching the magic and somewhat scary words **Global Warming** and **Climate Change** to any of their policies that this somehow absolves them from any public scrutiny.

Of course, political scaremongering aside, the core idea behind the Climate Change lobby of inciting people into lifestyle changes in order to use our resources more efficiently is laudable; anything we can do to save and not waste the precious resources of this planet is a good thing, but

- the green tax,
- the carbon tax,
- the extra fossil fuel tax,
- the flying tax and now
- the recycling-rubbish tax recently introduced in the UK

...are all just token taxes which will do nothing to intrinsically modify people's behaviour or impact on the issue of 'saving the planet'. On the other hand, they will do a wonderful job of covering the shortfall in the politicians' blatantly mismanaged budgets and help in no uncertain manner to refill the empty coffers of many an incompetent, irresponsible and unscrupulous central government.

Indeed, former Labour Chancellor Alistair Darling even admitted that the flight taxes had nothing to do with Global Warming or Climate Change.

So the Climate Change issue is not only a **scientific issue**, it is a **political issue** as well, but that is not all; it has become an **economic issue** too.

This is because - revenue from taxes notwithstanding - the carbon management industry and all that surrounds it is now big business, becoming an integral part of the political and corporate jigsaw.

The green agenda has brought with it a whole new sector of growth providing so many jobs these days that even the politicians who didn't believe in it in the first place, can no longer ignore it.

They might know that it is all a scam…but unemployment is such a political hot-potato for any politician that they would probably err on the side of self-preservation if faced head-on with the issue rather than try to curb the green band-wagon…even if they knew that many of the jobs that have been created are built on logic as sound or as shaky as that used to explain the wonders of sub-prime mortgages – i.e., thin air.

Now, nobody is denying the existence of Climate Change but history, archaeological and geological studies all tell us that it is a natural, ongoing occurrence, a cyclical phenomenon, a gradual evolutionary process which has been taking place for over 400 million years.

Our planet is constantly evolving; fluctuations in temperature are a natural trend and while our current climate is undoubtedly changing, could it not just be simply the precursor to the next metamorphosis of our planet as it transitions into its new age.

That is evolution; it is inevitable and there is nothing we can do about it; it is not man-made and people should wake up to the political scam.

I believe that we may well be at the dawn of a new age, a new phase in our planet's evolution and if that is the case - rather than taxing our lifestyles, impoverishing us all a little more every day - why aren't the politicians concentrating their efforts on finding more renewable energy sources; why aren't they being more pro-active in consolidating or restructuring our low-lying shorelines to take into account the raised water levels which will inevitably occur with the melting ice-caps?

Why?

Because like many of us, politicians are selfish, self-serving individuals who would rather tax people now in the short-term – during their lifetime and their terms in office, so as to balance their current deficit-riddled budgets - rather than plan for the future, because in the long-term, when the water levels do increase and people do get flooded out it will not be their problem, they will be long gone and no longer in a position to be held accountable.

A summit <u>was</u> held recently in Copenhagen during which the politicians decided unilaterally that we should limit any increase in the planet's temperature over the next ten years to two degrees...which is an honourable resolution I'm sure, but it is completely delusional.

It is simply unrealistic to suggest that we – the human race - have any control over the rise of global temperatures; planet earth has been heating up and cooling down for millions of years without any interference from politicians or mankind in general; who are these pretentious politicians who believe they can legislate against evolution and the universe?

How presumptuous, arrogant and typical of their own warped sense of self-importance that they believe we can influence the universe or control nature in this way.

Is mankind really so pompous and so self-absorbed with his own importance that he believes that by his actions he can change the cyclical occurrences in the wider universe?

The universe is completely indifferent to our existence, so when are these deluded politicians going to realise that the forces of nature and the forces of the universe are far greater than anything that we humans could ever muster; just look at what happens when a tsunami strikes, when a volcano erupts, when a tropical cyclone or an earthquake hits land or when something so inane as a heavy fall of snow blankets our towns and cities; we are completely helpless; we are insignificant in the universe and the sooner the politicians reign in their egos and come to terms with the fact, the better.

———

Incidentally, most of the climate change prophets don't bear much moral scrutiny; when they gathered together for that summit in Copenhagen, to discuss the global warming crisis, they all flew in on their private jets – Tony Blair, Gordon Brown and Prince Charles among them – how hypocritical is that?

And even more ironically; the Energy and Climate Change Committee recently spent almost £50K of taxpayers' money flying six MPs to China to assist at an inquiry into lowering carbon. How self defeating is that?

Surely a video conference would have been the better option.

———

In conclusion, I do understand people's concern about Global Warming and Climate Change and I completely agree that we should do anything we can to save resources and not waste what we have, but these depressing doomsday-advocates and scared, environmental zealots who have been taken in by the politicians alarmist subterfuge that the problem is man-made do nothing but contribute to the hysteria and the panic of the world's populations.

…and who <u>are</u> these environmental activists anyhow…who want to save the planet; peaceful demonstrators who want their voice heard or just mindless militants whose only goal is to rampage, disrupt and destroy?

If these people are pacifists, then why is it that every time one of these UN summits is organised to discuss environmental issues, the host city has to deploy a military task-force to protect / defend its town centre against the invasion of these fanatics, boarding up their shops and windows and lining their streets with barricades, turning them into ghost-towns, against the threat of violence from these unruly mobs, many of whom belong to groups which were only created by concerned citizens on the back of the scare-mongering hysteria of Al Gore and his acolytes…but have since been infiltrated by some very violent thugs.

These are not peaceful demonstrators; these people are not interested in the question of Climate Change; they are groups of organised, well-trained mercenaries and hardened criminals who plan their operations like military interventions, deliberately exploiting the volatile situation that, once again, they create, for their own ends, dressing to avoid being recognised with their hoodies and face-masks while they go around causing as much havoc and disruption as they can; they have little or no interest in the talks; their only interest is in thuggery, violence and opportunist thieving.

Indeed, much of what these so-called environmentalists believe has little - *if any at all* - basis in science; their unscientific objections being no more than urban myth in most cases.

I would suggest that if anyone is that passionate about a cause, however misguided that cause might be, then he / she should have the courage of his / her convictions, stand up for what they believe in and defend it proudly, with dignity and integrity – not hide behind masks and scarves like terrorists.

People will never follow a leader who hides behind a mask because of the mistrust that it breeds and because of the over-riding suspicion that the person behind the mask actually has something to hide; indeed, any law-abiding citizen will tell you that anybody who hides their identity for whatever reason is up to no good, whether it be on a street corner or a public demonstration and therefore, he isn't credible and will never have his message heard.

Wouldn't it be wonderful though, if we could mobilise these same people in just as huge numbers to bring about World Peace.

———

One last point which concerns me greatly; If our world leaders are not in league with the scare-mongers, if they are not involved or complicit in any way with this sham, then how come those people we consider the most intelligent amongst us, those we have elected as our moral guides, are behaving so naïvely, like the notorious King Canute trying to turn back the tide.

Do they really and honestly believe that in the great scheme of things, in the vastness of the universe, that taxing people's lifestyles here on planet earth, doubling the price of our air-fares and forcing us to change our light bulbs (based on unsubstantiated findings) is going to somehow reverse millions of years of evolution; because if so, we need new leaders and fast!

In fact, what the world desperately needs now, is for somebody to emerge, a real statesman to step up to the plate – a voice of reason to rise up and show the way - an iconic leader with irreproachable morals, someone like Nelson Mandela who would stand up to the onslaught of misinformation and not get swept along with the ludicrous hysteria.

We need a wise man, a sage, a prophet of sorts to step up and restore some sanity to the madness that the politicians and their corporate lackeys are burdening us with; someone with broad shoulders who speaks with authority and gravitas - and someone who will stand out from the spineless, point-scoring, headline-grabbing political lightweights who currently occupy the world stage and who so obviously lack the moral stature of statesmanship…

…and only when we find this special person will the human race be able to move forward confidently, in serenity and peace, putting the foolishness of this last period of political greed and subterfuge behind us.

———

NB1 – The decarbonisation policy enshrined in the Climate Change Act by David Cameron will go down as his greatest folly. The EU only wanted a 20% reduction by 2020 but Cameron imposed a 35% reduction on the UK putting us at a huge disadvantage in comparison to other countries just so as to satisfy his proclamation of being the 'Greenest government ever'.

This self-imposed folly is economic suicide because the reality is that we simply do not have the technological knowhow to achieve such over-ambitious targets...and in trying to take the lead on the issue the UK has saddled itself with a fanatically outrageous green energy policy which does no more than sacrifice British households (through extortionate energy bills) and forfeit British jobs (through companies and manufactures relocating to countries which don't have such extortionate green taxes and ridiculous emissions targets) in the race to useless oblivion.

The Climate Change Act itself which commits us to reducing emissions by 80% by 2050 will cost the UK £18 billion a year to implement...and will surely render the country bankrupt - sooner rather than later - if we pursue with such folly, but in any event, it is futile for us in the UK to try to cut carbon emissions on our tiny little island, if the rest of the world and notably those who pollute it the most, i.e., the USA, China, Russia and India are not doing the same; and the recent summits in Kyoto and Copenhagen suggest that the political will in those countries is not there to do it.

NB2 - The concept of reducing our carbon footprint by planting trees and off-setting carbon emissions through random calculations is again no more than a feeble attempt by those with more money than sense - and who pretend to be fashionably green - to massage their egos, ease their moral conscience and appease the virulent deluded zealots who point the finger - but in reality the offset charge is no more than just another stealth tax.

References;

The bullying political classes and the obnoxiously, single-minded environmental lobbyists only push their side of the argument but if you wish to find out more and gain a more balanced view of the issue than the one being fed to you by the politicians, here are some of the references I used to research this subject;

Heaven & Earth; global warming; the missing science by Ian Plimer
Nature, not human activity rules the climate   by Fred Singer
The Real Global Warming Disaster   by Christopher Booker

US Senate Minority Report

Catastrophe   - TV documentary by Tony Robinson
Earth; The Power of the Planet   - TV documentary by Dr Iain Stewart
The Great Global Warming Swindle - TV documentary by Channel 4 UK which shows that the carbon problem has been created and perpetuated by politicians despite scientific evidence to the contrary because it now keeps hundreds of thousands of people in jobs.

Other fallacies exploited by the zealots that are not true according to Professor Stanley Feldman and professor Vincent Marks in their book 'Global Warming and other Bollocks; The truth about all those science scare stories'.

- CO_2 levels in the atmosphere are not at unprecedented highs
- Polar bears are not dying out...neither are penguins
- And the Maldives aren't sinking.

———

Of course, Global Warming and Climate Charge are not the first fallacy concepts that the human race has been sold – the God concept is another – and both concepts use the same irrational dogma to control people, the same scare tactics elaborated very carefully to exploit the inherent naiveté of the masses –

'Control people's fear and you control them'

Tell them stories about an imaginary afterlife
which offers them the choice between;

- **A heaven / paradise / nirvana** filled with angels, harps and a cornucopia of good living

Or

- **A Hell** blackened by fire and misery under the stewardship of a scary guy with horns, dressed in red and carrying a trident

... and they will choose heaven every time.

Then you add the condition; in order to get into heaven you have to spend your whole life believing that an imaginary supreme being is looking down on you and watching your every move so that when you die you can be judged on your actions.

Religion is all about exploiting the fear of not getting the nod into heaven when the time comes and the same concept applies to Climate Change;

Tell people apocalyptic stories about how the ice-caps are melting, how we are all going to die and how the world as we know it is going to come to an end unless we all pay more taxes, and we will all queue up to pay more taxes – out of fear, because we are afraid of what we don't understand and what we cannot control.

It is simple psycho-manipulation.

That said, while I believe that the religious bandwagon is still rolling - even though it is losing speed – the Climate Change chariot doesn't seem to have religion's astonishing endurance and is already slowing down.

Therefore, people of the world – heed this warning - expect the grey-suits to come up with a new scare-mongering tactic pretty soon – something like, if you don't pay double your taxes, little green men will visit you in the middle of the night and you will never be heard of again.

...and you know what; people will queue up to pay double their taxes because they will not want to risk the possibility of receiving a visit from the little green men.

Scare tactics work; they prey on the naive, the insecure and the gullible.

But of course, this tactic only works in countries where people actually pay taxes; where the men in grey-suits hold all the aces; the rest of the planet where people don't pay taxes will just carry on living regardless, in blissful ignorance, as they have done for more than 400 million years; what does that tell you...?

Initial PDC solutions to combat 'Climate Change';

Firstly, even though some people seem to be unaware of it, the UK is an island with a finite coast-line and that coast-line, despite some effort on out part, is slowly being eroded by the sea, which means by definition that, as the process continues the land mass will gradually reduce.

At the same time, the sea-level in our oceans is continuing to rise due to the melting polar ice-caps, and as a consequence of these two phenomenons, the low-lying areas around our country will slowly be whittled away or submerged leaving even less of this great land for us to inhabit.

However, rather than succumb to the hysteria of the 'we're all going to die' Climate Change lobby the PDC would act calmly and intelligently by firstly erecting some kind of natural barrier around our most exposed coasts - to slow down the erosion process - and then organise a gradual and orderly withdrawal from the inhabited parts of the shore-line. No more new builds would be sanctioned on land at the current sea level and a new safety exclusion zone would be enforced.

Then we would have to look at how we live, and apart from the oxygen that we need to breathe the next thing we need to sustain ourselves is food and water.

Water is an essential element for life and for that reason the PDC would immediately increase investment in the development of new desalination techniques so that we might use the ever-increasing natural resource of the sea as drinking water.

As for food, we would have to look into our agricultural policies because; at the moment we only produce 56% of our food needs. The other 44% is imported and if our land-mass decreases as it surely will, we will have to look very carefully at those figures in order to strike a balance between the number of people living on this island and the number of people it can sustain.

It is simple economics; if we allow the population to continue to rise - inexorably - as is currently the case, the demand for food will increase and our percentage of home grown food would inevitably decrease as we use the land available to build homes for that ever increasing population rather than agriculture.

This is why I believe that we should slow down the population growth (as set out in population chapter) because inevitably, unless we do something, we will end up being overcrowded on this island and dependent entirely on imports to survive which is not a sustainable or a long-term peaceful situation.

———

Energy

Author's comment;

The politicians have made more of a shambles of our energy policy than they did of the economy...and because they have lacked any foresight, any gumption or any creative innovation they have mortgaged the health and the well-being of the British population for generations to come, all to appease the misguided eco-zealots of today.

Wind –

The reason our economy is not growing is because energy costs are being held artificially high in order to finance the wind-turbine scam which is the greatest example ever seen of 'get-rich quick' companies exploiting ridiculously generous subsidies and tax-breaks offered by spineless politicians.

And why are politicians doing this;

- Firstly; to appease the Green lobby - who have completely hi-jacked our energy policy - in the hope that, when the time comes, the votes of these people would swing the next election
- and secondly; to get on the right side of the voracious, money-laden corporate conglomerates - who are gorging themselves on government subsidies - in the hope that they would be offered a directorship on one of their boards once they have finished fleecing the taxpayer.

Wind-power as a concept sounds very ecological and very new-age but in fact it was never about producing the necessary energy to power the country or making energy cheaper for the consumers; it was always about the politicians pretending to have a green agenda in order to appeases the environmentalists while at the same time lining the pockets of the scam's promoters who negotiated the construction contracts entitling them to billions of taxpayers money in the form of ridiculous government subsidies.

People need to remember that politicians have only one goal in life; and that is, to get themselves re-elected again and again, so as to keep their place on the gravy train; they will say anything you want to hear and they will do whatever they think is necessary – not <u>what is right</u> but what is <u>necessary</u> – for that to keep happening and they will give away taxpayers money by the truck-load if they have to, if it means them keeping their cosy lifestyles and their seat on the gravy train. After all, it's not their money that they are giving away; it's just a means to an end...and that end is... their feather-bedded retirement.

People also need to remember that politicians are not the intelligent ones; look at the mess they are making of the world's economies; the intelligent ones are the businessmen and women who create wealth and jobs and who are prepared to do anything <u>they</u> have to, in order to enhance their NP; these people are ruthless and <u>their</u> only goal is to cultivate / create the right environment worldwide for their particular portfolio to flourish - Rupert Murdoch is a great example of this.

———

The Corporate Motto;

- politicians don't matter (they can be manipulated or bought)
- and people don't matter either (they only serve two functions; to produce or to consume)

———

Comment;

Wind-farms - which incidentally are the most expensive form of energy ever devised - are deeply unpopular with the majority of the British public; indeed, many of them think the climate-change argument itself is a scam but developers will keep building them as long as the grants and subsidies keep flowing from the government...and the grants and subsidies will keep flowing from the government as long as those same developers have the politicians in their pockets; it's a closed circuit of greed. Who cares what the British public thinks...right?

Selfish greed and the patent lack of morality have no bounds for these people.

And of course, the politicians have the perfect foil; the deluded green lobby with all their scare stories and irrational dogma of how the world is going to come to an end unless we give all our money to huge exploitative corporations and construct a wind-turbine every hundred yards.

According to one source, in the UK we are handing out £400 million a year in subsidies to renewable energy companies...though another source suggests that that figure could be as high as £7.6 billion which in itself shows the alarming lack of transparency and scrutiny that surrounds this matter.

Meanwhile another £850 million of British taxpayers' money has been handed over in bribes to 'reluctant' landowners for the right to impose these hideous monstrosities on our landscape...and not to be outdone, the DECC, the government's own department (Department of Energy and Climate Change) waded into the mêlée, by handing out millions of pounds in bonuses to already overpaid bureaucrats as a reward for them imposing their questionable green policies on the British public.

This is all very generous, but let's stop and think for a moment;

Any start-up industry has to pass a viability test at some point in order to check its potential for success and wind-farms should be no different.

There are thousands of people trying to set up businesses in this country every year only to be told by the banks that their business plan is flawed and therefore not viable.

Meanwhile, the wind-turbine industry which depends solely on government subsidies and grants to survive is allowed to flourish; how is that a viable business-plan?

The reality is, of course, that it is a complete folly, a massive investment for very little return and I believe that this is just a visible ploy by the politicians to show that they are doing something to appease and placate the green zealots so as to win their votes in the next election without them (the politicians) having really understood the costs or the implications of this foolishness; especially, as wind power costs three times the price of nuclear or gas power.

———

Wind-farms are just an indulgent pipedream of the deluded greenies because not only are they ugly and not only are they a blight on our landscape but they are;

- costly to produce
- costly to maintain
- unreliable,
- and wholly dependant on the vagaries of atmospheric unpredictability which offer no guarantee of regular or constant production

...and when they <u>do work</u>, they produce trivial amounts of energy in return for this massive investment.

In fact, figures show that they barely generate 19% of their potential capacity, contributing only 2% of energy to the National Grid.

———

And what's more, apart from the fact that they are aesthetically unappealing and a hideous eyesore on the rolling landscapes of our green and pleasant land, these lavishly funded white elephants have to be turned off at times because there is <u>too</u> <u>much wind;</u>

So, to sum up;

- they are ugly
- they don't work in extreme weather conditions
- and they don't work when its not windy enough

That leaves a very small window of opportunity when the wind might be blowing at just the right speed.

Surely, anyone can see that this is not a viable solution to power a whole country.

These turbines are not cost-effective, they are inefficient and they are unreliable.

Irony; several propellers on wind-turbines have been snapped off or spontaneously set on fire...by the wind.

...and one last thing; these turbines not only effect the lives of those living nearby by their mere presence and constant noise, they are also responsible for shredding between 75000 and 275000 birds in their blades every year.

Comment;

Now, throughout this manifesto my biggest preoccupation has always been my inherent dislike of hypocrisy in all its forms and here is another example;

Amongst others, both Prince Charles and Prince Philip have condemned the wind-turbine paranoia but despite their public outrage on the matter they are nevertheless installing 45 turbines on Crown Estate land in order to rake in £1m in subsidies every year.

One last thing; I really hate to see the collusion between the politicians and big-business (the energy companies in this case) as it can only ever be detrimental to the taxpayer.

To see how the spineless politicians have slyly buried the cost of financing the renewable energy scam inside the energy bills of the everyday consumer through increased taxes is outrageous...and very, very devious.

To make the faceless energy companies takes the heat for all the extra charges, thereby absolving themselves from any responsibility - yet again - in exchange for the guarantee of continued subsidies to build more turbines shows the politicians complete lack of moral integrity.

And of course, it's a closed circuit, revolving agreement where everyone wins but the poor consumer;

- big business keep getting multi-million pound tax-payer subsidies,
- politicians keep their promise to the climate change lobby in exchange for their votes

...and the poor consumers, the people at the end of the chain, just keep getting higher bills to pay...or they go without heating.

Is that the result that our political leaders should be working towards?

Nuclear;

Despite being twice or even three times more cost-effective than wind-power, nuclear power is being slowly strangled out of existence in this country because the EU has banned nuclear industries from receiving any EU subsidies to either maintain or develop it further.

This means that we are depriving an industry of investment, an industry that <u>could</u> keep the lights on…while offering exorbitant subsidies to hare-brained schemes and initiatives which <u>will not</u>.

So, when the lights do inevitably go out in Britain and we have to introduce power-cuts in order to cope – we can all thank Mr Ed Miliband who while Minister for Energy and Climate Change sold off our last world-class nuclear construction company in October 2006.

How short-sighted was that?

(This is the same man who came up with the idea of reducing green-house gas emissions by 80% - instead of the 60% being requested – by 2050… and who pushed through the Climate Change Act in 2008 that instigated the crippling green taxes that are now being added to the energy bill of every household)

Indeed, his lack of foresight and his tenuous hold on the reality of people's lives is inconceivable for somebody who hopes to lead the country one day, although he does have one 'redeeming' quality, one saving grace.

He did push forward the idea of developing smart-meters to manage the inevitable power cuts that will occur because of his short-sightedness… at a cost of £7billion.

The irony is that it would have cost less to build the nuclear power stations necessary to provide the extra energy that we require, thereby avoiding the need for power cuts in the first place.

The PDC solution - in the medium-term - would be to carry out the necessary up-grades on our existing power-stations so that they might stay in production beyond their current decommissioning dates - in order to keep the lights on - while at the same time developing new sources of energy.

Fusion and fission could also be explored as alternatives.

NB - I understand people's concerns about nuclear power after the incident at Fukushima in Japan, but we are up against the wall here and as long as we put in place the right protocols as far as security is concerned and carry them out correctly any future disasters should be avoided.

———

Meanwhile, an EU anti-pollution directive is also forcing us to close down six of our coal-burning power-stations...and while I agree that we need to faze them out because fossil fuels are not infinite, I believe that we should be able to do so, in our own time and only when we have suitable replacement capacity, not because of some unilateral bureaucratic diktat from Brussels which doesn't take into account the problems involved in closing down power-stations without having the necessary energy-producing replacement solutions in place.

———

Comment on the Green Party & Environmentalists;

The OED (Oxford English Dictionary) defines the word 'green' as; unripe, immature and undeveloped which pretty much sums up the 'green' movement.

I would also add clinically naive and gullible to that definition to describe those deluded individuals who believe that somehow we can power the whole planet with a couple of windmills – like the hippies in the 1960's who thought that by spreading the message of peace and love, the world's problems would somehow, by some strange magical miracle, suddenly be resolved...but hey, guess what; we are fifty years down the line from that period of hope and nothing has changed.

Utopian ideology is all very well in the mind of its creator or believer but in the harsh reality of everyday life, it's as useful as a bucket with no bottom.

Yes, it would be wonderful if we all lived in an ideal world, living off the land, making our own clothes and stopped using cars, petrol or electricity – but its not going to happen any time soon – so those who just constantly harp on against nuclear power and off-shore oil production should just be grateful that we do still have petrol to run their cars and electricity to light and heat their homes.

We are trying to find new solutions – it just takes time, and in the mean time we need oil and nuclear power to avoid a total collapse of our economy.

I do applaud the work that environmentalists do in protecting the world's wild-life (within reason) and I also applaud their fight against pollution from the oil–producing industry but their systematic rejection of nuclear energy and fossil fuels in favour of inefficient renewable energies is narrow-minded, short-sighted and destined to failure because until we discover another viable, sustainable energy-source that can power our society we have to work with them.

Now I don't know if their rigid ideology is post-modern apocalyptic or simply a return to the Middle Ages but if all these doom-mongers *who are so hostile to the use of any kind of fossil fuel but who shiver like frightened lambs being led to slaughter when confronted by the reality that their flawed ideologies don't take into account* are not happy living in their heated and lighted houses, travelling to work in their cars and buying their food in supermarkets then I suggest that they get together and create a separate commune of their own with a single wind-turbine to provide all the power they need. Only then, when they were faced with reality, with the fact that wind turbines do not create enough energy to supply everyone on a regular basis would they begin to see the extent of their folly;

- they could all live off the land maybe,
- make their own clothes,
- travel around on bicycles
- and collect their water from a well
- they could even heat and light their homes with candles,

- but they would only have electricity when the wind blew, because they refuse to use petrol or gas.

This sounds like a nightmare to me but if that's how these people want to live, in the belief that they would somehow be saving the planet - Amish style – in some sort of pre-industrial 'Survivors' time-warp, then they are welcome to do so.

What they would eat, I have no idea, because;

- they could not eat meat; too much methane production,
- they could not eat fish because apparently fish suffer pain when caught,
- they could not eat vegetables because those vegetables feel pain too when unceremoniously ripped out of the soil,
- and they could not eat fruit as I imagine fruit feel that same pain when stripped from the branch.

I suppose they could eat the fruit that had fallen from the tree naturally but wouldn't that fruit still feel the same pain when their flesh was punctured by razor-sharp teeth.

I wonder; could these people really survive wearing hemp shirts and eating organic muesli?

Meanwhile the rest of us will go on searching for new and renewable technologies to develop our society and make it more sustainable.

———

Of course the above is extremely patronising, but that is where we would be if we listened to all their ridiculous demands and silly ideas; these supremely naive individuals need to face the facts and start living in the real world.

———

The EU

The FUBs (faceless unelected bureaucrats) in Brussels seem to believe that their way is the only way, that they are infallible – but the danger with this arrogant stance lies in the fact that while they are imposing their way on everyone in the EU – their way is based on theories that have been shown to be flawed – and that is where the problem lies.

Now despite what we might think, these people are human beings and while they have the same propensity to make mistakes as the rest of us, they believe that as the all-powerful EU executive they cannot be seen to be weak, vulnerable or wrong.

This is where their arrogance, their stubbornness and their pig-headedness comes into play because even though their model has been proved to be flawed they will not change their alarmist predictions.

Their self-centred egotism will not allow them to be seen as weak, so they are pushing on regardless with all this costly investment in renewable energies, bankrupting economies and ruining energy production for the next fifty years, just so that they don't have to admit that they were wrong;

...and yet; the man who initially championed the cause through his Gaia theory – James Lovelock - now qualifies the idea of sustainable development as 'meaningless drivel' – indeed he freely admits he went too far in his theory and now says that he is a firm supporter of nuclear power.

Meanwhile, this retreat from rationality will be seen by generations to come as the most extreme example of how collective naiveté, misinformation and a political system with no backbone can be exploited by multi-national corporations - through cleverly manipulating the hysteria and nurturing the paranoia - to earn themselves billions of dollars in profit.

———

Author's comment on EU Hypocrisy;

As part of its Green / Environmental Policy, the EU is imposing draconian renewable-energy targets on its member states committing us all to unreasonable and unattainable goals. (32% of energy must be provided by renewable by 2020)

Meanwhile, it has an army of 484 chauffeurs driving cars around Brussels and Strasbourg which are empty most of the time – the driver aside.

This makes a complete mockery of the EU's supposed commitment to reducing its carbon footprint.

PDC Solutions;

The water in our oceans and the sun up above our heads are two of the most powerful energy sources known to man and yet we have barely tapped into that massive potential in the search for our energy needs. These two naturally occurring elements are right in front of us and yet for some reason we don't seem to see it.

Water;

71 to 80% of planet Earth is water (depending on which expert you listen to) and yet somehow we still suffer from droughts; how and why does that happen if we, the human race consider ourselves so intelligent?

We should put more effort into desalination research so that we can draw as much water as we need from the sea and have systems put in place to clean it again before it is returned to the ocean, especially as the projections looking into the future suggest that our weather is going to get progressively warmer, thereby drying out the land and the crops to a greater extent.

In Barcelona, they are leading the way, having just built the biggest desalination plant in the world after several years of drought, but that is only the start.

We should also invest more in hydro power from both barrage and turbine projects.

In France they have sunk huge turbines off-shore (north coast) to harness tidal energy.

We, in the UK must do more to harness wave and tidal power.

––––––

Sun;

The sun is a source of eternal energy. It produces 386 billion billion megawatts of power every second – that's the power and the energy we need to be tapping into; we need to do more to utilise <u>that</u> energy.

We need more investment in perfecting the capture of solar energy.

In Spain they have 'Solar Centrales' (solar farms) producing huge amounts of energy and there is even a factory in Alicante turning algae into petrol but why not take it a step further.

Oil and gas are finite, so why not invest in the French idea of sending up satellites to soak up solar energy and then laser it down to earth.

This would be hugely expensive in the short term and might need a concerted international effort to put in place but eventually it could provide all the energy we need at a fraction of the price we are now paying for fossil fuels.

––––––

Wind;

As for wind-farms; the PDC would impose a moratorium on any new wind-farms and shelve any future land-based wind-farm investment indefinitely.

Then, as new power stations were built and came on-line the PDC would order those who profited from putting up on-shore wind-farms to dismantle them, recycle them and return the countryside to its previous natural state at their expense.

Off-shore sites; if they were to somehow end up being self-sufficient and sustainable – without any further subsidies - because of the more prevalent and advantageous weather conditions out at sea, then they could be maintained as back-up until no longer needed.

––––––––

Author's comment;

I might be repeating myself here but I find the way that the politicians are hiding green taxes in energy bills, more than a little contemptuous; allowing the energy companies to take the heat for price hikes in exchange for guarantees and ongoing funding shows a clear lack of integrity and honesty; especially as those stealth taxes have surreptitiously added 15/20% to everybody's energy bill.

Surely, if the energy companies are convinced that wind-power is the way forward, then they themselves should be funding the infrastructure necessary to accomplish that state of affairs, not the British consumer; after all, it is they who will be taking the profits from those investments.

As it stands the British public is paying for the investment in green energy and they will be fleeced again in their future energy bills...while Energy Company shareholders simply sit back and rake in the profits; that is simply not right.

––––––––

Energy notes;

- Power / energy companies need to be called to rights. Breaking into a person's home to install a meter while the person is out... and leaving that person without heating, hot water and hot food because they don't know how the meter works...is despicable; especially as the person in question in this particular case, didn't actually owe the energy company anything
- We need more schemes like the 'Big Switch' scheme recently championed by 'Which Magazine' where consumers got together, using the power of their numbers as leverage to drive down their bills and negotiate a better deal for themselves – the same schemes are being tried out in Belgium with great success.

Europe; The European Community

Why it doesn't work as a concept

The general concept of centralisation might sound very appealing in theory – a single entity deciding policy for all those who sign up to its charter - but in reality it is far too fragile a concept to be a lasting success - especially on this scale - as there are way too many working parts to such an enterprise, any one of which could go wrong at any moment; the most significant - and potentially the most unreliable - of which, is, of course, the human component.

A physical structure is only as strong as its weakest link and in any theory or technological conjecture, the unknown element - and therefore its weakest link - is usually the unpredictable human component; that is where reliability and trust issues usually occur.

Mankind is naturally greedy due to his 'survival instincts' and despite the safeguards and the fire-walls put in place by those who conceived this project, that innate greed will inevitably surface at some point, invariably weakening the structure;

- One day, somewhere along the line, someone will see an opportunity to exploit which will compromise the integrity of the project putting it at risk
- Then, a while later, somebody else will take advantage of another opportunity which will weaken the structure further
- ...and eventually, little by little the whole project, the whole structure will collapse like the proverbial house of cards...

...and that is why the centralisation of government on this scale is dangerous and riddled with the potential to fail...because it depends on mankind for its integrity.

I draw a parallel here with the ill-fated Titanic.

The Titanic was the most prestigious ocean-going vessel of its time built to the highest standards known to man and theoretically capable of resisting anything that nature could throw at it.

Indeed it was unsinkable if its much-heralded promotion was to be believed - and yet, despite the best laid plans, the best architects, the best builders and the best raw materials that money could buy...which should all have guaranteed its enduring success, the Titanic sank with the loss of 1500 lives.

Why...because of its weakest link; mankind;

- *because of the corners that were discreetly cut in construction, in the quality of the rivets that held it together, for example*
- *because of the lack of sufficient life-boats,*
- *because of the over-confidence of the owners*
- *and because of the smug, misplaced pride of the captain who steered it inadvertently towards its tragic destiny.*

The EU is a similar vessel and who wants to be aboard a ship steaming inexorably towards the rocks and almost certain oblivion?

Of course, the original idea - to try to create a European Union of member states with political and fiscal unity, where we would all live by the same rules, united as one nation in order to be a force on the world stage is a very laudable concept, (even though it is based on cold-war politics which no longer have tenure) but unfortunately, implementing it was always going to be a utopian nightmare waiting to happen - just like globalisation is now proving to be a nightmare for industries and workforces alike - because it depends inherently on its weakest component – mankind - not to let it down and unfortunately, therein lies its downfall.

The EU is built on compromise which is the basis of any contractual agreement between opposing parties and it is a wonderful demonstration of what the human race <u>can</u> achieve when it puts its mind to it, but sadly the EU State project <u>is and always will be</u> an idealistic pipe-dream because the very concept of compromise doesn't stand the test of time.

...and why; because, alas, it relies on the morality, the honesty, the integrity and the loyalty of mankind to uphold it...and that is where it all falls apart, because we all know that the allegiance of mankind can be bought, sold and twisted to conform to any number of selfish, self-serving ventures.

———

Author's comment;

Trying to marry the idealistic dreams of man with his inability to overcome his natural human failings is a whimsical folly and this project for a European State will ultimately and inevitably impoverish every nation that participates in its deluded idealism for decades to come, both morally and financially.

———

Why it doesn't work in practice -

Identity; the psychological importance and significance of **colour** and **allegiance;**

This is another reason why the EU experiment was doomed from the outset.

The grey suits in Brussels only had to look at the failure of **ESPERANTO** – the common European language idea – to see that while an idea can sound good in a brain-storming exercise in an anonymous office, high in the upper floors of a non-descript sky-scraper somewhere on the outskirts of Brussels, the reality of implementing it in practical terms on the ground is something completely different.

- Did these faceless bureaucrats not see the national fervour and the emotion displayed by every team's athletes when representing their country during the recent Olympics and the Paralympics in London 2012?
- Did they not see the pride and the passion shown by sportsmen and women alike when hearing their national anthem being played as they stood atop the various podiums?
- ...and did they not see the thousands of young children waving their arms and coloured flags...or singing along, feeling that same sense of pride and that same patriotism as their parents, delighted to be joining in and celebrating being part of a particular culture.

———

Author's comment;

It certainly made my heart swell with unrestrained emotion to watch such endeavour being recognised and rewarded...and furthermore, might I take this opportunity to say how wonderful it was to witness the strength of friendship and fellowship demonstrated by the Olympic athletes during the 2012 London Games (Olympics and Paralympics).

The respect that the athletes have for each other was clear for all to see and I have to say that I was humbled by both their modesty (despite years of gruelling effort in relative obscurity) and by the absence of any overt displays of vanity that the overpaid, over-pampered footballers with their over-inflated egos would have treated us to had they been the focus of the world's media. If we could only instil that same sense of pride, passion and dedication into the rest of the country we would indeed be a proud nation.

———

...and what about other major European sporting events?

Have the grey suits never seen the enthusiasm, the patriotism and the pure unadulterated joy of the thousands of people who dress up in their vibrant national colours and wave their multi-coloured flags with gusto as spectators?

People like to belong, they like to have an identity; they like to be part of something; it's tribal – look at how they wear their football clubs' colours to matches; look at the fervour and the passion that that engenders.

It may only be symbolic but colour is part of their identity, a part of who they are; it is what stirs the passion and inflames the sense of pride.

———

Author's comment –

Beethoven's 'Ode to Joy' might be a wonderful piece of music but it would pale into insignificance if played at the Millennium Stadium in Cardiff alongside the Welsh national anthem; 'Land of my Fathers' or at Twickenham alongside the English national anthem.

———

People are viscerally attached to their origins, their culture, their history and their national colours - and this has always been the case - but the grey suits in Brussels or the FUBs as I like to call them – **F**aceless, **U**nelected **B**ureaucrats - with their bland, misguided ideology clearly cannot see that.

They are determined to cover Europe in a swathe of metaphorical beige, painting over - if not eradicating completely - centuries of evolved culture, diversity and history without a second thought, all in the name centralised equivalence.

- No more yellow and red for Spain,
- No more red, white and blue (tricolours) for either France or the UK,

- No more red, yellow or black for Germany
- Or green, white and red for Italy etc…

…just 'homogenous beige' for everyone; bland, boring beige; all so that the self-absorbed suits in Brussels can pretend to exist in their tiny one-dimensional vacuum…

…and if it is not bland, boring and beige the FUBs immediately bring out a ruling against it, no matter how petty or futile that might seem; indeed, if they could insist that oranges be beige, they would bring out a ruling to that effect.

It's sad to see but once again – as is so often the case in human history – the self-righteous few are imposing their will on the unsuspecting masses… and yet, how presumptuous it is of these FUBs to believe that they can magically homogenise 28 different cultures, each with its own distinct history, tradition and national identity into one single entity.

…and anyway, why would they want to do that, why would these meddling busy-bodies, obsessed with their own self-importance want to sweep away centuries of culture and history? It's madness.

'Vive la difference' I say; (even if it is out of context; the French apply this phrase to women).

———

The FUBs vision of the future is Europe as one united federal state whether the people of these individual countries want it or not…but the reality is that there is no unity, there is no political consensus between all the different member-states to do this, and it is only logical; how can the FUBs possibly expect each of these different cultures to see a problem from the same standpoint when every problem impacts differently on each of their respective economies.

Preferential trade ties, maybe, but a unified monetary and justice system together with the removal of all national borders, all run through a centralised governing body in Brussels was only ever going to be a recipe for chaos.

You simply cannot wipe away people's deep-rooted identity and thousands of years of history and culture with a summary diktat handed down from Brussels or Strasbourg.

People will not accept it...or at the very least, they will resist.

But there again, maybe the FUBs have seen all that...and decided quite simply that they couldn't possibly have people being passionate about something that they didn't control...

...and that, my friends, is what is called autocracy by committee.

Indeed, the more sinister-minded among us would see the European Charter as the EU's way of subtlety but deliberately erasing any sense of national identity, creating a melting pot of nationalities so intermingled with each other that the only thing they have in common is their European identity.

Their idea, to reduce our whole existence into a series of neat and tidy bureaucratic accountancy boxes lined up on a gigantic spreadsheet that they control like megalomaniac puppeteers from Brussels; their rule being the 3B's; bland, boring and beige.

Now this might sound a little far-fetched to the uninitiated but in fact, the EU **directive 2004/38** clearly suggests that this is indeed one of their fundamental objectives.

There is a paradox here however, because while the FUBs in Brussels are desperately trying to homogenise Europe in a swathe of metaphorical beige they are simultaneously promoting multi-cultural societies. Surely that shows a lack of coherence and forethought at some level during the conception of this project.

...and one final note; isn't it curious that the more the FUBs try to homogenise us all, the more people are defending themselves, re-affirming their culture, their traditions and their innate sense of identity? The Walloons, the Flemish, the English, the Scottish, the Welsh, the Catalans, the Basques and the Bretons have all lobbied the EU to demand recognition for their particular culture in one way or another, so clearly, not everybody is prepared to lose their individuality in the great melting pot of Europe.

———

Brussels; *the home of the EU*

…or as some would say; a place where all useless, washed-up politicians go to die in the hope of perpetuating their money-grabbing lifestyles for a few more years at the tax-payers expense

———

The idea of creating a huge continental society based on the communist-style brotherhood of man where everyone is equal and every economy runs smoothly on the exact same template probably looked amazing on paper during that crazy brain-storming session all those years ago, but the reality is that it will only ever be a pipe-dream and a very costly pipedream at that.

Why?

Firstly, because of the innate weaknesses of the human race, as mentioned earlier;

Men and Women lie,

- they cheat, they steal and they betray each other,
- they plot and scheme against each other
- they are inherently conceited and deceitful,
- they are unreliable, unpredictable and irresponsible
- they are jealous and covetous,
- and most of all, they are greedy and selfish

...and these are just a few of their failings.

And secondly; because just like our ancestors the apes, we are a species based on hierarchy and leadership, and as a consequence, there will always be;

- those at the top giving the orders and enjoying the privileges of their position...and
- those at the bottom - the majority - struggling to survive...

...just look at China, North Korea or any of the other 'communist' states.

...but what is worse; is the fact that the EU as a concept is anti-democratic.

Look at how Greece and Italy have had their democratically-elected leaders removed and replaced by Eurocrat puppets without a second thought for their respective electorates...

*...although in a belated show of defiance the Italian public has since disowned Mario Monti who came **LAST** in a subsequent election.*

The Republic of Ireland too was warned - in no uncertain terms – about its position.

The Irish voted against the Lisbon Treaty when it was put to them in June 2008 and were promptly told to vote again in October 2009 - and to get the right result - or decisions would be made that would wreck their economy.

That is not democracy, people; that is pseudo-dictatorship.

Even the French whose politicians have always been at the forefront of EU policy voted **NO** to the EU Constitution on May 29th 2005 - as did the Dutch on June 1st 2005 – and yet it still went ahead.

It seems that the EU has a fixed and fast rule when it comes to referendums;

There will be NO referendums (unless the result goes their way)

This is unacceptable. The very notion of democracy is being completely ignored.

Referendums are being organised but the FUBs do what they like whatever the result.

Surely, this is not what the people of Europe signed up for; to be bullied into following a particular political line without having the right to question it.

It is certainly not what the British people signed up for and I believe that, given the choice, none of these countries would have given up;

- their proud history,
- their heritage,
- the diversity of their culture,
- their money or
- their intellectual independence.

The people of Europe are simply being held hostage by their political classes who believe – with no shortage of arrogance - that they are infallible and that they somehow connect with each other on a higher plane than the rest of us...and to this end they are forging ahead with a constant stream of creeping legislation which is slowly unifying every aspect of our lives whether the people of Europe agree with it or not... sucking the joy of human existence out of the many for the benefit of the few – i.e. themselves and their own personal gravy train.

Indeed, the EU's only role seems to lie;

- in being used as a masochistic exercise in atonement for the Germans to assuage an understandable but misplaced obligation to expunge the misdemeanours of previous generations as they strive to rebuild their reputation and be accepted once again as a nation within the bosom of humanity

- in providing subsidies for the inefficient French farmers who receive a disproportionate amount of funding
- in issuing a constant stream of petty diktats (ten thousand regulations, directives and decisions have been imposed on us since 1973)
- and finally to give hundreds if not thousands of bureaucrats, bean-counters and also-ran politicians the chance to squeeze yet another salary out of the tax-payers' pocket; the whole system is run by – and for the benefit of – those troughing officials who work in and around Brussels.

Meanwhile, it has completely destabilised whole economies and disrupted thousands of lives, through the relocation of entire factories and hundreds of businesses whose management structures rightly refuse to abide by the draconian decrees being imposed on every aspect of their business by these self-serving bureaucrats.

The result is a net loss of hundreds of thousands of jobs.

The EU as a bureaucratic project has been a complete disaster for most European countries; just look at the devastated economies all around us that have lacked the visionary leadership necessary to avoid - or find a solution to - their economic woes.

This is because the FUBs are completely clueless and their decision to remove all border controls - under the Schengen Agreement in 1995 which allows the free movement of all EU citizens within the EU zone – without putting in any mechanisms to regulate the flow from country to country is just another example of their incompetence. It probably looked good on paper...but the Schengen Agreement has had a catastrophic effect on European society in more ways than one.

It is an easy target but criminality is one area where the Schengen Agreement has been systematically exploited. Criminals convicted in one country are simply taking advantage of the freedom of movement to wander with impunity into the next country...and then the next...in order to avoid arrest and continue their activities.

The UK has definitely seen a marked increase in foreign-based criminality from both individuals and organised gangs since the borders were removed.

However, the influx of criminals from all over the EU is not my only concern. The Schengen Agreement has also led to hundreds of thousands of Europeans arriving on Britain's shores looking for work...which would be a good thing in a time of economic boom, but unfortunately, like most economies, the UK is still feeling the effects of the World slump and the arrival of all these people has done nothing but exacerbate the already swollen unemployment figures;

...a trend which has in turn swamped;

- the benefit system,
- the health service,
- the education system
- and the housing market

The UK's infrastructure simply hasn't been designed with such rapid expansion in mind.

―――――

Author's comment;

What the FUBs should have done was; cemented their fiscal and judicial harmonisation programme first - which was always their ultimate goal – and then opened up all the borders...not the other way around, as the free movement of shifting populations has clearly destabilised most EU economies.

Again, the lack of fore-thought and planning on this matter is clear for all to see

The FUBs   (*faceless, unelected bureaucrats*)

Now these FUBs with their self-appointed superiority complex should be the most intelligent among us; right? How else would they have been able to conceive of such a vast if somewhat costly and ultimately futile project?

The reality is that they are not; as neither their arrogance nor their 'superior' grey-matter stands up to any scrutiny.

This is because despite all the power that they can wield there is no real consensus or leadership among them.

These people - who worryingly hold the destiny of millions of people in their hands - are not erudite scholars, they are not visionaries, master tacticians or even strong-willed civilians prepared to defend their convictions with firm and decisive action; they are just a collection of self-indulgent bureaucrats with a penchant for politics muddling through as best they can every day just hoping that no one will ever question their decisions or pick-up on their ineptitude and incompetence.

Indeed, they are no more than a group of glorified pen-pushers, hiding behind the anonymity of a vast bureaucratic machine in order to impose their will on the unsuspecting citizens of Europe using a constant stream of useless drivel to distract them like some antiquated dictatorial committee.

However, it's all a masquerade; a smokescreen, a facade.

There is no real game-plan...

- other than to keep up the illusion that they are working towards the hypothetical goal of making Europe one big bureaucratic dictatorship sometime in the future –

...and their incompetence, their inability to manage a budget and their failure to eradicate the inherent corruption within their own ranks clearly demonstrates that they are not fit for purpose.

Author's comment;

Each year, the EU produces its Official Journal which sets out the laws agreed to by its member states. It comprises 34,000 pages and lists 10,000 regulations, directives and decisions that every member must abide by.

This is bureaucracy out of all control and I find it inconceivable that we as a sovereign nation are not 'allowed' to protect ourselves in any way from this constant onslaught of EU drivel...sorry, legislation.

I don't believe for a moment that any of these bureaucrats really believe that a Federal Europe, a single EU State will ever become a lasting reality.

No doubt, there are a few idealists among them with honourable - if somewhat naively deluded intentions – but I believe that the vast majority of those who haunt the corridors of power in Brussels have absolutely no belief in the project; they are simply there to dangle the vision of Europe as a single state in front of an unsuspecting European public like a tantalising mirage while they help themselves surreptitiously to as much of the taxpayers' money as they can, much like the politicians do in Westminster.

Personal gain is the only motivation for these people and thousands of them will make a fortune out of pretending to support the illusion having seized on the opportunity to exploit the ideal for their own ends?

Sadly, this insatiable cupidity is human nature...and that is why such a vast project can never work...because we humans have a hard time disassociating the innate human instinct to look after No.1 from the need for honesty and integrity that a vast machine such as this needs in order to function correctly.

The depressing thing is that while the FUBs and the MEPs are getting richer and richer they are simultaneously bankrupting whole countries, without so much as a second thought for the citizens of those countries suffering the consequences of their (the FUBs & MEPs) actions.

———

Idealism and altruism are wonderful concepts but the EU is not an altruistic endeavour; just ask the Greeks, the Italians, the Irish or the Portuguese, who are all struggling to keep their heads above water in this time of crisis...

Each of these countries has looked to the EU for help only to have their pleas of support met with a request for more money through an increased budgetary contribution.

BTW; *the EU has recently asked the UK for an extra £1.4 billion to cover* <u>*over-spending*</u>*...because despite all their economists and all their financial experts they still have no idea how to stick to a budget.*

———

Typical example of a FUB (faceless unelected bureaucrat)

Baroness Ashton (Lab) is the UK's highest-ranking FUB and in her position as High Representative of the Union for Foreign Affairs and Security Policy... and Vice President of the European Commission, she wields a great deal of power in Brussels...and yet she has never once stood for election.

In fact, does anybody in the UK know who she is or what she does? Could anybody pick her out of a line-up of self-serving Eurocrats? I sincerely doubt it and yet she is the highest paid female politician in the world.

Baroness Ashton earns £250K a year working in Brussels (the Prime Minister of the UK earns £142,500) and can look forward to a gold-plated pension

*when she retires...and yet nobody knows who she is or what she does...
because if she <u>was doing anything of worth</u>, that was changing our lives in
any way for the better, we would surely know about it; the press would be
all over it, and they are not. So why is she so deserving of such a generous
salary, especially as in a survey of more than 320 EU policymakers she was
voted the least useful of all the EU commissioners and some senior diplomats
even referred to her as 'a joke'*

*Now, Baroness Ashton is not the only one in this position, but as invisible
as she is, she is nonetheless the most 'high-profile' of our FUBs; so what does
that tell you...?*

———

Okay, now that we have established that the FUBs are just glorified
office-workers with nothing better to do with their time than find new
ways of wasting hard-earned taxpayer money and handing down silly
diktats about the size and shape of a fruit, lets look at more examples
of their ineptitude, of why these people really shouldn't be the guiding
council of so many peoples destinies.

- **Firstly**; they cannot manage a budget; in each of the last eighteen
  years the financial watchdog that monitors EU budgets - known
  as the EU Court of Auditors - has failed to sign off on the
  budgets put before them because of concerns about fraud...
  *everybody knows that profligacy and abuse of taxpayers' money is
  way out of control in Brussels...*
- **Secondly**; they are incapable of reaching any consensus. The
  sheer size of the EU apparatus works against consensus and
  because of all the bureaucratic protocols and the complexity
  of getting anything done, it just lurches from one crisis to the
  next...*apart from when they have to decide how much to increase
  the member states budgets by to cover up their profligacy and their
  exorbitant salaries, expenses and pensions; then there is usually more
  consensus.*
- **Thirdly**; Because of a lack of good, strong leadership these
  people have absolutely no idea how to deal with a crisis; they
  are incapable of making the hard decisions. They present an

imperious facade – posturing and fist-shaking in the Brussels Council Chamber – but all these bureaucrats really know how to do is ask for more money to squander.

True, they can talk, they can organise summit upon summit, costing the taxpayers of Europe millions if not billions of Euros every time in travel, hotels and food costs...but ask them to make a real decision, whether it be political or financial and they all look at each other waiting for somebody else to react.

Nobody is prepared to stand up and take the lead because nobody really wants to shoulder the responsibility or face up to the consequences of any decision they might make.

We should be able to trust the 'superior' knowledge and judgement of these people but we cannot, because these so-called learned experts do not possess the ultimate truth, they do not have a crystal ball; they are no wiser than the rest of us.

Sure, they can hand down diktat after bureaucratic diktat to complicate the lives of the little people, but actually stand up and do the job they are getting paid a fortune to do – no way!

Just look at the way they dragged their feet over the wars in Iraq, Afghanistan and Libya...and look at the mess they made of the banking crisis and the subsequent issues surrounding the Euro; not one of them had the gumption to grasp the nettle by the thorns – they all just looked to their neighbour and stood back as country after country sank into the mire.

The truth is that the FUBs are just accountants, bad accountants, second-rate accountants but accountants all the same, and all accountants know about is money; it's all they are interested in; it doesn't matter that the world's economy is on life-support...they just want more and more money to spend on their deluded pipe-dream.

Why else would they impose a budget deficit of less than 3% of GDP on their member states knowing full well that the majority of their members could never adhere to it?

The answer is simple; they attached a penalty of 0.1% of GDP to the policy meaning that any country that was already in financial difficulty was punished twice.

This is the same flawed reasoning as used in the justice system; why impose fines on people who are already in financial difficulty?

...because it's all about the money!

So I ask; why should we listen to these people when it has been proved time and again that they have no greater insight into how to resolve an issue than any other career politician making a career out of milking the system?

Author's comment;

As mentioned earlier; in each of the last eighteen years the financial watchdog that monitors EU budgets - known as the EU Court of Auditors - has failed to sign off on the budgets put before them because of concerns about fraud.

And how has the EU Commission reacted to that reality check?

It has decided to cut the EU Court of Auditors budget for no reason other than to spite it for not condoning their profligacy.

That is what happens in Brussels if you don't play ball with the FUBs

----

EU FINANCES

Income;

The EU Budget is €150 billion a year.

That is a huge amount of money to manage but with all the financial expertise at their disposal you would expect that the FUBs would at least manage to balance the books.

Sadly, that is not the case as every year, despite an army of accountants and a multitude of financial 'experts' they get it wrong time and time again... forcing them to demand increases in budgetary contributions - or top-up payments – on a regular basis from each of their member states in order to cover up their immeasurable profligacy and unbounded incompetence.

It is outrageous, especially when many of those member states are on the brink of complete economic meltdown themselves...

This is highway robbery; it is 'stand and deliver' economics on a monumental scale because if the member states refuse to pay-up to cover the profligacy of Brussels they are immediately threatened with sanctions or the withdrawal of the meagre subsidies and support that they do receive.

I ask myself; why do these deluded bean-counters believe that they should be immune from the austerity that most of their member countries are suffering?

It just shows how out of touch these people are in their ivory towers in Brussels.

Now, of course, there are variables in every budget, but to get it so badly wrong year on year...for eighteen years straight...surely there must come a time when we have to question the competence or the accountancy skills of these people.

Expenditure;

Capital investment

The FUBs spend taxpayers' money like it is going out of fashion and when it is not on themselves it is on outrageously expensive real-estate projects.

- £280million was recently spent on the Europa building in Brussels and
- £850million was spent on a new building in Luxembourg

This is extraordinarily extravagant expenditure in the middle of a recession but of course the FUBs have no concept of restraint; it's not their money.

Salaries and expenses

Any reasonable person can see - without having much insight into the inner workings of this relatively closed community - that the EU and its control centre in Brussels is totally corrupt...and that the FUBs and the MEP's are simply there to milk the deluded dreams of a small minority of well-meaning but ultimately absurd technocrats...and reap the rewards for as long as they can before the whole thing collapses.

There is no game-plan, the people who populate all those offices in Brussels and Strasbourg are not really motivated by any selfless, altruistic desire to broker world peace; it's all about the money; about the gravy-train; about making sure that 'my pot is bigger than yours'.

Just look at their salaries and expenses. They are extortionate in comparison to the average wage earned in their member states...even by politicians' standards.

There are 27 **unelected** EU commissioners in Brussels earning £194,000 per annum who are also entitled to claim back their expenses on any number of other 'activities'.

Then we have thousands of EU civil servants earning up to £81,000+ per annum and they too are entitled to claim back any expenses they might incur.

...and finally there are 52 different Quangos which collectively receive £2billion a year in funding from the EU coffers in order to pay for still more civil servants and FUBs

———

Average annual salary of EU member states in British pounds;

Top; (cited most often)

Germany	£ 37,421	(ref; 2012)
France	£ 29,178	(ref; 2009)
UK	£ 24,252	(ref; 2012)

Bottom;

Lithuania	£ 6,552	(ref; 2012)
Romania	£ 5,163	(ref; 2013)
Bulgaria	£ 4,168	(ref; 2013)

Compare these with;

FUB / MEP salary	£ 81,000 + expenses

———

Brussels is the golden goose that just keeps giving. It is a gold-mine for washed-up politicians, mediocre number-crunchers and hopeless bean-counters; a place where they can quickly feather their retirement nests without ever being accountable for their actions or taking any responsibility.

In fact, over a five year period an MEP can make up to £1m, between the salary on offer and the expenses he / she can claim; Mr & Mrs Neil Kinnock for example made over £10million during their time in Brussels.

I ask myself; were they really in Brussels for the sole purpose of defending the interests of the British people...?

NB; the incessant transfer of the assembly back and fore between Brussels and Strasbourg also costs the taxpayer another £145million a year in travel expenses and hotels etc

---

To sum up;

The EU as a single, independent state is a fantasy, an illusion; it is never going to happen because of all the reasons given previously but until the real intellectuals and the true, un-biased scholars figure that out...the FUBs in Brussels will keep topping up their bank-accounts and living off the beast...

...which takes us back once again to the fallibility of mankind;

Greed has been an over-riding feature in much of the research undertaken for this manifesto and none more so than in the EU. It is the one constant and reigns supreme wherever we look in the bureaucratic machine from the top all the way down to the bottom.

- We see it in the way lucrative contracts are attributed to influential friends
- We see it in the way huge taxpayer-funded grants and subsidies are distributed to 'co-operative' and 'sympathetic' partners,
- We see it in the way the FUBs and the MEPs are shamelessly pocketing salaries and expenses far in excess of their worth

...and we see it all the way down to the bottom of the pile where badly-paid clerks in the smaller, less-affluent countries are selling EU passports and visas to non EU citizens so that they can migrate all the way across the EU continent and into the UK without ever being challenged.

Every stage of the EU process is an opportunity for someone, somewhere to make money.

In my eyes, the EU is just a lumbering giant incapable of efficient government and...

- because of its size,
- because of the eclectic mix of its cultures
- because of the different priorities of each of its members
- and because of its lack of a clearly defined mandate

...it will never work; it is simply impossible to keep all of the people happy all of the time and keeping such a huge entity viable with so many different components was only ever going to be an idealistic nightmare.

In simple terms, the EU is just an over-sized auditor's office that is so big it cannot keep a check on what is going on in its <u>own head office</u> (Brussels) and yet it is forever correcting and reprimanding the mangers of its regional offices who are just trying to do their jobs.

It's a typical, do as I say, not as I do scenario.

One final recap;

1) The people running the EU are incapable of consensus
2) They are hopelessly out of touch in their Brussels bubble
3) They are indecisive in a crisis

4) They are obsessed with money yet unable to manage a budget... and

5) They have no real game-plan other than the insidious creation of a supranational Euro-state...which is no more than an illusion that is never going to materialise

...and yet we - the citizens of Europe - are all expected to put our lives and our destinies in the hands of these people...?

I'm sure I'm not alone in finding that a worrying prospect.

The UK and Europe –

One of the great tragedies of modern Britain is that our leaders are not honest with us... and then they wonder why there is a disconnect, a fracture between them and us.

All the British people want - in fact all any population wants - is for its politicians / leaders to tell them the truth and stop going behind their backs in order to pursue their own agendas.

When the British people signed up to the EU or the EEC (European Economic Community aka the Common Market) as it was known in 1973, it was supposed to be purely a free-trade agreement. It was all about improving relations and promoting trade with the other EU countries in order to grow our respective economies...or at least that was the line we were sold in order to obtain our approval.

Author's comment;

Little did we know that the 'Trade Agreement' was a Trojan Horse and that the intention of the bureaucrats in Brussels all along was to create a one-state Europe with full integration including fiscal union, judicial union and political union.

The politicians of the time simply had to spin it as a trading agreement for a few years because they knew that the British people would never have signed up to give away their sovereignty.

This is the kind of sly, underhand dealing that makes the people despise politicians.

So, trusting their politicians not to betray them, the British people signed-up to this Trade Agreement, not realising the insidious nature of the political agenda and not knowing that for the next forty years the politicians would never again consult them on an issue that ultimately defines their whole existence, taking it upon themselves (*the politicians*) to sign up to the subsequent treaties unilaterally without any popular consensus;

- The Maastricht Treaty in 1993
- The Schengen Agreement (free borders law) in 1995
- The Amsterdam treaty in 1997
- The Nice Treaty in 2001...and
- The Lisbon Treaty in 2007

...were all signed by the politicians without the British people having a choice...

...and herein lies the problem, because all these treaties have really done is restrict our free will a little more each time, putting the British people in a metaphorical straight-jacket that allows them less and less room to manoeuvre with every subsequent strap that the FUBs tighten.

This is a blatant betrayal of the British people and just another example of how the ruling classes do one thing while the people want another;

- just like we weren't consulted about going to war in Iraq and Afghanistan and
- just like we weren't consulted about the mass immigration that has changed our communities forever.

As a result; the UK is now in a straight-jacket shackled to a corpse...but none of our political leaders was ever truthful enough to tell the British people that they were leading them into such a perilous situation, a situation where they would ultimately lose their independence and their sovereignty.

And why...?

Because they knew that the British people would never have signed up to the idea...that the sovereignty and the independence – that they have fought so valiantly to preserve for centuries and through two world wars - would be given away one diktat at a time by their spineless politicians.

So, as mentioned above, it was the politicians who took the UK into Europe telling the people that there was no need for a referendum as <u>they</u> were our elected representatives, that <u>they</u> knew best, and that <u>we could trust them</u>...and yet this is the same body of self-serving, untrustworthy miscreants who have shown for decades that they lack any kind of moral decency or integrity - their blatant exploitation of the expenses system being the most recent example of that - so why should we give any credibility to the judgement of these people?

They clearly don't have our best interests at heart – at least not those voiced by the majority of the British public.

Now these 'self-proclaimed, super-intelligent, Oxbridge-educated' politicians might consider that...what we, the British people want...is wrong; that we don't quite understand the complexities of the conceited world of international political intrigue...and that might well be the case...but <u>that is not their call</u> to make.

This is where the politicians get it wrong; their opinion doesn't matter; it doesn't count.

They are not elected to represent their own opinion or even that of their party; they are elected to represent the voice of those who voted for them; that is their privilege, to humbly represent the voice of their electorate. That is the essence of democracy.

Politicians would not exist; they would not have a job if not for that proviso.

When are they going to realise that...?

It is that self-obsessed arrogance that the British people so abhor; the idea that they the politicians believe that being elected somehow elevates them to a higher plane where they always know best...when quite clearly in many cases, they don't.

Time and time again they have allowed the FUBs to undermine our history, our heritage and our way of life, without ever standing up for the values we hold dear, allowing themselves to be railroaded systematically into submission by the bureaucrats in Brussels without so much as a challenging disagreement...

...while at the same time always being careful to prevent the voters of this country from being able to voice their opinion.

That is not democracy and ultimately, even if the politicians believe that the UK voters are wrong in their thinking, it is their duty - as the people's elected representatives - to act as the people's voice, not to put forward their own personal opinions or party agenda...and if they cannot do that objectively, then they should not be representing us.

Successive governments have buried us in European legislation, handing over our sovereignty little by little without ever consulting us.

Like a virulent cancer the EU is inexorably eating away at our way of life a little more every day;

We have already lost control;

- over our laws,
- over our foreign policy,
- over our defences
- over our fishing grounds...and
- over our own frontiers.

...and now the EU is looking to take over our coast-guard too, not forgetting its constant meddling in our Health Service.

Our once proud nation has been brought to heel - if not to its knees - by a torrent of ridiculously petty diktats and trivial laws, often bereft of any common sense, from the colour of our passports to the use and re-use of jam-jars and our spineless politicians have allowed it to happen without so much as a whimper of discord.

Indeed, the EU now regulates everything from the way we dispose of our rubbish (landfill policy) to the size and shape of the envelopes we can use in our postal service and they will not be content until the UK is completely humiliated and servile...on a political level at least...

———

Author's comment;

How ridiculous is it that there is an EU directive that actually <u>prevents the discussion</u> over whether breast milk or formula is best for new-born babies?

Who are these smug individuals who think they know better than nature itself?

Are they on the baby-formula pay-roll?

Whatever did new mothers do in the thousands of years before formula or the EU?

It frustrates me so much that people who I did not elect, with whom I have no particular affinity and with whom I disagree on almost every issue are imposing their will on my life and taking the UK in a direction that many of its citizens do not agree with; it's time to call a halt to this madness.

ECHR (European Court of Human Rights); see also chapter on Human Rights

...and when it is not the FUBs themselves dictating to us, it is the ECHR and its self-appointed judges that are ceaselessly trying to extend their sphere of influence over us, over-stepping their mandate and creeping inexorably from the fundamental issue of human rights for which the court was created, into the social and civic rights of our everyday lives – to a point where it too is meddling in our sovereignty.

I am so tired of these people interfering in our justice system, trying constantly to supersede or undermine our authority with their wishy-washy liberalism.

The UK is being bullied left, right and centre by these bleeding-hearts and it is time that somebody took up the mantle of defending this country from this constant...and often pointless...onslaught of liberal idealism.

Author's comment;

There is nothing wrong...or extreme...or bigoted about

- *wanting to defend your country*
- *or about wanting it to govern itself and uphold its ancient traditions and laws*

- *or for wanting its sovereign justice system to protect those who would do its citizens harm. Indeed it is one of the most fundamental roles of government; to keep the citizens in its charge safe.*

Now, in addition to all the pernickety little diktats that we have to deal with on a daily basis, the UK also has to hand over vast contributions to the EU for purposes over which we have absolutely no control.

In fact, it costs us over £20 billion a year to be a member of the EU – the UK is the second largest contributor after Germany – and what do we really get back out of it other than the constant stream of toxic drivel?

I do not expect parity from the EU; that we should systematically get out what we put in, as we are one of the EU's more fortunate countries and should understandably be prepared to help those in more precarious situations…but nonetheless it is worth noting that only once in forty years did the UK ever have a surplus in its dealings with the EU…and that was in 1975 when bizarrely the UK was voting on whether or not to stay in it; which in itself offers an insight into the way the FUBs operate.

The more cynical among us might find that a little too 'convenient' to be a coincidence but those who have followed my reasoning will recognise the pattern; the FUBs only argument; money (*they are accountants; it's all they know*)

Our one saving-grace however, during all this time, has been to keep hold of our currency which will at least save us from getting drawn too deeply into the inevitable collapse of the self-imploding Euro, be that in the short or medium-term.

I don't doubt that we will be affected in some way by this impending catastrophe but at least when the time comes we will be in charge of most of our monetary levers.

———

Summary;

The British people are not averse to change or to progress but in the case of the EU they feel as if they have been duped by the politicians and the bureaucrats...and as a proud nation which has always decided on its own destiny they feel as if they are being dictated to, by people who they never elected to govern them...rather than the EU project being a joint venture of shared endeavour...

...and that is why they will never fully embrace it.

The politicians might have auctioned off our sovereignty to Brussels - while calling those who disagree with their policies 'wild alarmists' - but the British people will never reconcile themselves with the idea that they must be slaves to the men in grey suits in Brussels and as with the Climate Change rebels who suffered the same abuse, year by year, those 'wild alarmists' are slowly being proved right.

———

Referendum –

In a reflection of the ECHR (**European Charter for Human Rights**) - which is no more than a charter for cynical opportunists and their grubby compensation lawyers to exploit for all its worth - the EU has strayed from its path and overstepped its original remit as far as the British people are concerned.

It is sucking the life-blood out of this country and it will only get worse if we do nothing to halt it.

**Remember people...look back thirty years...
...and then look forward thirty...
...do you like what you see?**

The British people have been patient, they have been indulgent and they have been supportive of the EU project – if only financially for forty years now, but enough is enough. It is time for us to reclaim our independence, before the EU and its creeping federalism removes or replaces all our institutions leaving us without the necessary structures in place to rule over our country and decide our own destiny.

I believe that the EU's influence on our lives and on our society has been more detrimental than beneficial to us as a nation…and even if that was the only reason - without all the political and economical interference - I believe it would already be enough of a reason for us to set in motion the process of a referendum to decide whether or not we should break the EU shackles and reclaim our independence.

The **European Union act 2011** stipulates that in the event of another change to the European treaty the British voters would get a referendum on whether to accept it or not but that could be many years from now.

We have to act NOW.

The choice is simple;

If we stay;

- It is equivalent to a 2nd class ticket on a rudderless Titanic, with no compass, an uncertain future and an ever decreasing hold on our destiny.

If we leave,

- we would reclaim our pride and the Sovereignty that we should never have given up in the first place
- we would reclaim our independence as a nation of free-spirit and enterprise, liberated from the restrictive shackles of Brussels
- we would reclaim our integrity and our autonomy as to the decision-making processes concerning international matters

- and we would reclaim control over;
    - our laws,
    - our justice system,
    - our foreign policy,
    - our defence policy,
    - our immigration policy and
    - our health service

Independence would also allow us to develop our economy and increase international trade agreements with emerging markets around the world, which is now such a small place, thanks to globalisation...

...and finally; it would mean £20 billion more to inject into our own economy allowing us to;

- Redirect the subsidies currently being given to the French farmers to our own farmers who are struggling just as much
- Stimulate job creation through new investment and development ideas
- Re-define the NHS 'mission-statement'
- Build thousands of new homes; we currently have 1.8 million people on the housing list...and finally we could
- Re-configure the public sector wage-template which is way out of sync.

In fact, if we were to leave the EU the whole country would wake up after forty years of torpor and steady decline...

Now, of course, the risk-averse hand-wringers and the inveterate Europhiles will tremble at the prospect, pointing to the fact that a large percentage of our trade is with the EU; they will say that if we leave we would lose all that trade and all the jobs that come with it...but that is just nonsense, typical of any scare-mongering initiative.

We would not automatically lose that trade or those jobs because the Lisbon Treaty takes care of that.

Sure, some EU countries might be churlish at first, shun us and even cancel a few contracts, but that's life and eventually things would settle down again...and we would either regain that trade or replace it with alternatives contracts from other emerging economies around the world.

Author's comment;

The EU and its propagandists have always been effective at pressuring the member states into believing that leaving the union would be catastrophic for them – but it is simply not true as in the **2007 Lisbon Treaty** (article 50) it states that any country which decides to leave should be offered a free-trade agreement...and that is all the PDC would be advocating.

That said; the political elite of this country are well aware that an overwhelming majority of the British public want a referendum on Europe, but because it doesn't fit in with their agenda, they are wilfully refusing to accept the glaringly obvious sentiment of the people.

They do the same thing with capital punishment - it's just another example of political cynicism, of how the ruling classes over-ride the democratic views of the people when they don't suit the party agenda.

Is it any wonder the British voting public feel disenfranchised?

...and here is the hypocrisy; all three of the UK political parties promised the voters a referendum in their manifestos before the last election... **all three**...

...but predictably and with an inured inevitability they have all since dodged the question.

That is what is so frustrating about politicians; the lies, the hypocrisy and the inherent cynicism.

Of course, I know that manifestos are just throw-away guidelines; they are not binding in any way but the British people are sick of broken promises from mendacious politicians.

David Cameron, the current Prime Minister, says that a debate on the EU would be a 'distraction'.

A distraction...?

How can he possibly describe an issue that is so huge that it affects the fundamental way in which we govern ourselves as a country...and the way in which they spend £20 billions of our money...as a 'distraction'?

Surely, the fact of denying us the right to decide, denying us the chance to vote on issues that directly affect our lives and have done so for over forty years qualifies as more than a 'distraction'; it is a scandal... and unquestionably undemocratic...but of course, the truth is that the political classes are horrified by the prospect of a referendum as they fear that they would not receive the response that <u>they</u> would want...

...and they also fear that a referendum would reveal the depth of mistrust and ill-feeling that exists in Britain towards the EU which is why they will not give the public a vote.

———

The proof;

Forced by ordinary people to have a debate on holding a referendum through an 'e-petition' on 24/10/2011, (a concept which the Conservative party invented) all three major parties instructed their members to vote against the idea despite each of them promising it in their manifestos.

That is where the fracture between the people and the ruling elite is so clearly evident.

Where is the democracy in that kind of underhand manoeuvring?

The PDC Policy;

The PDC would not suggest an immediate withdrawal from the EU but a suspension of our allegiance as it currently stands until we can re-negotiate a better deal from Brussels, during which time we would regain control of the main levers of our economy and our society.

The people would then be given the choice to decide via a referendum if they wanted to continue participating in the EU project or not.

For information;

The EU treaty itself says that 'the EU must respect the essential state functions of member states' and even Jacques Delors, architect of the EU has acknowledged that the UK could remain part of the EU without having to fully integrate into its federalist ethos.

Now, naturally the scare-mongerers and those defending their own interests (*probably because they are in the pockets of big business conglomerates enjoying the huge EU grants and subsidies coming their way*) would go to work suggesting that leaving the EU would;

1) ruin us economically,
2) dry up foreign investment and
3) leave us isolated in our island paradise

...but I would counter those arguments immediately with the following;

1) The Lisbon Treaty allows us to leave and renegotiate a trade agreement which Jacques Delors himself has advocated...while the emerging markets around the world would offer us a myriad of new trading opportunities

2) Recent figures published by UK Trade and Investment show a steady rise in foreign investment; up 11% last year...and

3) I would suggest that those people fearful of being isolated look at Switzerland, a country which is right in the middle of Europe but has not joined as a member, preferring the same kind of Trade solution that we would be advocating...

Alas, I understand why those with no moral substance, who have no real convictions or vision for the future, would argue to stay in the fold where there is safety in numbers...but while they huddle together in their pen like frightened lambs - or on the decks of the Titanic as I suggested earlier - convinced that they are secure I would rather that Britain re-emerged from the mists of this European chimera and re-affirmed itself as a strong independent country full of;

-   ambition,
-   self-belief,
-   resilience,
-   ingenuity,
-   innovation
-   creativity and confidence,

...sailing proudly towards a brighter and more prosperous future.

Britain has stood alone before...for centuries in fact...because as an island nation we are used to deciding our own destiny, so, rather than being penned in and dictated to, or stuck on the Titanic waiting for the inevitable to happen, I believe that now is the time to be bold, strong, decisive and determined.

We need to reclaim our independence and our sovereignty, and get back to being a world trading nation, leaving behind those who still wish to believe in the illusion to their own devices, wondering which direction to take and when the iceberg is going to hit.

It will require an Act of Parliament to break free as we would have to repeal the European Communities Act, but if that's what it takes and that's what the people want, let's go for it.

Alas, I have no solution to the EU's woes as I believe the whole experiment is destined to fail...but what is more worrying for the EU member states, is that the FUBs in Brussels have no idea either...and that is why I believe that the UK should pull out of this self-indulgent apparatus of incompetence as soon as possible.

To borrow a concept from the USA, It is time that the 99% make sure that they never allow the greedy, self-serving 1% (i.e.; politicians and bankers) to lead them down the road to oblivion ever again.

NB; Our membership of the G8 and G20, our seats on the UN Security Council, the World Trade Organisation and the IMF are not dependent on us being in the EU so lets negotiate that trade agreement, open-up our markets and re-connect with the wider world, safe in the knowledge that we are in charge of our own destiny.

Stop press –

David Cameron has just promised a referendum on Europe...in 2017... but only if the Conservatives win the next elections in 2015.

However, this announcement has nothing to do with any moral epiphany that he might have had, nor was it the result of any cultivated reflection or any spontaneous recognition of the public mood on the matter, because David Cameron himself is a committed Europhile.

No, he has done this purely and simply as a political ploy; it is a knee-jerk reaction to counter the emergence of UKIP as a political force on the EU issue, Cameron believing quite selfishly that if he were to dangle the possibility of a referendum in front of the electorate, he might have a better chance of winning the next election.

It's a recurring ploy used time and again by politicians for decades but **NONE** has yet to keep his word....

That is the level of insincerity and cynicism that embodies our political class.

The big picture doesn't really interest them; all that matters is staying in power and keeping their seats on the gravy train...

...and sadly David Cameron is no different to all the rest in that respect.

So while this is the right decision – albeit a little too far down the line - his motivation is not one of democracy in action but one of self-interest and political expediency.

The emergence of UKIP has merely forced his hand.

It's just another example of party politics and the conservation of power taking precedence - in the thought process at least - over the legitimate rights of the people to decide.

So, in the run up to the next election expect the PM, who is demonstrably pro-Europe to

- posture at regular intervals,
- organise a rally here and there and
- constantly remind the electorate of his promise of a post-election referendum in order to win the ballot vote

...masking his real intentions in the usual patronising artifice.

Summary;

If the Conservatives lose the next election, the promise falls logically by the wayside and if they win the next election, it will still not be honoured due to 'unforeseen circumstances' that the politicians will conjure up accordingly;

i.e.; if the polls suggest that the 'STAY IN' vote does not have a positive 60/40 split, allowing for a huge margin of error, we can expect them to invent some trite excuse in order to renege on the promise. Much like the Irish vote; we will let you have a referendum as long as you vote for the result that we tell you to.

That is the devious nature of British politics.

As for New Labour, they too promised us a referendum in 2007 under Gordon Brown only to renege on it...and the new Labour leader Ed Miliband has already announced that he would not be in favour of a referendum...so there is no hope there...

Then we have the Lib-Dems who are very pro-Europe but having betrayed their supporters and their values so unashamedly in exchange for a taste of power in the current coalition government, they will not be a deciding factor in British politics again for a long while.

NB - Remember people; if the politicians don't feel that it is <u>in their interest</u> to hold a referendum, there will be no referendum...so don't hold your breath. They will have absolutely no compunction about reneging on a promise; they are politicians; they have been doing it since time immemorial.

Author's comment;

Those who are fighting for a renegotiation of the terms of the treaty that binds us to the EU – who are not insane or alarmist as the Europhiles will try to make out – will need to offer just as good an argument against those who want to stay in, as those called sceptics and alarmists back in 1973

———

Conclusion; why the PDC would not be a part of the EU

Using the problems with the Euro as his argument, David Cameron has said that now is not the time to discuss the EU issue – but like in most things in life, it's <u>never</u> the <u>right time.</u>

However, I believe that there comes a time when you just have to make a stand, especially when it comes to our most precious and fundamental principles – the right to run our own country and our own economy on our own terms...

...and as a result I believe that now is definitely the right time for somebody to stand up for Britain, while the EU itself is in flux over its own future...

We have to ask ourselves what future do we want for this country?

Do we want to be run by a body;

- that operates on un-British principles,
- that is undemocratic,
- that is unelected
- that does not serve our interests
- that compels us to do an increasing number of things we do not wish to do...and which may not be for our benefit

...or do we want to reclaim our sovereignty and our independence?

There is no doubt in my mind where my vote would go.

———

However, if the British people did decide to stay in the EU, here are a couple of ideas that might help to swallow the pill;

Employment –

- Jobs should be advertised locally before being offered to Europeans and then only granted on a structured and controlled work-visa system. The freedom of movement concept – as far as employment is concerned – is too anarchic and the ever fluctuating migration patterns do not allow any government the time to adjust its budgetary provisions in consequence, leaving it constantly chasing its tail

Industry –

- When discussing EU contracts, the rule should be that the best priced offer gets the contract but if the offer of the company that is native to the country concerned comes within a 2% margin of the best price then a little national favouritism could be exercised in order to promote employment in that country.
- The EU needs to get real; allowing employees who fall ill during their holidays to claim the time back from their employers is insane; who are these people? Businesses on a tight budget cannot afford this kind of luxury.

———

World Affairs / Foreign Policy

It is unfortunate but undeniable, that over time, the British people have developed a rather haughty arrogance and a misplaced sense of superiority towards the other nations of the world, linked no doubt to a bygone age when Britannia ruled the waves with its armadas and its armies...and even today, despite some progress being made, there are those who still suffer from that affliction, that typically-British quirk of self-importance, synonymous with a time when Great Britain <u>was</u> 'Great' and <u>was</u> a force to be reckoned with on the world stage...but...

Britain is no longer that world force; it is no longer 'Great' and therefore this inherited nostalgia of superiority no longer has any tenure or legitimacy.

In fact, according to recent figures, the UK is now;

- 23rd in literacy
- 28th in maths
- 16th in science
- 13th in life expectancy
- 25th in infant mortality
- 8th in household income
- 17th in labour force and
- 10th in exports

And yet, in spite these figures and despite it being a throw-back in time, this stubborn sense of superiority still lives on in the minds of some British people, in the minds of some politicians and in those of the more gentrified families who still to this day continue to live in the past and crave the time when they had servants and underlings...

However, these people need to come to terms with the fact that this is the 21ˢᵗ century and that Britain is no longer at the helm - nor indeed in the vanguard - of world affairs despite what these deluded politicians and nostalgic aristocrats would like to think.

In fact, as a citizen of this once-great country, I find it somewhat embarrassing at times to witness the current crop of inept political-wannabes - still afflicted by this innate sense of superiority and arrogance – floundering hopelessly and striving desperately to exist in a world where their word - indeed the word of the British government as a whole - carries less and less weight...especially as five of their colleagues (four MPs and a Peer of the Realm) are currently being detained at *Her Majesty's pleasure*, for various reasons proving that our political community can hardly claim the moral high-ground in this area.

We need to stop deluding ourselves.

———

Author's comment;

More worryingly, in what appears to be another vestige of this superiority complex, today's younger generations would prefer to live off the State than do jobs that they consider are beneath their station.

———

Britain is no longer <u>Great</u> Britain because, through no fault of its people, we have lost the respect of many other people worldwide...

The Eurovision song contest - although a frivolous example of this - is a clear indication of how the rest of Europe views us...arrogant and pompous...

...and this is all down to our politicians, who, desperate to enhance their own reputations and build on their personal legacies have often gone against the collective wishes of the people and led this country down a number of questionable paths...knowing full well that if they had consulted the electorate, we the British people would never have agreed to them engaging our integrity or our reputation on their ruinous escapades. (Iraq, Afghanistan etc)

They ignored this reality, betrayed the people's trust and continued in their deceit...which is why, we as a country are now paying the price; why we are not well-liked on the world-stage.

———

Of course, Britain did once hold a position of power in the world but times have changed; we are now in a new era and we should stop trying to act as if our opinion still matters – it doesn't matter any more...at least not to the same extent.

We have been overtaken in that respect, most notably by China and Russia (among others) and so now is the time for us to rein in that irritating arrogance, accept that we no longer rule the world and deal with the fact that the 21st century is a very different place.

Britain still has its place on the world stage...but we are no longer a leader in the world as we once were.

That said, we can be grateful that we still have a seat at the table; a vote in the UN and in NATO, but that's all we have, a vote as part of a consensus.

Let's stop the posturing and stop trying to be something we are not any more.

We can no longer go around thinking that 'we, the British' can solve all the world's problems, be it through waging wars or offering aid; we cannot.

We no longer have the military capacity or the financial clout to do that.

Besides, why should anybody listen to us, and why should we believe that we have any right to a voice in the world when our recent leaders have been seen to be riddled with corruption and lies (WMD, expenses and torture flights)?

Is it any wonder that there are so many people around the world who despise us?

———

That said; the past is the past; we cannot change that and while it's true that we did some horrible things, we cannot go on apologising indefinitely for those mistakes.

This is the 21st century and we can only be held responsible for our own actions.

It is worth mentioning here that we also did some good things too.

———

Foreign policy

———

Commonwealth;

The Commonwealth as a concept is an anachronism and therefore the first action of a PDC government - as far as foreign policy is concerned - would be to contact each of these countries that we have plundered and abused over decades if not centuries and offer to draw up plans with them - if they so desire - to withdraw sovereignty in order to restore their integrity and their independence.

This would of course be done over a period of time, on a set timetable so as not to destabilise their economies.

We cannot deny or redo the past, but it is no longer right for us to try to impose ourselves over those people we have no right to govern.

Realistically, we could never compensate them enough for what we have taken from them, but we can hope that in return for their riches, we have at least tried to give them something back through our culture and our language; it may have been an unbalanced exchange but it was an exchange of sorts.

This initiative would hopefully draw a line under the past and allow everyone to look to the future with a more positive outlook.

Of course, nothing would be imposed and if trade agreements could be maintained so much the better.

At home;

We need to change the world's perception of us as a nation, and that begins at home.

I am tired of seeing British tourists making a fool of themselves while on holiday; the binge-drinking, the promiscuity and the general lack of acceptable behaviour displayed by these people has tainted our reputation immeasurably on the international stage over the past decade or two.

Some places around Europe have come to accept that behaviour and even adapted to it in order to keep the tourist money flowing in, but I believe it is an area that needs to be addressed if we ever hope to regain a measure of respect and standing within the international community.

The PDC would immediately attack the booze culture here at home - as set out in the Justice Chapter earlier - and then introduce stricter guidelines for those who go abroad, potentially obliging those that get convicted of criminal or unruly activity in other countries to spend a month or so in one of the new correction-facilities - that we would be building - when they get back, to remind them of how to behave.

The rest of the world;

As for the rest of the world, the PDC would have an ethical and coherent foreign policy which reflects and respects the values that we hold dear.

We would therefore start with a blank slate and review every agreement with every country currently in place - irrespective of previous allegiances and understandings – with a view to clarifying our position on the world stage and producing a solid base on which to found a new 21st century society.

This would mean updating and overhauling our relations with every single country...based on their current status...and while the past and historical entente would naturally be considered and taken into account, it would not be allowed to cloud any future agreements.

No more hypocrisy or double-standards.

At the same time, the PDC would have no dealings with any dictators or any repressive regimes, and any assets held in this country by those people would immediately be frozen and returned to the rightful people upon request by an official and legitimate representation.

—————

Visas;

Rules governing the granting of visas in foreign embassies and consulates would be tightened...and to make things perfectly clear before these people travel to our country applicants would be issued with a copy of the new immigration rules and justice laws.

—————

Extradition; (see also Justice)

As part of the general foreign policy set out above, which would include deportation agreements as well as health care for visiting foreign nationals, the PDC would review every extradition treaty currently in place, in line with its ideals based on common values;

Agreements would be made clearer, fairer and more transparent...and no UK citizens would ever be handed over to any foreign country without one of these new agreements in place.

Our position as far as the USA is concerned is one that would need special attention as the PDC would not accept the double standards currently being displayed by our spineless politicians over rendition flights and extraditions (Nat West 3)

The PDC would not want to be party either to any deliberate misinformation for political expediency such as what happened over Iraq and the WMD files.

That kind of political jeopardy rightly impacts on our integrity and our credibility within the wider world and it is simply not acceptable.

NB; we would uphold the right of any **British citizen** to challenge an extradition order concerning him or her in the High Court.

As for war-criminals who might ask for asylum in this country, the PDC would systematically side with the victims rather than the perpetrators. Therefore, if a country was to ask for a person's extradition in order to put them on trial for war-crimes, according to the laws of their country, we would not stand in their way...as long as verifiable proof of the person's guilt was produced.

The UK cannot be seen as a haven for criminals.

This decision would mean withdrawing from the EU Human Rights charter which doesn't allow repatriation of criminals if there is a danger that their human rights would not be respected...but that charter would no longer have tenure under the PDC as we would replace it with a new British Charter for Human Rights, adapted to our own laws.

Now, I understand that the woolly liberals who defend the EU Human Rights charter will be outraged by this, but I would remind them of the victims…and ask them if the human rights of those victims had been respected by the 'alleged' perpetrators.

Foreign aid –

Foreign aid is always a contentious issue but it shouldn't be; it's a simple question of priorities.

The Prime Minister, David Cameron said that 'we have a moral obligation to help people in other countries even when times are tough'. That may well be true, but what he omitted to say was that we should look after our own citizens first; that should always be our priority, our first moral obligation, before we help others.

I would remind him of the safety-rules on airplanes; 'always put your own oxygen mask on first…and then help others if you are able'.

Charity is a wonderful thing and foreign aid is no more than government-funded charity – with the added factor of political influence – that is used to help those 'in need' in other countries.

My problem is this; we have people 'in need' in this country too; poor people, homeless people living on the streets, dependent on charity and relying on food-banks to survive…and while I understand that we should, as a prosperous nation, do our fair share to help those around the world less fortunate than we are, our priority as a country should nevertheless be to help those living amongst us.

At the moment, because of the economic down-turn, all government budgets are being cut - by up to 40% in some cases - meaning that British citizens and taxpayers are being denied urgent operations and deprived of vital drugs because the budgets are no longer there to provide them.

Meanwhile, the government has increased the international aid budget by 40%, just to satisfy David Cameron's moral grandstanding on the world stage; it is simply not logical economics.

Of course we need to continue with overseas aid; I am not suggesting that we shouldn't but we need to stop trying to ingratiate ourselves with the rest of the world by throwing money at them.

I cannot understand for example, why we are pouring millions of pounds into climate change programmes in Africa for example while the UK is facing economic meltdown...and a majority of its citizens are suffering hardship on a daily basis.

This is a question of priorities and I believe that we should concentrate on sorting out our own problems and our own economy first, before giving away money that we don't have.

Here is the paradox; as a country we borrow billions of pounds on a daily basis, increasing our national debt exponentially, only to give that money away in foreign aid...

Can somebody please explain the logic of that situation to me...?

———

Comment;

The PDC's main goal would be to weed out the hypocrisy and double-standards in politics.

We cannot preach a civilised humanitarian message in this country while at the same time sending £1.3 billion of UK taxpayers' money - in the form of foreign aid - to countries such as Ethiopia where it is used to prop up a corrupt, single-party government, finance its army and decimate its population. It is simply not ethical;

The people of Ethiopia are being slaughtered on a daily basis, women are being subjected to mass rape by gun-toting soldiers and gangs, whole villages are being displaced from fertile lands to arid refugee-camps and if anyone dares to protest on the street, they are shot on sight, while dissidents and journalists who try to reveal these atrocities are often locked up under new, draconian anti-terrorism laws...

...and all this is being done with British taxpayers' money.

International politics is a tricky business, it is a delicate business but our foreign aid programme should not be underwriting this kind of repression no matter what the derivative gains might be in mineral extraction or terrorist monitoring.

At the same time, we cannot black-list countries run by tyrants and then sell arms to them worth £12 billion as has recently been reported.

We need a consistent and coherent foreign-aid policy.

PDC Policy;

After the banking fiasco most western economies are suffering enormous hardship and because we are experiencing that hardship here in the UK too, I believe that we should reduce or even suspend our foreign aid budget for a year or two and divert that money into getting our economy back on its feet.

Then, once we are on an even keel again, we can restart the process having made a couple of important fundamental changes.

Firstly, we need to reconsider **who** we give the aid to, as the world has changed so dramatically over the last 15 years.

India for example;

The British government has been sending British taxpayers' money to India for decades trying to absolve itself of our colonial past, but if India can now afford a space programme of its own, and can afford to spend £10 billion on new fighter jets, then why should it still be down the British tax-payer to save their poor.

Surely the Indian government should now take on that responsibility – especially as the Indian government has announced that it doesn't even need our aid any more.

In fact, the Indian economy is doing so well that it now offers its own aid to other countries; more than we give to them if truth be told.

Nigeria too, has announced a space programme and yet we are still ploughing millions of pounds into their economy too.

The PDC would revise all these agreements.

Then we need to consider **how** we give our aid.

The UK sent out £11billion pounds in foreign aid last year - more than Germany, which is considered Europe's most affluent economy - with absolutely no control over how it was spent.

That needs to change because UK taxpayers are sick of seeing their money misappropriated. They want the money they send to these countries to be spent on humanitarian projects and economic development, not siphoned off by corrupt regimes to spend on Malibu mansions, gulfstream jets or fleets of luxury cars.

I believe that all humanitarian aid should be channelled through an accountable international agency to avoid corrupt officials or unscrupulous politicians stealing it, creaming it off or pocketing it for themselves, before it can get to those who really need it.

Better still, rather that giving cash, it might be an even better idea to find out what these countries need and then manufacture those items here in the UK, thereby targeting exactly what is needed while at the same time creating jobs in this country.

Maybe we could even give the jobs to prisoners, teaching them a trade at the same time.

Perhaps we could also nominate an envoy and send him/her to these countries to see what was needed. He/she could then report back with a comprehensive list of the items required.

Then, rather than send the money, the British government could place orders with British companies to supply those needs. This creates jobs in this country and prevents our foreign-aid money being siphoned off by unscrupulous politicians and military leaders; it's a win / win situation.

NB; with mechanical projects we must also remember to provide the training (more jobs) and technical support on how to use and repair the machinery because without that knowledge the machines would quickly fall into disrepair. We also have to work out some kind of spare parts supply clause for the same reason. There is no point delivering equipment to these countries without the necessary logistical and technical support to make it viable.

War and conflict –

My first observation on war and conflict has to be this ambivalent paradox;

The United Nations was set up as a force for world peace and yet the UN's five most prominent members produce and deal in ninety-five per cent of the world's most deadly weapons.

Personally, I am against the act of war unless it is against the megalomaniac dictators of this world and their repressive regimes.

However, those who choose to sign up to lucrative contracts to act as mercenaries and fight in these countries, to deliberately put themselves in harm's way, should not expect the government of this country to bail them out if they get into trouble.

———

There are three points I would like to make on war and conflict –

Firstly –

In the past, the West has had a different agenda when getting involved in other countries 'difficulties'.

Stabilising their economies and their political systems was usually the initial, stated goal of the western forces, but self-interest quickly took over, playing a key role in the decision of whether or not to get involved.

Political influence, access to oil and commerce (weapons etc) were the major drivers but things are different now; the game has changed and every area of the world should now be responsible and accountable for itself within its region.

In the Gulf Region, for example, I believe that the Arab league should stand up with more conviction if it wants to be seen as a major player in resolving disputes amongst neighbouring countries. Knowing the culture and the sensibilities of the different warring factions would be such a help in finding compromise, because as it stands, <u>whenever there is a problem</u> in that region and the people of a country call out in distress, it is inevitably the West that comes to their aid – USA, UK, France and Germany etc.

However, this is a double-edged sword because when the West does get involved and tries to help, it is immediately criticised by some for being an invasion / occupying force.

It is a catch 22 situation.

If the West goes in to help, they get panned and if they don't go in, thousands of people die; that is often the dilemma that western politicians face, and that is why I believe that the Arab league and the Gulf States need to stand up and administer the area themselves.

The West - and notably the USA - got its fingers burned in Afghanistan and Iraq and in future it will be loath to intervene unless they have a clear mandate from the UN.

NB - The war in Afghanistan was always pointless and unwinnable; more thought should have gone into that invasion. The knee-jerk reaction of George W Bush after 9/11 was understandable but he should have looked at what happened when the Russians invaded a few decades earlier and were sent packing.

———

Secondly -

The UN should announce to the world that we, the international community, are prepared to withdraw all international troops from every country currently being patrolled, on the condition that the people of those countries has chosen their leader and the way that they want to be governed.

These countries don't want UN personnel 'occupying' them...and we in the West certainly don't want to be there putting the lives of our military personnel at risk, so if these countries can show that they don't need us – I know they don't want us – then we should leave them to it.

Besides, resources are being stretched all around, both financial and logistical and an organised withdrawal would clearly ease those pressures.

———

And thirdly –

Now, while suggesting that each area of the world deals with its own conflicts and proposing the withdrawal of unwanted UN personnel from areas where they are no longer required might seem idealistic, and it is, I am in no doubt that conflict will continue somewhere in the world. It is in man's nature to fight and therefore conflict is inevitable**.**

That is why I believe that we need to strengthen the international Security Council.

The **UN / NATO** has to grow a spine and some balls and in order to do that, we need a global agreement – with teeth – signed by every country on the planet which allows an international task force of specially trained commandoes to intervene wherever, whenever required, at a minute's notice without being bogged down by any overly-cautious bureaucracy.

This task-force – if sanctioned by the international community – would be mandated to operate without the fear of political meddling, in-fighting or recrimination and its mission would be to counter any threat to the international community, to conduct anti-terrorist operations and carry out kidnap recovery assignments (pirates) wherever they might occur around the world.

Its mission could also include the removal of blood-thirsty tyrants and dictators who do not respect the humanitarian protocols currently in place.

Meanwhile, we would still have mandated UN inspectors who could be sent in to assess a volatile situation before or during a conflict...and the blue-helmeted peace-keepers to help in stabilising a situation after a conflict had been resolved until a new government has been elected... but I firmly believe that the UN / IC (International Community) should have an intervention force for situations where diplomacy is just not going to cut it.

It might also act as a deterrent to those projecting future unrest.

NB – Decisions would be made on a majority vote to avoid a stalemate situation where no action could be taken because one or two members don't agree. We all live on the same planet and the well-intentioned majority has to prevail over the selfish interests of the few; what was it that David Cameron said; 'we are all in this together'. Those countries who disagree for whatever reason would simply have to stand down and abstain from participating in whatever action was endorsed and those who refuse to sign up to the protocol for whatever reason would be subject to a trade ban from the rest of the IC on non-essential commodities until they complied.

Author's comment;

As a race and supposedly the most intelligent race on this planet, we are told growing up that LIFE is the most precious thing that we possess, that it is all that matters and that we should do whatever we can during our lifetimes to save and protect it.

Well, if we human beings cherish life to that extent, surely we cannot possibly accept a situation where we have to sit back and watch innocent people get slaughtered by the thousand just because there is no international agreement in place to prevent it.

It is simply unpalatable that a motion put before the international Security Council which could save the lives of thousands of people can be blocked by one or two countries in order to defend their own self-interest.

That politics and self-interest should trump the saving of innocent lives shows that some people have their priorities in the wrong order.

What is more important in life; life itself...or money, power and influence?

There is no discussion, because without life...money, power and influence have no meaning.

Dictatorships –

As recent events along the Mediterranean basin have suggested, it is time for the autocratic dynasties of the past to be swept away.

Tunisia and Egypt have set the precedence, although Egypt is still a little unsettled but it is now time for all those countries that have lived for centuries shrouded in ignorance and religious repression to get with the programme; this is the 21st century.

All the remaining ***dictatorships and military juntas*** around the world, all those regimes based on brutal repression and deprivation need to realise that their time is up.

They no longer have tenure in the 21st century; they are an anachronism.

The time when ignorance and naiveté could be exploited is gone and democracy should now reign supreme throughout the world.

Any head of state that has to use tanks and chemical weapons on his own people in order to maintain his grip on power should automatically lose his legitimacy in the eyes of the rest of the world (Saddam Hussein in Iraq, Col. Moammar Gaddafi in Libya and Bashar al-Assad in Syria are three recent examples but there are many others around the world)

––––

Author's comment;

There has to be a line that we – as human beings – do not cross; an act of barbarism that is so inhumane that it triggers an automatic reaction from the rest of the world's populace without the need for prolonged debate.

––––

Here is a list of the Dictatorships and repressive regimes still operating in the world today

List One: the most repressive nations and territories

Burma
Chechnya, *a disputed territory controlled by Russia*
Cuba
North Korea
Somalia
Sudan
Tibet, *a disputed territory controlled by China*
Turkmenistan
Uzbekistan

List Two: all other nations and territories judged 'not free'

Algeria
Angola
Azerbaijan
Belarus
Bhutan
Brunei
Cambodia
Cameroon
Chad
China
Congo (Brazzaville)
Congo (Kinshasa)
Cote d'Ivoire
Egypt (*currently undergoing change*)
Equatorial Guinea
Eritrea
Guinea
Iran
Iraq
Israeli-occupied disputed territories
Kashmir, the portion of the disputed territory controlled by Pakistan

Kazakhstan
Kosovo, *a disputed territory controlled by Serbia*
Laos
Maldives
Oman
Pakistan
Qatar
Russia
Rwanda
Saudi Arabia
Swaziland
Syria
Tajikistan
Thailand
Togo
Transnistria, *a disputed territory controlled by Moldova*
Tunisia
United Arab Emirates
Vietnam
Western Sahara, *a disputed territory controlled by Morocco*
Zimbabwe

Other international issues –

Disarmament;

The strike teams mentioned previously are a necessary deterrent for now - human nature being what it is - but the first role of the International Community should always be one of diplomacy and mediation...and one area where it should be more pro-active in the medium to long-term is that of disarmament and the destruction of WMD.

A UN resolution was passed recently which forces Syria to destroy its chemical weapons but why doesn't this accord cover every country in the world including the major players who are dictating the policy.

This is a prime example of the inherent hypocrisy of humanity, the bigger states dictating to the smaller states under the threat of sanction while doing exactly the same thing themselves. The 'super-power' states dictate to other countries that they cannot have nuclear or chemical weapons, but they themselves have enormous stock-piles of both types of weapon squirreled away and ready for use. So, why is it okay for the USA, Russia and China etc to have nuclear and chemical weapons but not the smaller states? It's no wonder that the smaller states rebel and kick back against the bullying 'super-powers' from time to time.

Now, preventing unstable regimes from having WMD is of course a positive step as far as the International Community is concerned but if we are really intent on making the world a better place, why stop there... we already have an initiative in place that covers the non-proliferation of nuclear weapons but why not go one step further and agree the complete abandonment of WMD worldwide...to be followed eventually by the eradication of all other weapons great and small...because as long as we keep producing them (guns, grenades and bombs) war-mongers and those with a criminal tendency will carry on using them.

Of course, I realise that this is idealistic thinking but I do believe that the International Community has a duty to itself and to mankind as a whole to do all it can to rid the world of dangerous weapons, so why not start now...before we get to the inevitable apocalypse...that so many of our celebrated visionaries have foreseen for us.

Surely, this has to be the goal of mankind at some point...before it's too late.

———

Population;

I am afraid for the future of mankind when I see short-sighted countries like China, Pakistan, India, Vietnam or Afghanistan suppressing their female populations at birth...

- through abortion,
- infanticide

- or giving them away for adoption in the West

...while rewarding and celebrating male births

I understand the cultural imperatives at the root of this tradition but unfortunately, without realising it, these countries are unwittingly skewing humanity and their respective societies by promoting male offspring as the only acceptable choice.

What will happen in a few generations time when men outnumber women ten to one?

What will be the future of mankind then...when there is an abundance of men and not enough women to produce the next generation; what happens then?

Surely the leaders of these countries can see that if this misguided practice continues – with every generation that passes – there will be fewer and fewer women...and that eventually there will not be enough women alive to continue populating the planet.

What then for humanity...?

As time goes by, men will get more possessive...and frustrated...and this will lead to more arguments and more testosterone-fuelled aggression; women will most likely be hidden away like prized possessions (undoing decades of self-empowerment) and ultimately more war will break-out leading to the inevitable destruction of the planet.

Just look at the increased number of rapes now happening in India; this is a catastrophe waiting to happen.

Meanwhile, as a consequence of these blinkered policies a culture of kidnapping has developed in these countries with children as young as a few days old being sold by unscrupulous human traffickers.

I believe that we, in the international community should be doing something more positive to help these countries move into the 21ˢᵗ century, before it is too late.

———

Space;

I believe that it is wrong to be investing billions in astronomically-priced space exploration...and travel...when there are people on this planet who are dying of hunger and have no access to clean water.

Then, there are all those people who have lost their homes and everything in them after a forest fire – or after a tornado has ripped through their town laying waste to everything in its path including infrastructure worth billions...or entire villages that have to be rebuilt from scratch after devastating floods.

These are the projects that we should be investing in; not space exploration. If governments have money set aside for space research then I would suggest they consider redirecting it into rebuilding the homes of these people and improving the environment of everyone else living on this planet first.

That said; we do need to get rid of nuclear waste and increase our energy sources; so, if we do have to pursue space technology, why not develop a system for taking waste up into space, to be dumped on the other side of the universe in a capsule that would then soak up solar energy on its way back and bring that energy back down to earth...or...maybe it could laser it down to strategically placed energy reception centres placed at different sites around the planet.

———

Pirates;

The pirates, terrorists and criminals around the world who carry out un-just kidnapping operations involving British citizens need to know that no ransoms would ever be paid by a PDC government; quite the opposite in fact; we would take a very dim view of this kind of activity and perpetrators of such crimes would be 'reprimanded' most severely.

Oceans;

And finally, I believe that the UN should do more for the environment.

They should create a fleet of ships to scour the oceans and trawl up all the plastic flotsam that is currently washing around our planet, polluting our water and killing the marine life.

Teams should also be organised in every country to go around and clear up the debris which is being thrown up onto our shore-lines and beaches...

...and finally the UN should set up a network of re-cycling plants where all this waste could be treated and transformed into an energy-source or re-usable items that could then be re-cycled *ad-infinitum...*

The UN should also encourage greater research into bio-degradable products in tandem with the initiatives mentioned above.

Meanwhile, those countries found to be deliberately or excessively polluting the oceans should be sanctioned.

The Military

The first thing I have to say about our military is this;

- Anybody who is prepared to fight and put their life on the line for their country deserves to be treated with added respect.

They should not be treated in the way that New Labour treated the Ghurkhas for example; those brave people fought for this country and yet they were threatened with deportation by the New Labour government; only being allowed to stay here – on reduced pensions – after the intervention – *in extremis* – of actress Joanna Lumley.

That kind of politics is unacceptable and unbecoming of this country.

- **Secondly**; I believe that our military personnel should get a decent wage. Why should a politician who sits in his cosy office in Westminster earn <u>eight times</u> that of a soldier who puts his life on the line for his country? It doesn't equate.

And why should 55000 pen-pushers at the MoD share £40m in bonuses as they did recently, while serving soldiers were given a measly 1% pay-rise.

How is that fair and justifiable?

- **Thirdly**; I believe that soldiers serving on the front-line should be exempt from paying tax while they are deployed...and should also be rewarded for their commitment and devotion to duty with a tax-free bonus when they return.

A life-insurance policy of some kind should also be set up to cover those on active duty, to be paid out to the families in the event of their loved-ones not surviving a mission.

- **Fourthly**; when they do get injured fighting for their country, I believe that every soldier should get all the care and attention they need, no matter the cost, together with a comprehensive care package and pension.
- And finally, we should stop neglecting our service personnel once they return to civilian life.

I know that there is some help available for those leaving the service but it is somewhat inadequate and I believe that it is only right that we do more to re-integrate our military personnel when they leave the service.

For example;

- they should go to the top of the list for council housing in the area of their choosing when they leave the armed forces,
- they should receive more help in finding jobs and...
- those still suffering from PTSD (post traumatic stress disorder) or any other psychological pathologies should receive on-going care despite their new civilian status.

As for those who are injured, with physical traumas to overcome, we already have Headley Court Rehabilitation Centre, the Queen Elizabeth Hospital in Birmingham (which has recently replaced the old Selly Oak hospital) and the new British Legion Centre in Lilleshall but I believe we still need a dedicated hospital to take care of retired soldiers.

Cynical politicians want to take away their disability benefits but maybe a better solution would be to offer these people the help they need. Something along the lines of the Royal Hospital, Chelsea where the veterans forfeit their pensions in exchange for the care they need and a roof above their heads.

The new War Memorial (National Memorial Arboretum) constructed in Staffordshire as a mark of respect to those who have made the ultimate sacrifice for their country is a wonderful idea, and a poignant reminder that we should never forget those who laid down their lives so that we might live ours in the way we choose...but personally, I would have preferred that we spend the £7 million that it cost, taking better care of the living, and those who have come home injured.

A memorial by all means; that goes without saying but £7 million was far too much.

We need to get our priorities right and to that end the PDC would look into creating a dedicated ministry to look after military veterans and the issues concerning them.

A word for the 'Help for Heroes' charity;

I have to commend the work carried out by these people and those who represent them.

Everything they do seems to reflect the same fundamental values, the same determination, the same courage and the same devotion to duty that our military personnel has always displayed, without fail, whenever it has been called upon, wherever it goes in the world.

Bravo.

Compensation;

Compensation claims by military personnel should be consistent and coherent and should reflect the degree of trauma a person has suffered when being considered in a way that is fair and reasonable – if we can talk about fair and reasonable when soldiers have lost the use of limbs or worse.

It is not right for example that a lesbian soldier was awarded £200K for 'hurt feelings', when;

- one soldier who lost an arm and a leg was only offered £161K
- another who lost a leg was awarded £57K

- another, who was almost totally paralyzed from the neck down after being hit by machine gun fire was awarded £201K
- and another who lost both legs and an arm only received £214K

In comparison, the MoD awarded an injured Kosovo soldier £2.4 million in compensation which is 18 times what a British soldier can expect to get.

How humiliating and soul-destroying it must be for our wounded servicemen and women to see that the MoD looks after others, to a far better degree than it does its own.

The penny-pinching AFCS (Armed Forces Compensation Scheme) needs a root-and-branch overhaul and should be aligned at the very least with Civil Court payouts.

Ministry of Defence;

The British Ministry of Defence is outrageously over-subscribed in civil servants.

Look at this comparison;

- we have over **23,000** procurement personnel in this country
- while Israel, which has a similar defence budget, has only **400** staff…and the situation in Israel is far more volatile than our own.

This is clearly untenable and the PDC would immediately reduce these numbers to a more manageable and accountable level.

However, not only is the MoD over-staffed, it is also unduly profligate with taxpayers' money, hiding systematically behind the well-worn doctrine that 'National Security has no price', to justify its outrageous spending.

For example; spending on consultants soared from £6m to £270m in five years during the New Labour years which is a 45-fold increase... and as mentioned previously, during the same period, MoD staff gladly shared in £40m of bonuses...while front-line troops faced a pay-squeeze and job cuts.

Surely, handing out bonuses to the pen-pushers while simultaneously laying off operational personnel is a clear indication that the Ministry of Defence has its priorities in the wrong order.

———

But that is not all; not only is the MoD over-staffed and profligate, it is also 'institutionally incompetent'; according to the National Audit Office;

- £5 billion of equipment has been either mislaid or stolen
- £6.6 billion has been wasted on unused kit and supplies
- £2.5 billion was squandered on the 'wrong equipment' under New Labour
- And bungling MoD officials even managed to lose track of the 'last wills and testaments' of many of their serving personnel.

This is bureaucratic incompetence of the highest order and it might only be anecdotal but the fact that the dysfunctional MoD spent £40K on calls to the 'speaking-clock' as was recently disclosed, reveals a glaring disregard among their staff for the innate British reflex not to waste other people's money.

———

Other examples of profligacy and incompetence;

- The MoD recently spent £40million rehiring the thousands of civil servants that they had previously spent £70million making redundant, handing them pay-offs of more than £30,000 each
- They gave away property worth £1.5billion to Germany after our withdrawal from the area...without any form of compensation

- They over-paid tax to the tune of £1.5million and never bothered to claim it back
- They 'wrote off' £743,000 in 'lost' field generators
- They 'misplaced' missile parts worth £527,000
- They wasted £393,000 in cancelled rental agreements on buildings rented for training and then not used
- They 'lost' £390,000 of kit in Canada
- They 'wasted' another £277,000 buying the wrong ammunition

And finally they 'wrote-off' **£33.6million** in 'unsupported balances' which is bean-counter language for 'we can't account for any of this missing money; we don't know where it's gone'.

Ref; Daily Mail 8th of September 2013

———

One final note; the MoD procurement service and the arms manufacturers that provide the hardware are in bed together; that is too cosy.

The MOD procurement programme is currently £6.6bn over budget; they already have a shortfall of £38bn from previous years and they have wasted billions more buying equipment that remained unused.

This inventory mismanagement needs to be addressed and more accountability needs to be put in place.

———

Author's comment;

The MoD also demanded two aircraft carriers from the New Labour government at £3 billion a piece and desperate for good-will from wherever they could find it, irrespective of the cost, the New Labour government signed off on it.

This was a complete folly because anyone looking forward can see that this kind of conventional military hardware will almost certainly be out of date before it is even launched, probably replaced by technological advances in long-range un-manned weapons systems, such as drones etc.

To their credit, the new coalition government recognised this error of judgement and the clear evidence of what warfare in the future will look like, but rather than cancel the air-craft carriers - in a desperate attempt to save money after the banking crisis - they decided instead to abandon the harrier jump jets used to fly missions off of those kinds of ships, which effectively compounded the folly. (The harrier jump-jets have since been sold to the USA)

But that wasn't all...and in another short-sighted cost-cutting exercise, they then proceeded to scrap the Nimrod programme worth another £3.6 billion <u>without those aircraft ever having taken to the skies</u>;

Now, the logic of these decisions can be debated until we are blue in the face but the reality of the situation is that we now have two aircraft carriers on order with no planes to fly off of them.

Where is the coherence in these policies...?

One option would have been to cancel the air-craft carriers but apparently we cannot do that because when negotiating the contracts the hapless New Labour government tied us into very expensive retraction clauses – which would I have read cost the country more than the ships themselves – and so now, we are in a position where we are having to go ahead with the construction of two hugely-expensive ocean-going aircraft-carriers for which we have absolutely no use.

Hindsight, I know, is a wonderful thing...but sometimes a little sober reflection and fore-sight would not go amiss in the corridors of Westminster.

Of course, in this ever changing world we might yet find a use for <u>one</u> of these ships between now and the completion date...we might even decide to convert one of them into a prison ship while we renovate and up-grade our prison network...but the only option for the second vessel would seem to be to sell it (if we can find a buyer) or to scrap it at great loss.

I have to ask; is this really the best way to be using hard-earned taxpayer money...?

Now, granted, this is not all the MoD's fault but it does highlight the profligacy and the lack of pecuniary control in the MoD's finances...and I believe that it is time that we put an end to it; someone, somewhere has to be held accountable.

―――――

But that is not all; not only is the MoD;

- over-staffed,
- profligate and
- incompetent

...it is also lacking in the innate qualities of respect and moral decorum that the British people expect from their governing bodies; especially from its military ranks.

An example; The MOD is currently appealing against the compensation claims made by a number of its injured personnel.

There are currently 279 dossiers being processed through the system, but again I have to ask; how can the MoD betray our soldiers like this... appealing against their compensation claims...?

Words fail me to explain why these pen-pushing bureaucrats in their cosy little offices would want to contest these claims from soldiers who have served on the front-line – if indeed, these claims are genuine...and they must be genuine because our wonderful New Labour government had these men spied upon, just to make sure.

Is there no integrity these days...?

...and finally, I believe that we need to review redundancy procedures for military personnel; it is not in the spirit of the military covenant or in the spirit of the British people to axe people only days before their pensions kick in, just so as to save the government money.

That kind of political manoeuvring suggests a lack of respect and compassion...and is unbecoming of our proud military traditions; that we should put financial concerns before the human considerations of those who have dedicated their lives to the cause is unacceptable in my eyes.

It is a cynical stunt that happened under the intrinsically amoral New Labour government...but much to their shame the current coalition has allowed it to continue...and it is not right.

A compromise must be found on this issue because to renege on those pension contracts is immoral and a complete betrayal of everything that the British military has ever stood for.

Budget –

The latest MoD budget of £37.5 billion is the 4th largest in the world and while it is only 2.6% of GDP, it is money that could clearly be better spent. (*see section on profligacy*)

We need to use that money more wisely – to benefit everyday British citizens – not to fight other people's battles around the world.

The PDC would revise the MoD budget to reflect the reduced role of the British military in world affairs, and the surplus would be redistributed between...

- the Justice system – to facilitate the building of the new prison and reform camps

- the Police Force - to fund its increased capacity and to contribute to its new, revised pay scale
- the new Border Police Force – to set up this vital new service which will be comprised mainly of ex-servicemen and women
- and finally, to improve facilities in military rehab centres

———

The PDC Military Policy;

Over the years, the British Military (Army, Navy and Air Force) has forged its reputation and earned the respect of most every nation around the world.

Indeed, the British Military has often been considered one of the world's most professional fighting-forces because its efficiency, its integrity and its willingness to stick at a job until it is done, come what may.

It has intervened in numerous conflicts around the world and in many cases it has proudly succeeded where many others would have failed.

However, now is the time for change because despite our glorious military past – if going to war can indeed be expressed in such noble terms – I believe that the age of military conquest through mass invasion is a thing of the past.

This is no great revelation; it is a simple statement of fact, of reality in the 21st century and while it seems harsh to consign all that glory to the history books we have to accept that we have now entered a new era where the idea of conventional warfare – of mass-invasion needing thousands upon thousands of fighting troops ready and waiting to respond to the country's call – is redundant.

Conflicts will inevitably continue to flare up – that is the nature of the human race - but when this does happen in future, technology will almost certainly be at the forefront of any action; un-manned drones replacing boots on the ground in both reconnaissance and in strike missions...and as a consequence of this 'brave new world' we will no longer have any need for the numbers in military personnel that we used to.

———

Therefore we need a more modern approach to military issues... and I believe that this begins with us withdrawing from our role of international problem-solver alongside the USA.

After all;

- The Cold War is over
- The Empire has been given back for the most part
- Nuclear disarmament is on-going around the world...'allegedly'
- and the idea that a super-power still wants to take over the world through military force has largely faded away in the minds of most people

So now is the time I believe for us to stop being Uncle Sam's side-kick in policing the world's problems and concentrate our efforts on more pressing, more immediate problems closer to home.

Besides, I do not see why this country should feel obliged to act as the world's policeman alongside the Americans. Who appointed us...or indeed the Americans...to the role of the world's fixer?

We have to stop interfering - with military interventions – in the affairs of other sovereign states; especially as, for the most part, we are not wanted or welcome in these countries. That task should be left to the International Community, not individual states like ours because, as we have seen time and time again, unilateral or bi-lateral interventions inevitably backfire on the perpetrators.

Consequently, under a PDC administration, while we would naturally continue to fulfil our commitment to the international effort as part of a joint Task Force, Britain would no longer be taking the lead - unilaterally or bi-laterally – in any military action...unless it was specifically asked to do so by the International Community because of our specialised knowledge.

———

'Britain is not an outpost of the UN. We have to put the people in this country first', said **Lord Glassman** recently. (Lord Glassman is an advisor to Ed Miliband)

———

Author's comment *on politicians obsessed with self-aggrandisement, their legacy and their standing on the world stage.*

Why is it that whenever an international crisis blows up the politicians of this country act as if it is our national destiny to intervene...which usually involves the country in great expense and sacrifice...and very little positive return?

Why do we always have to get involved in conflicts that do not really concern us...and why do our narcissistic, war-mongering, publicity seeking, legacy building politicians always have to appear front and centre on the international stage whenever there is a problem...like Zorro riding to the rescue on his black stallion?

Why? I suppose that question is rhetorical if not redundant really...because...

...they are narcissistic, war-mongering, publicity seeking, legacy building politicians.

But I have to ask; is the need for global recognition really that irresistible for these people? Is it really indispensable for a politician to go down in the history books as some kind of global liberator? Why so much political vanity?

I understand the attraction of international ego-stroking and self-aggrandisement on the world's stage but I believe that, for UK politicians at least, it is time to stop the pretence.

Our politicians should be more realistic about the limitations of our current military potential and stop posturing, stop harking back to the past when <u>we were</u> a global military power. That time is gone.

The British people have had enough of the half-hearted attempts of their politicians to keep up the facade of our illustrious past with their smoke-screen policies of sending our troops to intervene abroad, just to save us from the international embarrassment of revealing that we are no longer the force we were — even though that is the reality of today's world.

Especially as our recent New Labour government clearly failed in its duty to provide our military personnel with the necessary equipment and logistical support to defend themselves or carry out the missions they sent them out to achieve last time around.

Indeed, I find it more than a little cynical of our political leaders to send our military personnel into harms way knowing full-well that they were under-equipped — while they themselves stayed at home in their cosy Westminster offices...just to save us from the international embarrassment of revealing that we are no longer the force we were.

Of course, our army still performed magnificently despite the lack of equipment — we would expect nothing less - but if we cannot give them the tools to do the job, then we should not be sending them in the first place.

Besides, the international embarrassment to our lily-livered, light-weight leaders could never be any greater than the glorious ridicule with which they cover themselves on a daily basis here at home.

Tony Blair was a great example of this political self-delusion. He was desperate to be seen as a leader, as a statesman on the world stage but sadly, his career will only ever be remembered for one thing. The fact that he, as the New Labour leader ignored the wishes of the British people and took the country to war based on a dodgy dossier and a pack of lies...

It is a damning personal legacy for the man himself...but sadly he is not the only one tainted by his action...and the deception he masterminded, his lies, his bogus claims and the betrayal that the British public felt over this saga means that <u>all British politicians</u> are now tarred with the same brush.

Anybody involved in politics in Britain today, however small that involvement might be, is immediately mistrusted and reviled by the British public on the back of what Tony Blair did; so not only did he let the country down as PM, he also let his colleagues down too by poisoning the well of trust that needs to exist between the political classes and the people...

...although the political class hasn't done itself any favours either with its recent, contemptible expenses scandal...

It is a sad conclusion to his political career in Britain but in trying to ingratiate himself in the eyes of President George W. Bush - as a way of raising his profile on the world stage - Tony Blair managed to single-handedly destroy the trust of the British people and tarnish the reputation of politicians in this country for generations to come...the repercussions of which are already being felt in the Syrian conflict because now that it has been broken, that crucial trust between the politicians and the British public will no doubt take a very long time to re-build.

I believe that before trying to sort out the problems of the world and give others lessons in how they should run their countries, we should get our own house in order and concentrate on righting the wrongs in this country first.

It is time to re-deploy our huge military budgets to areas of our society in greater need... rather than spending it on ill-advised military incursions into other countries.

Needless to say, I am not suggesting disbanding the Army completely; we will always need to maintain our capacity to defend ourselves. However I am suggesting that we scale it back and re-deploy the excess capacity that we currently carry, in a civilian role in this country as part of a policy to regain control;

- of our borders,
- of our streets and
- of the growing number of criminal elements now operating here

We currently have 227.000 military personnel and 174000 reserves; that is far too many in this time of reduced military threat.

(We also have 40 admirals and 260 captains in our Navy for only 19 ships… while the Army has 256 brigadiers and generals…and only 200 Challenger II tanks; clearly we are over-staffed in hierarchy)

Its time to bring our soldiers home to fight the real fight; the fight to save Britain from itself and the mess that successive governments have created over the last thirty years – because, if we allow the current politicians to carry on as they have done, for the next thirty, then this country is doomed.

Remember the motto people;

**Remember how things were thirty years ago…
Look at how things are now…
and think about how things might be in thirty years time
if we don't do something to change things.**

Going forward;

Naturally, the new streamlined British military would retain a reasonable defence force in order to guarantee the security of all British citizens… and all those with important military skills and tactical knowledge would of course be integrated into the new model;

- The SAS and Special Forces would also be retained <u>and properly funded</u> so that they might carry out the special operations and

precise surgical interventions that they might be called upon to accomplish as part of the international alliance...and
- We would also retain enough personnel to fulfil our commitment to NATO and the UN Security Council

However, under the PDC the rest of the military would be scaled back dramatically.

This means that tank regiments and parachute regiments (SAS excluded) for example would become obsolete.

Now I understand the nostalgia and the debt that we owe to such regiments from previous campaigns, but mass invasion is now a thing of the past, and to have all this capital tied up in machines that no longer have a purpose – especially in the current economic climate – is not practical, reasonable or logical; it is simply not cost effective.

———

As a consequence of this re-structuring programme we would have a number of demobilised military personnel to re-integrate into civilian life but rather than seeing that as a problem the PDC would use it as an ideal opportunity to reorganize Britain's law-enforcement agencies.

The PDC would be creating a new Border Police Force for example, and with 30,000 service personnel being repatriated from Germany in the next couple of years, we would have a ready-made well-drilled, disciplined corps of men and women ready to serve their country and defend its borders.

Ergo, the Border Police Force could be crystallised and put into service very quickly using this trained personnel and financed by a part of the MoD's revised budget.

Other demobilised military personnel could go into;

- the prison service which we would be strengthening or
- the fire-service or

- the regular police force which the PDC would be reinforcing or
- they could join the new Community Officer programme that the PDC would be introducing.

Some might choose to be trained to run the reform centres (Youth Training Camps) or be employed as bus and train controllers which would also be re-introduced as part of the new civic-charter.

The PDC would also encourage injured and invalid soldiers to integrate one of the above services in some capacity while they go through their rehab...before potentially going on to forge a career elsewhere.

(Opportunities would be made available at checking desks and in clerical positions adapted to the specific needs of these people.)

We might even study the possibility of introducing a revolving contract for the Border Police, the Reform Camp Personnel and the Military which would allow an exchange of key personnel every eighteen months or so to keep everybody on their toes and up to speed with the latest techniques and technological advances in each area, just in case they are ever needed.

Lastly; the PDC military policy would be one based on defence;

Therefore, we would scrap the submarine missile programme (Trident) which is costing £100 billion and replace it with a less costly intercept programme based at various strategic locations around the country.

Of course we need a deterrent for those who would want to threaten us on our own soil, but we do not need nuclear weapons to go around the world posturing and threatening to invade others.

NATO & the UN

As stated in the chapter on Foreign Policy, I believe that we should leave it to NATO, the UN or a new International Alliance to mediate and co-ordinate any future interventions around the world.

We all live on the same planet and that is why - in my vision of the future - all international conflicts - **involving humanitarian abuse** - should be addressed and dealt with by the International Community as a whole.

It may be a radical step but I believe that we need a new world-body with a new mandate that encompasses the Geneva Conventions, the Chemical Weapons Convention and the UN mandate.

Every country in the world would have to sign up to this New World Charter which would give its executive universal jurisdiction on the planet allowing it to intervene on **HUMANITARIAN ISSUES** wherever they might occur around the world. Its reach would even over-ride individual sovereignty if that sovereignty was found to be violating the New World Charter.

However, unlike the current world organisations – such as the UN and NATO - this new world executive would have some backbone and some teeth as well as some of the greatest diplomatic minds.

Of course, diplomacy would always be the first tool used, but at their disposition this new executive would also have a multi-national intervention force of highly-trained strike teams that would – given the green light by the executive - target and surgically remove any dictator or any despot, together with his close associates, who was not upholding the protocols laid out in the New World Charter.

This new executive would also have the authority and the power to freeze the personal assets of these tyrants - invested around the world - until any situation involving them had been resolved. After that, all assets would be returned - if legally acquired - or confiscated and returned to the country's new legitimate executive after an election overseen by the IC (International Community)

This task force would eliminate the need for individual countries to have their own massed armies and negate the arguments about invasion and occupation that currently beleaguers our disjointed international interventions. The only military obligations these countries would still have, would be to provide their allotted number of personnel to the international task force and to organise their own defence in case of external threat.

NB; these missions - based on precision and stealth - would only ever be carried out for **HUMANITARIAN REASONS**; they would not be on the table for cavalier regime change.

BTW; any country that did not sign up to this New World Charter would immediately be the subject of a trade ban from the International Community on non-essential commodities until such a time as they saw sense.

Author's comment;

We, the human race, have been found shamefully wanting on many occasions throughout our history, often standing by while our fellow men are abused, enslaved and slaughtered with impunity.

Now, sadly, there is nothing we can do for those who have already perished but what we can do, is learn from their horrific plight.

It is a cliché I know, but this should never be allowed to happen again.

The human race should never again stand idly by and watch another dictator massacre the innocent citizens of his country – with military or chemical weapons – in order to cling onto his executive power. (I say HIS, because this megalo-manic behaviour seems to be exclusively a male preserve)

The Monarchy & Pompous Elite

Before Charles 1ˢᵗ was beheaded, Oliver Cromwell stated the following;

'...it hath been found by experience, that the office of a King in this nation...is unnecessary, burdensome and dangerous to the liberty, safety and public interest of the people'...

I wouldn't go that far...but I do believe that the time has come to retire the concept of monarchy and royal families who reign supreme over a sovereign nation. This idea of inherited privilege handed down from generation to generation is an anachronism and just as it is time to put an end all dictatorships and autocracies around the world, it is also time to abolish this medieval institution.

It may be quaint and typically British but all those people with pompous titles and privileged positions who look down on the unwashed masses from the lofty perches of their ivory towers and gilded cages while feasting on the public purse should now be consigned to history; even those who now only perform a figure-head role.

There *is* no divine right or destiny – nobody has any divine right of superiority over anybody else – we are all human beings - we are all born equal – we are all the same.

The citizens of a country should not have a royal family imposed on them any more than they should have a dictator imposed on them – it should be every citizen's right to choose who leads them from the top.

Of course, there was a time in centuries past;

- for Kings and Queens
- for Kingdoms and Empires
- and even Imperialist Dynasties and Colonies

...as they gave structure and order to emerging societies...but democracy has now superseded these autocratically installed institutions – apart from in those dreadful computer games that is - and just as we are seeing the dictators of the world (Mubarak, Gaddaffi and Saddam Hussein) being deposed one after the other, we must now turn our attention to that other anachronism; the monarchy.

The concept of class, of *us-and-them* belongs to the past; to that age when the ignorance of the masses could be easily manipulated and exploited...but this is the 21st century and it is time to move forward.

The class divide between the rich and the poor will always remain an issue until the chasm that now exists – and which is growing daily - between the '*haves and the have-nots*' is reduced to a more equitable level...and while it will never be perfect because it is human nature to always want more than the next person, we clearly have to work towards it in order to avoid future unrest.

———

Now, self proclamation as ruler of all that one surveys is one thing, but I have to take issue with the presumption that a royal is somehow a better person than the rest of us, more intelligent, more honourable and more morally upright...especially as the idea is clearly a fallacy.

Throughout the ages, royal families have pretended to abide by some ancestral rules in order to protect the purity of the royal lineage, inventing a myriad of pompous protocols and pretentious etiquette in order to restrict access to their inner court...but in reality, because of generations of in-breeding within the walls of their palaces - they are no more than the biological product of all humanity just like the rest of us.

Indeed, it is well documented what went on in the royal palaces and how the royal house-holds have produced any number of illegitimate children down the years.

Samuel Pepys for example wrote endlessly about the goings-on in the royal court in 1660 and reported regularly on King Charles II (known as Merry Charles at the time because of all his mistresses), his entourage and what they all got up to; notably the rapacious Lady Castlemaine...

...and this licentious behaviour has continued all the way down to the present day where Camilla Parker-Bowles who was married herself, continued her affair with Charles while he was married to Diana whose own great-grandmother Alice Keppel had herself been the mistress of Edward Albert in 1898.

It is also said that George III had 58 grand-children, only one of whom was legitimate.

This turns out to be a slight exaggeration after much research but Queen Victoria's uncles – the Duke of Clarence (later William IV) with his 10 illegitimate children by the actress Mrs Jordan and the innumerable mistresses of the Prince Regent show a complete disregard for propriety within the royal family; even Prince Edward, Victoria's father lived with his mistress Mme St Laurent for 27 years.

So where is the purity of the royal lineage amongst all that?

Where is the shining example of morality?

Author's comment;

The royals make such a fuss over protocol and convention, over who can marry who, because of their links to the church etc - as Wallis Simpson found out to her detriment – and indeed, in the 1950's you weren't allowed in the Royal Enclosure at Ascot if you were divorced - but if that rule were still enforced today, half of the royal family would be excluded, as High-court judge Sir Paul Coleridge recently remarked.

———

I hate hypocrisy in all its forms, especially the snobbish hypocrisy and the false façades of the promiscuous upper classes who remain faithful to their spouses just long enough to produce an heir before continuing their affairs.

I also hate the self-serving hypocrisy of the so-called upstanding landed gentry who hand down lessons to the lower classes while scandalously transgressing and abusing every one of those rules themselves.

———

Many will argue that we should never retire the monarchy; that it promotes social cohesion, a rallying point for the country in times of trouble.

Really?

Let's look at that idea.

After all; what is the monarchy; how can we define it; what does the monarchy actually represent?

It seems to me that the concept of the monarchy is just one of ordinary people believing one after the other that by God's grace (however they conceptualise that particular idea) they are somehow extra-ordinary and therefore entitled to a life of inherited privilege as some kind of 'God-given' right.

It has been going on for centuries with people constantly squabbling and battling it out with each other for the right to sit on the gilded throne and wear the ceremonial crown that designates them as ruler, while at the same time;

- Ruthlessly waging war on anybody who might threaten or dispute their legitimacy

- Cruelly assassinating, beheading or taking vengeance upon anyone perceived as an enemy or a threat...family members included
- Having to broker convoluted alliance after convoluted alliance with potential adversaries...and sign political allegiances with people who cannot be trusted, who subsequently renege on the undertaking as soon as another more lucrative / beneficial pact is presented to them
- Having to thwart the incessant conspiracies of their conniving entourages; examples of humiliating betrayal, back-stabbing, jealousy and treachery are plentiful in the history books, almost an everyday occurrence in fact
- Keeping usurpers, imposters and the ever-present whiff of scandal and in-breeding (needed to protect the succession line) at bay
- and finally, having to deal with the constant scheming and plotting of 'holy men' and church representatives who desperately crave the supreme power for themselves

So, seriously; are these people really good role models; do they really promote social cohesion or are they just selfish, self-indulgent, power-grabbing tricksters?

Of course, this last point doesn't really apply to the current royal family which only fulfils a constitutional role....but the monarchy itself, as a concept dates from the middle-ages, it is an anachronism and one that's consignation to the history books is long overdue.

Monarchy and inherited privilege no longer have tenure or credibility in the 21st century.

The Windsor Family –

The Royal Family as a concept represent everything that is wrong with the class system – living in the past as they do, with their servants and their valets etc

Much like the fictional Crawley family of Downton Abbey, they belong to another era.

As a premise they are an anachronism, out of touch with the reality of today's world, and Her Majesty aside, they are a pointless drain on the state's resources.

They are pompous, ungrateful, penny-pinching, stuck up and like the youth of today they seem to suffer with a sense of entitlement which no longer has tenure.

Another reason to bring an end to the monarchy is all the silly protocol that goes with it. New guidelines suggest that William's wife, Kate Middleton should curtsy in front of Beatrice and Eugenie (Prince Andrew's daughters) because of their blood-line.

How very 17th century of them!!

Do these people not know that this is the 21st century?

These protocols are four centuries out of date; four centuries!

Another example of how out of touch these people are; they tried sending a decree down from above in an attempt to ban the pictures of Harry's nude romp in Las Vegas, not realising that the Internet was already buzzing with the photos and that everyone who wanted to see them, had already done so.

They did the same to Mrs Simpson in the 1930's; the whole world knew what was going on but the British people were kept in the dark because of a royal diktat.

Alas, trying that same thing in 2012 with the Internet in most people's homes was ludicrous – and the buttoned up reactions of some of the special royal correspondents as well as those of some journalists was equally embarrassing.

HRH Queen Elizabeth II;

As I have made clear by now, I believe that it is time for a change, for a new 21st century leader but that said, I do feel that the current Queen deserves to see out her reign without contest, as a thank-you from the people of Britain for the way she has conducted herself and devoted her whole life so tirelessly and selflessly to her task.

She has been dignified throughout her reign and apart from a small wobble when Diana died she has been a tower of strength and a rock of stability for the British public.

Charles;

Where do I begin...?

In a nutshell; I really abhor the utter and complete hypocrisy of Charles' whole life.

His relationships with two married women - Dale 'Kanga' Tryon and Camilla Parker Bowles clearly show that the man has never grown up and was only ever looking for a mother figure to carry on where his nannies had left off.

And how intolerable was it that the spineless husbands of these two women allowed these charades to carry on unchecked and unchallenged just because of the royal connection.

And then came the marriage to poor, naive Diana who said of her wedding day that...'it was the worst day of her life' and that '...she felt like a lamb to the slaughter'.

What a scam that was.

There was never any love there; 'whatever love is' as Charles remarked so romantically on the day of their engagement.

That one remark told the people of this country that Diana was never to be more than a vessel for his succession.

The man had no respect for his wife. Look at how he treated her, carrying on his relationship with Camilla Parker Bowles while they were married, seeing himself as above the law and untouchable just like many of his philandering predecessors, though I doubt he had their gusto for the more passionate side of human inter-action if the Camilla-gate conversation about 'Tampax' was anything to go by.

Charles once said to Diana on a walkabout; 'they are not cheering you, you know, because you're you – they're cheering you because you are married to me - get that into your thick head'. How humiliating that must have been for Diana and how callous, pompous and uncaring it was of him as her '*pseudo-husband*'.

Diana once told this story to Paul Johnson (historian and writer); Charles once complained that his valet had put three shirts out for him to choose from but that he didn't like any of them, even though they looked perfectly alright to her; anyway, he rang the bell and when his valet came into the room he greeted him rather abruptly with; 'don't like those shirts'; so the valet immediately walked across the room and picked out two or three others from the shelves and laid them out instead – When the valet had gone, Diana asked; 'why did you ring for that man to come all the way up here when all you had to do was walk across the room and pick out a shirt that you do like?' – Charles answered fiercely, 'because he's paid to do it'.

That kind of pedantic behaviour and petty arrogance is one of the many reasons why the concept of royalty needs to be abolished.

Charles is a complete wimp so imbided in privilege that he has no idea of the real world; he is a petulant man-child who has been allowed to let opportunity and entitlement go to his head to such a point that he is in no way connected to reality.

He is a spoilt child in a man's body who has never so much as learned to dress himself and who has spent his whole life in a selfish, self-centred bubble waiting desperately to fulfil a hypothetical role that might never ever materialise.

How preposterous is it that Charles has never picked up his own clothes or undressed himself; the man has three valets to look after his clothes for him, one of whom even irons his shoe-laces every time they are used;

...and I thought slavery had been abolished.

Sadly, Charles represents all that is wrong with the class system and his behaviour as described in the two situations above is a perfect illustration of why we need to consign the monarchy to the pages of history.

All the royals have left is their pride and their pomposity but do we really want somebody like that leading our country?

So, citizens of Britain please beware; Charles has already started meddling if his recent letters and meetings with government ministers are anything to go by... despite the constitutional status of our monarchy...and he has yet to accede to the throne...

As for Camilla; I abhor the scheming way in which she dedicated her whole life to obtaining the position she so desperately coveted / craved... and has now achieved...in order to go down in history – stepping on whoever got in her way, her rivals, her husband and whoever else to get it.

Anne;

The only one of the Queen's children who has enjoyed her privileged position and lived her life with dignity, without rubbing it in the faces of the British public.

Andrew;

After a reasonable career in the Navy, flying helicopters Andrew has become a figure of fun in later life.

He is 'affectionately' known by the popular press as 'Air-miles Andy' as all he seems to do is fly around the world enjoying a life of inherited privilege, with no responsibility or accountability, posing as an unofficial trade envoy and mixing with questionable individuals who are drawn to the idea of rubbing shoulders with him and his royal entourage.

Sadly, he doesn't seem to serve any real purpose.

Incidentally, the way the Royal family disowned Sarah Ferguson and left her to fend for herself after her divorce from Andrew was disgraceful and callous – it's no wonder she went off the rails.

Edward;

It is said that the Earl of Wessex is so pompous that he doesn't ever allow his chauffeur to turn his head, even when the car he is driving is stationary; enough said.

William, Kate...and George

I have already voiced my views on the monarchy...but paradoxically, if it is to survive – through the will of the British people – then I believe it will need to rely heavily on the younger generation to carry it on... because without this influx of new-blood and modernity, the crusty old institution is undoubtedly doomed.

William, Kate...and Harry have been like a breath of fresh air for the British public over the last couple of years and they...and their off-spring will clearly be instrumental in the perennialisation of the institution.

The 'fairy-tale' wedding and the birth of their son George have made William and Kate headline news for the last couple of years and for the foreseeable future they will be steady fodder for all the society magazines, for who they are, for the way in which they parent their child / children and of course for Kate's taste in fashion.

However, I do wonder whether, after playing such a vital and fulfilling role - that of helicopter rescue pilot – the dreary, mundane existence of glad-handing hundreds of people every day until he and Kate slide slowly but inexorably into the sedentary lifestyle of middle-age will really suit William?

Kate meanwhile, after a rather inauspicious and unflattering start due to the 'Waitey Katey' epithet bestowed upon her by the British press has now morphed seamlessly into the Duchess of Cambridge and become a wonderful role-model for her young admirers...both as a mother and a fashion icon.

Strange isn't it how the British people take to non-royals like Diana and Kate.

Maybe they just don't like the pomposity and pretentiousness of inherited privilege.

Author's comment;

It was clearly wrong of the paparazzi to steal photographs of Kate sunbathing topless in France last year but while it was commendable - if a little naive and 19th century - to see William trying to protect his wife from the glare of the press, he needs to realise that this is the 21st century and that most everybody nowadays carries a mobile phone with an integrated camera-lens.

His intentions were of course very noble but sending diktats down from above - as in a bygone age - ordering people not to take photographs of his wife, shows a surprising lack of maturity and understanding of the modern world. The reality is that for the rest of her life Kate will have to keep her clothes on or accept the consequences of having her photo taken.

It's just one of those things that comes with the territory and the privilege of being a public figure in the 21ˢᵗ century.

Harry;

I didn't agree with the fact that William and Harry were allowed to lead 'Hooray Henry' lifestyles in their teenage years - borrowing helicopters for a stag night to impress their girlfriends for example - just because of their privileged position, but they have grown up since, and while they still live in gilded cages, both have now morphed into fine young men.

William has become the country's most popular father...and much to his credit Harry has genuinely embraced his military career. Indeed, the obvious passion that he puts into his charity work in order to gather recognition and funding for his injured colleagues - and ex-colleagues - among others is most admirable.

Pompous Elite;

Titles lead to a sense of entitlement in those who use them and create tension and a class divide - albeit artificial - with the general public, thereby flying in the face of the concept that we, as human beings, are all equal.

The PDC would be trying to create a fair society, a classless society, a society based on equality and equal opportunity for everyone and as a result we would look into disposing of all these pompous and pretentious titles which do no more than breed entitlement, snobbery, jealousy and class distinction.

We would also phase out the pompous titles and accolades handed out in the Queen's and New Year's honours lists. These awards for political or financial cronyism are so anachronistic and yet another throwback to our colonial past.

We cannot create equality while, simultaneously creating an artificial class of titled entitlement.

Recognition is a good thing; fatuous titles and cronyism is not.

Consequently; instead of the Honours List, the PDC would create a new set of Merit Awards for Service to the Country...whether on a national or a community level, crystallised in a discreet coloured pin to be worn proudly on the lapel. (No ribbons and no clunking metal medals)

...and while we are doing away with all the superfluous and unwarranted pomp and ceremony that surrounds the elite – we should also stop referring to MPs as 'the honourable or the right-honourable' gentleman; that is a title wholly undeserved; these people have not been 'honourable' for quite some time.

———

Finally; I would suggest that we change the national anthem;

For the UK as a whole, I propose...   Land of Hope and Glory

...and for England itself, I propose...   There'll always be an England

After all; each of the other three nations has its own anthem

———

The Emotional & Moral Wimpification of the British Public by the Overbearing Nanny State

The British public and the British establishment in particular has traditionally been geared towards producing men of a steadfast disposition and a stiff upper lip.

Men were always taught to stand up straight and not to articulate their emotions...but I have to say that the wimpification of the male gender that has taken place in this country since the feminist uprising in the 1970's makes my blood boil.

Ever since the velvet revolution, men have been harangued and constantly goaded into getting in touch with their feminine side so that they might understand what these new 21st century women want.

It began with them becoming metrosexuals, wearing make-up, moisturising their skin morning, noon and night...and then grooming their hair into fanciful styles in order to follow the latest trend...

...but it has all gone too far now.

Men, especially the younger generation (the fact that they are badly-educated, work-shy and have a raging sense of entitlement aside) have become prissy and precious...to the point where they now have more grooming products in their bathrooms than the women do.

Hygiene is important, I am not contesting that but what I cannot condone is the way that 21st century British men all act like **whipped puppies** around the women in their lives, afraid to do anything to upset their female counterparts, frightened to stand up for themselves and show any gumption...for fear of being called racist, sexist or simply opinionated.

These days, it is not unusual to see sullen-faced young men with their hair in their eyes and their trousers around their knees, being dragged around the town centres of Britain like pets following obediently in the footsteps of their owners.

Sometimes they are allowed to hold hands with their female partners but mostly they are just there to carry the shopping bags. It appears that 21st century women see the male gender as simply extensions of themselves with two more arms.

It is frightening to see how docile and clueless these young men really are. All that is missing from this scenario is a ring through their noses (a real one, not those cosmetic piercings) and a lead on the collars around their necks and the domestication of men as women's pets will be complete.

It's 'yes dear, of course dear, you're right dear,' (sorry; you're ALWAYS right dear).

What a bunch of wimps – the young men of this country have no b... bottle or self-respect.

Equality and respect by all means, but the pendulum really seems to have swung too far...

———

It is time to put an end to the wimpification of this country.

The justice system, the police service, our institutions and even the ordinary members of the British public have all been wimpified over the last thirty years by a constant avalanche of bleeding heart liberalism... and castrated by a growing collection of naive idealists who are afraid of their own shadows and so desperate not to upset or offend anyone that they have transformed the country into one big risk-averse nursery.

These PC (political correctness) zealots using H&S (health and safety) concerns and the HR (human rights) legislation have over the last thirty years managed to completely remove the moral backbone of this country and eradicated every hint of discipline from our society... and it is time that stopped.

The Nanny State is also to blame of course.

We have become a country incapable of doing anything for ourselves; we are unable to cope with any kind of pressure or deal with any kind of crisis on our own. We need assistance in everything we do from how to cook, how to eat, how to dress, how to arrange our homes and how to tend our gardens.

The majority of our TV programmes are now no more than instruction videos on how to live our lives; how to cook, how to buy a house, how to dress correctly, how to organise a wedding etc, etc

Meanwhile, we are warned before every news item, that there may be some flash photography or that some people might find the images offensive, disturbing or distressing – and when the report ends, we are immediately given a number to call, just in case we have been adversely affected by what we have just seen and need comforting.

People don't think for themselves anymore; common sense seems alien to most people and the first thing they do when faced with a problem is to call somebody to sort it out for them.

Britain has gone soft – we don't discipline our children, we don't confront rowdy teenagers (for fear of reprisal), we no longer ask others to respect the rules...or the law (feet on seats, noise in libraries). In fact, we seem to have renounced all personal responsibility, relying solely on the state to micro-manage every aspect of our lives.

Where has the backbone that made this nation great gone?

———

Moreover, ever since Diana's death in 1997, which was the first time I noticed it, this country has become a soppy, sentimental mess submerged constantly by a wave of watery emotion.

We lost 8million working-days last year because of people staying at home to mourn their dead pets, their dead PETS and more recently we had a group of mothers and children crying over the culling of a school's pet lamb.

Grow up people; enough of this emotional incontinence.

The British emotional psyche is now so fragile and so shallow that people are constantly breaking down in floods of tears, either watching films, being interviewed or having performed on a reality TV show; everyone is crying. Even our Olympic champions joined in.

How annoying it is to live in this wimpish society; this over sentimentality has to stop.

Life is full of interruptions and complications; dealing with them is what makes life worth living.

Our national identity should be rooted in our history and our culture.

Where is our pride, our dignity and our patriotism?

Where is the Churchill-ian stiff upper lip which won the day all those years ago?

I understand that privacy, restraint and modesty are seen as old-fashioned ideas these days but;

- let's stop the mass-mawkishness;
- let's stop the instant shrines that pop up outside houses where a crime has been committed...and
- let's stop marking the place where an accident has occurred on the road.

If people want to show their support, let them offer it in person or make a donation to a deserving charity; the flowers and the fluffy toys that get ruined by the rain are a nice gesture but ultimately they are a waste of money and a pointless reminder of loss.

It's time to reclaim our dignity and our self-respect.

Author's comment;

This lap-dog mentality, this wimpification of men born out of the systematic and ongoing feminisation of our society in order to appease the liberals and the feminists, does not bode well, for the future of the male species or indeed for humanity itself. (See chapter on ethics)

Political Correctness

Author's comment;

Our society is overly burdened by Political Correctness and Health & Safety issues. We need to free ourselves from the tyranny of the PC Brigade and the H&S zealots. The Political Correctness madness and the fatuous Big Brother / Nanny State / Health and Safety culture has to be curtailed.

The PDC would not pander to any PC agenda; that particular folly has already gone way too far.

Respect for the fundamentals of life using the PDC's three guiding principles

Nature
Logic...and
Common sense...

...most definitely...

...pandering to every lily-livered, hand-wringing social activist? Out of the question.

Surely I am not alone in this; in feeling sick to death of hearing about this sterile, risk-averse society that the PC and H&S brigades have imposed on us.

Political Correctness was invented to make us better people...but the irony is that it has created prejudices in walks of life where they never existed before, thereby increasing the social fracture.

The constant over-emphasis on Political Correctness which persistently ties our hands as we strive desperately in any way possible to spare other peoples feelings in whatever situation we might find ourselves is frankly ridiculous...and what's more, we are deluding ourselves if we believe that it has made <u>everybody</u> a better person; because while we are busy shooting ourselves in the foot, trying to respect every one of these ridiculous PC diktats to the letter - like any good, law-abiding citizen should - behind the scenes, others with more covert agendas, unburdened by the self-inflicted psychosis or sensibilities of the buttoned-up British people;

- who don't wish to offend
- who don't want to speak up out of embarrassment
- or who don't want to stand up for fear of being pointed out and labelled a racist, a homophobe or a sexist

...have been secretly exploiting that non-confrontational naiveté, manoeuvring furtively in the background to slowly position themselves in all the key areas and corridors of power in our society (doctors and councillors etc; remember Glasgow airport, those two men were 'doctors').

The British people are ignoring religious extremism for fear of causing offence to minorities etc, but while they are doing this, those who disagree with our culture and our lifestyle are using our attempts to be **right, fair and just** as weapons to infiltrate our society and take advantage of it, multiplying and spreading their own poisons in an effort to accelerate their end-game.

These people have no interest in integration or Political Correctness; their goal is simple...subtle, gradual and progressive overthrow of the British culture and the British way of life...and because the British are too afraid to stand up for themselves – having been infantilised and brow-beaten by the overbearing Nanny State and various pressure groups – they are succeeding.

They are taking advantage of the British people's compassionate nature, their indulgence and their innate kindness to further their cause and accelerate the process and we are submissively handing these people the metaphorical baton to beat us with.

These people do not care how long it takes because they believe it is their destiny to become the dominant culture on this island…and meanwhile, the lily-livered politicians in Westminster – who should be monitoring this activity – are afraid to act for fear of being called racist and losing their place on the gravy train…which of course these people are relying on to happen.

We need to get away from this hysterical PC culture as quickly as possible or it will inevitably lead to the complete destruction of life in Britain as we know it.

In this country, it has become a constant round of the Rights of the individual versus the Responsibilities of the Government to run the country…and every problem that is now tabled is immediately considered through the kaleidoscope of sexual equality or human rights abuse…and if neither of these arguments provides a solution, the Health and Safety zealots get involved hoping to benefit in some way from the compensation culture - imported from the US - which now blights our society.

Whatever happened to common sense?

Here are a few examples of Political Correctness that border on the absurd

- A couple of gay people were offended by the label homo-sexual
- A five year old girl who was applying for a passport was refused because the photo she had tendered showed her bare shoulders, and this was considered as potentially offensive to Muslims – she was <u>five years old</u>

- A job offer for a white-collar job was advertised asking for applicants to speak English and the company was condemned as being racist
- A Lib-Dem MP suggested banning school sports-days in order to avoid hurting the losers' feelings
- A man was prevented from flying the flag of St George because it might upset Muslims by reminding them of the crusades
- Another job was advertised in a museum, which excluded **WHITE** people from applying.
- Christmas lights which have been installed in Britain's streets over Christmas for decades are now known as festive lights – when they are not removed completely - so as not to offend other religions
- In prison, the word prisoner is no longer used - prisoners are addressed as Mister A,B or C
- In school; our children are being taught nursery rhymes where the original lyrics, written hundreds of years ago, are changed in order to be politically correct and non-racist – e.g. Baa, baa rainbow sheep or baa, baa happy sheep – <u>not black sheep</u>
- In school; the black-board is now called the chalk-board to avoid being racist
- In school; the study of British culture has been removed from the teaching curriculum so as not to alienate other cultures
- New Christmas rules have been introduced for staff parties; no raffles to avoid offending Muslims who are anti-gambling – no meat or alcohol as prizes in case they offend – no 'gay' comments - organisers must make sure that any music is mixed to avoid discrimination claims and above all, they must carry out a risk assessment survey before hanging any Christmas decorations which must also be anti-inflammatory
- The Black police museum – where infamous criminal weapons are displayed – has been re-named...so as not to offend
- The name 'Wendy house' for a toy-tent has been changed to 'Play-house' because it might be considered sexist
- The phrase 'Cheeky little monkey' has been banned by both the RSPCA and RSPCC as offensive to animals...and to children
- There is now a list of words that cannot be used in our justice system to avoid causing offence. Words such as immigrant,

Asian and West Indian (smacks of colonialism) are banned for fear of causing offence

- Two men were taken to court a few months back for inciting racial hatred by threatening to bite the heads off of a couple of Black Jelly Babies

Now, of course these are only a few examples, there are many, many more and at the risk of repeating myself; WHATEVER HAPPENED TO COMMON SENSE

———

Health and Safety

Taking risks, calculated risks is what takes us forward as a race; it also teaches us about boundaries and anybody who has ever taken a risk will tell you how good it feels to be alive when doing so.

Whether it be succeeding in a particular endeavour, conquering our fears or simply pitting ourselves against an opponent – taking risks gives us the opportunity to learn and grow as individuals, and sometimes we lose out, but that does not stop us from trying again; we learn from our mistakes and our failures and move on with more experience for next time.

The human race didn't get where it is today by not taking risks; risk is a part of life in all its forms, a part of being human and part of the constant striving we have undertaken over the centuries to get to where we are...but thanks to the PC zealots, we now live in a risk-averse society, a society which is contrary to the fundamentals of the human existence which has thrived and gotten us to where we are today, by taking risks.

We have always taken risks – that's how we invented airplanes, discovered the North and South poles, conquered Everest and mastered space-travel.

The H&S executive was introduced to regulate heavy industries such as mining and pharmaceuticals – its rules were never meant to be applied to our everyday lives...but nowadays every single aspect of human activity in the UK must have a Health & Safety certificate if there is the slightest possibility of anybody getting hurt.

We now have a vast, incompetent, feather-bedded state, presided over by unelected quango-crats and overpaid busy-body officials delving into every aspect of our lives, private, personal and public.

These people are stifling the human race's natural inclination to take risks in order to push boundaries and improve themselves and their lives which has led to the entire British public becoming infantilised by a Nanny State constantly meddling and telling them what they can and cannot do. Personal responsibility has been eliminated and every action we accomplish is now micro-managed by the state and accompanied by a Health & Safety certificate.

In fact, we now live in an almost pathologically over cautious, over sensitive, risk-averse society where creativity is reined in and fun is outlawed for fear of us experiencing reality.

Who wants to live in this bubble-wrapped world?

Whatever happened to common sense?

This ludicrous madness has to stop.

Compensation; (see also Justice Chapter)

Of course the real reason behind the risk-averse obsession that has swept through our society is the compensation culture that the New Labour Party imported from the USA in 1999 which allows people to sue each other by shifting responsibility.

This was just one among many bad-calls made by that New Labour government but the combination of fault, blame and money is clearly toxic...and the 'No win; No fee' arrangements which underpin the compensation culture has done nothing but enrich the ambulance-chasing lawyers - who sue for both real and imaginary injury – ever since.

This is an insidious by-product of the Health & Safety folly.

Meanwhile, employers who desperately want to avoid these claims wherever possible are implementing the most draconian H&S protocols and applying the most stringent rules to every work-related assignment to the point of ridicule. (See examples below)

What these petty bureaucrats - who are well-paid by the public purse - don't seem to realise is that not only are they complicating the work-place environment with time consuming and expensive risk-assessment procedures they are also stealing the childhoods of a generation of young people who are no longer allowed to participate in the most basic of childhood activities in case they get hurt.

Under the PDC, all those bureaucrats - on committees and sub-committees in charge of inventing one of these ridiculous new rules every day...simply to justify or validate their existence and their salaries - would have their positions re-evaluated, their usefulness determined and their field of intervention re-aligned with a policy based on logic and common sense.

I am sick of all these jobs-worths and quango-crats just coming up with more imaginative ways of keeping their jobs and their desk-seats warm.

Those who persisted in promoting scatter-brain policies would be retrograded and re-trained or re-assigned to roles more in keeping with their aptitudes...and those unable to use common sense or logic would simply be relieved of their duties.

This obsession with Health & Safety has wrecked our society or at the very least it has ruined the part where we inter-act with each other...and it has to be stopped for our children's sake and their future.

We need to get rid of this cotton-wool culture which has led to all manner of activities being banned in the name of eliminating risk.

Let our children be children and learn by their mistakes
Let our adults act like responsible adults and role models

Let's get rid of all this self-evident absurdity...and
Let us live our lives

We need a return to common sense, especially in health and safety issues

---

A few examples of the compensation madness
in school due to H&S concerns

- A pupil was paid £4,000 after tripping and grazing a knee
- One boy received £6,500 for damaged teeth after a friend accidentally hit him with a tennis racket
- A young girl received £10,000 when her hair was burned by a Bunsen burner
- A child was paid £1,800 after slipping on an icy patch of Astroturf
- One pupil received £15,719 for slipping and falling down a bank
- Another received £10,000 for a finger trapped between two desks
- A pupil received £3,500 after being hit by a discus
- Another received £11,500 for injuring their back during a dance lesson
- Another £10,000 for injuring a hand
- Another £14,329 for climbing a tree and then falling out of it
- And another received £26,500 after hurting themselves putting away a trampoline
- One pupil received £16,000 for slipping on wet leaves...and
- Another £10,000 for tripping over a tree-root

Ambulance-chasing lawyers with their constant advertising and no-fee promises are fostering a culture of compensation greed and, much like every other sector of society, from the bankers down parents are falling into the greed trap.

Irony - the H&S Executive has recently admitted that 'the cotton wool culture' that they helped to create has eroded children's freedom to play outdoors – though fear of litigation still prevents many from loosening the rules.

NB – the PDC would revise and eliminate any preposterous Health & Safety rules – in conjunction with its root-and-branch reform of the Legal system in order to eradicate the Compensation Culture while still protecting those with genuine litigious claims.

————

Specific H&S rules for schools;

These activities are now banned –

Egg and spoon races
Football; in case someone scrapes a knee
Hopscotch
Making paper planes
Nature walks
Running in playgrounds in case someone falls
Sack races and three-legged races at sports-days
Snowball fights

————

And;

- Pupils are also banned from using toilet-roll tubes as an art-material or shaving foam in case they **'drown'** in it (actual term used)
- They are forced to wear safety goggles when handling 'blu-tack'
- They are forced to wear fluorescent high-visibility jackets when participating in pancake-races
- They are forced to wear heavy jumpers in the summer to avoid getting skin cancer
- They are forced to wear safety goggles to play conkers

- They are not allowed outside without a hat and sunscreen
- They are not allowed to wear plastic hair-bands
- And the use of Vaseline on dry lips is also banned

School ties have also been banned for fear of accidental strangulation or catching fire during a science experiment; clip-ons only

Teachers cannot apply sunscreen or plasters for fear of being accused of abuse or paedophilia.

There are many more examples I could cite; too many for me to list here in fact, but I believe I have made my point.

NB - It has recently been revealed that risk-averse parents who raise their children 'in captivity' – i.e. wrapped up in cotton wool - are potentially creating mental-health problems for their offspring. Anxiety disorders and depression are becoming more common because these children, who are never confronted with a problem to solve because of an overbearing, ever-present parent, lack any emotional resilience and therefore they cannot cope with life's everyday challenges.

They are not being taught how to assess or manage risk and the paranoid culture which protects them from every possibility of danger is leaving them unable to function in the real world, recent research into their psychological development revealed.

...and here are a few examples of the absurd Health and Safety Rules

---

- £15.000 was spent on a pamphlet on how to cross a road; another pamphlet was produced called 'The code of practice for pet-owners'
- 25 firemen scrambled to save a bird from a 3ft deep pond refused to wade into the water because of H&S regulations

- A 59yr old man with grey hair and a walking stick was prevented from buying a packet of cigarettes because he didn't have identity papers proving he was over 18
- A choir was asked to do a risk assessment of a church before being allowed to sing
- A clock-winder lost his job – a job that had been done for over 200 years – because it meant him using a ladder
- A four-page leaflet has been produced on how to sit on a toilet called 'Good Defecation Dynamics'
- A group of Russian trapeze artists was informed that they would have to wear protective helmets if they wanted to perform in this country
- A local council told a mother that if she wanted to put a paddling pool in her back garden she would need to employ a life-guard and upgrade her insurance
- A pensioner was banned from his allotment in case he hurt his hip
- A teacher was recently awarded £70K for unfair dismissal; she had been sacked for pruning a bush without following the correct health and safety procedures
- A veteran spitfire pilot was prevented from climbing into the cockpit once again after 70yrs in case he injured himself
- A young boy climbed up a tree to rescue a cat stranded for 5 days while firemen stood by and did nothing because they didn't have H&S clearance to use a ladder
- An actor re-enacting 'Nelson' at Trafalgar was forced to wear a life-jacket over his 19th century uniform
- An outside swimming pool was closed because of rain which had the potential to obscure the life-savers' vision
- At a school sports-day pupils were offered the choice of opting out of the sprint races in case they felt embarrassed at losing – instead they sat around drinking fizzy drinks and getting fat – parents too were prevented from filming those that did participate – as they are from school plays – to avoid the pictures being seen by paedophiles
- Boating lakes have been banned
- Bouncey-castles have been banned

- Candles on birthday cakes have been banned unless a risk assessment has been carried out
- Children are not given sweets for fear of choking
- Climbing trees has been banned
- Conker collection is banned for fear of hurting someone as they fall to the ground - councils have even started ruthlessly chopping down chestnut trees to save us all from the peril of a falling conker
- Councils have banned frying eggs outdoors for fear of splashing
- Councils have banned kite-flying for health and safety reasons
- Crash helmets must now be worn when riding donkeys on the beach
- Firemen have been advised not to use poles and ladders to avoid twisting their ankles
- Firework displays are banned and H&S officers confiscate sparklers from children even when they are being supervised by their parents
- Hair-dressing apprentices are not allowed to hold or use scissors even under supervision in case they cut themselves
- Hanging baskets are banned in case they fall on someone
- Hats in pubs – a seventy year old woman was refused access to a pub because she was wearing a floppy hat
- Headstones have been laid flat in cemeteries in case they fall over
- In public parks; benches have signs on them 'caution; seats may become wet when rain falls'
- On Bonfire night, people were forced to watch a virtual bonfire on a screen because of H&S worries, air pollution and the possibility of trees in the surrounding area being scorched
- One man was banned from using a tooth-pick in a restaurant in case he pricked the inside of his cheek
- One school demanded that parents get a CRB check, costing £28 before they could watch their own children play sports
- Pantomime performers were prevented from throwing sweets into the crowd in case they hurt someone
- People have been banned from hanging up Christmas decorations unless they complete a Health & Safety assessment course

- People have been banned from planting flowers in case they hurt their wrists
- People have been prevented from swimming lengths in a pool in case they drown; widths only
- People working on the **night-shift** on the railways were provided with sunscreen in order to comply with H&S rules
- Police and firemen have been banned from climbing 3ft ladders without the proper training - Ladder awareness courses cost £230
- Refuse collectors have been banned from pulling wheelie-bins because of fears they might suffer from musculoskeletal injuries (injuries to their backs)
- Sadly, because of recent tragic events, scouts have been told not carry pen-knives
- Safety railings have been imposed inside churches
- Some pick-your-own fruit farms have closed to the public; the risk of pricking a finger is too dangerous
- Swings, slides, climbing-frames and roundabouts have all been banned in children's playgrounds
- The army was asked to put handrails up the Brecon Beacons to stop soldiers falling over while out on manoeuvres
- The Chitty-Chitty Bang-Bang car was banned from a street parade for H&S reasons because it didn't have a valid MOT
- The H&S executive also wants to ban pall-bearers from carrying coffins in case they hurt their backs
- The police have banned charity bed-races because of H&S issues
- The women of the WI were banned from tending flowers on a roundabout in case they were run over
- Two parents were prevented from taking their three children into a paddling pool because H&S decrees there should be one adult per child
- Two volunteer football coaches were banned for allowing youngsters to compete in a football competition – the rules state that games <u>must not</u> be competitive, <u>no-one should win</u> and <u>no-one should lose</u> to save them from suffering any disappointment
- Two young girls were banned from a museum for safety reasons

- Welcome mats were banned because they could be a 'trip-hazard'
- Window cleaners are banned from using ladders and must construct costly scaffolding to reach first floor windows instead

...and on a more serious note;

A father was drowning in 18ins of water but police, firemen and paramedics were told it was too risky to rescue him – he died.

A man feeding swans was left to drown in 3ft of water because emergency services can only go into water ankle deep.

A woman fell down a mine-shaft where she was left for eight hours because the winch that could have saved her was restricted to being used for rescuing trapped miners – the mother of two died of a heart attack brought on by hyperthermia.

A young girl collapsed on a cross-country run but paramedics did not intervene because the ground was too slippery and one of them didn't want to hurt her back carrying the girl; the girl died

During the 7/7 terrorist attacks people were left to die in agony because firemen weren't allowed to go into the Underground tunnels without first doing a risk assessment.

Emergency crews were held back for 90 minutes - for H&S reasons - when a man went on a killing spree in Cumbria; several people who might have survived their injuries had they been reached in time, died.

Two police community support officers stood by while a 10 year old boy drowned in a pond after diving in to save his younger sister. They weren't 'qualified' to intervene and feared rebuke if they did so without having completed the proper training.

The PDC argument;

H&S aside, and irrespective of them being emergency services the natural instincts of these people as human beings should have been to try and save those in danger.

However, desperate not to transgress the egregious H&S rules, they allowed these people to die.

Surely, anyone can see - even the lily-livered H&S zealots - that what they are doing is counter-productive and morally wrong.

They are trying to protect people but in fact they are making peoples lives more difficult and as in the cases cited above, people are even dying in order to respect their silly rules.

Police officers in this country used to be obliged to be able to swim and if they couldn't swim, they received swimming and life-saving training.

That training has been cut as part of spending restrictions but surely if these H&S campaigners wanted to help, they should be demanding that this training be re-instated, rather than advocating that emergency services not venture into water deeper than 18 inches.

Once again, they are attacking the problem from the wrong stand-point.

The French have a rule for this which I believe we should adopt in this country in order to over-rule these H&S idiots; it is called '*non-assistance a une personne en danger*' - anybody who does not help a person in danger can themselves be prosecuted, as well as those who, by their asinine rulings, prevented that person from being saved.

———

Society / Social Issues

'Modern Britain is an angry and cruel society
which no longer cherishes old-fashioned virtues'...Helen Mirren

---

Author's comment;

I want to live in a society where people respect the law, each other and the world around them.

What is wrong with celebrating traditional values such as courage, resilience, integrity, loyalty, honesty, kindness, altruism, respect, responsibility and self control...or everyday qualities such as politeness, punctuality and good manners?

It might not be in keeping with today's selfish, hypocritical and immoral society based on greed and self-obsession...but wouldn't it be wonderful.

Something else to think about... the OECD (organisation for economic co-operation and development) recently put the UK at the bottom of a list of 21 countries in terms of family breakdown, drink, drugs, teenage sex and fear of violence.

Alcohol / 24 hour drinking

The first objective of the PDC would be to eradicate the binge-drinking culture from our society and restore some sanity to our streets.

The decision by Tony Blair and the New Labour Party to de-regulate the alcohol supply laws and allow 24 hour drinking in this country was the single, most irresponsible action I have ever witnessed from a politician or political party; especially knowing the tendency of the British people as a whole to abuse alcohol.

Author's comment;

At one point, a 12 year old boy was found working behind a bar because New Labour had quietly changed the law covering children serving alcohol – how outrageously irresponsible is that?

Here are a few facts;

1) Since the laws were changed, alcohol abuse has been proved to be the root cause of an increase in violent assaults in this country – 56,000 NHS staff were attacked last year within the confines of the A&E service by irresponsible drunks
2) Dealing with alcohol-related problems now costs the NHS £3.5 billion a year and costs society as a whole £11 billion a year in crime-related incidents.
3) 500.000 sick days a year are being lost because of hangovers
4) Murders generally, have more than doubled; life-threatening woundings are up by a fifth...and while they cannot all be directly linked to alcohol abuse it has surely played its part.
5) Common assault committed by foul-mouthed, inebriated and violent '*ladettes*' has soared by 151%. Indeed, shocking figures recently released reveal that women are being convicted of violent crimes at the rate of more than 200 every week – an increase of 81% since New Labour introduced the 24hour drinking laws. That violence is being fuelled by alcohol - more often than not - as women make the most of the extra hours.

These figures relate to violent crime but the number of women being fined simply for being drunk and disorderly in public has risen by nearly a third in three years – the cumulative figures up from 6098 in 2005 to 7930 in 2007, a much sharper increase than that seen in men – and what is more disheartening is the fact that the biggest rise of all was seen amongst very young women – the number of girls aged between 16 and 17 increased by 47%, from 438 to 642.

The chairman of the Police Federation Paul McKeever even released a statement recently confirming that 'There has been a real and unacceptable rise in the number of offences committed by young women'.

Now, there are those who have tried to blame this phenomenon on drink-spiking but figures on that argument prove that this is largely an urban-myth; a modern scapegoat for a generation of irresponsible women who cannot face up to the fact that the vast amounts of alcohol that they are consuming could in any way be a factor in their losing control.

It is displacement; women shifting responsibility, transferring the blame onto someone else for their own lack of self-control...because there is little doubt that women underestimate the dangers of excessive drinking...and sadly, as there is no shame in being drunk and out of control these days; it is almost seen as a vital part of a good night out in our city-centres.

...but surely, this cannot be right; this cannot be good for the future of our country.

———

Author's comment;

It is a sad indictment of the binge drinking culture in Britain today when the main head-line in the morning papers is the announcement that people will be able to get easier and cheaper access to alcohol – delivered to their door via the internet.

(This idea was ultimately blocked but nevertheless it reveals the irresponsible thinking and the selfish mentality of those behind it.)

The PDC solution –

We need a return to a restricted 8 hour law whereby pubs and clubs can choose when to open. It is a shame that we have to do this but unfortunately, our inherent drinking culture does not allow us the luxury of European hours...because we, the British people, simply do not know how to self-moderate.

The PDC would start this process by removing alcohol licenses from supermarkets as the easy accessibility of alcohol has clearly encouraged abuse and teenage drinking. (Punitive fines would be imposed on those who transgress).

We would then redistribute the licences if necessary to a new revitalised pub-industry, re-introduce adjoined off-licences and impose a minimum charge for every measure / unit of alcohol sold which would be surcharged for alcohol sold in the new off-licenses in an effort to reverse the trend for home-consumption and encourage people to frequent the local pub where hopefully we would begin to rekindle a community spirit.

Clubs opening late would have to pay an extra tax for late-night policing and in return for the re-introduction of off-licenses the alcohol industry would be mandated to provide and fund late-night transport within a reasonable radius of their establishments – between the hours of 22h30 and 00h00 - in collaboration with local councils through extended bus-timetables or minibus provision at designated pick-up spots.

Again, this measure would be accompanied by the threat of closure or license withdrawal if businesses failed to comply...because unfortunately, as with everything in life, every carrot has to be accompanied by a stick.

However, on the up-side, as a by-product of this policy, more jobs would be created in pubs - behind bars and in off-licenses; not to mention in the late-night transport-service industry.

An idea from Miss Ann Widdecombe MP; 'as it is still an offence to be drunk and disorderly in public, why not round up all the drunks in the streets and those clogging up the A&E services and arrest them all – then, when they appear in court, print their names and post their mug-shots'.

Drugs –

I believe that a government should never put itself in a position where it can be identified as being hypocritical.

We all know the dangers of tobacco and alcohol and yet we tolerate them in our society because of the tax-revenue they generate...and because of the laws on democratic, personal and cultural choice.

Meanwhile, we ban cannabis, and yet cannabis when broken down to its component parts is just a plant that we put a match to, in order to inhale the fumes, much like tobacco.

Now, while some people say cannabis is dangerous, others say it is therapeutic.

The former would argue that it can cause heart-attacks, lung cancer and problems in pregnancy much like tobacco, and that its decriminalisation would create an extra burden on the already overstretched resources of the NHS, while the latter would point to the USA where cannabis is already prescribed for medical purposes in 17 states and has recently been decriminalised in a few others.

Both sides of the argument have produced positive recommendations and organised any number of clinical tests and trials to prove or disprove their theories over the years, but let's now make a decision one way or the other.

Personally, I believe that taking any drug - other than those prescribed by a qualified medical professional is harmful to the human body – and even those prescribed drugs can be dangerous – but I also feel that it is up to the individual to decide what he or she wants to put into their body – much like what they eat - and that the government should not systematically interfere with that freedom of choice.

Of course, it is the government's role to advise and inform on dangerous and delicate issues but it should not systematically impose its beliefs on the public any more unilaterally or dogmatically than religion should be allowed to do.

A government that says you may drink alcohol and smoke tobacco because it brings in tax-revenue...but you may not smoke cannabis because that does not bring in any tax-revenue would be showing itself to be hypocritical and that is what the PDC would want to avoid.

We have to pull back on the Nanny State and Big Brother.

The PDC solution –

I believe that because we have been confronted with so much conflicting information over the past few years from both sides of the argument, we should now put into place a ten-year plan during which time cannabis would be decriminalised and made available in a controlled environment; cultivation, production and dealing on an industrial scale would of course still remain outlawed.

This would allow us to test both the arguments for and against, but at the same time it would also take the initiative away from the drug-traffickers and the dealers who have been making fortunes out of their illegal activities.

Moreover, it would give the authorities the necessary time to dismantle all the illegal farms and houses currently being used to grow these plants and to prosecute and / or deport all the people currently involved in this activity as they would have been doing so illegally.

Once we had done that, we could then concentrate our resources elsewhere, on those dealing in the harder Class A drugs.

...and then, in ten years time, having cleaned up all the illegal activity, we could set up a panel to review the findings and to answer all the claims and counter claims... before ultimately coming up with a consensus and a new policy going forward which would satisfy all those concerned.

Author's comment;

I would like to see the therapeutic benefits or marijuana analysed and re-produced in a cream, a patch or a pill...but before we decide one way or the other, I suggest people read **'Hash' by Wensley Clarkson** which explains the multi-billion pound trade in marijuana and hash in this country...about the gangs of hardened criminals from Albania, Turkey and Morocco who control and distribute it...and about the penalties dished out by them to anyone who treads on their toes; it is chilling.

One final thought; as Ecstasy exists and the side-effects of taking it are relatively minor; why not produce a legal version of it to take out all the dealers and the toxic / deadly pills made from rat-poison currently being peddled to our teenagers?

It might also counter the increasing number of legal-highs being hawked around to our unsuspecting teenagers, the contents and the effects of which are often unknown.

NB – The PDC would be bringing in a zero-tolerance for drivers who drink alcohol but that zero tolerance would also apply to drug / cannabis use.

...and naturally, all the Class A drugs (cocaine, crack, ecstasy, heroin, LSD and magic mushrooms) which have <u>no proven therapeutic value</u> and only have a negative effect on the body – would still remain on the banned-substance list.

Thugs –

We have a generation of violent, illiterate, lawless young men in this country with a blunted sense of right and wrong and they are slowly corrupting the whole of society.

These young and not so young hoodlums are cowards who stand around in groups on street corners frightening people - looking threatening with their hoodies pulled up around their faces to shield their identities and scowling at anyone that crosses their path as they wait for someone to mug. Indeed, some even wear two different coloured hoodies deliberately, in order to change their appearance quickly in case anybody witnesses them doing something they shouldn't.

For example; a group of thugs stood outside a man's house for two weeks terrorising him and throwing rocks at his car because he asked them not to sit on his wall – the police eventually moved them on – but a few months later they bumped into the man at a supermarket and in their words 'kicked the shit out of him' almost killing him – is that the society we want to live in?

These people are dangerous...but they are dangerous not only because they threaten violence on innocent members of the public, they are dangerous because they have not been taught about what is right and what is wrong; they know nothing about boundaries, about morality and self-discipline, about respect or empathy or even about the consequences of their actions...and it is this lack of knowledge that is sadly more dangerous than their fists because these young people will ultimately go through life with no values, no ambition, no aspiration and no hope – living off benefits and becoming a burden to society their whole life long; a lifestyle which leads to low self-esteem and inevitably to taking drugs which is sadly financed by further criminal activity thereby perpetuating a vicious circle.

These petty thugs are unable to make the transition into manhood and unless we do something to straighten them out now, they will remain petty criminals and outcasts for their whole lives and that has terrifying implications for us all.

The PDC would put this untamed tyranny under the microscope, scrutinise its core components and find a solution.

––––––

Parenting -

Children -

These days, parents don't allow their children to play outside because of the risks from cars and paedophiles. Instead, they prefer to sit their little ones in front of a TV or a computer screen where they are safe.

Safe...? There are more paedophiles online than in any public park...and the mind-numbing virtual-reality games they play on their computers could traumatise them for life.

The paedophile hysteria that has gripped this country over the last decade has been blown out of all proportion and it has denied a generation of children access to the gardens and play-areas where they used to get their exercise.

This situation is unacceptable and what has made it worse is the short-sighted actions of the politicians who have used the psychosis to sell off many of the school playing fields for profit, thereby adding to the ongoing obesity problem.

––––––

10.000 playing fields were sold off between 1979 and 1997 – and when they came to power New Labour announced that they would end the previous government's policy of forcing schools to sell off their playing fields.

They then went ahead and sold off another 203.

And how is this for hypocrisy – only days after the 2012 Olympics had ended – even though their slogan during the Games was 'inspire a generation', the Conservative / LibDem coalition decided to sell off still more school sports playing fields.

How short-sighted and contradictory is that, especially as we have a growing obesity problem which will only get worse with nowhere for the children to play or exercise.

———

We need to provide a safe environment for our children where they can grow up happy and fulfilled, so, let's stop the neurotic hysteria and reclaim the parks and playing fields from the scare-mongers.

Let's free people to live their lives again thanks to a better, more efficient justice system that will deal with the '*paedophile problem*' more effectively...and most importantly, lets get our children out playing again, being children.

———

Author's comment;

A child allowed to play and dream will grow up to be an imaginative adult.

———

Children's Fashion –

It seems to me that the clueless liberal elite have absolutely no idea about what is going on in the rest of today's society...because while they live their lives in their blinkered, buttoned-up little microcosm of a world centred around middle-England, big business, has taken advantage of the general lack of discipline - and the ever-growing vacuum in morality that currently blights our country - to exploit and cheapen our whole existence.

From the fashion adverts on the billboards and in the weekly magazines to the children's clothes-lines which blatantly encourage small girls to dress like tarts, the pornographication of our society is well on the way to completion...and somehow the politicians, out of touch and oblivious to reality, haven't seen it happening.

The PDC would reverse this creeping, insidious trend.

The PDC Solution –

Our children should be allowed a childhood...and because of the current climate and the hysteria over paedophiles I believe it would be a sensible course of action to discourage parents from sexualising their children before their time – i.e. below the age of puberty...

...and to that end, I believe that parents should avoid activities such as beauty pageants which groom young girls and have a tendency to make them vulnerable and attractive to paedophiles. France for example has already banned these events.

We need some common sense here; we need to educate parents and make them responsible and aware of what they are doing, showcasing their children and offering them up to abuse and ridicule.

Under the PDC, all fashion for pre-pubescent girls would be reviewed and if necessary we would impose stricter guidelines on retailers.

It is outrageous to see;

- padded bras, bikinis and thongs advertised for six year olds

- earrings on five year old boys
- shops selling baby clothes with slogans like 'I'm a babe' and 'my mum is hot'
- and worst of all, pole-dancing kits for ten year old girls

...this should <u>not</u> be happening.

The PDC would also ban children - especially young girls - from waxing, using fake-tan, piercing their bodies, wearing perfume, jewellery or adult fashions until they are of a more cognisant age.

Reality TV - Tiaras and Toddlers / Baby Beauty Queens

I believe that 'Miss Teenage Beauty' pageants where girls as young as 14 take part are wrong.

It is clearly unhealthy for these girls - at such a vulnerable stage of their development - to reinforce the shallow stereotype that the way their bodies look is all that counts.

I understand that it might boost self-confidence in some, but it could also quite easily destroy those of a more fragile disposition.

Being judged on the way they look at that age can only magnify a young girl's insecurities and bruise her fragile self-esteem which really needs nurturing during those difficult transformative years.

Who are these silly, naive, short-sighted child-women who try to live out their own dreams of being pageant-queens vicariously through their poor toddlers and young daughters?

I really don't understand these misguided mothers.

Do they not realise that by painting their nails and dressing their daughters up in mini-skirts to look older than they really are, they are sexualising their children and offering them up as fodder for paedophiles?

I understand the feminine attraction to 'glitz and glamour' but it is not age-appropriate for girls below the age of puberty to be sexualised in this manner and these mothers who appear to still be little girls themselves should be interviewed about their parenting skills, their responsibilities and their motives.

We should never forget Jonbenet Ramsey.

Silly / immature mothers –

There are many different kinds of mother in Britain but there are two types of mothers that I find really infuriating;

- **Mother One** - The teenage mother who gets pregnant through her own ignorance or simply as a way out, in order to live off of the child-benefits system
  ...and...
- **Mother Two** - the pushy, over-protective but ultra-competitive school mother who wraps her children in cotton wool and tries desperately to protect them from living in the real world.

Mother One;

The breakdown in education and social morality / discipline in this country has led to an explosion in immature adolescent girls with poor educations giving birth to children without even the slightest knowledge of child-care or parental responsibility as proved by the teenage pregnancy rate which is the worst in Europe; if not the world.

Clearly the message about contraception hasn't been heard and now we have a situation in Britain where children are giving birth to more children.

These young women want babies because they're cute and cuddly, like their dolls, and having seen their favourite celebrities having one, as part of the generation that just wants everything it sees, they want one too, believing somehow that by having a baby they would resolve all their problems.

However, they don't really want to be parents as such; they don't know the first thing about it, they just want something to change in their lives and they know that if nothing else happens for them, socially or professionally, they can always get pregnant to give themselves a purpose and rely on the state benefits system to provide for them and their child, thereby improving their situation, if only marginally.

...and as for young men it is even worse; they want the fun of casual sex but they definitely do not want the responsibility of a pregnancy or fatherhood.

But of course, this issue doesn't stop there. As these children get older, their naive and uneducated young mothers - totally influenced by the shallow celebrity culture that surrounds them – start treating them like designer dolls, dressing them up like Barbie or Bratz.

Then, a few years later, they begin to sexualise them by trying to follow the fashion bandwagon and dressing them as mini-adults (taking them to salons for pampering, dressing them up for beauty pageants etc).

This cannot be allowed to continue.

This trend by intellectually-challenged young mothers...and it is young mothers who do this; they have no need for any male input on this matter...to turn their pre-pubescent daughters into sex objects with overtly sexual t-shirts and padded bras is outrageous and degrading.

They are sexualising their children far too early and in an ideal world they would be arrested for moral and emotional cruelty just as those who ignore health warnings by feeding them junk food (which leads to obesity) should.

We need to educate these young women, and these young men, offer them courses in good parenting, in morality, in respect and what is socially acceptable; give them a set of values that they can live by and pass on.

We could of course prosecute them for negligence, for child abuse and parental abdication – ultimately taking away the child to be placed in a more acceptable environment but that would have to be a last resort.

We could also offer free sterilisation to those who simply cannot act responsibly for whatever reasons, be it medical or behavioural but clearly, that too would be controversial.

Mother Two;

These are the doting helicopter mothers who push their offspring into baby yoga, ballet, swimming and piano lessons from the age of three onwards while indulging their children's every whim.

Little do these women realise – because they are so wrapped up in their child-centric universe – that they are making a rod for their own back, not to mention bringing up a generation of spoiled, over-indulged prima donnas with a sense of entitlement that far exceeds their station.

And more importantly, their overbearing, over-indulgent parenting runs the risk of de-motivating the children completely because they (the children) simply feel that they are no more than a passive project being constructed against their will by their parents.

They are not being allowed to develop their personality, their awareness or their social skills because at every given moment, every step of the way, their mothers are there... constantly fussing, checking, organising, ferrying them to and from school, to and from a friends house, or following them at a discreet distance in the street ready to intervene if ever they need their noses wiped.

These children, infantilised by their parents and the over-reaching nanny-state are being brought up in a non-competitive world where nothing is unfair or difficult or uncomfortable, but unfortunately that is not the real world.

And herein lies the problem because, between the parents at home who molly-coddle and spoil them trying to be their friends rather than their educators – and the schools that don't allow them to participate in anything competitive for fear of being sued or sanctioned by the H&S zealots, this generation of children is growing up;

- with a complete lack of respect for themselves,
- or for others and their property,
- with no discipline,
- no boundaries,
- no structure...and
- no idea how to behave in society.

...while at the same time becoming arrogant, self-centred and selfish adolescents devoid of any moral fortitude.

They should - at the very least - be doing household chores on a regular basis to ground them in the real world; it is for their own good, for their own future – children need boundaries, structure and a little discipline.

What are these mothers thinking?

- 10yr old girls are getting body waxes and saving for boob-jobs
- 13yr old girls are posing provocatively on their Facebook pages
- 16yr old girls are being offered tummy-tucks by their mothers as birthday presents
- 27% of young girls are losing their virginity below the age of consent

- 3yr old girls are getting pole-dancing lessons and taking part in beauty pageants dressed in bikinis and high heels; their painted faces making them look grotesque
- 5yr old Suri Cruise has a multi-million-dollar wardrobe and already wears high heels
- 75% of teenage girls admit to having been the victim of sexual or physical abuse from boys because of the way they dressed
- 7yr old girls are riding in stretch-limos and helicopters, wearing dresses that cost £800 to their primary school dances
- 8yr old girls are getting manicures and pedicures
- One mother wanted her 4yr old girl to get breast implants to improve her chances in her beauty pageants
- Children as young as ONE year old are being offered spray tans and facials in a beauty parlour normally reserved for under 13's
- One 3yr old gets a spray-tan from her mother every month
- One 7yr old girl was given Botox by her mother
- One mother refused to give her child a gender until he was five...and another family indulged a 4yr old boy who wanted to be a girl – because he had seen 'Dora the explorer' on the TV - thereby making him an object of ridicule and public humiliation – what tosh – I know the British can be eccentric but should these people really be allowed to be parents
- Pole-dancing kits were being sold at one point for 10yr olds
- The mother of one 9yr old suggested that her daughter participated in beauty pageants because she might want to be a topless model when she was older; how desperately sad is that; where is the aspiration?

Meanwhile; Teen magazines are constantly sexualising young girls with their articles on sex, boyfriends, flirting, kissing-tips, make-up and fashion. Even Vogue magazine featured a 10yr old girl dressed up like a vamp on its front page

What is wrong with these people?

The PDC solution –

This is a carousel of fools

The **PDC** would ban the sexualisation of children at all levels;

We would ban pamper parties for kids

We would ban make-over tents for children at school fairs

We would ban make-over parties for under 10's

We would ban Prom dances at primary schools

We would introduce a ban on companies involved in fashion (clothes, magazines) who promote dangerously unhealthy size-zero clothes and ranges of clothes targeting the sexualisation of small children

We would also ban airbrushed photographs in magazines targeting under-16's to protect their health and self-esteem

I also believe that organising teen night-clubs between 8pm and midnight is wrong – it is putting vulnerable young teenagers in danger and exposing them to life's vices much too soon (drink, drugs and sex) and besides, they should not be out on the streets at that hour

The organisation of a school dance at term's-end in a safe, secure environment is very different from the inappropriate / immoral commercialisation and exploitation of very young people's social lives by unprincipled businessmen motivated by greed, even if aided and abetted by naive and gullible parents unable to say no to their offspring.

We would look into working with people like Anna Richardson from the Sex Ed Show as a consultant – her slogan; 'Stop pimping the kids' and Tanith Carey, the author of 'Whatever happened to my little girl' who also champions the fight against the sexualisation of children.

Actual Parenting –

The concept of family life, so cherished by Mrs Thatcher, was systematically and wilfully undermined by the New Labour government when it was in power, its 'misguided' ministers believing wrongly that the Nanny-state would somehow be better at bringing up children than a married man and woman.

Of course it isn't; bureaucracy and legislation will never completely trump nature, but by taking away parental responsibility without putting the necessary safeguards or practices in place to structure our society New Labour created a social vacuum where <u>nobody</u> takes responsibility for anything anymore.

It is a bit of a cliché but there is no hand-book for bringing up children... and yet ironically, because of the situation we now find ourselves in - where the family dynamic has been so dramatically and so permanently altered by those misguided Labour politicians - I believe it is now time to write one.

The PDC would thus create a parenting book - offering advice and explaining coping strategies in a friendly, non-judgemental way - for every new mother which would be given to her as she left the maternity unit, for her and the child's father to learn all about their responsibilities and what the state expects them to do with their child in their new role as parents.

The handbook would offer help and advice on a variety of subjects;

- right and wrong,
- respect,
- morality,
- boundaries...and
- behaviour in shops, restaurants and on airplanes

...but it would also warn of the consequences if the parenting role was not taken seriously or carried out to a satisfactory level.

The PDC would also broaden the role of health visitors using ante-natal and post-natal classes – which would include birthing information and parenting guidelines – to prepare new parents for the strain a new baby will place on their relationship.

(These classes would be given by real people who could assess a situation in real terms...and not via internet tutorials)

And after the birth of their first child, new parents would be followed regularly and given regular lessons on positive parenting for at least the first year of their child's life by social services. Then, after that period, any cases that might need prolonged or sustained monitoring would be flagged up and given extra help.

These lessons would be mandatory and failure to attend would regrettably have an incidence on any benefits being claimed. It is unfortunate but this sanction has to be put in place and enforced in order for people to comply; otherwise they simply wouldn't bother.

Furthermore we would offer parents a parenting booster-class when their child starts primary school to update them on their new responsibilities.

———

Moreover, in addition to the basic rules of teaching (respect, manners and the six key words that we all should know; please and thank-you - hello and goodbye – sorry and excuse-me), parents would also be told to hammer this vital message into their children;

'If you are old enough to do the crime, you are old enough to do the time'

...explaining to their children the difference between right and wrong from an early age; under the PDC there would be no place to hide no matter what age.

Social and civic rules would need to be taught too, <u>assiduously</u>; no spitting in public, no littering, no feet on seats, respect for others and their property etc etc.

This all sounds very menial but unfortunately good manners are just another casualty in the ongoing collapse of our society and the breakdown is so glaring that unless the next generation is instilled with these rules and boundaries during their formative years they will reproduce the behaviour of the current generation again and again.

Parents of young children would also be made aware that - if their children did get into trouble that was clearly foreseeable and could have been avoided - any benefits they might be claiming would be affected; this would hopefully encourage them to keep their children in check if they weren't motivated to do so otherwise.

NB; **Parents** of older children who display violent social behaviour such as happy-slapping etc would be reprimanded for bad parenting with community service orders.

Facts –

Young children are starting school not even knowing their own names and this lack of communication at home is translating into a major handicap outside the home in a social setting;

One mother explained – *'he might only be two years old but he doesn't speak to me so I don't speak to him'.* How irresponsible is that?

Some children start school unable to use a knife and fork properly – others do not know how to use a toilet properly or dress themselves.

Teachers have become surrogate parents, feeding, clothing and changing nappies of children neglected by their own parents' lack of parenting skills.

However, teachers are not social workers; this is not their job but they are being obliged to fill the void vacated by parents.

The phrase; '*I never stayed at school and I manage*' will not be accepted as an explanation or an excuse.

Author's comments on single parents;

There is no longer any stigma attached to one-parent families in the UK but we are going down the road of more and more one-parent families and I believe that that is not good for children or for society as a whole.

That said; single parenthood is not to blame for the breakdown of society – that has happened since women abandoned the family home with their 'I want it all attitude' fed to them by selfish narrow-minded feminists.

Discipline –

Positive parenting is all very well and the protection of children in the home is vital.

However, the reason we have brought up such an unruly generation over the last thirty years is because of the Nanny State and a multitude of well-meaning - but ultimately misguided - pressure groups which have tied our hands in so many areas of everyday life.

Author's comment;

Personally, I have no time for those daft people, who claim that correcting children will damage their self-esteem and hinder their sense of achievement; who are these limp-lettuces?

Life-skills need to be taught and the sooner the better.

The real world doesn't make exceptions for wimps.

———

Children need a combination of firmness and love but these days, parents are afraid to discipline their children because of all the new regulations...and unfortunately it has created an unruly generation for us all.

We now have teenagers throwing the tantrums of two year-olds because when they <u>were</u> two years old they weren't taught that that kind of behaviour is unacceptable.

It would be a wonderful utopian state of affairs if we lived in an ideal world but sadly, the new-age, liberal approach;

- of not disciplining children,
- of trying to bribe them into behaving,
- of trying to befriend them
- or systematically giving in to their outrageous demands

... isn't realistic and hasn't worked.

The proof can be seen every day in our homes, in our schools and on our streets.

This doesn't mean to say that I am recommending a return to corporal punishment in schools; a more psychological approach should be used to address discipline in that specific area of our society but I do believe that a slap on the wrist to correct a young child's indiscipline in the home should not be considered an offence in law.

Indeed, it should be a parent's duty to instil good manners and respect in their offspring during those first years. (*What would be acceptable and what <u>would not</u> be acceptable would be included in the parenting hand-book and revisited in the parenting lessons*).

Parents must have the right to correct their children when they do wrong, so that those children learn right from wrong; though parents would also be made aware that any over-use or abuse of that parental function would logically be punished most severely.

Of course, the mealy-mouthed, new-age do-gooders will criticise this approach to parenting, but it is clear that the softly, softly approach hasn't worked and I would suggest that we look to nature for the solution.

Author's comment;

We have to disassociate a corrective tap from smacking and child abuse. I am not advocating violence against children; however I do believe that a parent should have the right to correct a child who might be doing the wrong thing; the curious hand and fingers, playing with an electric socket is the easiest of examples to comprehend

---

Look at it this way people; in many of the species that inhabit this great planet of ours - including bears, tigers and lions - the young are kept in line and learn what to do and what not to do, thanks to a complex behavioural template, which covers gentle encouragement all the way through to admonishing chastisement.

Animals use nudging, prodding, nuzzling and any other form of physical display they can think of to impart their knowledge on their young but when the fractious offspring doesn't get the message, a well-placed nip or controlled swipe usually does the trick and brings them into line.

So, why shouldn't we, as humans use the same template?

… after all…we are just another species.

Note to parents;

TV's, computers and tablets should be banned from children's bedrooms and should not be seen as surrogate parents...because they are ill-equipped to do so; there is no control, no filter and no censor to the content on these electronic devices.

And here is another idea;

I will explain later on, why I believe families should be doing more for their elderly relatives but in the mean-time, here is something to think about; **Mamie au pairs**. If people with children do not have an elderly relative that they could take in, then maybe they could take in a 'mamie au pair' who could look after the children in exchange for room and board. This is another idea already in use in France.

Teenagers in Britain today;

The '**Why Bother**' generation or the Caveman generation as I prefer to call them - that is anyone from the age of 5 to 25 currently living in our midst – have absolutely no concept of the discipline or the work they need to put in to achieve their dreams; they simply expect everything to be handed to them on a plate.

Indeed they have almost regressed to a Neanderthal mentality where;

They **grunt to communicate**;

- and when they do deign to look up from their mobile phones and speak, a look of utter contempt and disdain on their faces, their only conversation revolves around alcohol (getting drunk), soap opera storylines or the shallow, vacuous celebrity culture which has now crept insidiously into every corner of British society

They are **lazy;**

- due to a lack of exercise and a lack of motivation

They are **intellectually challenged;**

- because of the failing British education system

They are **deluded, unknowingly ignorant and obnoxious;**

- believing systematically that they know best when in fact they have absolutely no experience of life to draw from

They are **mindless;**

- because they have not learned or been taught how to behave in civilised society

They have **too much licence;**

- too few **boundaries** and not enough **discipline or respect**

They lack any kind of **social or moral compass**

They have **no manners, no inhibitions, no morals** and **no interest** in learning

They are **lawless, unruly, verbally abusive and threatening**

They **are inherently violent;**

- through the frustration of their situation and their lack of opportunity, their addiction to blood-thirsty virtual reality games...and their overall outlook on life which they perceive as offering them 'no future'

They **carry weapons;**

- and are prepared to use them with absolutely no thought of the consequences that will arise from their actions

They walk down the street without a care in the world as if they are all starring in their own personal reality TV shows;

- indeed, they are fed on **reality TV** shows like Big Brother, Towie and the X-Factor which have manufactured careers for their participants and sent out the message that you can be rich and famous without an iota of talent

...and they have a pretty tenuous grip on reality; the luxuries of the past being considered essentials by today's pampered generation.

The girls dream of being WAGS simply for the lifestyle (money, houses and cars)...and some among them are even dropping out of university in order to set themselves up as escorts. That is a sad indictment of today's shallow instant gratification society.

The young people of Britain want **everything for nothing** expecting to access **instant affluence** without ever having to work for it...as if they somehow have a divine right to a life of entitled luxury much like the inherited privileges of the royal family

...and finally, they prefer to **join gangs** and roam around the streets looking for trouble rather than work (or do good in the community), behaviour which brings them into contact with drugs and more bad people which in turn leads to more bad behaviour and more crime etc, etc and the self-perpetuating circle of life goes on and on.

And because of all the above, **the current generation of young people is;**

UNEMPLOYABLE

But it is not **ALL** their fault; this situation is a direct consequence of;

- the Nanny State spoon feeding them all their lives,
- their parents own lack of maturity as far as parenting skills are concerned (discipline and guidance)...and

- having their reality blurred by a society which has allowed them to grow up without any boundaries, moral or otherwise.

Of course there are exceptions but the whole point of creating a society is so that we can get together and enjoy each others company.

That is a basic human need; to interact, but nowadays, most people are afraid of the younger generation because with their hoodies, their posturing and their crude behaviour, they have no boundaries, no respect, no moral reserve and no sense of right and wrong to hold them back from doing whatever; they have no concept of responsibility; they just want what they want and are prepared to do whatever it takes to get it without a thought for others or any consequences that might ensue.

...and sadly, they are not alone in this, because by the same score – the compensation culture that has swept over to Britain from the USA has exacerbated the natural greed of our adult population too; we have all become potential frauds these days, as our first reflex whenever anything happens is not to take personal responsibility for our actions but to ask 'who can I sue and how much compensation can I get?'

The Lost Generation –

The Jeremy Kyle generation is actually the Blair / Brown generation; the generation that was promised so much, and yet received so little.

Everybody will remember Tony Blair's triumphant 'education, education, education' speech and yet many of those who were in education during his time in office now lack the most basic of skills; illiteracy rates have sky-rocketed and a whole generation of young people has now left school with no future because they haven't been given the basic tools they need to get themselves a job.

This has led to a generation of disaffected, feral youths frustrated with their lot.

Tony Blair would of course say that this is not true and he would no doubt produce statistics to support his case, but everybody can see what is happening on our streets and we all know that statistics can be manipulated and made to say whatever one wants them to say.

Indeed, Blair's spin-doctors Peter Mandelson and Alastair Campbell made a living out of producing the right statistics to support whatever argument the Labour leader was trying to put forward - whether they were true or not - and they had absolutely no qualms about manipulating and massaging the numbers - or even lying to the British public - as long as it meant Tony Blair saying the right thing for him, New Labour, and by association, they themselves to stay in power.

Psychological explanation of youth problems –

Studies in Holland and Italy have shown that puberty is occurring earlier these days – around 10 years old. This echoes the findings of endocrinologists (doctors who specialise in hormones) such as Dr Richard Stanhope from Great Ormond Street Children's Hospital who have registered a surge in the number of early puberty cases and the fact that youngsters are maturing so much faster physically than they are emotionally is creating huge tensions and a great deal of conflict in the home and on the street.

The problem is that two important life events – puberty (where we develop physically and sexually) and adolescence (where we mature emotionally and psychologically) are now happening separately for many children, instead of coinciding as they did in the past, leaving their psyche out of balance.

These young people are now physically ready for sexual reproduction but they are unready mentally which has opened up the potential for sexual abuse and teenage pregnancy.

Research suggests that this early increase in testosterone levels is leading to aggression in boys unable to control their impulses while at the same time girls of 13 are wreaking havoc at home demanding to wear revealing low-cut clothes and make-up even at school in response to these hormonal changes.

———

The PDC Solution –

Okay – so having knocked them down – what can we do to get the young generation standing proud once again?

We need to move past this fashionable mood of victimhood, infantilism, vulgarity and self absorption.

We need to eradicate the greedy and selfish nature of our society which misguidedly drives the aspirations of our expectant youth to want everything they desire without ever having to earn or work for it.

The fact that they cannot always have what they want whenever they want it has fuelled their frustration and their perceived feeling / sense of injustice which in turn has led to the violence and lawlessness we witness on a daily basis (riots).

Young people need some motivation; they need some real inspiration and what better inspiration than the recent Olympic Games in London which made us all so proud.

When you see what the young people <u>are</u> capable of, what they <u>can</u> produce in a sporting arena, it just goes to show what <u>can be</u> achieved - with a little hard work, a lot of dedication and a dose of discipline - if their talent is nurtured in the right way by those who believe in them, be it parents, family or teachers offering their guidance and their support.

These are the young people who should be the role-models of today's youth. They are the ones setting a good example for the others to follow through their exploits in the sporting arena.

There is one exception however and that is the football arena, which really is an arena of self-indulgent aggression, just as the Romans designed it, populated by arrogant narcissists, pampered prima-donnas and petulant 'twenty-five year old teenagers';

- *who cynically cheat whenever they can to get the upper hand,*
- *who are verbally-abusive to each other and to the officials,*
- *who still act like schoolyard bullies,*
- *who throw childish tantrums when decisions go against them,*
- *who are scandalously over-paid for what they do,*
- *who are sexually and morally incontinent off the field*

...and who, while being manoeuvred and manipulated by their money-grabbing agents are blinded by their privileged lifestyles and the indulgence afforded them by their coaches, managers and owners alike, leaving them with only a tenuous grasp on the reality of everyday life for those in the stands who pay their wages.

Sadly, because of the win-at-all-costs mentality in football honesty and integrity are considered a weakness, both on and off the pitch; even the ball-boys, who look up to the players as role models – are encouraged to cheat, to hold onto the ball when it should go to the opposing team or deliberately waste time to ensure their own team's result. Football is no longer about fair-play and respect for the rules but about doing whatever it takes – cheating if necessary – in order to win.

So alas, because football, or least the men's game, is morally corrupt from top to bottom I would not hold it up as a good example to our young people which is unfortunate – because while princeling footballers might not want the responsibility of being a role model - it inevitably comes with the territory when you are a public figure.

Paradoxically, in complete contrast to the men's game, in women's football, no-one dives to win penalties, no-one feigns injury or writhes about on the floor trying to influence the referee; the girls don't spit crudely on the ground or empty their nostrils as soon as the camera focuses on them; there is no wrestling in the penalty box during corner kicks; they don't bad-mouth the officials, they don't cynically kiss their badges and nor do they perform silly, tediously-choreographed routines when scoring goals; they just enjoy the game and that is so refreshing to watch.

These women <u>are</u> good role models.

...but back to teenagers...

Some have called them hoodie-wearing half-wits, others have called them feckless, lazy, irresponsible, useless, selfish, disenfranchised...or any number of other derogatory names but despite the poverty of aspiration that seems to blight so many young lives today, we have to remember that they are nevertheless the future of our society.

I too, hate the feckless, self-centred, materialistic over-indulged and ungrateful youngsters of today with their intellectual ignorance and defiant sense of entitlement, but we have to wonder where they got that attitude.

Nobody can say for sure but - the general lack of structure and discipline mentioned earlier notwithstanding - I believe that it was handed down to them by the 'we want it all - and we want it now' feminists.

This is because today's youth culture is driven mainly by naïve, easily influenced young girls, who are the children of the children of the feminist generation, and having been told by their mothers and their mothers' mothers that they can have it all – that's exactly what they are demanding.

Of course the spineless, feeble-minded politicians, reluctant to challenge the wave of pressure from any number of hand-wringing do-gooder organisations allowed it to happen, but the ruthless fashion, beauty and media industries were quick to spot this culture-shift and immediately began targeting these young, impressionable teenage girls using the shallow veneer of Hollywood's celebrity culture to blind them...

...though gadget-crazy boys were not forgotten either by the electronic and technological revolution in gaming consoles, I-pods and mobile phones.

———

The cult of the individual as championed by the feminists and spread by the celebrity / fashion business has become so strong in this country that many people, especially the young, now seem to believe that all that matters is what they want.

We have raised a generation of vapid clones for whom looks and appearance take precedence over everything else.

What's more, a greed mentality has been allowed to develop and flourish in this country – encouraged by the consumer life-style and the celebrity culture – which has morphed rather insidiously into a sense of entitlement that everybody should have everything whether they can afford it or not.

This is another almost inevitable consequence of the 'me-first' culture which has become so endemic in our society.

All this is the inevitable result of the culture of instant gratification which for more than a decade now has glorified fame and money and devalued family and love; a shallow 'all-that-matters-is me' celebrity culture which has led to the majority of the country just wanting one thing 'to be on the TV, to be rich and to be famous' and if at all possible without having to lift a muscle to achieve it.

The younger generation and especially young women, but not exclusively, has experienced a culture shift over the last 20/30 years and they have been seduced by the emphasis put on;

- *material wealth,*
- *physical appearance*
- *and celebrity worship*

through the internet, reality TV, easy credit, our consumerist, competitive and individualistic society, and a generation of indulgent, helicopter parents who have raised their children to think that they are special, amazing and perfect.

Our young, teenage girls are under almost unbearable stress these days to mirror the glossy images of beauty that appear in their sphere on TV, in magazines etc...and yet these images are unachievable and only exist because of air-brushing and photo-shop intervention.

This all means that we now have a warped sense of reality with phoney rich people (who are crippled by debt), phoney beauty (plastic surgery), phoney celebrities (reality TV and YouTube), phoney geniuses (due to grade inflation) and phoney friends (social network sites).

It's a sad state of affairs when modesty, restraint and good-taste no longer have any tenure in our modern society.

———

However, it is time to put an end to;

- this peer-pressure mind-set,
- this must-have way-of-life,
- this culture of entitlement where unappreciative, narcissistic youngsters, suffering from creative inertia - and yet demonstrating an unrivalled cultural arrogance - believe that somehow the world owes them a living without them having to lift a finger.

Enough of these self-obsessed layabouts, of this spoon-fed, assisted generation who - without any experience of life - ignorantly (*through a lack of knowledge or respect*) over-rule and frustratingly undermine their elders with their misplaced and hollow arrogance.

That said; no matter how much we, as the older generation might have a problem coming to terms with it, the reality of life, of our human existence is that it is our duty to take care of the generation that follows ours and despite our understandable disappointment and the natural prejudices / jealousies that come with the on-set of age, no matter how we look at it, because of the circle of life, the young will always be the future.

So, let's show some unconditional altruism here and try to instil in them a sense of personal pride by giving them an education which teaches them how to behave in a civilised society while at the same time arming them with the knowledge they can use to make something of their lives.

Discipline and boundaries are what is needed for this increasingly resentful (resentful of their elders trying to teach them) generation.

That is what they need and that is what they will respond to – not this pally-parenting. There is no point in trying to reason with the unreasonable or with hormonally-charged teenagers stressed-out by a multitude of unresolved issues, who throw tantrums and punches over the contents of party gift-bags, or hit out their parents in supermarkets because they have been refused their latest selfish demand.

We also need to do something for the 'lost generation' – those from the Blair / Brown years which produced a generation of illiterate or badly-educated youngsters with no morals, no discipline, no boundaries, no hope, no aspirations and no possibility of bettering themselves.

Those young people, almost forgotten by society, are also in dire need of a mix of education and training; they too need to feel as if they can be part of a better future and therefore we have to offer more apprenticeships tied to top-up education for the 16 to 25 yr olds.

In France they have 'L'ecole de l'armee', where young people are given a second chance to make something of their lives; they learn about discipline and respect, they top up their education and they are made to get in shape physically through a daily run and regular sport. Then, to reward them they are given swimming lessons, driving lessons (tests) and follow apprenticeship courses (electronics, plumbing, electricians, cooking) – it is a voluntary system but it could be adapted to this country.

––––––––

And for children younger than 16, we need to give more help and direction to their parents, offerings them courses on parenting / discipline and helping them to structure their children's lives.

In exchange, as a reward, we should offer access to sporting facilities and free tickets to sporting events for families who keep with the programme.

It is an old cliché but the carrot and the stick really does work.

We should also organise more sports facilities in schools and communities to keep them occupied and off the streets and encourage youth groups like the scouts and the girl guides...and other sports groups where they learn social skills.

These young people have to learn that honesty and endeavour will pay in the end.

––––––––

However, for those that;

- don't want to learn,
- don't want to work,
- don't want to be part of society,

who just want to live off benefits or worse, join gangs and get into crime, then they should know that the PDC would be setting up a programme especially for them.

They would be rooted out and taken to a special facility where they could not hurt society or the hard-working, law-abiding citizens who make up that society.

The thugs, the thieves, the drug-dealers, the gang-members and anybody else motivated by crime and violence would also be removed and subjected to that same justice; an eye for an eye is just as powerful a concept for criminals as the carrot and the stick is for those who want to make something of their lives. (See Justice Chapter)

The Coming of Age policy –

As part of its Social reforms, I believe that the PDC would need to introduce some kind of structure to the chaotic lives of our young people.

We need to create ambition and aspiration.

Therefore the PDC would introduce a 'Coming of Age' policy which would revolve around the theme of responsibility and everything that a young person aspires towards at that age.

That age would be eighteen and on reaching it, every teenager would be encouraged to celebrate it.

- It would be the age of responsibility – in everything;
- It would be the age of consent
- It would be the age when young girls were given the option of removing the contraceptive implant (see contraception) and undergoing their first pap-smear
- It would be the age up until which their parents would be alerted if they were held in Police Custody
- It would be the age when alcohol could be legally consumed
- It would be the age when they could apply for their first credit-card
- It would be the age when they could freely choose their religion
- It would be the age at which they could sign up for organ donation
- It would be the age when they could legally get married

- It would be the age when they would have the choice to gamble... or not
- It would be the age when they would start paying taxes...and
- It would be the age when they would start voting

Other components of the 'Coming of Age' Policy;

Transport -

As part of their coming of age package, young people would be able to apply for free public transport within an agreed radius (10 miles for example) around the nearest big-city to their home.

This would be to help them look for jobs essentially but it would also allow them to get home in the evening - while the public transport service was still running - and not find themselves out on the street or thrown off a bus / train because they were 20p short of the fare.

This initiative, jointly-financed by central and local government, would run from their 18th birthday to their 21st by which time they should logically be earning a salary consequent enough to absorb their own transport costs.

Cars –

As for driving licences; young people would be able to apply for a provisional licence at 17 in order to become accustomed to driving with a responsible driver in the passenger seat.

They would then be able to apply to take the driving test itself (written and practical) on reaching 18 as part of their 'coming of age' celebrations.

Successful applicants would subsequently have to drive with a 'new driver' (ND) warning badge on their car and a maximum of two passengers at any one time until the age of 21.

This stipulation would save on accidents where 5 or 6 young people pile into a car and end up hurting themselves.

Also, during this period between 18 and 21 years old, young drivers would only be allocated half the number of penalty points on their licence in order to make them more responsible and make them think twice about losing them.

Insurance -

These days, because of the exorbitant costs, many young people drive around without any insurance – or tax – preferring instead to pay the fine if they get caught.

Clearly that is against the law but more importantly, it doesn't protect other road-users so the PDC would introduce a credit-card style presentation system which would force all drivers to present tax and insurance proof – which could be scanned with facial recognition software - before they could fill up with petrol; anybody caught in fraudulent activity would be arrested immediately and the car would be impounded.

NB – the PDC would be looking into working with car manufacturers in order to produce an electric or a hydrogen fuelled car specifically geared to new drivers (18 / 21 year olds).

This car would have its engine automatically restricted to 50 MPH and would be eligible for a reduced insurance premium for the probationary period of a new young driver.

Then, when the young driver trades the car in for a newer model he would be offered special terms by the insurance companies to reward him or her for not having an accident etc during the probationary period. (see industry chapter)

This is all about learning to be responsible and if successful we might look into restricting young drivers (18/21yr olds) exclusively to this type of car – whether through a hired-arrangement or outright ownership.

Another idea would be to roll out the new monitoring device – in conjunction with the insurance companies - which imposes curfews on younger drivers by dramatically increasing the cost of insurance after 11pm.

Jobs –

Those young people who find some kind of employment between the age of 16 and their 18th birthday would be exonerated from tax.

Employers would also pay a reduced rate in taxes for employing a young person...but restrictions would be put in place on the number of 16-18yr olds they could hire, to avoid abuse.

Military –

Those who join up to military cadet training schemes would not be allowed to perform any life-threatening activity in any official capacity until their 18th birthday.

Education –

Coming of Age at eighteen should mean just that and the thinking behind it should be integrated into the education system alongside sex education.

There would be a few restrictions however;

- No benefit handouts for under 18's - that budget would be reassigned to training courses
- No botox or cosmetic surgery before the age of 18. Young girls should not be cosmetically indulged without a valid medical reason until reaching that age.
- No sun-beds for the under 18's
- No tattoos or piercings (ears excepted) before the age of 18

...and there would be <u>no more</u> humiliation on national TV for under-18's in the desperate chase for celebrity and fame.

If young people want to perform in talent shows then they should do so at a local level with the support of their friends and family. This would allow them to build up an immunity to rejection in a safe environment, while enjoying the reward of any success.

Then, when they are 18 and a little more mature, they would be able enter the national competitions and step into the spotlight with confidence, self-assurance and the emotional strength to deal with the inevitable consequences, both positive and negative.

Author's comment;

It is not appropriate for 11yr olds to be singing about sex and drugs...or one-night-stands...as contestants on the BGT show did recently. I do not expect TV executives to act with any moral conscience; their role seems to lie solely in the exploitation of people for the sake of entertainment and their own self-interest, but parents and society must take the lead in proffering the necessary moral guidance.

Various other society-based issues

Elections – the PDC would introduce mandatory electoral participation – those who wish to vote 'blank' would be able to do so, but they would have to turn out. Fines would be imposed on those who didn't vote.

———

Holidays - 28 days paid holiday + 8 public holidays

As there would be no religious component to the PDC manifesto, the **Christmas** period - *which has largely lost its religious symbolism anyway, in favour of commercial exploitation and culinary excess which unbelievably begins in August* – would be replaced by a two week period called the Winter Festival from December 25th to January 5th when people would be encouraged to celebrate their family, their fellow man and the dawn of the New Year.

Easter would be known as the Spring Festival and two of the public holidays would be used for cultural initiatives such as an Open-house Heritage day – where stately homes and government buildings would be thrown open to the public, so that the people might look around and feel a part of the country. This would help them in understanding the wheels of government and hopefully reduce the disconnect between the ruling class and themselves.

A sports initiative or a music-based initiative might also be considered.

At the same time, the PDC would eradicate the yob culture 'yob-fest' by banning the socially irresponsible Pagan festivities such as Halloween and Mischief night (the night before) which have been hijacked and turned into an excuse for anti-social behaviour where groups of feral youths go around harassing and frightening the elderly, terrorising and intimidating homeowners with threats to vandalise their homes pretexting 'trick or treat'.

Similarly, Bonfire night would be restricted to official events and the sale of fireworks would be limited to those qualified and registered to handle them.

Housing – The PDC would enforce the law against squatting introduced in September 2012

We would then look into the actions of those heinous / unscrupulous / immoral / rapacious land-lords who have no sense of decency, compassion or humanity and who exploit the poor and unfortunate in our society. These people would be forced to apply the same official guidelines and building regulations to their properties as the rest of us under threat of serious sanction.

Fashion – Young girls are fed a constant diet of totally unrealistic airbrushed and photo-shopped images that no-one, not even the model who posed for the pictures originally, could ever possibly attain in real life – that has to change.

We need to stop the body-image madness and the obsessive celebrity culture and while I know that it would be impossible because of the internet, I believe that we should also try to ban photographs of anorexic celebrities.

...and another thing; suggestive clothing and explicit music videos are eroding society's values – I believe that t-shits with 'playboy bunny' and 'porn star in the making' are inappropriate and unacceptable.

The PDC Solution;

As the average size of a woman in Britain is 16, why not recalibrate all sizes so that 16 becomes the norm – i.e. size zero – and below that becomes -1, -2 etc, to show young girls that they are not overweight and could actually gain weight and still be within the norm – bigger sizes +1, +2 etc would also alert women of those sizes that they need potentially to be aware of possible 'spread'.

And another thing ladies; stop wearing such ridiculously high heels. If vacuous celebrities and model-types want to make a fool of themselves, teetering on sky-scraper heels trying to outdo each other as to who can wear the highest heels without falling over; just let them get on with it.

They can afford to pay the doctors bills to treat their metatarsal injuries, their ankle-sprains, the angry bunions and their spinal injuries.

The PDC would suggest the following guidelines;

- a two-inch heel; this gives the appearance of narrower ankles and is a suitable height for the working environment
- a three-inch heel; this accentuates the posture and elongates the calves; suitable for a night-out...and
- a four-inch heel; this is for a 'special occasion'...but that is the limit
- Anything above four inches and made of clear plastic...no comment!

———

Obesity - rather than impose an extra fat-tax on fast-food which would only increase the hardship on struggling families, the PDC would try to <u>promote healthy eating</u> by reducing VAT on a wider range of basic foodstuffs (pasta, rice, flour, eggs etc) and healthy options thereby offering the less-well-off the chance to eat better.

We would also ban <u>super-sized</u> sugary drinks in fast-food outlets and adapt BFI's to normal-sized human beings.

———

The British and Sex –

The slogan 'No sex please, we're British' is quaintly old-fashioned but it clearly reveals an alarming lack of maturity within the British psyche about anything relating to sex, which borders on outright naiveté.

The **British** are such an enigma; for a country, a people that has travelled the world for centuries, conquering and colonising as they went, seeing all the sights and experiencing all the different cultures, they are still so insular and unworldly when it comes to some of the most basic areas of human existence.

These people, so full of grit and determination, who have proved themselves to be so stubborn and resilient over time when faced with a challenge or a crisis...and who are renowned the world over for their stiff upper lip in both the field of conflict and the sporting arena, still seem so very immature and juvenile when confronted with the realities of a number of key areas of life.

Sex and Death are two subjects that immediately spring to mind.

Why are the British so coy, so self-conscious and so inherently embarrassed by any form of discussion on these subjects?

Any mention of anything, in any way controversial or taboo is immediately swept under the carpet amid a chorus of noisy throat-clearing and head-shaking.

What is wrong with these people that they are unable to discuss sex and death in an adult manner?

The British culture thrives on innuendo; they love to titter and giggle... and yet they are so uptight and burdened by the religious shame and guilt of centuries past that the slightest mention of the word sex in open conversation transforms them instantly into bumbling buffoons;

- they start to feel uncomfortable,
- they start shifting self-consciously in their seats,
- they avert their eyes or look down at the floor
- and if all that fails, they begin to shake their newspapers with deliberate intent while mumbling incoherently under their breath

In fact, the British will do absolutely anything to distract attention or avoid an awkward conversation...and when they do get cornered and have no choice but to respond in some way to a direct question, they are so self-aware that they are barely able to mouth the words before they have to turn away coyly, a hand raised to the mouth, as their cheeks begin to glow with the guilt of a thousand imagined indiscretions that they would never ever dare to indulge in.

But here is the reality people;

Human beings and the human body in particular have hardly changed throughout the ages...and during all that time they have enjoyed sex, whether to procreate or simply for the pleasure that it procures; that's why we are all still here.

It is a perfectly natural and healthy part of our physical and psychological make-up and more importantly, it is fundamental to our continued existence on this planet.

That is why I really don't understand this inherent embarrassment and the almost enforced naiveté of the British public; in fact I find it more than a little galling that my fellow compatriots are so repressed when it comes to sex and talking about it...because the hidden consequences of such deliberate avoidance-tactics go much further than the awkward silences.

It leaves a vacuum in both ours and our children's education which is having an insidious and stigmatising knock-on effect on related issues such as teenage pregnancy, reporting child-abuse, cases of rape and incidences of paedophilia (the Jimmy Savile case is a prime example).

So, lets clear this up once and for all; it happens people; it happens a million times over every day, all over the planet...and burying your head in the sand and pretending it doesn't exist as some people try to, is very naïve and shows a worrying lack of intellectual maturity and worldliness.

Of course, religion probably has a lot to do with it; religion has skewed everybody's mind all over the world but the British people have been dragging this hereditary guilt around for long enough; it is time for them to grow up and deal with the fact that we are now in the 21st century and that sex is an integral part of human nature.

After all, as human beings we are only here once; why be frightened of knowledge; knowledge allows us to make informed decisions – I don't understand why people would be afraid of that.

———

Now, I do understand that this is a difficult subject for some...and we have to take into consideration the conservative nature of those brought up in sheltered homes where parents were unable to broach such 'delicate' subjects.

We must also be aware of the shame-based reticence and the guilt-ridden embarrassment that religion has imposed on others - a guilt-complex which can easily be traced back to the Bible and its malignant concept of original sin (Adam & Eve)... but religion cannot legislate against normal human behaviour any more so than the politicians and the Nanny State can legislate on instinctive parenting as mentioned earlier.

What comes naturally to a human-being comes naturally; we are living, breathing creatures and there are certain functions in the human body that no amount of bureaucratic paperwork or damnation-based threats can veto.

———

Author's comment;

In centuries past, the church and its leaders believed that by controlling the human sex-drive they could control the masses. It invented the notion of shame; it invented the guilt-complex for those who had 'impure' thoughts and it classified <u>normal human</u> <u>behaviour</u> as 'sinful' in order to enforce its inhumane philosophy.

Because of religion, people were banished from their homes; they were punished, mutilated and killed even, just for indulging their bodies with what comes natural to us all, even to the hypocrites who were persecuting and killing their fellow men at the time.

And even today, the church is still trying to maintain its control over human sexuality with its antiquated ideas...but here is the contradiction or is it blatant hypocrisy?

The bible says; 'be fruitful, go forth and multiply' and yet the Pope says 'sex is a sin'.

It's no wonder that those who believe in religion are confused.

———

Of course, religious guilt is one thing but I also feel sorry for the puritanical, beige cardigan wearing middle-England brigade; who misguidedly see themselves as the guardians of Victorian morality and values.

These uptight, narrow-minded prudes who were brought up in the 1950's when sex education consisted of one phrase, 'as long as you know right from wrong', who see sex as wrong and grubby and who hold sway in the centre ground of British public opinion...are the bane of a progressive society...

...and what is so paradoxical is that they seem to be under some kind of misguided illusion that the Victorians were more chaste and more ethical than today's generation, when in fact, the Victorians were just as promiscuous as any other generation, if not more so.

It is absurd that the British people has been brainwashed by this repressed minority into thinking that sex is wrong and that nudity is dirty – it is not – it is our most natural state; we are born naked and it really exasperates me to witness this shame-based culture full of ageing prudes who demonise sex because of their own inhibitions and repressed natures...or present what is the most natural of human behaviour as a sin, as religion would have it with its guilt complexes.

I also feel sorry for the sanctimonious, buttoned-up Mumsy women like those at Mums Net / the Girls' School Association or the Mothers Union who still believe in the prim and proper world of Queen Victoria, where butter didn't melt in the mouths of women who knew nothing about sex and whose naiveté bordered on complete and utter ignorance...allegedly.

If there is one thing that I find intolerable it is adult naiveté and the ignorance and lack of knowledge which subsequently engenders moral indignation and judgementalism.

I'm sorry but the 21st century has no time for this joyless Puritanism; the world has moved on and we need to grow up in this country and relegate these antiquated, Victorian ideas to the annals of yesteryear.

This is the 21st century – lets stop being so immature and morally timid about this perfectly normal adult issue.

Naturally, we should respect the wishes of those in the minority who do not wish to be enlightened – for whatever reason – it is their absolute right to remain ignorant if they so choose but a government <u>has the duty and the responsibility</u> to inform the remainder of the population on all issues, social and political.

Victoria Wood summed up the British and sex brilliantly in this joke; a couple are having sex on a train; all around them, the other passengers shake their newspapers and avert their eyes modestly while mumbling under their breath – this goes on for a while and then, having finished their embrace, the couple who were having sex get up to go for a cigarette – as you do... afterwards... – at which point, several people stood up and shouted – I think you'll find this is a no-smoking carriage.

The irony of the British attitude towards sex is that despite their prudish, straight-laced approach, they try constantly to extrapolate whatever is said in whatever context, into some kind of tortured pun, twisting any allusion to sex, however remote the link might be, into some kind of risqué innuendo.

They might still raise their eyebrows in horror whenever anything pertaining to sex is mentioned - as they did in Queen Victoria's day - but at the same time they titter and snigger endlessly at the most tenuous extrapolations revelling in every prurient detail they can find out, which does no more than highlight their inherent repression.

...and when they do talk about sex, in comedic situations for example, it is always awkward, crude and vulgar; it becomes toilet humour; there is no 'sophistication' or sexiness to British sex-talk because of their unease with the subject.

Contraception

So, as a consequence and a by-product of our inability to talk about sex...and despite numerous advertising-campaigns and initiatives costing millions of pounds, teenage pregnancies in the UK are still sky-rocketing.

Recent studies have shown that sex-education has failed to impact on pregnancy in the UK; in 1969 there were 6.9 pregnancies per 1000 girls between the ages of 13 and 15...and in 2009, that figure was ostensibly the same at 7.5.

This is unacceptable. It needs to be addressed and while I am in favour of the idea of introducing discreet clinics in schools which hand out information and advice on sexual matters to pubescent teenagers - because unfortunately, the parents aren't able to do so, which is sad – I have to draw the line at them handing out 'the morning-after pill' to pupils as young as twelve years old as was recently revealed.

The abandonment of parental responsibility has meant that schools have had an increased role to play in the social and sexual education of our younger generations but that is a step too far. It is outrageous and irresponsible.

I also believe that it is wrong on so many levels for the NHS to offer over-the-counter contraception pills to 13yr old girls without any consultation, either medical or parental and I also have to disagree with the contraceptive pill being available to anyone, especially teenagers, over the Internet without any professional advice or support whatsoever.

Therefore, in order to radically cut down on teenage pregnancy the PDC would introduce a cervical cancer jab and contraceptive implant for all girls as they reach puberty to arrest the current cycle of children giving birth to more children.

Then at eighteen, as part of their 'coming of age' celebrations young women would be given the choice of removing the implant or renewing it through their university years.

Simultaneously, the PDC would also launch a sexual-health programme which would include young women receiving their first smear test at the age of 18 yrs old, to be repeated thereafter on a regular basis throughout their lives.

———

We do not want any more of this –

- A 12yr old boy and a 15yr old girl had a baby together
- A 12yr old girl gave birth

- A 13yr old boy got a 14yr old girl pregnant
- One 15yr old girl is already a mother of two; her feckless boyfriend having fathered not only her two children but several others around the town where they live
- Another feckless teenager had ten children by ten different girls
- Two sisters of 15 and 17 gave birth simultaneously

What are these children thinking, and what to say about the parents who allowed it all to happen and then hawked the stories around the newspapers and TV channels to make a quick buck out of it?

Where was the education, where were the moral boundaries and whatever happened to raising your children to be responsible adults?

———

Prostitution

Currently, there are 80000 prostitutes working in the UK earning in excess of £770m a year and according to the statistics 2.3 million men use those prostitutes every year at least once.

So, clearly this phenomenon is not going away any time soon and until science finds a way to completely rule out the need for men as a gender - which they are well on the way to achieving - it will continue.

Therefore, without getting side-tracked by the old clichés of 'it's the world's oldest profession' or the feminist agenda of outlawing it completely, which would almost certainly lead to an increase in rape-cases, I believe that we should clarify our position on the matter, instead of hypocritically brushing it under the carpet and pretending that it doesn't exist.

Again, I ask; why do we have such a problem in this country being mature and adult about anything to do with sex?

Truthfully, I have no time for the stuffy, frowning classes with their narrow minded, petty morals or their repressed, puritanical and frankly naïve view on life; we need to deal with the hypocrisy and the double standards around this issue.

As stated previously, sex is part of who we are, and prostitution will always exist; why not admit to the fact and try to regulate it with the aim of protecting the women who – for whatever reason - work in this trade. Protect them on a health level with regular check-ups etc, but also protect them from the abuse and the exploitation of minders and pimps.

I believe that we should license premises to a 'moral person' who would have to provide all the necessary information (proof of identity, DNA, fingerprints etc to avoid organised crime taking over) and then tax them on their earnings like any other business...especially as brothels and consensual sex-work is recession proof.

Naturally, safe-guards would have to be put in place as far as the location and opening times of these premises are concerned (e.g.; not within 500 metres of a school) but we need to find an adult solution to this question.

––––––

Sport; (not necessarily a political issue but a social comment)

Boxing;

I am against anything that I see as an anachronism; religion and the monarchy are two examples already cited and boxing is another. Now, I have nothing against sports which are a test...

- of human strength (Greco-roman wrestling),
- of technique (martial arts) or
- of tactical awareness

...but I do have a problem with boxing which is the last legal activity that reduces humanity to its basest instincts; that of survival through self-preservation; I cannot accept that hitting another human being until that person can no longer defend himself or hit back is an acceptable sport.

It is barbaric and while it might be the ultimate one-on-one, testosterone-filled challenge, the ultimate gladiatorial experience I simply cannot conceive that hitting a person around the head until he is unconscious qualifies as a sport – it might appeal to the blood-thirsty troglodytes amongst us but personally I have no time for this slug-fest or the circus that surrounds it. Humanity needs to move on from this savage spectacle...but I am under no illusion. I realise that greedy promoters and even greedier TV executives will not be sacrificing the golden goose any time soon.

Hunting;

I don't agree with fox-hunting either but I have no issue with trail or drag hunting which perpetuates the tradition without the need for unnecessary bloodshed.

The New PDC Social Charter
based on individual responsibility

The vast majority of ordinary British people instinctively want to belong to a world in which people care for one another - Whatever happened to manners and morality?

We need to stop the erosion of our common decencies and re-establish some boundaries, some semblance of structure and respect for those around us.

We need a return to personal responsibility.

A combination of the riots in 2011 and various other instances of drunken, aggressive behaviour have left the citizens of this country in despair. Everybody recognises that there is an undercurrent of violence and aggression in today's British society - fuelled by binge-drinking on the one hand, and outright despair that life has nothing to offer on the other. It is time to correct that anomaly.

The PDC would put forward a new Social charter based on respect and good manners;

Respect on the street –
No drinking on the streets
No dropping litter in the street...or from car windows
No spitting in the street
No swearing in the street

Dress sense in public -
No slobs allowed; let's bring back dress codes and school uniforms
No cheap grey stretch-jersey track-suit bottoms on the high street (acceptable in a sporting context, not on the street)
No hoodies
No underwear on show (wish-bones or boxers)

Respect on public transport -
No feet to be put up on train and bus seats
Laptops, rucksacks, shopping and handbags should not be used to claim ownership of the seat beside the one you are using

Chivalry might be dead because of the feminist movement but that doesn't mean that we shouldn't be polite and respectful; holding a door open might be considered too patronising and contemptible for some women but surely they would agree to people being courteous and offering a pregnant woman or an old person a seat.

In addition, the PDC would look into introducing a system to jam electronic devices (phones and bombs) on public transport. The mobile phone has taken over our society and had a harmful effect on our ability to interact and communicate with each other; this needs to be addressed.

Manners generally –
These need to be improved both at home and in company (clear your own plates at home, clear your own tray of junk in fast-food restaurants etc)

We need to respect other people's right to silence in libraries; why not reserve a floor for quiet people? No phones and no talking.

We need to be more patient when queuing and not jump in front of those who were there before us. (at checkouts, at bus-stops, at taxi-ranks or in traffic)

And we need to respect the designated parking spaces that have been allocated to the disabled and parents with children in supermarkets etc.

I also believe that cashiers and shop-assistants should talk to their customers and not to each other...and that customers themselves should show more courtesy and respect; if you must take a call, step out of the line until you have finished with it. Why are people so rude and obnoxious these days?

Education

This country is not only going through an economic recession – it is also going through an intellectual recession with the dumbing-down of school lessons and the ridiculous grade inflation fiascos of the last few years which have been attributing A-level passes - and grade A level passes at that - to even the most mediocre students just so that the politicians can revel in their falsely-enhanced, deviously-manipulated statistics and league tables.

However, this academic recession is not only a problem in school as the knock-on effect of the reduced level of education of the wider population means that through a lack of intelligence and common sense our society is slipping back into the 18th century;

Take for example the duplicitous nature of our morality; girls are getting pregnant younger (we have the worst problem in Europe), single mothers abound, one-night stands are the norm and at the same time there are people pushing for the water-shed on TV to be put back to 10 p.m. because they are offended by the odd swear-word and pseudo-explicit content; this is down to ignorance and a lack of intellectual maturity.

'Education, education, education'; that was Tony Blair's rallying cry when he came to power in 1997 and what happened; we now have more people leaving our education system with illiteracy problems and a lack of culture than ever before.

In fact, while New Labour was in office, every year, more and more children were leaving school without even the most basic knowledge of how to read or write.

Author's comment;

I hope Tony Blair is proud of that, and of his wonderful idea to introduce 24/7 drinking which has led to this country developing the worst booze culture in Europe.

———

We in the UK now have a generation of young people - which a recent survey confirmed - whose intelligence, as far as mathematics is concerned at least, does not exceed that of a nine / eleven year old, while our school literacy level has plummeted to an all time low in the world league; indeed, 10% of our children now leave school without mastering the three R's.

Moreover, the number of failing schools has gone up 4% and overall UK schools have dropped from 7ᵗʰ place to 22nd in literacy...and from 8ᵗʰ to 21ˢᵗ in maths in comparison to other countries.

New Labour saw this happening - having deliberately engineered it, more or less – but rather than trying to rectify it as any responsible administration would have done, they decided instead, to fiddle with the SATs (scholastic achievement test) results and lower the pass-rates in order to avoid exposing the tidal wave of failure that they had presided over.

They brought in an American company - at great cost to the taxpayer - to oversee this rather cynical process and as expected it duly devalued the marking system in order to save Labour's reputation; the whole exercise was a sham and proved to be a complete debacle.

I mean, come on people; there is no way, absolutely no way that our schools were turning out a 98% success rate; not if the levels of marking were of a decent standard.

The teachers knew it, the parents knew it, the people on the street knew it; in fact everybody knew it...and sadly, many of the children who were given grade-A passes during those New Labour years - but still cannot read and write properly - knew it too.

The lack of integrity displayed by our egocentric politicians...and dare I say by those in charge of our children's education has been disgraceful. These young people are our future; they are not just pawns on the political chessboard to be used as statistics on a graph in the next party manifesto.

So, let's stop all the lying – let's stop listening to the deluded politicians who keep producing these imaginary statistics claiming that education is getting better.

If we as a nation are honest, we all know, everybody in British society knows that the level of education in this country has been declining for years. We see it and hear it on the streets every day. Everyone knows that more and more children are leaving school without any proper qualifications and with no real plan for the future.

It's only the calculating politicians, motivated by self-preservation - and desperate to keep their places on the gravy train - who are still trying to keep up the facade.

———

Truancy in schools is soaring too, and this is probably linked in some way to the fact that, when they are in school, children are constantly under threat from the increasingly prevalent culture of violence that is now inherent within;

- physical bullying is on the rise...and
- violence with mobile phones is becoming endemic (they are either stolen or used to threaten violence via text, e-mail or social media)

Children no longer feel safe in our schools - or on our streets for that matter - and that is why they have taken to carrying knives and even guns. We have to put an end to all this behaviour before it becomes too ingrained.

Teachers too are quitting in their droves because of the pressures of meeting targets rather than actually teaching...though the constant threat of violence from pupils and the lack of support from their hierarchy when their authority has been called into question is also forcing many others to rethink their careers too.

New Labour did make one half-hearted attempt to address the problem, throwing £650M at Juvenile Rehabilitation but like many of their policies it was more for the tabloid headline than for any actual credible intervention. In fact, in just over ten years, New Labour managed to wash away all the educational structure and discipline that had been instilled in generation after generation of British people over hundreds of years, turning our young people into a bunch of knife-wielding alcoholics with no respect for the law or their elders.

...not to mention all the teenage abortions, which went up by over 25% during the New Labour years.

That is their legacy and that is the toxic inheritance they left for the coalition government to pick up.

It's no wonder that today's younger generation feels useless and frustrated.

They are completely lost. Their whole education has been botched by politicians more interested in producing statistics and league tables than they are in producing well rounded individuals ready to take their place in society...and as a result they (the young) see no future for themselves.

It is not their fault, but alas, this situation has made many young people turn to anti-social behaviour in a cry for help; <u>that cannot be the solution</u>.

We need to address this problem now. Our education system needs a complete overhaul with earlier detection of those that need help, apprenticeships for those that are less academic and for those who do go on to university, a more structured and honest exam-marking system that will be recognised for its diligence and its quality, because without a new direction the spiral that we are now in, will just continue on its inevitable path downwards.

―――

Some Literacy facts –

33% of 11yr olds in the UK fail to grasp the 3R's - Cuba, Estonia, Poland and Barbados all boast higher literacy rates than the UK

- English is now a foreign language for one in seven primary-school children
- English is only a second language for over one million children in the UK
- Five million British adults are functionally illiterate and seventeen million cannot add up properly
- Illiteracy leads to a life-sentence on the edge of society

In 2009 nearly a quarter of a million children left primary school unable to read, write or add up properly.

The link between illiteracy and delinquency is beyond doubt.

Some cities in the UK are becoming racially segregated and their populations are leading parallel lives to the rest of society; the language barrier is creating dangerous divisions in society.

―――

New Guidelines

―――

The social chapter of a PDC government would be founded first and foremost on responsible parenting, and therefore under a PDC administration, parents would have to sign up to a charter when signing their children up to school which would outline their responsibilities and detail what the school would require of them.

The agreement would of course set out what the school would expect of the children...but as importantly, it would also set out what it would expect from their parents including standards and behaviour; parents would also be made aware - in front of their child to avoid any misunderstanding - of the sanctions facing unruly students...and they would also be informed that after roll-call every morning – they would be sent an e-mail or text to inform them of any absence.

This would be done for the student's own safety but it would also allow for a record to be kept in order to support any disciplinary action further on down the line.

23,000 primary-school pupils play truant every day in the UK; that has to be addressed.

Parents would also be warned that their own behaviour and their interaction with the teaching staff would be monitored and linked to any decisions concerning their child.

NB; any hint of violence or threatening behaviour on the part of a parent towards any member of the teaching staff would lead to the immediate exclusion of the child and a visit to the parents home by the relevant authorities...

...and if parents declined – for whatever reason - to sign up to the school charter, then they would be put under a parenting order forcing them to take parenting lessons that they would have to pay for, under the threat of financial sanction (fine; benefits withheld)

However, this policy would be about individual responsibility; the PDC would not be asking people to snoop on their neighbours as New Labour suggested they do; that was unforgivable and downright reprehensible – we should be trying to build a community not destroy it by isolating everyone and setting them against each other.

At the school-gates –

Naturally, it goes without saying that pupils / students should always arrive on time, be dressed correctly, and be in possession of the books and the basic equipment necessary to learn (pens, pencils, rulers, rubber).

> We need to re-introduce a level of discipline
> in behaviour and attitude.

So, the first measure that the PDC would re-introduce would be that of compulsory uniforms - adapted to the children's age group - on the condition that a deal could be struck with the retail industry and supermarkets to maintain the current value ranges.

These uniforms would be checked at the school-gate to ensure that;

- they were the proper / correct attire (colour, design etc)
- they were modest and tidy
- they were clean and not torn, even if fashionable and...
- they were straightened to look presentable (ties, skirts etc)

...and only then would access be granted to the school-grounds.

If a uniform was unsatisfactory in any way, the pupil would be sent home; the parents would be given <u>one</u> chance to correct the problem and if the issue was not addressed, then the parents would be asked to meet with the principal to explain why, so that the matter could be resolved.

———

When age-appropriate; only discreet make-up would be authorised; and as for earrings, only stud earrings would be allowed (no large rings)

Outrageous hair-styles and coloured hair would be banned and no chewing-gum would be allowed within the school premises or its grounds.

...and finally, outside school; let's set a good example, let's leave the hoodies and the gangster clothing to the criminals – so...

- no more hoodies
- no more underwear flashing
- no more low-slung jeans...and
- no more ugly thong-wishbones

———

Let's create The PDC Generation; a generation that respects itself and others.

BTW; let's also get rid of this 'namby pamby' society where children do not go to school because of an inch of snow; it sends the wrong message.

Today, its school, but tomorrow these children will not bother going to work if the weather is at all inclement.

———

In the classroom –

The PDC would also re-install discipline in the classroom, starting with the tried-and-tested concept of forward-facing desks.

Children's attention is focussed on what is right in front of them and that needs to be the teacher and not a friend who is giggling, making funny faces or distracting them in any other way as with the current square-tables concept.

This silly child-centric dogma of sitting pupils in groups where teachers are just facilitators is ridiculous; this is why our education system has gone to pot.

The introduction of these silly new-age concepts has basically allowed the government to opt out of any guiding influence in education. New Labour basically adopted an out of sight, out of mind policy which has done nothing but drive down standards - and the levels of learning by removing the structure, the boundaries and the discipline needed to teach children how to learn and grow up to be decent, law-abiding citizens.

It is outrageous.

Its a bit like the hippies of the sixties and seventies who believed that all you had to do was lay around in a green field making daisy chains until enlightenment came to you.

Of course, it never did and it doesn't; intelligence has to be nurtured and taught directly, within a framework, with boundaries and dare I say it...with a measure of discipline.

It cannot simply be infused into the mind, in a rule-free chaos where pupils are never challenged or stretched. Children need to be challenged and stretched; they need to strive in order to develop.

They need the grounding and structure that classical teaching imposes on them; a teaching that gives them boundaries, both moral and social.

The liberal educationalists - obsessed with child-centric learning - have destroyed the futures of a generation of young people and its time to recognise that.

We now live in a society that knows the price of everything but the value of nothing and its time that we did something to change that; discipline needs to be re-introduced from the top; discipline in dress code and in the respect we should have for tutors, teachers and the elderly.

We need to change the failed policies that have blurred if not inversed the roles of teachers and pupils and paradoxically allowed the students to take over the schools.

The PDC would also introduce sound-proof lockers into each classroom where mobile phones would be deposited before class and retrieved after class, under the supervision of the teacher (some kind of personalisation would help in recognising which phone belonged to which student (name tags or coloured pouches)

Parents would be advised during the induction interview that in case of emergency they should contact the school which would then relay any urgent messages to students / pupils following an agreed protocol.

I believe that we need this mandatory ban on mobile phones in the classroom because students are using them to threaten each other, to threaten staff-members, and to take suggestive photos of female teachers which they then post on the internet, totally undermining the teacher's authority.

Mobile phones are also used as weapons to send bullying texts, to swap pornography or other images of violent acts – and instead of interacting with each other during breaks, young people do nothing but stand around pressing buttons, their noses glued to their phone-screens.

This ban would extend to all electronic gadgetry brought into the classroom by students, with the proviso that teachers would not be infringing any students' rights in enforcing it. This would remove the temptation from those mischievous students looking to create problems by reporting teachers to the police.

NB – any mobile phone found in class would be sanctioned severely - especially in an examination situation, which would lead to an immediate exclusion (all exam papers would be headed by a phrase attesting to the fact that the student had been made aware that mobile phones were banned and every student would have to sign the paper after a secondary (verbal) affirmation from the moderator before commencing the paper)

**A copy of the following would be posted
on the wall of each classroom,**

and every day after roll-call – Monday excepted - ONE
of these rules would be discussed for ten minutes

Rules for finding fulfilment

---

1) Be courteous, be punctual, always say please and thank-you, be sure to hold your knife and fork properly; others take their cue on how to treat you from your own manners

2) Be kind, considerate and compassionate when others are in trouble, even if you have problems of your own. Others will admire your selflessness and will help you in due course

3) Show moral courage. Do what is right, even if that makes you unpopular. You need to be able to look in the mirror every morning with a clear conscience

4) Show humility. Stand your ground but pause to reflect on what the other person is saying, and back down when you know you are wrong. Never worry about losing face; that only happens when you are being pig-headed

5) Learn from your mistakes. You will make plenty so use them as a learning tool. If you keep making the same mistake over and over, you're doing something wrong

6) Avoid disparaging someone to a third party; it is only you who will look bad; if you have a problem with someone, tell them face to face

7) Hold fire. If someone crosses you, don't react immediately. Once you say something, it can never be taken back and most people deserve a second chance

8) Have fun; if this involves taking risks, so be it. If you get caught, hold your hands up

9) Give to charity and help those who are less fortunate than you; its easy and very rewarding

10) Always look on the up-side; the glass is half-full, never half-empty. Every adversity has a silver lining if you seek it out

11) Make it your instinct to always say 'yes'. Look for reasons to do something rather than excuses not to. Your friends will cherish you for that

12) Be canny; you will get more of what you want if you can give someone more of what they desire. Compromise can be king

13) Always accept an invitation; you might not want to go, but the person organising wants you there; show them that courtesy and respect

14) Never let a friend down but choose them wisely

15) Always tip for good service. It shows respect, but never reward poor service. Poor service is insulting

16) Always treat those you meet as your equal, whether they are above or below your station in life. For those above you, show due deference but don't be a sycophant

17) Always respect age as age equals wisdom

18) Be prepared to put the needs of others first

19) Be proud of who you are and where you come from, but open your mind to other cultures and languages

20) Be ambitious and back up those ambitions with craftsmanship and hard work

21) Live every day to its full; do something every day that makes you feel alive, smile or laugh; avoid procrastination

22) Give your best at school

23) Always pay the most you can afford. You get what you pay for

24) Never give up

25) Never feel sorry for yourself; at least not for long

26) Look after your body and it will look after you

27) Learn a language

28) Cherish your parents and your siblings

———

Typical timetable breakdown;

08.30 - 09.00 - Breakfast club

09.00 - 11.00 - Morning session

11.00 - 11.30 - Break

11.30 - 12.30 - Mid-morning session

12.30 - 14.00 - Dinner break (lunch first, then recreation); this should be organised in such a way that half the teaching staff supervises while the other half eats and vice-versa

14.00 - 16.00 - Afternoon session; later finish plus journey-time calculated to coincide with parents getting home from work thereby leaving children less time alone to get up to mischief

16.00 - 18.00 - Extra-curricular activities

Author's comment;

The last hour of the afternoon period could be used to recap the day's work and to clarify any subjects that might need it, thereby removing the need for regular homework and allowing students more time in the evenings to spend with their families.

———

School layout;

The PDC would also insist on separate conveniences for boys and girls – the idea that we should have unisex toilets in schools is simply ludicrous. We cannot have pre-pubescent 11yr old girls sharing toilets with 18yr old boys – it's just unacceptable.

———

Junior / Primary School

At the start of every school day, after roll-call, Monday excepted, the PDC would introduce a 10 minute period of reflection based on one of the **Rules for finding fulfilment** which cover morality, dignity, respect and good and evil etc.

On the Monday morning, the national anthem would be taught during that same time slot and once it had been learned, it would be sung every Monday morning in order to start the new week with a rousing swell of inspiration.

However, as the PDC would be an advocate of a republican state, this would not be the royalist 'God save the Queen'. The song to be sung in England would be 'There'll always be an England or Land of Hope and Glory', while in other parts of the UK, their respective national anthems would be sung.

As for the curriculum –

The PDC would take a leaf out of Finland's educational model by concentrating on the three main subjects of **reading, writing and mathematics** which would be interspersed with age-appropriate lessons at intermittent times in the following subjects according to the teachers' assessment of the pupils;

- Art / drawing / painting
- Age-appropriate lessons in computers – keyboards etc but also the dangers of the internet, face-book
- Discovering nature / going outside
- Geography
- History

- Music – singing / introduction to playing instruments. The PDC would like to restore access to musical instruments to every child from 7yrs old – in Venezuela they have created the 'el sistema' programme which teaches youngsters from all walks of life to play an instrument – this has led to a drop in crime and the creation of the Simon Bolivar Youth Orchestra which is now recognised throughout the world for its talent
- Social integration / respect
- Sport / exercise

As stated previously religion would not be taught in school but it would be explained...and as for climate change, we would broach the subject from the standpoint of an ever-evolving planet. We would not be teaching children that the world is overheating, causing massive floods and killing polar bears just because of human activity when it simply is not true.

...and finally, there would be no pressure for results; no tests or examinations up until the age of nine. Primary-school children are in school to learn, to build up their self-confidence, to develop their character and their personality; not to tick boxes.

Some have suggested that sex-education should be introduced for children a young as four; others have proposed lessons in trans-gender for five year olds or even lessons in swearing. I believe that this is quite inappropriate. It is ethically questionable at best - and immoral at worst; therefore those kinds of initiative would not be pursued.

Instead, children would be allowed a childhood, and junior / primary school would be all about learning the basics, about confidence building and about encouraging and igniting aspiration in a pleasant and relaxed environment where they can play and develop at their own pace and where everyone is equal and has an equal opportunity.

I would also like to see the return of milk being offered to children up to eleven on a daily basis – this would not only help with their calcium intake and their general welfare, it would also help the dairy farmers who have a glut of milk that they are unable to sell.

Life should not always be about the bottom line; it should sometimes be about helping each other as part of the national fabric that holds us all together, so with this in mind I believe that we should offer a helping-hand to hard-pressed dairy farmers by reversing Mrs Thatcher's ruling and organising a daily glass of milk for every child, thus helping both with the child's health / growth and the dairy-farmers livelihoods.

...and from time to time, when the season permits, we might even provide the children with an apple a day - or every other day - alternating it with the milk.

Author's comment;

We have lost 40% of our dairy farmers since 2000 and I believe that, as a nation we need to support them by offering those that remain, a reasonable price for their milk; we need to support them and by supporting them we will preserve their livelihoods and their families.

Where is the sense of community?

The price of milk is currently set by the milk processors but going forward the PDC would suggest a two-tier price structure – one for school milk and the other for commercial businesses which is a fair reflection on cost.

We, the public need to support the dairy farmers but we cannot do that when milk costs 29p to produce and the huge supermarkets only offer the farmers 25p to take it off their hands; simple economics / maths tells us that that is not financially viable and cannot work long-term.

A two tier pricing system where the farmers sell to the government (for the children) at cost and to the milk processors at cost +3p could make everybody happy – the children would get their milk, the farmers would be able to sell all that they produce without any waste and the milk processors could negotiate with the supermarkets to find a price that suits both of them - and if the milk processors did not listen to reason over this, the PDC would set up a parallel system of national suppliers – milk shops - in conjunction with the farmers thereby creating jobs in distribution and eliminating the exploitative middle men altogether.

We need to break the stranglehold that huge multi-national chain-stores have over the farmers, so that they can survive and their families prosper.

Secondary School

The three main subjects **reading, writing and mathematics** will be maintained at all costs – without which **NO** child can move forward.

Then there are a variety of other subjects which all need to be tackled as part of a child's progression into adulthood;

As youngsters have fewer and fewer male role-models these days, we need to maintain the teaching of **history** in school; we need to teach them about men of stature and inspiration, be it in the field of science, or in politics, in a military context or in a sporting situation.

However, rather than teach them about dates and events, I would suggest that we concentrate on the characters and the personalities of the past, Nelson, Wellington, Churchill etc; strong role models whose life-stories could teach the young about the past while simultaneously introducing them to good character-traits that they could imbibe and still use today. (Dedication, determination and pride)

This will help to give them a good grounding, to remind them of their roots and then expand their knowledge as their awareness grows and develops.

The PDC would also introduce **Citizenship lessons** which would include traditional values...or maintain them in schools where they have already been trialled. We would teach students about;

- **Respect** for one's elders and other people's property (this should also be taught in the home and as a consequence these guidelines would also be included in the new parent booklet handed out in the maternity unit) We would teach them social skills to look after the elderly thereby allowing them to interact and learn to respect them more

- **Manners** - Shaking hands – speaking clearly – not interrupting; wouldn't it be nice to have polite and helpful youngsters rather than the surly and hostile thugs we currently have...and
- **Social etiquette and responsibility** (on right and wrong, how to behave in cinemas, on trains, on buses, in the streets etc)

———

As part of the **social skills** programme, we would also re-introduce **Cookery classes** and classes on nutrition for all - Domestic science was dropped by liberal educationalists on the grounds that it was sexist and demeaning to young girls; how wonderful that sexual equality meant that they no longer needed to know how to cook or eat healthily. That really worked well didn't it. We are now facing an epidemic of obesity as more and more mothers fill their children with fast food because they haven't been taught how to cook; and might I remind everybody and especially the feminist zealots that the most renowned chefs in the world are men, so there is no stigma attached to boys learning how to cook. (e.g. Alain Ducasse, Albert and Michel Roux, Gaston Lenotre, Joel Robuchon, Paul Bocuse; **and in the UK**; Heston Blumenthal, James Martin, Jamie Oliver, Jean Christophe Novelli, Marco Pierre White, Raymond Blanc etc)

———

The PDC would also introduce **Anti-gang** lessons in collaboration with the Police who would talk about bullying in school and via social media.

Teenagers might also be shown extracts from the TV series Brat-Camp to show them what their behaviour does - to themselves and to their families. The camp might also offer them a gentle reminder of what awaits them if they choose the wrong path.

We would also produce a film of life in a BCF (Behaviour Correction Facility) showing the muscle-bound team of ex-militaries ready to welcome wayward teenagers. This film would be taken around the schools to scare those unruly elements and potential criminals into mending their ways. We might even organise day trips to the boot camps in order to convince those who need that extra little push.

———

Another lesson might include **media awareness** and **the pitfalls of the internet** including a lesson on the effects of online bullying – We might even show students the nine-minute You-tube video made by Canadian schoolgirl Amanda Todd who killed herself at 15 because of the bullying she received via Facebook and perhaps make them read the poem written by 14yr old Izzy Dix who also took her own life after months of bullying.

———

The PDC would also re-introduce practical skills classes in **DIY** from learning how to change a plug to plumbing or building a shed. These classes were also curtailed because of the Health & Safety zealots but some children who are not academically-minded often shine in manual work and they might find a calling in this area which could subsequently lead to an apprenticeship.

———

We would also teach students about **financial responsibility** and the value of money.

———

We would teach them the advantages of a **second language**; French, Spanish, German or Cantonese.

———

The nanny state has infantilised a whole generation of people to the point where they have no idea of parenting skills so we need to put **child-care and parenting skills** on the curriculum too, alongside the sex-education classes. This might also include baby-sitting skills and first-aid.

We might also provide them with an introduction into **fashion** to prevent the girls dressing too provocatively, too early – low-cut blouses, short skirts etc.

This might also help to root out the mixed signals that young women are giving off and hopefully reduce the number of sexually motivated aggressions.

We would also introduce lessons on the **Highway Code** for those hoping to pass their driving test.

We would make sure that **sport** and **music** figure prominently in the curriculum while banishing the ridiculous trendy diktats of 'no winners and no losers' – the reality of life <u>has</u> to be faced.

Meanwhile, we might also introduce some age-appropriate **dance lessons** (to deal with social awkwardness, overcoming inhibition, and interaction with the opposite sex;) this would also highlight respect issues, involve exercise, and improve rhythm and coordination while building young people's self-confidence.

The PDC would also offer potentially life-saving **swimming lessons** to all children which would, once again, help with obesity issues.

We would also re-introduce school trips – with safe-guards for the children but also for the teachers, which prevent them from being sued by over-zealous parents when unfortunate accidents happen and it is not their fault. No more compensation and guilt culture.

...and finally, we would ban initiation ceremonies (hazing) with a suitable sanction for those who transgress.

Furthermore...

From the age of 14 onwards the PDC would look into introducing – by increments – work experience and apprenticeship schemes for those pupils who do not have the potential for higher education so that they might transition more smoothly into the working environment.

Maybe we could link this to a mentoring programme where those heading towards retirement reduce their hours and use the extra time to introduce new apprentices to the workplace, thereby creating a balance at either end of the workforce; perhaps we could even tie it to the Magnet Centre scheme.

There must also be a way of identifying bright kids from ordinary backgrounds and giving them a world class education in our best universities.

For difficult students –

The PDC would introduce anger management classes that might include psychological evaluations.

This would act as a safety valve and hopefully combat the unreasonable outrage or the backlash of the pampered, over-protected, over-indulged generation who lack any restraint, cannot accept criticism or disapproval of their actions and cannot be taught anything because they think they already know it all.

Discipline and boundaries are what is needed for this increasingly resentful (resentful of their elders trying to teach them) generation; that is what they need and that is what they will respond to.

However, those who could still not conform would be assigned to one of the special reform schools or BCF's (Behaviour Correction Facility) that we would be setting-up. These facilities would come complete with a stricter syllabus and an intensive physical workout programme designed specifically for these people to work out their issues and their aggression.

———

Health / Sex education –

The ethical degeneration and moral confusion of today's young people springs from their lack of sexual morality and this can all be traced back to the seventies when the rise of feminism threw open the doors of entitlement.

They tore up the rule-book during those years and ever since, as far as sex is concerned, anything goes;

- there is no longer any moral awareness,
- there is no respect (for oneself or for others)
- there is no personal responsibility
- and there are no boundaries

This has led to teenage boys;

- whose minds are warped by the constant wave of pornographic images thrown at them on a daily basis by the media, magazines and advertising
- and by the easy access they have to pornography on the internet

...now having a very misogynous attitude towards girls and young women.

There is no respect - sex to them is just sex, a mechanical, physical release.

There is no interest in getting to know the girl or making an emotional connection with her; she is seen purely as a sex-object, there to fulfil his fantasy and if she doesn't consent to that she is inexorably bullied into it through social media and peer-pressure.

I wonder how many of these young people actually understand the biological consequences of their actions and the repercussions of such sexual promiscuity.

Author's comment;

Two 13yr olds were recently expelled from a private school for having sex... while another was expelled for stealing a bottle of whisky

---

So; sex-education needs to be improved in our schools for all the reasons above...and to reduce our woeful record on unwanted pregnancies.

Teachers already have enough responsibility in the classroom, so rather than add to that already heavy burden the PDC would introduce a sex-education programme for all teenagers - using age and language-appropriate terminology – to be dispensed by employees of the social services.

This would create a certain distance from the teaching staff (embarrassment issues) while allowing a degree of anonymity for students if they needed to seek further information.

I believe that regular visits to the schools by a recognisable, responsible adult would also help to weave a thread and firm up community bonding.

Topics to be covered using age-appropriate guidelines;

- **sex** – the mechanics and biology

- **pregnancy and motherhood** – in the UK we have 40,000 teenage pregnancies every year which is the highest in Western Europe and in order to stem this tide the PDC would look into rolling out the Straight Talking Peer Education scheme which is an initiative where teenage mothers go around schools talking about teenage pregnancy and motherhood. Teenagers and teenage mothers in particular also need to be made aware of the advantages of **breast-feeding** which is the most natural way of feeding a baby and has been for thousands of years.

- **contraception** (Pill, condoms, vasectomies, sterilisation, coil, and diaphragm) - Unfortunately, contraception still has to be the woman's responsibility for the most part as women will never be able to rely on men to be 100% truthful and honest in those circumstances – and if an unprotected dalliance results in pregnancy it's her and her body that has to carry the developing child – however young men should receive more applied educative advice too

- **STDs** - cases of cervical cancer have risen dramatically in recent years – scientists blame the rise on young girls having unprotected sex at a younger age and with more partners – the HPV jab is available on the NHS to those between 12 and 13 and cuts the risk of cervical cancer by approximately 70%. The PDC would recommend its use, but not only to young girls; - it should also be given to boys as its benefits against cancer growth are not gender-specific

- **relationships and respect issues** - At a time when teenage girls are under unprecedented assault from our increasingly sexualised culture 75% of them admit to having been the victim of sexual or physical abuse from boys because of the way they dressed. Boys need to be taught about respect, they need to be taught how to handle their emotions so that they don't become jealous, obsessive, possessive and violent towards girls. They need to be told that bombarding girls with texts and phone-calls demanding to know where they are and who they are with at any given time of the day or night or stalking them is not acceptable behaviour. That kind of insecure / immature behaviour needs to be addressed.

- **information on financial obligations and child support for young men who become fathers** - Teenage fathers should be forced into acting responsible – taught social skills – (the recent case of an unemployed feckless young man having 7 children with 7 different teenage girls all living off the state is unacceptable and should never be repeated)
- We also need to inform young people – especially young girls - about **the dangers of rape and street grooming** – either via the net or by bribes in the street using alcohol, drugs or money – including the consequences for boys (on a legal basis) – but also the consequences for girls who make-up false accusations
- **social media** - Girls must be made aware of the dangers of sending naked pictures of themselves to boys – they may not regret it immediately but most will do so, long-term – those pictures are shared between boys and put on the internet and when a relationship ends, they are used to blackmail or humiliate the girls, leading to depression and a loss of self-worth – young people need to learn about self-respect – texting or posting topless photos of themselves on social networking sites is not acceptable behaviour.

Of course, we would need to constantly update the message being given to young people, in order to keep up with the times, but that message has to maintain the integrity of the established moral code.

———

Extra-help (after school term) –

For those who miss out on their exams, the PDC would organise summer camps where students would study for half the time and engage in sports during the rest of the time.

These camps would be constructed to the highest specifications, their internal structure and monitoring procedures would be beyond reproach…and every safety measure would have a fail-safe mechanism so that the spectre of being sued by cupidinous parents was permanently removed from the shoulders of the teachers and monitors, if ever an accident was to occur.

NB; Naturally, this concept would only be put in place once we had curtailed the outrageously pernickety H&S zealots and reviewed the compensation culture.

Author's comment;

We should look at the template of sports academies like Marcoussis in France which takes promising young rugby players and teaches them both the rules of the game and - by extension - the rules of life

---

Discipline –

Every day of our school-terms, almost 900 children are suspended from the classroom for appalling behaviour. Indeed, a recent study also showed that up to 90 pupils every day were sent home for violently attacking or verbally abusing their teachers or classmates and police records show that between 26 and 65 serious assaults take place every day with pupils regularly throwing chairs at teachers.

(Official figures show that 8030 children between the ages of 5 and 11 received a sanction in 2010/2011)

This tidal-wave of ill-discipline has to stop and the balance of power which has been so undermined of late by a series of useless liberal initiatives needs to swing back in favour of the teachers.

Sadly, violent crime is rife in our schools.

Teachers are treated with contempt and threatened with being stabbed on a daily basis but nevertheless we cannot allow unruly youths to hold the power in the classrooms any more so than we should allow them to, on our street corners.

This inherent violence within the school environment is driving good and experienced teachers away from the profession and the worrying trend is that 66% of teachers are now considering leaving the profession altogether.

This cannot continue and under a PDC government new discipline procedures would play a major role in redressing the balance.

———

The lack of disciplinary rigour extends throughout the schools system as it does throughout society, for many of the same reasons...because teachers' hands are tied by the Health & Safety zealots, the Political Correctness lobbyists, and the ubiquitous Human Rights activists.

It is a sad state of affairs, but due to the endemic family breakdown in this country and the poor parental guidance that is given at home, some children have a complete and utter disregard for rules and regulations leaving us, as a nation, with a generation of feral youths with no manners, no morals and no boundaries.

Children need structure, they need rules, they need boundaries in which to develop their personalities and their characters but because the short-sighted, lily-livered liberal elite decided to abandon all discipline over the last three decades, we have to start again right from the beginning.

It is a mammoth task but if we start small by disciplining;

- those who swear at teachers
- those who refuse to listen
- or those who refuse to obey an instruction

... in the fullness of time we might succeed in re-educating our whole population.

———

Swearing is endemic in some classrooms as is general insubordination and supercilious behaviour.

In fact, these days, boorish kids are proud to swear...and bad influences like the Lauren character and her 'whatev-ah' or 'am I bovvered?' retorts...or the foul-mouthed Nan character in Catherine Tate's TV sketches...or the vulgar Vicky Pollard character in Little Britain sketches do nothing to help.

Alas, coarse language is only part of the problem.

Aggressive, defiant anti-social behaviour is everywhere; just look around; look at TV programmes like East-Enders and Big Brother. Vulgarity and uncouth behaviour are now the norm in 21st century Britain.

Indeed, it has almost become acceptable in this country to act like a Neanderthal and I'm pretty certain that anyone who dares to complain is immediately slaughtered by the internet trolls and the social network bandits as an old fuddy-duddy.

However, under a PDC government, this unnecessary vulgarity and aggression on TV would not be considered acceptable before the 9pm watershed.

It is time to make a stand for decency.

No more leniency, no more lax attitudes; the mocking sneers need to be wiped off the faces of these thugs.

Aggression, brutality and disrespect must be addressed; the muttering of profanities in class – even under the breath - will not be tolerated.

NB; Under the PDC, students who stand around and goad others into hitting teachers would suffer the same punishment as the perpetrators themselves and be subjected to a disciplinary procedure based on learning about respect.

––––––

NO MORE OF THIS

- In 2010, 44 teachers were hospitalised after classroom assaults
- Two 10yr old boys raped an 8yr old girl in the playground
- Another 10yr old boy head-butted one teacher unconscious and kicked another, fracturing her leg
- Yet another 10yr old boy stabbed his teacher in the chest with a pencil
- A 14 yr old boy was convicted of carrying a gun to school
- One 15yr old boy raped his teacher as she marked books in her classroom
- And another 15yr old boy in Hartlepool kicked his teacher and then grabbed him in a headlock

At the same time...

- the father of one pupil abused and punched a headmistress for telling his son off for racially abusing another pupil...and
- another father defended his teenage son who refused to stand up for his headmaster 'because the headmaster hadn't yet earned the boy's respect';

Who are these parents?

––––––

The PDC Solution –

- We would authorise teachers to detain students after school for misbehaving without giving parents 24h notice; although they would of course be informed in some way as part of the process (by phone, text or e-mail). Teachers must have a measure of control in order to assert their authority...and that must not come with the fear of persecution or prosecution from either the establishment or the families of their students.

- School discipline panels which have paralysed attempts to maintain order will be abolished so that unruly students could be expelled without delay.
- All thuggish elements would be removed from the school environment **and it would not be against their human rights or any other rights for this to happen.** The rights of teachers and pupils to evolve in a safe, non-threatening environment must trump those of violent, disruptive thugs.
- A procedure would be put in place – at the school gates - to remove potentially dangerous weapons and the PDC would give school personnel the right to restrain students who fight in class without fear of reprisal
- We would also authorise teachers to confiscate any pornographic material and to initiate a disciplinary procedure against a student in collaboration with their parents.
- Any student found making false claims or bullying outside of school on social-networks would be suspended immediately and his / her parents called in for a meeting to discuss the student's future presence at the school. Parents would be given ONE chance to correct any dubious behaviour and if that was unsuccessful or if the behaviour continued beyond the realms of normal social integration, then more radical measures would be enforced...

...and finally, violence in the school environment would be considered in the same light as violence on the street with the same punishment, just like violence on the football field is now being taken to court. *(See the Justice section for sanctions)*

Teachers (priorities) -

More men;

- The fear of being seen as potential paedophiles has driven male teachers away from teaching in primary schools; in fact, between 20 and 25% of primary schools in the UK have no male teachers teaching in them whatsoever which means that many young children are growing up in this country without any recognisable male role models in their lives...as quite often there is no father-figure at home either.

- This paranoia driven by the feminist movement which has demonised men in every sector of society has created a situation where young men – often being brought up by single mothers - have absolutely no male role-models, while at the same time, over-protective young mothers are reluctant to leave their offspring with male teachers because of unfounded suspicions.

- This demonization of men has to stop.

- Sadly, we are already producing generation after generation of fatherless young men in this country but if they do not get more support many of them will be destined to a life of crime and failure; they need more male role models and not footballers or actors or wannabe reality TV contestants; they need real role models, successful businessmen, Olympic athletes or maybe just a responsible adult they can turn to...like a teacher.

More mathematics teachers;

- We desperately need more quality mathematics teachers in this country; inadequate subject knowledge bedevils the English education system, but especially in mathematics - Teenage mathematics skills are no better than they were thirty years ago according to a study by Kings College London and Durham University...and that cannot be deemed acceptable.

Regular assessments;

- To keep them up to date and on their toes, teachers should be re-assessed every five years; Trainee-teachers who have to take a mathematics test 37 times – as one did - before passing need to be guided into another career.

Author's comment;

I would also suggest that teachers live as close as possible to their school to avoid any disruption due to bad weather. We recently saw that teachers were unable to get to school because of the bad weather, forcing schools to close unnecessarily.

Complaints –

Four thousand complaints are made against teachers in this country every year but the vast majority of these complaints have very little or no foundation; often they are just retaliatory acts made by immature, embarrassed students.

These days, in this media-savvy age, children and young people are very aware of their power as potential victims and witnesses...and it's clear that unscrupulous parents too are playing the system trying to get compensation...but how can it be right for a head-teacher to be suspended and hauled before a public tribunal for trying to make her students do their homework, obey the school rules and behave honestly?

How sad it is that pupils know their rights but not their responsibilities... or their times-tables.

This culture of trying to get teachers into trouble has to stop. I am sick of reading about good, honest teachers having their reputations needlessly besmirched, sullied and dragged through the mud by a system that systematically believes often mendacious and vengeful pupils over the word of a professional adult.

At the last count, one in every four teachers has been the subject of false accusations by pupils; that is unacceptable.

Teachers shouldn't be treated this way; they should be treated with more respect.

Now I understand that we have to protect the children, but why do we systematically take the word of immature, often intellectually-challenged but devious young children over the word of mature adults, who are seasoned, experienced professionals?

It cannot be right that teachers' rights, including their human rights, should be ignored in this way when even the most frivolous charge from a pupil can lead to their suspension or the loss of their career.

Indeed, it is scandalous that we have reached a situation where teachers are presumed guilty until proven innocent.

This injustice and the tipping of the scales in favour of the children cannot be allowed to continue because, unless it is reigned in, it will only get worse.

We need to reform child freedom laws in order to retake control – no more suing of parents and teachers by scheming, disaffected children.

Shouts of 'I'll get you sacked if you come near me' or 'my parents will sue you' cannot and would not be tolerated by the PDC.

Of course, the erosion of teacher power in favour of the students rights coincided with a generation of parents who were not enforcing logical rules at home either...and this abdication of responsibility by a generation of parents who were no more than children themselves has sadly created a society where nobody respects any rules and loud-mouthed students have been allowed to exploit the situation – but this emasculation of teachers has to stop.

Authority has to remain with the responsible adults; the alternative is uncontrolled anarchy in our classrooms.

Some examples of complaints from pupils –

- A 13yr old complained to the police that a teacher had punched him, when in fact <u>he</u> had punched the teacher – the teacher was suspended and his marriage was threatened by the stress caused.

- In another case, a dedicated head-teacher was forced to resign for pinning a violent boy against a wall to stop him from striking other pupils
- One teacher was sacked for misconduct because he grabbed a disruptive pupil's arm in art class – the boy replied 'get off or I'll stab your eye out'.
- A respected deputy headmaster with an unblemished 41yr career was forced to resign after a 7yr old accused him of assault.
- Another teacher with 25yrs experience resigned because a female student made a complaint that he had touched her bottom when pushing a stool out of the way. Naturally, brainwashed by the compensation culture, the parents immediately threatened legal action, but the worst thing is that once the teacher had resigned, the girl admitted that there was no truth to her complaint; it was just a prank – a malicious prank that ended the career of an honourable man
- Yet another exemplary teacher was prosecuted for excluding a pupil who was continually telling racist jokes and sadly, one teacher died amid allegations by <u>her colleagues</u> that she had tried to give <u>too much help</u> to her students
- And finally, a dinner lady was suspended and charged with gross misconduct for revealing to a girl's parents that she had rescued their 7yr old girl in the playground from four boys who had tied her to a fence and were whipping her with a skipping-rope.

This example was symptomatic of the New Labour years <u>when the only crime you could get sacked for, was telling the truth</u>. Indeed Tony Blair and Gordon Brown had a shameful record for persecuting whistleblowers and dissenters who dared reveal institutional lies, their own wrong-doing or their incompetence; we must not go back to that time.

The PDC Solution –

I believe that we should maintain the anonymity of teachers who are accused of misconduct – in the same way that I believe that we should withhold the identity of rapists and rape victims – to avoid any adverse publicity ruining their careers or impacting on their trials.

Today, because of the lack of structure in the lives of young people, combined with the insidious compensation culture which has simply added to the problem, more and more frivolous cases are being brought against teachers by unscrupulous pupils and their parents...and yet, recent statistics show that only 2% of claims against teachers turn out to be true.

It is time for head-teachers to take a firmer stance – to defend their staff and not to buy into the idea that all teachers are bad and that all children are good.

I believe that school governors too, should be a lot more supportive of their teaching staff and that those who, for whatever reason, cannot back the head-teacher with common sense and reason need to be removed. I would also suggest that spineless board-members who cannot stand behind a teacher falsely-accused because they do not have enough gumption or perspective to see what is happening in the bigger picture need to stand aside.

The police and local councils also need to look at the way they deal with these issues – of course we have to protect the children but systematically blaming the teachers and ruining their careers by announcing their names and providing the press with their photographs should not be the norm.

It is not always that black and white and immature children who know their rights while not knowing the difference between right and wrong should not be systematically believed.

Of course, if the allegations are proved to be true, then the teacher must face the consequences but until such time that a verdict is pronounced the anonymity of all concerned must be preserved.

Parents also need to be included as part of the plan to avoid confrontation between them and the school. Turning up at the school and threatening teachers with intimidating behaviour is unacceptable and does nothing but undermine the teachers' authority.

Exams –

Over the last decade or so, rather than acting like responsible administrators exam-boards in the UK have been acting like supermarkets giving customers what they want.

Well, I believe it is time that we changed that inexcusable state of affairs; it's not fooling anyone.

We have to stop pandering to this silly New Labour idea that everyone's a winner even when they are not because to do so, devalues the whole system.

We have to start giving students what they are asking for…and that is an honest appraisal and a realistic assessment of their potential; a true reflection of their academic ability.

What is wrong with being honest? Doesn't it fit into a politically-correct dogma?

No sector in any industry progresses inexorably year in year out – peaks and troughs are inevitable, they are a part of life and for that reason there is no way that exam results could be systematically better every year over a sustained twenty year period without someone somewhere having tweaked the system somehow.

Nobody will ever convince me that students have been getting progressively and steadily better every year for the last 20years – every year better than the last.

It is simply not possible to sustain such constant progress…and when I see the results and the quality of the generation that those twenty years have produced, where some of them have left school without even mastering the basic 3R's, it is clear to me that something in our education process is very wrong.

Of course there will be a chorus of disapproval from 'over-anxious parents' and 'weedy teachers unions' to my statement but it is time to face reality and redress the balance. Our education system has been short-changing children for decades, sending too many 16yr olds out into the world with very poor literacy and numeric skills – not to mention a total / complete and utter lack of aspiration.

Here is the perfect example; when a class of 12 year olds was asked recently if they knew who Churchill was; everybody put their hands up; impressed, the teacher asked the star pupil in the front to eulogise about the great man, expecting a clever, reasoned response. However, she was left flabbergasted by the girl's answer, as every one the students responded in chorus – Miss, everybody knows who Churchill is, he is the dog on the insurance ads; that, my fellow citizens is the level of our children's intelligence.

Sadly, much of this folly is down to different exam-boards competing with each other to offer the easiest paper so that the schools in their area rise up the ludicrous league tables…but we really need to stop sacrificing our children's education in the race to fill government targets and appear higher on these pointless league tables.

Education, while it should be competitive in the classroom and on the sports field should not be a competition between school governors for validation from politicians but sadly schools are judged on how many A-C results they achieve in GCSE not in the number of disadvantaged bad-boys they manage to redeem. There is a real anomaly there that needs correcting.

Our children's education is not a commodity; it is too important to be used and exploited for political gain and back-slapping.

It is not a myth; grade inflation does exist – the public knows it; they can see it every day with their own eyes; it is only the politicians and the education quango-crats who are in denial…and to a lesser extent the teaching profession who fear losing their jobs if they speak out.

There is absolutely no way that over 90% of our intellectually challenged young-people are deserving of an 'A' Grade in their exam results – I would like to believe it is true but the fact is, it's a complete contradiction of the reality that we see every day on our streets.

We have to stop dumbing it down; nobody is being fooled. Children are leaving school as A-students when in reality they cannot even read or write.

In the small town of Bury, they even give out certificates to youngsters who 'know how to get on a bus'.

This cannot go on, and therefore, in order to stop this race to the bottom, the PDC would introduce a national syllabus to stop exam-boards competing with each other to be the easiest.

BTW; Ofsted (the **O**ffice **F**or **ST**andards in **ED**ucation, children's services and skills) which costs the taxpayer £207 million a year, is in need of a complete overhaul – it is hopeless, toothless and wholly ineffective.

PDC Policy –

Education is fundamental to a society's capacity to prosper.

A decent education broadens horizons; it provides authority, moral leadership and through sport, an appropriate outlet for aggression.

The PDC would install a results-driven ethos which promotes respect for the teachers and each other; no blaming society, no culture of victimhood and no bad teachers.

Moreover, as girls now regularly outstrip boys at every stage of education - and working-class white boys in particular - it has become imperative that we address the same issues of discrimination and exclusion for boys and men as we once did for women.

School standards are woefully low but rather than blame teachers, we should blame the bureaucracy which forces them to meet targets instead of doing their jobs properly; we need a war on red-tape.

Tony Blair wanted a multi-cultural society and his open door policy on immigration has led to an increase of 57% in the number of ethnic pupils in our schools.

This is a staggering influx and the make-up of our society - and the direction that Britain takes in future - will be forever changed by that decision.

Now we could sit and discuss the cynical reasoning behind Tony Blair's decision until the cows come home but the reality is, we cannot turn back time; those children are here now and we have to help them and help them integrate.

We have to do more because without an education the boys take to crime - we all need money to survive - and the girls get pregnant in order to claim the benefits and the financial incentives that come with them.

We need an ethos that inspires respect, success, effort and ambition; we need to teach our young people more about self-awareness and acceptance of responsibility...but most importantly we need to renovate our decaying education system – a system that has been depriving our children of a decent education for far too long.

Sport –

Schools are offering 60% less sporting activity these days because of Coalition funding cuts and yet this was the last thing that they should have done when childhood obesity is on the rise.

Thousands of playing fields were sold off between 1979 and 1997; Tony Blair sold off another 200+ while he was in charge and now another 30 more are up for consideration.

We need to stop selling off our playing fields.

Now I understand that space is at a premium and that the number of pupils is constantly increasing because of an immigration-fuelled baby-boom but taking away physical activity from our young people is very short sighted.

We need another course of action.

Does logic and common sense never enter into the minds of our posturing politicians?

The weedy New Labour dogma of abandoning competitive sport in school so that nobody ever experienced the pain of loss had a devastating effect on sporting and academic standards in this country and the introduction of fun-sports such as cheerleading, yoga and circus skills (juggling) to replace the pitch-based sports which could no longer be practiced was the most woeful attempt at sticking-plaster politics.

The PDC would promote competitive sport with winners and losers... and would support anybody trying to give our children a healthy lifestyle.

Other Issues –

School-places; we need to end the Post-code lottery for the attribution of school places; make it more flexible. It is ridiculous that in some cases two children from the same family have to go to two different schools at opposite ends of the town.

Faith schools; the PDC, as a secular administration, would phase out any government funding for faith-based schools...but naturally, if people still wanted to maintain these schools because of their religious beliefs then of course they would be free to do so through their own means as long as they integrate the basic curriculum that we would be setting out alongside their religious teachings. I do despair however, that these schools not only educate but also indoctrinate their children leaving them no objective choice as to their beliefs.

Holidays; we should do something about those who exploit special events and school holidays to triple their prices.

Travel firms, hotels, and air lines all exploit captive markets unfairly.

I understand the concept of supply and demand but it should not equate to extortion.

Could we not stagger school holiday periods between regions to prevent travel agencies from hiking up the prices unduly for families?

The PDC would champion any travel company which did not hike up their prices during school holidays with a new 'seal of approval' scheme.

CCTV; the PDC would look into introducing CCTV into the classroom. This would be done not only to weed out unruly students and truants but also to protect teachers from harm and false accusations.

It would also combat bullying, aggressive behaviour and vandalism and bring back a sense of security to what has become a difficult and challenging environment.

It could also be used as a constructive aid offering feedback about ways of improving teaching techniques using actual real-life examples of good-teaching.

However, it would not be judgemental or performance linked in any way...although bad teachers would naturally improve or be released.

Access to the images would be restricted to the school's board of governors and the images would be destroyed every month if no incidents of any note were reported.

NB; We shouldn't have to use cameras in the classroom but until we get the next generation of young people through, having instilled upon them the difference between right and wrong and a value and respect system that they can follow, there is no other way.

―――――

...and finally...here's an idea...

Maybe we could create an incentive scheme that rewarded personal responsibility among sixteen and seventeen year olds. Any students who got a job during the summer holiday would receive an extra credit at the end of the year that might just tip the balance in their favour.

A simple letter from the employer would act as proof of what they had done and that letter could subsequently serve as their first reference, the first evidence of their burgeoning responsibility and maturity when they go looking for a job after graduation.

―――――

University

Firstly; let me make this clear...

Under the PDC, all education establishments would be secular and this would naturally include all universities too, unless they were specifically funded and independently run by a particular religious persuasion.

This means that the rules on wearing ostentatious signs of religion as set out in chapter three of this manifesto would apply...because I believe that universities are for learning and not for indoctrination, sectarianism or conflict.

Religion and cultural choices derived from religion must be left at the gates of our educational establishments, and if a student or a teacher cannot observe or respect those rules then that student or teacher would have to find an alternative solution to their respective situations.

A new British Bill of Human Rights adapted to British Law would reflect this ruling...and include any other official institutions (court-rooms, hospitals, town-halls, airports etc) where the verification of a person's identity is an imperative.

Author's comment;

I have to say how much I am saddened by the fact that, in this country;

- we champion people with no talent,
- we lionise people who are prepared to humiliate themselves on any number of inane reality TV shows,
- and we idolise people who live in the fatuous world of celebrity that has swamped our collective consciousness over the last decade or so...

...while at the same time, vilifying anybody displaying a modicum of intelligence.

For example; a young woman who recently helped her team win the University Challenge programme on TV was panned by the internet trolls and the social network sites for being too intelligent, rather than being held up as a shining example for her peers.

This is just another example of the direction that this country is going in; down and down...dumber and dumber.

———

Now, aspiration is a wonderful thing and should always be encouraged... but the deluded New Labour policy of trying to get 50% of teenagers into university was always going to be a pipe-dream.

Of course I understand the thinking behind it, to give as many people as possible the chance to go to university - unless it was just another cynical ploy by New Labour to gain the youth vote - but unfortunately the reason for university education is not just to spend three years partying and chilling - a lifestyle that I'm sure most of us would enjoy – it is to nurture and support the most intelligent amongst us so that they might go on to improve all our lives in some way in the future.

The 'access for all' policy sounds good as a socialist ideal but sadly it has totally diluted the value of a university qualification these days to the point where they have become almost meaningless to employers, resulting in the glut of unemployed graduates that we now have on our unemployment register.

The PDC would have a different approach.

———

Funding;

Our universities and our seats of learning should not just become businesses offering their renowned teaching-skills to the highest bidders from abroad; they should also be there for OUR young people, to educate them and prepare them for the future.

Everybody understands the need to finance the running of educational establishments but the recent dilemma we faced concerning the funding of university education is as much a moral issue as it is a financial one.

I do not agree that university educations should necessarily come with a price-tag. Our young people are our future and as a generation we have a moral obligation to do whatever we can - no matter the cost - to help the generation that follows ours;

- to go forward with confidence,
- to improve the society we are all a part of...and
- to ultimately perpetuate the human race

...thanks to the education and the knowledge that we as the previous generation will have passed on to them.

That is the perfect model of course and in an ideal world I am certain that it would be the case; however I am very much aware that after decades of mismanagement of the nation's purse by any number of bungling politicians, we are now in a position where we have to do all we can to balance the books...and sadly even our education system has to contribute to that national cause.

Nevertheless, I do not believe that those who choose to work in vocational public service industries should begin their careers with £27K of debt simply because they wanted to receive the necessary training to accomplish that task.

At the same time, I believe that we need to reverse the trend of bringing in people from abroad to work in the service industries. It seems preposterous to me that we have so many unemployed young people in this country who are desperate to validate their lives through employment and yet they are not being given the chance or the tools to do so. Meanwhile, the number of foreign workers increases year on year.

––––––

Author's comment;

Hospitals are recruiting Spanish and Portuguese nurses in record numbers while British applicants are being refused places on training courses. Bosses say that there are not enough British-trained nurses to meet demand; well let's start training them rather than paying foreign recruitment agencies to send us people who might not have the level of training we should insist upon.

5000 training places have been axed since the last election; this is so short-sighted and does not reflect the reality of an aging population needing more and more care.

––––––

The PDC would rectify that state of affairs by educating and training our own **Nex-gen** to take on the responsibility of these jobs while at the same time offering them a structured start to their professional careers.

And to begin with, the PDC would provide funding and university places for anybody wishing to pursue a career in one of the public service industries such as;

- nurses (hospital / community)
- doctors
- midwives
- dentists / hygienists
- teachers
- clerical / support staff for any of the above
- childcare experts to work in crèches etc
- care-home workers
- engineers (to research desalination and coastal erosion etc)
- plumbers and electricians

...although a cap might have to be introduced if particular courses were significantly oversubscribed.

These courses would be fully funded but there would be a pre-arranged condition attached to each place granted.

For example; to qualify as a dentist takes 5 years; the government would fund that training for those five years on condition that - once qualified - the graduate then worked within the NHS for an equal amount of time – on a 'starter' salary.

In this way, the qualified graduates would gain experience in a controlled environment and the government would recoup some of the costs from its initial outlay.

Then, on completion of that obligation / residency - and only on completion of that obligation / residency - could the graduate then leave and go abroad...or set up in private practice if they felt it was in their best interests.

This policy would slowly flood the country with a new generation of qualified personnel offering reasonably priced treatment - along the same lines as the low-cost service in France - and once we have enough capacity to cover the dental needs of the British people, we could then expand our services to include paying health tourists.

These contracts would naturally be binding, and if broken – for whatever reason - the student would have to repay the university fees with interest.

NB; For those tempted to go abroad before the 'obligation period' had been concluded; payment would be demanded before any emigration visas were validated.

Of course, those who were able to pay the fees normally – without the government's support - would not be subjected to these constraints.

––––––

On the other hand, those who opt for careers in more lucrative sectors of the economy such as the law, politics or banking - *and who could look forward to earning 10x, 20x or 50x the 'Emgee Ratio' at some point in their careers* - would have to pay for their university tuition at the going rate...as their generous future salaries would easily absorb the incurred cost without much hardship.

No subsidies would be provided - no matter the community or background of students - in these sectors, as we already have an over-capacity of lawyers and bankers.

One exception would however be considered; I do not believe in positive discrimination but I do believe that it is time that women were more involved in the political process...and as a result the PDC would look into sponsoring young women who want to study politics so that, as time went on, their numbers would become more representative.

––––––

No funding would be provided either for 'Mickey Mouse' courses such as 'how to audition for the X-Factor' and indeed the majority of such courses would be quickly phased-out.

We would also streamline university education by reducing the number courses or modifying others...maybe introducing a university degree in police law for example – as an alternative to judicial law that would concentrate on police forensics (CSI). The same contractual obligations would apply; the course would be paid for – locally or centrally - and then graduates would have to 'work off' the cost as an intern in community policing – allowing more on the job training - before being officially posted.

One last point; university courses would need to be redesigned; 12 hours of tuition every two weeks spread over four years is wasteful, inefficient and completely unrealistic. We need better working timetables and shorter, more productive courses.

NB; We would need to increase capacity in technical colleges to prepare young people for the small business revolution that we would be promoting (see industry chapter) and we would also need to create or overhaul the Regional sports academies (based on county lines and population density) that would be providing the education and training for the sports animators to be employed in the Magnet Centres. (see industry chapter)

University academics and professors;

We all know that the standard of education has declined over the last thirty years and that fact – as it is intrinsically linked - cannot be disassociated from the standard of teaching.

Therefore, those members of the teaching profession who have lost the drive, the motivation and the commitment needed to teach their respective subjects to the best of their ability would be invited to stand down in favour of a more...enthusiastic colleague.

Fees;

British students

For those universities offering courses in law, politics and banking etc, (where graduates will earn very high wages upon graduation), there should be no limit on what they can charge.

For other universities and technical colleges where the qualifications will lead to a 'standard' wage, the fees could be set by the universities themselves with a ceiling according to their individual criteria put in place in their mission statements and based on potential earnings after graduation.

However, for those who cannot afford to pay but deserve to have the chance of a university place because of their unique ability and rigorous exam results, the PDC would put in place a bursary / scholarship scheme to help them.

This idea could also be introduced on a local government level. Funding could be organised through local authorities on condition that students work in the community that has funded them – under specific rules that would have to be set out beforehand - for three years or so after graduating. This would allow the community that had contributed towards the student's education to benefit from it for a while through a little *quid pro quo*.

At the same time, the PDC would create or support a charity that finances under-privileged children in university.

———

Foreign students –

Foreign students who want to benefit from our education system would have to pay the full rate.

However, we would probably have to maintain a quota policy on overseas students in our top universities so that UK students were not squeezed out completely. A percentage of places would have to be set-aside for top British students.

NB - Hundreds of foreign students - mostly from the EU - currently owe £75 million in unpaid loan repayments, effectively getting a free education in the UK and leaving the British taxpayers to pick up the bill.

This has to be addressed.

Why can't we ask their governments to advance the fees and let them claim the money back through their tax system as we do, once their citizens are back and working in their own country?

———

University places –

We also need to apply some logic to the university applications and admissions procedure.

Why can't we offer university places on the basis of mock A-level results taken in January and then confirm those places once the real grades are known in August.

This would surely reduce all the fraught-ridden clearing work undertaken at the last minute.

———

Benefits

Author's comment;

> The British people will always fight the corner of the underdog
> but there is no place in a fair and just society
> for the idle and the ungrateful.

The original purpose of the benefit system was to support people genuinely unable to work...and to help others survive during spells of unemployment; it was never meant to be a lifestyle choice.

The concept is highly commendable but sadly, over time, this laudable ethos has been corrupted and exploited...and allowed to expand and drift without any guiding direction by a succession of unethical and weak-willed politicians afraid to tackle its core failings but happy to use its capital for political gain whenever possible – much like the NHS - to the point where it has lost all sight of its founding principles.

For example; in a deliberate ploy to sway the electoral balance the New Labour party allowed vast swathes of the UK to become dependent on very generous benefit payments, calculating that, come election-time those claimants would inevitably vote for them. This was as cynical a measure as their nefarious open-door immigration policy - which flooded the country with more than our fair share of the world's misery – and completely unworthy of a party that wants to govern this country.

There are many words in the English language that annoy me, but none more so than the words...entitled and deserved...two words that have – over the last thirty years - formed the basis of a whole new sub-culture of British society.

The Benefit system was intended as a safety net for those who through circumstances beyond their control - genuine unemployment or disability - were unable to care for themselves...but human nature being what it is, we now have any number of people in this country from illegal immigrants, to gangs and people who don't even live here exploiting the UK benefit system, not to mention those who do live here and just work the system because they have no moral conscience.

£1 billion is scammed from the Benefits budget every year and this cannot be allowed to continue.

———

The load being supported by the British taxpayers – in order to look after those in our country who <u>are deserving</u> and who <u>are entitled</u> to those benefits - is already putting a huge strain on the country's reserves, so I believe that those areas of abuse which are creating an extra burden on the public purse need to be addressed;

To begin with;

Overseas -

The benefits paid out in this country by this country's taxpayers should go to those people who live here and contribute in some way to this country's way of life. The benefits budget is not a bottomless pit to be plundered with impunity by the rest of the world.

Therefore, I believe that we should clamp down on the amount of Child Benefit being sent to Europe every year for children who have nothing to do with this country.

Figures vary, but the latest estimation suggests that up to £4.9million of British taxpayers' money is sent abroad every day by immigrants claiming for their families who will <u>never ever</u> have anything to do with this country.

The British people are amongst the most generous and charitable people on this planet...but it is not the role of the British taxpayer to feed or look after the rest of the world.

The UK already sends billions of taxpayers' money abroad every year as part of its foreign aid package and for that reason I consider that we are already doing our part for the world's population.

Of course, we would like to do more, we would love to help each and every one of the world's poor...but that is just not feasible; it's not realistic. Their own governments, the EU and the world's humanitarian organisations need to do more to help these people.

It is not the British taxpayers' responsibility to do this.

Lets use some common sense here and get our priorities right. We still have people starving and living on the street in this country; <u>let's help them first</u>.

Obviously, we would have to throw off the shackles of the EU before we can do this - because it is EU policy to allow EU citizens to claim these benefits - but as set out previously, jumping from the Titanic would be one of the first measures that a PDC administration would enact.

Secondly, we should clamp down on the extraordinary amount of disability payments being sent abroad every year; over £52 million in 2007. Who are all these disabled people?

...and finally, we should re-examine the case of 'ex-pats' who are claiming the annual heating allowance for homes in France and Spain; if these people remain in this country, all well and good; if they choose to go and live abroad in a warmer climate then they should forfeit the <u>UK heating allowance</u>, no matter their 'entitlement'.

Benefit payments which are sent directly abroad every year (excluding those claimed here and then sent abroad)

Figure from 2007

Attendance allowance	-	£3m
Bereavement benefits	-	£18m
Carers' allowance	-	£1m
Disability living allowance	-	£11m
Employment and support allowance	-	£1m
Incapacity benefit	-	£41m
Jobseekers allowance	-	£1m
The winter fuel allowance for ex-pats	-	£16m
Total	-	£92m

Pensions – the PDC would also review the widow's pension arrangements for spouses born abroad and living abroad...who have never contributed anything to this country or even set foot here.

Child Benefit –

This planet only has so many natural resources and in order to make those resources stretch for as long as possible we need to do something to limit or reduce the demand on those resources.

Over-population is a global problem and needs to be addressed (see chapter on immigration)

The PDC would suggest that the UK could do its part by limiting child benefits to three children and no more; a measure that would contain the overall expansion of the population and reduce the growing number of irresponsible people having large numbers of children just to claim the extra benefits.

———

Now, some might say that all child benefit should be scrapped; that if you cannot afford to raise children, then you should not have them. I believe that that is a little too draconian but I do believe that the current system is too generous and doesn't encourage responsible parenting adapted to people's circumstances.

Therefore the PDC would continue to extend a helping hand to young parents but only for the first three children.

- The first child would receive the full benefit amount
- The second child would receive half the amount...and
- The third children would receive a quarter of the amount.

The decision thereafter, to have any further children would then have to be made by the parents in a responsible manner taking into account whether or not they could afford it.

We have to start living within our means.

This measure would of course have to be phased in over time to avoid any undue hardship on existing families whose benefits would slowly be reduced - incrementally - year on year...but these transitional arrangements have to be put in place to wean people off state-dependence.

———

To ease the transition and off-set the loss of money, we would raise the threshold for those in the lower tax bands to compensate for the reduction. This would make it more profitable to work and help not only those with children but everyone in that lower-income tax bracket.

We would however, for the sake of coherence and to link up with the 'Coming of Age' policy that the PDC would be introducing, maintain child benefit for 'children' up to the age of 18, unless of course the child leaves school and takes up full time employment before that milestone occurs.

―――

Families would of course have to be managed sensitively while the adjustments back to a more logical standpoint were being made...and any family adversely affected by the new rules would naturally be taken care of and dealt with on a case by case basis.

For some in the wider community this might appear unfair in the short term but the children already here should not suffer during the transitional period back to sanity.

It will be difficult; I understand that...but we have to increase personal responsibility and reduce the child-benefit budget.

The PDC would also look into restricting child-benefit payments to those in the lowest tax bracket rather than offering it universally...and as these claims would have to be made initially in person, hopefully only those who really need to, would attend.

―――

Childcare – along with the not-for-profit day-care centres that we would be introducing as part of the Magnet scheme (see industry and commerce chapter), the PDC would also consider George Osborne's idea on child-care vouchers...but rather than giving the vouchers to homes where both parents are working, we would look into giving them to people and particularly single parents whose earnings are below the first tax threshold in order that they might use the free-time to look for work or pursue some kind of further education, even part-time.

The scheme would be limited to two children per family.

Those house-holds where both parents <u>are working</u> would not be forgotten either as they would be able to use the new 'not-for-profit' day-care centres mentioned above for a nominal fee.

––––––

Examples of benefits abuse –

- A couple with twenty children got divorced so as to obtain two separate houses.
- One man who had a wife, a mistress and 14 children complained about not getting enough money in handouts…or a big enough house.
- A mother of six invented 15 foster children in order to claim benefits for them
- Then we had two recent cases of 13 and 15 children families qualifying single mothers for free housing, transport and tax exemption.
- And finally most recently we had a feckless father of twelve who, having been given a new super-home to house his family, ranted indignantly that he could have fifty children if he wanted to - because the State would pay for them - when he was criticised for his lifestyle choice.

In the UK, there are currently 190 families with ten children or more receiving over £60.000 a year each from the benefits pool…and there are countless other cases of feckless men producing numerous children with numerous different women besides; indeed, one man has sixteen children with fourteen different women.

This in intolerable and I cannot begin to express how deeply I abhor the shameless arrogance of ignorance…and the lack of responsibility shown by all these people.

Author's comment;

There are also large families who work and who do not rely on the State to support their lifestyle...which only goes to prove that it can be done... and confirms that those mentioned above have by their own actions made a lifestyle choice to live on benefits.

It is unfortunate but we have reached a point in this country where we need to enact 'revolutionary' change in our behaviour in order to remedy these kinds of situation and that kind of mentality.

When it comes to a point where people are 'breeding' children - as in the recent Philpott case - with the sole aim of claiming the benefits that those children generate...we have all lost our moral compass...and the benefit system has gone too far.

We have to encourage more personal responsibility.

It cannot be right that a family can be better off claiming a benefits-package than working.

Reminder;

Bigamy is illegal in this country.

Therefore, in the interests of fairness - and in order to respect the law which applies to each and every citizen equally - Islamic claimants who practice polygamy would not be allowed to claim married benefits for each of their four wives under a PDC administration.

Author's suggestion;

In conjunction with the supermarkets - maybe we could introduce some kind of card-system – similar to the top-up cards for mobile phones where a percentage of a person's benefits is credited every week and has to be spent on food...and not on alcohol or cigarettes – the USA uses food-stamps but surely a more modern approach could work.

Young women –

Every year in this country we have 40.000 teenage pregnancies which is the highest figure in Western Europe.

This is unacceptable and I believe that the Government needs to re-think its policy of handing out money for teenage pregnancies. I have already addressed this issue from a moral standpoint in the chapter on education but as far as the financial element of the problem is concerned, we have to stop providing young girls - and they are young girls, not mature women or young men – with a life-style based on what they can claim on benefits as soon as they produce a child.

These girls get pregnant – deliberately or not – knowing full well that the British government and its taxpayers will provide for them when they give birth no matter what, with an array of different benefits.

- They are given council houses to live in (taxes and utility bills paid)
- They are given food and money for their children's care...and
- They are given travel expenses to help them get around

The State has, to all intents and purposes, taken over the role of provider for these young women...and their children...and sadly, because there are no fathers around to help them, these girls become dependent on the benefits they receive and go on to live their whole lives trapped on or just above the poverty line.

A worrying new statistic shows a generation of young mothers living in this country with no jobs, no money, and no partners; very few of them work and most live on benefits.

We need to reverse that trend; we need to help these young women out of this spiral of hopelessness by offering them a solution...and not by giving them more benefits.

The 'coming of age' policy that the PDC would introduce (as set out in the chapter on education) would undoubtedly reduce teenage pregnancy and increase personal responsibility...but first of all, we have to stop rewarding fecklessness and irresponsibility.

Perhaps we could start by raising the age at which the housing allowance can be claimed. This would force teenagers to stay at home longer...in a hopefully more moral and controlled environment.

Comparative example –

Two girls leave school at the same time –

One takes a job as a trainee hairdresser; the other becomes a single parent.

Five years down the line, the first girl, having finished her apprenticeship is earning £200 a week as a qualified stylist.

The second girl, having had five children from five different fathers, has never worked a day in her life but is earning £440 a week from the benefits system.

It cannot be right that we reward this fecklessness more than we do hard-work.

And as for the young men who get these girls pregnant;

We need to root out the irresponsible behaviour and the 'who cares' attitude of the young men of this country born out of arrogance and ignorance.

There is a young man somewhere in this country <u>who is still in his teens</u>; he is unemployed and has had 7 children with 7 different girls...all of whom are living off the state.

This cannot be seen as acceptable behaviour.

We need to improve attitudes and education, especially sex education.

People need to be made responsible for their actions.

Ignorance, loose-morals and underhand logic used to circumvent the benefit system should not be tolerated.

———

Author's comment on benefits and fertility;

The fertility landscape in Britain is changing;

- sensible middle-class women are choosing to have fewer children and they are choosing to have them later in order to concentrate on their careers
- while at the same time, the feckless that live on benefits are having more and more children in order to increase the number and the amount of benefits that they can claim...because of those additional children.

Hence, the bearing and raising of children has largely become the province of the lower classes.

What is happening in Britain, because of the benefit system, is a kind of **reverse Darwinism** where the intelligent minority is retreating and the intellectually-challenged - **but sexually potent** - are thriving.

It is a downward spiral back to intellectual oblivion.

———

Incapacity benefit; this is another area that has to be addressed;

There are currently 3.3 million people in this country claiming over £13 billion a year in incapacity benefit...and latest figures suggest that over half a million of these claimants are in reality, fit to work. This is unacceptable and the PDC would reinforce the Fraud Investigation Units in order to combat and reduce this abuse.

A few examples of those found claiming incapacity benefit under false pretences;

- A man who claimed he could hardly walk without assistance due to a bad back was caught Moto-cross riding
- Another who was claiming £17,000 a year in disability benefits was caught participating in a triathlon
- Another who had claimed over £300,000 in disability benefits, because he was supposedly confined to a wheelchair, was caught hula-dancing
- One man sailed the Atlantic while claiming incapacity benefit
- Another who claimed he couldn't walk following a knee operation was caught playing badminton and another was caught playing Widow Twankey at his local theatre
- One man who claimed to be paralysed from the neck down and who had received £400,000 in benefits was caught dancing at his own wedding
- A woman who claimed her back pain made it almost impossible for her to walk or get out of bed was caught playing golf
- Another woman who claimed her bad back meant using crutches was caught sky-diving and another who claimed she could only crawl around her house because of mobility issues was caught doing judo
- One woman who claimed she had to use crutches to get around was caught in a bikini on a monster pool-slide in Spain and another who claimed she was so weak she couldn't dress herself or cook a meal was caught running marathons

- Another woman who said she was too weak to climb stairs was caught scuba-diving
- One man who was claiming for crippling back pain was caught lifting a car off the ground as a stunt and another who had claimed £4,000 in incapacity benefits because he had a 'balance problem' was caught tiling roofs, checking chimneys and clearing guttering on several occasions

...and finally; one person in eight involved in the riots of 2011 was claiming disability benefit...although it never stopped any of them carrying TVs and laptops out of looted shops.

These people have all been caught but there are many many more out there for the fraud repression agencies to catch and the PDC would prioritise these benefit recovery operations.

Unemployment benefit –

The PDC would look into raising the age at which teenagers could apply for benefits to 18 in line with the 'Coming of Age' policy and claims would be means tested to include their parents' situation. (A copy of the parents' most recent tax return would have to be presented when registering)

If this confuses people, please re-read the first paragraph of this chapter.

Criminal gangs –

This is another area for the fraud repression agencies to target and prioritise because every year we pay out up to £2 billion to foreign nationals who are working the UK benefit system.

These people are running any number of illegal schemes in order to milk the benefits system...but one of the most horrendous of these scams involves the trafficking of children into the country simply to claim benefits for them...and when the traffickers cannot get enough children into the country, they simply forge a number of birth certificates in order to top up their claims.

This is happening on a regular basis and proof of this activity was revealed recently when a Ugandan gang was convicted and jailed for creating hundreds of false birth certificates - with the help of a corrupt registrar - in order to claim £4 million in child benefits over a 20 year period; one man was actually claiming benefits for more than 100 children.

In another case a family of Czech migrants pocketed £500,000, using over a hundred different bank accounts to harvest the cash.

These people have no morals and no boundaries and need to be processed out of our society.

PDC solutions –

The PDC would provide extra funding to extend the network of benefit-fraud inspectors working for the DWP (Dept of Work and Pensions).

These inspectors would target the organised gangs who are bleeding the system of millions of pounds, as well as the incapacity cheats and any other area of abuse.

For example; Heroin and crack cocaine addicts claim £1.6billion in benefits only to spend it on their habits. This is not acceptable use of taxpayers' money.

Of course, justice for all would be the PDC's first priority; then when people knew what they risked for cheating the system I believe a sea-change would occur in their behaviour.

Secondly; although it would be very costly and very time-consuming initially, all social benefit claims would be means-tested and the entitlement rules tightened up.

Once again I am convinced that the long-term savings would be worthwhile.

This task would be undertaken by the army of bureaucrats and civil servants in local council offices currently getting paid to send each other e-mails, twitter feeds and 'selfies'.

In addition to the social benefits I believe that the universal allowances such as child benefit and fuel / heating subsidies should also be means-tested.

This would be done by deferring them for a year and refunding them as a tax rebate once people's tax returns had been processed according to whether the person qualified or not – i.e. his / her tax bracket.

In the intervening year, those that really needed the allowances would be able to apply for them alongside their other benefits...and I would like to believe that the added layer of bureaucracy would dissuade all but those who really needed them from applying.

All other benefits would also be reviewed and updated.

Housing benefit;

The PDC would review the rules governing housing benefit to avoid teenagers claiming the money simply to set themselves up in homes at the tax-payers expense.

This does not mean that we would abandon housing benefit; we would simply push back eligibility a couple of years until people had reached a more mature and responsible age.

Subsidised housing;

People who live in subsidised housing, who depend on the taxpayer to pay for their accommodation and who do not pay market-price for their lodgings must realise that their situation can be reviewed at any time, especially when their family-situation changes.

It cannot be right that a person - or a couple – whose children have flown the nest – still inhabits a house with extra bedrooms that they no longer require at the taxpayers expense.

If it is their own home that they have paid for…there is of course no issue but for people who live entirely off the state, it must be a rule that their accommodation is adapted to their minimum needs.

One exception would be made however; people of retirement age would not be moved out of their homes or their neighbourhood during their last years (though hopefully, they would already have been down-sized by the time they get to that age).

Subsidised housing for foreign nationals;

Firstly, it is unacceptable that people come to this country - for whatever reason –

- simply to take advantage of our generous benefits system…or
- to obtain subsidised housing…and living conditions that they could only ever dream of in their own country - all at the British taxpayers' expense.

Secondly; it is completely out of order for those people to then complain that they are not being given enough support...while at the same time trashing and disrespecting the very homes they have been given to live in.

This lack of gratitude is a kick in the teeth to the British public who have offered them a safe haven; especially as in many cases the British taxpayers themselves could never afford to live in the homes that these people are given.

What is more; I find it unreasonable that 'foreign nationals' come to this country demanding to live in a certain area (city, town or suburb) and are indulged in those demands by over-sensitive local officials.

It cannot be right that foreign nationals living on benefits are housed in mansions in London for example - at the taxpayers' expense - simply because they '*want*' to live in central London.

Who wouldn't 'want' to live in central London? The problem is...most of us cannot afford it.

Of course this example is an anomaly - or *at least I hope it is* - and probably says more about the council that allocated the house to these people than anything else but henceforth – or at least *under a PDC administration* – all councils would be instructed to find more suitable and less controversial living arrangements for these people.

Sure, I understand the reasons why these people would want to live in a particular area - family ties and cultural links being the most obvious - but councils should not be dictated to by those asking for help; we can offer these people a choice of where they would like to live on the forms that they have to fill out...but if there is no available housing in those chosen areas, within the council's budget, then I feel it is only right and proper that they accept what is offered to them, even if it is in another part of the country.

It is a horrible cliché, I know...but 'beggars can't be choosers'.

That said; if any foreign national felt that the solution being offered to them was unacceptable, unsatisfactory or below the level of their expectations then they would always be free to return to their country of origin...and the PDC would gladly put a protocol in place to help them with their repatriation.

For information;

In a recent case, a Latvian single-mother of ten who was already claiming £34,000 a year in benefits <u>demanded</u> a bigger house just because the one she had been given, in which she was living free of charge was, in her opinion, too small. I wonder how a British person with ten children would be treated in Latvia.

However this woman is not alone; a jobless British mother of eleven who is already receiving £60,000 a year in benefits is having a £400,000 house built for her and her children, at the taxpayers' expense, saying that if it isn't big enough she will demand an even bigger one.

Local Government / Councils

Comment on decentralisation;

We have seen throughout the history of mankind that the concentration of power in one place heightens the risk of megalomania and increases the potential for executive abuse. This is why I believe in decentralisation. Decentralisation reduces the possibility of centralised authoritarianism while increasing the level of democracy in the regions. I believe that if we are all to move forward together, it is imperative that power and responsibility should be delegated, shared and spread around, rather than monopolised by a small group of self-indulgent policy-makers huddled together in their Westminster bubble.

Scotland and Wales have both negotiated devolution pacts with England and yet British politics still revolves around Westminster. We must break this stranglehold.

Firstly, I have to say that I find it encouraging to see that there is still some community spirit left in this country – residents willing to rise up and rebel against abusive council rules – just as it is reassuring to see some constituents holding their politicians to account if they do not do what is required of them.

This is why I believe that we need more local MP's – people who will be and feel accountable to their own communities – rather than anonymous strangers parachuted in by this or that political party.

I also believe that Local Councils should participate a lot more...and play a greater role in managing their respective communities...and I suggest they do this by providing a greater variety of services than they do currently...thereby not only creating jobs but also promoting community spirit and a bustling hive of activity in our city-centres which are slowly being deserted.

We have some amazing architecture in this country full of splendour and nostalgic grandeur - much of which houses our establishment and our civic institutions - but I believe that in many cases these wonderful buildings are under-used. In my opinion it would be much more sensible and much more practical if they were used more productively as part of the community rather than standing idle as a reminder of our former glory.

Westminster has taken away all responsibility from local communities, counties, towns and villages to become a faceless autocratic machine with which the public cannot relate but the PDC would hand it all back under a new charter;

So, as well as being in charge of hospitals, schools, highways and the usual council services (refuse collection etc); I believe that councils should also be put in charge of several other areas of responsibility;

Each local council should have a...

Fiscal department;

- This department would correlate all the necessary information and paperwork for car registration, driving licenses and passports before that information was sent – once approved - to a regionalised office for rubber-stamping and issuing. Hopefully this would eliminate errors and save the time and money currently being wasted in sending incomplete or wrongly filled-out paperwork back and forth.
- This department would also be authorised to rubber-stamp house sales; we need to stop fleecing home-owners with obligatory payments to lawyers just for making these transactions legal.

- This department would also have a permanent desk – open to the public - to deal with tax queries and offer advice on any fiscal issues that people might have
- and finally, this department would collaborate with the new Border Police to fulfil their part of the protocol concerning immigrant registration and work permits

---

Family department; (children / elderly)

- This department would be responsible for **child-benefit payments**. Under the PDC parents would have to apply to their local council to claim child-benefit in person...and the information given at that point of contact would then be used to link it to other possible benefits and entitlements. It would also be used to control and check council tax payment. This would be a separate service leaving the job centre to concentrate exclusively on employment issues, though the databases would be linked to correlate payments.
- This department would also be linked to social services for child visits, parenting courses and elderly care.
- It would also handle **adoption** requests. I believe that councils and child-services need to be more pro-active in finding adoptive parents to avoid children being left in the system; two years and seven months which is the current average is not good enough.
- This department would also oversee school placements in order to avoid a situation where children from the same family are separated and sent to different schools at either end of a town or city. Common sense must prevail.
- This department would also be in charge or issuing winter fuel payments to the elderly while at the same time offering them loft-insulation and boiler maintenance as part of the national economy drive to save on energy use.
- It would also deliver free bus passes to the elderly, indexed on the retirement age. This policy would not be means tested; if a person was eligible all that person would have to do is turn up at the town hall with proof of his / her identity, date of birth,

NI number and proof of address. However, we would strongly recommend that those who do not need to make use of this facility refrain from doing so (millionaires, people who have their own cars etc). The hidden benefit of this policy is not only that the elderly are mobile and playing a part in society, it also means that they are able to get into town to spend their money in shops that desperately need their custom.

- This department would also look after the provision of temporary safe-havens for young women - In collaboration with social services, I believe that local councils should provide shelters for women and children where they might find refuge and be safe from a violent, threatening or abusive boyfriend, husband or father. This service would also be extended to young women being forced into marriage and those who might be potential victims of honour killing.

Community department;

- This department would be responsible for the administration of the 'tradesman charter' and the operation of the people's hot-line (see chapter on Industry and Commerce)
- It would also be responsible for co-ordinating the 'late-night' transport service in collaboration with the alcohol industry... and
- Other duties would include the creation of the position of Sports Co-ordinator (this person would be in charge of the different Magnet-centre sports facilities and the organisation of inter-communal sporting challenges)

This shake-up in local government would create a whole host of new jobs but before this revolution could take place, the first priority of a PDC administration, as in Westminster, would be to get rid of the army of unproductive officials currently warming the seats in council offices waiting desperately for their retirement packages to kick in.

Local government in this country is blighted by a multitude of petty, self-serving civil-servants who all seem to have been lobotomised of any common sense and logic, and whose only task seems to be to interfere with the lives of everyday people, using any number of inane schemes dreamed up by the pen-pushing PC / H&S brigade.

Consequently, under a PDC administration, all these misguided jobsworths would have their positions and their roles re-assessed.

Those that could be re-trained would be reassigned and allocated new duties...and those who were unable to carry out due diligence, for whatever reason, would be guided towards another path of fulfilment more appropriate, more in keeping with their intellectual potential.

After that, going forward in its new streamlined form any future local government bureaucracy would have to pass the test of the PDC's three guiding principles – the respect of nature, common sense and logic.

In addition, anybody in a position of responsibility who felt that he / she was unable to apply these three simple rules would be asked to step aside so that someone with the right attitude and approach might step in. They would then be offered a less demanding role more in keeping with their aptitude and a salary more commensurate with their intellectual competence.

Alternatively, if no agreement could be reached, these people would be suspended without pay while they made their case against dismissal through the newly reformed Justice System.

Under the PDC, the 'jobsworths' and the people working in Health & Safety or Political Correctness who came up with any of the diktats mentioned below - or any similar rules which persecute the innocent for no apparent reason - would be immediately suspended and re-trained... or given a new role more commensurate with their IQ.

Author's definition of a jobs-worth*; any person who says 'It's more than my job's worth' (to act with commons sense, logic or reasoning)*

I really have no time for these stroppy, inflexible, petty, pedantic, self-important little officials who stroll around with a set of keys or a clip-board pretending to be some kind of all-powerful authoritative figure.

These box-ticking bullies are the bane of our lives and will have to go.

—◆—

Some examples of how council officials have been abusing their authority;

- A council warden fined a couple for parking outside their own home while they went inside to fetch their seriously-disabled son
- A grieving mother was ordered to remove a memorial bench from her son's graveside and lease one from the council for five times the cost (impose a style by all means so that anarchy doesn't rule, but don't exploit people; its not right)
- A man was fined for putting a letter in a street-bin; the council went through the bin and found his address
- A mother was accused of fly-tipping by her local council when she dropped off some clothes at an overflowing charity recycling bank
- A pirate flag put up for a child's birthday was banned as unauthorised advertising
- A woman was fined by council workers for feeding the birds in a park
- An 85yr old woman was told to drag her old TV to the kerb (H&S rules prevented the council from walking up her path to pick it up)
- Another council wanted to make 80yr old pensioners drag their dustbins for 1½ miles before they would empty them
- One woman was taken to court for putting rubbish in the wrong bin; this frivolous action was later quashed

- Bin bullies put a council ban on a 95 yr old, half-blind war veteran for mistakenly putting a bottle in the wrong bin.
- Litter police fined a child for dropping a piece of sausage from a sausage roll
- Officials at Argyll and Bute council hounded a schoolgirl for posting pictures of her school dinners on the Internet
- One council contractor only filled-in half of a pothole because the other half bordered a private access road
- Another council equipped their traffic wardens with tape-measures in order to fine motorists for parking too close to or to far away from the kerb
- Another threatened to sue an 82yr old widow for brushing some dead leaves into the gutter
- Retired-pensioners were threatened with prosecution for not cleaning up graffiti in their back alley
- Surrey county council took legal action against a couple for removing weeds and rubbish from in front of their home

Similarly;

- It was wrong for Westminster Council to pull the plug on the electricity supply when Bruce Springsteen and Paul McCartney were singing in concert last year...
- and a little more diplomacy could have been used during the 2012 Olympics when an officious little busybody snatched the relay-baton out of Usain Bolt's hand after he and his team had won the world-record breaking 4x100 relay – Usain Bolt wanted to keep the baton as a souvenir but the unbending official 'only following orders' would not allow it.
- And finally; it was very close but a national embarrassment was narrowly avoided last year at Wimbledon when Andy Murray was about to serve for the match at 23h.02. The 'jobsworths' were ready to turn out the lights but thankfully at the last minute someone used some common sense and the debacle was avoided. Nevertheless, the threat was there...and it was real.

Now, of course I understand that there are rules against noise at certain times and that health and safety issues make everybody in this country paranoid but in exceptional circumstances people must be able to make a judgement call without fearing for their job.

Nobody should ever be put in a position where he feels that his job is on the line if he makes a judgement-call. Logic and common sense should always prevail.

> The PDC would always support anyone who
> used common sense and logic;
> the 'jobsworth' on the other hand, would be managed 'appropriately'.

———

BTW; The PDC would put forward direct elections for the position of Mayor so that the person elected could be held accountable by the local community. However, this would not extend to Police Chiefs as they need to follow a national directive.

———

Salaries and bonuses –

The way that council chiefs and their staff are remunerated needs urgent attention as abuses of the system are costing the tax-payers huge sums of money in expenses, pay-offs, redundancy and pension packages.

As a country, we have been in the grip of recession for the last five years and yet thousands of council chiefs – whose salaries are paid by the very same taxpayers who are struggling to keep their heads above water - are earning over £100,000 a year; that is almost four times the average wage.

Indeed, 70% of council chiefs earn more than the Prime Minister (source; Telegraph) and some have even continued to receive salary increases of up to £17,000 in recent years while at the same time cutting front-line services including libraries, care for the elderly, youth clubs and refuse collection.

In fact, one chief executive recently received a pay rise of £40,000 while driving through deep swingeing cuts to front-line services. That has to be wrong, especially as ordinary council workers have had their salary rises capped at 1%.

These people have to start living in the real world, they have to start getting their priorities in the right order and if they are unable to do so, they should step down.

It is time to move beyond this selfish Greed Generation with its elitist tendencies...and re-introduce a more collective, all-inclusive approach to community life which includes incorporating a measure of sanity into the public purse.

Currently;

- 42 council staff earn more than £250,000 a year,
- 636 council officials earn more than the Prime Minister who earns £142,500
- More than 2500 council staff earn over £100,000
- and another 30,000 town-hall pen-pushers earn over £50,000 a year each

Council taxes are constantly rising but they are not rising to improve or increase services for the tax-payers; they are rising in order to finance these bloated salaries for council jobsworths and that is not right.

These practices and these salaries need to be reviewed It is time to divide up the wealth pie more evenly, more equally and more fairly.

I for one, would much rather see;

- 1000 people gainfully employed on salaries of £25,000 a year

...than...

- 500 on £50,000 a year or
- 250 fat-cats on £100,000 a year

...and I would also much prefer that they reinstate the discretionary services that have been abolished...than pay additional bonuses to these fat-cat civil-servants just for doing their jobs.

Greed cannot be the only motor working society's levers as we go forward and in order to rein it in we need more accountability; nothing tempers a man's greed more effectively than the magnifying-glass or the microscope of accountability.

———

Therefore, just like in Westminster, the PDC would roll flat the wage structure of local government and implement a complete overhaul of pay and salaries, including any bonus system among civil-servants and local government representatives – thereby re-distributing the salary-budget, creating more jobs and getting rid of the 'something for nothing / reward for failure' culture.

Under a PDC administration, being a local councillor would no longer mean spending four totally unaccountable years on a publicly funded ego trip.

Salaries would be capped for the majority of executives, although the basic salary for those at the very top in larger town and cities would include an incremental supplement depending on the size of their municipality in order to take into account the extra duties and responsibilities.

This cap would effectively mean that the £200,000 a year salaries and more that some council executives are currently enjoying would become a thing of the past. Local government should be about serving the people, not about personal gain and if these people disagree with that idea they are welcome to go and work in the private sector.

The PDC would also force councils to publish their employees' salaries - including bonuses - so that the taxpayers paying those salaries and those bonuses can verify whether they are getting value-for-money or not.

Transparency is the only deterrent to temptation.

––––––

Compensation –

The PDC would also clamp down on fatuous / trivial compensation claims being made by council staff;

Recent examples include;

- one person claiming compensation for falling out of bed,
- another was compensated for back strain after carrying six tins of baked-beans,
- one person was compensated for being trapped in a lift,
- another complained of back-pain after putting some paper in a printer and another from carrying a bag of dog faeces

Local councils also paid out up to £15 million in compensation to car-owners whose cars had been damaged by pot-holes.

This is another area that has to be addressed as once again, I would much rather see 300 people employed to fill in pot-holes, thereby making life better and easier for us all – and providing jobs for them and income-tax revenue for the Treasury - than see tax-payers hard-earned cash being used to feed the compensation culture.

––––––

Funding –

Local councils are funded by government grants, council tax and business rates.

They account for 25% of all public spending and while central government imposes some mandatory services in exchange for those grants, each council then decides on what discretionary services it will provide.

———

Now, the extra work-load created by the services mentioned earlier would increase the number of staff needed to carry out these extra duties and this would need to be financed.

Restructuring the pay system would be the first measure helping towards the funding of these new missions as we redistribute the available budget, but other measures would also contribute.

- The TV license money which would no longer be handed over to the BBC (see media chapter) would be collected at local government level and used by a newly-created department in each town council to help fund the investment in sporting-facilities in each of the Magnet centres (transparency)
- The fines recovered by speed cameras would also contribute towards financing the community police force and not just disappear into central government coffers.
- Savings would be made by councils being more pro-active in recovering uncollected taxes; a recent estimate suggested that £2.3 billion was still outstanding in uncollected taxes

...and finally, the endemic profligacy and free spending of council officials would be reined in...and any frivolous use of funds would be outlawed.

The spending on council credit-cards is absolutely staggering –

- £30 million has been spent in the last five years on chauffeur-driven cars
- One council spent £6000 on Sat-navs for their lawn-mowers.

- Council officials regularly go on all-expenses paid global jaunts in order to learn how to raise extra money. (I'm sorry but that kind of information does not need an all-expenses paid trip.)
- Taxpayer money has even been spent on golf lessons

...and of course, £262 million has been spent on 'compromise agreements' which effectively act as gagging orders to prevent people from revealing the murkier side of council-life.

———

Under the PDC, this kind of folly would cease.

We would introduce an auditor's office for each region to comb through their accounts, financed out of the £114 billion budget that is currently handed over to local councils.

These auditors then would report directly to the cabinet with a mission to highlight any local official – **by name** – who they suspected of using or abusing taxpayer money unwisely; for gagging orders for example.

The details of that official would then be forwarded to HMRC for further scrutiny.

These auditors themselves would also be subject to a performance review and impromptu visits from the HMRC to keep everybody on their toes...and the appropriate sanctions would be put in place to avoid any questionable activity / behaviour.

———

Other Issues -

Snooping;

The PDC would also clamp down on any abuse of the snooping / surveillance laws introduced by David Blunkett (Regulation of Investigatory Powers Act 2000 aka RIPA)

Ever since these laws were introduced in 2000, local councils have been over-reaching their powers and making wholly inappropriate use of this anti-terrorist legislation to snoop on citizens who are just going about their daily lives.

345 local councils went on 9600 spying missions in the last three years in order to monitor such threats as;

- dog fouling
- litter dropping
- people fishing illegally
- people flaunting the smoking ban
- people making fraudulent applications for a school place
- people putting out their dustbins too early
- and people with planning issues

That is nine spying missions a day.

Of course, the majority of these trivial matters never come to anything... but the cost of organising them comes systematically out of the tax-payers pocket.

We need more responsible and cost-aware leadership;, because at the moment spineless, incompetent council officials are handing over tax-payers money far too readily.

The coalition recently introduced the condition that councils should obtain the permission of a magistrate before launching any more of these misguided missions but I believe a more rigorous tightening of the law is needed.

Under a PDC administration, those councils that make a request would have to name the person making the request and that person would then be held responsible if it was deemed that his / her spying mission was unfounded, unwarranted and a waste of public money. A sanction would then be handed down and anybody found to have abused the system would be vetoed from further access.

This protocol would hopefully encourage a more responsible attitude.

The British public does not want a council snooper on every street-corner trying to catch them out as they go about their daily lives - *the idea is reminiscent of Cold-War Russia where KGB informants were stationed on every floor of every hotel to monitor movement in and out of the rooms* – and those in charge need to be aware that if they continue to hound and badger the people of this country in this Orwellian-style regime the British public will eventually react; look how the youth vented their frustrations in 2011.

It might take time but the British <u>are</u> capable of revolt.

Housing –

The housing policy in this country is a mess because, like in so many other areas of British politics nobody has had the gumption to grasp the nettle and deal with the problem;

- because it is too complicated,
- because it is too expensive...and mainly
- because there are no votes to be won in it, which is all politicians are really interested in.

The PDC would put in place a new building initiative for social housing financed by both central government and local investment - in conjunction with the Magnet Centre project - to replace the millions of council houses sold off under Mrs Thatcher that have never been replaced...despite the exponential increase in our population.

The shortfall in the market is huge.

Therefore, as a first step, the PDC would ask each council to compile a list of all the boarded up streets in their sector and all the schools, hospitals and other council / government buildings that had been closed down or were no longer in use...and together we would come up with a comprehensive plan to re-develop these areas and create new communities, new jobs and new hope.

Any existing brown sites would also be cleared and any unfinished construction sites would be either completed or re-designed to accommodate more living-space.

The PDC would also support the recent initiative that suggests councils sell off any top of the range houses and use the money to build more affordable housing in greater numbers. Estimates suggest that this initiative could raise around £4.5 billion.

However, while creating new capacity the PDC would also clamp down on existing council-house tenants who sub-let the properties and pocket the difference. That activity would be rooted out and offenders would be processed out of the system.

We would also introduce rent-control in certain areas, on a regional basis to clamp down on exploitative landlords.

———

Meanwhile, another area of concern would be the handing out of building certificates to developers in areas with a flood-risk which leaves those duped into investing in those areas devastated when their homes are flooded. This is the equivalent of legally sanctioned fraud and it cannot be tolerated.

———

And finally, the PDC would maintain planning permission and respect for building regulations for conservatories and house extensions. We cannot have a free-for-all in this sector as the coalition has been suggesting because to do so would lead to anarchy; building regulations have to be respected for both safety and insurance reasons, because human beings being who they are, they would quickly start cutting corners and the results would be catastrophic.(remember the Titanic)

———

Refuse collection and recycling –

I really have a problem with the fact that just 9% of all the waste generated in the UK comes from domestic households, and yet those same households bear the brunt of all the government directives concerning recycling. House-holders are constantly threatened with fines and their bins don't get emptied if they don't comply...and yet those who produce the other 91% of the waste are never bothered. This has to be addressed.

The PDC would put a programme in place to promote innovative re-cycling ideas - looking into ways of using our rubbish to produce electricity - and this increased investment would not only create jobs, it would also create a demand for recyclable material thereby prompting the re-introduction of weekly refuse collection which in turn would help in the prevention of fly-tipping and the spread of urban foxes that we are currently experiencing.

In addition, the PDC would ask local governments to come together and produce a cohesive and unified policy on re-cycling...because at the moment the public is completely foxed by the disparity in information.

We need a coherent and consistent policy for recycling waste where the same sorting criteria and the same coloured bins are rolled out throughout the country in a universally standardised policy.

Local councils simply have to get together to produce a clear and concise re-cycling leaflet that everyone can follow and abide by. Then, as part of their policy to re-build community spirit trained local officials could visit every home in their area to explain the policy - and the fines that would be handed out to those who refused to comply.

In conjunction with the above and in order to reduce litter further… and to minimise the use of plastic in all its forms…the PDC would also encourage a return to the use of glass bottles for soft-drinks. Discussions would take place and in partnership with the supermarkets we would re-introduce the 'deposit' system where bottles could be returned to a collection point in exchange for the deposit paid. The bottles could then be re-cycled.

This would add another layer to the general sense of personal responsibility that we would be trying to re-create.

———

The PDC would also revise the money-grabbing New Labour initiative of doubling the land-fill taxes for councils which had the knock-on effect of increasing council taxes for everyone…

…and finally, as part of our plans to encourage a community spirit, we would also address the problem of people dumping rubbish in their front gardens; sofas, fridges or car shells etc. This slovenly behaviour is unacceptable. It blights a neighbourhood on so many levels and drags down the tone of the whole community.

In some areas, a service already exists to remove large and cumbersome items from anyone's front door upon request and this service would be rolled out throughout the country as part of the re-cycling policy.

We need to have more pride in our homes and anybody who would disregard this initiative would be disrespecting his or her neighbours and their whole community.

Sadly, of course, as with any human pedagogy, the enforcement of these rulings would have to come with a warning…followed by a hefty fine for repeat offenders as human behaviour is not easily reformed.

———

Cars –

Parking;

Cowboy clampers have been fleecing motorists in the UK to the tune of £58 million a year.

The PDC would outlaw this exploitative independent private enterprise.

However, in an effort to avoid errant and illegal parking, we would recommend that local councils invest in a fleet of tow trucks themselves and create a pound where cars that had been illegally parked could be stored until a fine (high enough to be dissuasive) was paid.

Of course, this activity could be sub-contracted out but under the PDC the ultimate responsibility and the liability of any grievance would always stay with the local council and its representatives so that they remain locked in and accountable to the taxpayers that they represent.

———

Local councils would also need to sort out the problem of rogue taxis. This could be done using the new trade-identity card scheme which features in the Industry and Commerce chapter.

———

Speed-camera fines -

Up until now, local councils have been told to send all receipts from speed-camera fines into central government – to help with the general shortfall and cover up the financial incompetence of those in Westminster – and if they (the local councils) needed finance for their own wasteful spending programmes, they were told to raise the funds themselves by milking the motorist in other ways; hiking up the prices of municipal car-parks and stationary violations etc.

However**,** many Councils are now using traffic-enforcement powers simply as a lucrative revenue stream which borders on exploitation and even entrapment in some cases.

This anomaly has to be tackled.

I have already addressed what would be the PDC policy on speed-cameras in the Police chapter but I would suggest that the actual receipts from speed-cameras be devolved to the local councils, thereby adding to their overall budget and helping to finance the new community police-force.

Given the choice, the British public would much prefer to see more police on the streets than more cameras; speed or CCTV.

————

Parks and Streets;

I believe Local Authorities should be encouraged to do more about keeping their communities clean.

Street wardens and park attendants could be introduced or re-introduced to impose new cleanliness laws thereby creating jobs (maybe for the older generation).

Currently, just like the police - who are plagued by a target based revenue culture - park wardens – where they exist - are incentivised to issue litter fines.

However, the mission of these new wardens would not be 'zero tolerance' as currently being imposed in the Welsh Valleys creating a backlash from the public. It would be one of common sense, guidance and information; these wardens would not be target driven but community spirit driven.

Of course, the sanction has to be there to dissuade the deliberate or repeat offender but more discretion should be used.

These wardens could also monitor;

- the dog laws (fouling, breeds, behaviour)
- the by-laws (spitting, swearing, urinating in the street etc)
- the community rules (tree / bush encroachment, bins etc)...and
- the anti-dumping initiative in people's front-gardens.

Weather Management –

Local government needs to manage cold weather better.

We need a better network of heavy duty 'gritting-trucks' and because of our changing weather patterns, we also need to invest in a machine / tractor that farmers could buy for their use all-year round but which was also adaptable in some way so that a snow-plough fitting could be easily attached to the front of it allowing the farmers to help clear the snow in their local areas. (Some kind of tax relief could be offered to farmers if they invested in this equipment)

We should also have a contingency plan where those who have access to 4x4 vehicles can be called upon in a crisis. (maybe we could register them for some kind of road-tax rebate if they were called upon)

We also need more solid grit boxes (anchored firmly into the ground to avoid thieves); I'm sure that a modern design could be found to blend in with local infrastructure.

We should also look into developing non-slip, non-freeze pavement surfaces and insist on people performing their civic duty of clearing the snow from the pavement in front of their homes; if everyone does a little, life is made easier for all.

Supermarkets and garden centres could help in this by stocking bags of grit so that, in the event of an emergency, everyone could be prepared.

These measures should take care of any local problems but **Central government** would naturally have its own national policy in place too, where the Army could be called in to clear any strategic areas, airports etc.

———

One final point...

Libraries;

I believe that knowledge and the transmission of knowledge is absolutely vital to society and crucial to the future of humanity...and whether that knowledge is transmitted via a computer, a tablet or any other electronic gadget I believe that the essence of that knowledge is in the hard-drive of our literary heritage. Therefore, libraries – or at least a multimedia outlet that offers access to that knowledge - should be integrated into the Magnet centre concept (see industry chapter)

———

Big Brother

Author's comment;

The Big Brother culture is going too far; we need to pull back before it's too late.

Over the last ten or fifteen years, because of the ongoing terrorist threat, the personal liberties and the fundamental right to privacy of the British people have taken an absolute hammering.

Using the terrorist threats to scare people – government after government – has slowly but inexorably eroded our personal liberties – one after the other - with any number of costly and labour intensive screening schemes.

We are no longer ordinary citizens going about our lives, enjoying the quiet freedom of our democratic choice. Instead, through a kaleidoscope of presumed guilt-by-association and derived suspicion we have all become potential suspects.

An institutionalised surveillance system now watches over our every move regulated by the police, the politicians and the civil servants who now have an entire arsenal of surveillance powers at their disposal with which to carry out their pernicious activities.

CCTV follows our every move; we are photographed constantly, our finger-prints are taken, the irises in our eyes are scanned and the very make-up of our genes, of what makes us human beings, is taken and filed away forever, just in case, all in the name of security.

However, in many cases the manpower needed - both physical and in the number of hours necessary to do the job properly - far outweighs the benefits and the results that have been obtained...and more importantly, it never redresses the balance of the democratic rights infringed in order to carry them out.

This is yet another example of the ridiculous reverse thinking, so typical of the New Labour years; let's punish 99.9% of the people (at great expense both in material and man-hours) in order to catch the 0.1%

I do not subscribe to the idea or to the ethos that if we can catch one person then it's all worthwhile; why should millions of people be penalised and have their whole lives blighted and dissected in order to catch one person?

It's like a *needle-in-a-haystack* viewpoint; burn down the haystack and you will find the needle...but by burning down the haystack you will have lost the sustenance which could have fed a population.

I do not agree that we should systematically punish 99.9% of the population in order to catch 0.1% of criminals. It's just not logical; it does not compute and it installs a constant and unhealthy atmosphere of suspicion throughout the country which feeds on people's fears, their insecurities and their prejudices.

This presumption of guilt that hangs over every adult person cannot and should not be tolerated in a democratic society.

Of course, when the 0.1% succeeds in its endeavour – whatever domain that might be in – the majority of us will be horrified and outraged (whether it be a terrorist attack, a case of paedophilia or whatever) but that rare outrage is the price we must pay to live in a true democracy; the alternative is a Big Brother State.

Ominously, the Nanny State is creeping ever more intrusively into every aspect of our daily lives, and their latest idea of allowing tax inspectors into peoples homes to count the number of TV's they have, to value the jewellery they own and to appraise the paintings hanging on the walls in order to tax them on it is clearly wrong.

The new Census rules too, asking people to reveal their earnings, their sexual proclivities and whether other people stayed in their homes overnight is again a complete invasion of privacy, which encroaches on their personal liberties.

We must resist the constant attempts by government to invade the sanctity of our homes and our private lives. It is anti-constitutional and a step too far.

The PDC would revisit each and every one of the 1043 'snooping laws' brought in by New Labour to invade our homes and our privacy...and we would re-affirm Sir Edward Coke's majestic judgement of 1604 in which he stated that '...an Englishman's home is his castle and as such a haven from those outside who would harm him or his family'.

...or as David Davis, a more recent politician once said; 'the slow but ceaseless encroachment of the State into our daily lives must come to an end'.

We need to make the distinction between individual security and national security clear – people protecting their homes or their businesses is one thing, intrusive state surveillance is another.

Political paranoia –

The lily-livered politicians who are so desperate not to lose their jobs on the gravy train and so anxious to be appear politically correct in whatever they do - *to the point of stupidity in some cases* - have allowed themselves to be influenced by so many civil liberties groups and minority pressure groups that they have backed themselves into a corner...and the society that they have created as a consequence, is one filled with paranoia, suspicion and obsessive surveillance, one which is destroying our land of freedom by stealth.

British society is now full of officially sanctioned mistrust, a mistrust that allows almost anyone to insidiously access our most personal information.

Indeed 800 agencies, each with a different agenda, currently have access to our personal details, or at least they can apply to have access to those personal details.

These include 474 local councils who not only have access to our 'private' information but also to a chilling array of snooping powers, each more devious than the last in order to catch us out going about our daily lives.

Today, every minute a request is made by one or other of these agencies to snoop on someone's phone records or e-mail account...and in 2008 alone 504,073 requests were sanctioned.

This is what 12 years of New Labour did to this country. It installed an endemic culture of suspicion which is clearly manifest in the 3500 new crimes it created during those same 12 years.

The whole country has been infantilised by micro-management and fear.

-   Police regularly stop anybody who photographs a public building
-   Jacqui Smith (former Home Secretary) wanted to introduce finger-printing in Post-offices and pharmacies; she maintained that it was only for passports and driving licences but the potential for abuse is unthinkable
-   One local council insisted that all taxi-cabs install CCTV and microphones to listen to conversations; people be warned; when jumping into a cab, ask first if you are being filmed and listened to...

- But the most sinister of these concepts is that we are all potential paedophiles and that anyone working with children however near or far has to be CRB checked at a cost of £64 per person;
  o Music tutors
  o Babysitters
  o Sports coaches
  o Volunteers working in church halls
  o Grandparents who take their grandchildren to the parks and swimming pools
  o Parents who give lifts to neighbours' children and school-friends
  o Parents who welcome exchange students into their homes and...
  o even in school – during school plays and sports days – parents and grandparents are told not to photograph <u>their own children</u> and <u>grandchildren</u> to avoid being suspected of paedophilia

This is not only wrong; it is unethical and I wonder whether in reality the grasping New Labour government was more motivated by the revenue from the £64 fee for each person...than actually protecting the public.

Nevertheless, we are losing our national identity and too many people have too many powers to snoop on innocent people; that situation really has to change.

In this country we are innocent until proven guilty – not the other way around - but that is how the 'liberty-destroying' New Labour government twisted our society.

Whatever happened to our centuries-old traditions of freedom?

Breaking news;

A new scheme has been devised to monitor every one of our e-mails and phone calls via the GCHQ (Government Communications HQ) in

Cheltenham. This will mean that freedom as we know it, will no longer exist; we will all just become potential threats to Big Brother.

CCTV – overview

The UK has the largest CCTV network in the world; we have a system in place which catches people on camera up to 300 times a day...and yet a recent Scotland Yard report admitted that for every 1000 CCTV cameras installed, only one crime is solved every year.

The police themselves freely admit that the <u>one million</u> cameras in London have helped with barely <u>1000 crimes</u>.

Surely, these figures alone demonstrate the limitations of CCTV.

In fact, studies by Privacy International over the last 15 years have consistently shown that CCTV cameras don't work as either a deterrent or an aid in solving crime; they just film it and as Crispin Blunt (the National Security spokesman) once said; 'CCTV can be a useful tool against crime and anti-social behaviour but it is no substitute for having real police presence on our streets'.

...and herein lies the problem because it is not the Police's fault.

The only reason that the Police are multiplying the number of cameras being installed around the country is because they see it as a stop-gap solution to the fact that governments are constantly cutting their recruitment budgets while at the same time increasing their workload with mountains of extra bureaucracy.

The whole costly experiment needs streamlining and re-focussing.

In fact, a major re-think is necessary as the ineffective network has already cost £500 million out of the Home Office Crime Prevention budget with very little return in reduced crime rates.

Another factor should also be considered; public perception.

Not only does CCTV do very little to prevent crime, conversely it is extremely intrusive into ordinary peoples lives, invading their privacy at every turn.

There is already a crisis of confidence between the police and the British public - for any number of reasons - but this feeling that we live under permanent surveillance only exacerbates that 'them and us' mentality.

The British public simply does not trust its institutions or its authorities because those institutions and those authorities are either betraying that trust or snooping on them constantly, making them all feel like criminals.

David Smith (Deputy Information Commissioner) once said; 'Use of CCTV must be reasonable and proportionate if we are to maintain public trust and confidence in its deployment'.

...and Chris Grayling admitted in April 2009 – 'the big problem is that the government has built up a culture of surveillance which goes far beyond counter terrorism and serious crime'.

The consensus – as far as I can see – is clear; we need to review and re-assess the Big Brother issue.

Specifics –

While I agree with CCTV systems being installed in shops etc as a deterrent for thieves...and on major streets in order to monitor crime I do not agree with a ruling that forces blanket coverage of every single establishment.

Of course, businesses that could be targeted by criminals need some kind of protection, if only for insurance purposes but forcing everyone to install it in every commercial location just feeds the paranoia.

BTW; Schemes like Crime-watch and Crime-stoppers have my full backing.

I have no issue with them being used on roads to control traffic and speeding...as long as they are not being used solely as cash-traps...but I believe that motorway CCTV cameras that read your number plate and track your every movement is a step too far.

These cameras are taking away our fundamental right to freedom which is an absolute right that must be defended at every possible opportunity if we don't want to go down the road of becoming a database-society.

Now, of course I understand that it allows police to track potential criminals but it is the same - 99.9% / 0.1% - argument as before; punish everyone in order to catch the one person doing wrong.

I do agree however that public servants who might come into contact with crime or anti-social behaviour (police officers, traffic wardens - *and can we please forget the PC names; civil enforcement officer -*, park wardens etc) should be kitted out with CCTV – on the condition that those images are automatically destroyed after a 60 day period if no complaints were made or no crime was committed.

One last point; the PDC would look into installing CCTV in classrooms for a trial period, to protect teachers from threatening students. This would however, only be a temporary measure while we work through straightening out the current generation of children whose parents have not 'parented' them correctly.

And the real crux...?

As in so many cases, it's the politicians with their usual arrogance who are not listening to the public.

They think that they know best...but of course, they don't because they have no connection to the real world outside the Westminster bubble. These people are just accountants and not very good accountants at that, who lack any symbiosis with the reality of life in 21st century Britain.

The public want more police on the streets protecting them; they don't want them sitting in darkened rooms looking at banks of screens... but of course the politicians / accountants whose priorities clearly lay elsewhere - cannot equate with this logic.

I repeat; the British public would much rather see uniforms on the street – giving men and women jobs (*the police after all are human beings who have to earn a living and provide for their families just like the rest of us*) than see billions of pounds invested in electronic surveillance systems controlled from afar that are extremely costly to run and maintain and whose effectiveness is clearly minimal.

Why is this so hard for politicians and accountants to comprehend?

I understand that because of cuts in the budget the Police are trying to replace the officers on the beat with CCTV cameras but this policy has and continues to prove ineffective.

It is time to roll it back and reverse the trend with the backing of a new government.

Surely it would be better to recruit the officers they need to do the job properly and to provide a human presence on our streets.

It might be a more costly solution to train and pay new officers than it is to buy, install and monitor CCTV cameras <u>but that is what the public wants</u>...and not only would it answer the public's concern;

- it would provide these people with jobs that generate income tax for the treasury
- it would provide them with a way of looking after their families... and
- it would help with stitching back together the fabric of our society that has been allowed to crumble, every day a little more, for far too long.

Why can't the politicians see this?

Let's look further than the balance sheet; let's look at re-building a community spirit - not one of a '1984 variety' where we are all just disconnected from the ruling elite, given a number and monitored in our every movement – but a real community spirit where we all live together, in harmony, in the respect of the law, safe in the knowledge that everyone is playing his or her part and fulfilling a role in the community jigsaw.

Databases -

When they were in office the New Labour Party was obsessed with personal data-collection which cost the British taxpayer billions, persistently infringed on their privacy and put them all at risk of identity theft.

They spent £16 billion a year on these schemes and planned to spend another £105billion...which needless to say would have been another £105billion not going into frontline services where it is really needed.

This is classic over-compensation, typical of our current generation of politicians born out of a deep-rooted paranoia and a chronic sense of ineptitude and insecurity. These are people - living in fear that they are not competent enough or morally strong enough to fulfil the role that they have been attributed - adding layers of metaphorical protection to their actions in order to avoid blame or responsibility in case of failure.

It's classic overkill.

New Labour was also behind a flurry of other new databases and the scale is vast and very, very expensive; up to £32 billion.

These included the DNA database, centralised medical records, the e-borders database (which will require you to provide 53 pieces of information before you leave the country) and the children's database Contact-Point.

How long would it have been I wonder, before we all had to have bar-codes branded across our foreheads?

———

Sadly, the unfortunate coalition (Conservative / LibDem) that has succeeded the hapless Labour Party has no more moral fibre than their predecessors, tabling the idea to listen to every conversation, read every e-mail and check every website that we ever visit.

I wonder how costly and labour intensive that particular folly is going to be?

Imagine the infrastructure needed to listen to every single conversation.

This is once again a question of ridiculous reverse thinking; let's punish 99.9% of the people (at great expense both in material and man-hours) in order to catch the 0.1%

The creeping paranoia epitomised by New Labour has now gained the other parties too and it is out of control; those in charge are abusing their position and I believe that the people need to rise up and refuse this intrusion into their lives in order to safeguard their privacy, especially as Professor Ross Anderson (from Cambridge University) suggested that; 'eleven of the data-bases *currently in use* are almost certainly illegal'.

Besides, in the current climate – all the Big Brother paranoia aside – should we really be spending £2 billion trying to spy on everybody's e-mails, phone calls and text-messages when we do not actually allow intercepted evidence in our courtrooms?

Author's comment;

The New Labour Government also spent £30 million to snoop on smokers – their priority clearly to recover money through fines, as it was with speed cameras and CRB checks. I might be repeating myself but in my view the Government should not appear to be <u>interested only in money.</u>

I also think that it is pretty significant that politicians have exempted themselves from being included in databases. It shows that they don't trust the system that they themselves are putting in place to be secure...and more disturbingly, it breaks the most fundamental rule of free society; that the same laws should apply equally to everyone and crucially to the law-makers themselves.

DNA database –

Over 6 million people are in the UK DNA database making it the largest database in the world.

It includes over 400,000 children aged between 10 and 15.

I have to ask; is it right that two young girls, <u>arrested for drawing a hopscotch-grid in chalk on the pavement</u> have had their DNA taken and added to this database.

Is that really what we want? Is that really the society that we want to live in?

...and another thing; 850,000 of those people in the database are completely innocent.

I find it morally wrong for governments to keep the DNA samples of innocent people - who have not been charged - under the premise that they might potentially offend in the future.

DNA from innocent people should be destroyed. If the police want to regain the trust and the respect of the British public, then they cannot be seen to be covertly building up their database with the DNA of innocents.

Incompetence -

This attack on our personal liberties and their cost is one thing but what is even more worrying is the incompetent way in which the Authorities are handling out personal data once they have collected it...

For example;

- Terrorist information was left on a train – <u>twice</u> in one week
- Child Benefit information for 25 million people was 'lost'
- Revenue and Customs information on 15,000 people was 'lost'
- The Health Service 'lost' discs containing the confidential medical records of 1.8m people
- A lap-top containing Army recruitment information was 'lost'
- A computer disc containing the DNA of murderers and rapists was 'lost'

...and a special mention for the DVLC which not only 'lost' data about peoples driving-licences, it actually sold people's private information to the highest bidder... which is clearly 'wrong and improper use of that private information'.

Hardly a week goes by without another scandal concerning the mass leak of private data or sensitive information by a government source... and meanwhile, a recent 'Freedom of Information' act revealed that nine local authority staff-members had been sacked for illegally accessing personal records.

This all shows that while they are obsessed with hoarding our personal information the politicians cannot be trusted to keep it private.

―――――

Author's comment;

We have all seen films where paranoid politicians or nebulous corporations try to control the lives or the minds of the world's population, to the point where people are no longer individuals, but just a series of coded numbers in an all-knowing computer that knows our every movement;

- *Enemy of the State*
- *Minority Report*
- *The Bourne Trilogy*
- *The Conversation,*
- *The Matrix,*
- *Three Days of the Condor or*
- *Total Recall...*

...are all good examples.

Needless to say, it never ends well for anybody; someone always dies...or life as we know it is completely destroyed by one or other of these psychopathic, power-hungry organisations...and the planet becomes a wasteland.

Now, of course this is all fiction, but it does give us an insight into what might happen - in the future - if we go too far down the road of Big Brother and allow all the surveillance legislation that is currently being tabled, to be brought in.

―――――

Conclusion –

Ultimately, it is the cost of our freedom that we have to calculate.

Do we live in a free democracy where our private lives are our own, aware that once and a while that freedom will be challenged by some other ideology or do we go down the Big Brother route and just become numbers in a huge database with code-bars burnished onto our forehead?

I would suggest that those who favour the second idea have no faith in humanity or in its capacity to defend its existence.

A final thought (inspired by Hazel Hargraves from Essex); if the politicians had suggested twenty-five years ago that every citizen should carry around - at all times - a monitoring device which recorded their location, the details of who they communicated with and a whole host of other personal information, there would have been uproar. However, these days people carry around Smart-phones which do exactly that... monitor a person's every move... and nobody blinks an eyelid.

Dogs

The British have a reputation as an animal / pet loving nation.

However, in 2011 the RSPCA (Royal Society for the Protection of Cruelty to Animals) received 1.3 million calls...mostly about cruelty or the mistreatment of animals...and it takes in 120,000 animals a year that have been abandoned or whose owners can no longer afford to look after them.

These figures show that the mood in the country has changed, that the violence that now haunts our streets is also being visited upon the defenceless animal population.

This cannot be allowed to continue unchecked and those people found to be harming animals should be made aware that under a PDC administration there would be a custodial sentence waiting for them, should they transgress the law; a message that should also be relayed;

-   to those reckless people breeding violent dogs
-   to immoral back-street breeders who use animals as a meal ticket...and
-   to irresponsible owners who use dogs as status symbols or to fight

---

Now, dogs are considered by many to be Man's best friend but nevertheless they are still animals and can be highly unpredictable; a point proved recently by the Queen's normally-docile corgis when they attacked Beatrice's terrier.

This is not un-common with dogs and a recent report from the Post Office highlighted the fact that there has been a marked increase in the number of postmen being bitten by aggressive canines...so there is clearly a problem here that needs to be addressed...especially as sixteen people have actually lost their lives over the last eight years as a result of one of these attacks. That is an average of two people a year being killed by dogs; a statistic that I find unacceptable, particularly as the majority of those victims have been children.

Therefore, under a PDC administration, all dogs would have to be officially chipped within a set time of their birth and registration.

If not, they would be confiscated and destroyed - and the owner would be fined and billed for the procedure and costs. (To enforce this, the PDC would equip the new Street Wardens with scanners)

———

Author's comment;

After the most recent death; that of a 14yr old girl who was attacked by four out-of-control dogs, I believe that it is time that we changed the law so that the owner of a dog that injures or kills a human-being is considered liable and criminally responsible wherever the injury takes place...with one exception; if it occurs in the context of a criminal act (e.g.; burglary)

Perhaps a Category Three (five year) sentence for owners of dogs that kill would make these people more responsible.

———

The Dangerous Dog Act 1991

This legislature banned four breeds of dog but has yet to be fully enforced.

We need that to happen and we need the law to be strengthened to include even part breeds of those four which have already been banned.

Indeed, any dog that poses a clear threat to people should be banned and under the PDC **ANY** dog that drew human blood would be systematically destroyed, no matter its breed.

———

Statistics from the ITV programme 'Barking Mad';

- 210.000 attacks were recorded in the UK in 2011
- That's 575 people injured or maimed by dogs every day

There were 6000 hospital admissions for dog attacks (the number has doubled in the last ten years) and the cost to the NHS - £3.3 million

———

Breaking news; as I write this page, news arrives that yet another 4yr old girl has been mauled to death by a dog...this cannot be allowed to continue...

NHS / Health / Hospitals

'*No society can legitimately call itself civilised if a sick person is denied medical aid because of a lack of means*'; Aneurin Bevan

---

Hospital

The NHS was New Labour's next big project and if you listen to any New Labour politician, they will tell you that they poured millions if not billions into this sector of society in an attempt to put it right.

My question is...where...where did all the money go?

- into the creation of tax-guzzling quangos,
- into management consultants...or
- into another layer of inefficient, incompetent bureaucracy

...because it certainly didn't go where it was needed most; the front line; our hospitals - those that have not been closed down - are filthy; MRSA is rife and it has been found that C-diff is killing patients on a regular basis.

A Tory spokesman recently announced that – 'three times as many people are now dying through infections in hospital as are killed on the roads each year'.

That is intolerable, but cleanliness isn't the only issue. At the same time, pressured by the accountants in Whitehall and their targets-based culture hospitals have also been putting cost cutting initiatives above patient care and safety; a practice which has led to a number of serious errors taking place as hard-pressed doctors and over-worked nursing-staff try to keep up with the relentless rhythm.

In fact, things are that bad that health professionals such as doctors and nurses are actually advising their loved ones to stay away from the places where they themselves work…and a recent survey also revealed that 80% of patients would not recommend the hospitals where they had been treated.

That is the New Labour legacy.

Author's comment;

The reputation of any establishment in the service industry hinges on three basic criteria;

- *the cleanliness of its environment*
- *the competence of its personnel…and*
- *the quality of its service.*

The out-sourcing of the cleaning duties in hospitals was the first mistake that our politicians made, because private companies, desperate to make a profit themselves, have clearly been cutting corners and not providing the level of service required of them. Our hospitals are filthy…but as nobody has been holding the cleaning companies to account, they have – being human like the rest of us - quietly eased up on every aspect of the job they have been employed to carry out (fewer personnel, fewer visits etc, etc) and the result is there for all to see.

The cleanliness of our hospitals should be paramount to all those concerned. It should be beyond reproach and it should set the standard by which every department in the hospital runs its service.

Waiting Times;

At the same time, waiting times have increased inexorably - despite the virulent denials of a string of dithering politicians - and when people do eventually get to hospital, they are often made to wait for hours in ambulances parked on the forecourts of A&E or on trolleys in draughty corridors.

That is a sad state of affairs...but what is worse...is that when patients are finally admitted to the hospital and allocated a bed, the care and attention that we would expect them to receive isn't there, as any one of the numerous scandals that have rocked the NHS over recent times has exposed.

Indeed, a recent report revealed that elderly patients had been left in their hospital beds in their own faeces for days on end...and that some had even had to resort to drinking the water in the flower-vases beside their beds in order to hydrate themselves…simply because there was nobody around to take care of them; meanwhile, others have been dying of malnutrition and in one case a man was bitten by a rat as he lay in his hospital bed.

To say that that is unacceptable is an understatement; it is outrageous and yet not a single person of any level of responsibility has been sacked or held to account for this state of affairs, even for the most scandalous incompetence.

This institutional inertia has to be addressed because undoubtedly the fault lies in the very ethos of an NHS that has come to see meeting targets as more important than caring for patients.

I understand that our doctors are overstretched and that our nurses are at the end of their tethers but there is an inherent duty of care that has to be met in a hospital situation and we are clearly falling short in this department.

Of course, if they had any gumption, the politicians would be on the front line tackling these problems and offering solutions but sadly – as in most cases these days – these pseudo-leaders of our country are more concerned in keeping their jobs and their seats on the gravy train than actually getting involved in any kind of politics... and as a result, rather than grasp the nettle by the thorns, their first reaction to evidence of this appalling inhumanity has been simply to cover it up...or to pay people off with huge compensation payments and gagging orders for the sake of political expediency.

This culture of collusion is still prevalent and will remain so, until real change comes about.

Oh for a real politician with a spine and a set of principles!!

———

Author's comment;

At this point, I would however draw attention to the fact that there are still many NHS staff who remain highly motivated and totally committed to the cause, who are driven by the most deeply-rooted ethical principles; it is just unfortunate that their number diminishes with every passing day...

———

Staffing;

Successive budgetary restraint measures have also meant that front-line staffing levels have been cut to the bone – *while paradoxically... and gallingly...the number of management personnel has increased dramatically* – creating a situation where conscientious staff have to prioritise tasks rather than complete every one; a state of affairs which is inevitably and inexorably lowering the overall standard of care being provided.

However, these reductions in staff have not only impacted on the quality of the service provided, they have also and predictably had a knock on effect on the number of beds available because there is simply not the staff to look after them.

Fewer beds of course means less capacity and therefore greater waiting times...and so the problem just keeps getting worse.

This is an ongoing problem that has been getting steadily worse for decades but rather than address it and find a solution the mealy-mouthed answer of our politicians to this challenge has been to simply close-down the hospitals...despite a growing and an ageing population.

How morally irresponsible and lacking in political resourcefulness is that?

———

The solution is of course very simple in theory; it's a question of rebalancing the whole organisation;

- fewer administrators, fewer management personnel and less interference from politicians on the one side
- and more doctors, more nurses and more basic support staff on the other.

———

Author's comment;

Of course, the chaos in the NHS can be attributed to many different factors, but I believe that while those on the front line shoulder much of the blame - because they are the visible part of the iceberg - the real culprits are those who make up the bulk of the iceberg, who are unseen by the public but who make all the decisions; the civil servants, the accountants and all the other self-serving bureaucrats that feed off the NHS budget.

The NHS is overflowing with professional managers and consultants. We have 264,012 administrators and 175,646 beds. That is 1.5 managers for every bed, not to mention the 42 quangos which also live off the health-care budget.

This needs to change. We need to work towards a target ratio of 1 manager to every 12 beds and furthermore, we need to install a mandatory 'patient to nurse' ratio when planning staffing levels as they do in Australia.

———

An example of bureaucratic excess; *in 1981 there were 8 NHS press officers to cover the whole of Britain. There are now 82 in London alone. Now I understand that in the 21ˢᵗ century Media and Communications have become vitally important...but I can't help thinking that this level of staff multiplication is somehow abusive.*

———

It is imperative that we remedy this state of affairs as quickly as possible and indeed treat it as a priority, because many of the trained professionals who currently work at the sharp end of the NHS are leaving the country to go and work abroad, having had their fill of working in conditions that they feel are inadequate and unacceptable.

This phenomenon is on the rise and it is compounding our problems, creating a situation where we have to import more and more doctors from the third world - many of whom don't speak English – in order to cover the ever-increasing shortfall.

Fact; 33% of our doctors are now of foreign extraction and while we are grateful for their contribution I feel that it cannot be right that in 21ˢᵗ century Britain we have doctors treating patients;

- who do not speak our language,
- who have issues with our culture…or
- who have a problem treating women

…clearly, this needs to change.

We have to recognise the quality of our teaching in this country and tie our graduates into contracts which oblige them - initially at least - to work off the taxpayers' investment in their training (see education chapter)...and then encourage them to stay for as long as possible within the NHS with incentives and structured career plans...rather than let them leave, only to bring in doctors from abroad who do not have the same level of basic training.

———

Of course, it has to be said that we have brought many of these problems on ourselves. This is because – over the last thirty years – nobody, not a single politician has come forward with a long-term plan for the NHS. No-one has come up with any prescient thinking or visionary ideas for the future that incorporated both the flexibility and the need for adaptability required to face the challenges of a growing and an ageing population while also being financially viable.

Instead we have had a succession of disastrous, wasteful and short-term policies put in place by transient governments and inter-changeable Health-Ministers whose quick-fix solutions never project any further than the next election.

The PDC solution –

As with most of the areas of British society that have been allowed to spread unchecked like an uncontrolled mass of self-indulgence over the last thirty years, I believe that it is time to re-introduce some structure and some limits to the NHS covenant while at the same time removing the wastrels and parasites.

However, this needs to be a long-term plan and not one geared solely to the gaining of political capital in the run-up to the next election.

I believe that nobody in the UK should ever be more than 30 minutes from a hospital bed - or a maternity clinic for that matter - and as a consequence the PDC would develop a network of hospitals, using the best of what is currently available as a starting point and complementing that with a vast renovation, overhaul and construction plan based on a ratio between population and bed capacity.

Each regional hospital (offering primary care) would then have a specialised unit which would in turn be supplemented by a number of dependant satellite rehabilitation, recuperation and care homes (offering secondary care) to help with bed-management.

515

A third level of care (offering tertiary care) would also be integrated into the community as part of the Magnet Centre concept replacing the gimmicky, sticking-plaster solution of Urgent Care Centres that I believe have proved unsuccessful. These new units – staffed by community nurses - would provide non-urgent medical-support and a day-care programme for the local community to allow family carers some respite. They would also be linked to;

- the ambulance service (999),
- the social services (child / elderly)...and
- the local doctor's surgeries (which would of course still deal with all the more problematic injuries and illnesses)

The PDC would also maintain the 111 phone-service...although it would be streamlined, refined and upgraded after review as part of a Cross-European accord for the standardisation of emergency care... and incorporated into the community service set out above to enhance its local profile.

The introduction of this buffer-service would also ease the burden and the pressure on hard-pressed doctors' surgeries and on A&E departments.

Now I am well aware that the NHS is constantly being re-organised but unlike the short-term, politically-motivated polices of the major parties in recent years, this would be a thirty year project which would take into account our growing and our ageing population.

Looking to the future; New Hospitals -

Any new hospitals would have an A&E service on the ground floor – next to the reception area - for immediate access and then be divided into two distinct wings; one for women and one for men...as I believe - despite what some might say - that each gender has its own specific complications and needs.

In a recent survey 80% of those asked wanted single sex wards and I would tend to agree that that should be the case.

The top two floors of any new hospital could then be floating wards – and interconnected in the building's design – to accommodate an overflow of either sex…or an epidemic / disaster scenario. (A roof-top helipad would also allow for easy access to these wards and allow for a security lock-down or an isolation / quarantine protocol to be put in place quickly and efficiently if needed)

———

In the meantime, the first thing to do, in existing hospitals, is to re-integrate the cleaning services so that those given the job can be held responsible and accountable for the cleanliness of the wards and the hospital itself.

That would be followed by improved security and the hiring of security personnel to monitor A&E units…because sadly we make over two million trips to that service every year, mainly with alcohol-related issues…and as a consequence A&E personnel are constantly being harassed, threatened and attacked by belligerent drunks.

This needs to be addressed; we need to provide A&E personnel with protection.

———:

Design ideas that could be incorporated to improve security in A&E;

- CCTV cameras linked directly to the local Police Station
- A panic button behind the reception desk linked directly to the Police
- The main entrance could be fitted with buttons that close and lock the doors in case of an emergency or a threat and reinforced glass should be used for windows in the immediate vicinity

- The security post should be situated in close proximity for easy access to the A&E department and include a holding cell for violent or confrontational individuals.
- We might even offer A&E personnel lessons in self-defence

Security personnel would also be put in charge of reducing the amount of theft from our hospitals…because at the moment almost £13 million of hospital equipment is being stolen every year.

Of course, I realise that this initiative would not eradicate either problem completely - drunks or thieves - but hopefully it would shrink it…and I would much rather see people trained and employed as security guards protecting hospital staff from belligerent drunks…and preventing thieves from helping themselves to public property…than sitting around doing nothing in the unemployment office.

Now, this proposal might well cost as much to implement as what is being stolen, but it would nevertheless be positive economics because, while it might not stop all the theft, it would be providing jobs and disposable income for people who wouldn't otherwise have had any while at the same time creating income-tax revenue for the treasury.

The PDC would see the A&E issue as a priority and once it had been sorted and secured, we would work our way through every other service.

A lightening Time-and-Motion study would be carried out in each department to evaluate and determine the relevance of every position and every member of staff…and the Organigram of every service would be deconstructed and rebuilt around a new set of principles and priorities, because at the moment we are running a five day operation over a seven-day period and that cannot continue.

Everybody knows that the potential for dying in hospital increases over the weekend when junior staff and skeleton teams are manning the hospital...because their more senior colleagues are absent or out golfing; that too has to change.

The PDC would insist that a senior A&E doctor be on duty at all times; 24/7.

———

Author's comment;

I also see the re-introduction of the matron-role or floor manger as an imperative if we are to get any structure and improvements in care going forward.

———

Various financial issues that need to be addressed (non-exhaustive)

The NHS is haemorrhaging money at an alarming rate and as a consequence the following issues need to be addressed;

1) 30 NHS Trusts have racked up £300m of debt – a lot due to the costly and exploitative PFA initiatives set up by New Labour which are fleecing the NHS left, right and centre...and bleeding us all dry. This is the result once again of savvy business-men taking advantage of incompetent politicians and callow, bungling bureaucrats...and of course, it is the British taxpayer who is paying the price for it – this needs to be addressed.

2) Officially unpaid health tourism costs the NHS £24 million a year…but the figure is wildly under-estimated in my opinion; this needs to be addressed.

3) The Head of the Care Quality Commission earns £435.000 a year in salary and bonuses and yet our hospitals have never been in a worse mess. These outrageous salaries and bonuses have to be curtailed. Under the PDC a new pay structure would be put in place and incompetence would not be rewarded.

4) David Nicholson, the current NHS chief earns £211,000 a year; his replacement who will step up next year has been offered

£189,900. That is a slight reduction in salary but it is still excessive in my opinion.

5) 48 NHS quango-crats who have absolutely no responsibility and are not accountable for what they do or say, are currently paid more than the Prime Minister who earns £142,500; surely, this has to be unjustified and unjustifiable abuse of the public purse.

6) Recently, the NHS paid out £1.4billion in redundancy payments; 950 people were given lucrative six-figure pay-offs... and 3,200 managers who also received pay-offs have since been re-hired. This is very bad management; we need more coherence and more responsible supervision of the public purse.

7) 45,000 NHS staff call in sick every day costing the taxpayer almost £1.7 billion a year. This latent but widespread abuse needs to be investigated and addressed

8) Many hospitals are paying over the odds for their supplies. There is clearly a lot of abuse of the public purse in this particular area and it would be a priority for the PDC to clamp down on the army of middle-men taking their cut.

9) Fraud costs the NHS up to £3 billion a year; mortgage payments, iPods, digital cameras and computer games are all being paid for with NHS funds. The PDC would also target this abuse.

10) We also need to reduce the compensation bill for 'medical blunders and staff accidents' – two reasons;

  (A) They shouldn't be happening in the first place and certainly not in such great numbers (this shows that the personnel is stretched)...and

  (B) The NHS simply cannot afford it. Last year £1.4 billion was paid out in compensation. That is simply unacceptable.

...on the positive side;

The influx of a new generation of doctors and nursing staff would slowly remove the need for 'agency staff' to be drafted in from abroad to cover shifts, thereby saving the NHS £1 billion every year; money which would then be used to cover the salaries of the new generation...

...and with this new potential and the expansion of the number of doctors and qualified personnel that would be graduating from our universities, we would also be able to multiply the number of out-reach initiatives – like those currently being tested in China and the Middle East – to other places around the world, thereby generating more cash and recognition for the NHS through the spreading of our knowledge and our medical expertise.

———

In the mean-time, while the above policy is being filtered in, we would also have to look at the cost of the LOCUM GP's that we would still be employing; £1,350.00 per shift as is currently the case, is simply immoral.

———

The NHS is also sitting on over £2 billion of empty space in buildings that they no longer occupy...but continue to maintain and pay for. This is an outrageous waste of public money and doesn't sit well in a time of swathing cuts to front-line services and jobs in healthcare.

The PDC would call for an inventory of these sites and if it was considered that these buildings had no viable use and couldn't be modernised or upgraded with the latest technology – because of the expense that that would entail – then they would be sold off.

The money received from these sales would then be re-invested in upgrading existing hospitals or creating new facilities where there is the greatest need...and of course as a by-product of this initiative more jobs would be created in demolition, in construction and in other related areas.

———

Other 'non-financial' issues that would need to be addressed;

- **Obesity** – The NHS spends £85 million a year on obesity itself (gastric bands / bypass surgery etc) and £5.1billion a year on obesity related problems; in fact surgical procedures for the obese increased by 70% between 2008 and 2010 – this is clearly an issue and needs to be addressed but firstly we have to revise the BMI criteria which is qualifying perfectly healthy children as obese

- **Alcohol** - The NHS spends almost £3 billion a year on alcohol related problems and yet it keeps getting worse; we certainly need to address this problem.

- **Breast-cancer** - The 'Jade Goody effect' of inciting young women to get tested for breast-cancer is wearing off so we must re-enforce the message

- **Maternity wards** – child kidnapping from hospitals is a reality and therefore we need to introduce a system of security anklets for new-borns to avoid abduction scenarios – these are currently in use in France and proving very successful

- **Blood** - I disagree with the idea that our blood and blood-plasma stocks should be managed by private enterprise; what are the politicians going to sell off next; our souls? This is a very sensitive issue and one that should remain within the realm of national supervision. We should not be applying commercial principles to what is a voluntary and altruistic act. Blood donation is to help people, not to make profit.

- **Blood transfusions from homosexuals**; new tests should prevent the transfer of AIDS but there is still a risk; we must work on eradicating that risk

- **Doctors** - The PDC would provide regular refresher courses for doctors so that they were always up to date with the latest technology...however...

- **Doctors** who have been struck off need to be policed more strictly

- **Health-checks** - The PDC would look into introducing a bi-annual health check to monitor the population's general health and catch illnesses in the early stages

- **Ethics / Code of conduct** - Nurses must not be allowed to talk about patients on their Facebook pages as was recently the case; there has to be some kind of confidentiality agreement in place.
- **Charges in hospitals**; let's stop taking advantage of patients in hospital, charging them extortionate prices for TV and phone lines. I understand that there is a cost to this but let's show a little more compassion and make it a little more reasonable.
- **Car parking in hospitals** – car-parking fees for the families of long-term patients who visit on a daily basis should be addressed.
- **Viagra** should not be prescribed free on the NHS to men with a history of paedophilia, as was recently the case.

Foreign Visitors –

Health tourism costs the British taxpayer £20 million a year according to David Cameron; it costs £200 million a year according to Jeremy Hunt...but the reality is ten times greater; the real figure for health tourism in the UK is more in the region of £2 billion a year.

This is because, as a result of the EU Treaty, all EU citizens are guaranteed freedom of movement between EU member states. This edict was put in place to encourage and promote workforce mobility…but instead it is being used by the whole of the EU as an excuse to come to the UK for free health-care...and predictably the phenomenon is swamping and over-stretching our resources.

However, it is not only people from the EU who are coming here. People are coming here from all over the world – in their droves – in order to receive free medical treatment on the NHS. In fact, they even organise regular flights in some countries - twice a week - for people with illnesses who want to fly to the UK for free treatment.

My question is this...

How come these people can pay for their flights in and out of the country – which shows they have means - but they can't pay for the treatment they receive while they are here?

Does anybody else see the anomaly?

Does anybody else see that the gullible British taxpayer is once again being exploited?

Does anybody else see how once again, the well-intentioned - but ultimately naive - British public is being taken for a ride; that people from all around the world are taking advantage of our generous and charitable spirit?

———

Maternity health tourism is a major problem. Expectant mothers are arriving at Heathrow airport on almost a daily basis and going straight to the nearest A&E / Maternity ward for free treatment and child-birth. Philippine women, for example, although very affable, are clogging up the maternity wards in many of our hospitals without ever having paid a penny into the system.

Other people are flying in for costly cancer treatments, for transplants and for dialysis sessions etc, and then flying straight back out again without ever paying a penny towards the treatment they receive.

Is that morally right; is that fair on those who actually fund the service?

———

Of course, we would like to be all things to all men but we simply cannot afford all these health-tourists. The NHS is not there to provide free treatment and healthcare for all the sick people from all over the world. We simply do not have the resources in this country to cure all the ills of the world <u>free of charge</u>.

———

The result of this phenomenon;

- In hospitals; British citizens are left on trolleys in corridors, while overseas visitors are given priority treatment due to the urgent nature of their conditions...and
- Elsewhere in the country, live-saving drugs are being denied to genuine British citizens and taxpayers because the NHS budget is finite and the emergency treatment given to overseas visitors is using up all the available resources leaving the NHS unable to cover the cost of these drugs or to provide for the very people who fund it.

Proof of the extent of the problem;

The NHS spends £23 million a year on translators alone covering 120 languages.

PDC Policy;

Firstly, might I remind everybody what the National Health Service was set up to do;

'To provide medical care, free, at point-of-need to all Britons'.

That was Bevan's philosophy; that was his mandate. The key word here is 'Britons'. The **National** Health Service is just that; a **National** Health Service...it is not an International Health Service.

It is time that we put in place, a system where foreign visitors – who have nothing to do with this country and have never paid a penny into the system - pay for any care they receive from the NHS. It is time to stem the flow of medical tourists flying in from all around the world to get free treatment from our NHS because the truth is, we simply cannot afford to carry on doing it.

Consequently, under the PDC, all non-British citizens would be asked to provide credit-card details when entering an NHS hospital. A deposit and proof of address in their homeland would then be taken against future treatment before any health-care could be provided...unless of course we had a reciprocity agreement in place with their country of origin beforehand which guaranteed that our citizens would receive the same level of care free-of-charge if they fell ill there.

Now I don't for a minute believe that this practice would stop all fraud immediately but I do believe that it would slowly reduce the abuse and eventually change the attitudes and the minds of those looking to exploit our system.

British citizens would simply have to present their NI Number to prove that they are British taxpayers. (Residency must be a factor in gaining access)

Of course, we would still continue to provide any urgent treatment or emergency care to anybody who needed it - wherever they might come from, without prejudice or discrimination, in line with our international and humanitarian commitments - without these formalities being carried out beforehand...but as soon as the patient was stabilised, the protocol would have to be enacted by the person himself / herself or a relative.

We simply cannot afford **NOT** to do this!

———

Surely, in the interest of fairness it is only right that we prioritise – in some way – those who actually fund the NHS; i.e., the taxpayers of this country.

The alternative is to privatise healthcare completely and make everybody pay no matter where they come from...but unfortunately that solution is one that would immediately penalise the vulnerable and the disadvantaged who would no doubt opt out of healthcare altogether because of the cost...leaving us back where we started when Bevan first began his crusade.

Author's comment;

In the USA, when you walk into a hospital with an injury or an illness; the first question you are asked is; 'Do you have health-insurance?', if not...the second question is; 'what is your credit card number?'

We would simply be doing the same thing.

One final point; the savings made on treating people who do not fall within the purview of the NHS - and the revenue generated from those visitors who still want to take advantage of our medical expertise – would not only allow us to provide better care for the citizens of this country, it would also allow us to invest in new medical infrastructure or new equipment and / or pay for hundreds of new doctors.

Women;

Women's health, because it is so vital to our very existence, should be monitored constantly from puberty through to the menopause and beyond...in special female-friendly clinics (situated within the main hospitals or within the community depending on its size).

These clinics would provide information and advice in areas such as contraception, STD's, pregnancy and motherhood and also offer advice and screening for breast cancer and other gender-specific illnesses.

Young women meanwhile should have an initial pap-smear at 18 as part of their 'coming of age contract'. This delicate procedure would be carried out in conjunction with the removal or the replacement of the contraceptive implant put in place during puberty and should then be repeated regularly on a three-yearly cycle...unless of course that initial test revealed a potential risk in which case the doctors would advise.

———

No

IVF Treatment;

The NHS was created as a safety net for those in need; it was not set up to pander to the whims, fads and vanities of today's self-absorbed society's constantly evolving and ever-changing maxims; that was never Aneurin Bevan's intention...and for that reason I do not believe that the NHS should be in the fertility business; it should not be providing costly IVF treatment *ad infinitum* to anybody who asks for it.

This state of affairs is not conducive with the NHS's mission-statement and therefore I do not believe that we – as a society - should be holding the NHS to ransom in this way.

IVF is a very costly and drawn out procedure and I do not believe that selfish women should be allowed to demand it on the NHS just because of their gender.

Procreation is not a Human Right; sometimes it is just not meant to be.

We need to get away from this culture of 'I want it all and I want it now' that self-centred women and their feminist movement have imposed on our society over the last thirty years.

Women cannot have it all; it just isn't possible. Choices have to be made.

A woman's female condition does not guarantee her the right to motherhood and despite medical progress in this area, there is no divine right to be a parent...however desperate a woman might be.

Just look at what happens in nature; in most species, if not all, there is a dynamic of natural selection which means that not all females are impregnated.

The analogy might be crude but I believe that future spouses should take a fertility test before going through with a marriage...and then accept the results of that test... which would indicate whether they had the potential to conceive and produce offspring or not.

It happens in all species; not every individual gets to procreate and when it comes down to nature we are no different to all the other species that inhabit this planet.

To be a mother <u>is not a human right</u> as some have suggested, so if women put off motherhood until their careers are well and truly established, ignoring their biological clocks through personal choice then I believe that they should have to pay for the procedure privately when they do finally decide to start a family.

Otherwise they should accept the vagaries of nature like the females of any other species.

Of course, I understand that starting a family is a very big decision and that every woman has to make that decision according to her circumstances but that said, it should not be the taxpayers' role to support her in that decision - through NHS funding – because it is a lifestyle-choice that goes against the natural order of human biology.

It is not the role of the NHS to get involved in such matters.

The PDC would naturally support pregnancy and maternity in its natural happenstance but it cannot be right to expect the taxpayer to pick up the cost of IVF treatment for women who make a life-style choice to deliberately delay child-berth and motherhood until after their natural child-bearing years.

Besides, there are alternatives; such as adoption for example.

Author's comment;

Perhaps women who decide to prioritise their careers could plan ahead by taking out an insurance policy of some kind to pay for the IVF treatment they will need when the time comes.

Caesarean birth;

Once again, this is a costly and potentially dangerous procedure and the NHS should not be pandering to the 'caesareans-for-all brigade'.

There is too much choice and too much political correctness in our 21st century society.

Caesarean birth should be a last resort and not a lifestyle choice to fit in with a busy social schedule.

Cosmetic surgery;

The feminist mantra of 'we want it all and we want it now'…and the sense of entitlement that that phrase has engendered in all our everyday lives has now spilled over into the NHS.

Driven by the shallow celebrity culture that now plagues our society women have begun to demand more and more procedures for themselves… none of which was ever part of the NHS remit when it was created.

Cosmetic surgeries comprising breast augmentation, breast reduction, botox-injections and rhinoplasty (nose-jobs) etc were never on Aneurin Bevan's mind when he dreamed up the NHS…and the ever-increasing demand for these treatments as well as the costly IVF procedures mentioned previously from self-obsessed women using the Human Rights argument to demand them have contributed in no small way to the NHS budget spiralling out of control.

In recent years, 250 girls under the age of 16 have been given breast enlargement treatment on the NHS while girls as young as 11 are having breast reduction surgery; I find these statistics abhorrent; surely, it is premature to be doing anything to these young women before their bodies have even finished developing?

I believe that it is time for us to re-focus and re-define our priorities as far as the NHS is concerned.

For example, it cannot be right that we refuse an operation to a child with cerebral-palsy that would help him to walk...but accept to carry out frivolous requests from young women for 36DD breast-enlargements so that they can look like Page 3 models.

Might I remind everybody once again what the NHS was set up to do 'to provide <u>medical care</u>, free, at point-of-need to all Britons'.

That statement doesn't really make it clear but the sub-text is that the NHS was created <u>to help people who were ill</u>, not to provide all manner of service for perfectly healthy, self-indulgent people who simply want to follow the current trend.

If people want cosmetic surgery then they should find another way of paying for it, which doesn't involve plundering the taxpayers' pocket.

NB; this does not, of course, include essential reconstructive surgery for people recovering from major trauma.

Warning;

I believe that the cosmetic surgery business - <u>and it is a business</u> - which is no more than the indulgence of vanity – needs regulating with specific qualifications and a code of conduct.

At the moment anybody can set up shop without any professional qualifications and start performing surgical procedures on people.

This cannot be right or acceptable when people's health is at stake.

Gastric band surgery;

Gastric band surgery - or any other cosmetic surgery for that matter - based solely on vanity should not fall under the NHS remit.

These procedures have nothing to do with illness; that <u>is not</u> what the NHS was set up for – to pander to social engineering or the latest craze.

Tattoos;

Tattoo removal is another procedure that should not be covered by the NHS.

People pay out of their own pocket to have these garish stamps put on their bodies; why should the tax-payer then be expected to pay for them to be removed?

That said; I would encourage any budding entrepreneurs out there looking to set up a new business to get involved in this service.

Once people get over the current fad, realise their mistakes and start getting their tattoos removed, tattoo-removal will become a boom-industry.

Sex-change surgery;

Now, while I understand the psychological distress of people in this situation I cannot see how sex-changes fit into Aneurin Bevan's mission statement which was 'to provide medical care (for illness), free, at point-of-need to all Britons'.

Sex-changes on the NHS have trebled in recent years and while it was judged to be a human right by the Appeal Court in 1999, is it really what Bevan intended?

People are being denied life-saving cancer drugs while costly IVF and trans-gender treatments are being performed on a daily basis...and are clearly on the rise.

Is that really what the NHS is for?

In a related case, a trans-sexual person recently demanded breast-enlargement surgery on the NHS; is that really where our priorities should lie?

I suggest that Charities - who specialise in these matters - should group together and fund these treatments which are understandably crucial to those involved, but are not, as I see it, covered by Bevan's philosophy.

A human right...is not an illness!

I know that there will be those who will criticise me for this, for being controversial, callous or uncaring but I simply believe that the NHS has lost its way over the last thirty years, it has lost sight of its mission-statement because a succession of spineless politicians have allowed themselves to be pushed around by any number of lobby groups - each with their own selfish agenda.

In fact, every time that they have been challenged by one of these pressure groups the politicians have caved in, probably hoping that their indulgence would be seen as courageous and garner more votes for them, thus allowing them to retain their seats on the Westminster gravy train for another term...

Meanwhile, the NHS deficit just keeps spiralling further and further out of control.

People of Britain; we simply cannot afford to fund all this non-essential treatment. If it is not life-threatening or a recognised illness then it should not be covered by the NHS covenant.

Alcohol, Drugs and Smoking;

It is estimated that up to 1.6 million people in the UK have some degree of alcohol dependence...and recent figures show that the British government spends over £3 billion a year in dealing with alcohol related issues.

Meanwhile, 44,585 drug users were hospitalised last year out of a total of 206,889 who needed treatment of some kind...

...and finally 1 in 20 hospital patients are there because of a smoking-related illness.

These figures are staggering and a sad indictment as to the state of our 21st century society.

However, these 'conditions' are not illnesses they are mind-sets, based on bad choices.

Nobody forced these people to start smoking or drinking...or to take drugs...in the first place; it was their choice.

This is why I believe that people who deliberately harm their health through their own life-style choices, people who consciously choose to indulge in these habits - i.e.; alcohol, drugs and smoking - should not expect the NHS to provide medicines to help them give up.

On the contrary, I believe that these people should be weaned off their respective drugs through abstinence based recovery programmes and the money saved put towards the funding and research into unavoidable illnesses such as cancer and Alzheimer's etc.

Alcoholics and smokers will always argue – in order to justify their addictions - that they finance their care through the VAT that they pay in feeding their habit throughout their lifetimes...and that therefore they are entitled to all the care that they subsequently receive.

However, that argument does not equate. The cost of the intensive care needed to treat alcohol and smoking-related illnesses far outweighs any amount of VAT that an alcoholic or a smoker could ever generate in his or her lifetime and therefore this argument is invalid.

...and as for drugs, they are illegal and hence, do not generate any VAT whatsoever, so their treatment is clearly 'un-financed'.

Pro-active and not reactive measures need to be taken. (Refer to Justice Section)

General Policy;

To sum up; the PDC would re-focus the NHS on the reasons for which it was created in the first place; to help the needy and the vulnerable.

Funding would be maintained at the same level but by concentrating on essential services and reducing the number and the range of services being provided we would - as any decent economist would concede - realise a net increase in real terms (quality and efficiency) for the services that we would continue to support...which would be an improvement all round on the current state of affairs.

GPs -

Opening hours / appointments

As doctors appointments are getting harder and harder to obtain in local medical centres (and don't listen to high-handed professionals or conceited politicians who protest that this isn't the case; listen to those who know; the British public), A&E departments in hospitals are being inundated with people who only have minor ailments.

In fact, 30% of patients who currently go to A&E should really be seen by their local GP but sadly they cannot get an appointment...and the knock-on effect of them going directly to A&E has led to an increase in A&E waiting times of over 40%.

This situation is unacceptable and the reason it has come about is mainly because GP's have become too attuned to office hours. They no longer work or do house calls after hours...or on weekends, and this despite earning salaries of over £100.000 per annum which is – if we refer to the Emgee Ratio (see chapter on Salary) – almost four times the average wage.

Indeed, a recent report by the Health Department noted that 93% of doctors' surgeries were not open when it was convenient for patients, but only when it suited the medical staff. This is proof sadly, that the vocation to help cure people which used to be the doctors motivation has today been replaced by the same selfish, greed-based dogma that the politicians use for themselves.

How can these medical professionals simply 'opt out' of doing their job?

This seems to me like a 'dereliction of duty' almost... and would not be tolerated in any other public service where the public's health and safety is a priority.

We need to redress this imbalance created as a result of New Labour's ridiculous decision to allow GP's to opt out of 'out-of-hours' care...and at the same time we need to relieve the strain on A&E services by giving them the staff and the equipment they need to do the job properly.

Doctors surgeries need to be re-organised and their opening hours revised...and the PDC with its new university education policy for essential sectors would help with this re-organisation in two distinct ways;

- Firstly, we would flood communities with a generation of new young doctors ready to fill the consultation rooms that are currently under-utilised or stand empty most of the time, like supermarket checkouts, post-office counters and bank cashier points...and this extra capacity would also allow us to re-integrate the 'out-of-hours services' that have been contracted out to the private sector.
- ...and secondly...the PDC would introduce a new generation of community nurses as part of the new Magnet centre concept (see Industry chapter). An initiative which would no only ease pressure on doctors' surgeries but also on the A&E departments in hospitals...acting as a buffer between the two hard-pressed institutions.

(As we would be promoting service-based courses in universities, the same policy would also apply to hospital doctors, midwives, dentists, and opticians etc.)

This would mean more doctors and more nurses available to more people for longer.

However, as part of our overall ethos on personal responsibility the PDC would also move towards making a charge for doctor's appointments. This would only be a small contribution but it would be put in place in order to stop people taking advantage and missing appointments... in the belief that there is no consequence to their lack of consideration.

It is only when people are hit in the pocket that apathy becomes awareness.

There would of course be exemptions to this charge for under 18's, the unemployed and the elderly (within reason).

Of course, the BMA and the doctors themselves would not be happy with these proposals ...and no doubt they would resist the changes initially, hoping to hold onto their golden goose...but I'm pretty certain that the British public would much rather see six doctors working in a medical centre earning £50,000 a year each and covering extended hours...than three earning £100,000 a year and barely keeping office hours...which is currently the case.

Author's comment;

This flood of modern young doctors with their new PDC contracts would also break the BMA monopoly and stop them wielding the threat of strike action to protect their pensions while the sick languish in queues in hospital corridors.

I am sick of seeing the British public - through their timid political representatives - being held to ransom by bullying, self-serving unions.

Complaints –

Complaints against GP's have risen by 24% in recent years and most of those complaints are from patients saying that they are;

- being ignored,
- shown no respect...or
- lied to

This phenomenon suggests that communication and the understanding of our cultural sensitivities is clearly an issue in our 21st century doctors' surgeries; a fact which is born out by the number of doctors who have been struck off by the General Medical Council in the last five years. Out of a total of 669 doctors 'struck-off', 420 had been trained overseas.

This is an indication, and another reason for promoting English-speaking, British trained medical personnel...which would be one of the PDC's major priorities.

However I have to mention new technology here.

The advent of the computer has made it so much easier for the medical profession to consult patients' files and x-rays these days...but sadly the computer screen has also created an invisible barrier between the medical profession and the patient.

It is unfortunate, but nowadays, doctors have so much information available to them on the computer screen that they often forget to make eye-contact with their patients... conducting entire appointments at times without ever looking away from their computer screen.

This is why people feel that they are being ignored. The information is being shared but the lack of human interaction makes the experience cold and uncaring.

We must be wary of this; we are already becoming file-numbers because of technology...but we must never lose the human component of medical care; we must never as individuals, as human-beings, be reduced simply to a list of bar-codes.

———

Salary;

While we all respect our doctors and the work that they do, it is clear that they have now joined the gravy train of greed, following the outlandish example set by our MPs, our bankers and our energy companies.

They have caught the greed disease but I suppose that it is a natural human reaction;

> '**They** (the politicians and the bankers...and
> the energy companies) **are doing it,**
> **and getting away with it; why shouldn't we'?**

After all, any one of us offered a hike in salary and easier working conditions - through a reduction in hours and obligations - would undoubtedly do the same.

This is all down to New Labour who offered GP's a 45% increase in salary with the choice of opting out of all the awkward 'out-of-hours' work...and of course they jumped at the opportunity; who wouldn't?

However, unlike many other areas of life, Health is not a 9 to 5 job and cannot be treated in office hours exclusively.

The average GP salary in the UK is now over £100,000 a year for doing less work than they did ten years ago (£104,100 in fact, if we take into account the bonus system set up for them for treating particular illnesses)...and as much as we respect what they do and the years they have spent qualifying for their positions, I feel that it is wrong for GP's - and dentists for that matter - to be earning such vast amounts from the public purse.

There are cases of people earning between £300,000 and £400,000 a year working for the NHS...and in two extreme cases, one person earned £750,000 and another £1.8m.

That is anything from **12** to **72** times the average wage...paid out of the taxpayer's pocket.

Does that sit right with a moral conscience?

For information;

In a recent survey it was announced that British GPs are the best paid doctors in the Western world, earning 3.4 times the average wage, whilst British nurses lag way behind their counter-parts in other countries and are among the least well paid in their sector earning only 0.9 of the average wage. The PDC would look to redress this imbalance.

———

Performance linked salaries and bonuses were also introduced to reward doctors for taking better care of their patients – but surely **that is their job**; does the greed and the bonus culture know no end; is it right that people should be asking for bonuses on top of their salary just for doing their job? Is that fair?

That doctors even demanded bonus payments to administer vaccines is outrageous; their salaries have gone up almost 55% in five years and yet they still have their hands out for more...?

What world are they living in?

Does the BMA not comprehend the concept of morality?

These people seem to have lost sight of the NHS's vocation.

The NHS was not created to make doctors rich; it was created to help people in the community who were ill...and in an ideal world the doctors would even be volunteering their time and their service for free...as they do in the Third World but sadly in greedy, self-serving 21st century Britain such noble ideals have no tenure.

In my opinion, people who choose this career-path – who depend on the public purse for their salaries - should not be motivated simply by financial gain. The vocational aspect of healthcare might no longer have tenure, **but why so much greed**?

———

PDC Solution;

Firstly, we have to recognise that the extra-ordinarily generous contracts (pay and conditions) handed out to doctors by the New Labour Party were flawed to say the least...and need wholesale revision and adjustment.

I can hear the GPs screaming and howling already...but the truth is that the spineless and incompetent New Labour party made a monumental mistake in agreeing to the terms of these contracts...and sometimes mistakes simply have to be rectified if not reversed.

Author's comment; *Isn't it strange how people always complain at the thought of having something taken away but when it is given – even if it is given mistakenly – they barely register the fact?*

Secondly, the PDC would roll-flat all public sector pay-scales – including the NHS, the Civil Service and Local Government - and re-construct them on a new, fairer and more sustainable basis with the goal of levelling the playing field across a comparable knowledge segment.

Transparency and logic would be the guiding factors in creating these new templates...although...the tried and trusted 'points and bands' scheme currently in use throughout the NHS would probably be maintained...with just a few minor tweaks and adjustments to the incremental detail.

I believe, as a citizen of this country, that a goal of three times the average wage - plus a small contingency to allow for hierarchy - should be the absolute limit for people living off the taxpayer...and as a result, the PDC would look to respect that ceiling throughout the public sector.

Any more than three times the average wage is an abuse of the democratic principle of receiving a fair wage for a fair day's work.

NB; for the specific attention of the new generation;

Through its new education policy, the PDC would offer hundreds of university places to medical students, but in exchange for that place and that tuition newly qualified medical personnel would have to fulfil certain conditions, including a five-year contract upon graduation which would tie them to the NHS for the duration of that period.

This policy would not only allow newly qualified medical personnel to continue gaining valuable on-the-job experience while still being supervised, it would also go some way towards paying back the British public for financing their training.

The salary offered during this period would also be subject to certain conditions...but it would be commensurate with the newly qualified person's position in accordance with the revised pay-scale that the PDC would be putting in place for all areas of the public sector.

Conclusion;

The GPs never complained about getting paid double - for half the work - which created an almighty mess in our health service - and especially in A&E - but their decade of being over-paid by the public purse is now over and it is time for them to cut their cloth more frugally.

I am certain that they will all be howling at the injustice of it all but it doesn't matter – the corrective agenda that the PDC would put in place would be a fairer deal for the whole country.

However, these new conditions might not suit everybody and those doctors;

- who felt unable to accept the new, fairer conditions and,
- who felt that they needed or deserved to earn £100,000 a year and more...

...would be more than welcome - and indeed encouraged even - to set themselves up in private practice – like they do in the USA – on the condition that they gave enough notice to the relevant authorities before relinquishing their positions.

In such cases, the PDC would simply de-register these doctors from the NHS index, allowing them all the time and space they needed to concentrate on their new situation, taking advantage of the free-market; a state of affairs which would clearly make it far easier for them to finance the lifestyles that they felt they 'deserved'.

Now; this might lead to a period of instability at first, but I believe that the new generation of GPs with their new sensible contracts, their youthful desire to achieve and their eagerness to take up the challenge put before them would quickly take up the slack and make the transition between the previous generation and their own, quite a smooth one.

I believe in the next generation.

Pensions;

The British taxpayer is funding 80% of doctors' pensions to the tune of £83 billion...while the doctors themselves are only contributing £13 billion.

This arrangement allows some medical professionals to retire on pensions of up to £140,000 a year.

Meanwhile, ordinary working-class taxpayers – who have funded the above pensions – only receive £5727.80 a year from their retirement pension;

Is that right...?

Is that fair...?

Perhaps this is another area that needs to be addressed.

―――――

Dentists & Opticians

These are two more areas that need reform.

Why are those who work in the dental care industry and the ophthalmic industry surprised that people are reluctant to use their services?

The answer is simple; because they are far too expensive.

People cannot afford to go to the dentist, so they do without. Even the smallest intervention costs a fortune and when prosthetics are involved, the price sky-rockets instantaneously.

The same applies to opticians; the average person cannot afford £200 for frames as is currently the case.

I would like to see both these sectors reformed to allow greater access for all at a cheaper rate...and the PDC policy on university education should remedy this by swamping these sectors (dentists and opticians) with new recruits which would multiply the number of dental practices and ophthalmic clinics available...and push up the need for equipment providers, stimulate competition and drive down costs.

Those at the high end of both these services would then have to concentrate on their rich patients, align themselves with the new order... or simply cease trading.

―――――

Author's comment;

Surely, it cannot be right...that it is cheaper to go to Europe to get dental treatment - including travel and hotel expenses – than it is to get treatment in this country.

The quality of the work might not be the same but in a world where budgets are tight; people adapt their expectations.

Hygienists;

The work of hygienists is largely unknown in this country but I believe that it will soon become as important a profession as a doctor or a dentist.

A recent survey shows that half of our children are at risk of rotting teeth due to a lack of regular cleaning and programmed check-ups...and while the 'traffic-light' scheme used by dentists – to rate dental condition - is a start, I believe that we now need to integrate regular dental care into our busy lives through the introduction of hygienists into our collective consciousness.

At the moment hygienists have to work 'under the supervision' of a qualified dentist but I would suggest that we allow qualified hygienists to set up 'walk-in' businesses in supermarkets or shopping centres offering simple and limited services without them having to go through dentists whose controlling influence is clearly restrictive and undemocratic.

Fraud;

Doctors have been charging the NHS £162 million a year for 'ghost' patients who have;

- moved,
- left the country or
- who have been dead for up to 40 years

...and thanks to yet another inefficient and costly New Labour initiative dentists too have been allowed to do the same, billing the NHS;

- for 'ghost' patients who don't exist...and
- for treatments they have never carried out

In fact fraudulent claims by dentists are costing the NHS £73 million a year.

That is a total of £235 million a year of fraudulent activity from these two sectors alone.

Some of the worst cases of abuse include;

- one doctor who claimed £61,000 in overtime <u>after</u> she had stopped working
- a dentist who charged the NHS £200,000 for work he never carried out
- another dentist who billed the NHS for £600,000 for people who were dead...and
- yet another dentist who charged the NHS £1.4 million for work that she never carried out

People; with the money from those four cases alone (£2,261,000) we could pay the salaries of 115 nurses for a year and they are just the tip of the iceberg. Therefore, the PDC would pay particular attention to this fraudulent activity because, in my eyes, it is the ultimate betrayal of taxpayers' trust.

Health Business;

I hate to see greed masquerading under a thin veneer of altruism.

Pharmaceutical companies are insatiable monsters with voracious appetites that gobble up research funds...and when there is a lull in their finances they simply create / invent diseases / illnesses in order to sell us the solution to our problems in the form of a new and improved – and more expensive – wonder drug / cure.

It is not right that commercial considerations are allowed override decisions concerning people's health and it is not acceptable that the bottom line is always prioritised by these companies to the detriment of people's lives.

The passive corruption of medical professionals should also be monitored and checked. Pharmaceutical companies often offer 'consultancy fees' to doctors as a way of promoting their products but these payments would be considered as bribes in any other sector.

———

Secondly, the scandal involving the banking sector showed the greed that Mankind is capable of...but the next big scandal in the UK will undoubtedly be linked to either the new 'Police and Crime Commissioners' who are already under scrutiny...or the new commissioning groups that have been created to oversee the NHS budget.

This is an accident waiting to happen and it beggars belief to anybody with a brain that the government would introduce this travesty into the NHS...because the potential for conflict of interest and corruption is absolutely colossal.

The very idea of health service staff profiting financially from commercial NHS decisions is more than a cause for concern, because the stench of corruption will not be far behind.

We just cannot have a situation where people running an organisation stand to make substantial personal profit from contracts awarded by that same organisation.

These people will have £65 billion of NHS money to share out...and there is every possibility that morally weak human beings – as many of us are - will be tempted to abuse this arrangement for their own personal gain.

Anybody working for the NHS making any kind of profit on the side will be to all intents and purposes siphoning off public money…which is possibly worse in some respect than what the bankers did.

———

Other Notes;

- Up to 1200 people died unnecessarily while in the care of the Mid-Staffordshire NHS Trust and nobody of any rank was held accountable; that is unacceptable. The PDC would reintroduce a regional body to oversee the running of hospitals in their area with a named CEO who would be held personally responsible and accountable for any misconduct in the hospitals under his supervision…if issues highlighted by staff, patients or the public were not dealt with. These CEO's would report directly to the Health Secretary and the appropriate sanctions would be put in place to avoid any questionable activity / behaviour.
- The PDC would also compose a database of those working for the NHS in order to monitor those who have been struck-off and those who have received redundancy payments (a three-year period would have to be observed before re-hiring or the redundancy payment would have to be forfeited) We cannot continue with a situation where people are being made redundant with huge pay-offs and then being re-employed – albeit in another capacity - four weeks later – The revolving door has to be closed
- Under the PDC, no women more than seven months pregnant would be allowed to fly into Britain. All airlines flying into the country would receive a communiqué explaining that if they allowed a pregnant woman onto one of their flights, and that that person had to undergo immediate delivery upon arrival in this country, then they would be billed with the cost of her hospitalisation. This would hopefully stop the 'delivery-room tourism' and the abuse of the NHS that is currently going on. British women for their part would not be allowed to fly out after the sixth month of gestation for their own safety.

- The PDC would also introduce new guidelines on hygiene and safety for tattoo parlours and those involved in the Cosmetic surgery business.

———

Whistleblowers

'There comes a time when silence is betrayal'...Martin Luther King

---

In an attempt to hide the truth from the British public, a culture of deception and bullying has been allowed to spread across officialdom in this country.

We all know that corruption and incompetence is widespread within our society...and sadly in recent times those in authority - who might possibly be implicated or embarrassed by the revelation of certain of their activities, on a personal level or within their departments - have become inured to covering-up those shortcomings in a variety of different ways;

- Firstly, they try to bully and harass the people who would reveal the truth about their inadequacies...
- Then, if the bullying doesn't work they proffer threats of legal action against potential informants...
- ...and finally if neither the bullying or the threat of legal action manages to dent the integrity and resolve of the honest employee, then immoral management resort to bribery and the offer of a rather large severance package...which naturally comes with conditions, most notably a gagging-order that prevents the potential whistle-blower from making public what they know.

Of course, none of this is very ethical for a principled society...but sadly we no longer live in a principled society, we live in a hypocritical society... and as a consequence this kind of corrupt behaviour is happening more and more often.

Incompetent management personnel - who are paid with public money – are simply using more public money to cover up their incompetence, their misconduct and their shortcomings…and until somebody puts a stop to it, it will continue…because incompetence is widespread and the culture of pay-offs is now rooted firmly in our administrations.

For proof;

Over the past few months we have had six cases in the UK of people being bullied, paid off…or prevented from coming forward to reveal incompetence, mismanagement or inappropriate behaviour by their colleagues or superiors. This proves – *de facto* - that this behaviour is endemic across the spectrum of authority.

There have been…

- Two cases in the NHS,
- One case in the Liberal Democrat Organisation,
- One involving a Police and Crime Commissioner
- another in the investment banking sector …and finally
- one case in the BBC

The worst of these cases;

The chairman of the Care Quality Commission, Dame Jo Williams not only wrote to the Department of Health urging that Ms Sheldon (the person who came forward) be suspended immediately from her job, she also sought to have Ms Sheldon declared mentally ill!

That is absolutely criminal and should not be tolerated!

…although the Police and Crime Commissioner having the whistleblower arrested for reporting him runs a pretty close second in the 'abuse of power' ratings.

People of the UK, we live in a democracy...and legitimate grievances must be heard;

- it cannot be right that decent men and women of this country are metaphorically gagged and vilified when they dare to speak the truth?...and
- neither can it be right that despite all the evidence of institutional breakdown revealed by the cases mentioned above, not a single official from any of the organisations cited has been sacked or prosecuted.

...that is simply unacceptable and creates a vacuum in the integrity of our pseudo-leaders where suspicion of corruption and mistrust can fester.

Author's comment;

Why is honesty and telling the truth...having a decent and moral outlook on life considered wrong?

Whistleblowers are regularly gagged or even arrested these days simply for revealing the truth; why?

Do the politicians and those in charge consider themselves above the law?

Do our governments have the right to keep the truth from us?

They are clearly working behind the scenes to protect us but does that give them the right to decide what truth we should know about and what truth they would rather keep from us?

Surely the truth is the truth?

- maybe if more people were honest and told the truth we wouldn't need all the surveillance we now have spying on our every move…and
- maybe if governments and politicians came clean about what they are doing in the shadows, there would be no reason for suspicion and conspiracy theories either…

…but of course politics is more complicated than that.

The world of politics is opaque; it is grubby, it is ugly, it is a shady area of human interaction which is riddled with self-interest. It is a world of aspiring megalomaniacs and continuous power struggles between multinational conglomerates each of which acts like a puppeteer controlling politicians and policy through their economic and financial clout.

Politics is all about power and inside knowledge.

———

Now, I understand that;

- Edward Snowden (who leaked the information on how the USA and the UK have been illegally collecting the personal data of millions of people around the world)
  and
- Private Bradley Manning who through Julian Assange and Wikileaks leaked thousands of documents containing USA military secrets

…abused their positions - and betrayed the trust of their nation - in revealing what they revealed…**but what they revealed was the truth**.

Surely to prosecute them for telling the truth is a strange way for a civilised society – based on justice - to react.

How can a government defend sending out the message that if you speak up about its wrong-doing or its incompetence, it will put you in prison, **even if what you say is the truth**?

Where is the democracy in that?

Where is the integrity in the idea that telling the truth can be punishable with prison?

That is cold-war politics.

———

This is very dangerous territory and it takes us one step closer to a society built around the psychosis of central governments being constantly suspicious of the individual and his / her free-spirit...and if we allow ourselves to continue along this path and we feed / encourage this madness, then all the nightmare scenarios involving Big Brother – foreseen in fiction over the last few decades - will slowly be realised.

We cannot allow our privacy and the intimacy of our everyday lives to be monitored constantly by central government; every conversation, every text, every e-mail, every click we make on our computers to be analysed on the pretext of terrorist prevention...because, if we do, one by one all our civil liberties and all our individual freedoms will be removed until in the end we are just numbers following orders against a backdrop of the threat of imprisonment for disobedience.

———

Now, of course, those who betray their country should be reprimanded in some way for their transgressions...especially if they have signed a confidentiality agreement which contains a non-disclosure clause, but if their 'error' was to tell the truth how do we reconcile that 'error' with a democracy based on justice which relies on the truth to operate.

It's a weird dichotomy.

———

We all know that our governments do things behind our backs, we all know that they cover-up their mistakes and their security breaches under the blanket of 'classified information or national security mantras' but we simply cannot have a situation where telling the truth makes you an outcast, a pariah or *persona non grata*.

When governments not only stop listening, but persecute, arrest and imprison people for telling the truth, society and democracy as we know it is in trouble.

The people need to keep this in mind at all times; we must never let those who govern us ever acquire a level of power that allows them to take away our freedom if we don't agree with their policies or reveal their shortcomings.

That would be a step too far...and the beginning of the end for our democracy.

Politicians and the political machine must always be answerable to the people, not the other way around. The faceless machine cannot be allowed to control the human spirit; we cannot allow the security obsession - and an increasingly-intrusive Big Brother paranoia - to undermine the freedoms that we have fought so hard to attain.

———

Author's comment;

There is corruption at every level of society...because there are human beings at every level of society...but if you believe in something, you have to fight for it. You have to have the courage to follow your heart and your convictions so that your voice can be heard, because the alternative is resigned acceptance and submission.

———

The PDC Solution; Democracy in Action

You cannot take on the State as an individual – even if you believe that you are in the right and you have proof of the State's wrongdoing. The State will crush you every time if it feels threatened.

Many have tried before...and found that out to their cost, notably;

- Bradley Manning & Julian Assange,
- Edward Snowden...and
- Dr David Kelly

...who have all paid the price for revealing information that the State didn't want their citizens to know about.

We need an organisation where people with concerns can go and receive non-judgmental advice on situations that they feel need to be brought to the public's attention...without any fear of retribution.

The PDC would therefore create the Public Awareness and Concern Agency (PACA) where people with these concerns could voice them anonymously…and be heard.

...although a safe-guard would have to be put in place, to prevent people using the service for personal gain or to settle a grudge...and systematic prosecution would have to be enforced for those who break the rules.

This should deter most scammers.

Social Services

Because of our ageing population and the problems that our social services have faced over recent years, I believe we need a new approach to caring in the community.

Child Services and Child Protection;

Lest we forget;

Five years after the death of 8yr old Victoria Climbie who was brutally murdered by her 'family' in the most horrendous of circumstances – the same authorities in Haringey - led by Sharon Shoesmith - allowed a 17 month old boy, Peter Connolly – aka Baby P – to be brutally tortured to death by his 'parents', the authorities failing to pick up on the 50 different injuries that had been inflicted upon the boy's tiny body despite 78 visits to the house where he lived. (I hesitate to call it his 'home', as a home is a place where you feel safe and secure)

It beggars belief that this poor child was used as a punch ball by his mother and her sadistic partner over a period of time and yet Haringey social services never once detected this abuse.

What a shambles; if that is not incompetence, what is…?

Our social services and our child services in particular need urgent root and branch reform and the memory of that little boy's suffering will be all the motivation we need to make certain that change happens.

Author's comment;

The final insult of this harrowing affair is that while the perpetrators <u>were convicted</u>, they were cleared of the child's manslaughter; how does that work? How is that justice? We have to stop failing the citizens of this country with a justice system that just doesn't deliver on its mandate.

Surely, if ever there was a case for the re-introduction of capital punishment, this would be it; for this kind of person, for this kind of man who would torture a poor baby and throw him against a wall inflicting terrible injuries on him before putting him across his knee and breaking his back, ultimately killing him.

Surely, even the wonderfully naive activists who stand up against any form of punishment do not want this kind of person living among us?

Surely, there is a politician out there with a spine who will stand up to the bleeding-heart liberals and the deluded moral campaigners and defend our right as a society not to have these monsters living amongst us...or is there...?

Now, this case is by far the most high-profile of those that we have had to endure in recent years but it is by no means the only one. As mentioned previously the case of Victoria Climbie preceded this one and the cases of Daniel Pelka and Hamzah Khan for example have come to pass since, so there is clearly an ongoing problem within our society, concerning the abuse of children.

We need to address this issue. We need to address the systemic and abject failure of our social services to deal with these cases in the right and proper manner...and more importantly we need, as a society, to eradicate the morally-reprehensible people who perpetrate them.

In recent years our social services have often missed out on the children they should be protecting while focussing on the wrong areas;

For example;

-   they took a **two hour** old baby from her mother while ignoring the case of a 4yr old girl killed by her parents and found with over 100 injuries and cigarette burns to her body...and also
-   failed to protect all the young girls who were being groomed by the Asian sex-gangs right under their noses (although the police who held back in their investigations for fear of being accused of racism were not entirely blameless in this matter either)

———

Now I understand that they are under pressure from all sides but with their oft-misplaced moral judgementalism the social services in this country are clearly falling short in fulfilling their role of protecting the young and vulnerable. However, this failure is not due solely to the intrinsic incompetence of certain individuals; there are a number of other contributing factors that impact on the quality of the service provided;

-   budget,
-   staffing-levels,
-   training (the proficiency to deal with unusual and difficult situations)
-   the target culture that pervades throughout our public services... and
-   the availability of alternative solutions

...but there is also the fear factor...

-   the fear of making a wrong decision
-   the fear of a backlash from the media if they make a wrong decision
-   the fear that the Political Correctness Brigade will disapprove...or

- the fear that the Health and Safety Executive will criticise their methods

People are afraid to do their jobs properly because they are afraid of the tempest that will rain down on them if they get it wrong.

People are afraid of being vilified but this fear of criticism and reprisal leads them to be overly cautious in some situations and too 'laissez-faire' in others.

We have to change this 'cover your back' mentality and rebuild confidence among our care-professionals by reigning in the numerous, interfering pressure groups and allowing these people to do their jobs without the constant pressure and scrutiny on their every action.

Of course there has to be a code of conduct but there also has to be room for flexibility, for a judgement call, because no two cases are the same and we have to trust our professionals to make that call.

However, any social-service professional seen to be under-performing in their duties - or on the contrary being over-zealous in their actions - would need to undergo strict redress.

The PDC would undertake a review of all social-service procedures and provide better funding, better training and better solutions / alternative actions for our social-care professionals to put into practice. (See below)

I believe that babies and young children should be accompanied by social services in conjunction with their parents from the maternity ward up until their first day in primary school, where teachers would then take up the relay as society's monitor.

This policy would be put in place, in liaison with the pregnant woman's doctor after she had had the 20-week anomaly-scan to check on the baby's development.

A 'doola' would be assigned to the pregnant woman and this person would then accompany the future mother through the latter stages of her pregnancy offereing her advice and guidance with child-birth techniques, early parenting skills and all-round moral support.

The 'doola's' contract would run for six months (three months before and three months after the birth)

Then, at three months a social-worker would be assigned to the family and he/she would help the new parents with any follow-up questions concerning the health of the child and its nutrition (to hopefully anticipate / avert the early on-set of eating disorders (anorexia / bulimia).

This would take the form of a weekly visit and continue until the child was enrolled into primary school when the school's teachers would become society's monitor.

Other issues involving children that need to be addressed;

- We need to review the rules about the persecution and prosecution of parents for un-explained cot-deaths as our understanding of this phenomenon has greatly improved
- we also need to review the rules about child-protection and the removal of children from abusive parents; more common sense needs to be applied
- the adoption rules also need to be revised...and any misguided bureaucrats – in decision-making roles – who took babies and children away from their parents under the false pretension of child protection in order to meet adoption targets - which if reached would trigger extra bonuses for them – would be severely sanctioned.

- We also need to look at kinship carers who take in children. They need to receive the same level of support as foster parents instead of councils hiding behind 'residence permits' to absolve themselves of any responsibility.
- The PDC would look into winding up the CSA (Child Support Agency) and giving fathers more access to their children through fairer judgements in divorce settlements. Psychologists have discovered that good mothers make their children feel safe and secure, but that it is good fathers who are vital for their offspring's self-esteem. We need to encourage that.
- ...and finally, teenagers; Under the PDC no young girls or women in care would be placed in areas where there is a high concentration of Pakistani immigrants. Recent events have shown that there is a real danger of abuse from people of this culture and until the elders of the Pakistani community take responsibility for their constituents the PDC would not allow these vulnerable young girls to be exposed to this salacious exploitative culture. Moreover, those that have already been placed within such communities would be relocated as a priority to an area out of harm's way, out of the reach of these repulsive 'groomers'.

The Elderly and the Infirm;

'Respect for our elders is probably the biggest casualty
of our selfish, me-first 21st century culture'

With improvements in health-care and living-standards, life-expectancy these days is far greater than it has ever been...which is wonderful... however, that state of affairs brings with it a whole new set of challenges that we will have to resolve going forward and after the series of scandals that have rocked our hospitals and care-homes in recent times, the PDC would take a completely different approach to elderly care.

Firstly, as people, we should be respectful of our elders; after all they brought us into this world. We should respect their life-experience and learn from it. Other cultures integrate their elderly, often living, several generations, under the one roof. Why shouldn't we?

At the moment, here are the choices open to our elderly people;

- an NHS hospital where they risk dying from a lack of care and a culture of covering up anything that goes wrong...or
- a care-home run by cold, uncaring accountants that slowly but inexorably bleeds them dry, until they can no longer pay.

We pretend to be a civilised society...but is that really how we should treat our elderly people...especially as the current generation of pensioners are the men and women who fought for us in WW2?

NO IT IS NOT; our elderly people should be taken care of and treated with respect...and as an antidote to the care-homes fiasco, the PDC would promote a policy of families looking after their elderly relatives... which always used to be the case in generations past...by offering those house-holders who did take in an elderly or dependent relative a tax break or an extra benefit to help them with the additional cost.

This would hopefully reduce the need for so many care homes and thereby improve the quality of care provided in those that remained which would be monitored through regular check-ups.

This initiative would help everyone;

- It would help ease the strain on NHS hospital bed occupation
- It would help the elderly in all manner of ways to still feel part of a family and part of society
- It might help parents too, to have a presence in the home and someone to rely on

- And it might even benefit the children / grandchildren to have a matriarchal / patriarchal figure around the house

---

Grandparents can help;

- with babies (care and mothering advice)
- with children (care, education, babysitting and school collection)
- with parents (listening)
- with the cooking
- with the housework...and even
- with the gardening...
- they can show love,
- they can make children behave better
- they can make adults less likely to argue...and
- their mere presence in the home can have a calming influence on everyone,

...until of course the time comes when they need to be looked after themselves.

These are all very positive notions and hugely compassionate aspects of the policy...but most importantly, including the elderly in our everyday lives would go a long way to recreating the family unit and rebuilding the community spirit that has been exploded by recent governments.

Other cultures manage it; why shouldn't we?

Author's comment;

OAP's are now taking self-defence courses, using their walking sticks to defend themselves against aggressors. This is a new phenomenon...

and while such initiatives are to be applauded and encouraged, they are sadly an indication that there is a serious malaise at the heart of our society. The expansion of these classes also proves that the elderly feel abandoned by the government and suggests that they don't trust those in charge to protect them.

———

The PDC Solution;

Care in the community including hospitals, doctors and social services would be centralised regionally and each of these organisations would oversee every aspect of care within their area;

Social services would be re-organised thus;

- Each town would be divided into sectors and each sector divided into manageable areas.
- a qualified care-worker would then be put in charge of a group of people within a particular area
  o some new-borns / babies,
  o some small children
  o some elderly people living alone who need home-visits…and
  o some elderly people living with families (those registered under the tax-rebate scheme)

…to monitor their health, their care and their well-being.

———

Example of the social-worker contract;

Each social-worker / carer would work 8-hour days and have 12 visits to carry out daily (12x30mins = 6 hours) which would allow two hours for travel time and flexi-time if necessary for unforeseen dramas.

They would work eight hours a day / five days a week = 40 hours.

Twelve visits a day / five days a week = 60 visits a week.

———

The PDC would abandon the pointless 15 minute visits which don't allow the care to be properly administered and replace them with 30/40 minute visits allowing the carer ten minutes to greet the patient, to check in and to read their care history, and at least thirty minutes to actually carry out the work.

———

Perhaps – if time allowed – they could also make a weekly visit to the local Magnet centre to liaise with the nurses there and promote a more inclusive community.

Then, at the end of each shift, they would file an electronic report to central office flagging up – possibly through a colour scheme – any incidents that might have occurred during the day where urgent action might be needed...so that the relevant authorities could be alerted and the necessary protocols put in place. This would include reporting any ill-treatment or suspicious behaviour.

The salary on offer would be based on the Points and Bands system – currently used by the NHS – which allows for seniority and promotion through recognition...while encouraging commitment, dedication and aspiration – although there would be no guaranteed annual rise.

———

As for the weekends; relief teams would be put in place to cover those, to step-in, in case of illness and to deputise during holiday absences... and naturally these positions would be remunerated at a slightly higher hourly-rate than the weekly-rate to compensate for the unsocial hours and the issue of 'permanent availability'.

———

I understand that this is a costly policy - but unfortunately, it is a necessary one which would have to be developed and rolled out around the county as our population continues to expand and the number of our elderly continues to increase.

The slow transfer of the state pension over to the private sector should act as a funding stimulus for this policy in the years to come.

———

Other services;

- We would also need a team of qualified professionals to go around the country inspecting care-homes and making sure that they conform to the legislature in force.
- We would also need to introduce some joined-up thinking and develop communication between the NHS hospitals and social services. Not so long ago, a man was found dead in his bed; he had been there for almost two years before his neighbour thought to knock on his door...and finally
- We would have to create a network of committed professionals – trained in teaching – who would go around our schools offering advice and giving lessons / speeches in sex-education to teens. This department would also be in charge of the parenting lessons set out previously.

———

Care Homes

Sadly, I knew that the Care System was in trouble twenty years ago when some very dodgy local businessmen from my home town began investing in nursing homes.

They had absolutely;

- no health qualifications,
- no knowledge of care or medicine,
- no interest in people's welfare or well-being...and
- every interest in making a lot of easy money for themselves

...which told me that there was going to be trouble down the line...and sure enough that is what has happened.

People's health should not be about the bottom line but about dignity, respect and a duty of care towards 'those in need'.

However, in privatising elderly healthcare, those responsible have made people, real people...a commodity; a number on a spreadsheet.

Accountants should not be in charge of people's health; they should not be running care homes because it is simply not their calling and their promotion to the front line in recent years has sadly led directly to the catastrophic events and the calamitous situations that we are now dealing with on a daily basis;

- poor quality of care
- poor standards
- badly trained and inexperienced staff...and most importantly of all

- the wrong kind of staff, lacking in the compassion, the kindness and the communication skills necessary for this kind of work.

Ever since care-home management was opened up to the private sector, businessmen and equity funds - <u>whose only goal is to make money</u> - have milked thousands of elderly people out of their hard-earned savings... and forced many others to sell their homes to pay for the spiralling costs of their care. However, as the successive scandals that we have witnessed have proved, the care that those people have been receiving in return for their life-savings has been scandalously inadequate.

We need to exercise greater control over these 'exploitative' nursing and retirement homes which are fleecing our parents and our grandparents - not only out of their nest-eggs - but also out of their dignity, their pride and their self-respect...and while it is not illegal as such, it is nevertheless immoral in my eyes that some people have become billionaires on the backs of other people paying these extortionate fees for their care.

For information;

Some care-homes charge up to £1000 a week for a bed and board...which is more expensive than many of the world's top hotels.

PDC Policy concerning Care Homes -

The PDC would introduce an 'accountability charter' for the management of private care-homes with an individual responsibility clause for the person in charge – much like a licensee has to display over the door of a public house.

This person's name would have to be displayed clearly in the reception area of the care-home together with a number to call in case of complaint.

This would ensure that the person in charge knew...that if they did not make certain that the charter and the code of conduct was being respected...and that good practices were laid down and carried out to the required level / standard by their personnel...then they would be held responsible...personally; it would be their reputation and their livelihood that was on the line.

Nothing encourages respect for the rules better than a named person being held personally responsible and accountable for their implementation.

The PDC would also insist that a qualified supervisor - in charge of care - be present at all times. *(At almost £1000 per week, per resident, this should not be a problem)*

The PDC rules would also insist upon the following;

- a greater subject knowledge (care / medical) for all employees in direct contact with residents...together with an officially recognised qualification
- CCTV in every room to monitor safety, neglect and abuse...and finally
- The care-home licence would be tied to its management respecting an index-linked cap on charges after an industry-wide consultation to discuss and fix the initial base rate of service to avoid a repeat of the current exploitative practices.

NB; we also need to look into not splitting up elderly couples when the time comes to look after them. If families cannot take them in, as a nation we have to step up and re-house them together.

Humanity

"What we are doing to the forests of the world is but a mirror reflection of what we are doing to ourselves and to one another." Mahatma Gandhi

---

I am truly saddened by the depth of evil and depravity that exists in this world;

- from the blood-thirsty dictators
- to the murderers and paedophiles
- to the human traffickers (the pimps and the organ harvesters)
- to the cartels and the drug traffickers
- to the criminal underworld

...and all the way down through the gang culture to the little thugs on the street corners and the bullies in the school-yards; there just seems to be so much evil around, to the point where our 21st century YouTube generation with their selfish arrogance and their ubiquitous camera phones are now actually proud to openly display their lack of compassion and humanity.

It is a sad reality but these days, people would much rather stand around and film those who are literally dying before their eyes - than offer them help.

These days people film executions, they film people dying in accidents, they film people fighting in the street (men and women); they film anything and everything but nobody...nobody ever steps in to help; what is wrong with people? Where is the empathy?

I have seen how people around the world treat each other;

- how the Mexican cartels summarily execute and dismember their enemies,
- how the Guatemalans and Brazilians deliver street justice by beating people to a pulp and then setting them on fire,
- how the Africans (Rwanda) machete people to death by the thousand
- how in Syria, snipers deliberately target pregnant women in a macabre point-scoring 'game'
- how in Saudi Arabia, Pakistan, Iran and Iraq they still hang people in groups from makeshift gallows and cranes...and stone people in the streets
- how the Chechens and the Russians kill each other without a second's thought,
- how those same Russians chastise inmates in prison with sadistic beatings just as they do in Venezuela...and
- how the ruthlessly savage Afghan Taliban line up innocent civilians and then summarily mow them down with Kalashnikovs...or mercilessly decapitate them in cold blood (it's all there on the Internet)

———

No, we are a long way from my idea of humanity.

There are people in this world with no morality, no integrity and no compassion; who have no sense of honesty or justice and no idea about what is right or wrong, who are prepared to take everything and anything from you without even batting an eye-lid; that is the reality of life...that is the underbelly of humanity.

Mankind as a species is not innately good; he has learned compassion and morality over time – through a painstakingly slow process of socialisation - but it is not inherent in his animal nature to be good, as the ubiquitous criminality that exists worldwide clearly demonstrates.

———

The human template is pretty easy to understand; in fact it is very basic because under all the BS of what is socially acceptable, underneath all the airs and graces and behind all the facades and pretences of sophistication that are drummed into us over time, we are all running on the same caveman software...wired to hunt for food in order to survive and to procreate in order to pass our genes onto the next generation.

It is as simple as that.

We have been trying to improve ourselves over time, to throw off the shackles of our violent nature - through an on-going process of behavioural conditioning - and sometimes, on the odd occasion, we have actually succeeded in doing so, but sadly, all attempts at definitively taming or even controlling our inherent natural aggression are doomed to failure because we simply need that drive as a race in order to survive.

We just have to make sure that those among us who might be tempted to use that force for evil or to exploit the weak (physical and moral) are kept in check.

What is wrong with humanity? (2)

We consider ourselves the most evolved species on the planet and yet we behave in a way that is so undignified that we really do not deserve our lofty position at the top of the evolutionary tree.

Human beings are fundamentally selfish, self-centred and greedy; character traits that might have allowed us to survive over time but which will inevitably contribute to our own self-destruction.

Just look at life; look at how we treat each other – to begin with...we lie, we cheat and we steal......but then we are also aggressive and violent towards each other;

- we abuse each other
- we betray each other

- we fight and kill each other
- we consider ourselves civilised and yet we allow people to be massacred by their leaders without intervening
- we make refugees of people in their own country for political gain...if we are not killing them or using them as human shields
- we kidnap, buy and sell **other human beings** to use or sell for sex or profit
- while allowing others to starve to death
- a woman is raped every second of every hour somewhere around the world...and finally...
- we force children and young children at that, to work down mines or in sweat-shops

It is quite chilling how human beings can be so completely exempt of all humanity without actually having to be cold-blooded killers, psychopaths, sociopaths or paedophiles.

———

Humanity as it stands is not a representation of what is good; on the contrary noble traits such as truth, compassion and honour are seen as weak these days and instead of applauding them, people would rather exploit them.

That is where humanity is right now; on the road to oblivion because as I said above, human beings are fundamentally selfish, self-centred and greedy and being selfish, self-centred and greedy we will continue to plunder the planet's finite natural resources with impunity until there are no more.

Then, we will simply die out because we are inherently selfish and greedy...and incapable of reneging on those fundamental characteristics.

We believe that we are the most evolved creatures on this planet but the reality is that we are still savages looking out for number one, who turn a blind eye to other people's misery when it doesn't concern us.

Indeed, we are more often judgemental and critical...than caring, altruistic and kind.

Humanity is not innately good; it is hardly a shining example of decency and integrity and quite frankly, we do not deserve to be in charge of the destiny of life on this planet.

The evolution of humanity;

It has been a long process but the evolution of humanity is following the same path...as a whole entity...as we do as individuals;

- from childhood; where we were ignorant and knew nothing
- through our teenage years; where we think we know everything when we don't
- to our adult life when we are content in the knowledge we did the best we could

---

I see the history of humanity in a similar tri-partite evolution;

- **Stage one**; the prehistoric age (un-evolved)
- **Stage two**; the learning / evolutionary age (the current age; from the gods and goddesses of ancient Greece and Rome, through the religious theologies and wars used to manipulate the masses and all the way through to the spectacular advances in medicine, science and technology)
- **Stage three**; the enlightenment age (this would be a hypothetical era where everybody lived in peace and harmony, but sadly I fear that we will never reach this stage...as religion, human stupidity and the politics of greed will have wiped us out long before the genesis of this can take seed)

The Future;

As stated previously, I am afraid for the future of mankind.

The violence and our self-destructive nature aside, we are compromising our future on other levels too;

- with short-sighted countries like China and India suppressing their female populations at birth (promoting male offspring as the only acceptable choice; a policy which has - by the way – spawned a rise in the kidnapping and sale of children as young as a few days old)
- and now the Gays and Lesbians obtaining the right to get married,

...humanity is being skewed out of all proportion, beyond all recognition.

Ethical Issues

The fundamental rule;

As human beings we are all equal; therefore we should all be treated the same... and any natural proclivities that we might personify - whether it be our sexual orientation or the colour of our skin; things that we are born with and can do nothing about - should never be legislated for or against by society.

However, as a human being, I have to say that I abhor the way we are skewing / distorting humanity in order to bow to the selfish demands of any number of minority groups who are using the ridiculous European Human Rights Act and the folly of the political correctness lobby to bully spineless politicians into consenting to their demands, even when those demands are contra-nature.

I believe that it is fundamentally wrong to tamper with the natural order of things.

Nature has been doing fine for hundreds of thousands of years without the meddling of mankind, but between society's desire to be all things to all men...and man's natural tendency to interfere where he shouldn't I'm pretty certain that we will mess up humanity...and no doubt the rest of the planet...sooner rather than later.

Homosexual Issues –

Gay marriage;

This is a conundrum for me but here are my thoughts.

I believe that people should be allowed to love whoever they want; however, that said, looking at the bigger picture and the ongoing future of the human race, I worry that we might be compromising that future in the way we are artificially engineering our society in order to appease, mollify and placate any number of minority pressure groups and Civil Liberties organisations.

Everybody knows that trying to please all of the people all of the time never works; choices have to be made...and while I respect everybody's right to do as they feel, on this particular issue I have to come down on the side of humanity and the perpetuity of the human race as my guiding principle.

Critically, the concept of marriage is a religious invention that was dreamed up by the church at a time when it was trying to control people's sexuality, in the hope that it would create the best environment possible in which to bring up young children.

However, that concept has since been recognised by the rest of society and written into the social contract as an indisputable paradigm...which is sadly, where the seed of discord takes root...because whenever religion and the state are inter-twined the consequence is almost inevitably confusion and conflict as the two ideals simply cannot co-exist.

This is because...

- the state represents all its citizens; it cannot choose which part of society it wishes to represent...it represents everybody within its purview
- while on the other hand, religion - whichever that religion might be - only represents those who sign up to its particular dogma, leaving those who do not follow its teachings to one side.

This duality of ideals creates tension within the state and the constant struggle of the two entities trying to work within the same framework... but with different agendas... is what ultimately fills our history books and our graveyards.

That is why there would be no religious component to the PDC manifesto and why the only requirement that the PDC would insist upon, as far as marriage is concerned, irrespective of gender would be a small ceremony in a designated government building in order to sign the civic register, as a way of legitimising the event.

If couples then wanted to go and celebrate their marriage in a religious setting then they would be welcome to do so, no matter their sex, their race or their religious beliefs...and as for the conundrum of whether or not certain establishments would be prepared to celebrate or bless such unions within their walls, let's be sensible and pragmatic about it.

Let's decide that every establishment should be free to choose whether or not they would be prepared to celebrate such unions...and as long as they made it clear what their position was in advance of any booking, finding an alternative venue to host an event should not be too difficult a task.

———

This separation between religion and the state concerning the marriage contract would also allow the PDC to remove the incentive of a preferential tax arrangement for spouses...because up until now, because of the influence of religion on the state, marriage had been used as a sweetener to encourage people to stay together in order to benefit from a better tax rate.

The gay-community saw that arrangement as going against their Human Rights; they challenged it and quite rightly won their case on the grounds of equal rights for all.

So now that the gay-community has equality in respect of the law...and quite rightly so...the PDC would revise the tax laws concerning married people and remove any direct fiscal advantage tied to the concept.

Married people, whoever they might be, whatever their gender would pay the same rate of tax as anyone else in their wage bracket...and any 'advantage' they might receive from the state as a couple would be linked entirely to the children that they might nurture.

This means that people would be marrying for the right reasons; for love...and not for a reduced tax-bill.

Gays and IVF;

In writing this manifesto, all my thinking, all my reasoning as a human being, on whatever subject, revolves around **Nature**...and this particular subject goes right to the very heart of nature, of our nature.

The fundamental role of a woman on this earth is to give birth to the next generation so that our species might continue *ad infinitum*. However, there are circumstances, as in every species, where – for whatever reason – a woman cannot accomplish this task.

This could be down to natural selection as it is in many species...or infertility...or any number of other complicated medical conditions, any of which could preclude a woman from getting pregnant...and homosexuality is another logical explanation of why a woman has not conceived.

However, some lesbian women are not prepared to accept nature as their guide in this very sensitive matter and they have forced the issue of motherhood and children onto the front stage, demanding that as women it is their human right to be parents in order to respond to an innate maternal instinct.

These women even went to court on the matter and they won the case, arguing that because they were female it was their human right to fulfil their maternal role.

This is a very selfish argument because <u>it is not a human right to be a parent</u> - indeed many heterosexual people never become parents - but it is what it is in this egotistical 'me,me,me' society.

Nevertheless it was a landmark case and because the women won it, it then allowed gay men to jump on the bandwagon to demand that their rights to be fathers be respected...although <u>they</u> didn't use the human-rights argument that the women had used as their leverage. Instead, they used the equality laws; laws which had initially been drawn up to protect women and their right to equality in society.

The argument was simple; if lesbian women could demand to be mothers then why shouldn't homosexual men demand to be fathers?

Once again, the matter went to court and once again the decision was made in favour of the plaintiff; i.e. gay men.

Now this all sounds very logical...and very legal, which it is...but the fact remains that while we are creating laws and adapting society to the whims and selfish desires of the individual, we are scaffolding a false reality for ourselves through legislation...while at the same time skewing the natural course of humanity.

Just because we pass a law that says BLACK is the new WHITE, it doesn't change the fundamental fact that BLACK is still BLACK.

The simple fact is that by pandering to all the different pressure groups that are demanding that their voice be heard we are...as a race...skewing humanity beyond all recognition.

Children should not be conceived in test-tubes and Petri dishes.

It is not what humanity is about in my opinion.

The human race has two sexes for a reason, just like any other species... and I believe that the selfish, short-sighted generation that currently inhabits the planet with its 'I want it all because I can' attitude, doesn't auger well for the generations of dysfunctional individuals that will follow them in the next few decades.

I do not wish to condemn or judge people of the gay community for wanting to be parents but my problem is this;

- the reason we are all here today is because our forefathers procreated for generation after generation in order for it to be this way...

...and if we go too far down the road of single sex relationships, what is the future of the human race, where are the next generations going to come from;

Are genetically-modified / test-tube births going to become the norm?

Is that the future of humanity?

I do hope not.

Conclusion;

In conclusion, as stated previously I believe that all people should have the right to love whoever they want.

However, I am against two lesbian women - even those who have a 'married' status - being granted IVF treatment on the NHS in order to have children when there is no male / father-figure involved...just as I am against two men using surrogacy to fulfil their selfish desires to be parents without the involvement of a female / mother-figure.

It is not nature's way...and it is not the end of the world for a woman not to be a mother...or indeed for a man not to be a father.

Gay people are now free to pursue a same-sex relationship in this country in the full acceptance of the law which is a huge evolution in our mind-set considering that homosexuality was still illegal in this country up until 1967, but it is nevertheless a lifestyle choice of the individual's choosing and that choice should include an understanding that there would be no 'artificially-created' children as part of the relationship.

This mirrors another PDC policy which would oblige potential heterosexual spouses to take a fertility test before walking down the aisle and to accept the results of those tests if they established that the future married couple would be unable to conceive for whatever reason; a situation which would mean that people were entering into the sanctity of marriage fully aware of whether there would be the possibility of children with that particular partner...or not.

Now I understand that I will be vilified for this by all the Civil Libertarians but my only goal here is to respect Nature and defend humanity.

In many species, not every female has the right to procreate and not every male has the right to sire...that is what the law of nature tells us... and that is what I believe should be our guiding principle too.

It is not an absolute right for a woman to give birth and indeed, as mentioned previously, many heterosexual women don't have children either...so for those lesbian women who do have a pronounced maternal instinct and are desperate for a child, I would suggest they turn their attention instead to adoption as a more 'natural' solution to their dilemma because to deliberately create children...outside the normal parameters of nature... is simply not <u>natural</u>.

We have to stop twisting nature in order to bow to these unrelenting lobby groups.

Author's comment;

Over 5000 children have been born in the UK in the last decade through IVF treatment to lesbian and single mothers...none of whom has a father.

Is that how we see the future of humanity, devoid of any male role models?

———

Gays and adoption;

My goal in writing this manifesto is to suggest a way forward for the British public but also to suggest ways that people and humanity as a whole might go forward in peace and harmony...and my guiding precepts on this journey are;

- the respect of Nature,
- Logic and
- Common Sense

As stated previously, I believe in equality for all...but once again on this issue I am faced with a conundrum;

I would like to see gay couples able to adopt like any heterosexual couple because at the end of the day it is the children's needs that should be considered first.

However we cannot get away from the fact that our species comprises male and female components and therefore, the ideal situation in my eyes – looking at the bigger picture and the future of the human race – would always be one based on a heterosexual family unit.

Nevertheless, while I would prefer Nature to be respected I feel that it is only right that I compromise on this very delicate issue - using the third of my guiding principles; Common Sense - because while I draw the line at creating children artificially I do believe nonetheless that homosexual parents are just as capable of showering love and affection on an adopted child as their heterosexual counterparts.

Heterosexuals and IVF –

Having researched the IVF question in quite some depth the biggest and most reductive sentiment I keep getting is one of selfishness.

Now I understand that Nature can be very fickle and even cruel at times but I do not believe that it is every woman's <u>right</u> to have a child. In other species the females don't always get to mate and they calmly accept it with dignity and grace (without complaint).

Why can't women, the human female accept that rule of Nature too?

It is just another example of this 'have it all society' that the feminists have imposed on us over the last forty years filled with selfish, self-indulgent women - who just want what they want – and will not even accept Nature itself dictating to them.

There are two segments of the population desperate for IVF treatment;

- Women of a naturally child-bearing age who cannot - for whatever reason – conceive...and
- Women who are post-menopausal and yet still want to conceive

The first group deserve a little sympathy because the truth can sometimes be hard to face and to accept...but the second group are just...selfish.

Of course, I understand the over-whelming desire of a woman to be a mother but in matters of procreation my ultimate guideline has to be the respect of nature.

These days, just as children have no boundaries because of a lack of decent parenting, women have no boundaries either.

Often no more than overgrown children themselves, they are encouraged - by the frivolously dangerous feminist slogans of 'we want it all'...and...'because we're worth it' - to continue to demand their own way even when Mother Nature has told them that they have left it too late or that it's not medically possible for them to get pregnant, for whatever reason.

These self-obsessed people are de-constructing society one selfish demand after the other until one day nothing will make any sense anymore and anarchy will prevail.

For example;

- A 57 year old woman had a baby through IVF because the science was there to do it...but now, several years later that same woman regrets her decision because the child will have to be brought up by her niece when she dies.

Surely with a little forethought and some professional guidance this outcome could have been foreseen and avoided before getting to the point of no return.

Author's comment;

Just like celebrity adoption, IVF is the ultimate act of selfish 'I want it all' feminism – but it is not only selfish, it is morally wrong, not to say reprehensible for post-menopausal women of 50, 60 and why not 70 to still be demanding the right to have children when nature has told them that their time is up.

Giving birth should be ruled by Nature and a study of Nature tells us that a woman's fertility declines rapidly after thirty five.

There is a reason for this. It is Nature's way of saying, you've have your chance to procreate and you have taken up that opportunity or not. However, it is not an open-ended offer...and just because we now have the science to go beyond that natural barrier it doesn't necessarily mean that we should.

It is not every woman's right to give birth – in every other species, the female has no guarantees; some just have to learn that it was not meant to be.

The menopause is nature's way of drawing a line under that part of a woman's life and she should accept that state of affairs.

The menopause is nature's birth control model and we should respect it...because tampering with it will only get us into trouble as we have already found out to our cost on previous occasions when we have tried to interfere with nature.

––––––

We have to stop messing with humanity;

- Women are now freezing ovarian tissue to be used at a later date
- those who are unable to carry a child are asking to use their mothers' wombs
- others want to donate their eggs to their children meaning that a girl would effectively be giving birth to her own sister
- one woman has already used her sister's egg, and had her sister-in-law act as the surrogate before <u>she</u> (the first woman) then became the legal parent
- meanwhile post-menopausal women are having ovarian grafts
- ...and cases of women demanding to use the sperm of their dead husbands or ex-partners in order to have children are on the rise.

––––––

These methods which defy natural science and normal human biology are all being perfected in laboratories around the world...all to satisfy the selfish desires of women who want more than what nature has intended them to have, and while I understand the maternal instinct and the desire that many have for children, **this is not natural**.

It is, on the other hand symptomatic of our selfish society that even when nature tells us **NO** we still want what we want.

Its 'me-me-me' all the time...but what about the children being born to sixty year old mothers who can't cope with the physical demands of 24/7 motherhood and potentially won't be around long enough to see them grow up....

Who is thinking about them?

Do these people know nothing of the biology of the human race?

It's twisted.

If these people are so desperate to be parents then they should adopt an orphan from Africa or elsewhere in the world where there is a great and growing need for loving parents.

So in conclusion; I have to side with humanity on this issue.

It's not always because we can, that we should.

———

Wombs for hire;

Meanwhile, a lucrative new business has sprouted in India; baby farms or baby factories.

These are places where rich couples from the West...unable to conceive on their own but desperate for a child...can either adopt or provide their own 'genetic matter / DNA' to be implanted in a surrogate and handed back to them after the gestation period.

Once again, I understand the 'parents' desire to have children but is this...should this be the future of humanity...renting the wombs of women whose social situation leaves them no other choice?

This is just another example of the selfish, self-indulgence of those wanting more than what nature had decreed was their due.

It is also alas, money which is shaping humanity because these poor Indian women who cannot support themselves financially in any other way are being exploited for their bodies almost in the same way as prostitutes...and of course money paves the way.

I cannot agree with the commercialisation of childbirth in this way, treating human reproduction as a business and this constant manipulation of our genetics makes me more than a little uncomfortable.

IVF and the NHS –

I have already addressed this issue in the NHS chapter but for those who missed it

---

Why should women be allowed to demand very expensive IVF treatment from the NHS just because they are female; <u>it is not a human right</u> despite what they might believe.

If these women want this treatment, then they should pay for it privately or they should accept their situation like any other female in any other species.

The NHS was not set up to pander to this female vanity.

This is just another example of the selfish 'I want it all because I can society' that the feminists have imposed on us all over the last forty years or so.

Even couples who already have children are asking for free IVF treatment on the NHS which is scandalous.

The NHS cannot afford to offer this service *ad infinitum* to everybody that asks for it; it is a very costly and drawn out procedure and an unsustainable drain on limited resources.

We need to get away from this feminist driven culture of 'I want it all and I want it now'.

Women cannot have it all – their female condition does not automatically guarantee them the right to motherhood and despite medical progress in this area, they have no divine right to be a parent; it doesn't matter how desperate they might be.

Just look again at what happens in nature – in most species, if not all, there is a dynamic of natural selection which means that not all females are impregnated – the analogy might be crude but it is a fact born out of thousands of years of evolution.

We should not be holding the NHS to ransom, demanding that they carry out fertility treatment as a right to all women to have children.

Some women and some men too will simply have to accept the fact that they will never be parents; it happens in all species.

After all, when it comes to Nature we are no different, even though we sometimes think we are.

————

Author's comment;

The ultimate irony; we have now passed a law to allow women over forty to sue the NHS if they are refused IVF treatment.

I wonder; are these people deliberately trying to bankrupt the NHS, just so as to satisfy that small group of women who consciously chose not to have their children during their fertile years?

This is once again outrageous and needs to be curtailed forthwith.

––––––––

Sperm donation;

Sperm donation has become a contentious issue these days because of new legislation which removes anonymity for men and forces them to reveal their identities so that any future offspring can trace them.

Meanwhile, women can frivolously choose to put any Tom, Dick or Harry on the birth certificate of their child as the father – male, female, animal or plant.

This legislation lacks coherence; if men have to stand up and be counted then there has to be coherence in genetic tracing.

It is no surprise that sperm donations have dwindled as a result - because of the quagmire of paternity issues that this new legislation has thrown up - and unless we reinstate anonymity for donors that situation will only get worse.

––––––––

Another legal minefield has also been created by women obtaining the right to use the sperm of their ex-partners and dead husbands in order to get pregnant, because, as much as the women want to be mothers, the men want that same right, <u>not to be fathers</u>.

I believe that any sperm donation should be anonymous as it is an altruistic act to help someone – much like giving blood – and I also believe that any sperm that remains unused upon the death of the donor should be destroyed unless prior consent had been agreed.

Artificial sperm;

Sperm donation is one issue but scientists are already hard at work trying to produce artificial sperm.

However, here is my hypothesis on this; if the scientists manage to create artificial sperm, thereby forgoing the need for men altogether, they will also have to address the male sex-drive and develop bi-laterally an anti-testosterone drug because men who find themselves sexually redundant with no outlet, and no means of expressing themselves would get extremely aggressive.

This would leave humanity with a very serious conundrum because if we take away their testosterone, men would not develop their manly traits and characteristics. They would not develop the muscle strength needed to carry out any physical tasks and as a consequence they would all become redundant wet-lettuces transforming society as we know it into a crumbling wasteland.

Scientists of the world beware; you might just be programming the end of humanity with your meddling.

Going forward –

Even if we accept that the nuclear model for family life is a thing of the past – what is the future of humanity?

Is the future of humanity going to be reduced to biological anarchy – to an experimental mix-n-match swap-shop with no genetic links, no chemical bond and no maternal instinct – just a mechanised procedure or monetary transaction managed by technology and developed through a process of impersonal test-tube conception or cloning in a post-coital world, or will it be created in a series of Petri-dishes thanks to the random donation of sperm and eggs which will have been frozen in time and kept for years...or

…is surrogacy the way forward…like they do in the United States of America where super-rich celebrities with super-sized egos who don't have the time or the patience to gestate for nine months get somebody else to do it for them and just have the package picked up from the hospital by their chauffeurs like the latest accessory...

Is that what we want for ourselves? Is that the future of humanity?

A hybrid / mutant society where nobody has the same blood type as their parents…with no roots and no genetic ties; just imagine the compatibility problems with blood-transfusions and the issues of rejection related to organ donation...or will we just grow those extra organs in separate Petri-dishes too?

All I'm saying is - because we can doesn't necessarily mean we should - and because we can put legislation in place to legalise these procedures and pander to this selfish fad, it doesn't necessarily mean that we should.

I do not see it that way but if we continue to pander to these selfish individuals for long enough...and allow the scientists free-reign to manipulate the composition of our very existence, then the future looks bleak for us all.

The future;

However we do it, whether in a Petri dish, a test-tube or by actually having sexual congress we will always need to mix the human male components with those of the female in order for the human race to continue to exist.

Now, science is progressing every day and maybe in the not too distant future we will actually be able to create life artificially...but is that really what we want our future to be?

By reducing human procreation to a biological assignment, picking and choosing the components out of a database without any actual input from the future 'parents' seems to me to be skewing humanity out of all recognition...and as I see it such dispassionate and clinical engineering of our genes, of our very essence in fact, will do nothing as time goes by but create generation after generation of individuals with no roots, no emotional connection and no innate identity; human traits considered superfluous by the supercilious geneticists of the future will slowly be phased out one after the other and all those silly little quirks and foibles that make us human will be eliminated progressively as the scientists of the future try to create the perfect specimen.

However, what is possibly more worrying is that other human traits such as empathy, emotions (embarrassment), our sense of morality or our innate sense of right and wrong might also be removed or at least compromised.

All that will be left is a race of perfect automatons...and that is why I believe that scientists need to be careful with how they mess with humanity and its genetics – both in artificial conception and in the reprogramming of our DNA.

———

Gender choice needs to be resisted too, because if people are allowed to choose the sex of their offspring through genetic manipulation it will quickly ruin the natural ratio and create an imbalance leading to an excess of men and not enough women to continue producing subsequent generations of the human race.

Just look at how the Chinese have created an artificial imbalance through their one-child policy and how it is beginning to affect their population. Their approach was less scientific than what I am suggesting above - they simply drowned female babies at birth so that the parents could try again for a male descendant – but this imbalance between the two genders will ultimately come back to haunt them.

This might be a good thing for the rest of the world as it will put a brake on the evolution of the Chinese population - *India is experiencing the same phenomenon* - but if it is replicated in other countries around the world this imbalance will inevitably lead to unrest in many areas as men become frustrated and possessive over 'their' women-folk. This would then lead to more aggression and fuel more arguments as the men fight over the women. (it happens in every species that males fight over females, especially when they are scarce)

This scarcity-factor would then put women at greater risk of sexual attack which would in turn lead to them hiding away from society, voluntarily or being forcibly hidden away by their male 'guardians' for their own protection, a situation which would replicate the medieval practices of fundamentalist religions today and reverse decades of struggle for the affirmation of women's rights.

Meanwhile, other women would simply be enslaved and exploited by men for profit as they are the world over.

For information;

Cases of rape are already on the rise in India for example where the number of available women has declined considerably.

And another clear example of imbalance is the Lebanon where there are four women to every man. Now this is mainly down to war casualties but the imbalance between the sexes has clearly impacted on life there.

Therefore, scientists of the world I would remind you of your responsibilities and of the dangers of pandering to the selfish 'we want designer children' generation...and about allowing people to choose the sex of their children...because, as a consequence of your actions, rather than liberating the women of this world, you will be guiding them - as a minority - towards a reclusive future where they would have to constantly hide from the amorous advances of the hoards of testosterone-filled men roaming the streets.

Author's comment;

Maybe Mary Shelley's **Frankenstein** was prophetic; '...that science might one day be misused by those who wish to alter or tamper with nature...'

...and we have all seen the mutant results of that particular experiment... albeit fictional.

————

Conclusion;

Between the one-child (hopefully male) policies of China and India, the manipulation of our genes by the scientists and the explosion in same-sex relationships exacerbating the phenomenon, it is clear that the overall balance of humanity is slowly being altered...and the fact that we are skewing humanity a little more every day leads me to believe that by messing with nature on so many different levels we are ultimately putting ourselves as a race on a self-made path to oblivion.

————

Breastfeeding; (*not really an ethical issue but still...*)

Breast-feeding is good; it is nature's way of nourishing the very young. How can it be wrong, as some suggest when so many other species inhabiting this planet have developed the same method?

It is only the human race that thinks it can do better than nature.

How arrogant are we? How arrogant are the pharmaceutical companies that have been brainwashing people into believing that their products are better than nature's own?

My question is this; what came first, nature or exploitative big-business?

The NHS has spent £40 million in recent years curing illnesses in young children that could have been prevented had they been breast-fed; that is outrageous, that we would put big-business before the health of our children is absolutely scandalous...but sadly it does prove my point.

The PDC would promote the natural solution that has sustained our species since the beginning of time...and not one that is being imposed on us by big-business which has only been around for a few decades... though not in communal work-places or boardrooms as was recently suggested.

Adoption;

The PDC would look at the long, arduous and costly process of adoption.

We need to make the rules of adoption a lot easier because prospective parents are being put off by all the intrusive checks and invasive questions from over-zealous 'I must cover my back' social workers.

That said; I believe that there should be an upper age limit on anybody adopting.

Common sense and logic must prevail on this sensitive issue.

Abortion;

Under the PDC, all pregnancies would be monitored and scanned at regular intervals in order to detect any fœtal deformities or potential problems which would ultimately lead to that individual becoming a burden on society after its birth...

...and if it was decided by the medical specialists that there was no possibility of that individual leading a 'normal' existence as part of society with a decent quality of life, then the PDC policy would be to terminate the pregnancy, to pre-empt those future difficulties from ever arising.

Pregnancy scans;

Early scan;	6-10 weeks
Dating scan;	10-13 weeks
Anomaly scan;	20 weeks (abortion limit)
Growth scan;	28-38 weeks

That said; the progress in post-natal technology which now allows us to save very premature babies would motivate the PDC to reduce the number of weeks during which an abortion could be performed from 24 to 20 weeks...although gender-specific abortions for cultural / socio-economic reasons would never be tolerated under any circumstances.

Teenage Abortion;

In the UK we perform 200,000 terminations a year, 40,000 of which are teenage pregnancies (the highest in the western world) and 4000 of those procedures are on teenagers who have not yet reached the legal age of consent. Some were 13, 12 and even 11yrs old.

New Labour spent £300 million trying to address the issue of teenage pregnancy but the number of underage pregnancies still went through the roof as the £1million that the NHS spends on repeat abortions every week testifies; *one teenager has had eight abortions!*

So there is clearly a problem still to be addressed.

Some specialists suggest fitting 11 and 12 yr olds with the coil but I would prefer another method of avoiding teenage pregnancy – **more and better education**.

However this does not mean shifting responsibility onto the teaching staff in cases of teenage pregnancy. Teachers need to be reminded that schoolgirls up to the age of fifteen are still considered children in the eyes of the law and therefore still under the guardianship of their parents who must be informed of any situation concerning their children. I understand that this is a very delicate conversation - which needs to be handled with the utmost sensitivity - but it must nevertheless take place. It is then up to the parents of the teenager to make a decision, with their daughter's accord…and depending on their particular circumstances.

We have to stop blurring the lines of the law with all this woolly Political Correctness / Human Rights nonsense.

The PDC would however be in favour of qualified school nurses using their discretion - in exceptional circumstances – to hand out a morning-after pill to a student who had made a 'mistake' the night before… although this arrangement would have to be carefully monitored and not used as a form of contraception as some grown women seem to be doing.

Stem cell research –

Scientists and biologists will always push the boundaries; that is how they make discoveries and advance our understanding of the universe. However, on certain matters, because they have no boundaries, it is the moral duty of our political leaders to protect us and set those boundaries for the scientists to respect.

- Stem cell research into blindness, cerebral palsy and multiple sclerosis for example, is wonderful.

- Work on the elimination of hereditary diseases and the regeneration of organs that can subsequently be implanted into the human body is fantastic.
- but research into genetic manipulation, into cloning and the creation of hybrid embryos is far more controversial and brings with it fundamental and ethical issues that have yet to be assessed.

So while I am right behind the research into solving the mysteries of our most debilitating illnesses, I am totally against the manipulation of our genetics surrounding childbirth and the creation of life.

That is where I have to draw the line because when mankind gets too cocky or too arrogant Nature has a way of putting him back in his place; just look at how nature confounded and tamed the arrogance and the over-reaching ambition of men during the Titanic disaster. We think we know better than nature but we underestimate her at our own peril.

―――――

Transplants;

I believe that transplant operations in Britain should prioritise British patients over patients from other countries...and I also believe that we should take that idea one step further by making an exception for blood relatives; in a recent case a mother was refused her daughter's organs (kidneys) and died. That, in my eyes, is unacceptable.

Of course, I understand the 'waiting-list' concept but in such cases I believe that it would be ethically correct to consider an immediate family member who might need the organ of a loved-one...before a complete stranger.

―――――

Death;

This is the 21st century; everybody knows about the cycle of life. Death is a part of that cycle and I really do not understand why those who govern us cannot see through their blinkered political agendas to the reality which is; that people want to be in control of the way they leave this world just as much as they want to control every other aspect of their existence.

How I hate the hypocrisy of the current situation which allows British people to go to Dignitas in Switzerland to die...but doesn't allow them that same right in their own country.

When are we, as a nation, going to have a grown-up conversation about the circle of life?

Why are we in this country, so afraid to discuss any topic that has been labelled 'taboo' by the repressed middle-classes ...topics like sex and death...which are perfectly normal components of life?

I have no idea whether it is naiveté, a lack of intellectual maturity or just our legendary reserved nature that stops us from taking informed decisions based on common-sense and logic...

...or whether again it is just the lily-livered politicians not wanting to upset the exasperating 'bleeding hearts' lobby...

...but given the chance, I believe that many people in this country would much rather stay in their own homes, surrounded by their own families, for the final days of their lives... than have to undertake the arduous journey to Switzerland to the Dignitas clinic in order for their wishes to be carried out.

What is wrong with self-determination?

We shoot horses...don't we...to put them out of their misery?

We put down cats and dogs humanely...and yet we force our fellow human beings, those we love and cherish the most, to stay alive whether they want to or not...through a cocktail of drugs and medicines...

...and when those drugs and medicines no longer have any effect and their bodily functions break down because they are simply worn out and can no longer sustain life on their own, we attach machines to those bodies to prolong the indignity of their existence for even longer.

You have to sympathise with fierce 'right-to-die' campaigners such as Tony Nicklinson and Paul Lamb...and indeed anyone in a similar situation who is forced to carry on living, often in the most horrendous circumstances...simply because the lily-livered conservatives who systematically oppose 'assisted-dying' refuse to move into the 21st century.

Of course, life is our most important possession but we all know that it is naturally finite.

We use our intelligence to try to prolong life in many ways but why shouldn't we also use that same intelligence to be dogmatic about self determination.

People know when they are ready to go; they know when their bodies can no longer cope with or sustain life.

———

Now I understand the conflict of interest that doctors are faced with – they have a code of ethics framed in the Hippocratic Oath which states that their role is to save people's lives and not help to end them...and of course that oath must be respected whenever possible.

However, some people get to a point in their lives where they simply cannot be saved, where their bodies can no longer function, where they have no quality of life and would not survive another minute without a tube thrust down their throats or a needle in their arm.

Life is sacred but if there is no quality to that life, patients should have the choice to die with dignity rather than live every day with the embarrassment and the humiliation of having every one of their bodily functions taken care of by a carer or a machine.

We are all finite, we know that and therefore I believe that if ever we arrive at a time in our lives where we no longer have our faculties, where we no longer control the quality of our life or even our bodily functions – then there is no longer any point in being here.

Of course, rules would have to be drawn up - after consultation - and a consensus would have to be reached but this is the right thing to do and a discussion on this issue must take place.

Why should we be made to live a life with no quality?

I believe that the only person, who can judge if his / her life is worth living, is the person himself / herself...so why should our right to die with dignity be taken away from us just to satisfy the timorous 'life-at-all-costs' brigade, however noble and laudable their argument might be?

This is the 21st century and choices have to be made.

———

We need to grow a backbone in this country when it comes to taking difficult decisions and therefore the PDC would introduce a **Living Will** for everyone over the age of fifty.

This would be a statement of fact witnessed by a family member and a legal representative...renewable every five years...that would indicate a person's position on assisted suicide and confirm their wish to be resuscitated or not if ever they were in a position that that question would be asked.

The Living Will would also include a clause that would give the medical profession – under strict supervision and in the presence of family and legal representation – the right to turn off a machine keeping a person alive if that was their last wish.

People, this is not euthanasia; euthanasia implies somebody else making the decision for you.

This would be the person himself / herself letting his / her wishes on assisted suicide be known before any illness ever took hold, while they were still compos-mentis.

NB; The Human Rights Act would be amended in the new British version - which the PDC would be introducing - to reflect this modern development and avoid any confusion.

Post-life arrangements;

With the number of visits to cemeteries on the decline...and the need for land to build houses for the living steadily increasing, the PDC would look into re-structuring our post-life arrangements.

This is a very delicate matter and has to be handled with great sensitivity but I believe that it is time to phase out the concept of cemeteries altogether and introduce compulsory cremation for everyone.

The cost of funerals and burial arrangements in the UK has soared in recent years - increasing by over 80% between 2004 and 2013 - and as burial plots become more and more elusive...and therefore more and more expensive...an average funeral now costs over £7,000; £2,160 of which is administration fees.

Ordinary people are reaching a point where they simply cannot afford to die.

We have to rein in these spiralling costs, especially those administration fees, and as a first step the PDC would impose a fixed-rate charge on all local councils for the provision of this service, with a view to preventing the more callous and unscrupulous amongst them from exploiting the grieving families of recently deceased loved-ones by hiking up the costs of their burial arrangements; an ongoing situation which has been widely reported of late.

The PDC would also look into creating a number of Memorial Parks and landscaped gardens - based on the same concept as the Military Arboretum – where memorial plaques could be placed for those wishing to grieve their dearly departed or simply spend some time in a reflective mood.

NB; these plaques would be made of a very durable but non-precious compound, in order to discourage the wilful desecration of these areas by metal thieves.

———

One final point;

We also need to update and modernise the current laws governing Wills and Testaments. Their execution needs to be much clearer, much simpler and far less costly.

———

Salary

Author's comment;

This might be an outdated philosophy or ideal, but I believe that for any society to prosper and function properly, each and every sector of that society needs to feel part of it – needs to feel that at their level – whatever that level might be – they are being treated fairly and with respect.

We cannot hope for a society based on equality for all if we promote a social elite.

PUBLIC SECTOR PAY;

The greed generation is over.

The public sector cannot - and should never have tried to - compete with the private sector on salary because their respective mission statements are completely opposed;

There is a clear distinction between the two;

- one is there to provide a service to the public...while
- the other is their to make a profit for their shareholders

These two models have completely different priorities...and completely different goals...and therefore it is only logical that they have completely different remuneration guidelines.

Public sector salaries are dictated by central government while private sector salaries are wholly dependant on the economic forces in play adapting naturally to those circumstances in order for the company they service to survive.

———

Now I realise that people will never be satisfied; they will always want more; it's who we are...but the public sector which is financed by the taxpayer has to be administered with strict guidelines within a framework that is fair, realistic, affordable and most importantly...accountable to the taxpayer who funds it.

However, in recent years, because of a lack of political steel and a dearth of moral guidance among our managerial classes, salaries in certain areas of the public sector have been allowed to deviate from what could be considered an honest and deserved level.

That situation has to be corrected.

It is not right that people holding public office should be fleecing the taxpayer for all they can get. (We currently have local government officials with fancy titles earning over £400,000 a year).

That is not what public service should be about. It should be about receiving a fair salary in return for a decent day's work, providing the best service possible - within a particular sphere of competence - to the tax-paying British public; no more, no less.

———

Under a PDC administration every organisation in the public sector would have its accounts audited going back to 1997 which I see as the beginning of the 'greed generation'.

Every sector's pay structure would be deconstructed, each salary would be scrutinised and any faction that appeared to have gained an unfair advantage over the rest of society since 1997 in respect of what they offer and the level of service they provide would have its salaries revised and adjusted to a more reasonable and sustainable level.

That said; anyone who could not accept the new revised pay-scales that the PDC would be putting in place, who felt that they deserved more or that they could earn more by moving to the private sector, would be summarily invited to go and do just that.

The bankers threatened to leave for Hong Kong or New York after the financial crash of 2008 but they didn't follow through on the threat, because they knew they had gone too far and deserved to have their wings clipped. However, if the doctors and dentists for example wanted to go private without the guarantees of the NHS behind them, they would be welcome to do so...and if the fat-cat local councillors felt that the grass was greener elsewhere...the door would be wide open for them to exit too.

Under a PDC administration, anybody in the public sector who could not accept having their greed reined-in would be welcome to move to the private sector...but whatever these people decided to do, empty threats and blackmail would not be an option – because under the PDC's new education policy there would always be a queue of people waiting in line to learn their trade and take their place.

I repeat once again; the **Greed Generation** is over

———

Salary;

If we consider a salary in terms of a pie-chart or even a horizontal indicator, we would see it divided into four distinct parts;

1) The **necessity portion** (this is the part of the salary that pays for mortgages, basic services (water, gas and electric) and food.
2) The **comfort portion** (this is the part of the salary that pays for satellite TV, the latest mobile phone and cars etc)

3) The **disposable portion** (this is the part of the salary that pays for luxuries; holidays, designer clothes etc)...and finally...

4) The **surplus portion**; what I would quantify as the greed portion (this is the part of the salary which goes above and beyond the realm of necessity and comfort in relation to the average wage)

Of course the percentages of each portion depends on the level of salary and the socio-economic situation of those involved but I would like to see the **necessity portion** in lower incomes increased and the **surplus portion** in higher incomes reduced; a rebalancing of the country's wealth...in other words.

The New Public Sector Pay Structure;

It is incomprehensible that some local government officials should be earning up to four times the salary of the Prime-Minister. Surely, the Prime Minister, as the person who actually runs the country, should sit at the top of the public sector pyramid…and therefore earn the highest salary.

I believe that the public sector wage system should be a pyramid structure from the 16 year old work experience newcomer right through to the very top and the Prime-Minister's office…because I am convinced that a pyramid structure with an organised hierarchy encourages both stability and aspiration.

This is why the PDC would review every public sector salary in order to rebalance the excesses that have been allowed to go unchallenged since 1997.

It would not be an easy task; in fact it would be very complicated initially but all major change is complicated initially…until it is in place…and the PDC would not shirk from this challenge on the basis of its size.

We are not talking revolution here, just a timely re-adjustment to remind people, especially those at the top who have been enjoying life on the public purse just a little too much, of their responsibilities and their priorities.

The new pay-structure would be based on the 'Bands and Points system' currently in use in the NHS as this would provide a proven platform on which to build.

However, the above system would only be a template as the PDC would henceforth introduce a number of modifications to it, reducing the the size of the increments, the grades and the number of these grades in order to conform to the new rules.

I repeat; it will not be easy but I believe that this new configuration of the public-sector pay structure – *which would extend to all areas of the public sector that have been allowed to increase their salaries excessively in recent years thanks to spineless politicians* - based on solid principles of reward for hard work – would not only be transparent and easy to understand, it would also prevent any more greed-induced phenomenon creeping into the system.

Under the PDC, employers would offer jobs on a Basic Grade Level and use the incremental flexibility within that grade-level to organise seniority, promotion and personal growth…and…

…as part of the restructuring programme…and to help with the upheaval and readjustment…all public sector salaries would be index-linked for five years so that the cost of living would remain relatively stable for a period of time, although outside forces would always remain an unknown quantity and have to be taken into account if necessary.

However, after that five-year period, anybody working in the public sector who was still earning less than the 'Emgee Ratio' of 1.0 (average wage) would continue to have their salaries index-linked year on year during a PDC administration.

Of course, promotions during that time would also allow those motivated to succeed to increase their salaries accordingly.

As for those at the top, the PDC would impose a salary cap of £200,000 a year (ER; 8)

That is a fair wage in anybody's book for somebody being paid from the public purse.

This revised and simplified wage structure would hopefully reintroduce a measure of sanity and fairness to the public-sector salary system after years of self-absorbed greed, the goal being to reduce the disparity between the 'haves and the have-nots' in our society that has been allowed to open up by weak leadership...

...and besides, decent salaries for all would mean that those on the lowest salaries would no longer need tax-credits and housing benefits... so it's a win/win situation all round.

Extra note;

When calculating a salary, employers should always keep in mind the average annual wage of the ordinary man in the street and how his salary compares to the salary that they are about to offer; i.e., using the 'Emgee Ratio', if the average salary is £25,000 a year, does the position they are about to advertise warrant twice that sum, three times that sum...or four times that sum...etc, etc?

Situations that annoy the taxpayer;

- Many taxpayers would be outraged to learn that the head of the Royal Mail is paid a £1million a year salary (ER; 40) while the Post-Office is closing down 2500 post-offices all around the country. I am certain that the taxpayers who pay that salary would much prefer the money be invested in providing the service that is being abolished than paid to a fat-cat bureaucrat.
- Recently, a person was appointed to take charge of the HS2 project at a cost of £750,000 a year. (ER; 30) I believe this project will never go ahead so to be paying a person £750,000 a year (ER; 30) out of the taxpayers pocket for a project that has no future is absolutely immoral.
- Incidentally, there are a number of other quango-crats earning up to £300,000 a year (ER; 12) from the public purse and the total amount paid out to these people every year is £100 million; is this really justified?
- Meanwhile 331 managers at the BBC earn £100,000 a year (ER; 4) or more with the DG himself earning £838,000 (ER; 33.5) a year.
- Similarly, there are people working in 'not for profit' companies funded by the taxpayer who are earning salaries in excess of £850,000 (ER; 34). That is simply dishonest.

Surely the British taxpayers should be getting
better value for their money!

The Emgee Ratio;

Firstly let me explain what I have called the 'Emgee Ratio'.

The average wage in the UK today - <u>not the minimum wage</u> – the average wage is £24,252 a year and I believe that if that is the average amount of a British wage – in order to be as fair-play as possible - then the salary scale of every area of the public sector should relate to that average amount.

However, over time, that figure will fluctuate…so to avoid having to constantly update the published figure I have given it the appellation 'Emgee Ratio' to make it easier to refer to.

(To demonstrate the mechanism and to simplify the calculation I have rounded the average wage up to £25, 000)

The average wage in the UK – after qualification – is £25,000 a year…so in future when deciding on a salary – and where it sits within the company profile and society as a whole – potential employers would be asked to consider the implications of the position using the following concept;

If £25,000 is the average wage; does the position on offer and the responsibilities attached to the position sit right within the company's individual, self-contained structure…and also in comparison to a similar position elsewhere in the marketplace?

Here are two examples;

- Does a politician deserve an 'Emgee Ratio' of 3; (3 x the average wage)
  o i.e. £75,000 a year…or
- Does a footballer for example deserve a ratio of 624;
  o i.e. £300,000 a week x 52 weeks. That is £15.6 million a year just to kick a piece of plastic around a field. <u>The equivalent of 624 average salaries</u>

That is the question that I would like potential employers to ask themselves.

Of course there are specific considerations that have to be taken into account in the above examples;

- the first is in the public sector, the second in the private sector,

- the first has public responsibility while the second has to consider the longevity of a footballing career...but I have to ask...can any one person really justify earning the equivalent of 624 salaries just because he can kick a ball? Talent is one thing but <u>is it right that a footballer can earn in one week what an average worker earns in twelve years</u> even taking into consideration the short duration of a footballing career?

Now, these examples are simply to illustrate the purpose of this mechanism but its goal (no pun intended) is not to criticise; it is to make people think, to temper their innate greed and make them aware – make them realise their position within society as a whole.

———

Humility Factor; (to be added to all pay-slips)

Under the PDC, the 'Emgee Ratio' would appear as a percentage in a box on every pay slip next to the figure indicating 'gross salary';

Example;

1) for a person earning £12,500 a year, the figure in the box would be 0.5
2) for a person earning £25,000 a year, the figure in the box would be 1.0
3) for a person earning £100,00 a year, the figure in the box would be 4.0...and so on...

The reason for doing this would be to incite those earning multiple times the average wage to take the time to examine their conscience and ask themselves one soul-searching question;

With what I do...with what I produce...do I really deserve to earn 10, 20 or 624 times the average UK wage?

———

Further Illustration in Table Form

	Lowest pay	Emgee ratio	Highest pay	Emgee ratio
Civil Service	£57,300	(2.3)	£178,709	(7.15)
Local Gov.	£14,844	(0.59)	£400,000	(16.0)
Military	£17,689	(0.71)	£100,973	(4.04)
NHS	£14,153	(0.56)	£97,478	(3.90)
Police	£19,000	(0.76)	£181,455	(7.30)
Prison Officer	£17,744	(0.71)	£78,732	(3.15)
Teachers	£15,817	(0.63)	£105,097	(4.20)
BBC	£14,177	(0.57)	£838,000	(33.5)

(Figures based on an 'Emgee ratio' index of £25000 as the average wage)

For information;

Average annual salaries of EU countries in British pounds;

Country	£'s	Date of reference
UK	**24252**	**2012**
Austria	25057	2010
Belgium	32518	2010
Bulgaria	4168	2013
Croatia	10934	2013
Cyprus	22618	2012
Czech Rep	9497	2013
Denmark	52326	2011
Estonia	9276	2013
Finland	31484	2012
France	29178	2009
Germany	37421	2012
Greece	12355	2011
Hungary	7752	2012

Ireland	29707	2012
Italy	27126	2012
Latvia	7523	2012
Lithuania	6552	2012
Luxembourg	44755	2010
Malta	12757	2012
Netherlands	30331	2012
Poland	9300	2013
Portugal	11542	2011
Romania	5163	2013
Slovakia	8092	2013
Slovenia	15876	2012
Spain	19357	2012
Sweden	31184	2010

General comments on various sectors;

A&E -

I believe that the pay-scale for those working in A&E should be modified slightly to take into account the extra stress put on them in the environment in which they work.

I would suggest an incremental nudge for these most under-appreciated of our public servants.

Firemen –

I believe fire-fighters should receive a decent wage but because of the physical component to their work I also believe they should be allowed to retire early when their health or their physical strength wanes.

However this early retirement and subsequent pension payment would have to be reflected in the salary.

Lawyers –

Lawyers have been feeding off the taxpayer-funded Legal Aid system for years, earning hundreds of thousands of pounds from the public purse.

This voracity will be reined in through the PDC's new capping-policy.

Teachers –

The teaching profession is an important part of the fabric of any society but I believe its wage structure needs a fundamental, root and branch overhaul.

Teachers in the UK are among the best paid in Europe earning almost double what teachers earn in France for example but the disparity between those at the bottom of the scale earning £15,817 a year (ER; 0.63) and those at the top earning £105,000 (ER; 4.2) a year is too great.

That imbalance needs to be addressed.

We also have more than 800 head teachers in this country earning £100,000 or more and that trend too, is simply unsustainable. Do head-teachers really deserve to earn more than 4 times the 'Emgee Ratio'? They are important I know; but I feel that the current wage is excessive... especially as teachers also benefit from 13 weeks holiday a year.

The public purse is not a fathomless pit to be ceaselessly plundered.

The BBC –

The PDC would put an end to the steady flow of fat-cat BBC executives who have been gorging themselves and their crony friends on tax-payers' license-fee payments in both salaries and eye-watering pay-offs for far too long now. (See chapter on media)

———

Railways -

It is outrageous that Rail-bosses, already on salaries of between £348,000 (ER; 13.92) and £577,000 (ER; 23.08) a year are being rewarded with bonuses worth up to 60% of their basic income linked to, of all things... performance.

How can this possibly be justified when the service they oversee is considered one of the worst in the developed world?

Rail companies have been fined £75 million for missing punctuality targets, their trains have never been more crowded, they are constantly introducing inflation-busting fare-hikes and everybody agrees that their overall performance dismal.

...and they are being rewarded for this debacle with bonuses based on good performance!

The company says that these bonuses are intended 'to recognise outstanding and exceptional performance'; the people who came out with that statement need a reality check.

We must stop this culture of reward for failure.

As stated above, the rail-companies were fined £75 million for missing punctuality targets...but as I have said previously, why fine a person or a company that is already in financial difficulty, if that is indeed the case of the rail-companies.

The people running these companies do not care if the company itself gets fined; it is not their money, just like the politicians who spend taxpayers' money with unrestrained profligacy, accountability does not enter into the mind-set of these people.

The emphasis in this situation is wrong and until the sanction of responsibility is placed firmly on the shoulders of those in charge, and not on those of the company, these people will just keep drawing their cheques and letting the company take the fall for their incompetence time after time.

Public Sector pay rises;

Politicians see themselves rather arrogantly as a class apart in our society, but they are nonetheless civil-servants like the rest of the people, paid out of the public purse, and as public servants, under the PDC the politicians...and the civil service...would only get a pay-rise as part of a general hike for all those working in the public-sector – and to the same degree.

This would be fair to everyone; it would avoid conflict, it would avoid misunderstandings or jealousy and most importantly it would allow the PDC to dismantle the IPSA (Independent Parliamentary Standards Authority) which currently sets MPs salaries, thereby saving money.

A review of Public Sector salaries would then be carried out on a five-yearly cycle.

NB - When considering wage-rises, employers should always remember that the rise has to cover...and go beyond...the amount which would mean the recipient earning less in real terms through a change of tax-band. (refer to table in Tax section)

Public Sector bonuses;

A bonus is not a systematic due; it is, and I quote the OED on this,
'A sum of money added to a person's wage
as a reward for good performance;
an extra and unexpected advantage'

―――――

The bonus culture in the public sector needs to be phased out completely.

A salary is a salary. It is what you should be paid for any given function and I find it illogical and morally wrong to be giving greedy, fat-cat executives bonuses – and excessive bonuses at that – while;

- front-line jobs are being cut,
- targets are not being met...and
- investment is desperately needed in new technology, training and renovation

Under the PDC there would be **NO** bonuses in the public sector for people simply doing the job they have been employed to do as it is laid out in the job-description.

I just do not believe that people should be incentivised for simply doing their job properly.

That said; I have nothing against an occasional bonus as a goodwill gesture in the right circumstances. However, when it becomes an entitlement, the word 'greed' immediately springs to mind and that word has no place in PDC policy.

―――――

Public Sector pay-offs;

The PDC would not pursue anybody who had benefitted from a huge salary or a huge pay-off from the public purse in recent years – if, of course, those salaries and those pay-offs had been contractually agreed, but nevertheless, we would be compiling a list of those people we considered 'unfit for purpose' and 'persona non grata'.

This would include anyone who had already taken advantage or profited - whether unduly or unfairly – on a previous occasion from the public purse...and being on this list would subsequently preclude these people from any future appointment in the public sector under a PDC administration.

After all, it would be greedy to win the lottery twice, wouldn't it?

This 'Greed List' would not be published, nor would it be in the public domain but the PDC would not tolerate any cupidity and all those in a position to nominate future candidates would be instructed to consult it – via a designated protocol – before offering any new posts.

NB; any future pay-offs in the public sector would be limited to three months salary and anybody who received a pay-off from the public purse would then have to observe a three year cooling off period before they could be re-employed therein.

This clause would figure in all new contracts.

If however people are dismissed for misconduct or forced out of their jobs for presiding over a scandal, they would forfeit the right to any bonuses and to any golden handshakes... and their super-sized pensions would be replaced with a basic state-pension.

Lying and malpractice would henceforth nullify any contractual agreement.

Reward for failure;

The PDC would also review the process of selection and nomination for positions of authority within its remit. We cannot keep rewarding incompetence and irresponsibility in public office with promotions, pay-offs and lucrative pensions;

For example;

Cynthia Bower who preceded Sir David Nicholson at the now shamed Mid-Staffs hospital, was promoted to the CQC (Care Quality Commission) where she presided over yet another catalogue of failure, but her position was never questioned until she was finally caught up in the **<u>alleged</u>** NHS cover-up and bribery allegations alongside Jill Finney, Anna Jefferson and Tony Halsall

Dame Helen Ghosh known as 'Lady Calamity' around Westminster, was regularly 'confounded' during her time in Whitehall, and yet she was subsequently put in charge of the National Trust

Lin Homer – aka 'Ms Incompetence' made a complete muddle of the Border Agency but was then rewarded with a promotion to the Tax Office...and

Sir David Nicholson – who was in charge of the Mid-Staffs NHS Foundation Trust where up to 1200 people died because of poor care was subsequently promoted to Chief executive of the NHS

Surely I am not alone in finding this incestuous game of bureaucratic musical-chairs unpalatable.

———

Personally, I am sick of seeing people being given high-ranking positions through nepotism or the 'old-boys club' when they are clearly not up to the job...and I positively abhor the subsequent lack of accountability that these people demonstrate when things go wrong...as they inevitably do when people do not have the right credentials to fulfil a role.

If these people want the money, the perks and the pension that these jobs provide, which is after all their goal, then they should be made to read the job description before accepting the position. It has to be made clear to them that they cannot simply accept the salary...and then opt out of the responsibility intrinsic to the job when it is called into question.

They have to be held to account for their mistakes...and certainly not rewarded for their incompetence with another post.

We have to put an end to this Westminster merry-go-round.

To sum up –

I want people working in the Public Sector to have a set of principles and a set of morals. I want them to respect the positions they hold and I want them to perform their duties to the best of their ability without every action they might undertake needing to be rewarded in some way or another.

Those whose motivations lie elsewhere than the development of our country as a proud, respectable, tolerant and independent nation should not be working in the public sector.

Public service is not for everybody because the very idea of public service, of serving our fellow man inevitably involves a part of altruism which many cannot find within themselves and cannot be expressed in monetary terms. Public Service is not for the selfish or for the greedy but it can nevertheless be exceptionally rewarding.

The new PDC salary scales would be fair and balanced, rewarding hard work with a commensurate salary but they would in no way try to rival, compete or compare with salaries in the private sector because the two sectors are completely different.

We would pay a fair wage for a fair day's work and every salary would be subjected to the same scrutiny and to the same question.

Does the person doing this job deserve X times the 'Emgee Ratio'?

If it can be justified and passes that test, all is well and good. If it is considered that the job deserves more...or less...then the salary would be adjusted in accordance with the rules.

The Private sector;

The overall pay scale in this country has become top-heavy and as a consequence the gap between the 'haves and the have-nots' has widened dramatically with the potential for unrest amongst the population growing daily.

This imbalance has to be addressed. It cannot be right that 10% of the population controls 90% of the wealth.

We need to reduce the disparity between those earning millions and those who are struggling to get by, because if we don't, some kind of social conflict is sure to erupt sooner or later.

Currently, there are hundreds of companies in the UK with a salary ratio of over 120 – which means that those at the top earn at least 120 times what those at the bottom are earning.

I believe that this ratio is disproportionate and greedy, and can only lead to a measure of jealousy, resentment and strife among those who struggle to make ends meet at the lower end.

We have to temper this galloping greed; it is out of control.

Individual companies are independent and autonomous and the PDC would not interfere with the free-market concept of private enterprise... but it is clear that in recent years the executives of all big businesses have been helping themselves to as much money as they could possibly grab in salaries, bonuses and pensions.

Corruption seems to be rife in many areas of big-business, in the banking sector, in the energy sector...and in many others...and of course it is those at the bottom who are just trying to make ends meet with less and less at their disposal who are paying the price...as usual... which is why the PDC would encourage those bosses who <u>pay themselves</u> more than eight times the 'Emgee ratio' (i.e.; £200,000) to ensure that their employees at the other end of the scale earn at least a living wage that does not require tax credits for them to keep their heads above water.

This will not happen overnight because greed is as addictive as any other drug but we must move toward a re-balancing of the financial scales if we want to avoid a catastrophic social revolt in the medium term.

———

For multi-national companies - as part of the PDC's Fair-play Charter - we would also suggest that a salary ratio be considered; somewhere between 20 and 25 for example to begin with.

This would mean that the people at the very top could not earn more than 20/25 times what the person earning the lowest salary in the same company is being paid. This would have the effect of raising the salaries at the bottom of the scale...not because the bosses would feel in any way more benevolent towards their staff - but because if those at the bottom were earning more then they (the bosses) would be able <u>to pay themselves</u> <u>more</u>, while at the same time respecting the ratio.

For example; if the lowest wage in a company is £25,000 (ER; 1.0) – which is currently the average wage – using a co-efficient of 25, the MD's salary would be limited to no more than £625,000 a year which is more than a fair wage.

Above and beyond £625,000 a year is just greed. It might be within the terms of a company's wage structure but it is not justifiable.

———

Author's comment;

All those seniors executives who throw tantrums like spoilt children because they have not been given the latest Blackberry or free tickets to Wimbledon or the Cup Final…on top of their huge salaries, their outrageous bonuses and their generous pension plans…really need to be given a reality check

…and the irony; companies bought millions of electronic gadgets to help their staff be more productive…and instead these people spend all their time texting each other and sending each other silly pictures of themselves (selfies).

———

That said; if companies then considered that their top-executives and board-members deserved still more money, in bonuses for example, they could put it to their shareholders who could then rubber-stamp those bonuses…or not. This would prevent any scandalous abuse of the bonus-system and put a stop to fat-cat salaries and the bonuses themselves spiralling out of control.

At the same time, if a company - or a bank – fails and hits a wall; why not hold the board of directors, the CEO and all the executives to account; in that way they would have a vested interest in keeping the company afloat rather than just milking it for all they can get out of it.

———

Obviously, these policy ideas would have to be phased in over a period of time but I believe that we have to act on this matter…and by setting a finite target for the integration of this policy…and keeping to it…I also believe that the future of our society as a whole would have more coherence.

———

For information;

As stated previously, the PDC would not interfere with private companies' internal affairs but we would make a point of flagging-up those companies which signed up to our Fair-play Charter.

———

Bonuses;

> A bonus is not a systematic due; it is, and I quote the OED on this,
> 'A sum of money added to a person's wage
> as a reward for good performance;
> an extra and unexpected advantage'

———

The bonus culture needs to be revised.

I have nothing against companies running an incentive scheme for their employees but a systematic annual bonus completely defeats the object of a bonus as a motivational tool. (*Read the definition above*)

A bonus has to be performance related and should only be paid to those that have earned them and deserve them; they should not be just an accepted annual occurrence.

In addition, bonuses should only be awarded at the end of the financial year on the condition that the following criteria have been fulfilled;

    1) the company has made a profit...and
    2) the shareholders agree with it

Incompetence...complacency...recklessness...and downright failure <u>should not</u> be rewarded. I do not understand these companies who sign off on contractually-agreed bonuses that do not respect the above criteria. Mercantile avarice is no excuse.

Furthermore, applying the same logic here as I have throughout – I believe that any bank that has received taxpayers' money from the government in order to get itself out of trouble should be banned from paying out any bonuses or golden handshakes whatsoever...until such a time as the money borrowed has been paid back.

No discussion, no argument and no compromise...and any future bonuses should only be granted once the bank has returned to making a profit.

Allowances;

Because the cost of living in London and Greater London is considerably more expensive than the rest of the country I believe that companies in the London area who value their employees should be able to add an allowance to their employees' salaries in order to compensate them for this higher cost of living.

However, to ensure fairness, this allowance would have to be on a flat-rate basis, not a pro-rata basis (salary) and limited to pay-grades below a certain level.

Why not offer companies a tax-rebate to sign up to this idea?

Bonuses and Tax;

In order to reign in the outrageous amounts currently being handed out in bonuses, especially in the banking sector, the PDC would impose a 100% tax on any bonus over £50,000 as part of the corporation tax system so that the bonus pot is shared more evenly between already rich executives and shareholders...and the government which would then invest its share in public services.

This would hopefully make companies more reasonable...

...and moreover, the PDC would also insist that any bonuses over £50,000 were not paid in cash but in bonds and held over for at least a year, until the bank's or the company's financial report came out proving its positive results.

If, however, a company's balance sheet showed a loss in its annual statement, then those bonuses would be forfeited and those at the top would also forfeit any bonuses that they were due, irrespective of whether those bonuses had been agreed and rubber-stamped by their friends and colleagues in the boardroom beforehand.

It is obscene that chief executives who are already earning multi-million pound salaries, then double or triple their income thanks to outrageous annual bonuses.

Let's stop this self-indulgent greed.

One final note;

Minimum wage –

We have to introduce a minimum wage.

Now I understand small and medium sized businesses pushing back against this idea because they rely on unpaid interns, zero-hour contracts and incredibly cheap labour to survive but I believe that... if these businesses need to pay a pittance...or if they can only survive as a going-concern thanks to a form of professional exploitation...then their business model is clearly not viable, and as a result they do not deserve to survive, despite of the number of jobs that they might be providing.

We have to have a bottom line with a minimum wage - for a set number of hours-work - as a foundation on which to build our commercial economy as it would go a long way towards lifting people out of poverty.

It would also eradicate the need for tax-credits and housing benefits… and hopefully stem the growing tide of people having to use food-banks to survive.

NB; Another component of this 'fairer deal for those struggling to keep their heads above water' would be a cap on rents. We have to stop greedy landlords from milking people of their dignity as well as their money.

———

Minimum wage;

The PDC would set the minimum wage at £6.00 an hour.

On the basis of 40 hours a week, that equates to £240.00 a week.

52 weeks at £240.00 = £12,480 a year which is just below the first threshold for income tax (£12,500.00) in the PDC model

That has to be our goal as a minimum living wage for all.

———

Tax

Personal Tax –

Every population complains about budget cuts and tax increases; complaining is an intrinsic part of human nature...but it seems to me that while the majority of law-abiding citizens are complaining with a defendable justification, there are others who are selfishly pulling more and more of the blanket to their side of the bed.

Taxes are a necessary evil for a democratic society to function because without them democracy cannot be sustained.

Just look at Greece and how their economy failed because no-one was paying their taxes and everyone was abusing the system. It is sad to see, but the Greeks got themselves into that mess by trusting the wrong people to lead them – i.e. selfish, greedy politicians who allowed a free-for-all as long as they were first in the queue.

A fair tax system that is well structured and well monitored, that doesn't penalise one section of the community in relation to another...or offer an unfair advantage to a select few to the detriment of the majority...is the only way to govern a multi-faceted society harmoniously.

The PDC would apply a simplified Tax-band system that would be fair to all;

Income Tax bands

Grade 1a -	£0	to	£12,499	-	0%	Tax
Grade 1b -	£12,500	to	£24,999	-	10%	Tax
Grade 2 -	£25,000	to	£37,499	-	15%	Tax
Grade 3 -	£37,500	to	£49,999	-	20%	Tax

Grade 4	-	£50,000	to	£62,499	-	25%	Tax
Grade 5	-	£62,500	to	£87,499	-	30%	Tax
Grade 6	-	£87,500	to	£99,999	-	35%	Tax
Grade 7	-	£100,000	to	£249,999	-	40%	Tax

The politicians will say different but it really doesn't have to be any more complicated than that.

Extra Notes;

- the raising of the tax threshold at the bottom of the scale would be accompanied by a reduction in benefits to encourage people into work rather than staying at home...and
- at the top of the scale, together with the 100% tax on bonuses over £50,000 offered by companies anybody earning over £250,000 a year would be taxed at 50% on that extra amount.

However there are areas that would need to be addressed;

- we need to make sure that tax avoidance / evasion is stamped out and that the methods used by the mega-rich to live in this country without contributing to its economy are squashed. The PDC would set up a team dedicated to recovering unpaid taxes.
- we also need to close the loophole that allows people to pay themselves through a personal company - thereby paying the corporation rate of tax - rather than the income tax rate relative to their income bracket
- we also need an added tax for excessive capital gains returns
- we need to increase the pressure on benefit cheats and council tax dodgers...and finally
- we need to re-educate the general population on VAT fraud.

Small Business;

Cash-in-hand culture –

We need to stop the very British culture of 'cash in hand' transactions to avoid paying VAT.

To do this, the PDC would introduce a Professional Recognition Scheme.

This would be a government-issued calling-card which would;

- prove a tradesman's identity (with photo)
- confirm his or her credentials and competence…and
- guarantee his or her legitimacy.

Potential customers would simply have to ask the tradesman for his or her card to prove that he or she was genuine and qualified to undertake the work being discussed (gardener, plumber, locksmith, mechanic or repairman).

Then, they would be able to verify these credentials – if need be – through a hot-line set up in the local government offices or on an official government website before they went ahead and accepted his or her quote for the work.

And finally, any transaction that took place between the two parties would then be paid through this card so that the tax was paid and recovered by the government.

NB; the advances in 'smart-phone' technology would facilitate this process.

I would also suggest that - as a bonus - this system would eliminate any number of 'cowboy' operators and impersonators who go around knocking on peoples' doors.

Comment on Business Rates -

These rates need root and branch reform.

Why can't we simply do away with the Valuation Office Agency and allow local councils to apply a rate per square metre using a banding code to differentiate between city-centre premises and those in the suburbs.

Bus companies use a system of zones radiating out from the centre of town to organise their fare-structures...and indeed local councils themselves use a similar method to calculate rates on housing; so why can't the same method be used for business premises.

It would make things much simpler for everybody and if greedy councils charged too much for the privilege of running a business in a particular area, then businesses would simply move elsewhere. A natural balance would soon be found.

The current system is far too complicated and the two sets of figures – one from the Valuation Office Agency and the other from the Local Council - leave most people completely bemused…

…and of course, whenever there is complication and bemusement, there is room for error…and corruption.

———

Big Business;

While the politicians are always first at the trough when it comes to tax-avoidance, expenses and bonuses, huge multi-nationals are never far behind.

Giant corporations and huge multi-nationals like Google, Amazon, Starbucks and IBM are not charitable organisations; they do not have any moral obligation to act in a certain way and we should not expect them to.

However, they do have accountants; teams of them whose sole job it is to find loopholes in tax-legislation that will reduce the company's tax liability…and as a result we cannot and should not expect any spontaneous commitment or unprompted ethical gesture from these people to pay any more tax than they are obliged to; it just wouldn't be company policy in a free market.

Now, this might seem immoral to some but sadly morality is not a word or a principle that we can associate with big business. These people deal with hard facts and numbers, not ethereal values or human sensibilities and therefore we cannot blame companies for exploiting the system and using it to their own advantage if the system allows them to do so. That is just common sense and good business practice in the world we live in.

———

For information;

Figures show that major companies have avoided paying over £25.5 billion in UK corporation tax in the last year.

Apple, for example, made £6 billion in the UK last year but only paid £10million in corporation tax – Amazon and Google did the same. This is not acceptable.

———

People in multi-national conglomerates follow the rules - for the most part - and if the rules allow them not to pay tax, then they will not pay the tax; it is as simple as that…which is why we have to change the rules and close the loopholes that allow these companies to escape a proper level of taxation.

It may take a sea-change in behaviour…or some kind of international agreement…but the multinationals have had it their way for far too long…using their 'multi-national' status to transfer capital from one country to the next and back again, or onto another tax-haven…and then another in order to cover their tracks and not pay the due tax on their operations.

We need to force companies to pay their taxes in the country where they have made their money before they are allowed to send their profits abroad…and not the other way around as is currently the case…and the G20 and the OECD (Organisation for Economic Co-operation and Development) need to legislate for that circumstance worldwide.

Author's comment;

It is absolutely scandalous that over the last decade, indeed since 2004, that the Water companies have only paid £1.7 billion in corporation tax between them while rewarding their shareholders with dividends worth £11 billion.

At the same time, these companies, many of which are foreign owned are racking up debts and writing off the interest on those debts against their corporation tax payments, so that their capital and their company assets remain firmly in their hands and not in the hands of the British taxman / taxpayer.

The profits they do make are then transferred off-shore to their shareholders.

Now, this might be legal…and good business practice…but in my opinion it should never have been allowed to happen.

These companies, having been allowed to invest in our essential services sector – which was, I repeat, a disastrous decision - are now bleeding this country dry and draining of its wealth like a horde of voracious, insatiable vampires.

Investing in the UK's essential services sector was a very shrewd move on their part but it should never have been allowed to happen because these companies have absolutely no obligation or responsibility towards the

British public. The British consumers are just a host and these blood-sucking leeches will keep pumping blood from that host until it is dry.

They have no reason not to...that is business and if we don't like it we should never have let them take control of our essential services.

The same applies to the electricity companies; because of spiralling bills many British citizens are having to choose between eating or heating their homes but the cynical if not callous response of these companies - which once again are mainly foreign-owned - to those having difficulty paying their constantly rising utility bills is this; 'just put on another jumper'.

———

Privatisation was supposed to improve on the State's running of certain industries but these companies are enforcing greater and greater hardship on more and more British consumers with every turn of the screw, be it on electricity bills or on water rates and they are doing it with relative impunity because they are not accountable to the British people...as the State would have been; the only goal of these companies is to make as much profit out of the British people as possible for their shareholders... and sadly we, the British people cannot do anything about it because we invited them in.

This is another reason why I believe that all our essential services should be brought back under the control of a British-based tax-paying company.

We are being held to ransom.

———

Multi-nationals exist for a reason, much of it based on economies of scale and financial trickery (artificially inflating their internal monetary transactions between parent companies and its franchisees resulting in the franchisee never making a taxable profit) but the concept is finite and will self-implode eventually when these companies over-extend themselves, become too big to manage...and errors – human errors or technological errors – occur.

The current phenomenon, brought about by the internet, of people, individuals creating their own products in their own homes and selling them online will accelerate in the next few years and the lumbering multi-nationals with their greed, their exploitative business practices and their scandals will eventually crumble…unless of course they sanitise their operations by creating individual companies in the countries where they are implanted and adhere to the rules of those countries, pay their taxes in those countries and participate in the development of those countries as an integral part of their business plan, rather than just exploiting them, their workers and their tax systems.

––––––

Author's comment;

We must simplify the tax system and enforce a rule where every company that trades in this country, is registered to trade in this country and declares the fruit of that trade in this country so that it can be taxed accordingly…before it disappears into the complex labyrinth of planetary deception that is the international banking system, in order to avoid detection.

––––––

It is ludicrous that companies can do billions of pounds worth in trade in one country and then declare those sales in another country…a country of their choice…where the corporation tax is at its most beneficial for them.

I believe that every country should receive the tax it is due from the business done on its soil and that is why;

- it is time to stop the multinationals and their greedy executives exploiting tax loopholes
- it is time to force them to set up holding / clearing companies in the countries where they set up shop so that they pay the due tax on the turnover they generate in that country…and

- it is time to make the world a fairer place for all by closing tax havens worldwide

―――

If multi-nationals want to operate in the UK, let's insist on this;

**You earn money here; you pay tax on that
money here, multi-national or not.**

―――

The PDC going forward;

- Our priority would be an international agreement which would force companies the world over to declare their earnings and pay their taxes in the country where they do the business before exporting any profits.
- However, we would start on a national level by insisting that every multi-national company established in the UK set up a holding company as part of their conglomerate - which would be bound by British law - through which all foreign transactions would be channelled so that any taxable receipts could be controlled and verified, before being transferred offshore.
    o Those companies who did not comply or who were found to be not paying their taxes would have their licences-to-trade in the UK rescinded.
- Tax cheats overall, cost the British economy at least £32 billion a year – 25% of our current deficit. Imagine people; we could wipe out our deficit in 4/5 years if everyone actually paid the taxes that they owe...which is why the PDC would systematically audit companies that specialise in tax-avoidance...and any company that was clearly acting against the common good would be targeted in the same manner. They would also be excluded from tendering for government contracts.
- The PDC would also look into the amounts we write off in tax receipts by establishing a designated task-force geared specifically to dealing with the major multi-national corporations who

have been legally avoiding paying their fair-share in tax using loopholes and high-powered lawyers for years and if these companies refuse to discuss a compromise on their obligations we would look into ways of restricting their field of interest here; cancel permits, licences to trade etc. Perhaps we could publish their tax records to show the British public the facts and use consumer power to boycott their products

- The PDC would also produce and publish a list of 20 companies every year who do not pay their fair share of taxes…and a second list of companies who do – thereby encouraging the public to give their patronage to the latter while discouraging them from using the former
- We would also look into reducing our Corporation tax-rate to encourage investment; currently the UK has a corporation tax rate of 21%; that is not as low as Ireland's (12.5%) but it is lower than France (33.33%) and Germany (29.48%), and therefore we should be able to attract more business to these shores. However, I do believe that 20% should be our optimum target.
- VAT fraud and counterfeit goods fraud would also be targeted

---

On a positive note;

- The PDC would invite large companies to invest in the community by sponsoring a Magnet centre - in its entirety or just the sports component for example – and in return they would be offered a tax-reduction
- We would also offer tax relief to companies in exchange for more apprenticeships, more investment in technology and the development of new ideas…and finally…
- The PDC would look to promote enterprise creation in deprived areas by offering tax holidays up to five years to help new business get off the ground

However, the PDC's most important goal in all this would be the eradication of selfish greed…individual and corporate…so that once again our society as a whole can prosper and flourish.

Other Tax Issues;

VAT;

In recent years excessive taxation has been used to shore up the budgetary mismanagement and incompetence of our political 'leaders'... but excessive tax stifles free-enterprise and therefore the PDC would reduce VAT to 15%.

This would have the effect of not only stimulating growth but more importantly it would make people feel that the government wasn't trying constantly to squeeze every last penny out of them.

Besides, lower taxes will encourage more investment and more enterprise which in turn leads to more jobs, more production, more happy people and a greater taxable volume for the treasury. It's a win / win situation for everyone.

There would be a few exceptions however; the VAT on healthy food options would be fixed at 10% for a period of five years in order to analyse its benefits and the VAT on sugary, fizzy drinks would be set at 20% for that same period in order to discourage their consumption at too great a volume.

As for essential food-stuffs; a number of these would not be subjected to VAT, although the current VAT exemption list would be reappraised.

VAT on imports;

I believe that we should tax imports while promoting home grown goods; that we should rehabilitate the 'made in GB' label – using tax incentives (limited in time) which would be sanctioned severely if abused.

This might provoke calls of protectionism or a backlash worldwide against our exports but if we create and produce more and more of our own needs then the effect and the impact of the world market's retaliatory measures would be greatly reduced.

No doubt the EU would take issue with this but our withdrawal from the over-reaching EU would be one of the PDC's first priorities and therefore the irritation from the EU would be minimal. (See chapter on EU)

Fuel;

The PDC would introduce a variable tax on a sliding scale to stabilise the price of petrol during times of difficulty...and we would also look into lightening the fuel-tax burden on the transport industry – which is the life-blood of our economy - through improvements in technology.

Gambling; (see section on gambling)

We need to reinstall the tax on winnings

Marriage -

In a perfect world the PDC would have liked to abolish child-benefit completely in favour of offering more tax-relief to married couples who stay together but...now that we have thrown convention to the wind and re-invented the Christian definition of the word and the concept of marriage – i.e., no longer the union between a man and a woman coming together to bring up the fruit of that union in a safe family unit, but just any two people of any combination who want to commit to each other – there is no longer any need for married people to benefit from special arrangements for tax purposes, which were supposed to ease the burden of bringing up that family; everybody who works will simply pay the same amount of tax as anybody else according to the tax-band that corresponds to their salary.

The savings made by the government would be transferred to the child-benefit budget so that everybody was treated equally.

––––––

Housing;

We need to abolish Stamp Duty on properties of less than £250,000 to help people at the lower end of the market.

––––––

Inheritance;

An inheritance tax is fundamentally unfair because it is a tax on money that has already been taxed somewhere else along the line.

However, it is not unreasonable to put a tax on inheritances over £1 million because this money is often a result of property appreciating over time, rather than money earned from actual work...and therefore it is more a capital gains tax on un-earned wealth than a sanction on a hard-earned bequest.

Ideally there would be no tax on inheritance but I believe that this is a fair compromise for the whole of society. We should not punish people for working hard and saving.

It is unfair that people who work hard all their lives...and save all their lives...in order to pass something on to their families, people inhabited by the most basic instinct of all, that of wanting their children and their grandchildren to have a better life than what they might have had, should have that aspiration taken away from them by an overreaching inheritance tax.

––––––

Reminder; when making budget cuts and increasing taxes; we must always remember to thoroughly investigate how these measures will impact on the poorest and the working-class families that will be affected by them most – the recent spate of fathers / husbands pushed to the brink and killing themselves and their families out of desperation cannot be an acceptable by-product of government cuts.

———

Pensions

The concept of retirement from working life was first launched in 1880 by Otto von Bismarck in Germany although it was a rather cynical move on his part as he set the retirement age at 65 when most people were dying at around 61.

In the UK it was Lloyd George who first introduced the idea of State-funded pensions in 1908 and the USA followed in 1935...but the state-pension has never become a universal right worldwide and sadly I believe that the concept – although a brilliant idea in its time - has now run its course.

Current situation;

In the UK today, we have an ageing population…and because we are all living longer, it is clear that the current mechanisms used to calculate pensions – put in place at a time when people were retiring at 65 and dying at 70 – are no longer fit for purpose.

It was a wonderful innovation at the time but these calculations never took into account the idea that people would one day retire at 65 and then live a long and productive life for another 35 to 40 years.

However that is now the case; these days, people are not only living longer, they are often living longer after retirement than the duration of their productive, working lives; retiring at 55 for example, having contributed to the system for 35 years and then living to the ripe old age of 100 and more, which means claiming from the system for over 45 years, having only paid in for 35.

Simple logic and basic mathematics tells us that this situation is unsustainable but because no politician has ever wanted to be seen tampering with the pension arrangements of these people - *who had based their whole lives on retiring at a certain age and enjoying the fruits of that labour in their later years* – the situation has never really been corrected or addressed properly.

Self-preservation is always a politician's first priority, as opposed to actually getting stuck into an issue - *especially an issue like pensions which is such a thorny and emotive issue, and one that is such an integral part of everybody's lives these days* – and therefore, rather than be seen to be meddling in people's lives and possibly losing votes…and potentially their seat on the gravy-train…as a consequence of that meddling, politician after politician…and government after government has systematically kicked the pension problem into the long grass, turning a blind-eye to the debt it has generated…and continues to generate year on year…allowing that debt to spiral further and further out of control.

Nevertheless, it is an issue that has to be addressed and the British people <u>will</u> accept change if they feel that it is necessary and fair to all.

———

The British people are not stupid. They can see that the current rules are unsustainable and that something has to be done; all they need is for somebody to stand up and offer them a solution.

I believe that we need to tackle the pension issue in two parts; **short / medium** term...and **long** term.

In the **short / medium** term I believe that we will have to introduce a progressive retirement age;

- People of 60 today will have to work on until the age of 67
- People of 50 today will have to work on until the age of 69
- People of 40 today will have to work on until the age of 71
- People of 30 today will have to work on until the age of 73

…and those starting work today at 18 will have to go to 75

Another option short term would be loans from the government secured against properties to be sold after a person's death…but that would create inheritance issues for lawyers to exploit, and we really need to avoid that kind of bother at all costs.

In the **long** term however; with a population that is becoming increasingly more top-heavy, simply because people are living longer, I believe that the state pension as a concept will have to be phased out.

It is a wonderful idea but the state pension was brought in at a time when retirement years were calculated in single figures and not in multiple decades as is now the case.

It was meant to reward those who had worked hard all their lives with a few years of comfort and compassion before they passed on, but these days people are living to a hundred and more, and claiming pensions for thirty or forty years, often for longer than they actually contributed to the system…and that is simply unsustainable.

This is because the calculations made by Lloyd George in 1908 have never been properly adjusted or updated to take into account today's reality and <u>that</u> is due to our craven politicians reluctance to address the issue, despite the fact that tackling the problem, trying to manage the ever-increasing black-hole of debt that the pension pot has generated… and continues to generate…in our economy, is one of the main constants that has burdened and continues to burden every single political leader that walks through the door of No.10 Downing Street.

Pension reform has become the ultimate conundrum for any UK politician but in recent years not one of them has had the temerity to address the issue, simply because it is a prickly thorn so full of jeopardy that they know it could end a political career.

Besides, where would you start?

How could you reform it in a way that was fair for all?

The simple answer is that the pension-scheme cannot be reformed...as any changes made to it would inevitably mean someone, somewhere losing out...and moreover, it would be unethical for people who have spent their whole lives paying into it, not to benefit from it when they retired.

However something has to be done.

We need a long term plan for our pensions - with built-in stability - and not one that will be tinkered with every five years or so whenever the government in Westminster changes.

———

Of course, it would be political suicide for any one party to attempt this reform on its own, but because this is an issue that concerns us all, I would suggest that we set-up a cross-party commission, come up with a solution and draw up a long-term agreement that would be set in stone for all parties to abide by. This decree would state that no matter who was in power at any given time, the system agreed upon would not be tampered with for the foreseeable future, offering a stability to all the interested parties.

———

The PDC Solution –

Going forward, simple mathematics tells us that a shrinking workforce will not be able to sustain a growing population of elderly people with state pensions which is why I believe that personal provision in some form will have to take on the relay at some time in the near future.

I would suggest that - as of January 1st 2020, for example - those entering the workforce would no longer contribute to the state pension;

instead, each employee would have to make their own arrangements for their retirement years by taking out a rolling life-insurance policy.

The idea is this; people would take out life-insurance policies of 10 to 15 years (which would be renewed at the end of each term, to take advantage of the fiscal changes that might have occurred in the intervening period).

Then, upon maturity, the lump-sum earned from the policy would be re-invested for the next 10 to 15 years – hopefully at a better rate – and so on and so forth (the accrued interest could either be cashed-in or re-invested in the next policy depending on a person's circumstances).

The capital built-up from consecutive policies could then be used as leverage when negotiating a subsequent policy which would allow people to shop around for the best deal...and force insurance companies to compete with each other for the business.

This process would mean that people would have...

- an on-going capital reserve for the long term...but also
- a medium-term savings-pot in case of premature death...and even
- a short-ish term solution for their monetary issues in the form of an interest windfall at the end of each term.

...all of which offers an attractive alternative to the annuity schemes currently in place which, once contracted, cannot be altered or changed for the duration of a person's life.

Of course, a safe-guard would have to be put in place, so that the insurance companies could not play fast and loose with these funds on the stock market and another stipulation would ensure that the capital itself would not be accessible until a legally recognised retirement age had been reached...to prevent people from cashing it in and leaving themselves without their nest-egg when the time came.

For information; 25% of all council tax paid goes towards funding town-hall pensions but this slow osmosis into private-pension policies would instantly free up this money for use in the community.

———

That said; all employees would still continue to pay their NI contributions through their employers (for health, child and family support...and unemployment) but this contribution would be split into its component parts so that those starting out and paying for the new pension policies could be exempted from the state retirement fund.

Employers' contributions would also be reduced by the pension increment for those on the new scheme, which would ease their financial burden to some extent.

Those already working would continue as normal.

Of course, consultations would have to take place with the financial services sector to refine the details of these policies and to cover such issues as unemployment but this is the kernel of a 50 year plan which would hopefully, in due course be fair to everyone.

———

NB; the only people who would lose out under these proposals are those already in work...who would see their retirement age increase slightly. However, I do believe that their sacrifice would be compensated in the long run by the advances in technology and the improvements in healthcare which will mean that in the year 2070, when they retire, 70 or even 75 will be the new 60.

———

Other issues –

Pension rises;

In the meantime, I believe that public sector pensions should be re-evaluated every five years…and the necessary adjustments made after that process. Pensioners were recently awarded a 25p rise in their pension payments. This means that the administration costs to implement the rise cost more than the rise itself making it effectively a loss-making exercise. How pointless is that? Giving people a 25p rise is an insult… and for some of the more vulnerable members of our population, it is psychologically demoralising.

Final salary pensions;

Final salary pensions should be phased out. Rather than final year pensions, could we not calculate an average pay-out over the last ten years of employment so as not to penalise those who start their careers slowly or late.

———

Elderly Care;

By necessity we will also have to introduce a new system to pay for care in later life.

The PDC would introduce the Golden Years Scheme which would be a state-run insurance policy. Contributions would be made on a rising percentage scale which would kick in a £25,000 (not before to protect the younger workers and the more vulnerable) and be used to fund elderly care.

If however, UPON DEATH no care had been required the contribution could be added to the person's estate as part of his / her legacy / inheritance. It would not however be reclaimable before death.

This would hopefully encourage families to look after their elderly relatives and take them into their homes with the carrot of an inheritance as the key.

I understand that this is very cynical in one respect and very disheartening in another, but a financial carrot is what most people need these days in order to get involved.

Of course, I would rather people take care of their elderly relatives out of love, compassion and loyalty but in the world we live in, money is the only form of barter that people understand.

———

NB; a percentage contribution would also be integrated into…and withheld from… unemployment payments so that even the long-term unemployed would be financing their elderly care.

———

Charity

Firstly I have to commend the people of Britain for their charity work; their generosity of pocket and spirit clearly knows no bounds.

Whenever an appeal is made, the great British public is always amongst the first to respond, offering whatever it can to help, be it medical aid or financial aid ...or aid of a more basic nature such as food, water, clothes and blankets.

They might be hard-pressed to make ends meet in their own lives - because of the ever-rising cost of living here in the UK - but nevertheless the British public still donates its hard-earned cash every time without fail, proving time and time again its commitment the humanitarian cause.

Comic Relief for example collected £100 million in 2013 and Sport Relief, organised the previous year (2012) raised over £50 million.

Now, these are wonderful displays of generosity and altruism but nevertheless I do have a question;

- Why, after all these years of collective giving do we seem to have made so little progress? We keep seeing the same poor children, the same abused animals and the same poverty on our screens time and time again, that we have been seeing for forty years or more – so where, might I ask is all the money really going?

Author's comment;

I would also ask this; if we can collect 20, 50 or £100 million to help other people around the world, why can't we do the same for our own? Our youth is binge-drinking itself to an early grave and roaming the streets aimlessly looking for trouble…out of sheer unadulterated boredom.

Maybe if we tried to occupy them with jobs or apprenticeships or sporting facilities, we could improve their lot too!

Celebrities;

Another question I have to ask.

We often see pretentious celebrities and conceited millionaire presenters fronting campaigns…and presenting fund-raisers for 'deserving' causes…but I wonder; how many of these people actually donate anything financially to these causes?

Of course, they donate their time by participating – although some do get a fee for doing that - but do these people actually make a financial contribution to the causes they seem to be so desperately concerned about…

…or is it, as I suspect, more about raising their own profile and taking advantage of the 'all-expenses-paid, fact-finding missions' they are offered to '*see for themselves*' the poverty that exists around the world.

We all know that poverty exists; putting a celebrity in the middle of an African village to encourage more donations is not only patronising but a waste of time and money.

If these people were really concerned about the plight of those less fortunate than themselves, all they would have to do is make a substantial donation to the fund from their considerable personal fortunes. This would be a much better way of showing their support; the fund's total would grow exponentially and the TV companies would save huge amounts of cash on first-class air-fares and hotel bills.

The celebrities could then get back into their chauffeur-driven cars and retreat once more to their country residences.

Now, of course, I am being patronising here and it is commendable that these people do donate their time for these causes…but if they really want us to believe that they feel 'concerned' by the plight of these poor people I believe that celebrities should give more than just their time.

Besides; the average donation of a British citizen is £30.00, which is what celebrities spend on shoe polish or lip-gloss alone, so surely, it is not asking too much.

Salary;

Another bug-bear of mine; people getting rich from working for charities.

It cannot be right that the 'Save the Children' charity pays one of its employees £234,000 a year in salary…and…that another charity pays the £70,000 a year boarding-school fees of its chief executive's children…on top of his £210,000 a year salary.

For me, there is a moral contradiction here. I understand the argument that these charities are now multi-national organisations that need expert management…but do these people really know the definition of the word 'charity'.

It seems to me that the concept of greed has even permeated into the most virtuous of human activities; the world of charity.

What a paradox that is…that people are making a fortune out of managing other people's misery.

I believe that it would make a lot more sense for retired businessman and women to offer their services to these charities – if they were so inclined – as an alternative to employing 'current professionals' on these outrageous salaries.

Retired people wouldn't demand such high reward for their expertise and if they were willing to get involved, it would be for the right reasons. After all, charity is an inherently altruistic activity, not another get-rich quick scheme.

The salaries being paid to these people are outrageous and if it carries on for much longer, if the British public feels that fat-cats are creaming off their generosity they will simply stop donating to these charities.

———

A word on Poppy Fascism;

The reason we honour the memory of those who died in battle is to recognise how their sacrifice then, has allowed us to live our lives as we see fit, today.

The sacrifice those people made on battlefields all around the world is what allows us to enjoy the freedoms for which those valiant people fought; it is what allows us to make choices.

That is why I believe that the systematic obligation for everybody in the media to wear a poppy for the two weeks preceding Remembrance Day in order to be 'politically-correct' is wrong; it makes a complete mockery of that 'right to choose'.

That poppies are on sale two weeks before Remembrance Day is not an issue; the more that can be collected for this cause - *which supports all current and ex-military personnel* - the better but this 'poppy-overkill' on our TV screens is patronising and hypocritical; it is unnecessary and it undermines the solemn nature of the cause giving it almost a gimmicky overtone.

As journalist Jon Snow once remarked; 'they died that we might be free to wear a poppy whenever we wish — I wish to wear mine on Remembrance Sunday' ...and not every day of the two weeks leading up to it.

I could not agree more; to wear a poppy on Remembrance Sunday - and only on Remembrance Sunday - as a sign of respect is so much more poignant and dignified.

The PC Executive with its bureaucratic meddling and its misguided directives is completely devaluing one of our most treasured and respected traditions…and it must be reined in.

———

Finance

Author's comment;

*(This is not a sleight at any particular section of society
but simply a comment on the human race)*

In every aspect of life, wherever you look,
there are always people whose only thought is
how they can manipulate a situation to their own benefit;
that is human nature and sadly we have to
take it into account in all things.

Banking;

The global economy in which we live today is built on a deep history of top-down hierarchies that promote domination and control.

We live in a world where economic philosophies that celebrate greed and selfishness can be easily implemented - through a web of legal and financial tools - so that those individuals with a psychological tendency toward self- interest can be elevated and rewarded - handsomely in most cases - regardless of the consequences and the impact that those actions might have on the rest of us...

...and nothing illustrates this point better than the worldwide banking collapse that has ruined the global economy over recent years.

However, the same phenomenon is replicated in most hierarchal situations, be it political or business-related; domination and control are inherently linked to the way our society is structured.

The Meltdown;

The parallel banking system that the great minds of the banking sector constructed out of thin-air, with no solid foundation, no safe-guards and no plan B, based on;

- the sub-prime mortgage market
- the derivatives market
- the futures market,
- the equities market
- and potential growth investments...

...was no more than a racket, a mirage created with one goal in mind; to generate quick profit for those rapacious individuals involved...

...and the resulting meltdown has shown the international banking community as no more than a bunch of common criminals...with unfortunately the same flaws and fallibilities as the rest of us.

What else can you say when the 'greatest financial minds in the Western world' band together to speculate and create such an unstable house of cards - irrespective of the risk to the world's economy - based wholly on avarice, greed and quick profit.

It is called 'securitisation' in banking terminology – i.e. the selling of future profits for today's gain; David Bowie for example, calculated his royalties for the next ten years and then sold them on, making a profit today on potential sales tomorrow.

Elsewhere unsubstantiated loans were agreed and sold on without the necessary due diligence or control...creating a house of cards with no substance and no solid foundation.

Regulation was lax too, because of exponential growth...and the scheme worked for a while, mainly because a lot of people were making a lot of money (while not really understanding the mechanics of the concept), but there was a finite inevitability to it all, as there is to any scam that isn't based on solid groundwork, and it all came crashing down.

You can only sell thin-air and a promise for so long; it's not eternally exponential and eventually somebody has to pay up...

...and when the bubble burst and the bankers were called to account, they could not cover their obligations which led to the global collapse.

The unfortunate consequence of this particular scam is that these people, these financial wizards, these people considered the 'best in the business', were entrusted with millions of ordinary peoples' livelihoods and they abused that trust, exploiting it for their own cupidity, much like Bernie Madoff – formerly head of the Nasdaq – whose pyramid scheme ruined many thousands of people's lives.

Now this latest scheme might have originated in the USA but the financial sector is a global market and the politicians in the UK, who were quite happy to turn a blind-eye to regulation (indeed accepting deregulation) must accept their part of the blame for jumping on the bandwagon rather than looking more carefully into the financial implications of selling future potential without any guarantees.

Perhaps, the FSA (Financial Services Authority) should have seen the crisis on the horizon and questioned the veracity or the soundness of the thinking behind this financial delusion, but for whatever reason they didn't, and instead they just gave themselves bonuses too, replicating the excesses of the immoral bankers.

The British people and banking –

People in Britain need to wake up and realise what banks are all about.

Banks are private businesses whose only goal is to make as much profit as they can for their shareholders, using the capital of their account-holders.

It is as simple as that; banks are not your friends.

Here is an example which illustrates that phrase and puts it into context;

- *When a bank uses our money, <u>the money in our accounts</u>, they pay very little interest for the privilege…yet when we use 'their' money, through a loan or an overdraught facility they charge us up to 18% interest. It is a one-way profit arrangement. A bank is not there to do you any favours.*
- *One man who had £17,000 in his account was recently credited with 23p of annual interest. Conversely, had he wanted to borrow £17,000 from the bank for a year the interest would have been over £3,000.*

Banking is a cut-throat business where there is no room for sentiment and no place for consideration. Time is money and the only thing that counts for a bank is the bottom line.

Gone are the days when you knew the name of your bank-manager and could ring him with a query on your account (remember Captain Mainwaring in Dad's Army).

Gone are the days when loyalty meant something, meant that you were treated with a little more respect after 30 or 40 years than somebody who has just opened an account.

These days, it is all about the money; banks are ruthless, voracious sharks with no principles and no morals as the recent scandals have shown…

For example;

- Barclays Bank was fined £290 million for its part in manipulating Libor rates
- A number of British banks were forced to pay back millions if not billions of pounds for selling PPI plans (payment protection insurance) to their customers unnecessarily

- HSBC was fined £1.2 billion for turning a blind eye to large scale money laundering by drug cartels, terrorists and rogue regimes
- RBS was fined £390 million for its part in the Libor rate-fixing scandal
- Standard and Charter was fined $300 million for violating US sanctions on Iran, Burma, Libya and Sudan. Prosecutors said that by hiding 60000 transactions worth $250 billion it had been aiding terrorists, drug runners and arms dealers
- UBS was fined £940 million for its part in the Libor rate-fixing scandal...and of course the worldwide meltdown saw off Lehmann Brothers because of its 'unethical' practices.

Greed is what drives the traders and the speculators of these banks... while loyalty counts for nothing...and if the banks can charge you £30 for overdrawing your account by a single penny then they will do so without a second's hesitation.

People should know not to trust the banks that have lined our high streets for decades; these institutions have lost all credibility and standing in our communities because their only interest...is self-interest...

...and that is why the PDC would look into setting up an independent UK Investment Bank for small businesses which would rival the big four and break their monopoly.

New rules;

The banks abandoned client-friendly personal banking many years ago, turning instead to the sale of more lucrative but ultimately dodgy insurance and derivative products.

However, the shocking stupidity and the reckless behaviour that the bankers displayed in the years before the credit-crunch, fuelled by the voracious greed of their traders and speculators to make a fast buck, while completely ignoring the economic consequences of their actions long-term has shown that banks are not to be trusted without regulation.

Complacency breeds chaos...and incompetence and immorality cannot be acceptable in a sector that is so vital to the British economy and to people's lives

Now, of course everybody recognises that we are in this mess because of the combination of greed and incompetence of both the banking industry and the political classes but looking back and playing the blame game will not take us forward.

Yes, those that took advantage should be punished but I believe it is time to move on.

We <u>need</u> a financial sector in this country as our whole economy is based on monetary exchange...

...this is because, for a number of decades, consecutive, short-sighted governments who never look beyond the next election prioritised the quick financial gains of the casino-style banking sector...to the detriment of every other sector of the economy, especially the manufacturing industry, making our economy top-heavy and heavily dependent on the financial sector.

...however, going forward, we need a new sanity, a new integrity and a whole set of new rules.

I believe that we should start by reversing the trend of huge multi-national corporations buying up all the competition and sharing the market between just four or five brands...whether this be in the banking sector or in the supermarket trade.

No one company should ever be allowed to own more than 15% of any market and if we want to keep the banks in the free market and not have to re-nationalise them completely I believe that we need to separate their high street banking operations from the speculative banking (stock market) operations which caused the melt-down in 2008 in order to protect the public from any future meltdowns…as suggested by the Independent Commission on Banking.

Current Chancellor George Osborne has also proposed splitting up the banks, and reducing them down to a more manageable size; high street on the one side, and investment on the other.

This firewall has to be implemented because, as we see time and time again, human beings have a tendency to break the rules.

We see it everywhere and most noticeably in the banking sector where billions upon billions have been lost by rogue traders;

- Nick Leeson bankrupted Barings Bank
- Jerome Kerviel lost billions for the French bank 'Societe Generale'
- JP Morgan Chase suffered huge losses
- Lehmann brothers folded
- and more recently Kweku Adoboli lost £1.4 billion working for UBS

The bankers say that a separation of high street and investment banking would add a cost to the high street and this may well be true…but the fact is that a separation would remove the constant threat hanging over ordinary people that they could suddenly lose everything they have ever owned through no fault of their own.

I believe that when people or companies are entrusted with the lives and the livelihoods of millions of ordinary citizens, then they should err on the side of caution; better to be safe than sorry.

Speculation is dangerous in anything - especially in banking because of the sums involved - so we need fail-safe guarantees and contingency plans in place in the event of misguided human judgement taking us in the wrong direction…ever again.

If however, the banks do replicate their reckless behaviour once again – which is not beyond the realms of possibility because of the natural greed we all have to acknowledge is part of our human DNA, I believe that they should be allowed to go under - as long as their capital reserves cover their obligations towards ordinary citizens to a reasonable level; no more bailouts.

This threat will hopefully engender more responsibility, though there are no guarantees when dealing with people who lack any morality, integrity or principle.

And finally…the PDC would not accept any trite excuses from senior management in any future scandal. It would instead make the board of directors of banks…and any other company…personally responsible and accountable for what their employees did…and the risks they took. The excuse that they 'weren't aware' or 'didn't know' what was going on within their walls cannot be acceptable when reckless trading is bringing down economies.

For information; the new PDC justice system would make special provision for those involved in questionable and criminal activity within the financial sector.

———

Author's comment;

Putting all our eggs in one basket, relying on the financial sector alone to drive our economy was always going to end in disaster.

It was desperation politics which pandered to the inherent greed of the human race - in the guise of our politicians – while at the same time feeding the constant need of an incompetent and profligate government – focussed solely on the short-term - to have huge sums of money readily available to cover up that incompetence and that tendency to spend, spend, spend.

This kind of politics shows a lack of integrity, it shows a lack of ideas and it shows a lack of any vision for the future. It also shows a distinct absence of the qualities needed in a political class to run a country and its economy. We cannot and should not have a group of inveterate gamblers running our country or our economy…but in essence that is what we have had…and it was only a matter of time before it all exploded in our faces.

Financial de-regulation put the power in the hands of the bankers and ever since they have taken the country to the cleaners…time and time again…

They have feasted on the public purse and yet not one of our craven politicians has had the courage to stand up to them – *not one banker has been prosecuted for ruining our economy* - which is why these loathsome people continue to give each other huge salaries, outrageous bonuses and gigantic pensions…even when their banks are losing money… without so much as a thought for what the British public might think of their reprehensible actions.

Of course, finances are an important part of the economy, but providing people with jobs and the possibility of a livelihood on which to base their lives, their futures and the futures of their families is even more important.

The time has come to re-balance our economy.

It is a question of priorities and anybody wishing to run a country should make sure that he or she has those priorities in the right order before putting themselves up for election.

New Bank;

The melt-down was one thing but I believe that the four major banking institutions in this country have had it all their own way for far too long; these creaking old institutions are in need of a world-shattering wake-up call.

Their questionable practices and underhand dealings run like a gangrenous river of greed and deception throughout the banking sector and I believe that it is time to change that flow with an infusion of new, clean blood.

The PDC would look into the creation of a new banking institution; The Brit-Bizz bank; a British Investment Bank which would be backed by the Bank of England to help small businesses and start-ups.

This new bank would drastically undercut the Big Four banks at every level, forcing them to reconsider their exploitative business practices and obliging them to bring down their prices in order to compete;

The new 'Brit-Bizz' bank would begin online;

- It would have an upper limit to its guarantee and the guidelines would stipulate that any company which exceeded the cap put in place with its turnover would have to find a new financial partner within a set period
- Interest would be charged at the Bank of England base rate and used simply to cover the running costs, including the provision of the service and inflation making it a *de-facto* non-profit venture.
- The new bank would only offer a restricted number of services. There would be no long-term loans such as home loans (mortgages) or consumer loans (cars, household goods); only short-term lending.

Its primary objective would be to help small businesses, to encourage start-ups…and potentially to help students / future entrepreneurs.

However, if the demand was there we might eventually develop the 'Brit-Bizz' into a High Street bank; after all the British taxpayer already owns over 80% of RBS which has branches all over the country – and if the bank was deemed successful for small businesses, we might even open it up later to the general public with current accounts.

There would however always be a cap on the amounts placed on these accounts to limit the government's liability.

Of course there is a cost to all this…but if we can conjure up billions of pounds to bail out the crooks and the incompetents, we should also be able to find funds for a new scandal-free enterprise focussed on helping new businesses and young entrepreneurs; i.e., our future…

…and in the long run, I'm pretty sure that the British public would sleep better in their beds at night knowing that their savings and their livelihoods were safe and secure in the hands of a responsible institution that they could trust not to gamble it away.

———

For the future; a separate branch of the bank could be dedicated to students; I believe that a bank geared specifically to the needs of students with limited facilities and a tight grip on loans and overdraughts would be the best way to introduce the younger generation to responsible lending and greater financial awareness.

———

Author's comment;

Because of the high street banks tendency to increase charges inexorably and add them onto every transaction – anybody who could create a financial institution which would guarantee free banking and reasonable charges would soon corner the market.

———

Salaries and Bonuses –

Salaries;

Bankers say - in order to justify their outrageous salaries - that they have to pay these exorbitant salaries to each other in order to hire the best people…and the traders say that if their inflated salaries are curtailed in any way…or if their bonuses are reduced they would go and work elsewhere.

Let's examine this...

Surely if these people were the best at what they do, the world's economy would not have crashed as it did...or was that more down to;

- their incompetence
- their lack of integrity or
- their lack of morality...than their financial talents.

I say that if these people want to leave we should let them go...and good riddance.

No-one is indispensable.

Of course, it would take a while to replace these people - were they to relocate to the other side of the world - but adjustments would be made and the world would keep on turning...and while it would be a shame to lose their experience I am certain that an enthusiastic new generation of people - with more integrity and a better, more humble approach to life – would delight in filling the roles being vacated.

We do not want people motivated purely by greed...

...who we cannot trust...and

...who have absolutely no morals...running our financial sector.

Nobody is indispensible and a PDC government would not respond to selfish threats or be held to ransom by people who have proved that they have no morality.

The banks too suggest that if they are taxed too heavily they will move elsewhere.

Let them go; we will create new institutions with more positive thinking, more integrity and more shared community spirit.

Indeed, I would love to see our high-streets populated by an array of smaller businesses, all offering different financial services (*in order to spread the risk*) and all adhering to a new code of conduct that would respect the new guarantee structure of limited responsibility that the PDC would put in place in order to protect both them as a business and their customers.

Author's comment;

Five years have passed since the hubris, the appalling greed and the monumental mismanagement of the banks which helped to trigger the worst financial meltdown of our lifetime but those same bankers are still living in another world to the rest of us.

It was revealed recently that over 2700 bankers in the UK are still earning salaries in excess of €1 million a year (£830,000) which is 33.2 times the 'Emgee Ratio' and 12 times more than any other EU country.

Why are British bankers so greedy?

Bonuses;

A bonus is not a systematic due; it is, and I quote the OED on this,

> 'A sum of money added to a person's wage
> as a reward for good performance;
> an extra and unexpected advantage'

The effrontery of those who continue to pocket huge bonuses is shameful; we have to rein in this culture of greed.

Now I have nothing against an incentive scheme, but there should be no systematic annual bonus to any employee unless it is truly merited and can be proved to be so.

A bonus has to be performance-related and not just an accepted annual occurrence.

Incompetence, complacency, recklessness and failure **<u>should never be rewarded</u>**.

Furthermore, applying the same logic here as I have throughout – I believe that any bank that has received taxpayers' money from the government in order to get itself out of trouble should be banned from paying out <u>any bonuses or golden handshakes</u> <u>whatsoever</u> until the money it has borrowed has been paid back to the taxpayer.

No discussion, no argument and no compromise...and any bonuses thereafter should only be awarded once the bank had returned to profit.

———

For information;

One bank recently axed 3700 jobs but still paid out £1.8bn in bonuses.

In another case, a banker who claimed that his £1.6million a year salary (ER; 64) was modest by banking standards, begged to be allowed to keep his £780,000 bonus. This just shows how much these people are out of touch with the rest of society.

———

Author's comment;

Alistair Darling (former Labour Chancellor of the Exchequer) once invoked the Bankers moral responsibilities in order to stop them giving themselves hefty bonuses out of the tax-payers money – but they didn't listen and why; <u>because they are bankers; they don't have any morality</u>.

You cannot expect any morality from people who are innately immoral.

———

Promotions and pensions;

It is also sickening to see those implicated in wholesale corruption getting promotions, salary hikes and bonuses.

Incompetence should not be rewarded – and in any future contracts a clause must be inserted into the severance package / retirement fund payouts so that these awards can be revised retrospectively if found to be abusive.

For example; Fred Goodwin was put in charge of RBS and having received 350 billion pounds of taxpayers' money to bail out the bank, he then proceeded to lose another £24 billion before walking away with a £650,000 a year pension.

That is not reasonable, that is not logical and that is not acceptable.

Author's comment;

Perhaps the solution would be to get all the world's major banking organisations in a room together and hammer out a worldwide cap on salary and bonus schemes for bank employees...but of course that will never happen because the free market argument will always be used to allow greed to prosper.

Other Financial Matters;

Complaints;

The financial ombudsman in the UK receives a complaint every six seconds about one bank or another; surely the banking sector cannot be happy with this level of dissatisfaction.

Charges;

Firstly, we need more transparency in Bank charges. Any charges should be fair and across the board within the same institution; for example; it is not right that an overdraught at Lloyds should cost £200 for one customer and only £15 for another because that person is a Muslim and not 'allowed' to pay interest. The bank is using semantics and sharp practice to appease Muslims and help them get around their faith. This is both morally wrong and socially unjust...and might even transgress the equality laws. It has to be the same rule for everyone.

Secondly; could we not protect those with very small bank balances from bank charges that take them into the red and then subject them to even more charges for being overdrawn? This does nothing but exacerbate an already precarious situation for people on the lowest incomes.

———

Credit;

The banking institutions should adopt a more responsible attitude towards credit. In recent years it has been far too easy for people to access credit that they cannot afford.

This has created massive debt and a 'live today, pay tomorrow' culture, ultimately ending in bankruptcy for many people. Those banks generating more than X amount of credit per annum (as a percentage of their turnover) should be fined for being irresponsible. (X; *to be determined*)

———

Credit cards;

The hidden fees on credit-card transactions should also be outlawed (flights, holidays, health clubs and cinema tickets etc – even the DVLA imposes a charge). The exorbitant interest rates being charged by these companies are already high enough to cover their costs.

We need to prevent immoral and irresponsible bank practices such as offering Visa credit cards to 11 year old children; the PDC would insist on withdrawal cards only for anyone under the age of 18. (*Tied to coming of age policy*)

Loans;

Looking forward; the PDC would introduce a preferential rate for home-loans to those people who fall into the category of 'service-provider' professions such as teachers, nurses, midwives etc. These loans would all be tied to the loyalty and contractual obligations set out in the education chapter – and if that contract was broken for whatever reason - the loan would revert back to the market rate.

This is to encourage fidelity and stability.

Cash;

Our money needs to reflect our identity; it needs to remain traditional, patriotic and symbolic of whom we are.

Britannia is iconic and represents the institutions on which Britain was built;

Our notes can always be modernised and updated to keep up with new technologies... and one step ahead of the forgers...but I believe that it is still too soon to discard the concept of cash completely as some have suggested; that time may well come; but not yet.

I would also suggest, as we now live in a global, more inclusive world, that we should look into introducing Braille on our bank-notes as they have in Canada…or incorporating a plastic compound into the fabrication of our notes as they have done in Australia to help with longevity…and to thwart fraudulent activity.

———

Debt collectors / Money Lenders; (Pay-day loans)

We also need to introduce stronger controls on abusive financial institutions such as debt collection agencies that threaten and harass people with tactics similar to those used in organised crime in the last century.

…and similarly, we need to take a closer look at Loan Sharks and money-lenders – legal or otherwise – who prey on the vulnerable and use methods bordering on criminal to extort the money back off their borrowers…with excessive interest.

Greed

The study of human behaviour suggests that it is normal for a human being to be greedy - as by pulling as much of the blanket as he can to his side of the bed, he ensures that he stays warm...thereby guaranteeing his survival.

It is a question of self-preservation.

The same metaphor can be used for money...but not only money; it can apply to food and to water too...and the fact that others might go cold, hungry or thirsty because of a person's action does not enter into the primal cognitive reasoning process.

It is Nature that instilled this selfish mechanism in us all, and while it is not our greatest quality it is one that has probably contributed in no small way to us still being here today.

Nevertheless, this survival instinct was developed for the individual... before we learned to live in groups, in families...and today, in a civilised society...and I believe that it is high time we tried to temper it.

We, in the West, have now created a world where there is enough to go around (if only we would share it out properly) but the native instinct to make sure that we have enough for ourselves first – and if possible more than we really need - still exists and probably always will...as part of our instinctive nature.

However, as we in our 21ˢᵗ century modern society already have the food, the drink and the heat necessary to satisfy our basic needs... we express our natural instinct for selfishness in other ways, through the collection of material possessions for example, and the means to obtaining those material possessions...is money.

This means that the first reflex of any person who reaches a position of responsibility or power is to make sure that He or She feathers his or her own nest first...and with the best materials. (the analogy with nature is deliberate).

This begins with the negotiation of the best possible salary combined with the most lucrative pension-scheme and the most generous of golden parachutes - in case of a 'parting of ways' - and then, year on year perks and bonuses are added one after the other until the nest is fully furnished.

The next project is the nest-egg and so it goes on in a self-perpetuating and never-ending cycle of insatiable greed; these people will never have enough because they have allowed their greed to define who they are...

The worst passengers on the Greed / Gravy Train –

1) MP's in Westminster; who have the potential to upgrade to First Class as an MEP (*given first place in this list as they are taking their money from the taxpayers*)
2) Bankers,
3) City-traders,
4) Top executives,
5) Lawyers

...and the more recent additions

6) Doctors,
7) Dentists,
8) The new Police Commissioners...and their cronies...

...but the greed culture doesn't stop there because for those who do not have access to the actual gravy train itself, there is always the poor man's option; the compensation band-wagon.

This is an alternative greed stream set up by Vultures & Co which circles continuously ready to sue everyone and anyone - however frivolous, however immoral or however damaging it might be to the integrity of this once great country – in order to make a quick buck; their only motivation money, money and still more money.

The greed culture has no limits because people will never have enough, they will always want more and sadly the most recent adherents to this compensation greed culture are our teachers and our police force; as one teacher commented...

'Hey; everybody else is on board so why should we get left behind...... right?'

That is our 21ˢᵗ century society; what a wonderful image...right?

What a wonderful legacy to hand down to future generations.

Just one thing;

Do these people not realise that all they are doing by making all these compensation claims is driving up the cost of living for us all - because the pay-outs they are claiming have to be financed somehow and the insurance companies do this by simply increasing the cost of insurance policies for everyone.

Oh no, of course they don't...because this selfish behaviour has no altruistic component.

Whatever happened to morality, integrity and honesty?

When did we lose sight of our humanity, our dignity...and our self-respect?

———

Industry & Commerce

Author's comment;

Any society is in decline, if not in decay when it values profit and the bottom line over people and their needs. We need to keep that in mind at all times.

A recent example; *Russia chose to continue selling weapons and helicopters to Bachar al Assad in Syria – to use against his own people – in order to support its own industry.*

I would like to see our business sector have a more moral, a more ethical approach to commercial enterprise, not only via the Fair-Trade programme for producers but also in its approach to its work-force and its customers.

General Policy –

While the world's economy is in a mess and economic demand has stalled we should be looking to regenerate our own economy and our own country…

…and investment in infrastructure would be the best way of doing that;

- To begin with…we should start renovating and renewing the road-system because pot-holes are becoming a major issue
- Then we should be pouring investment into improving the rail-network which has been neglected for decades; renovating / renewing rail-lines and rolling stock
- After that, we need to tackle the flood-barrier issue which has become such a major problem in recent times…and finally…

- We need to start bulldozing abandoned buildings and run-down areas all around the country in order to replace them with new community-friendly housing that incorporates social / sports halls, small shops and a police community office (see **Magnet centres** later)

These initiatives would only be a start...but all this work could be contracted out to British companies providing thousands of jobs for the people of Britain, giving them a livelihood and more importantly a disposable income for the foreseeable future.

At the same time, we should also encourage new entrepreneurs to set up businesses with simplified business plans, tax advantages and preferential loans...offset for 5 years or so.

Then when the world economy does pick up, as it inevitably will, we will have not only renewed our infrastructure, but we will also be in prime position to take on the challenge of renewed international demand thanks to a new generation of tried-and-tested business initiatives.

Weapons / Arms –

What a sad indictment it is of the human race that our most lucrative industry is the one where we design and produce machines that can kill as many of our own species as possible at any one time.

Be it;

- Nuclear explosions
- planes that drop bombs...and fire machine guns or
- battleships that launch rockets or
- tanks that can hit a target a mile away or
- individual weapons for that matter...from RPG's to hand-guns

...we have any number of ways at our disposal to tear through human flesh and rip our fellow man to shreds.

———

But what folly it is that the most evolved species on this planet spends so much of its time…and money…devising new and more devastating ways of eliminating members of its own genus. The human race really doesn't deserve to survive the apocalypse; we are just too stupid.

However, in the meantime, we in the UK need to find a way of transforming and re-inventing this industry of death…because unfortunately as it stands, it provides too many jobs for too many people – and by extension their families – to be abandoned without provision.

-   The weapons manufacturing industry in the UK employs around 300,000 people
-   There are over 9000 defence-based companies around the country…and
-   Weapons manufacturing brings in £11.4 billion in export money every year

———

I am well aware of the economics and of the importance of this industry to our economy but I am just as certain that the metal and the technology used to make all these weapons could quite easily be adapted and put to better use in new or existing industries that have a more ethical and morally-acceptable template.

I believe that if the human race is to survive it is time to scale back on the manufacture and sale of killing-machines…or the inevitable apocalypse, as suggested previously will come to pass sooner rather than later.

Besides, mass invasions requiring thousands of armed troops, tanks and bomber planes are now a thing of the past...and our military is already being scaled down to reflect that change...so clearly the need for all this weaponry is already on the decline and as a consequence, rather than see this as an opportunity to increase our exports of these killing-machines why not see it as an opportunity for our country to start re-inventing itself.

Of course we will still need to produce the necessary weapons to arm the military personnel that we will be retaining...and to maintain the defence programmes put in place to protect our sovereignty...but for those companies not involved specifically in those two areas, why not offer them help in converting their business or transforming it into another area of commerce.

Weapons-sales are currently a large part of the UK economy, so it would be hypocritical for me to say that the PDC could change this overnight, but I do believe that we need a timetable to stop producing and selling these killing machines.

It goes without saying that we would have to continue producing enough to protect ourselves, but let's slowly turn off the taps on worldwide sales.

Humanity needs someone to take the lead; why shouldn't that be us?

———

Energy - Important;

I believe that there are certain strategic areas of British life that should always remain under the control and the stewardship of the UK Government.

Air-traffic control is an obvious example, much like National Security and Border Control...but there are other vital industries and utilities that help to keep this country running...and contribute to maintaining our independence / sovereignty...which I believe should also be run by the UK government or at the very least by British companies based in the UK.

Why?

Look at our energy industry.

Heat, light and water are basic human needs and yet the British people are being held to ransom in these areas by a small number of dominant private companies, the majority of which are foreign owned.

We should not, as a proud independent and sovereign nation, be in a position where a foreign country can hold us to ransom over our energy and water needs. It leaves us vulnerable on the world stage.

Foreign investment is fine in less essential areas but I believe that we should have maintained control over all vital services.

Would we allow the Germans, the French or the Russians to run our military; NO, of course not; then why should they control our access to power (electricity / gas) and water?

…and by the same score; would the Germans, the French or the Russians allow **us** to run any of their vital services…? I highly doubt it. They might ask us to participate in joint ventures…but they certainly would never allow us to take complete control of any of their critical infrastructure…and that's the way it should be. That is what being a sovereign nation all is about.

Giving up control of our energy supplies was a very unwise decision and we are paying for it through the nose but as re-nationalising the energy companies is currently out of the question, I believe that in the meantime we should introduce a new energy regulator - with teeth – which will stop these companies from constantly exploiting us with excessive and ever-increasing bills.

People of Britain; it is time to stop these people from draining our economy of vital capital…and expatriating that capital in the form of profit, leaving us all, as a population, worse off.

———

Manufacturing;

We have lost much of our manufacturing knowledge and industry over the last thirty years but should investors back British entrepreneurship, I believe that many British customers would be only too pleased to buy home-made British produce, as long as the quality was good and the price was reasonable.

I also believe that the British government should take the lead in this; act as our flag-ship by promoting British industry and British goods whenever possible, using British cars to drive around in, and wearing British clothes whenever possible.

However I do not agree with the £50 million of taxpayer's money that was paid out for campaigns to promote Britain. That is a superficial fix... and a very costly one at that.

Communications –

This is supposed to be the 21st century; the age of communication...and while we do have it all at our fingertips 24/7, 21st century technology has paradoxically meant human interaction taking a step back.

In fact it has created another layer between people that blocks direct contact and totally distorts the communicative process.

The art of conversation was already dying but the advent of technology has speeded up the demise of that particular human interaction quicker than anybody could have ever imagined. People no longer talk to each other directly...and even speaking on the phone is becoming a rarity.

Instead, these days, people just text each other...or read the person's answer to their question on a cyberspace wall...and when they want to be hurtful, cruel or spiteful to each other they simply sign onto one of the social networking sites, create a pseudonym and gaily spew bile to their heart's content about anybody and everybody, people they don't know and situations they don't understand.

It is a very cowardly activity but that is what people have become.

They walk around all day with their noses and their thumbs glued to their mobile-phones but they are not really communicating...sharing maybe, but communicating, most certainly not.

Which is why - when these people are confronted with an actual situation – something like having an actual conversation face to face – they are not equipped to do so;

- they have no self-confidence,
- they have no vocabulary…and
- they have no social skills to deal with actual reality.

There is nothing more annoying in my eyes, than seeing two people sitting next to each other on a bus...or opposite each other at a table in a restaurant... communicating with each-other via text-messages…

...and the worst thing is that companies have also adopted this non-communicative stance.

For individuals; it is a personal choice, but companies need to communicate to survive, and yet they are not doing so. Nobody replies to a question or a request for information or a job application, <u>especially a job application</u> and it leaves those at the other end of this dearth of service most frustrated.

I cannot change this moronic, borderline-obsessive behaviour…or the weird relationships that some people now have with their mobile-phones - which I find rather sad and depressing - but I would suggest that every company with over 50 employees hire a Communications Liaison Officer to deal with the small admin that is currently being ignored.

It doesn't have to be a full time job but – with the right training - it would give a youngster a start in life - in an area where they are comfortable - and it would defuse the frustration of all those people trying to get answers, information, or employment.

All these people are asking for is to receive an e-mail, a text-message or a call to say thank-you for their enquiry with a contact number for further information or an apology.

Of course, I understand the economic reasoning behind companies not employing 'unproductive' personnel but a good communications officer would undeniably improve if not boost a company's reputation and their brand awareness in the wider world.

***

Building / construction industry –

As part of our over-population policy the PDC would put an end to the social experiment of high-rise tower-blocks. This policy has proved its limits and shown that people don't live well in cages stacked one on top of the other.

These grey tower blocks are depressing to look at, they are depressing to live in and they have spawned much of the social unrest that now haunts our streets and our society.

People need to be allowed to have their pride...and if they lived in small two-up / two-down houses with a little patch of green out front as part of an inclusive community they would be so much happier.

So, in our urban regeneration programme the PDC would embark on an extensive rebuilding plan, based on neighbourhood design schemes which encourage social inter-action and community spirit.

We would impose a maximum of four floors for apartment blocks outside our major cities...and those would have to be limited to a percentage of the market so as not to re-create the problems we are trying to resolve.

***

For information; With the tendency for more and more people to live alone or in single parent families we need to build more and more one and two bed residences rather than three, four or five-bed homes.

I see these residences appealing to most sections of the population, from single professionals and single parents to young families...and even the elderly. Indeed I would suggest that the ground floor of every development be systematically reserved for the elderly and those needing wheelchair-access to avoid them having to use lifts or stairs.

The residences would be finished in a variety of styles from standard to luxury and designed around – or at least within walking distance of - a commercial hub which would provide the essential services that a community needs to thrive. (*see Magnet centre later*)

These new community designs would also prioritise people over cars; cars would of course be given peripheral access, but the priority would be given to pedestrians.

Now in order to create the communities above I would like to see any site which has been left abandoned or derelict for more than three years – so-called 'brown-sites' - demolished and cleared.

However, if a particular building was still sound…and of significant historical interest… it could perhaps be renovated or transformed.

This is a huge project that will take many years to complete but in the meantime it will be providing jobs and homes for an ever-increasing population while at the same time clearing unsightly eye-sores and maximising potential where space to build new housing is becoming more and more contentious.

Cost will inevitably be an issue but I am certain that private enterprise could work hand in hand with local councils to find a compromise and some common ground on which to base a solution to this challenge.

If we can encourage responsible industry experts with the carrot of cut-priced land / space in exchange for the demolition and clearing of useless eyesores then why not?

However, we would have to put in place the necessary safeguards to avoid the natural instinct of unscrupulous businessmen to cut corners for profit.

———

As part of this re-development scheme, the PDC would also look to accelerate the development of re-cycling techniques so that when factories, houses and high-rise flats are taken down the building materials recovered from them can be re-used.

We need to create a process of grinding down rubble and re-creating new building blocks from the resulting material rather than consigning dismantled buildings in their entirety to land-fill. We might also look into using the non-recyclable materials as part of our flood-barrier policy.

The PDC would also look into introducing Carbon neutral houses, although I am not jumping on the band-wagon of the hysteria whipped up by the 'global warming' issues here; I have already expressed myself on that – but I do believe that if there is any way that we can make adjustments in the way we live which help the environment, then yes, I'm all for it; *just tell the politicians to stop frightening the masses with 'the end of the world as we know it speeches' just to get another meal-ticket.*

Meanwhile, in inner-cities, solar powered emergency generators should be installed systematically on the roofs of all high-rise office blocks as part of their energy-efficiency plans.

———

Author's comment;

Semantics; it is time to rehabilitate the title of Engineer and return it to its rightful place with the status it deserves. We have become lazy in our speech today, describing anybody who wears a uniform as 'an engineer'…but from this day forward, let's give engineers the recognition they deserve…and prefer the title of 'technician' for all those involved in the maintenance and repair industries.

Building Regulations –

Studies have shown that living in cramped conditions affects our health and well-being, both physical and psychological.

In Britain today, we have the smallest-sized rooms in Europe and this is because over the last thirty years 'astute' builders have taken advantage of the lapse in building regulations and exploited it massively in order to build smaller and smaller rooms, packing more and more people into smaller and smaller houses in order to maximise their profits.

Human beings should not be living in hutches, we are not rabbits and yet statistically the legal rules for hutch sizes are proportionately more generous than those being offered for human occupancy in the UK.

That cannot be right.

We need to re-introduce the minimum buildings standards / regulations abandoned in the 1980's concerning space and the size of rooms. We have to return to a 10m2 minimum for our own health and well-being.

Cowboys –

In the last three years we have had over 2.5 million disputes in the UK with cowboy builders.

The PDC would address this scourge by introducing a government funded charter for tradesmen which would guarantee that they were bona-fide and have the knowledge and the equipment to do a job properly.

This would apply to plumbers, electricians, locksmiths, gardeners, handy-men, car mechanics and even estate agents; anybody, in fact who might turn up at your door, invited or otherwise.

- Each tradesman would be issued with a card guaranteed by his particular trade representative and the list of qualified / recommended local tradesmen would be kept in the Council Offices where it would be updated on a regular basis
- The public would be able to check the person's credentials via an 0800 number…or do the same via the internet…or if they preferred, in person at the council offices…before going ahead with any work
- We have a history of paying cash-in-hand in this country but cash-in-hand transactions offer no guarantee or insurance. These cards would include a professional guarantee and the carrier's public liability insurance as well as the possibility of accepting payment, thereby preventing any VAT issues.
- We would also introduce a universal guideline for prices for particular jobs because while I understand that each job is different, a ball-park figure or a guideline as to the potential cost would hopefully reduce the temptation to exploit the customer

---

For information; a call-centre operation would be set up in the local council offices for each region depending on size with access to a universal / countrywide website which would cover all the different trades. (*Cowboys tend to move around a lot so a regional policy would not be practical*)

Justice –

We all know who the cowboys are; most people will have encountered a scam-merchant during their lifetime, so the PDC would revisit all the stories brought to the public's attention on programmes such as Crimewatch, Watchdog, Rip-off Britain and X-ray in Wales to find out who is being scammed, in what context and what we can do about nailing the rogues, swindlers, scoundrels and con-men.

I suggest identifying these people in local papers with;

- their photos
- their company names
- their van registration numbers...and
- maybe a few photos of their handiwork

Metal thieves –

We need to make the scrap-metal industry a cashless business. Scrap-metal should be paid for by cheque or direct debit and a photo taken of the goods and the seller in addition to his identity details being logged.

Car industry –

The car industry...and all its sub-contractors...is an important part of the British economy. It provides so many jobs in so many subsidiary areas that we should clearly offer to support it...in the short to medium term...in any way we can, until the next innovation in transport makes it redundant.

We need to offer incentives to industry so that they can research, design and produce the next generation of cars and particularly the electric or hydrogen-propelled cars for teenagers that we would look to promote;

The 'Teeno' would be a hybrid car for young drivers based on the best features of the Ford Ka, the Nissan Leaf, the Renault Twingo, the Smart car, the Tata Nano and the Vauxhall Adam.

- there would be two models (compact and hatch-back)
- colour-schemes would be personalised (within reason) and a certain palette of colours might even be reserved for young drivers to make them more identifiable to other road-users
- they would however only have two seats (this is to reduce the number of youngsters piling into the car)
- the speed of the car would be restricted to 50MPH...and
- the price of the car – which would need to be subsidised initially - would include six months insurance with the offer of a reduced rate for the rest of the driver's probationary two-year period if no convictions were accumulated.

Naturally consultations would have to take place between the constructors, the insurance companies and the government before this project could go ahead...but if we could produce a car designed specifically for our young people, which allows them to take to the road and learn about their responsibility as a driver and road-user during their early driving years, then maybe it would go some way to reducing the current accident-mortality rate.

It would be a challenge, I know but we have the technology and the know-how in this country; proof, the majority of Formula One teams are based here.

Author's comment;

Perhaps we could organise a design competition, sponsored by the constructors interested in participating in the project and even include some aspiring young engineers in the planning and construction of these cars.

Maybe we could also launch a new Black-Cab design as the current supplier in China seems to be hesitating in its commitment.

Scooters;

We would also need to design, develop and produce a range of Vespa-style scooters for the new Community Police force; another big project.

Other ideas to develop –

Car-club; this allows people to hire a car by the hour…or more…in order to get from A to B.

Car sales; the PDC would also work with the constructors to offer incentives to get older cars off the road and get people to invest in cleaner, safer vehicles.

Emergency services –

We need to introduce designated petrol pumps on larger fore-courts and reserve them for essential services to be accessed by a professional chip-card and thumb-print or using facial recognition software.

Car Insurance –

New drivers; as part of the idea of moving the driving licence eligibility age up to the 'coming of age' limit of 18, we need to offer a new insurance package to younger drivers both for the probationary period and thereafter. Anybody completing the probationary period without having had an accident during that period would be rewarded by the insurance companies with the offer of special terms when they invested in a new car.

Claims; the UK is the whiplash capital of the world. We have to clamp down on all these fraudulent claims. When they outlawed compensation for whiplash in Sweden – except for cases that required hospitalisation – there was an 80% drop in claims. Maybe we should try that.

For information; bogus claims and 'crash for cash' claims add at least £50 to every policy in the UK. Maybe in future, to counter-act all this fraudulent activity we could integrate a front-facing camera as standard into the rear-view mirror of our cars to record these accidents / incidents.

Repairs – we need to break this circuit. Garages notoriously inflate the cost of a repair, and then the insurance company passes that information on to an approved repairer who repairs the car at the inflated cost, the insurance company pays out and then recovers the money they have paid out by inflating the policy premium of the driver. It's a closed circuit and it is the captive motorist who pays every time while each of the other participants takes their slice of the pie; that needs to change.

———

Life-insurance loop-holes need to be closed – insurance companies want your money but try every which way not to pay you back, even when you have a legitimate claim. This lack of integrity needs to be addressed.

Health insurance - We also need to introduce universal definitions for health problems; one man recently had a heart attack but as his symptoms didn't quite fit the insurance company's definition of a heart-attack, they would not pay out. This is scandalous. Insurance companies are constantly looking for a way <u>not to pay out</u> on legitimate claims and as a consequence we need to look into incorporating universal definitions or at the very least a margin of flexibility into the interpretation of these contracts.

———

House insurance - People have been tied up and robbed at gunpoint; their wedding rings ripped from their fingers and still the insurance company would not pay out. These companies are very quick - and sometimes rather insistent - to set up policies for people but they are notoriously reluctant to reimburse those same people and painfully slow to honour perfectly legitimate claims. That needs to change.

———

Unemployment / Recruitment –

Interviews;

Firstly; please, please, please; no more bureaucratic box-ticking and pointless action-plans – whoever dreamt up this system of asking existential questions to candidates applying for a job needs sectioning.

'If you were a fruit, which one would you be…and why'?

What, by any stretch of the imagination has that question got to do with applying for a clerical job. We have to roll back on all this new-age nonsense and decide on a candidate's suitability using criteria relevant to the job-description.

Secondly, I hate to hear excuses like 'you are over-qualified for the position'. If the person has applied for the job, then it is safe to assume that they are well aware of the job description and have accepted its definition. If the person wants to work, give them the job.

And finally, employers; this is the 21st century; it is supposed to be the age of communication; people break up relationships and get fired by text message, so please, please, please make more of an effort to respond to candidates who send in their CV's with job applications. The lack of any kind of response or feedback is so demoralising for people desperate to find work.

On the plus-side; it is good to see eminent business people like Sir Terry Leahy (Tesco's) condemning the promotion of ruthlessness, selfishness and self-consumed bragging as seen on TV shows like The Apprentice. He suggests that it is a recipe for failure and that selfless teamwork is the way forward. I tend to agree.

———

For information; In Austria, everyone who doesn't have a job…or an apprenticeship…is offered some kind of training. Maybe we should take a leaf out of their book.

Their employment laws too, are a lot more flexible than ours - for hiring and firing - and their unemployment rate is the lowest in Europe. Surely, we can learn from this.

———

Employment contracts –

Idea One;

We need to devise a flexible working contract which allows a company to lay off staff when the order book is empty but to re-hire them when business picks up again – thereby avoiding unemployment and keeping skilled labour available for when its needed.

Compromise would have to be reached with the unions but if the employee accepted the idea, he could for example receive 70% of his salary while in reserve with the government picking up 60% of that 70% wage and the employer picking up 40%

For the government this might only be a little more than what they would have to pay out were the person claiming unemployment benefits and for the employer it would reduce the financial burden at a time when things are tough, while at the same time retaining his skilled workforce for when things do eventually turn around.

Of course the duration would have to be looked at, the number of times an employer could resort to it too, and the types of profession it could apply to, but flexibility has to be built into the workforce in order to take into account fluctuating markets.

Idea Two;

We need to organise a discussion between the bosses and the unions which would put in place contingency plans that would allow companies to reduce hours…and pay…for a limited period – maximum two years – during an economic downturn.

This flexible arrangement would have the goal of staving off redundancies during the bad times and would revert back to its original position once the economic climate picked up again.

Women –

While it is illegal to discriminate against them, women between the ages of 24 and 40 are regularly losing out on jobs because they might get pregnant and take up to a year off work – per baby.

Businesses on a tight budget just cannot factor in the cost of all this maternity leave and the extra cover needed to replace them during their absence…and therefore we need to work out a flexi-contract specifically designed for women or create an insurance policy that allows an employer to cover the cost of an employee's absence due to pregnancy…for a limited period.

After all, child-birth is an integral part of human existence…not just an inconvenience or a deliberate spanner in the works dreamt up by women to take extra time-off.

Youth –

Out of 1.7million jobs created since 1997, 81% have been taken up by foreign workers; we need to reverse that trend by shaking our youth out of their lethargy and their lack of ambition.

They need to be given a reality check; the perfect job that pays millions for doing nothing and comes with a beautiful secretary who deals with all your needs while you drive around blithely in the latest company car simply doesn't exist.

———

Temporary Youth Employment Programme;

Perhaps we could subsidise youth employment 50/50 between the Government and the local council – offering a wage-equivalent to unemployment benefit to see how many young people would rather work than stay at home.

These jobs would be in the public sector;

- Post-office workers
- Public park gardeners and wardens
- Sports organiser's assistant…or
- Crèche assistant in one of the new Magnet centres

…all of which would help in creating and cementing community spirit…

…and to make our younger generation more empathetic they could also be used;

- as Home-care assistants (visiting the elderly)
- in care homes and hospitals (on the ancillary side)… or
- trained up to offer a listening ear or to help with feeding in those same care-homes and hospitals to ease the pressure on nursing staff

These would be 18 to 24 month contracts with in-house training rewarded with an offer of permanent employment on completion of the programme...on the condition that there were no unfortunate issues along the way...and of course they would be supervised at all times and <u>would never have any medical responsibilities</u>.

Apprenticeships;

The Health and Safety Executive has strangled apprenticeships out of the work place while insurance companies do their level best to dissuade employers from employing young apprentices by ratcheting up the insurance cover.

We need to address this and encourage...rather than discourage... entrepreneurship in young people.

Business plans;

We also need to create a business plan specifically designed for industrious young entrepreneurs that includes a mentoring component, a funding component and a flexible employment component to attract both young self-starters and mothers who want to combine their parental duties with another rewarding activity outside the home.

I believe that micro enterprises, either set up in the home or in studio workshops situated within the new Magnet centres will form a growing part of our economy in the years ahead.

Elderly;

We are haemorrhaging skills and knowledge in this country at a phenomenal rate.

Let's re-introduce skilled seniors into the workforce in an educational / mentoring capacity to guide the less academic 16/18 yr olds into trades.

I suggest that we allow retired tradesmen to occupy the studio workshops in the new Magnet centres where they could pass on their knowledge and expertise to small groups of youngsters in the hope that they could then find themselves a permanent job.

The retired tradesmen would work for free but they would receive a rebate on their council tax in exchange for their time.

This policy would work on several levels; it would give seniors a purpose, it would give the young some kind of hope...and a trade...and it would also promote respect from one generation and understanding from the other, engendering community spirit.

Research and Development / Technology;

Energy –

As things stand, the French supply our electricity and the Russians supply our gas, but I believe that we need to find a way of regaining control of our energy supplies in this country to avoid being held to ransom by either of these countries in any future economic / military conflict. (*Price and supply are easy forms of leverage*)

We also need to reduce our dependence on the Middle East oil reserves as the beholden-nature of our relationship with these countries prevents us from behaving with the independence and the moral authority that a sovereign state should symbolize.

However, we can do none of this until we have an alternative power supply in place...and that is why I believe we need to invest in the technology that will allow us to develop a new form of energy production; one which would allow us to recover our self-sufficiency and re-establish our independence on the world stage.

It will take some time to do this and in the meantime, the PDC would invest in nuclear energy (*as set out in the energy chapter*) but the future thereafter will present us with an even greater challenge…with an increased and unending demand for power…and we will have to satisfy that demand if we are to continue, as a race, to prosper which is why the PDC would create a Centre of Excellence for the research and development of new technologies where new ideas would be cultivated, nurtured and brought into existence.

Imagine if every car in the country was electric…using new-age rechargeable batteries…and how much that would cut from the country's fuel bill, how much it would reduce the household budget and how it would free us as a country from the shackles which currently hinder our ability to affirm our independence.

Now, this preoccupation with the future…and with our future energy needs…might seem unreasonable to some, but I believe that it is vitally important that we plan today for tomorrow.

For information; the Germans are already developing a new material; Aero-graphite, which could completely revolutionise batteries.

For the future; the first privately financed rocket blasted off recently and…if that technology can be perfected…maybe we could develop rockets or satellites…or something of that nature…capable of soaking up solar energy and zapping it down to us. Then, we would have a permanent energy source…the sun.

Meanwhile we should continue investing in new technologies like those being developed at Swansea University where they are producing metal and glass panels which can be attached to the outside of buildings. These panels - or 'cladding' as they are being called - are covered with a special coating which can store energy and supply electricity to the building to which they are attached.

3D impression is another sector set to explode in the next few years - as is the production of Nano-paper, a super-strong cellulose-based product which is as strong as steel and is set to revolutionise the design of new cars.

These innovative ideas are the future and we as a nation need to be a part of this new technology.

Other areas where technology should be able to help; for example...

-   Could we not introduce automatic exit doors on public lavatories to avoid using the door handles? What's the point of washing our hands and then pulling on a handle used by thousands of other people who might not have been so hygienic?
-   Next; could somebody please invent a little black box that fits between the power source and the hard drive of a computer in order to block unwanted spam? This box could also scramble communications to thwart unwanted government snoopers.
-   Similarly, could somebody please invent another little black box that fits between the power source and the telephone hub to block cold-calls?

Cold calls or nuisance calls as most people call them are making peoples lives a misery. They are intrusive and distressing...and for some of the more vulnerable amongst us, cold calls are downright intimidating. In fact, over 3 million people in this country are now afraid to answer the phone.

This has to change.

The telephone providers should really be doing more to protect their customers from this constant harassment.

Now, many of these nuisance calls are from unregulated foreign firms, so why can't the telephone providers offer a discount to any customer prepared to receive these calls – using some kind of frequency modulation for example - while allowing those that don't want to be pestered to live in peace. This would an ex-directory kind of system that would remove the stress from people's lives…and if that was not a feasible solution then why don't they develop an easy-to-use answering machine that would allow people to filter out these calls and stop them from interfering in their daily lives…and finally

- Could somebody please invent an energy-saving, smart-charger that turns itself off when no longer charging a phone or similar electrical appliance?

Other industries;

Water;

Water-supply companies in the UK are 'losing' 300 million gallons of water a day through leaks and damaged pipes. This is unacceptable and downright incompetent.

It cannot be right, with the cost of water-bills currently being paid by hard-pressed British households that a percentage of those bills is to pay for water that has been wasted or allowed to escape the system.

Under the PDC the water companies would only be allowed to increase their prices again, once they had put their house in order.

Call-centres;

We need to repatriate call-centres from India which is now booming while our economy is struggling.

It's already happening to a certain extent but we need to offer companies more incentives to bring them back.

Let's give English-speaking workers the job of dealing with British people; this is in no way a sleight against the Indian people; they are amongst the most courteous, helpful and polite people I know, but unfortunately, the majority of British people simply do not understand their strong, Indian Delta accents.

The PDC would offer tax breaks to companies who bring back call centres from abroad, thereby creating new jobs here (*The cost of the tax breaks would be offset by the increase in income tax.*)

Pubs;

As part of our Community Re-creation Scheme the PDC would re-launch the pub-industry.

I believe that just like the post-office and the corner-shop, the pub has for many decades played a major role in our communities both as a meeting place and a place of relaxation.

However, in recent years, through greed and self-interest, the mega-breweries have short-sightedly sucked the life out of the pub-industry and squeezed the land-lords out of business with their excessive demands.

It is time to change that. We need a new industry of independent, local pubs that can purchase artisanal, locally produced beers and food products – and we need more independent local breweries offering quality beers with a local flavour.

No more tied houses, no more land-lords having heart-attacks because they haven't reached the unattainable targets set by the accountants of the faceless multi-national conglomerates.

The PDC would produce a business-plan designed specifically for people who wanted to set up a pub, and we would offer them loans and tax-breaks to start up their business on the condition that they were qualified to do so.

Then, I am convinced we would see any number of new enterprises popping up again like mushrooms, giving the much-needed life-blood back to strangled communities and jobs to local residents.

That said, the 24/7 drinking experiment introduced by New Labour which has proved to be such a monumental disaster would be immediately revoked. It was always going to be a folly to think that the British could somehow adapt overnight to 'continental attitudes'.

It was never going to happen.

———

Under the PDC opening hours would be re-introduced (each licensee would be free to open for a maximum of eight hours a day; either consecutively or split between lunch-time and the evening) and each pub would also be attributed a category;

Category A; - smoking; no fresh food (nuts and crisps only), no children,

Category B; - no smoking; food; adults only

Category C; - no smoking; food; children welcome (play-area)

In addition, all new premises would have the opportunity of creating an off-license service too, as the PDC would be removing alcoholic sales licences from supermarkets and other outlets which have clearly acted irresponsibly, using alcohol as loss-leaders to bring in customers, fuelling the boozy binge-culture as a result.

However, strict measures would be enforced around these off-licences to avoid, under-age drinking, thugs and thieves;

- CCTV would be compulsory
- re-enforced glass and bars would be obligatory on outside windows to counter the threat of theft
- every entrance would have to be fitted with a security door (SAS)…and
- proof of identity would have to be provided by the purchaser with every sale.

No identity, no sale – and any licensee caught not imposing these measures would be closed down immediately.

An extra tax of 5% would however be applied to off-licence sales to encourage people to drink responsibly in the pub rather than take the alcohol home.

In Ireland they have a Liquor Liability Law which prevents Licensees from serving Police in uniform and known prostitutes. It also forces them to send drunken people home in a taxi at the pub's expense. Perhaps we could introduce a similar law here?

The PDC would also insist that glasses in pubs were recalibrated; no more over-sized wine-glasses…

…and as stated previously; as part of this new system - in collaboration with local councils - pubs would have an obligation to participate in the provision of transport at closing time. (see social chapter)

The High Street –

The internet is killing off our high street shops but the one thing that the internet cannot provide is the human touch; the face to face selling and the personalised service of hairdressers, watch-repairers and seamstresses.

Author's comment;

Much like the CCTV policing situation - which cannot operate efficiently without the support of actual police personnel on the ground - the internet cannot provide the human touch.

———

We can buy anything online but what happens when what we buy goes wrong or doesn't fit anymore.

I would like to try an alternative approach and in keeping with the 21st century ethos of recycling, I would suggest that we move past the materialistic, throw-away society that we currently live in and rediscover the lost art of repair.

Nothing gets repaired anymore but a network of small businesses offering spare-parts and repairs for any number of household items would not only help in re-cycling, it would help with community spirit, it would offer manual jobs to talented young people with initiative and it would validate their existence by being positive, and productive and act as a source of pride rewarded by a job well done; *this could be tied to the Magnet programme where the elderly would pass on their skills.*

The idea would be to re-launch the economy with repair shops and services;

- shoe repairs,
- clothing repairs and alterations,
- TV repairs,
- Electronic repairs
- small electrical repairs…and
- Watch repairs.

Thousands of small specialised units all offering a service close to home that the internet with all its far-reaching commercialism cannot provide…and all creating jobs and networks between parts-supplies and communities who would spread the news of a good repair shop by the most effective of communications network ever invented; word of mouth.

It might seem outlandish to some but this sector is perfect for re-launching our economy because it can provide flexibility in working hours, it can offer job-sharing opportunities for those who so desire... and people could even work from home depending on their choice of commerce.

As for services; hairdressers, nail-bars, restaurants and coffee-shops can all provide the human touch and the personal service that the faceless internet simply cannot.

Napoleon once dismissed us a nation of shop-keepers – allegedly – well what if re-creating that nation of shopkeepers could be the precursor in our fight back to prosperity.

This new hive of activity on our high streets would be backed up by an army of retired tradesmen passing on their skills and knowledge to aspiring young entrepreneurs in workshops set up in the new Magnet Centres or in un-used local council buildings.

Of course heavy industry will also play its part in our 'renaissance' but if we can get the network working at a local level, we can then build on that regionally...and nationally.

Other Initiatives;

We need to help new businesses by making space for them on the High Street...and making that space cheaper. Perhaps we could promote Mary Portas's initiative of 'pop-up shops' in empty units; two or three micro-businesses could even work together in a single unit – sharing costs - if it was too big for one idea. This would give young entrepreneurs a feel of what it's like...and what it takes...to run a business.

Other issues –

- **Theft** - In order to cut down on the smash and grab culture, window displays in shops selling valuable merchandise should be bogus – jewellery, watches etc. – and their front doors should have a security door (SAS).
- **Promotional days** such as Black Friday need to be managed better or banned because they encourage frenzied behaviour and ugly scenes of violence and confrontation as people fight and grapple with each other over cut-price merchandise.

Magnet Centres

With the ongoing rise in internet shopping, city-centres as we know them are on the decline, and as a consequence the PDC would try to re-invent the social template by switching the public's focus from huge city-centre shopping centres to their own communities.

The idea would be to rekindle the community spirit and the civic pride of our elders by providing everyone with an 'out-of-town' shopping experience in the middle their communities…and to do this the PDC would create a network of 'Magnet Centres' each of which would be adapted to a particular community and provide all the essential services necessary to that community, hopefully becoming its beating heart.

Here is an outline of the plan;

Firstly, we need to restore trust and respect for the law in our communities…and on our streets…and I believe that we could do this by creating a Community Post at the centre of each neighbourhood.

The uniformed officers stationed at this post would be charged with patrolling the streets day and night within their sector looking out for any anti-social behaviour while reassuring the public by their presence. They would also be mandated to stop and check vehicles for tax and insurance.

Any arrests they did make would be centralised and processed through the Main Police Stations in City Centres where a dedicated force would still take care of city-centre policing (organised pro-rata according to size of towns).

This community post would be part of a Magnet Centre, a new modular concept of units that fit together in order to create a purpose-built hub adapted to the particular needs of each community, comprising a number of essential elements together with a variety of other component spaces which could be used to provide any services which might be lacking in the surrounding area.

––––––

Author's comment;

The design of the new Magnet centre could be opened up into a national competition.

––––––

A typical Magnet Centre would consist of –

- **the Community Police Office** financed jointly by central government, the local council and by the shops themselves instead of employing private security guards
- **a crèche for working parents** (run as a non-profit enterprise providing a safe environment and an age-appropriate teaching programme) – these crèches could be sponsored by big business against a tax deduction or maybe employers could subsidise employees use of these crèches in some way in return for a tax break; indeed family-friendly employers might even like to

offer to contribute to the cost of childcare as a 'perk', much like 'healthcare' is offered as a 'perk' – a percentage of places would also be reserved for the children of the unemployed so that they might have the time to go out and look for work.

These nurseries would be staffed mainly by women who are already mothers themselves…as they have the experience of dealing with young children…and they would run on a roster - co-ordinated by a full-time supervisor - based on part-time, job-sharing opportunities which would offer the necessary flexibility to 'stay-at-home' moms who would otherwise be ostracised from the workplace.

- **a children's play area** (children signed in and out by parents; limited in time while they do their shopping)
- **a sports facility** (basketball court, hard-surface 5-a-side pitch or an all-weather outdoor pitch which would be run by a small tight-knit team of enthusiastic, sports-minded young people (Regional sports academies - based on county lines and population density - would provide the education and training needed for these young sports animators)
- **a pharmacy / care-in-the-community relay centre** for the elderly and their families, offering help, advice and minor trauma care. These units would be linked to the ambulance network and to the wider Health Service
- **a public house**
- **a shopping area** with some quirky niche markets and independent retail outlets
- **a bank with an integrated post-office** (a service which is essential yet struggling to survive)…and
- **parking space**; either at ground level or adjoined.

Extra services that might be considered, depending on demand;

- a dental clinic
- a doctor's surgery
- a gym
- a health / wellness centre

- a few units could also be reserved for work-shops and micro-businesses (see below)…and finally…
- why not create a community hall with an internet library where the elderly could congregate, where youth groups and scout-groups could meet…but which could also be used as a transient market space from time to time.
- This Community Hall could also be used as part of a contingency plan, serving as a temporary crèche / refuge for schoolchildren when the weather forces the schools to close down but parents still need to get to work; staffing could be provided by local volunteers prepared to give up their time and parents would just have to pay a small fee to cover running costs and insurance.

———

Now, not every community would need every service as they might already have some very good local services in place in their area…and naturally we would not look to affect them.

The goal of the Magnet Centre would not be to supersede or undermine existing businesses and services…but to complement them in order to give every community a comprehensive array of essential – and non-essential when viable – services.

———

Work-shops;

As an added initiative, to promote community spirit, the PDC would suggest that we use a couple of units in each of the Magnet Centres to set-up a number of small, hands-on, artisan workshops to be run by recently-retired tradesmen who could potentially offer pre-apprenticeship skills to early school-leavers.

However, this idea is not exclusive and these workshops could also be run elsewhere in the local community (in church halls or in unused council buildings to avoid travel expenses) acting as another piece of the puzzle gluing the community together.

The instructors (retired tradesmen) would be unpaid, but they could be offered a rebate on their council tax or energy bill by way of compensation for their time and service.

The banks could also help out by offering sponsorship and sending advisors around to these workshops to meet these youngsters, to give them help and advice on setting up a small business and to make them feel that there is a future out there if they are prepared to work for it.

They could also offer access to capital for cooperative / community ventures...on preferential terms...and maybe, just maybe, by participating in these initiatives the banks might begin to restore their reputation and improve their moral capital in the eyes of the public after their recent 'troubles'.

...and finally...as an incentive, the PDC would look into offering these youngsters some kind of financial support in the form of an apprentice-benefit; similar to the EMA (education maintenance allowance) which was recently abolished.

———

Food;

Everybody knows that we should eat more healthily and that if we don't address the problem, obesity is going to spiral out of control in the next decade or so.

Jamie Oliver began the fight-back by introducing more nutritional, more well-balanced meals to the school canteen but that momentum has now slowed and we need to give it a new impetus.

However, looking at the bigger picture maybe it would be a good idea to use the recent horse-meat scandal to re-assess the whole way in which we eat and shop.

Clearly we cannot trust the huge corporations – driven only by profit – to put the necessary safeguards in place to protect us from being duped by unscrupulous middle-men so let's – as a country – pull back on the processed meals being imported from abroad, the contents of which nobody can guarantee, and turn the clock back.

- Let's start buying our meat from the local butchers. In that way, at least we will know what we are putting into our bodies while at the same time creating demand for more local enterprise.
- Let's buy our bread fresh from the bakers where the smell is real and not piped in artificially to tempt us.
- Let's start buying what we need, rather than falling for BOGOF deals and multi-packs that are constantly put in front of us to tempt us. If we only want to buy one or two of something why do we always have to buy four or six?
- Let's see more loose vegetables that we can buy according to our needs rather than the neatly packaged, nicely sized but aseptically produced and tasteless impersonations that currently fill the supermarket shelves.

In fact, let's all rebel against the supermarkets that have cornered every aspect of our lives and then served it up to us as cheaply as possible to maximise their profits; profits which they use to create more and more of the same, flooding our town centres, our corner shops and our shopping centres with as many of their outlets as possible as they expand their insatiable growth and market-share exponentially.

I understand that this would go against the EU rules of standardised and homogenised produce but the PDC would be advocating a withdrawal from the overbearing EU and hence we would be able to elaborate our own food-standards policy. (See chapter on EU)

It is time to take back our food…as well as our country.

BTW – Who are the irresponsible people at the Food Standards Authority who allowed the commercialisation of a soft-drink called 'Cocaine'? The PDC would review this organisation and introduce root-and-branch reform.

Supermarkets;

The theory of consolidation (buying out the opposition) to benefit from the ensuing economies of scale while choking off the competition might be the ultimate way of maximising profit in business, <u>but is the bottom line all that really counts?</u>

I would much rather see hundreds of corner shops providing local jobs and creating community spirit between generations, than three or four hypermarkets cornering the market, because in many ways the stranglehold of these voracious supermarket chains has ruined community life in the UK.

Small shops used to be an integral part of British life, but these days the Big-Four supermarkets act like a pseudo-cartel fixing prices between themselves to the detriment of consumers and any smaller independent trader who would dare challenge their omnipotent grip on the country's purse-strings.

I believe that business should not be completely single-minded. It should also feel that it has a responsibility to society; that it should not just feed off it but also be part of it, integrating itself in the community and offering those living nearby a chance to better themselves.

———

Issues;

- **Opening times** – while I understand that the supermarkets would like to open all-day every-day because their only god is profit, I feel that it is not in the public interest to have their lives revolve solely around these supermarkets 24/7. We have to maintain at least one day a week when smaller traders can trade without the overwhelming might of supermarkets breathing down their necks...and also allow time for those who work in these gigantic, faceless warehouse-style buildings to have some time off with their families to help with family and social cohesion. This is not a religious consideration but as most religions do practice on that day I believe that every other Sunday – on a rotation basis - should be preserved as a day when we change rhythms, we take some time to breathe, relax and do something other that what we do every other day.

- Maybe we could use the supermarket car parks for other community based activities on Sundays
- **Surplus** – I believe that supermarkets should work with charities to hand over produce no longer displayed on their shelves. Perhaps they could come to some arrangement with the government on this…because - as the rise in food-banks clearly shows - an increasing number of families are plainly struggling to put food on their tables. Food-poverty is becoming an issue in this country and it must be addressed.
- **Alcohol** - Supermarkets have become very powerful and very influential in our daily lives but driven by their only goal… profit…they have shown - much like the politicians, the banks, the police and the press - that they cannot be trusted to have our best interests at heart. That is why, as part of its 'rebalancing of society' programme, the PDC would take away alcohol-sales licences from supermarkets and other outlets (they have abused this right; selling alcohol at a loss to bring in the customer and it has had a devastating effect on society of all ages)
- In the meantime, all the big supermarkets should review their proof-of-age policies; recently, a 92 year old war veteran was asked to provide proof that he was over 18, a 66 year old man was prevented from buying a bottle of wine and a 21year old was prevented from buying non-alcoholic cider because it was stacked on the same shelf as normal cider.
- **Milk** - The PDC would encourage the supermarkets to renegotiate a proper deal with dairy farmers for their milk so that those farmers can earn a decent living. This arrangement could be integrated into the discussions concerning the re-introduction of milk in schools.
- **Accountability** - As the recent 'horse-meat' scandal proved once again that we cannot trust supermarkets to be honest as to the contents of the produce that they are putting into the food chain; the PDC would make the chairmen and executives of these companies criminally responsible for what they put

on their shelves for our consumption. This measure would undoubtedly make them more 'attentive'.

- Extra inspectors would only be a reactive measure once it's too late and the product exists. We need rigorous controls in place that make sure that supermarket chiefs do more, pro-actively and the only way to do that is to offer them jail-time as an alternative. Supermarket executives are human beings like the rest of us. They respond to the stick and the carrot like anybody else, whether they be a petty thug on a street corner or in charge of a multi-national heavy on every other street.

- **Technology** - I would also suggest that supermarkets roll back on technology to some extent. People need jobs to survive and look after their families. Give them the opportunity to do this. I would much rather see twenty cashiers lined up on cash-tills, each of whom would be earning a living and setting a good example to their children that hard-work is not 'uncool', rather than five cashiers and ten self-service till which are so impersonal and often malfunction. After all, the tills are there. Why install twenty tills and just use five? Service is the most easily forgotten commodity in our price-conscious, penny-pinching society - Let's bring back service instead of faceless technology

- Note - more and more people are walking out and leaving their purchases behind when confronted with a self-service till; yet another reason to bring back real people and a way for them to earn a living. Customers fear being accused of theft for failing to scan items correctly and the voice warning 'problem in the baggage area' irritates up to 80% of those questioned – I understand that the emphasis of a retailer is profit but helping the local community by providing jobs for people might also be a productive strategy

  I would suggest that petrol pump attendants could be beneficial to a supermarket's bottom line too, because not only would they add a smile and a friendly word to an otherwise stressful day as they run a clean cloth over the windscreen, they could also thwart those criminals who would fill up and drive off without paying.

- **Seal of approval** - Now it would be too much to ask for the Big-Four supermarkets to adhere to a code of conduct; they would just act like a cartel to maintain the status quo, so the PDC would create a 'seal of approval' that it would award to any supermarket that it felt was;

- o   offering value for money (putting aside any deception mechanisms)
- o   had an ethical policy as far as suppliers and food-sourcing was concerned…and
- o   rewarded its staff with decent salaries, working conditions and participation schemes.

Other supermarket initiatives;

- **Benefits** - Perhaps we could introduce a scheme where benefit-payments were credited to a card that can only be used to buy food and household products – not alcohol or cigarettes
- **BOGOFs** - To save waste on BOGOF deals – especially perishable items - supermarkets could issue customers with a voucher for a second article to be redeemed within a set timescale rather than making the customer take two items the same day. This would save on food being thrown out and bring in extra custom to supermarkets with return trade (this is an idea I read about; I cannot claim ownership)
- **Glass bottles** – as plastic cups and bottles have been linked with a number of health problems, the PDC would look into re-introducing glass bottles and the concept of deposit / refundable returns - possibly adding cans too - which could be collected and recycled rather than added to household waste. This initiative also has the added advantage of creating jobs in bottle production, distribution and cleaning as well as jobs for volunteers or retired pensioners in bottle-restitution points in supermarkets or in the new Magnet centres, perhaps in exchange for a council-tax rebate. However, no cash would be exchanged; deposits would be paid in vouchers to avoid any illegal scams being set-up.
- **Manners** - supermarkets should introduce a rule that cashiers will not serve people on mobile phones. We have to get away

from this selfish, self-centred, 'me-me' culture and restore a little common courtesy to our society. If people need to make a phone-call, then they can step out of the queue until the call is over. They don't have to be rude or obnoxious. The same applies to head-phones / ear-plugs and by the same token cashiers should not be chatting with each other while working

- **Plastic bags** –to help clean up the environment; let's make a point of no-longer using plastic bags; recyclables only!
- **Recycling** - could we not come to some kind of agreement with manufactures to put a little green or black coloured square on product-packaging to signal the recycling-bin destination of the wrapping to avoid confusion? We have been re-cycling for over a decade now but many people are still confused about what goes where. I believe that if we are serious about recycling, we should have some joined up thinking in the food chain…from production to the recycling bin; easy to read and clearer traffic light labelling should also be rolled-out.
- **Schools** - the PDC would look into re-introducing cookery classes into schools. This would be a costly initiative but if the supermarkets were motivated in the right way, perhaps they could help with funding equipment or providing ingredients.

Objections;

Could we also stop the practice of changing the composition of a product without warning customers…and could we also stop reducing the size / weight of a product while selling it at the same price. A recently bought, 30g packet of crisps contained three crisps and some crumbs. Retailers; you make enough money out of the consumers…so please give them <u>some</u> value for money…or you will find your trust index on a par with that of the politicians. Please stop the greed.

I would also request that retailers put an end to the ubiquitous 'odd-value' technique; selling articles at £1-99 in an effort to try to hood-wink customers; everybody knows that £1.99 is just £2 spelt differently.

(This 'suggestion' would be enforced eventually as the PDC would remove pointless 1p and 2p coins from circulation.)

I would also like to see the end of the guilt lanes stuffed with enticing treats on the way to the checkout…and more common sense used in layout-design; supermarkets should not be stacking the alcohol next to the chocolate.

––––

Conclusion;

My vision for the future would see local communities regenerated and rebuilt around a central hub; the Magnet Centre which would provide all the necessary services while reducing travel time and costs.

Meanwhile, town centres would be redeveloped and pedestrian-ised in order to concentrate on;

- Fiscal issues (town hall / tax office etc.),
- Business offices,
- Hotels
- Cultural and leisure activities such as;
  - o cinemas,
  - o theatres,
  - o restaurants,
  - o exhibition galleries,
  - o sporting facilities and events,
  - o pubs and clubs

…and out of town superstores and garden centres would concentrate on all the larger household purchases from furniture to cars.

––––

Idea; as greedy landlords, demanding exorbitant rents, have driven out small businesses from town-centres, why not make the vacant units the object of compulsory-purchase orders so that they might be transformed into affordable housing for the elderly.

———

...and finally...I repeat...the PDC would give its **Seal of Approval** to any company committed to policies in keeping with its philosophy.

———

Transrt

Air;

It is time to re-design and re-balance our airport system.

Heathrow is overcrowded but we clearly need more capacity to help us compete with other European hubs so if a third runway is not an option in the Heathrow area - because of all the opposition – then we need to consider building a new international airport elsewhere.

The UK is already too London-centric so rather than fight over a third runway at Heathrow…or the new HS2 train line…why not build a new transport hub for the future, between Kings Lynn and Peterborough for example (on the condition that it did not interfere with long-standing bird migratory patterns…to avoid the risk of bird-strikes).

This would not only provide easy access to most parts of the UK but it could also integrate sea access for both cargo and ferries.

Then, instead of the outrageously expensive north-south HS2 project which will save just 32 minutes in the journey-time between London and Birmingham at a cost of between £43 and £80 billion pounds depending on who we believe, we could build three new HS lines originating from the new international transport hub covering a much greater share of the country.

Line One would go north via Sheffield to Manchester and on to Liverpool

Line Two would go to Birmingham and on to Bristol and

Line Three would go to London, possibly connecting with the Eurostar and Europe

A further line connecting Manchester to Newcastle via Leeds could also be projected at a later date.

We could then develop Bristol airport to cover the south of England more efficiently and upgrade Manchester airport to cover the North of England.

In the meantime, Gatwick, Luton and Stanstead could concentrate their efforts on internal and charter flights…until they are ultimately phased out and redeveloped as new communities.

Now the above proposals might seem too progressive or too radical for some, but the simple fact is that we need to do something to ease the current congestion around Heathrow airport.

The Thames estuary was a good idea but as with any progressive ideas in this country, it was met with opposition from conservationists because its construction would encroach upon protected wildlife habitats…and herein lies the problem.

The UK is an island and space on this island is limited…so wherever we decide to build a new airport, there will always be opposition and detractors.

Whatever we decide, someone somewhere will not be happy; it's what we do in this country. We want it all; we want progress but we don't want to pay for it and we certainly don't want it in our own back yards. The NIMBY's are constantly holding this country back.

Therefore we should opt for the best solution - decided upon by a majority vote after consultation with those concerned - and forge ahead.

That would be democracy in action; <u>it will never make everybody happy</u> but that is the whole concept of a majority vote; it is rarely unanimous.

We have to get our priorities in the right order…and choices have to be made…if we want to look to the future and not lose more ground on rival European hubs.

———

Here is another idea; why not re-brand Heathrow, 'London International' and divert all internal and short-haul European flights to regional, satellite airports, thereby reducing the workload at our one major airport.

This would allow for a re-organisation of Heathrow's services while spreading the load and the jobs to other areas.

Then, once that system was operating smoothly, efficiently and cost-effectively, improving the quality of service in all areas at the same time – we could then develop Stanstead or look into the hub suggested above…or contemplate a 'Boris Island-type' construction-site…possibly on some reclaimed land, where we could build a new airport to share international flights going forward.

———

Other notes;

- Many countries apply an Exit Tax to help with the running costs of their airports; why shouldn't we do that?
- maybe it is time to introduce child-free zones on flights or even child-free flights for professional businessmen and older passengers who might appreciate and pay for the resulting peace and quiet.
- Money-grabbing airlines that charge for weight in the hold but allow that same weight in hand luggage are just revenue chasing, especially when obese people are allowed to take up their seat no matter their size. This weight issue needs clarification.

- **Airport Security** - the PDC would make sure that its new justice policy was in place…and make those who would transgress those rules aware of the consequences. Then – having consulted the international community - we would relax the draconian security rules that are currently in place in our airports…and make travelling a joy again…and not the nightmare it has become.

Rail;

The Crossrail tunnel project which will run from Maidenhead to London and on to Shenfield in Essex is costing £15.9 billion and might well improve transport across London; however, it is yet again more money for London after the Thameslink, the Olympics and every other major event.

Personally, I would much rather see more investment in the national network because while London is getting the new Crossrail tunnel and HS rail-links to the North and Europe, the rest of the country is still running on the framework of the original Victorian railway concept.

A lot of that aging infrastructure need replacing, rolling stock needs to be upgraded and as for the service, both on the trains and in the time-keeping department, it is a standing joke in this country - and has been for a very long time - going all the way back to when British Rail was running it.

Meanwhile prices have sky-rocketed, comfort has been reduced considerably – many people spending the whole journey stood up or squashed together like sardines – and the private companies now running our railways (TOC's (train operating companies) and FOC's (freight operating companies)) are all stretched between trying to satisfy the government, the customers and their shareholders…without having a solution for any of them.

Franchises have been sub-divided and fragmented to a point where often the right hand doesn't know what the left hand is doing and this lack of co-ordination and coherent thinking has led the mess we currently abide.

The Rail system in the UK needs a complete overhaul and ultimately I believe that it should return to the public fold.

Women –

Sadly, the question of security and personal safety has become an important issue for women in today's 21st century society - because of the constant threat of violence that exists on our streets - and therefore, when discussing transport policies I believe that this needs to be taken into account.

We already have pink taxis reserved for women in some areas, often driven by other women, so why not introduce pink buses too, as well as pink carriages on tube-trains and railway trains.

These carriages could be reserved;

- for women,
- for women with children…and possibly
- for pensioners…

…and could be designed with extra spaces to accommodate pushchairs. (*That same space being reserved for wheelchairs on other buses*)

Roads –

Firstly we need to do more to identify black-spots on our roads…

Black-spots are corners or junctions or roads which – for whatever reason – attract a higher number of accidents that what could be considered 'the norm'.

However, rather than simply modifying these locations with the introduction of a roundabout, a red-light or a speed-camera which just slows down the traffic, I believe that, on the contrary, we should look at maintaining the flow by redesigning the road.

The Health and Safety Executive and the Highways Authority are constantly introducing new measures to slow down traffic but these measures are always so repressive and negative in nature…and while I believe that safety should always be a priority I also believe that we should be looking at the issue from a more positive perspective.

Instead of simply clogging up our roads with roundabouts and red-lights…in an effort to slow down traffic…why not try to find alternative solutions; better designs for our roads, better signals and better circulation policies.

It won't always be possible…but I believe that many of the black-spots currently wreaking havoc on our roads could be eliminated quite easily with a little more forethought and application.

For information; we waste £20 billion of productivity a year just sitting in traffic jams; that cannot be acceptable or accepted as an 'inevitability' in 21st century Britain. We must address this problem as it will only get worse.

We also need to address the growing problem of pot-holes.

Speed; we need to review our speed-limits; the proliferation of road-signs and different speeds in different sections of the same road is just confusing people and the additional problem of speed cameras placed deliberately to catch people out whenever they exceed a speed-limit – even by the smallest margin - is making drivers drive erratically.

Motorways –

- **Speed**; the 70 MPH speed limit was introduced in the UK in 1964. However, the design of motor vehicles and the quality of the road-surface has improved dramatically since then. The introduction of seat-belts and air-bags inside the car...and the development of shock-absorbing bumpers and bodywork on the outside...have radically improved safety on our roads over the last fifty years and as a result the 21st century car bears very little resemblance to the cars which were on the road in 1964 when the 70MPH speed-limit was introduced. This is why the PDC would trial a new 80mph limit.
- **Road-signs**; the PDC would look into the multiplication and the proliferation of road-signs and advertising along our motorways. This constant distraction must inhibit concentration.
- **Repairs** - While local councils would be encouraged to concentrate on repairing and upgrading the secondary road system, including pot-holes, the PDC would work with professional road-builders to repair and upgrade the motorway system, negotiating an investment-linked toll system for each route. This would renovate the network while providing hundreds of jobs directly...and thousands more indirectly from the provision of raw materials.

New ideas;

- The PDC would introduce phosphorescent paint for road markings which lights up at night
- We would also look into a new concept currently being trialled in Holland where thermo-reactive particles are being incorporated into the tarmac. These particles then create symbols on the road's surface to signal falling temperatures.
- We would also plant more hedges along the motorways to stop animals running onto the road. This would not only create structure on our roads, it would also help with linear concentration (avoid distraction)

New rules –

At the moment, car manufacturers have to register a car with the DVLC when they sell it…with the purchaser's details.

The DVLC then monitors that car's usage 'big-brother' style;

- it makes sure that its owner pays road tax and insurance,
- it monitors congestion-charge payments…and
- it monitors any speed-camera violations that its driver might commit

The same applies to sales of two-wheelers; they too have to be registered with the DVLC.

However, the PDC would introduce a new system.

People purchasing motor-bikes and scooters would also have to register their new bikes with their local-community police. This would help with insurance violations but also with localised theft and crime…as more and more crime is being committed by criminals on two-wheels.

The community police - having registered a vehicle using its owner's post-codes to identify them - would then transfer that information to a national database.

NB – manslaughter is manslaughter – i.e. the killing of another human being unintentionally or by accident – and whether it occurs with a fist, a gun or a moving vehicle, it is still manslaughter and therefore the PDC would impose a category 3 sentence on anybody convicted of this crime. It is unacceptable that a person should only receive a six-month sentence for crushing another person to death under his vehicle because he was busy texting as was recently the case. The PDC would have a zero-tolerance approach to people driving and using a mobile phone at the same time.

Future –

In the future I would like to see our major city-centres served by an electric tramway system similar to the German model. This could be complemented by a system of satellite bus stations at the end of each line which would allow people to go further afield into smaller areas; the buses would also run electrically.

The design, construction and highway redevelopment needed for this project would provide jobs for thousands while getting rid of hundreds of buses which consume enormous amounts of fossil-fuel.

This again, is another initiative that would help the planet, save on our national fuel-bill and increase our self-sufficiency and independence.

Shipping – sea-trade is a big part off our economy. We need to revitalise major ports.

Trade Unions

Author's comment;

I have no time for Trade Union barons and firebrand mischief-makers whose only role – when they are not pursuing highly lucrative compensation claims or paying themselves huge salaries and bonuses - seems to be one of plotting the most destructive and disruptive way of crippling this great country of ours and bringing it to a standstill.

Their sole purpose seems to be;

- to ruin the lives of millions of people,
- to stop them getting to work,
- to stop their places of work from functioning,
- to stop their children from getting an education...and
- to stop everyone – themselves excluded - from going on holiday

...that for a Trade Unionist is a good day…

...and for what...so that they can satisfy their unquenchable thirst for power and their insatiable greed for influence...just like the politicians, the high-flying company executives and the bankers…?

Whatever happened to the good people, the honest people; the people with dignity, pride and humility, the people with a moral compass who don't see every situation that presents itself as an opportunity to screw the system; whatever happened to them?

People, if you have followed my reasoning this far, you will already know that I am no fan of any institution that I believe is an anachronism... and which I believe no longer has tenure in the 21st century.

Religion, dictatorships and the monarchy are flagrant examples - as is boxing in the sporting arena - but the next anachronism to be addressed has to be Trade Unions. (The BBC and the House of Lords will complete the collection later on)

The Trade Union Movement was founded in the 1800's in order to fight for better working conditions and better pay for their members… under the philosophy that unity and a massed rank would be a lot more effective than individual protest in circumstances of grievance and dispute with employers…and in that quest the TUM has been most successful…to the point where those rights and practices have now been written into the statute books…

…so while I believe that their struggle had to be fought…and won…I also believe that because their demands have now been met and essentially enshrined in law…there is no longer any real fight to be had.

Today –

There was a time when Trade Unions were worth their weight in gold to the working classes but nowadays - paradoxically - they simply oppress the poor;

- by holding them to ransom,
- by withholding essential services from them…and
- by demanding more and more money from an already struggling nation

The rules governing employment are pretty much set in stone now, thanks largely to the Trade Union Movement but I believe that the concept has now had its day.

In fact, the only time we ever hear from the Unions these days is when they hold a sword of Damocles over the government's head, in an effort to blackmail it into submission with the threat of strike action before every Bank-Holiday and every weekend that leads up to a school holiday.

These are the actions of desperate men who are losing their grip on the golden goose… and it is sad to see…but the Trade Union Movement nowadays seems to have become more an instrument of punishment… than the moral representative of the working class that its fore-fathers founded it to be.

Indeed, the once-great movement is now reduced to making outrageous compensation claims for its members…or organising disruptive strikes for frivolous grievances…which do nothing to hasten negotiations but cost businesses their livelihoods, workers their jobs and cause the public nothing but misery…while the self-righteous leaders who organise these disruptions sit back and enjoy huge salaries, wide-raging expenses and generous pensions.

…and now the final straw;

I have always read that turning to violence has to be a last resort in any situation, so I can only surmise that if the Trade Union Movement is now turning to bullying, to intimidation and to violence under the guise of their new 'last-resort leverage policy', then the movement is living its last few years of existence.

What is leverage?

According to the dictionary, leverage is explained by 'the application of pressure through menace and veiled threats'.

This is a new phenomenon amongst the Trade Union Movement which consists of them acting like bullies and thugs…and using tactics of intimidation not unlike those used by criminal gangs - such as the Krays back in the day - in order to put their point across.

Now, I understand that unions want to do the best for their members but intimidating senior managers <u>and their children</u> by sending groups of militant thugs or 'direct intervention teams' as they call them, to these people's homes - and printing wanted posters featuring their boss's face - in order to resolve an industrial dispute is a step too far.

These people describe themselves as industrial terrorists but the British people will not accept this threatening behaviour, this thuggery disguised as protest…and consequently these actions will do nothing but precipitate the demise of the union movement which has clearly lost its way and lost sight of its founding principles.

———

Author's comment;

We must – at all costs – avoid becoming like the French. In France, radical union members sequester management personnel in their offices against their will, depriving them of food and sleep for days on end. They humiliate these people…and intimidate them…and if they do not obtain satisfaction for their demands after a certain time, union members then proceed to wilfully destroy or vandalise the very workplace that they are trying to defend…

…and if they still do not obtain satisfaction, they then resort to more extreme measures, threatening to burn down factories or blow them up.

This is unacceptable behaviour in a civilised and democratic society and we must not allow it to happen here.

———

Conclusion –

Credibility is very important in all walks of life but credibility is based on respect and responsibility…and sadly the Trade Union Movement is losing that credibility because they and their leaders - nostalgic for the seventies when they did hold the balance of power - are now noticeably out of kilter with the rest of the population.

It is time for them to join the 21st century like the rest of us because the British people are sick and tired of being held to ransom by a minority of hard-line unionists nostalgic for a time when they were actually relevant.

At its outset, the Trade Union Movement was a movement for good, based on fraternity and solidarity, with an ethical policy and a moral charter, but these days, rather than defending the rights of workers, it has almost become a guerrilla organisation hell-bent on disrupting the lives of the British people for no other reason than to exist in a world that no longer sees its antiquated ideals as pertinent.

The Trade Unions were instrumental in effecting positive change in the work-place in this country and it would be a sad end…to a movement which was created for the good of the workers…if it was henceforth reviled by the British public as a disruptive, destructive and divisive force.

Salary –

Over the last thirty years or so, any number of unrealistic wage-structures have been scaffolded on the somewhat precarious ground of…management self-preservation and union blackmail…and sadly there is only one thing that motivates and unites both parties in these negotiations…and that is the 'greed factor'.

Not necessarily the over-exaggerated greed of the banking fraternity but just enough selfish greed to never be satisfied…and always want a bigger slice of the pie.

The unions always want a bigger slice from the management…and the management always want to keep as much of the pie as possible to themselves; it is the eternal struggle.

However; is it right that a union baron, whose only goal seems to be to wield power vicariously through the Labour Party like a pseudo-puppeteer…and to make the lives of the ordinary citizens of this country a living hell…should be paid £122,000 a year for doing so?

Let's refer back to the 'Emgee Ratio';

Does a person whose only activity seems to consist in two tasks;

- to demand wage increases…and
- to organise strikes when those – often outrageous – demands are refused

…deserve a salary with an ER of 4.88

Is what he does really worth the equivalent of 4.88 average salaries?

As far as I can see, the unions and their leaders just exploit and manipulate their memberships in order to exist and to feather their retirement plans, siphoning off huge salaries and expenses so that they might live the same luxurious lifestyle as the bosses that they are supposedly opposing and denigrating. What hypocrisy.

Meanwhile the workers on the shop-floor - that they supposedly represent - remain firmly rooted on the minimum wage.

I hate hypocrisy in all things, and it is the height of hypocrisy that these aging left-wing dinosaurs who are still trying to perpetuate a world that no longer exists – one of brotherhood and pseudo-socialist dogma – should be enjoying a lifestyle based on self-promotion and pure unadulterated capitalism, when those are the very ideals that they claim to despise.

Incentives and bonuses –

Author's comment;

Is the satisfaction of doing your job properly not enough any more; does it always have to have a carrot attached?

Whatever happened to professional pride in a job well-done?

I really do not understand why union-members should get bonus payments just for doing their jobs properly…as was the case during the 2012 Olympics when rail-chiefs were forced to cave in to militants who threatened to ruin the Games if they didn't receive a bonus just for doing their job. That is extortion…or at the very least blackmail… in any other situation.

People should not need an incentive to do their job properly beyond the receipt of their contracted salary – as long as that salary is competitive and in keeping with their position.

In fact, the only incentive these people should need to do their job properly is the line of two million unemployed people waiting to take their place…if they aren't prepared to do the job and would rather walk away.

———

Funding;

Of course, the demise of the unions would put an end to the generous salaries of those who run them, and put a dent in the Labour Party's finances as the unions provide 81% of that Party's finances but if they want to survive, I believe that trade unions should be self-funding.

Why should we - as taxpayers - pay £80 million a year to have trade union officials in state-run industries?

Did anybody ask us…and if they did, would we agree…?

In my humble opinion Union employees should not be the taxpayers' problem and I tend to believe that if any sector wants Trade Union representation, then they should have a structure in place to finance it…through voluntary contributions etc…

It seems incredible to me that the British taxpayer should be paying people a salary to organise ways of punishing those same taxpayers with strikes and demonstrations.

It borders on social masochism.

———

For information; we, the taxpayers pay £13 million a year to the Teaching Unions and £23.6 million a year to Whitehall…so that the unions might be represented in those sectors…

…just something to think about…

———

Going Forward –

Everything in life continues to move forward and as a consequence, I believe that the concept of trade unionism has to evolve too.

It should not be up to the tax-payer to pay for trade-unions but I believe there is still a role for a union-style representative in our business and industry sector who could act as a go-between in disputes…and a relay to explain management policy.

A union presence would also act as a control, to temper the management tendency to push boundaries a little too far.

I would suggest that in future, any company that employs more than a dozen people should have a designated person in the ranks - nominated by his or her colleagues - to represent the trade union ethos.

That person would then deal with grievances within the company, liaising with individual employees, the Human Resources Department and a Senior Management representative…and if no solution could be found in house, then this person could take the issue to a new Arbitration and Conciliation service that the PDC would set up to deal with such matters. An independent mediator would then be appointed to address the issue / grievance.

This solution would restrict the conflict to individual companies resulting in localised, contained disruption instead of national chaos.

These days, communication is so much easier through e-mail / Twitter / Facebook / text-messaging or even the mobile phone and as a result these representatives could quickly receive professional advice and support using that modern technology in order to find solutions to problems before punitive action need be considered.

They would still have to fulfil their contractual obligations to their employers as far as their job was concerned but they would be compensated for their time with a tax deduction on the basis of 5 hours a week per working week.

Now this might go against one of the unions guiding principles of 'collective bargaining' but as I see it, the major issues surrounding working conditions and acknowledgement of the workers' rights have already been addressed and written into law these days. Therefore the only issues that should arise are those related specifically to an individual company or to an employee of that specific company.

Naturally, the same rules would apply to national organisations or a company with two or more sites but the independent mediator would only be appointed in these cases when a pre-determined percentage of grievances had been reached on a pro-rata basis according to the number of employees…and any dispute involving a public sector industry would have to be accompanied by a contingency plan for the provision of a minimum service.

To sum up; disputes should be settled internally by individual companies rather than on a national platform – and when that is not possible for whatever reason – the grievance should be taken to an 'Arbitration and Conciliation Service'.

National organisations would also have their grievances addressed, but if this resulted in strike action, then a minimum service would have to be provided, in order to limit the disruption.

Author's comment;

I want people at the vanguard of this country with positive, progressive and inspirational ideas…and not obstructive or disruptive narcissists nostalgic for the past.

If we can reduce the potential for national strikes and limit disputes to a minimum, our economy would be much healthier and all our lives would run much smoother.

The trade union movement will no doubt endure for another generation or so, but I firmly believe that the British public will ultimately tire of its insidious, if not inherently confrontational ethos and will one day sweep it aside, to replace it with a more conciliatory concept based on fair and reasonable arbitration rather than conflict, mistrust and disagreement.

NB; Trade Unions are currently an unavoidable thorn in society's side and have to be accommodated but under a PDC administration, any profession which by its action disrupted the smooth running and normal function of society…or indeed threatened the national interest in any way…would be expected to put contingency plans in place to guarantee a minimum service.

If they did not comply with this measure, then the Military would be instructed to step in…and the union in question would be invoiced for the cost.

Strikes / demonstrations –

Those union bosses who are still making a living out of Trade-unionism are simply troublemakers who seem to delight in causing mayhem around the country and disrupting the lives of ordinary working people.

Their only weapon, strikes…but strikes do nothing to resolve issues;

- They do however weaken companies' reputations,
- ruin their productivity,
- make them miss dead-lines…and
- lose contracts…which ultimately leads to them closing down and <u>throwing everybody who did have a job out of work</u>.

What a paradox.

New rules –

As part of their working-rights, everybody in this country has the right to strike and to demonstrate if they feel they have a grievance against their employer; however, under the law, that right must be exercised and communicated <u>in a peaceful fashion.</u>

Now, I understand that the withdrawal of labour as a method of leverage is psychologically satisfying for some – to get one over on The MAN – but it is nothing less than industrial blackmail and suggests a tendency within the union ranks to flirt with crossing the line between legality and illegality in the defence of workers rights…

Indeed there are many examples of unions being infiltrated by Mafia-style people well versed in blackmail and extortion techniques, the most famous of which would be the Teamsters in the USA led by Jimmy Hoffa.

The London Underground drivers demanding more money during the Olympics so as not to ruin the Games was a prime example in this country, which is why, under a PDC administration, a couple of months before any major sporting event or any occasion of national importance the Unions would be summoned to appear at a gathering where their responsibilities would be laid out;

- 'Any union taking advantage or deliberately disrupting a situation which might be detrimental or damage the country's reputation would face the consequences through financial sanctions and 'personal reprimands' for their leaders'.

I am sick of the British public being held to ransom by a small minority of left-wing dinosaurs. We, as a nation should not be held hostage by these people.

It is time that the long-suffering British public were allowed to go about their lives without the constant threat of strikes being held over them.

The PDC would impose two rules;

- **Firstly** – eligibility; as stated previously, everybody has the right to strike but nevertheless exceptions have to be made in certain corps services – those involved in national security for example (military, border control, prison staff, police, emergency services and education (*children should not be exposed to Trade-Union dogma or the ethos of going on strike*). Meanwhile, other corps services should be obliged to provide a minimum service during a strike (tanker drivers, tube drivers, refuse collectors etc)

- **Secondly** – timing; strikes should be accepted as a basic democratic right – but as the general public usually lose out more than the companies being called into question, these strikes should not be organised during major holiday periods. The disagreement is with the individual employer...not the general public.

––––––

When strikes, demonstrations and marches do take place;

Under the PDC, the leaders and the organisers of these marches would be made responsible for the behaviour of those they represent. They would also have to ensure that their 'marchers' were dressed appropriately; no hoodies, no masks and no scarves covering faces…and they would also have to make sure that those marching were well aware that if they were caught wearing hoodies and scarves to disguise their identities they would be arrested and prosecuted under the PDC's new justice system.

If you really believe in a cause, you should stand up and be proud to represent that cause; you should not hide behind a disguise or a mask.

In addition, the PDC would ensure that any damage caused to private or public property during a 'disturbance' would be billed directly back to the organisers who would have to insure themselves against this eventuality.

––––––

Security –

In order to keep the peace and protect the law-abiding citizens of this country, the police would be authorised to use any of the following measures, if deemed appropriate;

- **Water cannons** – unruly crowds of demonstrators would be sprayed with Smart-water from water cannons. The ink in the water can be detected for days after - on skin and clothes - which would allow the authorities to make deferred arrests…if necessary
- **Paintballs** – loaded with indelible ink; these could be used for precision targeting and could also be traced back after the fact
- **Stun guns**
- **Tazers** – with a reduced voltage…and
- **Tear gas**

The destructive and criminal elements amongst the crowd (thugs, vandals etc) would be targeted and removed using the appropriate force.

The police would also scatter photographers in the crowd to photograph trouble-makers who could then be identified and picked up later.

Meanwhile, parents would be encouraged to turn in young thugs who have incited civil-unrest. Discipline and the respect of authority begins at home.

———

Media

Author's comment;

If there is one thing that I abhor, it is the way that the **media** in this country makes news out of nothing; the way they build everyday news items and shallow celebrity-based hogwash into a scoop to be sensationalised and splashed across the front pages.

Nothing chagrins me more.

These people are forever inventing new ways to celebrate mediocrity - and ignorance - and to say that I find it irritating is somewhat of an understatement.

Newspaper Journalism;

Journalism and the free-press is an integral part of democracy in general...and in British democracy in particular. However, those that work in this most noble of institutions are duty bound to do so within the boundaries of the law.

The recent 'News of the World' scandal, which uncovered and exposed the dark underbelly of tabloid journalism before that newspaper's untimely demise revealed a worrying trend in today's newspaper practices which are tainting a once great institution that is steadily losing touch with its raison d'etre,...all in the name of increased circulation.

Journalism should be about exposing corruption, reporting political agendas and informing the public on the social and community issues they need to know about...but in the cut-throat race for increased circulation in a shrinking market, values such as integrity, honesty and truth are clearly being lost and a creeping suspicion that certain details in what we read aren't entirely correct…or have been completely fabricated in order to sensationalise a story now haunts the British public.

People no longer trust what they read and it is a sad state of affairs when in the homes and on the streets of Britain, the phrase 'Don't believe what you read in the papers', is now a standard, almost throw-away commentary.

We should be able to believe what is written in our newspapers and those who run them should want that to be the case too.

We need people with integrity at the top of our newspaper industry; people with a strong moral-compass and a thirst for justice; people who are fit for purpose, because without those qualities being represented the pervasive lack of trust that is currently prevalent in our society will do nothing but hasten the industry's inevitable demise.

Possible solution;

Nobody wants the press to self-regulate – they have already shown that they are incapable of doing that…

…but nobody wants the politicians to regulate the Press either…for fear of them gagging free speech…

…so why not have an independent, tripartite watchdog made up of;

- three people nominated by the press,
- three people nominated by the politicians…and
- three people nominated by the media-unions to represent the people

The odd number would guarantee a result during any voting process.

Surely somebody with a moral conscience and no self-interest would ultimately emerge from that arrangement to make sure that we never, ever need another Leveson enquiry.

———

I would also recommend the imposition of a new 'Truth and Ethics Charter' on anyone working in journalism…and who knows, a case of integrity and morality might just break out.

———

NB; to maintain a spirit of independence, no one person should ever control more than 15% of our media…

…and when people are wronged by newspapers, they should receive an apology which…

- appears on the same page as the original story and in the same sized type…
- while the compensation received (*for damages to the person's reputation*) should be based on the number of copies sold on the day of the story.

———

Paparazzi

We need to curb the paper-thin - if not hollow - celebrity culture that the youth of today see as their only way of making anything of their lives.

One way we could to do this would be to introduce tighter, more restrictive rules on paparazzi, in order to protect the lives of those whose privacy is constantly being invaded by unscrupulous photographers. This would immediately reduce the number or tacky celebrity magazines.

I don't wish to go down the road of zero tolerance, as enforced in places like Monaco but I do believe that we need to meet up with the agency moguls to set out some new ground rules, especially as everyone has a camera integrated into their mobile-phones, these days.

———

The Internet

'I fear the day that technology will surpass our human interaction;
the world will have a generation of idiots';
phrase attributed to Albert Einstein

The internet is a wonderful invention and nobody will dispute that but people need rules and boundaries because without them, all our primitive instincts and our worst character traits are allowed to run wild.

Just look at how the lack of rules and the lack of boundaries on the internet has shone a light into the deepest and darkest crevices of human behaviour and revealed us as we truly are without the framework of a rule-book to keep us in check.

- we are animals,
- we are vicious,
- we are blood-thirsty,
- we are callous,
- we are selfish,
- we are jealous
- and worst of all, we are uncaring.

Look at how cowardly internet trolls – protected by the anonymity of a pseudonym – set up hate campaigns against innocent people 'just because'.

Look at the Facebook bullies goading children to kill themselves,

Look at the paedophiles surfing the web for children to abuse,

Look at the Twitter-trolls and the torrents of vitriolic bile that they spew out on a daily basis,

Look at the people with their camera-phones baiting fragile people to jump off buildings to their death just so that they can film it and show their friends,

Look at the people with their camera-phones filming other people dying in their cars or on the road after an accident rather than helping to save them…so that they can post the clip on YouTube.

THAT is Mankind; THAT is human nature without boundaries, without discipline and without a moral compass.

People need rules and boundaries and to back that up they need a real deterrent that warns them that if they step out of line there will be consequences.

———

This, of course, is going to need some kind of international agreement but it needs to be addressed.

———

Other Internet Issues;

Paedophiles – Paedophiles are targeting young girls on social media websites. We need to find a way of blocking them from gaining access to our children…so let's make internet site providers and those that advertise on these sites criminally responsible; Category 3 offence; (1/3/5 year prison term)

Morality / humanity - We need to find a way of blocking sites and closing them down if the material they are promoting is considered unacceptable by the majority of the population; those that can only do harm or those that promote or glorify any of the following;

Bomb-making	Racism
Sectarianism	Homophobia
Terrorism	Self-harming / Anorexia
Street-fighting	Suicide
Acts of thuggery and vandalism	Bullying

Of course, people should have the right to express themselves but it must remain within the letter of the law and if any content is considered particularly offensive the service providers should be forced to take it down as soon as it appears under threat of sanction. (This would of course rely on world-wide co-operation / agreements that are not yet in place but it will have to come if we are to maintain a notion of law, morality and boundaries)

Phishing – we also need to shut down copycat sites which imitate official government sites in order to exploit the unsuspecting public. Passport renewal, car-ownership papers and tax forms etc. It is illogical that official paperwork could be authorised by anyone but the government through official government channels.

Language – We need to do something about the language used on the internet –internet service providers need to be more responsible and more pro-active in blocking bad-language and crude comments (racist, sexist, bigoted, homophobic and most importantly bullying); these people have to be held to account for the content on their sites. (*This does in no way infringe on the right to free-speech*)

Violence – Janet Street Porter once pointed out the dangers of Facebook, noting that gangs use this and other social networking sites to post threatening material intended to impress rivals and scare off detractors.

The internet allows young people to glorify violence, to pose as soldiers in their version of urban warfare and intimidate whoever they please… but we need to be able to prosecute those exploiting violence in all areas – human rights and freedom of speech need to have boundaries imposed or anarchy will result…and finally…

Happy-slapping; we have to eradicate this gratuitous violence; the happy-slapping culture of our youth and those that exploit them has to be addressed before somebody dies.

Computers – We should sell computers with the parental control built-in and activated – the choice should be reversed – opting into particular services and not out.

Spam – We need to devise a better way of blocking spam, viruses and hacking. Why not launch a worldwide competition for all the computer wizards to come up with a little black box that could be fitted between the power source and the hard drive so that the good guys could win for once…

It wouldn't be compulsory so those who didn't wish to buy it wouldn't have to, but it would be a blessing in disguise for many while still leaving room for the advertising companies.

Internet Trolls

'The Internet is the Petri dish of humanity.
We can't control what grows in it, but we don't have to watch either'.
…Tiffany Madison

Author's comment;

The internet has become the underground playground for all those twisted inadequates who like to revel in others misfortune with odious spite…and nothing reflects the real face of humanity more clearly than the social media platforms which allow people to spew gratuitous bile 24/7 with no responsibility and no accountability.

Human beings will say and do anything if they believe that they will get away with something and not be found out.

All criminals use the same thought process; some elaborate intricate airtight alibis, others simply make up feasible excuses but the goal of all these people is always the same; to get away with behaviour that is unacceptable according to the established social template.

The simple fact is that people, human beings are cowards and internet trolls are the worst example of that cowardly nature because they hide their identities behind an online pseudonym to avoid being held to account or ridiculed for their gratuitous bile-spewing.

They criticise people they don't know, people they have never met and people they would never have the gumption to confront face to face. They are cowards and cowards deserve no more than disdain from the rest of us. They should be ignored and allowed to stew in their own putrid ignorance behind their computer screens.

Who are these people?

Is humanity really moving forward or are we regressing back to our savage state?

Social network sites were originally created for friends and family to keep in touch with each other but some of them – and notably Twitter – have subsequently been hijacked by these idiots and become no more than a platform for bullies, perverts, voyeurs and self-publicists to vent their spleen.

I have no time for those anonymous online bullies with their warped minds who spend their time posting vile messages about people they don't know and subjects they know nothing about.

There might not be very many of these callous, vicious, bullying, immoral degenerates but they are blighting the lives and ruining the enjoyment for everybody else.

That said; you have to feel sorry for these sad, lonely people sitting behind their screens all day with nothing better to do with their lives than to mock and criticise other people who they have never met and are never likely to meet...

...and to see them going to prison for their stupidity – as was recently the case - is unfortunate but alas they must be made to understand that there are consequences to their actions. Citizenship is all about responsibility and accountability.

——————

Social media providers –

The use of Twitter to outrage, bully and intimidate people has reached epidemic proportions in this country.

Social media sites should be made more responsible and more accountable. They have to be made to clamp down on the trolls.

This outrageous bile-spewing is simply unacceptable and has to be checked.

We need to set up sanctions for internet-service providers who allow their sites to be used to threaten, bully or abuse in any way; those accounts where abuse and bullying have been signalled should be closed immediately and the people behind them warned of serious sanctions if they set up another account to continue the harassment. The anonymity of the internet where people can hide behind a screen and incite the most vicious hatred cannot be tolerated in a civilised society.

——————

PDC policy on parental responsibility and accountability –

The PDC would not accept this casual cruelty and in a given situation, if it could be proved that the parents of an internet bully were found to be negligent in the way that they monitored their child's use of social media, allowing them to bully, stalk or otherwise abuse others repeatedly and maliciously over a period of time, then the PDC would prosecute those parents for moral or criminal neglect.

The child would also be prosecuted and sent to one of the reform camps that we would be setting up to learn how to behave correctly in society.

These people - both parents and children - need to learn about personal responsibility and what that means in the context of the social order.

We need to monitor the internet and social networking sites more vigilantly – cyber-bullying is on the increase so we need to tighten controls and clamp down on these people who are ruining other people's lives.

Under the PDC, if a case of bullying was reported, the ISP address of the perpetrator would be flagged up and the contract holder at that address would be interviewed. If the threats continued thereafter, the contract would be cancelled and an initial six-month ISP ban would be placed on that address.

The same controls would also apply to mobile phones and their contracts would suffer the same fate. The contract holder would be interviewed and the contract subsequently cancelled if any threatening behaviour continued – be it verbal or via text.

These are extreme measures but hopefully, once the parents have been alerted to the problem and have had their internet contracts cancelled they would keep tighter control on their offspring.

The PDC would also consider further fines and penalties for repeat-offenders.

Twitter –

Our behaviour in society, human behaviour, is learned behaviour, conditioned behaviour and while we are in a social context the majority of us are quite prepared to adhere to the principles of that conditioned behaviour.

However, remove that obligation to behave in a civilised manner as Twitter does, put it behind a screen, add anonymity and then you see what we really think of our fellow men, then you see that despite our position as the most evolved species on this planet, we are no better than any other species inhabiting our world.

In fact we are worse, because as human beings we have the possibility of making a conscious choice on whether to be vicious, vile and offensive or not, whereas most other species just follow their natural instincts.

The true character of humanity is plain to see in the amount of gratuitous bile that people spew out on a daily basis through this new medium; the hatred, the threats, the bullying, the criticism....that's humanity at its most basic level.

Of course, I believe in free speech - within the confines of personal responsibility - but this open-door to any and every idiot with an axe to grind clearly needs regulation.

We need an answer to the phenomenon of these social networking sites which allow predators of every sort to invade people's personal privacy without limit or restraint.

Twitter needs to introduce controls for those signing up;

- They should insist on a real identity behind the handle name backed up by a date of birth and they should add the country of origin (UK, US etc) to the handle to facilitate the identification of these odious troglodytes
- Twitter should also create a database of the ISP addresses of its adherents and create a list of 100 words or so that are considered unacceptable (swearwords, threatening words etc.)

- Meanwhile, advertisers should opt out of sites that allow threatening comments.

People who create these sites and the vehicle for these trolls to spew their disgusting bile should not be allowed to do so with impunity under the protective banner of 'free speech'.

Point of law;

We need to create a new law against bullying and stalking – as the current harassment laws were introduced long before the explosion of the internet.

Author's comment;

It is despicable that marketing companies are using product placements and incentives on social networking sites to encourage youngsters – some as young as seven – into promoting their products for them among their friends.

This is taking consumer culture and capitalism way too far; it is immoral in every respect.

Have these companies no shame…and no boundaries?

Games / Gaming

Why is it that game-makers do nothing but promote war and violence?

Every game I see is about killing people…all of the time…and I do not buy the argument that it is only 'virtual reality', because people are now so obsessed with these games that the line between virtual reality and actual reality has been more than a little blurred.

The adolescents who play these games are encouraged to murder as many people as possible with as much arbitrary violence as possible in as short a time as possible, under the guise of a game based on tactics.

They then watch TV where they see a constant stream of crime shows where people are constantly being killed and murdered…and it is easy to see the correlation when they go out in the street armed with knives and start killing people themselves.

Several studies in the past 30 years have linked TV violence to real-life violence; it's nothing new, and now computer games are compounding that effect, by de-sensitising these young people to the horrors of violence, erasing their moral judgment and instilling in them a worrying lack of empathy for their fellow man.

At the same time, I refuse to accept the other explanation that suggests that playing these games is a way of simply relieving aggression or displacing frustration.

On the contrary, I believe that there is a direct correlation between these games and the growing level of violence in our society.

These games play on the psyche and for those with a more fragile or disturbed disposition they can be tantamount to triggers that send them over the edge.

However these games are not only numbing our young people's sensitivity to extreme violence, they are also blunting their social skills and ruining their creative thinking, not to mention their health and fitness from the hours spent sitting on a couch in front of a screen.

But that is not all; our teenagers are not the only problem. These games are affecting our younger children too…impacting on their conceptual development and impairing their cognitive awareness. They are also making children rude and aggressive and in fact, children as young as four have been found re-enacting scenes from violent video games in the playground.

It is all very worrying but unfortunately, most parents are blissfully unaware of the content in these games…and yet the depth of depravity and the level of gratuitous violence contained within them are literally off the scale. Players take part in virtual killing sprees, actively maiming, torturing and murdering people…and the more they make their victims suffer, the more points they earn. They are even given 'fatality tutorials' to hone their killing skills.

It is grotesque and unpalatable for anyone with a moral conscience.

———

Who are the people behind these games creating so much carnage?

Are they human because they are clearly devoid of any human qualities that I would recognise or associate with humanity? In fact, there is not one redeeming quality in these games that I can see.

On the contrary, the people who make these video games have contributed to creating a generation of;

- selfish,
- self-centred,
- emotionally-stunted,
- de-sensitised,
- potential murderers who lack any sense of morality, manners, respect or boundaries

Technology by all means – teaching children to be proficient in killing or robbing banks…certainly not…and it would be immoral for any responsible authority to accept that.

———

The people making a fortune from this business say that video-games are not harmful.

They should consider this;

Norwegian killer Anders Breivik admitted that he perfected his shooting technique playing video games for 16 hours a day – before he went out on his killing spree, murdering 77 innocent people in cold blood.

Surely, what happened in Norway should act as a lesson to us all.

Author's comment;

Perhaps we should prosecute the computer programmers who create these violent and anti-social games which glorify crime and law-breaking. A charge of moral or criminal neglect would be a good starting point...

...and maybe we should ban games such as – GTA IV – Manhunt 2 – Hitman / Blood Money and Mortal Kombat which all glory in violence and vicious manslaughter.

That said; I believe that we should also ban sites that re-enforce gender stereotypes, such as the Bimbo web-site which targets young girls – encouraging the use of slimming pills and boob jobs etc.

Who are these twisted people that create and finance this rubbish?

Television;

The BBC –

The BBC (Biased Broadcasting Corporation) or the **B**iased **B**oys **C**lub to give it another name is an ageing institution that is rooted in the past with its leftist views and its antiquated Victorian attitudes; indeed, the general consensus among the British public is that the BBC is as much the unofficial Labour Party mouthpiece as the Guardian newspaper is, with its left-leaning politics.

But alas, the glory days of this once proud institution are over…and now the BBC is widely regarded by the majority of the British public as;

- ageist,
- sexist,
- out of touch…and most importantly
- overly profligate with the tax-payers money which it lavishes on both 'celebrity presenters' and innumerable executives who have job-titles that only an etymologist could decipher.

This is all very unpalatable…but what galls me the most is that the BBC management was advising its staff on <u>HOW NOT TO PAY TAX</u> through an offshore tax-avoidance scheme.

This is a corporation <u>funded solely by the taxpayer</u>, advising and encouraging its staff not to pay tax. What kind of moral person would dream up such a scheme?

This kind of corporate deceit is outrageous and it shows a complete lack of morality, integrity or leadership at the top of this once-respected institution.

Moreover, the sexism and the ageist issues aside, both of which have been proved to be rife throughout the corporation;

- the BBC clearly discriminates in its choice of subject matter; not allowing the anti-climate change argument any air-time for example because it would contradict <u>the establishment's views</u>. (re David Bellamy)
- and decides unilaterally on what the public should and should not be allowed to see. It recently censored Fawlty Towers – a much loved TV series – in order to be politically correct…while also censoring listeners views on The Archers racy plotlines

However, the most important issue that the BBC has failed to face up to…is the unpalatable truth of what had been happening within its walls over the last fifty years…and sadly, because of that lack of transparency and openness, the trust that had been built up between the corporation the British public, over many decades, no longer exists.

As stated previously, the BBC is an anachronism…because it has a culture of obfuscation and denial which is rooted in the attitudes of a bygone age…and in keeping with that mentality, it continues to present a hypocritically-prudish 1950's facade to the British public while at the same time covering up any questionable activities that might tarnish its reputation, like those of Jimmy Savile for example.

(*That kind of conduct is just so 1950's, to try to hide the truth for appearances sake*)

Nevertheless, the Savile case revealed that there was clearly a conspiracy… or at least a culture of tolerance of sexual abuse… within the walls of the BBC during those years…and the BBC's report on the case which had ninety of its pages redacted or blacked out to avoid any embarrassing revelations did no more than confirm its policy of non-disclosure and self-protection, showing the British public the same contempt and scorn as the politicians did with their outrageous expense claims.

Money Matters;

This creaking institution costs every household in the UK £145.50 every year which adds up to a grand total of over £3.6 billion.

My question is this; why should the British taxpayer continue to fund this archaic institution when these days they could just as easily tune in to any of a hundred other channels for a fraction of the price?

The BBC;

- is a 20th century organisation (created in 1922)
- based on 19th century attitudes (because those who created it were born in the previous century)
- trying to live in a 21st century world…

…and it simply cannot survive…at least not in its current form.

———

Even the concept of its hierarchy sounds dusty and outdated.

The stuffy people who run the BBC are known as 'the Board of Governors'…which in itself sounds so 19th century…and these people are so completely out of touch with reality that controversy is a regular occurrence, as is always the case when traditional 19th century ideas are confronted with the progressive ideas of the 21st century.

The BBC's nickname too, sounds as if it is a throwback to the past;

It is fondly known by many as 'Aunty'.

Meanwhile, its programmes, most of which are repeats and re-runs from the 1980's, have lost all their sheen…and any new programmes that they do produce lack the quality and slickness of previous offerings because of regular budgetary restraints on production costs.

That said…while production costs are being slashed, paradoxically salaries and perks for 'stars' and executives are constantly being flagged up and exposed as outrageously extravagant. Even Lord Patten, the new chairman of the BBC Trust admitted recently;

'The BBC is full of overpaid pen-pushers'.

This is clearly wrong; people should not be earning millions of pounds in salary from a publicly-funded organisation.

The Greed Generation is over; how can anybody justify earning a £1 million pound salary from the public purse, never mind 2, 3 or 5 million pounds.

£1 million a year equates to a ratio of 40 on the ER scale; that is 40 times the average wage.

£2 million a year equates to 80 salaries of £25K.

We could pay 80 nurses for a year with £2 million, giving them all a pay rise for the cost of one BBC presenter…and a BBC presenter only works a couple of hours a week…while nurses regularly work up to double their allotted 37.5 hours which often leads to burn-out.

How can we justify these salaries?

The Greed Generation must be consigned to the past.

Author's comment;

The BBC should reduce the size of these salaries so as to reduce the cost of the license fee…because if it can afford to pay its executives and its celebrities multi-million pound salaries then it is receiving too much from the public purse.

Pay-offs;

In the last eight years 7500 Corporation staff have walked away from the BBC with severance payments worth a total of £369 million, some being paid more than they were contractually obliged to receive.

- Deputy DG Mark Byford received £949,000
- Chief operating officer Caroline Thomson received £680,400, and
- DG George Entwhistle received £470,300 <u>for 54 days work</u> (double his entitlement)

More recent figures show that over the last three years 200 managers have been handed £100,000 or more in pay-offs and despite the outcry from the British public, the BBC has just handed another contract to a 'friend' worth £600,000 a year which also proves that cronyism and nepotism is still rife in this most outdated of organisations.

Will they never learn?

Meanwhile, the man at the centre of the 'Queen storming-off charade' quite rightly resigned for bringing his position into disrepute; that was most 'honourable' of him…but why was he given a pay-off of £500,000? Who are all these people being rewarded with bonuses and pay-offs for doing their jobs <u>badly?</u>

This culture of excessive pay and pay-offs has been tolerated for far too long and it is time for the purse-strings to be pulled.

Financial mismanagement;

Financial mismanagement is a specialty of the BBC and the reason why it is so profligate is easy to comprehend; it is somebody else's money – i.e., the tax-payers – and when it is somebody else's money, the need to be frugal and responsible somehow deserts even the most sensible of people.

Here are a few examples of the BBC's profligacy in recent years which is completely out of control;

- It spent £1 billion on the New Broadcasting House in London
- It spent another £1 billion on the Media City in Salford (which incidentally came in £55 million <u>over budget</u> and had to be – in part - revamped after 6 months)
- It spent £942 million on moving the whole organisation North
- It spent £24 million…to 'bribe' staff to move North
- It spent £60 million in pay-offs
- It spent £100 million on a useless IT system…and

- It spends £10 million a year on 'consultants' (this confuses me, because with the salaries they pay, the BBC should already have the best people…why do they need to spend another £10 million on consultants?)

And finally, it's greatest sin; the BBC uses tax-payers' license-fee money to gag and silence its staff when they threaten to reveal the truth of what goes on behind closed doors…

…and this is all on top of the outrageous salaries given to celebrities and executives.

The PDC Solution –

The big question is this; should we get rid of this archaic, anachronistic institution or not?

I personally believe that it is time to move on.

People of the UK; the Empire is long gone – and much like the monarchy, the BBC with its leftist attitudes is a lumbering relic from a by-gone age.

Britain no longer holds the position in the world that it once did, so why should we believe that we have still have a Post-Colonial duty to continue informing the rest of the world of what is happening in London.

I believe that it is time to retire 'Aunty' like an old spinster who is well past her sell-by date. She has abused her privileges (the licence fee) for far too long.

The BBC was created with good intentions at a time when Britain's standing in the world was very different than it is today but because of its bias, its lack of morality and transparency and its ongoing mismanagement of taxpayers' money I believe that it has brought about its own demise.

A lack of morality and integrity breeds mistrust and the taxpaying citizens of this country don't want to keep paying people that they do not trust; its human nature.

I believe that, as long as we secure a guarantee that the Crown Jewels of British Sport will be screened un-encrypted to the great British public by whoever tenders for the contract…then the BBC should be dismantled and its profitable elements sold off to private enterprise.

That said; the PDC would nevertheless maintain the licence-fee concept, replacing it with a screen-tax (TV or computer) which would apply to every home. This tax would apply to everyone, including pensioners but they would benefit from a reduced rate. I feel it is important that everyone in the community contributes.

This money, collected as part of the local community taxes, would be invested in cultural activities within the local authority's area and its usage would be made clearly transparent in the council's accounts.

… or it could be given to the culture secretary to invest in production companies as grants, some of which would come back in corporation tax if what they produce is successful.

However; should we choose to keep the BBC…

The first thing to do would be a wholesale purge of senior executives;

- To begin with we would need to abolish all those who do generic 'non-jobs', '*illico presto*'.
- Then, we would need to jettison all those considered incompetent and unfit for purpose and replace them with people who are competent and do have a moral compass.

The pay-structure would be the next priority.

- It needs a complete overhaul. The BBC should not be trying to compete with the private sector. They work in the same medium but they are completely different concepts. I believe that, if it is to survive, the BBC should concentrate on giving up-and-coming writers, artists and creative types the opportunity to make their mark, acting as a platform for the people who pay for it to exist...and not as a cash-cow for greedy executives and celebrity types.

Author's comment;

I personally would call in the BBC management and staff, one at a time, sit them down and ask them to justify their salaries, their pension plans and their pay-off arrangements.

The PDC would then restructure every department using logical and common sense guidelines on personnel and budget...and each department would be given a fixed objective to be achieved within a set time-period.

...and finally...the PDC would maintain three channels;

BBC 1 – for the mainstream public

BBC 2 – for cultural events and topical discussion (BBC 4's best programmes would be integrated into this channel)...and

BBC 3 – for the younger generation...as a proving ground

General comments on TV

While TV is an exciting and glamorous industry, the reality is that it is often shallow, pointless and puerile.

Stephen Fry once called the BBC's programming 'infantile'; I have to agree.

- Let's stop celebrating mediocrity and ignorance,
- let's stop perpetuating this cycle of self-destruction, of constant damage to our moral reputation,
- let's stop pandering to the vacuous, dumbed-down generation with their shallow, celebrity-driven inanities and their demands to all have their 'fifteen minutes' of fame…and
- Let's put an end to the ritual humiliation of junk / reality TV.

I believe that as a part of trying to repair our reputation abroad – we should ban the reality TV shows that champion the British tourist's lack of restraint when abroad.

Programmes such as 'Boozed-up Brits Abroad', 'Reps', 'Ibiza'…and the 'Bahamas Uncovered' are all filled with drunken sex and general promiscuity which does nothing to enhance our reputation on the world stage…and while we cannot stop it happening, not showcasing it on TV would hopefully have a calming effect and counter the desire of everybody wanting to be on TV no matter the cost to their pride, their dignity or our national reputation.

Sex in the Media –

The British public is cursed with Victorian propriety and the moral imperatives / restraints that that concept imposes on them, holding them back and preventing them from exploring and expressing their sexuality.

I am not suggesting that everyone should indulge in epicurean decadence all day, every day, but Britain needs to grow up in its attitude towards sex.

This ridiculous reputation that we have of being sexually repressed virgins who snigger like naughty little schoolboys at saucy seaside-postcards, St Trinian's, the Carry-on films and Benny Hill sketches is pathetic and needs to be consigned to the past.

The way we are scandalised by the slightest suggestion of anything sexual, calling the female-genital-area a 'front bottom' to avoid using the word 'vagina' while taking every opportunity we can to transform the slightest innuendo into a ' how rude' moment is risible.

With our old Victorian values we Brits are the laughing stock of the world.

How can we – in the 21st century – still be so self-conscious and uptight about sex that 64% of us still insist on making love with the lights out – while paradoxically, we have the worst under-age pregnancy rate in the world; that scandal itself is a contradiction in terms.

I pity stuffy, middle-England people of a certain vintage with their high-brow, hypocritical, Victorian values who…because they think we are still living in the 19th century…get outraged by a swear-word or are shocked at a naked shoulder on TV – then ring in to complain or write to the BBC or a newspaper to vent their moral indignation.

These people are sexually inhibited; morally repressed, uptight, obnoxious prudes and they need to join the 21st century.

That said; I do believe that the concept of a watershed should be maintained to differentiate content between what is family entertainment and what is for the more developed mind.

Advertising –

We need to review our Advertising Standards which seem to have lapsed of late;

Men;

TV is a heavily contrived medium but it seems to have a casual contempt for men – especially fathers who are often portrayed as feckless idiots.

This is inverse sexism, and reveals an underlying prejudice against men.

Indeed, some adverts are shamefully demeaning towards men...and yet if women were portrayed as these hapless idiots, the Feminists would be on the streets with their banners.

This reverse sexism is the unintended consequence of feminism and many psychologists agree that the drip, drip of negative images of fathers is having an adverse effect on our youth; they are starved of positive male role models.

Women;

Firstly; the advertising authority should systematically ban explicit slogans and campaigns gratuitously exploiting the female form when the product being advertised has no connection whatsoever with women.

For example; what does a woman draped over a car's bonnet in a bikini have to do with the car's efficiency, its economy, its safety or its cost? Nothing!

This ruling should also apply to street advertising as children these days are being confronted far too early by images of overt sexuality wherever they look.

I would also like to see a ban on the soft-peddling of prostitution on late night TV through blatant exploitation of mobile phone calls.

———

Other issues;

We should also ban any advertising which encourages children to want to look older than they really are; mainly clothes and make-up.

Meanwhile, I would like to see a ban on gambling adverts that appear throughout the day inciting people to gamble online; this is wrong and immoral…and

I would also like to see advertisers announcing and displaying the prices of their products more clearly.

———

Betting / Gambling

In 2005, desperate to fill the Treasury's coffers and to pursue their profligate, 'spend, spend, spend' policies, New Labour introduced the 2005 Gambling Act.

This was the latest in a series of bad decisions but in this case not from a political standpoint but from a moral standpoint.

I understand that our governing bodies are desperate to claw back money from wherever they can in order to shore up an ever-increasing deficit, and I know that this country has a history of betting on anything from a score-line to a royal baby name and on through horse-racing and the lottery…but making it easier for people to become gambling addicts so that the Treasury can increase its revenue is hardly responsible government.

The British gamble up to £46 billion a year which is why gambling is being championed in this country; not only because it brings in crucial revenue to our profligate treasury but also because it employs 40000 people…and we all know that politicians will do anything to keep unemployment figures down, even if it means feeding vices like gambling…or servicing white-elephant renewable energy projects as explained previously, in the chapter on 'Climate Change'.

However…as I see it…it is not the role of government to encourage citizens to engage in activities that are potentially detrimental to their wellbeing (mental or financial) – no matter how much tax these activities might generate for the Treasury.

I understand that gambling is ingrained in the British psyche; it has been for centuries, but nevertheless I believe that it is the role of a government to act responsibly in all matters…and for them to promote such folly seems counter-intuitive to that ethos.

Being in government is about having values, about making the right choices for the people. It is about being responsible…not irresponsible… and it is certainly not about encouraging people to indulge their vices; on the contrary, it should be about protecting its more vulnerable citizens from such vices.

––––––

The New Labour Gambling Act of 2005 which filled our High Streets with betting offices and fruit machines and our TV screens with constant publicity for poker competitions and other gambling possibilities was just another reckless idea to add to the list – much like 24hour drinking, the open-door policy on immigration and the overly-generous GP contracts…all reckless policies that have done nothing but create problems for this country.

Incompetence is one thing; a lack of integrity and morality is something else and something no responsible government should ever be accused of and yet.

- 9000 betting shops now litter our High Streets – lining the pockets of book-makers and payday loan sharks
- Publicity for gambling on our TV screens has soared by 1,444% in 8 years. In fact, it is reaching epidemic proportions.
- Meanwhile insidious specialist TV channels such as bingo sites, online casinos, poker sites and sports betting sites which all promote and cultivate the betting culture are selling the idea of gambling as fun and cool. They encourage children, housewives and the vulnerable to play all day, every day, fuelling addiction, depression, poverty and bankruptcy which then results in violence to feed the habit…and suicide.
- Facebook too, has any number of 'Las-Vegas' style casino games on its site.

Consequences – One man recently stole £1.5m from his company to pay for his addiction to online bingo – and in another recent case – a bank manager was convicted of stealing £176,000 to feed his online gambling addiction.

This is the legacy that New Labour left behind; a country full of binge-drinking gamblers.

————

Author's comment;

Sport too, has sold its soul by embracing the gambling industry as sponsors.

Football, for example has made a deal with the devil by allowing the betting business into their ranks…and someday in the not-too-distant future our national game will pay the price with a match-fixing scandal or two.

Cricket has already been tainted by match-fixing; boxing has always had problems with match-fixing and even the more sedate game of tennis has had its problems…football will be next…

————

News Flash; seven footballers have just been arrested in connection with 'alleged' spot-fixing accusations.

————

Westminster

Why are the British people so apathetic about politics?

This is why; because...

- they are sick of being lied to,
- they are sick of politicians promising and not delivering...and...
- they are sick of having the democratic process thrown in their faces by a group of self-serving hypocrites who just don't listen to their voice or their view.

On the 20th of April 1653, Oliver Cromwell stood in the House of Commons and announced the following...

'It is high time for me to put an end to your sitting in this place,
which you have dishonoured by your contempt of all virtue,
and defiled by your practice of every vice
…ye are a pack of mercenary wretches;
Is there a single virtue now remaining amongst you?
Is there one vice you do not possess?
Gold is your God;

which of you have not barter'd your conscience for bribes
Ye have no more religion than my horse…
…ye sordid prostitutes, have you not defiled this sacred place…
…and turned the Lord's temple into a den of thieves
by your immoral principles and wicked practices;
ye are grown intolerably odious to the whole nation…
…take away that shining bauble there, and lock up the doors…
…in the name of God, go!'

Author's comment;

Well, just like Oliver Cromwell all those years ago, I too, as a citizen of this country am sick and tired of all the corruption, the squabbling and the self-interest that is constantly being played out in Westminster.

Isn't it ironic that more than 350 years after Cromwell's rant the politicians of this House still have that same reputation?

I believe that a plaque should be made of Cromwell's words…and it should be hung with pride of place at the entrance to the House of Commons chamber as a caution to today's MPs and a reminder to them of their responsibilities.

Now, I myself would never be so presumptuous as to compare myself to **Oliver Cromwell** but if I manage to take this crusade for reform to its fruition I hope to show the same spirit and the same determination that he showed when ridding Parliament of its inherent corruption all those years ago.

Perhaps I could be a 21ˢᵗ Century version of the great man himself;

- but without the stain of dictatorship…or
- the execution of the monarch…or
- the Irish massacres…or
- the Damocles of religion hanging over me.

I would certainly be less puritanical than was Cromwell, but I do agree with him on one thing; that we should consign the concept of Christmas to the past; especially as the religious symbolism that it once represented has now waned irreparably and lost most of its apocryphal lustre.

In fact, in 21ˢᵗ Century Britain, far from being a sacred religious festival, the Christmas period has now become no more than a time of commercial excess to be exploited by marketing professionals of every ilk...

...and as a consequence the PDC would replace this pretence of a 'religious happening' with an end of year celebration built around family and fraternity.

Overview of politics;

It is a sad indictment of our democracy but unfortunately greed is the motor that drives western economies; it is greed that feeds capitalism – and never was it more glaringly obvious than during the banking collapse and crisis of 2007 / 2008.

...but what is it with politicians;

- why does the culture of politics corrupt them so;
- why do they become so greedy when put in charge of a country's finances and
- why do the concepts of truth, honesty and morality suddenly become so alien to them once they become elected officials?

Politics should be a noble profession filled with intelligent, altruistic people who are prepared to work hard for the common good, so why do we now mistrust them so;

Here are a few reasons why -

Politicians spend years in university learning communication skills but these days, when confronted with a question that requires a simple yes or no answer they are incapable of communicating a response with either of those monosyllabic words; why is that?

They also spend years learning about the intricacies of political rhetoric...but that just seems to mean that they have learned how to avoid answering a question…or telling the truth…while managing to keep a straight face…

…but is that really what we want from our politicians?

Do we really want everything that comes out of a politician's mouth to sound like misinformation sliding effortlessly off the slippery surface their forked tongues?

Is that really what we want…?

Wouldn't it be better if they just told us the truth?

What would be so wrong in that…?

It might be what they are taught at Oxbridge, but their shifty behaviour and their evasive answers do nothing but encourage our mistrust of them and all they represent; it is why we don't believe a word they say.

Whatever happened to honesty and integrity…and why are these virtues so elusive to the political elite?

For information;

The PDC would be decisive and bold; one simple rule would apply…

> If you have no **integrity** then you will have no **responsibility**
> **No Integrity; No Responsibility**

Politicians are elected and sent to Parliament to serve the people; they are not sent there simply to further their own personal ambitions.

However the current crop of INEPTS; that's…

- **I**ncompetent (bungling)
- **N**efarious (immoral and reprehensible)
- **E**gotistical (self-serving)
- **P**erfidious (deceitful)...and
- **T**wo-faced (hypocrites)

...seem to have lost their main focus...and the lack of integrity they display on a daily basis, on top of the well-publicised expenses scandal are both factors in the argument which - when exposed to the light of public scrutiny - begin to explain why the people of this country are so disillusioned with their political representatives; add to that the culture of spin-doctors who do nothing but add another devious layer to the politicians daily sugar-coating of lies in order to throw the public off the scent and we finally get a real understanding of how twisted our political culture really is.

Also, why is it that politicians can never say sorry or admit that they are wrong; why is that?

We are all human; we all suffer from human failings; we all get it wrong sometimes; so why is it so hard for politicians to show their humanity; is human weakness such a disadvantage in the scheming, cut-throat arena of front-bench politics?

...and finally; is it really that surprising that the British public mistrusts its politicians so...when they systematically whitewash any inquiry that would incriminate them and expose them for who they really are, while any other citizen who would do as they have done, would be hauled before the courts and thrown in prison for fraud.

These people suffer from a superiority complex and a misguided sense of entitlement believing that they are somehow immune to prosecution and above the rule of law simply because they have the letters MP after their names; that misconception has to be 'clarified'.

So, this is where we are in the UK today…and what a perplexing moral dichotomy that presents us with, as ordinary citizens, when we stand in the voting booth on polling day; proud to be exercising our democratic right on the one hand – and yet so frustrated on the other - in the knowledge that whoever we vote for will more likely than not, make his or her way directly from the polling station to the money trough to start filling up his or her pockets with tax-payers money quicker than Usain Bolt can run the 100 metres.

The City of Westminster –

The political system in the UK is intrinsically corrupt and full of scheming liars simply out to make as much money as they can for themselves from the public purse in order to feather their retirement years.

Politicians pretend to have morals and manners but these are just a veneer to distract the voters while they help themselves to the country's wealth. They don't really care what is right for the country or even for the people; they only care about what is right for them.

Westminster has lost the moral earnestness that it once epitomised. Today it is simply a den of vipers full of hypocrisy, back-biting and buck-passing; life in the Westminster village in the 21st century is all about entitlement, cronyism and nepotism;

- Passive corruption and unspoken understandings are commonplace…and in fact run throughout the corridors of power and across the political party-lines; especially when it suits a common purpose. Westminster is all about collusion and secret covenants where **MPs** quickly close ranks to deny the British people the truth if it's in their (MPs) interest; just look at how they banded together recently to block a motion for them to disclose their fat salaries and generous allowances. There is no real partisanship in Westminster because whenever anything threatens the golden goose – i.e. their pay and their expenses our wonderful MPs soon close ranks. It is time to unmask this charade.

- There is also a culture of calling-in favours and 'quid-pro-quo' arrangements (you scratch my back, I'll scratch yours) that goes on continuously…in and around the Westminster village.
- Nepotism too, is rife; it runs through politics as it always has, despite it flying in the face of modern equal-opportunities laws and anti-discrimination laws. Cases of nepotism in Westminster are up from 106 to 124 in recent years which show that shameless politicians have learnt nothing from the expenses scandal and are still not listening.

It is a sad reality but Westminster as an entity has been on the decline for a while now and it is decaying steadily a little more every day because there is nobody in that inner circle upholding the noble values on which it was founded.

- It is full of dead-wood, of career politicians and stuffy landed gentry who have been helping themselves to the public purse without rebuff for far too long.
- It is full of the greedy…and the amoral political elite intent on feathering its own nest at the expense of the British public…and
- It is full of tired, cynical 55year olds who just want to pick up their salaries and expenses and have a quiet drink at the heavily subsidised bar before returning home to the comfort of their taxpayer-funded retreats

That is what Westminster has become in the eyes of the British public… but Westminster is not alone in this; sadly, it is the way of politics the world over.

———

Author's comment;

The goal of the MPs in Westminster seems to be all about preserving privileges; <u>their privileges;</u>

- Whatever happened to honesty and decency and morality?
- Where is their sense of social responsibility, where is the altruism needed in order to represent others?

This is a depressing summary of life in Westminster and amongst the 'sharks' I am sure that there are a few 'allegedly honest' MPs...but sadly they (the honest few) can only swim against the tide for so long before being whipped into line by the tyrannical protocols of Westminster life.

Isn't it sad that we - as citizens of this country - have to depend on these people to rule over our lives, to run the country and sit in judgement of us, when for politicians, as for lawyers, it is given as read that lies, deception and dishonesty come with the territory?

Selective amnesia too, seems to be a pre-requisite for politicians...so why should the British public listen to MPs who shamelessly fiddle their expenses or bed other men's wives? Clearly, they do not have the moral authority to be handing out such lessons...and yet they do...

The lack of morality is staggering and the hypocrisy is mind-blowing.

The politicians of this country have completely lost touch with the voters and the gulf that separates Westminster from the people is ever-widening.

In fact, they often display an unpleasant and smug contempt for the electorate...until they need their votes to get re-elected that is; looking down at them from their plush offices in Westminster with disdain; disdain for the very people who are paying for them to live the lives they are living.

How ungrateful and arrogant is that...?

Author's comment;

The politicians recently demanded pay-rises of 32% while the country and its economy was in its deepest recession for almost a century…and the salaries of everybody else in the public sector had been frozen. That is not only insensitive; it shows just how much our politicians are out of touch with the rest of society.

Instances of Hypocrisy, **Deceit**, **Elastic morals** and **Nepotism** abound in Westminster;

Here are a few recent examples but there are hundreds more across all parties;

- **Hypocrisy – Ken Livingstone (Labour)** spent all his time attacking fat-cats who avoided paying tax but he himself avoided paying tax by getting his salary paid through an off-shore company
- **Deceit – Peter Cruddas (Conservative)** tried to sell access to the Prime Minister David Cameron and George Osborne; David Laws (**LibDem**) fiddled his expenses – Tony Blair (**New Labour**) lied about the Weapons of Mass Destruction and Gordon Brown (**New Labour**) as Chancellor helped himself to the people's retirement fund money to balance his tax cuts to the tune of £50 billion.
- **Elastic morals – John Hemming (LibDem)** – had been having an affair with his mistress for 13yrs and indeed fathered her child; then, in retaliation; his wife Christine broke into the mistress's flat and stole a kitten**;** infidelity is rife in Westminster and here's more proof; an internet website that offers extra-marital affairs recently revealed that it had received 52,375 hits in seven months from Westminster-based computers. Clearly our politicians would like it to be a den of iniquity but in reality it is just a nest of vipers.
- **Nepotism – Derek Conway (Conservative)** gorged himself and his family on taxpayers' money through his expense

accounts notably paying his son a salary when the boy was still at university. In fact MP's have been financing their families' lifestyles through their expenses to the tune of almost £8 million a year. One MP even employs both his wife…and his mistress.

This is not so much nepotism but married tandems who both have their snouts in the trough – **Harriet Harman & Jack Dromey + Ed Balls & Yvette Cooper**; both worthy successors to the **Kinnocks** who have since upgraded to the European gravy train.

The PDC Solution –

The first thing we need to do is change the mentality in Westminster; this noble profession has been abused for too long.

We need to get rid of the generations that have milked the system for far too long, the generations that have lived off the privileges of a time when the landed gentry believed they were somehow entitled, by inherited right to help themselves to the country's wealth in any way they desired and with complete impunity.

Then we need to drum it into those that remain that they are there because they have been elected to represent their constituents ideas, not their own, not their party's; <u>their constituents</u>.

This would mean an end to all the archaic protocols that regulate parliamentary life; the concept of bullying Whips for example.

It is time to phase out these megalo-manic enforcers who threaten independent thinking MP's with de-selection if they do not toe the party line…and allow those same MP's to vote in accordance with the wishes of their electorate…and not necessarily in accordance with the party they represent.

Politicians and the Young;

Westminster politicians set a bad example because the scent of entitlement hangs heavy in the air around them…and unfortunately this sense of entitlement is what they have transferred to the younger generation making them very poor role models;

- Politicians cheat (sexually incontinent),
- they lie (calling it political rhetoric)…and
- they steal (fiddle expenses), which is reminiscent of the riff used by wrestler Eddie Guerrero to promote himself.

But why is it…? Why is it that when they enter the House, these people abandon all morality?

Where is the ethical leadership; where is the expert guidance?

These people should – as our elected representatives - be setting an example to the disaffected youth of today but how can they when their own behaviour is so unbecoming?

Now they might not want the responsibility of that role - as a role model - but it comes with the territory when you are a public figure… and as a consequence I would suggest that all future MPs sign a code of conduct which forces them to behave with a little more dignity and reserve.

———

House of Commons – MPs as a group

Role –

At the moment, we have a whole bunch of pseudo leaders in Westminster, all delivered on a conveyor belt from Oxbridge with their sense of entitlement and privilege already in place, with no other agenda than to milk the system and continue milking the system as their fathers and their grandfathers did before them.

They can all talk the talk and walk the walk…but ask any one of them to stand up and accept responsibility or be courageous in any way and they all wither and shrivel like sultanas in the sun.

There is no courage, there is no fight in our politicians; sure, they can discuss the merits of why they deserve more money and more expenses until the cows come home but ask them to come up with a policy or to defend a policy that might entail some confrontation and they all pale into one of those faded ancestral shadows that haunt the corridors of Westminster, one of those faceless bureaucrats who have been feeding off the public purse for generation after generation.

These are not leaders, these people have no vision; they are just a collection of spineless wallies, a bunch of frightened cowards, petrified by the responsibility that they have inherited by proxy, terrified of the prospect of making a decision and frankly incapable of standing up for the people they are supposed to represent.

The celebrity/media driven world that we now live in means that politicians arrive in Westminster in pursuit of some very personal goals; self-promotion, glory and political stardom…they do not see representing their electorate as their main objective.

Bad MPs –

That said, many of our politicians know their short-comings, they know that they are incompetent; they know that they haven't got a clue, but despite what many might think, these people are not stupid.

The problem stems from the fact that they are career politicians; these are people who have no experience in the real world, who have progressed through university directly into the Westminster village… and therefore - as bad as they are - they have to carry on because they simply don't know anything else.

It's a shame but these people have to stay on the slow-train to oblivion because they don't have any alternative; there is no Plan B for people groomed to be in politics and I have to empathise with those who cannot make the grade…but my question is this…

How can people with no experience of real life or the real world be in charge of people who do live in the real world?

How can they sit in Westminster making decisions that affect us all – believing misguidedly that they know best in every situation - when they have absolutely no experience of running a business or making a real decision?

This is illogical and cannot be the right way to conduct our national affairs.

———

MPs are elected to Westminster to speak on our behalf; they are there to represent our view as the voters of this country but much like the EU, once elected our politicians treat public opinion as an obstacle to be overcome or ignored…rather than a reason for them to change direction.

Indeed, politicians seem to spend more time trying to manipulate public opinion than actually doing anything about it…to the point where it would appear that success in politics is all down to how well you can manipulate the system…because they clearly pay scant attention to the opinions and wishes of the people who put them there, doing as they or their party see fit and often pulling in the complete opposite direction to the people's wishes, arrogantly believing that because they have been elected they have somehow been invested with a higher knowledge, that they suddenly know better than the people who put them there in any given situation…even when they have no experience of life in the real world.

Politicians in Westminster underestimate the electorate because their default position is that they are better than them – both intellectually and socially.

This vanity-filled delusion…and the misplaced self-righteousness that goes with it…is plain to see in many politicians, but personal ambition in politics is like a gangrene that slowly consumes a person driving them towards either bitter senility or megalomanic dementia.

Our politicians are so wrapped up in their own parliamentary career plans that they have lost touch with the electorate and the gap is widening daily.

- When are politicians going to realise that they have been elected to serve the people and implement the policies that they (the people) have voted for…and
- When are they going to realise that they have not been elected to impose their own or their party's agenda.

Politicians seem determined to keep the public in the dark because they are convinced that they know what is best for us in every situation, but I believe that they should include the people more often, especially in major decisions through the referendum process.

We have had enough of our political 'elite' steering our destiny further and further into oblivion without asking for our approval.

———

Author's comment on the politician's mandate;

When is the political community going to stop treating the people of this country like fools?

The people of Britain are rational individuals; they can think for themselves; they don't need the politicians and the nanny state making every decision for them.

We live in a democracy; let the voters who represent that democracy decide;

1) Don't tell them what you think they want, trying to second guess them with your own agenda ; you don't know what they want until you ask them

2) As their elected representatives, listen to what they say, then act and try to deliver. It's simple mechanics…and finally
3) Don't make promises you know you can't or won't keep

The people are sick of politicians taking it upon themselves to make executive decisions without consulting them, for fear of them (the voters) countermanding the party line.

The political elite has ignored the wishes of the majority of the people for far too long in this country, pretexting that they know better and what is right for the country.

Well, we have left it up to them for a while now…and look where it has left us.

They have failed us all miserably creating a planetary mess of epic proportions.

———

When are the politicians going to realise that they have been put in power to implement the laws in accordance with the desires of the British voters and not their own or those of their party.

Yes, they have been voted in, and as our elected body they should be speaking for us, but they don't.

They don't listen to us…and instead of doing as we the voters have decided, they do as they like, making decisions inconsistent with the wishes of the people believing that as elected members they know better.

The most flagrant example of this being Tony Blair taking the country to war whether we liked it or not.

———

Smug quote attributed to Tony Blair;

'The British public decides every five years; in the meantime I decide what I like'.

———

Tony Blair took us to war because he personally believed it was the right thing to do.

He didn't consult us; the people.

In fact, not only did he not consult us, he deliberately ignored the millions of people in the street protesting against it because <u>he</u> thought it was the right thing to do.

This is where democracy is ignored and autocracy prevails.

Similarly, we were taken into the EU (in its current form) without being asked, and while other countries have since been consulted on subsequent charters, the British public has been repeatedly over-looked by the political classes because of this convenient assumption that they, the politicians, know best – when in reality, given the chance of a referendum on both of these issues the British public would more than likely have said, NO.

Politicians have made a mockery of democracy in this country over the last 30 years and it is time they realised that their role in parliament is to serve the people and not just to further their own personal ambitions.

They need to realise;

-   that they are OUR spokesperson in the world of politics,
-   that they are there to relay OUR ideas…and
-   that any personal leanings they might have should be put aside while they fulfil their mandate and defend what we, the people have decided

… and if they cannot do that, then they should not be in that position.

We live in a democracy in this country but it is a false democracy… for all these reasons…and what kind of democracy is it really when the politicians keep asking the same questions until they get the answer that they want to hear;

-   The Irish - for example - said no to the EU question but they were told to vote again until they said yes…and
-   Tony Blair was told by his advisors that invading Iraq was illegal but those advisors were told to go away and only come back when they had produced / invented a strategy where it would be legal.

Where are the democratic principles in these two examples..?

─────

Lack of gumption –

The politicians in this country have been in complete denial over some very major issues for far too long now, afraid to take the hard decisions because of their desire not to rock the boat - and this wishy-washy way of governing has led the mess we are now in – not just the financial mess, but also;

-   the immigration mess,
-   the education mess,
-   the social mess…and
-   the pensions mess

Our politicians constantly shy away from important decisions because important decisions are often controversial and as our lily-livered representatives only really care about their cushy lifestyles and their seats on the gravy train, they avoid putting their heads above the parapet.

Politicians are like impotent lambkins; they want the money, the power and the prestige but they are terrified of actually making any decisions that would put their privileges at risk.

We, in this country are not being governed, we are not even being managed; we are being patronised by a collection of gutless…and yet incredibly vain…men and women who play at being in politics in Westminster but who are - in fact - completely incompetent and wholly out of sync with the wishes of the people.

Indeed, it seems to me that most of the current crop of political and institutional leaders is either…spineless, incompetent or corrupt and instead of embracing reform on any issue, they simply dig in their heels, in order to protect their own interests and privileges.

Politicians have a voracious appetite for looking after no.1 and their priorities go like this;

- themselves
- THEMSELVES
- their families
- their cronies…and then
- their constituents (the voting public who finance their lifestyle)

Of course, they are not <u>ALL</u> viscerally corrupt but there are not enough of them with any backbone…and as a consequence even those that do have a little moral fortitude…are guilty by association of non-denunciation of the corruption and the incompetence that surrounds them, preferring instead to stand by and do nothing in order to protect their places on the gravy-train.

—————

Author's comment;

I have to say that I abhor the sheer gutlessness of many of our politicians who just sit on the fence protecting their pensions. They are cowards; they have no interest in guiding the country and its people towards a better future, their only interest is in filling their own pockets as quickly as they can with as much hard-earned taxpayer money as possible.

Individual MP's mentality and character –

Having witnessed the Waco siege against David Koresh and his followers, US comedian **Bill Hicks** said that all politicians and all governments are liars and murderers; I wouldn't go that far but I do believe that political office;

- corrupts,
- engenders egocentricity,
- leads to mild megalomania and
- taps deep into the human psyche's underlying need to dominate.

Examples of all four of these pathologies have been clearly in evidence in British politics since I began researching this book and through that research I have discovered a similar enmity for the current crop of politicians as that of Bill Hicks.

Hatred is too strong a word because I realise that politicians are only human, but strangled frustration almost sums it up; to see what they have done, how they have destroyed this country, dismantling it piece by piece and offering it on a plate to the grey suits in Brussels while filling their pockets with as much taxpayer money as possible is almost unpalatable.

Hand in hand, the politicians and the bankers have led this country down the road to ruin and economic disaster... and that frustrates me... but more than that, I am saddened at the way that these people have brought the mother of all Parliaments into disrepute...because instead of upholding the traditions and the reputation of the institution built up by their predecessors over centuries, the current crop of politicians have inexorably lowered its credibility almost beyond repair in the eyes of the British public – all through their own abject greed.

There is now a clear disconnect between the politicians and the people of this country and in barometric terms public opinion is at an all-time low.

Politicians should be beyond reproach, they should be role models, they should be shining examples of integrity and decency – not of greed and hypocrisy…and yet they are now held in lower esteem by the British public than the money-grabbing bankers and lawyers.

They have destroyed our trust and our faith…in them personally… and more significantly they have destroyed the integrity of the political office they hold.

They have brought the House of Commons into disrepute…and fundamental principles of decency, morality, humility and self-discipline have all been devalued by this bunch of greedy, self-serving egotists.

Politicians have always been driven by power, vanity and greed but the current generation has taken it to the next level with their parsimonious avarice.

In fact, the politicians in this country are now considered the high priests of hypocrisy, corruption, lies and spin.

That is the reputation that they have forged for themselves over the last thirty years and it is all self-inflicted.

The British people deserve better from their elected representatives.

———

For information;

Quotes from former MP Gyles Brandreth; this is typical advice handed down from the old-guard to new MP's arriving in Westminster;

- on the great national issues, take the moral high ground
- on local issues, keep your head down
- and on planning issues, don't touch anything

...more proof if needed of the endemic culture of self-preservation amongst politicians who spend more time scheming not to lose the privileges of their position than they do resolving the issues for which they have been elected.

Truth in politics –

Instead of an absolute, politicians view the Truth as just another concept, comprising a number of layers, each of which can be manipulated and twisted to any number of degrees until it fits the purpose they have mind.

For politicians truth is relative; they see it in terms of varying shades of grey depending on their party's position…and therefore the reality is that Truth, the real truth has no place in politics.

Now it is a given that politicians have always been economical with the truth when addressing the public;

- indeed, when asked a question; you can literally see them calculating, you can see the cogs in their minds cranking slowly into position as they try to gain as much time as possible before spouting the pre-endorsed party spin they have been told to apply to any given answer…or
- they cover-up their failings with smokescreens and mirrors
  - o   using duplicitous vocabulary and clever political rhetoric…or
  - o   they quote imaginary government stats that nobody can verify

…and then, when they do get caught out, they shamefully exploit the tactics of damage-limitation and fake contrition putting on performances worthy of the silver-screen.

Author's comment;

I just cannot understand how politicians can stand up in Westminster or in front of the media and deny something that reality clearly proves is untrue.

For example; during the New Labour years, successive Home Secretaries stood up in Westminster and denied that New Labour had an open-door policy towards immigration when everybody in the country could see their numbers increasing and their communities transforming.

(*Several New Labour MPs have since admitted that this was indeed the case, thereby confirming that the original party-line was mendacious*)

And in the same way I cannot fathom how politicians can stand up in Westminster or in front of the Press and tell bare-faced lies with a straight face, producing fictitious statistics to back them up when they don't even believe what they are saying themselves - *because they know it is not the truth* – and yet they expect the British public to swallow whole what they are saying without question.

What an insult to our intelligence!

Where is the respect for our democracy when politicians can stand up in the House of Commons, the seat of our democracy, and lie bare-faced to the country?

As for **the Speaker of the House** – we have gone from the corrupt and hopelessly out of touch - Michael Martin - whose attempts to thwart proper scrutiny and transparency of MP's allowances and expenses was a disgrace...to the pompously ridiculous and profligate John Bercow and his attention-seeking wife Sally.

Why can't we find somebody in this country who really stands for our values?

I once heard that **Politics** is not about the truth – it's about getting things done…and that **Democracy** only worked well when you have greed and corruption to finance it; what a sad state of affairs!

———

Meanwhile, political TV dramas such as;

- House of Cards,
- Party Animals
- Spitting Image,
- The New Statesman,
- The Thick of it…and
- Yes Minister / Prime Minister

…although fictional and in no way biographical – clearly illustrate the inherent lack of morality, the betrayal and the underhand conniving of typical self-indulgent politicians and their lackeys in the underbelly of the corridors of power.

It might be caricatured satire but I believe that these scripted dramas hit the nail on the head every time.

———

**Adjectives used in a number of recent
surveys to describe politicians –**

Abysmal
Aloof
Always believe they know best
Blinkered
Breathtakingly arrogant
Calculating
Can't be trusted
Complacent
Conceited
Condescending

Conniving
Corrupt
Crooks
Cynical
Deceitful
Devious
Disconnected / out of touch
Disgusting
Dishonest
Disingenuous
Disloyal
Don't listen
Egocentric
Egotistic
Full of hollow pledges
Full of s… / waffle
Grasping, Greedy
Hypocritical
Immoral
Inaccurate
Incompetent
Insincere
Intellectually barren
Irresponsible
Leeches feeding off the public purse
Malevolent
Manipulative
Manoeuvring
Middle-class
Misleading
Morally challenged bullies who simply crave control of the masses
Myopic – short-sighted poodles
Narrow-minded / parochial
Never answer a question directly (yes or no)
Obstinate
Often have glaring double standards
Pedantic and pretentious
People don't believe a word they say

People feel anger and alienation
Perfidious
Professional liars
Profligate
Publicity-mad parasites
Scaremongering (control tactic)
Scheming
Selfish / self-indulgent
Self-serving / in it for what they can get
Singularly ineffective
Unprincipled
Unscrupulous
Untrustworthy
Untruthful
Useless
Vain
Waste of space
Weak, while also being hollow and gutless

————

**Ten qualities thought to be lacking in our politicians
from those same surveys;**

Compassion
Dignity
Forthrightness
Honesty
Honour
Humility
Integrity
Morality
Sincerity…and
Truthfulness

The consensus among the public / voters is clear;

there is no TRUST; there is no CONNECTION

We need to reverse that state of affairs

Elections –

Author's comment;

For any leader to be legitimate he or she has to be democratically elected…and just like the position of PM, all cabinet members should be elected representatives too; we must never again be put in a situation where people like Gordon Brown, Alastair Campbell and Peter Mandelson are able to run the country without a single official mandate between them.

The campaign trail;

If there is one thing that I abhor – hypocrisy aside – it is the glaring dishonesty peddled by politicians today…and the self-serving arrogance with which they deliver their patronising election speeches filled with promises that they know they will never keep.

We all know that 'cast-iron, rock-solid, carved in marble' promises from politicians are as worthless as the expelled air used to formulate them.

Politicians make promises; it's just what they do. They offer short-term fleeting commitments while the focus is on them…or when an election is on the horizon…but once the cameras are switched off and the votes have been counted nothing substantial or tangible ever comes about.

This is 21st Century politics and in this age of 24 hour rolling news, it all about managing the present; a circumstance which has inevitably led to sound-byte journalism…and by-extension sound-byte politics.

- If only the politicians realised that the public aren't interested in cosy patronising sound-bytes,
- if only they could understand that people want real policies… with real substance and not just naked political ambition wrapped up in frothy candyfloss.

…and then of course we have the typical electioneering behaviour;

- the stage-managed rush to marginal seats in the hope of swaying the electors
- the hypocritical handshakes
- the photo-ops holding babies and children or
- posing with a hoodie, a baby sea-lion or an actual working person wearing a hard-hat.

Who do these campaign managers and spin-doctors think they are dealing with?

Do they not realise that the public see right through their cynical PR stunts and just laugh ironically at their pathetic and often desperate attempts to appear 'normal'?

…and do politicians really believe that we swallow their silly and somewhat, disingenuous PR spin…?

If they do, if they are naïve enough or gullible enough to believe that we don't see them for who they really are…then what does that say about the intellectual quotient of the person hoping to represent us…?

The voting public are not stupid, they can see right through these blatant, contrived antics.

My view is that a party's policies should be able to stand on their own merits without the need for any spin or ridiculous PR stunts…and if they don't do that, then the electors will decide on polling day.

My favourite definition of the word 'Spin' in a political context;

> *'A thick layer of malicious intent*
> *masquerading as respectability*
> *under a very thin coat of veneer'*

For information;

New Labour spent £1 billion a year on spin, but the Conservative/ Liberal Democrat coalition is still spending £93 million a year on the same rubbish and wasting at least £13.5million of that, despite warnings that such wastefulness is indefensible.

…and finally, when these people do get elected into office;

- having toured the country making empty promises and trying to pull the wool over our eyes…and
- having posed for countless selfies with the 'great unwashed', shaken their hands and grudgingly held their babies

…the first thing they do is abuse that privilege by taking care of themselves, their families and their cronies, while instantly forgetting or ignoring the wishes of those who put them there in the first place.

What hope is there for democracy when MP's pledge one thing on the soap-box to get elected – and then do the exact opposite once the voters have given them their trust?

If all the above is true – I think it is a sad reflection of our society and our democracy that we are forced through our electoral obligation, to vote in this twisted dichotomy where politicians run for office with campaigns full of lies and promises that they know they will never keep…and then do exactly the opposite when they reach Westminster.

———

Conclusion;

I have had enough;

- enough of self-serving politicians with no personal morality or integrity deciding the parameters of my future
- enough of egotistical, grand-standing politicians and pious moralising liberals
- enough of their theatrical, partisan speeches full of posturing and fist-pumping, delivered with as much belief and integrity as Pinocchio
- enough of lame speeches full of political rhetoric based on hypocritical spin and throwaway electoral promises that will never be kept
- enough of politicians constantly spouting inaccurate and misleading statistics; they all know that figures are not always instantly verifiable and use them as excuses to waffle on and not give straight answers
- enough of the lies and the mendacious hyperbole
- enough of politicians telling the people what they think the people want to hear without ever having any intention of following through on it, simply as a vote-collecting exercise for those still naïve enough to believe that politicians have anybody's best interests at heart other than their own. It is just pure demagoguery…and
- enough of populist bluster; we need concrete action with proof

———

Author's comment;

Political posturing and partisanship is pointless if there is no end-product.

Unless you are actually going to deliver, what's the point?

Let's ditch the spin, the hypocrisy, the skulduggery and the political hyperbole and instead install a new integrity to the political process.

IT IS TIME to modernise; IT IS TIME for change.

For information;

The PDC would introduce a mandatory fixed term for elections of four-yearly cycles and we would move the vote from Thursday to Sunday to improve turnout and avoid the disruption of closing down schools etc in order to turn them into voting / polling stations.

The new era of responsibility that we would hope to usher in would eradicate the excuse that we cannot hold elections on a Sunday because of 'Saturday-night hangovers'.

Money Matters -

Expenses; lest we forget their deception

It's an issue that was exhausted by the media for months on end but for posterity's sake and so that the politicians never forget - and so that the British public doesn't forget either - I have to mention the expenses scandal at this point.

During the expenses scandal many MP's claimed that they had made mistakes in their claims. How strange then, that every mistake they made was always in their favour – <u>nobody</u> ever claimed less; not once; it was <u>always</u> more; surely the law of averages would have suggested at least one had been underpaid if they were all being 'honest' and that was really the case.

Michael Martin, the Speaker of the House at the time has been described since as the worst Speaker ever, and because of his pivotal role in the scandal he was the first Speaker in office to be forced to resign for hundreds of years, losing his reputation and all the respect he had once enjoyed.

However, Michael Martin was just the shield, the man-hole cover trying to keep a lid on the bubbling corruption going on beneath him… and hiding behind his office motto 'duty of care', he tried desperately to prevent that corruption - and by extension the MP's - from being exposed to the light of day…and much to their joint shame all the lying, cheating, money-grabbing MP's gladly hid behind him.

Nevertheless, Michael Martin's reluctance to reveal the truth and his attempts to exempt MPs from scrutiny by introducing a non-disclosure clause to the proceedings clearly showed that a cover up was indeed being attempted.

Author's comment;

How downright deceitful it was of our politicians - led by the Speaker - to try to head off the Freedom of Information Act by introducing a non-disclosure / exemption clause into the proceedings which would prevent the law from being applied to them – so that they could hide their greed and incompetence.

How dare they try to acquire immunity from the law by which the rest of us must abide.

That was quite simply criminal and for it to be taking place at the seat of our democracy was patently outrageous.

These people are supposed to be our leaders, the most intelligent and most morally upstanding amongst us. However did they believe that it would be against the public interest for us to find out what they were spending our money on?

They must have been blinded by their own greed.

It shows a complete lack of integrity and the redacted versions of their accounts that were ultimately published were quite simply two fingers up to the British public.

Why am I not surprised then, that they decided not to charge Derek Conway MP for his outrageous accounting, preferring instead to destroy any evidence of his activity.

In fact, not only did they destroy Derek Conway's records, they destroyed all the records relating to their expenses for the previous ten years… once this first case had come to light…in an effort to protect themselves which to me suggests wholesale corruption.

Now, a normal citizen would be arrested for engaging in any of the above, but somehow, inexplicably fraud and deception are considered a normal part of the political process by MPs; that is wrong and this state of affairs will have to be addressed.

How I really feel about the politicians' expenses scandal;

I believe that ███ █████ █ █████ █ ██ █ ████ ████ █████ clearly █████ █ ███ ██████

no shame ██ ███████ ███ ███ ████ dishonest and immoral ███ █████ ██ █████

█████ right ███ ████ ████ allowed ███ █████ ██ ██████ █████ impunity ███ █████

unrepentant ▮▮▮▮ ▮▮▮▮▮▮▮...but I'm sure that there are a few good apples among them somewhere...

———

I have – by proxy - conferred upon our wonderful politicians their own signature tune...with a nod of course to the bankers; it is

'Everything Counts' by Dépêche Mode

(People of Britain; take a listen; this song sums up our politicians in a nutshell)

———

Now we all know about the duck-houses, the moat cleaning, the reclaimed mortgage payments…and all the other abuses revealed during the expenses scandal but here is a list of some of the more petty claims made by our rapacious MPs to show what kind of people we are dealing with;

(I have the names of these people but they are not pertinent in making the point)

5p	for a paper clip
7p	for a bulldog clip
8p	for a page marker
10p	for some drawing pins
17p	for a pack of staples
18p	for a mouse-mat
19p	for some Blu-Tac
20p	for parking
29p	for a packet of Hula-hoops
30p	for a doughnut
35p	for a ballpoint pen
41p	for a folder
46p	for some Post-it notes
49p	for a door-mat

64p   for a glue-stick
69p   for a dustpan
70p   for a stamp…etc…etc…

…they even claim for the milk they put in their tea.

How petty can these penny-pinching politicians be…?

Is that the kind of person we want representing us, leading our country; someone who is so petty he or she charges the taxpayer for every single drop of milk that goes into their tea? Where's the pride, where's the dignity, where's the statesmanship?

———

Expenses solutions -

Author's comment;

Politicians used to get elected in order to effect change…but these days they only seem interested in cementing their place in the history books (legacy) and salting away – by whatever means possible – enough money to cover their lavish expenses and fund their post-political retirements.

———

MPs, when they are elected, are supposed to show openness, honesty and integrity as laid down in the Code of Conduct but the current generation has clearly shown that it is not fit for purpose; they have played with… and lost…the people's trust, and while I do not believe that their personal addresses should be published for obvious security reasons, I do believe that their expense accounts should be published in their entirety as a means of providing transparency in how they handle and spend public funds.

This might seem a little extreme, but I believe that any refusal by our politicians to comply with this proposal would simply increase the public's already deep mistrust of them.

————

Greed and corruption – whether passive or active – are part of the human condition and we will never be able to curtail or separate these failings because of who we are, nor will we ever be able to eradicate people's selfish desires to further their own ambitions when in positions of influence.

However, we should nevertheless remain lucid and try our best to keep any abuse to a minimum by implementing regular checks - in order to weed out the bad seed - while at the same time demanding a maximum of transparency in all matters from the rest.

Politicians need to be held accountable for the way they spend taxpayers' money, just like the bankers should have been.

————

Now, despite being guilty of outright criminality during the expenses scandal some shameless MPs have nevertheless managed to cling onto their seats on the gravy-train and continue to draw parliamentary salaries and allowances.

Those people, under the PDC, would be 'quietly' notified of their moral obligation not to stand for re-election.

————

Going forward, we need to review and reform – if necessary – all the different entitlements and privileges that our politicians currently enjoy. In fact the whole workings of Parliament needs reform - top to bottom – in order to root out the corruption and the institutionalised abuse of public money that has built up there over the centuries.

We need to clear out the current crop of corrupt, self-serving thieves and tricksters…and we need to get rid of the old-guard – the generation for whom cronyism and nepotism are…and always have been…a way of life. It's not their fault; they are simply from a generation where that kind of arrangement was the convention but now…it is time…it is time to bring back the dignity, the honesty, the morality and all those other ethical qualities which used to symbolise our democracy and our reputation around the world.

―――

However, if the system remains the same…rather than adopting the 3+1 ER salary and expenses package that the PDC would put forward (see 'salary') we would nevertheless;

- impose a minimum claim of £25 (below that threshold MPs should be able to pay out of their own (deep) pockets)
- insist that no expenses over £50 should be paid in cash – although receipts would still be required as proof
- cut out second home allowances to those receiving 'grace and favours' homes (nobody should benefit twice)
- put an end to this free-spending, this cavalier attitude with public money being used to fund useless enterprise and free trips abroad for the boys – or imaginary jobs for close friends and family members…and we would
- put an end to ministers and politicians finding loopholes in the system to run two or three houses and receive grants from public funds in order to do so.

―――

Transparency;

After the MP's extraordinary and imaginative use of expenses during the scandal of 2009, during which they plundered the public purse for all they could get…any new government must commit to transparency and honesty on money-related issues and the Green Book (guide to Members Allowances) should be re-written or updated to reflect these changes.

At last, thanks to the Freedom of Information Act the country is going to be able to hold these contemptible rogues and the establishment they represent to account.

All those undeclared privileges that have been shrouded in secrecy for centuries, all those unspoken perks that politicians believed we, the public, didn't need to be informed about will now be aired in the open and held up to public scrutiny, just as it should be.

Hopefully we are going to see an end to the era of smug MP's with their arrogant sense of entitlement and their casual disregard for accountability; an end to the old-boys clubs where taxpayers' money was handed out on a nod and a wink to finance second home refurbishments and jollies abroad.

However, let there be no doubt; we, the people, will have to remain vigilant at all times because the politicians clearly haven't learned their lesson as the recent Maria Miller case plainly demonstrated. That arrogance and that superiority complex is still there and it will not change until the old-guard is retired and a new generation of younger politicians with a new set of values…and untainted by scandal…takes their place.

Transparency solution;

For many politicians, life in Westminster…and being an elected representative…is just a vast, subsidised ego trip; a chance to indulge themselves with impunity at the taxpayers' expense.

Well, that has to change; we need to roll the whole process flat and start again.

Firstly, the PDC would introduce an election pledge (**Transparency Charter**) that all political hopefuls who run for office would have to sign before taking up their seat in the new Parliament.

This would be an oath of truth, honesty and integrity in everything that they do and say – and it would be signed by the politicians in the full knowledge that if they ever breached the charter…or failed to uphold it in any way…their position would be revoked immediately and definitively without appeal – serious cases leading to up to 5 years in prison, no privileges, no early release and a life-time ban from public service.

Then, going forward, in order to regain the confidence and the trust that they once enjoyed…but so selfishly abused…MPs will have to address every issue with an unparalleled level of transparency, because anything less will leave them open to criticism and suspicion of corruption by the British people.

Now this might seem draconian…but sadly our politicians brought this on themselves.

———

Salary;

Author's comment;

Being an MP is not all about getting rich on the back of the taxpayer; it is about serving the people…so anybody whose first motivation is greed should look for another career.

———

Now, since their expense accounts were reined-in our MPs are finding £65,000 a year, a little tight…and I tend to agree with them.

Therefore, under the PDC, MPs would receive £100,000 per annum as their stipend.

This would comprise 3 x the ER Ratio for their personal expenditure (salary) on which they would pay tax like any other citizen…and another ER Unit for their expenses…which would have to be accounted for with verifiable receipts (VAT paid).

The amount they spend on actual expenses – open to public scrutiny - would then clearly reveal how much they were committed to the role and how much they kept back for themselves.

People might disagree with me, but this new concept would not be a reward for the current generation of MPs; it would - on the contrary - be an encouragement to the next generation of young people to get involved in politics whatever their background.

This system would be based on the Scandinavian system;

- where politicians are held to account for every expense they charge to the taxpayer
- where they have to declare every item in their patrimony…and
- where the Freedom of Information Act allows any member of the public to check on any of these issues with a simple request.

That is transparency and that is why the Scandinavian countries (Finland (1), Denmark (1), Sweden (4) and Norway (7)) fill the top slots on the Corruption Perception Index - which lists countries in order of transparency - while the UK is listed at No.17

———

Cabinet Ministers and Chairs such as the Speaker of the House would receive an additional and mutually identical benefit to recognise their extra responsibility while the PM would receive 4 X the Unit Ratio Figure plus 2 Units for expenses and an additional Unit on being elected to help settle into No.10.

I believe that, as leader of the country the Prime Minister should be the highest paid member of our political class…and as a consequence local councils would have to adjust and cut their cloth accordingly.

———

The ER Ratio / Unit Base figure of £25,000 which is an average wage, not a minimum wage would be tied to inflation (index-linked) in order to avoid the regular and often outrageous salary-increase demands of MPs that so exasperate the British public.

A similar pay-structure would be applied to all public service sectors, the difference from one Base Unit to the next allowing for the incremental recognition of hierarchy, promotion and advancement.

However, if any politician felt that these arrangements were not sufficiently rewarding for them to finance their multi-million pound homes, we would simply remind them that there is no obligation for them to stand for re-election.

The PDC would much prefer to have people who have the interests of the country and its citizens at heart running the country, rather than a bunch of smug, self-serving narcissists whose only motivation is to line their own pockets.

Note;

The gravy train has to be forced into retirement but reforming MP's pay and expenses has to be done by an independent body…because allowing the MP's to do it themselves would be like leaving the lunatics in charge of the asylum or like leaving the bank robbers in charge of the bank; they are not going to spite themselves or deprive themselves of anything they can get their grasping hands on.

The bankers are the same; they need to be threatened with sanctions and dismissal without parachutes because without the threat of sanction the human being simply doesn't learn; it is an anthropological certainty.

Additional allowances -

The PDC would make one concession.

We would introduce a 'London Allowance' to help with the exceptional cost of housing in London for those living within the M25 ring-road...

...and similarly we would introduce a travel allowance for those living outside the M25, for trips to and from Westminster...so as to be fair to all.

However, there would be;

- no more associated expenditure for home bills,
- no more claiming for parking charges, road tolls or congestion charges...and
- no more claiming for food (people earning far less manage to eat; why can't politicians?)

Meanwhile, office and staff costs would be reviewed; as would winding-up costs...

...and resettlement grants would be restricted to three months' salary.

For information;

British taxpayers will have to pay more towards MPs pensions in future after plans to make the MPs contribute more themselves were quietly dropped...

...are they being sly and self-serving again?

Naturally these new measures as well as all other pension 'arrangements' would be reviewed by the PDC as a matter of course.

Idea;

MPs do not need sumptuous five-star accommodation while they are in London attending Parliament. (*A privilege they abused so blatantly during the expenses scandal*).

Now, this might come as a shock to our entitled elite…but as I believe that it is now time to consign hereditary privilege and the monarchy to the past - once the reign of the present Queen has come to an end – would it not be a good idea to simply revamp Buckingham Palace - which has 775 rooms - and transform it into the requisite number of small studios for our politicians so that they might each have a 'pied-a-terre' while in London.

Buckingham Palace is after all the property of the state and it would be the perfect use for a building which has never really been used to its full potential.

Not only would it offer easy access to Parliament; it would also be easy to protect as far as security is concerned and because it would be in constant use, regular maintenance work could be carried out - and justified as an ongoing project - in order to protect our architectural heritage.

…or maybe we could renovate another landmark building in London and transform that into a hotel for our MPs…because frankly, any alternative would be better than the current arrangement of them billing the taxpayer for their overnight stays in luxury 5* hotels.

Of course; had we had more forethought we could even have accommodated them in the Olympic village once the 2012 Olympics had concluded…but sadly that ship has sailed…into the arms of Qatari investors?

The fact is; being an MP is a <u>temporary</u> job and therefore politicians do not need <u>permanent</u> second homes in London…and more importantly, the British taxpayer should not be subsidizing such lavish expenditure.

Other Westminster Issues;

Politics is a necessary evil but I believe that any future Government should re-assess and re-appraise its priorities.

We need a re-awakening of morality in this country – a return to the values on which it was founded…and to begin with…this section of British Law should be printed on the first page of the Member's Handbook(Green Book)which deals with MPs allowances and expenses.

The Fraud Act 2006 –

Section 2; Fraud by false representation

(3) A person is in breach of this section if he (a) dishonestly makes a false representation and (b) intends by making the representation to make a gain for himself or another
(4) A representation is false if (a) it is untrue or misleading and (b) the person making it knows that it is, or might be, untrue or misleading.

A person who is guilty of fraud is liable - (a) on a summary conviction, to imprisonment for a term not exceeding 12 months or to a fine not exceeding the statutory minimum (or to both); (b) on conviction on indictment, to imprisonment for a term not exceeding ten years or to a fine (or to both)

Budgets –

MPs must be held responsible for their budgets. No more blame-shifting, no more letting the Civil Service take care of it without some kind of oversight.

Under the PDC ministers would be made responsible for the actions of civil-servants who - while remaining impartial - are still under their orders and using their budgets; enough passing the buck when the time comes to take responsibility.

––––––

E-petitions –

Embarrassed by the success of e-petitions the MPs now want to re-visit the idea by increasing the number of signatures needed to launch a debate in Westminster.

They need to tread very carefully here…because to do so would go against the wave of democratic change and transparency that the British electorate is now insisting upon after the expenses scandal.

MPs need to regain the public's trust and trying to head off public opinion by stifling free speech because it doesn't suit their purpose will not help them heal the rift.

The coalition is also debating whether or not to do another u-turn – this time by dropping plans to allow voters to sack MP's who have misbehaved.

Again the politicians need to be very careful here because their paper-thin integrity is still very fragile.

The possibility that the electorate would be able to get rid of corrupt representatives was a key promise after the expenses scandal and to shelve it would send out the wrong message to the public – that they STILL cannot believe an MP's promise.

Clearly, the politicians have their sights set on returning to the way it was…once the dust has settled after all the scandals…but the PDC would most definitely support a 'right of recall' bill so that the voters could sack their MP between elections if their conduct was considered unbecoming.

Lobbying –

The PDC would also introduce a lobbyist register to monitor who is lobbying who, what they are lobbying about and how much is being spent by those lobbyists trying to influence the political process.

This register would be monitored for a ten-year period and if anyone was found to be abusing the democratic process in any way, if there were any cases of corruption or fraud during that ten year period, then the idea would be scrapped and lobbying rules would be restricted more severely.

We cannot have outside interests influencing policy-makers and the political agenda inside the heart of our democracy.

Second jobs –

Politics is a full time job and therefore nobody in public office should take up a parallel position which invites the perception of latent corruption or creates a conflict of interest with that primary role.

Second jobs or consultancy arrangements with lobbyists which leave a grey area that is far too easy to exploit by anyone with an agenda… and have the potential for influence to be abused…will always invite suspicion from the public, and the knowledge that some MPs are earning up to 50 times more than their constituents from those jobs on the side will always rankle with them, creating friction and an atmosphere of mistrust that should be avoided at all costs in the current climate.

This ruling would test their priorities and their commitment to the cause.

Furthermore, the PDC would impose a cooling off period between political responsibility and a post within the same sphere of activity in order to prevent ex-politicians cashing in on insider knowledge gained while exercising a confidential role.

I would suggest a three year ban on them taking up a position with any company that they had had 'significant dealings with' during their time in office…and companies who flaunt this rule would be banned from bidding for government contracts.

Accountability –

I believe that we should introduce permanent accountability in politics – so that the decisions taken while in power remain prosecutable even after the politician has left office…if found to be unethical or corrupt. It would keep politicians more honest if they knew that their decisions would follow them to their graves.

After all, we think nothing of prosecuting our soldiers after the fact and we still persecute war criminals from decades past…so why not politicians – e.g.; Tony Blair, for taking us to war on a lie.

Cabinet positions –

As part of a PDC cabinet, a department would be created and a person - who would be held responsible - put in charge of Administrative Budget Control to make sure that taxpayers' money was not being wasted.

He or she would also be charged with looking into credit card-transactions and expenses.

This person would be a 'Sam the Sheepdog' style character from the Wile E Coyote cartoons; a nice, charming individual who remains calm and vigilant at all times, who sees everything…and when asked to intervene…acts like a pit-bull.

We would also nominate;

- A Minister for Innovation and Research
- A Secretary of State in charge of ex-military issues…and
- A Minister for Re-industrialisation

Funding –

Funding for Political Parties should be discussed openly to avoid a repeat of the Tony Blair 'cash for honours' fiasco…though a cap on donations would have to be introduced to avoid any over-reaching influence.

Women in the House of Commons –

There is already a crèche in the House of Commons but we need to do more to encourage women to partake in the political process.

We need to change the poisonous, testosterone-fuelled male obsession with conflict and war…and the best way to do this would be to increase the number of women in representative office. It might seem frivolous to some but I believe that it is vitally important for the future of this country – and for humanity in general - that we promote the idea of women in politics because they would offer a much more moderate stance on many of the important issues that currently preoccupy the masses around the world.

That said, I do not agree with imposed quotas or positive discrimination purely for positive discrimination's sake; I believe that merit should always prevail to avoid dissent and recrimination.

However, in order to affect some kind of change why couldn't we set a precedent by having a male / female combination for each ministry rather than just one person – who is usually male – running the department?

After all, women represent more than half of the population; their view should have equal air-time and their presence in the upper-echelons of government would offer an alternative perspective on most issues thereby tempering the long-standing, masculine dogmatism.

Each issue could then be discussed on its merits within the department and once a mutually-agreed consensus has been reached, one of the two representatives – perhaps alternately - could submit their ideas and their proposals to the cabinet…and a majority vote would then decide on policy.

I understand that this might sound a little complicated…and no doubt, this mechanism would be top-heavy in men taking the leading role initially – because of the dearth of front-line women in politics – but I am pretty sure that that state of affairs would evolve pretty quickly as women are just as capable as their male counterparts and they are fast-learners.

Nepotism –

Cronyism and nepotism - both of which rouse suspicion and mistrust - have to be consigned to the past.

Paul Flowers - aka 'The Crystal Methodist' - has freely admitted in public that he was appointed to the chair of the Co-operative bank solely because he had 'friends in high-places' and David Cameron, the current Prime Minister has made a number of vanity appointments during his time in office.

This kind of patronage – on a nod and a wink - is unacceptable in the public arena; it riles the citizens of this country…and as a consequence the PDC would address the problem of cronyism by tightening the controls on relatives working on a family-member MP's payroll.

825

We need to widen the gene-pool in our political community and not concentrate it into a small incestual elite.

––––––

Political Whitewashes –

The PDC would put an end to bureaucratic white-washes; all the inquiries that are set up with the express mission not to find the truth… but to find an excuse or a reason not to prosecute;

-   Jean-Charles de Menenes,
-   The Lords selling their favours,
-   Various MP's with their expenses…etc etc

How many official inquiries have been set up in recent years to try to establish the truth about immoral behaviour in key areas of public life – and how many have produced results?

Look at how the Hutton inquiry into the death of Dr David Kelly and the Chilcot inquiry into the war in Iraq have failed, because politicians, civil-servants and anybody else that might be held to account has intervened to avoid any scandal.

In fact, not only does the civil-service interfere, it refuses to let inquiries publish key documents and it insists that anybody who might be implicated in those inquiries must be warned in advance so that they can act accordingly – i.e. erase the evidence.

Where is the justice in that…?

––––––

Author's comment;

The hypocrisy that surrounds Westminster stinks…because while they cash-in through their memoirs after they retire, politicians do everything they can to stop the public finding out the truth while they are in office.

The word 'confidential' in Westminster has been modified to mean 'anything they don't want the public to find out about'. It's all about the political elite protecting their own interests.

Now, of course I understand that when our national security is at risk some things must remain private, but it is a fundamental principle of democracy that the public must be informed about matters like those above for the sake of openness and accountability and transparency.

The public must realise that huge principles are at stake here because a political class that does all it can to protect itself from public scrutiny is not just a danger to itself; it is a danger to the country as a whole if… by its actions…it manages to escape accountability while constantly committing mistakes both here and abroad.

Sanction –

Under the PDC, the Parliamentary Commissioner for Standards – in charge of policing the MP's Code of Conduct - would report directly to the Cabinet, thereby eliminating the toothless Standards and Privileges Committee currently occupied by the old-boys-club, and a decision on any case brought before them would be taken by the Cabinet as a whole.

This measure would be introduced because the current crop of British politicians knows no shame;

- MPs who have lied to the House of Commons still sit there, some in very senior positions
- Others who have deceitfully fiddled their expenses still draw parliamentary salaries…and
- Peers of the Realm, who have been imprisoned for fraud blithely return to the House of Lords upon their release from jail

As I said, they know no shame.

———

Under the PDC;

-   any politician who misbehaved or who was caught up in a scandal …and <u>convicted</u>…would be banned from public office for life…and
-   any public figure who abused the system would be sanctioned severely…and that punishment would be exemplary and non-negotiable…and finally
-   when people in public office are sacked, as in the rest of industry, their pay-out must reflect the job they have done…and the results they have achieved; we should not be rewarding failure with massive redundancy packages and therefore a pre-emptive clause would be inserted into future contracts enabling this to happen.

———

Tax –

The PDC would maintain the 'ban on voting' for MPs and peers who do not pay tax in this country…until this anomaly had been corrected.

———

Conduct –

And while the wind of change is blowing I believe that we should also introduce new rules to govern MPs behaviour in the House of Commons chamber.

I'm sure that I am not alone in…

-   being constantly irritated by the sight of our party leaders at the dispatch box trying desperately to outdo each other…like two overgrown schoolboys…and

- being equally chagrined by the indecorous, school-boyish behaviour of those on the back-benches; the jeering, the tantrums, the heckling and the pounding on desks etc.

It all lacks the dignity with which such proceedings should be conducted…and completely dishonours the institution of democracy.

These are grown men, not schoolboys; it is time for them to grow up.

Let's get rid of the image of squabbling schoolboys and show…

- some reserve,
- some restraint,
- some respect and
- some self-control during the debates

No more hectoring, no more mud-slinging, no more quibbling like schoolchildren and no more petty, party-political point-scoring across the floor out of personal bigotry and resentment.

This is the seat of our democracy; a little decorum…PLEASE!

Other minor issues to be addressed;

- Politicians are inherently preoccupied with status, legacy and posterity. They love their titles and the status that goes with them within their inner circles but during the expenses scandal, where were the honourable and right-honourable men and women; where were the people with integrity, the people above suspicion? We need to do away with these pompous titles of 'honourable and right-honourable' because never was a group of people so undeserving of such deference – and going one step further, it might be tradition, it might have gone on for centuries but I believe that it is time to put an end to all the other pretentious titles too. The People are no longer interested in Sirs, Lords and Ladies, Barons, Baronets, Princes and Princesses... and it is also time to get rid of all the costly pomp and ceremony / pageantry that surrounds Westminster; the wigs, the stockings and the medieval robes etc. I understand tradition but this is the 21st century. Do we really want our official representatives looking like caricatures from a place time forgot?

- The PDC would also retire the Honours list; the people have had enough of cronyism. We would replace the Honours List with a new People's Champion award to recognise the efforts of real people without any political bias or entitlement

- We would also ban mobile phones and tablets during parliamentary discussions. Politicians are in the chamber to debate policy and not to e-mail or twitter. The British public would like to see them paying a little more attention to the matters in hand and not texting, twittering, snoozing or more worrying taking their orders directly from influences outside the chamber. BTW; Politicians have decided that 'tweeting' should be allowed during parliamentary debate and yet they continue to ban it in the public galleries; so much for equality then!

- The PDC would also look into reducing the number of MPs – 646MP's and almost 1000 unelected Lords is way too many and weighs far too heavy on the public purse

- The PDC would also stop squandering tax-payers money with hand-outs to B-list royals...and review the excessive costs of security and protection details; it is time for a new, modern society

- **Pets** - The PDC would introduce a ban on bringing pets to work in official government buildings – a professional environment is no place for pets and the distraction they bring

———

...and finally, for the un-initiated, here are a few definitions from the politicians' private dictionary to explain how life in Westminster works;

———

- **Bribery**;

In political and diplomatic circles, the word **bribery** is replaced by the altogether more palatable term of 'offering incentives' and **abusing the system for personal gain** is called 'enjoying the perks and advantages of life in office'.

- **Confidential**;

This is anything the politicians don't want the public to find out about.

- **Diplomacy and Political Correctness**;

Everybody knows that politicians never answer a question directly and are often very economical with the truth. They do this by using a method of speech perfected down the ages by their peers whereby they are able to skirt around the truth **diplomatically** with a great deal of **political correctness** while ceaselessly avoiding telling us what we really want to know; i.e., the truth. These concepts are all smoke and mirrors – a way of psychologically getting the better of someone by conveying a thought however unpleasant or offensive through the use of pretentious vocabulary rather than through a direct, honest exchange; it is just hypocrisy in another form - a means of lying without losing face.

- **Morality**;

In and around Westminster morality is measured or equates to 'not getting caught', whatever the context.

- **Spin and Political Rhetoric;**

Spin, a concept so prized by Tony Blair and New Labour is no more than a deliberate attempt to distort the truth; **spin-doctors** are no more than professional liars paid to twist the truth with political rhetoric - hiding behind the sick dogma of political correctness and other no-go areas which are currently afflicting our society - to avoid telling the public how it is. Alistair Campbell and Peter Mandelson were masters of this dark art; Mandelson often following the Goebbels principle that…'if a lie is big enough and is repeated often enough then people would come to believe it'.

Conclusion –

It is a sad indictment of our society that most of our political institutions are mired in corruption and injustice; everybody knows this is the case, but everybody also knows that while they are not perfect, these institutions are a necessary evil in the unstable fabric of our society.

Now, in order to restore the public's and more importantly the voters faith in them, all the politicians have to do going forward… is to actually follow through on their promises for once; give the people the right to choose their own destiny instead of imposing it on them and stop treating them like children incapable of making a rational decision for themselves.

Its time for real-world politics – not policies based on inconclusive and unattainable projections or potential growth in imaginary markets; previous governments over-extended their economies with these fantasy predictions and look where that left us.

Of course, forward planning has its place but we cannot live today on tomorrow's promise – the time for ill-considered risk is over...

Civil Service

The unofficial motto of the Civil Service;

'Bureaucracy is the art of making the possible, impossible'; **Javier Pascual Salcedo**

Overall, the Civil Service in Westminster does a sterling job oiling the wheels of government…but I believe that there are now far too many;

- pencil pushers, box tickers, jobsworths…and time-serving toadies

…haunting those hallowed corridors.

There are far too many parasites feeding off the Westminster flotsam; far too many risk-averse civil servants who tip-toe around issues just to keep their jobs – job security being their sole aim.

In fact, these days Westminster is literally over-run with overpaid civil servants, special advisors and self-important quango-representatives that do nothing but suck the life-blood out of this country…and while they have had a good run, I believe that the bloated bureaucracy of Whitehall with its endless red-tape and its unfathomable protocols is now in need of a new regime.

These people are masters of producing cynical smokescreens - and a tide of useless and irrelevant information - in order to distract and divert attention from the reality of a situation that might leave them vulnerable or call their positions into question.

They spend hours upon hours circulating mountains of irrelevant if not completely useless information to people who are not interested in the slightest in reading it…and sadly - influenced by the New Labour years - the Civil Service has now become so corrupt and partisan that the moral standards that reign in Whitehall are those of Blair, Brown and Mandelson which means that life is about what you can get away with and how you can make things look…rather than how they really are.

***

Comment;

Sir Jeremy Heywood - the Cabinet Secretary - recently admitted that lax standards in some quangos and government departments had meant that poor-performing officials had been allowed to remain unchallenged in their jobs for years. He also estimated that the performances of at least 10% of the 400,000 civil servants were below par.

***

I believe that the time has come to reform the anachronistic protocols that surround life in Westminster…and to shake up the bureaucratic inertia of the civil service which seems to prevent anything getting done anytime soon.

We need to put an end to any…and every… 'job-for-life scenario' in and around Westminster because 'job-for-life scenarios' breed complacency, apathy, contempt, and a tendency for corruption; just look at football which is run by an aging but resolutely immovable cartel of self-serving administrators anchored in the past.

Much like Westminster itself, the Civil Service needs to adapt to the modern world. There are far too many processes and far too many layers of bureaucracy to be considered, consulted or advised before anything gets done…which all slow down the decision-making process as each has a specific protocol to be observed.

It seems to me that the Civil service has created a whole labyrinth of bureaucracy simply to avoid getting anything done.

Now, these people will argue that they are hard-working and upstanding etc, etc…and no doubt some of them are…but the facts are there for all to see and the public perception of Whitehall is one of obstructive bureaucrats with hidden agenda simply milking the system.

The Civil Service should be more productive, more efficient and more value-for-money for the British taxpayer…and permanent secretaries should be unquestionably impartial and have the country's best interests at heart. They should not spend all their time protecting their own position or indeed those of the politicians they serve.

Staffing Numbers –

For information; the ranks of the Civil Service have swollen from 497 at its creation to 732,000 before Mrs Thatcher and 448,835 today.

The Labour Party tends to create non-jobs in the civil service - by their thousand - in order to sweeten the unemployment figures…and as a consequence, during their time in office the number of 'professional politicians' in Whitehall increased to 29000 costing the taxpayer £500 million a year which equates to the House of Commons chamber being filled 45 times over. How cynical is that?

In fact, during the Blair/Brown years more than 4000 civil servants were kept on the payroll – under the title of 'pre-surplus staff or redeployment pools' - even though they had no actual work to do - 3000 of them being tax inspectors. This is outrageous but this cynical manipulation aside, on a purely financial level, the £133 million cost of this underhand manoeuvring was…and is…simply scandalous.

New Labour spent £4 billion on consultants over a four-year period which equates to £1 billion a year to tell them how to do their jobs… and £340 million on press officers and special advisors increasing the Home Office staff from 19 to 157…and still they made a mess of it.

That said; I suppose somebody had to produce all the spin, the excuses… and the lies…sorry, the erroneous explanations.

Going forward –

- In recent years politicians have dumbed-down every area of British culture except their own, especially the one covering political rhetoric; their official gobbledygook dreamed up by the civil servants to bewilder the public is out of control. This must be rectified.
- We must change the rules that allow people of influence in Whitehall to negotiate lucrative contracts with large companies at taxpayers' expense and then take up a position on the same company's board. A cooling off period of three to five years should be introduced to replace the current three months
  o In one yearly-period 130 MOD officials quit the civil service to work in the defence industries; does anybody else smell a rat?
- We also need to enforce the Radcliffe rules which protect public servants from being embarrassed by employees who have recently left their service and prevent them from revealing sensitive information - butlers, PA's etc - I would suggest a cooling off period here too - of 10 to15 years after leaving office – before memoirs can be published.
- We also need to look into the 'leak-culture'; we need to look into how Damien Green, a Tory MP was arrested in his office in Parliament for leaking information that the Labour Party didn't want revealed.
- The PDC would proceed with independent reviews…and conduct speedy time and motion studies…for each sector of the Civil Service using structured guidelines that we will have put

in place…and any obstructive civil servants would be processed out of harm's way.

- We would also look at the number of civil servants working for the Trade Unions. We pay out over £92 million to civil servants working for the unions on top of the £21 million they receive in direct payments. This needs urgent review.
- The Civil Service 'jobs for the boys' culture means that only a fraction of Whitehall vacancies are ever advertised to the public. The Conservative/LibDem coalition promised to put an end to this 'closed shop' scandal more than three years ago but nothing has really changed which does nothing but perpetuate the idea of secrecy, of the public being kept at a distance from SW1

———

The PDC would remind the current administration of the four recommendations made by Sir Stafford Northcote and Charles Trevelyan in 1853 when recruiting Civil Servants;

1. Recruitment should be entirely on the basis of merit by open, competitive examinations
2. Entrants should have a good 'generalist' education and should be recruited to a unified Civil Service and not a specific department, to allow inter-departmental transfers.
3. Recruits should be placed into a hierarchical structure of classes and grades
4. Promotion would be on the basis of merit not on the grounds of 'preferment, patronage or purchase'.

———

Health –

As part of the employment process, the PDC would include a health check for potential candidates because - if recent figures are to be believed - Westminster seems to bring about…or exacerbate…health problems in civil servants.

The current average of five weeks off a year among civil servants - for sickness related reasons - is wholly unacceptable. We need people with a stronger constitution in Westminster who are dependable and reliable to avoid a breakdown in the smooth running of government.

The highly advantageous sick-pay benefits costing the taxpayer over £300 million a year would also be investigated and curtailed if found to be excessive.

———

Incompetence –

By common consent there has been a dramatic decline in the quality of senior officials in recent years and the incompetence that that has engendered is clear for all to see.

For example; an army of bungling bureaucrats whose job it is to administer public pensions didn't notice that public service pensions had been overpaid by £125 million.

They didn't notice either that they were overpaying civil servants to the tune of £1.5 million.

They were also responsible for axing 100 government officials who left with huge pay-offs only to be rehired at great expense to the British taxpayer.

Meanwhile, an IT system that should have <u>saved</u> £57 million in administration costs ended up costing the taxpayer another £81 million…while Whitehall has been paying £3,500 for computers that cost £250 on the High Street.

Can anybody explain to me why that is…other than because of incompetence or because it is not their money?

This catalogue of waste is endless…and this incompetence and this cavalier attitude with taxpayer's money cannot be allowed to continue. The procurement chain needs to be addressed as it does in the military.

The PDC would review this computerised payroll-system and remove incompetent staff forthwith.

Incompetence and poor performance must be considered 'sackable' offences.

Moreover, under the PDC, procurement would be centralised to take advantage of bulk buying / purchasing arrangements and each department would have to requisition new material from that centralised 'Administrative Budget Control office' which would then subtract that cost from the department's budget. Any excessive and repetitive requests for expensive new material would be flagged up and investigated thoroughly.

———

Author's comment on incompetence;

How can the person who made such a hash of the Border Agency – earning over £1 million while she was there – be promoted to run the Tax Office?

Why are these people who leave a catalogue of failure behind them rewarded with new posts?

The PDC would look into this as a matter of urgency.

———

Money Matters –

Salary –

While we want the best person for every job, economic realities must govern salary attribution; examples abound of people in the public sector earning mega-money without delivering value for that money.

For example; over 300 civil servants are paid more than the Prime Minister.

Do they really deserve to be earning more than the person running the country?

I highly doubt it.

The PDC would therefore review and revise all these salaries…and introduce a pyramid structure to the pay-roll based on responsibility… which would allow for more transparency and encourage aspiration.

Expenses –

We need to crack down on profligacy in all areas; so surely it is not unreasonable to cut-back on some of the outrageous expenses being incurred by the public sector; especially when police numbers are being cut, schools and hospitals are struggling to cope, and our transport system is failing.

Under the PDC there would be a curb on all government credit-cards and complete transparency would be demanded on all charges made; receipts would have to be produced…and checked as a matter of course…to ensure that any abuse was nipped in the bud.

Public servants racked up £1.15 billion on taxpayer-funded credit cards last year, a rise of £160 million despite David Cameron's pledge to cut spending on them.

This would have to be addressed and the PDC would also revise the second home allowance for civil-servants which currently stands at £50,000 a year. The country simply cannot afford these overly generous rewards.

Bonuses –

Recent bonuses to civil-servants show that the bonus-culture is still alive and kicking.

One civil servant took home £100,000 in bonuses over the last two years despite recent assurances from MPs that that would never happen again…and the list of bonuses that civil servants can pick up for just doing the job they are already being paid very handsomely to perform is seemingly endless.

For example, they received a £250 bonus last year… just for turning up for work…because it was snowing outside…and they managed – with great courage - to get to their desks.

WT…#$?...!!

Under the PDC performance related bonuses would be scrapped.

Why should we reward people for simply doing their job?

If these people are not happy with their situation, they are free to leave because somebody else would quickly take their place.

———

Pilfering -

The tendency in government offices to 'misappropriate' taxpayers' property is unacceptable…

During New Labour's time in office;

- 3000 computers were lost or stolen,
- 676 mobile phones were lost,
- 202 hard drives…and
- 195 memory sticks…simply disappeared.

…this without mentioning all the sensitive personal information that might have been lost together with the actual hardware itself.

The worst offenders were the MOD who lost 1044 lap-tops and 164 desk-tops...but the DWP were not far behind losing 828 desk-tops and 271 lap-tops (figures provided by Liberal Democrat Paul Holmes)

This woeful mismanagement of taxpayers' money is not acceptable and demonstrates a culture of 'carelessness' around Whitehall that cannot be tolerated; things go astray in all walks of life but this is negligence if not downright theft on a grand scale.

Quangos –

Successive governments have promised a bonfire of the quangos (quasi-autonomous non-governmental organisations) but as with the bonus issues and the expenses issues, these promises are just hot air, empty sound-bytes thrown out by cynical politicians to appease a disgruntled public.

There has been no such bonfire of the quangos; instead, many of them have simply been re-configured or re-named...because while 171 have indeed been abolished, 240 new ones have been created in recent years.

Author's comment;

When are politicians going to learn that there is no point in making promises if you do not follow through on them?

They promised to stop bonuses; bonuses are still being paid.

They promised to rein back on expenses; expenses are still being abused.

They promised to open-up the recruitment process for the civil service; it is still a closed-shop...and

They promised a bonfire of the quangos; there are now more quangos than ever;

What is the point of politicians if they never actually do anything… other than fill their boots and exploit the system…?

―――――

According to the Taxpayer's Alliance, there are now over 1152 quango organisations in the UK employing over 534,000 people and costing the country over £167 billion a year. (Figures from 2006)

Now I understand the concept of a quango but I have to question their relevance, their usefulness and their independence in some cases, especially as many of these quangos are run by Labour cronies put in place by Tony Blair and Gordon Brown as a 'reward for their loyalty'. In fact 77% of those appointed to these positions have an allegiance to the Labour Party.

It seems to me that all these consultations, inquiries and quangos just exist to keep incompetent MP's and bored civil servants in jobs at the taxpayers' expense…because the people nominated to these posts don't seem to have any particular intellectual qualities or guiding principles that make them the right candidates for these roles.

Their only motivation seems to be the salary, the perks that come with the job and how much the pension-scheme is worth; they are not interested in the mission itself, their only concern is what THEY can get in return. It's a boys-club concept based on political incest; you name me this time…and I'll name you next time so that we both get another slice of the pie.

The problem with quangos is that they pump money from the taxpayers' purse but there is no accountability in return.

―――――

The PDC Solution;

The tax-payer should not be subsidising the cosy lifestyles of these civil servants and therefore, under a PDC government, every Quango would be asked to present its mission statement and its results to an independent panel.

Careful consideration would be given to each and every operation…and then any project considered frivolous or surplus to requirements would be promptly wound-up.

For example - A police quango is spending £70 million on consultants while at the same time we are cutting front line services. Surely this money would be better spent on actual policing.

Waste especially would also be targeted;

- o the Environment agency for example squandered £13 million on expenses last year…while
- o Ofsted squandered £4 million on hotels and restaurants.

This careless and irresponsible waste of taxpayers' money has to stop.

In addition, the PDC would apply a no-doubling up rule to avoid the inherent abuse of recent years; ONE JOB; ONE SALARY would be our motto…because opening up the market and allowing more people to apply…and to have jobs in these quango organisations - as long as they are relevant - would not only widen the intellectual pool, it would also reduce the narrow and greedy 'jobs-for-the-boys' culture.

The new pay-scale that we would be putting in place would also apply to quangos.

We cannot have people working on these panels – with no responsibility and no accountability - earning more than the PM who is running the country.

That simply isn't logical.

At the moment, some of these people are earning over £1 million a year. That is not a public service salary in my book…and such rewards can only lead to abuse and corruption.

———

…and finally, the PDC would put in place an unbiased select-committee for dealing with appointments to quangos considered worthwhile and which serve a purpose.

They have had a good run but it is time to remove and replace all the leftist dinosaurs - installed by New Labour in key influential positions - who are clinging onto these posts - earning six-figure sums - without being objective or productive.

———

The House of Lords

The **House of Lords** has long been known as Britain's most comfortable retirement-home and it is time that that changed.

The most recent influx of cronies, which just took place, has taken the number of people sitting in this House to 836 which is more than the House of Commons (650) and more still than the EU (766) which oversees 500 million people.

In fact, this bloated chamber is now second only to the National People's Congress in communist China in the number of seats it comprises… but the Chinese Congress rules over 1.5 billion people…and the UK population numbers just 67 million.

How can that possibly be justified?

What's more; in a cynical move to sway the balance of power even further in his favour, David Cameron intends to appoint still more of his millionaire donor friends, cronies, lobbyists and schmoozers to this House in the next Honours List.

Well, I believe that it is time to put the sanctimonious political elite - with their out-dated sense of entitlement - out to grass.

Enough of the old-boys club…enough of the self-serving patronage.

It is time to retire all the bumbling old crones…and the numerous, insatiable leeches who have feasted on the public purse for decade after decade - expecting to have their indulgences as well as their homes paid for by the hard-working tax-payers of this country - and who don't take kindly to disadvantage or being called to account.

It is time to inform all those families with their mansions and their moats who - from generation to generation - have cannibalised the public purse, enjoying the myriad of inherited privileges handed down to them by their landed-gentry fore-fathers at the expense of the ordinary working-class citizen, that the gravy train has reached the end of the line.

Of course, there is still a need for a second chamber in a democracy… to temper extremist views or to restrain a government that gets carried away with its own importance…but it is time to sweep away;

- the hereditary pickpockets; crusty, musty and dusty
- those put in place as favours to friends…and
- those who have bought their way into the heart of our democracy

It is time to put an end to the sleaze-ridden generation put in place by Tony Blair and his cronies who sold their souls and bought their peerages.

It is time for the swindlers and the schemers to doff their top-hats and put away their canes for the last time.

The ruling class – as these men knew it – based on privilege for them and subjugation for everybody else is in its death throes; this is the 21st century and it is time to destroy the citadels of privilege that belong to a bygone age.

Author's comment;

I find it outrageous that a small number of <u>unelected</u> Lords (among them Lord Brittan and Lord and Baroness Kinnock) should be able to block any moves by the House of Lords as a whole that might entitle the British people to a referendum on Europe, just so that they can protect their EU pensions. This cannot be allowed to continue.

PDC Solution –

The House of Lords needs to be reformed and to do so we need to do away with inherited privilege in all its forms.

A healthy democracy requires a powerful second chamber in order to keep a check on the first chamber - in this case the House of Commons - especially as the House of Commons is increasingly packed with career politicians with no experience of life outside the Westminster bubble... and as a consequence I believe that this second chamber should be filled with people who do have some experience of life and who have made an exceptional contribution to the country and not just a load of old cronies there to milk the system as they have done for decades if not centuries.

The PDC would rename the second chamber 'The People's House' or 'the Chamber of Wisdom', but this House would not be restricted entirely to retired politicians...as to do so would allow parties and party whips to apply pressure to the chamber thereby influencing absolute democracy too directly.

Instead, we would introduce a council of intelligence and experience comprising individuals who have proved throughout their personal and professional lives to be upstanding citizens who represent the qualities necessary to be considered credible keepers of the country's destiny... and who would be prepared to uphold and defend those values in public office. These might well be retired politicians (though I am wary of old allegiances) but they would also be businessmen and women, professors, teachers and community leaders. In fact, anybody who had proved themselves to be a good person and who embodied the requisite qualities;

- Integrity
- Honesty
- Compassion
- Dignity
- Forthrightness
- Honour
- Sincerity...and
- Truth

This new chamber would be composed of the grey matter of the country that is not being used elsewhere - to avoid any conflict of interest - and those who sit on its seats would have the country's best interests at heart; they would respect its traditions, they would respect its heritage, they would respect the will of its people and they would not be there to fill their own pockets or to manifest their allegiance to a particular party.

Election process;

The people who would sit in this new House would need to be proposed by their fellow citizens…if they are a household name…or have their names put forward by the people in the community where they live.

They would not necessarily be ex-politicians or public figures, just people with intelligence, integrity and a moral compass who have proved themselves in one way or another within our society.

The goal would be an eclectic mix of people from all regions and all sections of society; from…

- business,
- commerce,
- science,
- the medical profession,
- academia,
- engineering
- journalism…and
- the legal profession…but also
- community leaders…and
- local representatives

…because…in our multicultural society…we need the wisest and the keenest minds from all areas in order to ensure equitable representation, although there would be no positive discrimination in candidacy.

The selection of these candidates would be conducted online - one vote per ISP address - and the first 300 people with most support - within a given time-frame - would accede to the new House.

Anybody proposed by a member of the public would be eligible... but this is not a popularity contest and every potential member would nevertheless have to be vetted by an independent panel to avoid any 'misunderstandings' at a later date. These are serious issues and the process and the integrity of the role must be respected.

NB; These elections do not need to be local or regional as these people will be representing the country as a whole.

Once selected, these people would be given a ten-year mandate which would include protocols for early and voluntary retirement...and for removal - even mid-term - or imprisonment if they were found to be transgressing the rules in any way.

It is not right that currently, a Lord cannot have his title revoked even when convicted of a serious offence (corruption or murder). Convicted criminals should not sit in judgement of the law-abiding.

This modern approach would put an end to the privilege of hereditary accession...and the removal of political partisanship would also mean that this new assembly would vote through what was good for the people - and the country as a whole - and not necessarily what the partisan politicians would want to impose on us.

Rules and Exceptions;

There would be no input or influence from Westminster on this matter and neither would there be any seats reserved specifically for religious representation.

We are constantly tying ourselves in knots in this country trying to play fair...but no other religion is represented in the current House of

Lords so why should the Church of England have an automatic seat in this new assembly?

Secondly, anybody with questionable morality or shaky integrity who had used the position he or she had achieved over the course of his or her career to influence or bend the rules / laws of the Land…would be excluded indefinitely from the new House. It would not be appropriate for somebody to sit in judgement of others, if it could be shown that that person's judgement had been flawed in previous circumstances.

And finally…the PDC would discard all the silly protocols; the wigs, the robes and the ridiculous medieval rituals, thereby bringing the new chamber into the 21st century.

Wales

(In four succinct points)

1) **Assembly**; there is now an elected house in Wales – but after the last elections, those that were elected weren't even capable of deciding…or agreeing…who should run the country…because of a split vote.

   In fact, it took those elected representatives several weeks of arguing and wrangling and negotiating to come up with a coalition arrangement…so I have to ask myself this; how much should we listen to these people and how much should we trust them with the public funds…when they can't even decide who should be in charge.

2) **Culture**; only 19% of the Welsh population speaks Welsh and yet those 19% impose their will on the other 81%. Is that reasonable?

   In this era of budgetary restraint…how profligate is it…to insist that all official paperwork be printed in both languages – Welsh and English – and that all road-signs be written in both languages…when 81% of the population doesn't have a clue what is written on the page or on the road-sign; all to appease a radical minority…? Where is the democracy in that…?

The majority of welsh people;

o   don't speak the language,
o   can't understand the language,
o   don't watch the welsh TV channel…or

> o   listen to the welsh radio station…and
>
> o   they can't read the road-signs

…so what really is the point? It's a complete waste of time and money; a pointless exercise in political posturing simply to satisfy a minority of militant radicals.

I understand the argument about heritage and culture but the Italians for example no longer speak Latin and their culture has survived into the 21st century; why shouldn't welsh culture survive in the modern world.

Languages and dialects have always evolved and died out; they have done for centuries…but humanity has always adapted and survived the upheaval…our cultures have always survived the change …so why does this fear of losing the welsh language have such purchase among the minority welsh population?

Again, I understand why they are clinging on; they are traditionalists who don't like change…but sadly…sometimes we simply have to let go of the past for the sake of the future. Unity comes from everybody pulling together for a common cause…and sharing the same language is part of building that unity.

———

3) **Society**; not so long ago there was a spate of hanging suicides among young people in Bridgend in South Wales. That was a horrendous situation and yet the response was to teach school-children how to write a suicide note and how to organise their own funerals. How wrong was that…?

———

…and finally;

4) **Sport**; Before an international rugby match in November 2006 at the Millennium Stadium, a small-minded WRU official made

a laughing stock of his country by antagonising the NZRU, resulting in a spat which forced the great All Blacks team to perform its world-famous pre-match 'Haka' in their changing rooms. This illustrates the lack of worldliness among welsh authority-figures and shows just how much the Welsh Rugby Union needs someone with experience and statesman-like qualities to take control of it, to guide it…and to set it on a more professional path.

(I will not go into the chaos and the overall lack of direction within welsh rugby at the moment (clubs and regions)…but the indecision and the lack of clarity that currently surrounds the game is typical of life in Wales)

Sports, all sports, should be run by people who are passionate about the game and respectful of tradition. They should not be run by obnoxious little jobsworths who put their oar in where it is not wanted.

Summary;

The people of Wales are a proud and passionate race…living in a country of myth and legend…but sadly they have been erring in the political wilderness for far too long… and Devolution hasn't really helped their cause.

The welsh people are renowned for their warmth and their welcome but they are desperate for a guide to emerge, they are desperate for somebody to represent them as a nation, for somebody with character who recognises the hardships of their yesteryear and the challenges facing them today, somebody with ideas that will regenerate and reinvigorate the welsh economy…and inspire their younger generations to fulfil their potential.

The welsh have always been a hard-working race - whether down the mines or in the dock-yards - making them natural supporters of the socialist ideas of the original trade-union-backed Labour Party, but sadly - despite holding a majority in Wales for more than anyone cares to remember - that 'working-class' Labour Party has never delivered on any of its promises or created any real prosperity for the welsh people…

Perhaps now, it's time for a change…

———

The British People

As a whole;

Guided by a succession of inept, self-indulgent political leaders - *who have all allowed themselves to be influenced by any number of bleeding-heart liberals in exchange for political support* - the British people have had their personal responsibilities taken away from them - one after the other - over the last thirty years, …to the point where;

- they no longer know their moral boundaries,
- they no longer know how to bring up their children
- they no longer know how to educate their children
- they no longer have a work-ethic…

…and because of a sustained period of irresponsible borrowing… and a tendency to borrow beyond their means…

- they no longer know how to run their own lives within the parameters of their resources

In fact, the British people - as a nation - has been systematically 'wimpified' over the last thirty years by an over-reaching nanny-state that cannot stop interfering in their private lives…to the point where the people have become emotionally fragile and unable to make a decision for themselves; a fact compounded by the ubiquitous benefit culture which encourages this dependency and supports this overbearing culture which is trying to regulate every waking moment of their lives.

At the same time, they (the British public) have been allowed to splurge in all directions without restraint…

look at…

- the obesity problem,
- the alcohol problem,
- the promiscuity problem,
- the increasing drug problem,
- the debt problem,
- the benefits problems,
- the anti-social behaviour issues…and
- the rise in lawless gangs

All this while being;

- fed a constant diarrhoea of petty rules and regulations handed down from Brussels… and a variety of other pressure groups *(environmentalists, health and safety, political correctness lobbies)*…
- and sold a never-ending torrent of drivel about celebrity culture and superstar lifestyles peddled by an insidious and manipulative media

---

The different generations;

The **younger generation** are all chancers; constantly on the look-out for something for nothing;

- they want everything…and they want it now; the newest phone, the latest fashion and all without ever wondering how their parents are going to pay for it
- they are selfish and have no idea of the meaning of the word 'altruism'
- they are often introspective and isolated in their virtual worlds… and of course
- they are obsessed by the inanities of life…and the pointless content of their social-network sites and their mobile-phones… to the point of addiction.

Moreover, they are infatuated by shallow reality TV shows - the superficial social template of which has led to any number of vacuous wannabes, unburdened by talent, being somehow adored and revered by their equally ignorant and intellectually-challenged peers.

Meanwhile, those in **middle-age** are squeezed from every side…and **the elderly**, having worked all their lives…and gotten us through a world-war…are considered a burden to be treated like debris and discarded at the first opportunity.

Of course these are all generalisations and not all the labels apply to all the people but mix them all together in multicultural 2014 Britain and that is what you have…a complete mess.

There is no respect anymore, for people, for property or for authority;

- there is no respect for parents at home
- there is no respect for the elderly
- there is no respect for teachers in the classroom…and
- there is no respect for the police on the streets.

Instead, society in Britain today is all about;

- corruption (in politics and in the police force)
- violence (in schools and on the streets)…and
- decadence (morality / alcohol)

…and the result of all this is a complete breakdown in the fabric of a society that generation after generation of great British citizens had so painstakingly put together…and sadly, instead of pulling together…as the generation that saw us through the war did so successfully …these days it is everybody for themselves…and that selfish, greedy attitude goes right the way through the system, from top to bottom.

The Political Class;

As for our politicians; we are being led by a generation of self-serving, lily-livered hypocrites; a group of career politicians with no back-bone who sway with the political opinion of the day and who crumble at the first sign of pressure from any lobby group with an agenda.

Just look at how all three parties suddenly became interested in the immigration issue once UKIP started to gain support.

Our 'leaders', educated in the privileged surroundings of Oxbridge are just a flock of frightened lambs who have never lived in the real world and who have never had to take any responsibility.

Moreover,

- they have no real beliefs (everything can be negotiated for a price),
- they have no core values,
- they have no vision for the future…and
- they have no clue as to the direction that the country should be moving in;

…and more importantly, they never stand up for this country or represent the views of its citizens on the world stage.

None of them has the interests of the British public at heart.

Now, they can spout political rhetoric for hours on end - in order to pull the wool over the eyes of the British public - but they will never actually make a stand or take the risk of saying anything controversial that might rock the boat and jeopardise their comfortable seats on the gravy train.

These people are in politics for one thing…and one thing only; to get out of it what they can; to line their pockets with as much of the taxpayers money as possible, in as quick a time as possible, in order to fund their retirement years…and to spend that time living in the lap of luxury at the taxpayers' expense.

———

It's a sad state of affairs but what is worse, is that the British public knows all this…and yet nobody is prepared to say or do anything about it.

This is because the British people have an overblown sense of propriety and an innate aversion to confrontation…of which the politicians are well aware. They know all about this British trait, this aversion, this unwillingness to cause a fuss or talk about the elephant in the room and they rely on it to bypass the real will of the people in order to impose their policies and pursue their own agendas.

Now this might sound a little conspiratorial but it is this widespread apathy towards the political process - and the politics that our politicians are preaching - that we have to change because, in typical British fashion we all complain and we all criticise from our armchairs, but if we say nothing, if we sit around and simply grumble at the TV without trying to change anything, our self-serving politicians with their misplaced arrogance will simply continue to impose their dogma on us and we will get everything we deserve.

———

John Cleese once said; '*Every Englishman rushes to his grave in the hope of never being embarrassed*'. I think that pretty much sums up the British character.

———

Author's comment;

People of Britain; our political elite and our privileged elite are not necessarily our intellectual elite…and they certainly don't have the monopoly on knowledge…so why should their views and their opinions always be held up as the standard…?

————

Now, the reason why nobody stands up in this country is because they feel that it would be too embarrassing to do so, especially as anyone who does dare to stand up and voice an opinion in this country is immediately labelled a bigot.

That is the problem.

In Britain, in 2014, if you have an opinion that is not mainstream and middle-of-the-road, you are immediately considered an extremist which shows a certain lack of worldliness among the general populous and a very blinkered state of mind.

Free speech in this country is not really free speech as it is hindered by the straight-jacket of the Political Correctness lobby, the Health and Safety rules and any number of other liberal sensibilities. Therefore free speech in Britain is not - in essence – free speech as it has to respect all these criteria.

————

Recent governments;

Recent governments have failed this country…and its voters…time and time again by bowing shamelessly - and hypocritically - to the proliferation of liberal advocates and fashionable feeble-minded moderates that have sprung up over the last few years.

This is a form of demagoguery where they turn with the wind like a weather vane in order to follow public opinion, listening to popular desires and prejudices rather than rational arguments. It is shallow, sound-byte politics.

Meanwhile, they have consistently failed to address any of the more fundamental problems blighting this country, which is why they are all now coming home to roost (NHS, pensions, immigration etc.)... and as the continuing scandals surrounding MPs expenses have shown, the British people have had enough of the narrow-minded supercilious arrogance of this smug political elite.

————

The New Labour years for example saw a series of incompetent, irresponsible leaders, each one a master of empty rhetoric presiding over fiasco after fiasco.

Every time that they were confronted with a problem, New Labour attacked it from the wrong angle, rolling out policy after policy to blight the lives of decent ordinary tax-paying citizens in the hope of turning up a newsworthy sound-byte for the media.

Each time, 99.9% of the population was penalised or punished in some way, in the hope of catching out the 0.1 per cent of offenders.

This is 'Hail Mary' politics; this is politics invented by people without a game-plan, who are hoping that by casting a net as far and as wide as possible they would trawl up something...anything that they could put in front of the media, and call a success.

It never works; it never did work and the repeated incompetence of the New Labour government to even implement its own policies before changing them again – *not to mention the U-turns, the lies and the spin* - created a bureaucratic nightmare that the subsequent coalition government is still trying to untangle.

————

People of Britain; we are ruining our freedoms in this country, one by one; we need to learn that sometimes we will have to take a hit, but that is the price we have to pay for democracy, for real democracy;

- enough of this 'wimpified', lily-livered, risk-averse society
- enough of the theory that if we save just one life, it's worth it

NO; I do not subscribe to the idea that in order to save one life, we have to blight the lives of millions of others. Why should we blight the lives of 99.9% of the population in order to potentially save the other 0.1% ; it is not right; any calculation includes a risk factor for potential losses etc. and we need to accept that.

We need to accept that the price of our democracy and our freedom to live our lives as we see fit comes with the potential for sacrifice; that is true liberty.

Religion;

Talking about religion is often discouraged in this country because a person's views on religion can easily be construed as biased against one faith or another, but I am not religious in any way, shape or form and as a consequence there is no reason for anybody to feel affronted by my position.

That said, I do respect the right of everyone to believe in what they will; some people believe in ghosts, others in astrology, others in the Yeti, UFO's, extra-terrestrials, Father Christmas and the tooth fairy; whatever gets you through the day, I say, but on a more serious point, the reason people are turning to Islam these days is not necessarily for spiritual reasons; it is because Islam offers guidance and structure to people's lives; it offers something that has been sorely lacking in the politicians of this country over the last thirty years; a vision and aspiration.

Politicians speak of broken Britain; well this rise in Islam is a consequence of broken Britain; a country which has;

- systematically let down its people,
- turned a deaf ear and a blind eye to their opinions,
- abused their democratic rights,
- ruined the prospects of a generation or two by dumbing-down their education in order to score cheap political points...and
- rewarded the greedy, the unscrupulous and the immoral few

That is Britain in 2014 - in a nutshell - and that is what needs to be addressed going forward.

PDC Solution;

This country will have to make some tough decisions going forward but in order to do that it will have to grow up.

Britain has a great history but its ironic lack of worldliness and the intellectual naiveté that religion and the gullible bleeding-hearts of middle-England impose on this country while the politicians play incestual political parlour games in and around Westminster are holding it back and preventing it from being in the vanguard of 21st century prosperity.

In fact, it is almost unbearable to witness how the British people bend over backwards to be politically correct, so as not to offend anybody, tying themselves in knots so as not to stand out or to contradict anybody in any way...and to be polite at all times so as not to rock the boat.

This is a laudable quality, or at least it would be in an ideal world, but in the harsh reality of world politics the rest of the world perceives the British as weak, as an easy mark.

We need to get tougher, we can still be polite but we need to put the steel back into our character and grow a backbone; only then will we gain the respect of other countries on the world stage.

Does anybody think the Chinese or the Russians suffer from this self-imposed, masochistic reserve?

Do the French or the Germans care what we think?

Of course not, they do what they believe they have to do for the good of their respective countries…and if it means ruffling a few feathers along the way, then so be it.

———

In this country, the concepts of courage and pride which were so ubiquitous during the conflict of world war have long been forgotten …worn away by wave after wave of lily-livered liberal pandering…but I believe, in my humble opinion…that the following concepts no longer have tenure in the 21st century;

- **Religion** – which is no more than a placebo to help people cope with the harsh reality of human existence
- **The concept of monarchy and inherited privilege (House of Lords)** which are clearly anachronisms in the modern, enlightened world
- **Dictatorships;** unacceptable in any circumstance
- The **Trade Union Movement**; which was started in 1871 after the industrial revolution and was vital in establishing 'workers' rights' but has now largely fulfilled that mission…and finally
- The **BBC** which was set up in 1927 and which is still run – as if it was still 1927 - by a handful of stuffy Guardian-reading ex-schoolboys in beige cardigans

We need to leave these old concepts behind and forge ahead with what is in front of us; a modern, 21st century future.

Today we live in a quick-fix society where we need an instant solution for each and every one of our problems…but sometimes it takes a little longer…and I believe that it will take a generation or so to undo the liberal chaos that currently reigns in this country and to restore order.

The PDC would set up a commission to re-examine every law brought in over the last 30 years and it would charge that commission to make the necessary adjustments and rectifications using its three guiding principles; logic, reason and common sense.

We need to erase the disastrous Blair years and the subsequent Brown administration – widely recognised as the most calamitous administration in living memory - from the history books of this great country…and we need to change things before the generation that saved us in the Second World War has passed on - because the pampered generations born since and brought up in a materialistic vacuum have no compass, be it moral, political or otherwise; they have no sustainable plan for the future.

For the last thirty years, this country with its free market ideas has been all about greed;

- greedy bankers,
- greedy politicians,
- greedy lawyers,
- greedy footballers…and their greedy agents etc.

…but these are not the only people; we were **ALL** gullibly caught up in the dream of never-ending prosperity fed to us by the politicians who got carried away with a booming economy which ramped up individual debt out of all proportion.

This repudiation of common sense and reason, in favour of self-indulgence and greed cannot be allowed to repeat itself. What was Gordon Brown's cry? 'No more boom and bust'? Well, we saw the result of that over-confidence and it is now time to learn the lesson.

I have no time for limp legislation or the lily-livered politicians currently warming the benches of Westminster; it is time for strong leadership…

and new, progressive ideas based on reality…and not on pipe-dreams for short-term political gain.

- Enough of the arcane and overblown language of Westminster and its worryingly meddlesome civil-servants
- Enough of the saccharine-soaked narratives of cosy, self-serving politicians

Plain speaking is what the British public wants…and plain speaking is what the British people deserve.

It is time to purge, it is time purify and it is time to clean-up the debris of our economy left behind by thirty years of spineless liberalism.

People of Britain; it is time for a new approach…

IT IS TIME for change.

Author's comment;

It is no wonder that the British people are disillusioned with politics and politicians; they feel that they have been ignored, betrayed and exploited after a decade or more of dishonesty, deceit and malicious mismanagement of the country's economy by a generation of demonstrably inept politicians; principally those in the New Labour Party…which during its time in office taxed many of them into poverty…and what they want now is a strong, morally-upstanding leader with a backbone who they can rely on, not to betray them or their country, at the first opportunity, either for personal or political gain.

So Now; Our Choices

The British political system, which is basically a bi-partisan system that alternates on a regular basis, is very easy to understand;

In a nut-shell;

- When the Labour Party is elected into office, they 'spend, spend, spend' like there is no tomorrow under the guise of populist socialism. It is irresponsible and short-sighted but they do this with one purpose and one purpose only in mind; to buy votes for the following election.
- *That said; how cynical and lacking in political integrity is it, not to have policy at the centre of government but just a desire not to lose the grip on power – and by extension the country's purse strings – by whatever means possible*
- Then; once the country's own coffers are empty the Labour Party turns to the international markets to borrow more money in order to sustain the rate of its profligate expenditure...and of course this - as you might expect - hikes up the national debt...
- ...and finally, when there really is no money left to spend; usually after a lot of dithering and a number of U-turns, the Labour Party calls an election...
- This is when, more often than not, the Conservative Party takes over...and because of the mess that they inherit from the outgoing Labour Party the new Conservative party usually has to introduce a series of austerity measures to try to rebalance the economy...which is why the Labour Party has attributed the epithet 'the Nasty Party' to the Conservatives.
- Now, of course, the country doesn't like the medicine that the Conservative Party has to dish out, so at the first opportunity they vote them out of office... again...and the Labour Party steps back in...again...
- ...and the whole process starts all over...

...but every time that happens, the national debt gets a little larger, because the Conservative Party can never make the necessary savings quick enough or make the inevitable cuts deep enough to put the economy back on an even keel before the Labour Party comes back in and starts spending again...reversing the momentum.

...everybody knows that it is easier to spend money than it is to save it...

That is what happens...and that is why the county has such a huge national debt; it is the never-ending, self perpetuating circle of British politics.

———

So here are our choices at the next election;

The Conservative Party –

This would be a difficult choice because sadly with their privileged backgrounds and their bold arrogance the Conservatives are somewhat out of touch...and lack the empathy to connect with the ordinary citizen.

These are career politicians from privileged backgrounds who have never lived in the real world. They have never had to take responsibility for anything in their lives and because of that they are lacking in ideas... and bereft of peripheral political insight.

Their education and their life-experience is too narrow...and moreover, their place among the 'elite of society' makes them inherently jealous of each other leading to constant bickering and in-fighting.

It's a sad fact but the Tory Party often loses its identity...and frequently self-implodes... through this constant bickering and in-fighting.

———

Author's comment;

I will never forget the way that Mrs Thatcher was betrayed by members of her own cabinet and Parliamentary party (Michael Heseltine, Kenneth Clark and Geoffrey Howe). That was a prime example of Conservative party politics in action and a lesson to us all never to trust a 'friend' in politics.

They say that there is honour amongst thieves but that obviously doesn't apply to politicians…or bankers having seen what happened during the credit crunch.

Mrs Thatcher was a great leader, even if she didn't always get it right (the Poll Tax fiasco was her undoing) and like most people, I didn't agree with everything she did; but there again nobody agrees entirely with anyone.

However Mrs Thatcher taught me one thing. She knew that being British was about standing your ground, not going with the tide when things got tough and fighting for what you believe in at home and abroad, even when the odds are stacked against you… and above all she taught me that you cannot spend what you haven't earned which is what the Labour Party does with wild abandon.

That said; like her or loathe her; Margaret Thatcher was the last real British leader with any backbone. She always set a clear course of action and believed in herself enough to see it through, even though - sadly - she became a little dictatorial towards the end of her career.

Since Mrs Thatcher left No.10 Downing Street in 1990 – the Conservatives have had several leaders;

- John Major,
- William Hague,
- Ian Duncan Smith…and
- Michael Howard

…none of whom was able to make his mark on the world stage as a statesmen.

David Cameron now holds that position and I have to say that he promised a lot when he came to the fore…but sadly his photo opportunities and publicity stunts;

- Bike-riding around London (followed by his car)
- Posing with huskies in the Arctic
- Fixing a wind-turbine to his house (subsequently removed because he did not have planning permission)
- Wearing trendy eco-trainers
- Promising to holiday ONLY in Britain (which he reneges upon regularly)…and
- Hugging a hoodie…etc,etc

…lead me to believe that he is more about spin than substance, in keeping with the rest of the lightweight, superficial suits currently swanning around Westminster.

So, people of Britain, we can either persist with the Toffs; with a crop of privileged public schoolboys from Oxbridge and Eton - those smug millionaire ex-members of the Bullingdon club - who treat running this country as their birth-right and personal plaything – just as their fore-fathers of the aristocracy and the Landowners Association did before them – while riding rough-shod over the rest of us…or

---

Liberal Democrats –

Or…

…we could choose the woolly Liberal-Democrats who spin without compass and blow with the wind like a weathervane … to take over our destiny.

They would certainly be an alternative...but sadly the Liberal Democrats have proved to be so hopelessly inept and hapless over the years...and their middle of the road policies - full of fluff and froth - designed not to upset anybody...ever...always lack one main ingredient...substance.

Their ideas might be idealistically rich - but sadly they are realistically poor.

Everybody knows that idealist rhetoric is wonderful in theory...but it is applying that theory to reality which is the real challenge of politics, and sadly the Liberal Democrats do not appear to have the courage of their convictions...nor more importantly the necessary support to follow through on them...and as a consequence they are too inconsequential as a political force to be considered a credible option.

Besides, any party willing to renounce its core values, its fundamental beliefs and its key policies in exchange for a taste of executive power is not a party worthy of comment or consideration.

———

New Labour -

Or do we go back to the New Labour Party?

- **A party** which, during its last tenure went behind the people's back and sent our military personnel to war in Iraq on the back of a dodgy dossier - a dossier that was all 'fabrication and lies' according to the latest investigation - despite millions of British citizens marching through London in protest.

They also compounded their transgression by sending our soldiers into war without the right equipment - which they initially denied - though it was later revealed that they had indeed withheld £1billion from the defence budget...

...and what was worse, they then took those same soldiers to court to contest their compensation claims when they came back injured.

- **A party** which came to power with the slogan 'education, education, education' and then proceeded to produce a generation of children incapable of mastering the three R's by the time they left school. In fact a recent survey confirmed, that we have a generation of young people in this country whose intelligence - as far as maths is concerned at least – does not exceed that of a nine / eleven year old

- **A party** which pledged not to sell off any playing fields and then promptly did so; selling off 203 playing fields as soon as they took office

- **A party** which deliberately flooded the country with millions of immigrants in a cynical political ploy to transform the make-up of our society without ensuring that there was enough housing and public services to deal with the influx.

- **A party** that didn't realise that 12,000 illegal immigrants were working in government jobs; some even working in the Home Office

- **A party** which systematically persecuted whistle-blowers who exposed their inadequacies, their incompetence and their ineptitude

- **A party** that suppressed warnings about under-performing hospitals, leaned on officials to keep the problems covered up and denied any responsibility in the scandals that have plagued the NHS over the past twenty years or so despite them being in office for much of that period.

- **A party** that presided over the MPs expenses scandal and tried to cover it up with the help of the then Speaker, Mr Michael Martin

- **A party** that sold off our gold reserves at the bottom of the market; robbed the elderly of their pensions and life savings and then denied those same elderly people the drugs / treatment they needed for cancer and Alzheimer's etc.

- **A party** that encouraged 24 hour-drinking which has led to us having the worst booze culture in Europe

- **A party** which allowed GPs to opt out of 'out-of-hours' care creating the chaos we see every day in A&E

- **A party** which strangled our identity out of us with its Big Brother obsession, its Political Correctness Rules and its Health & Safety overkill

- **A party** of irresponsible spend-thrifts who throw money at people to buy their voting allegiance

- **A party** that 'diverted billions of Lottery money away from the causes it was set up to help – art, sport, heritage and volunteer sector – and into its pet projects of education, health and transport' as former PM **John Major,** recently remarked.

- **A party** that promised an election and then reneged on that promise when it knew that it would lose

- **A party** that knighted Freddy Goodwin who went on to ruin RBS, costing the taxpayers billions before he retired with a £650.000 a year life-pension

- **A party** that offered bribes to the Irish Democratic Unionists in order to get the bill for 42 days detention through the House of Commons

- **A party** which filled our High Streets with betting shops, pay-day loan offices and pawn shops (cash for gold / cash converters etc.) and encouraged gambling on a huge scale

- **A party** which never stood up to the EU, waving through budget increase after budget increase up to 47% - while **Ed**

Balls was a treasury adviser - and gave away our EU rebate in return for reforms in the Common Agricultural Policy which never materialised

- **A party** which opposes holding an in/out referendum on membership of the EU

- **A party** that had the worst record of any government since WW2 for building new social housing; at least under the most recent governments of Tony Blair & Gordon Brown

- **A party** that has no strategies or vision of its own other than to constantly undermine and contradict the current coalition at every turn with shallow opportunism

...and finally, **a party** currently led by a man who was prepared to stab his own brother in the back (metaphorically speaking) in order to take up the position.

Clearly the self-serving Labour Party does not have the country's best interests at heart and therefore it is not fit for purpose.

More examples of New Labour's administrative and economic incompetence;

- Terrorist information was left on a train – twice in one week
- Child Benefit information for 25 million people was lost
- Revenue and customs information on 15000 people was lost
- The DVLC lost driving-licence data
- The Health service lost discs containing medical records
- A lap-top containing army recruitment info was lost
- Several discs with the DNA of murderers and rapists was lost… and
- According to conservative estimates,
    - o £24 million pounds was lost in Housing Benefit, although a more truthful figure would be £150 million

- o   £670 million was lost to 'error'…and
- o   £30 million was lost in Council Tax Benefits

…and finally;

£10 billion – enough to pay for the 2012 Olympics - was wasted or lost or misappropriated in the Tax Credits debacle over a four-year period.

(These are Audit Commission figures)

Furthermore;

During the Blair / Brown years, New Labour was a den of iniquity full of unscrupulous politicians and their government, based on spin, subterfuge and hypocrisy was suicidally corrupt.

They had thirteen dysfunctional years in office; thirteen years presiding over a shambolic mess of mismanagement, sleaze and traitorous incompetence, thirteen years of reckless spending while overseeing the steady attrition of our civil liberties.

Indeed, there seemed to be a culture of carelessness in the New Labour government, especially under Gordon Brown which engendered an unparalleled degree of recklessness that beggared belief as they all rushed to greedily fill their pockets with as much of the tax-payers money as possible.

New Labour brought this country to its knees while making its representatives very, very rich – notably Tony Blair, Gordon Brown, Peter Mandelson, Alistair Campbell, Jack Straw, David Blunkett, Margaret Beckett and Hazel Blears.

Are people's memories that short…?

Tony Blair and his band of merry-men were criminally irresponsible and should all be outlawed and held in contempt by the people of this country…just as they held the country in contempt by their actions while in power.

It is a disgrace what they did to this country – irresponsible and incompetent doesn't begin to describe these people; they are cynical, unpatriotic, grasping and corrupt without a saving grace amongst them.

In fact, anyone who was part of the New Labour cabinet during the Blair / Brown years, any of the 'yes-men' who colluded with Tony Blair and Gordon Brown on any of these issues and helped to betray the electorate both on the Iraq war and on the immigration issue cannot be trusted to have the country's best interests at heart and therefore should be prevented from holding any position of responsibility in the democratic process of this country ever again.

Here is a non-exhaustive selection of New Labour's roll-call of incompetence and dishonour

---

- **Alan Johnson**, a selectively-blind, hopelessly inept and clueless politician who was completely out of his depth as Home Secretary. Johnson finally admitted that New Labour had ultimately 'gotten it wrong on immigration' and also admitted 'we were complacent over louts'
- **Baroness Uddin** - fiddled her expenses
- **Bob Ainsworth** - Without going into his outrageous expense claims, Bob Ainsworth - who was Secretary of State for Defence - was another hopeless case when confronted by real military men like Sir Richard Dannett. So when Sir Richard exposed the government for the shortages of equipment in Afghanistan, Ainsworth gave **Lord Foulkes** the role of undermining and

smearing Sir Richard Dannett's name; that is how New Labour operated; anybody revealing the truth or shining a light on the lies circulated by the New Labour government was immediately targeted, their work undermined, their reputations smeared and their word dismissed as untrue; character assassination and demonization was the default position for New Labour.

- **For information**; Sir Richard Dannett, a man of undoubted integrity, claimed £19,291.00 in expenses while the man criticising him for those expenses Bob Ainsworth claimed £394,306.00
- **Caroline Flint –** caught up in the expenses scandal
- **Charles Clarke** was forced to quit as Home Secretary for releasing over 1000 foreign prisoners back onto our streets between 1999 and 2006 without even considering their deportation and his successor, **John Reid** described the department he inherited as 'not fit for purpose'
- **Dame Sally Powell** - who championed the 24-hour drinking plans under Tony Blair was banned from driving for being caught behind the wheel drunk; **twice** - she now believes that 24-hour drinking 'might not have been a good idea'.
- **David Blunkett –** another former Home Secretary – signed off on the extradition treaty - covering rendition flights - in secret, after 9/11 at a time when Tony Blair was George W Bush's poodle. He has also come out since and admitted that New Labour got it wrong on gambling
- **Dennis MacShane –** had to resign for submitting 19 bogus invoices for laptops and translation services
- **Ed Miliband** recently admitted that New Labour got it wrong on immigration and that to discuss immigration is not 'bigoted'. He also admitted that errors in the scheme to encourage off-shore wind farms will cost the British public £17 billion on their energy bills
- **Estelle Morris –** Education Secretary under Tony Blair – admitted in her resignation letter to being ineffective
- **Gordon Brown –** former Prime Minister; without going into his disastrous premiership, general dithering and numerous u-turns – Gordon Brown admitted to 'having doubts' about

24/7 drinking. He also admitted that New Labour never saw the recession coming

- **Harriett Harman** – a single-minded feminist zealot who considers that women are oppressed even though she has lived a life full of privilege; growing up in a posh home, going to a private school and a good university before falling into a series of cushy political posts; if there is one thing I despise; it's a hypocrite. Ms Harman was so confident that New Labour had the problem of security under control in her constituency of Peckham that she walked around wearing a stab-vest, protected by a police escort.
- I wonder if Ms Harman really believes her four maxims;
    1) all men are bastards
    2) all men are wrong, all the time
    3) all crime is committed by men…and
    4) all crime is committed against women
- That said; just like David Blunkett, before her, she too has since admitted that New Labour 'made a mistake' on gambling
- **Hazel Blears** – a staunch defender of the Labour party who regularly told untruths in her political rhetoric in order to defend the often indefensible party line, and was caught up in the expenses scandal dishonestly flipping properties to avoid capital gains tax. As Secretary of State for Communities and Local Government, she admitted 'we allowed a migrant free-for-all'.
- **Jacqui Smith** – admitted that she had 'never run a thing' before being named in the Home Office, and as Home Secretary she deported only 35 of the 7000 illegal immigrants found working as security staff, some of them in official government buildings. She too was caught up in the expenses scandal
- **John Prescott** – Deputy Leader – his affair with his diary-secretary aside – Prescott calamitously wasted £500 million of taxpayers' money restructuring the fire-service and another £2.2 billion bulldozing thousands of homes in his Pathfinder initiative. He also admitted recently that the invasion of Iraq was 'unjustifiable' and possibly 'illegal'.
- **Margaret Beckett –** Housing Minister – refused to pay back expenses when she was caught out
- **Margaret Moran** – also fiddled £53,000 in expenses

- **Patricia Hewitt** – another one caught out by the expenses scandal
- **Peter Mandelson** - built up a sizeable personal fortune from his position as Business Secretary while being careful never to actually say anything of any interest to the British public. He did once admit however that; '...too often we think we can act without explaining and take decisions without justifying them'....and more recently, in order to protect his lucrative EU pension, he also suggested that the British public should be denied their democratic right to vote on an In/Out referendum over the EU issue which **Neil Kinnock** - another ex-Labour MP who has been creaming in EU money for years as an MEP - quickly echoed. Surely if there was ever a case for us voting on the EU it would to show the self-serving individuals who ruined this country how wrong they are.
- **Phil Woolas** – Minister of State for Borders and Immigration - was humiliated like a little schoolboy by Joanna Lumley over the Ghurkhas fiasco and was just as deluded as his colleagues when announcing that 'we have one of the strongest borders in the world' when talking about immigration through France. Meanwhile, the French themselves admitted that at least 2000 immigrants a month were getting onto trucks in Calais. **Woolas** eventually came out and admitted 'we've got a problem; the public doesn't believe our claims ('lies') on immigration any more'.
- **Tessa Jowell** – caught up in financial scandal involving her husband
- **Tom Watson** – a former member of Gordon Brown's government recently admitted that 'we should never have licensed these machines' in the gambling act of 2005 when speaking about gambling machines.
- **Tristram Hunt**; Education spokesman admitted that exams had been dumbed-down during the last Labour government.

And finally...'**Teflon Jack**'...

As Home Secretary, Jack Straw was completely loyal to Tony Blair, and shielded his master from any flying flack on numerous occasions, often to the detriment of his own reputation. This was commendable from

Tony Blair's standpoint but sadly, Straw's loyalty to Blair often conflicted with what was right for the country.

Indeed, he once revealed that his and Blair's biggest regret was allowing the Freedom of Information Act to become law. That is a perfect example of how the corrupt mind of a politician works; it works against democracy in a self-serving and self-preserving vacuum.

So, the Freedom of Information Act did become law but despite that, Jack Straw colluded closely with Tony Blair in order to veto that part of the new law which covered cabinet minutes so that those relative to the days leading up to Britain going to war with Iraq were kept under wraps. Once again, this was done solely to protect Tony Blair.

Jack Straw also allowed rendition flights (the Libyan opposition leader – Abdel hakim Belhadj - was sent back in 2004) and more frivolously, he used his veto to avoid revelations about John Prescott's 'grace and favour' home.

The man was New Labour's truth-shield and how he managed to survive all those years...and avoid getting caught for his incompetence and his blatantly misplaced loyalty as he tiptoed through the minefields - and fielded the unexploded bombs that Tony Blair left in his wake - I really don't know; that is why I attribute him the epithet 'Teflon Jack'.

Last minute; Jack Straw, like Alan Johnson, Hazel Blears and Ed Miliband before him has now come out and admitted that New Labour's open-border immigration policy was a 'spectacular mistake'.

———

...and today's New Labour leadership; **Ed Miliband & Ed Balls**

When talking about the Conservative / Liberal Democrats coalition at the Labour Party Conference in 2012, Ed Miliband asked those gathered – 'have you ever seen a more incompetent, hopeless, out-of-touch, u-turning, pledge-breaking, make-it-up-as-you-go-along, back of the envelope, miserable shower?'.

Well, all he had to do was look over his shoulder (metaphorically speaking) to see the New Labour government that preceded the Conservative / Liberal Democrats coalition...which had - without doubt - been all of those things and more, and which <u>he</u> himself, along with Ed Balls, had been a part of.

Both Ed Miliband and Ed Balls were at the heart of the Labour government that wrecked the British economy and welcomed uncontrolled immigration into this country. In fact, Ed Balls was one of the chief architects of New Labour's disastrous economic policy under Gordon Brown coming up with the PFI fiasco which has now trapped so many establishments into almost insurmountable debt...and as Children's Secretary; he was also responsible for wanting to teach children of five about sex.

Sadly, **Ed Balls** suffers from the same sense of deluded entitlement as Gordon Brown did in his day and having watched from the political wings and seen how the former blustered, blundered and bullied his way to the top, Ed Balls thinks he can do exactly the same.

This man is driven, ambitious and believes like his guide Gordon Brown that he has some kind of divine right...that it is his destiny...to lead the country whether the country likes it or not.

The man is deluded. He claimed on the 3rd of June 2013 that there was 'no evidence of New Labour being profligate' and yet debt had soared from £350 billion to £900 billion during their time in office.

He is also a narcissist who conducted - and paid for - a survey to find out why people didn't like him.

Fortunately, for the British people, he has only blustered so far, but if he is allowed to get anywhere near No.10, he will no doubt blunder and bully like his mentor Gordon Brown.

However, in the next election, the alternative to David Cameron will more than likely be Ed Miliband, and yet he has yet to prove himself as a leader;

- he lacks gravitas,
- he lacks charisma,
- he lacks conviction…and quite frankly
- he lacks a political ethos.

All he does as leader of the Opposition is systematically contradict whatever policy the Conservatives are putting forward…and when that doesn't raise a cheer in the House, he simply resorts to making personal attacks on David Cameron.

The hypocrisy is startling because New Labour presided over our demise for 13 years and left this country in the worst mess in living memory.

Ed Miliband was a special advisor to Gordon Brown during that time and he was the person responsible for drafting the Labour manifesto, as well as being the person who put forward the ludicrous reduction programme for greenhouse-gas emissions which are clearly absurd and unattainable within the timescale he set out…and which are forcing unnecessary hardship and financial ruin on many of our fellow citizens.

Ed Miliband also sold off our only viable nuclear development company.

People of Britain, we should never forget that the economic mess that we have lived with for the past few years was caused in part by the gross incompetence of the last Labour Government in which Ed Miliband and Ed Balls were major figures…

…and one last thing…

Should the British public really trust a person who was prepared to stab his own brother in the back (metaphorically speaking) in order to get the leadership of the Party?

Author's comment;

Unfortunately, I believe that the current generation of Labour Party MPs, tainted by association with the toxic Blair and Brown governments will have to forego the idea of regaining power for a few years while they re-build their reputations, install new leadership and come up with some new policies.

———

So people of Britain; these are our choices in the next election…

- the Toffs
- the Windmills
- the Inveterate Spendthrifts…or

OR…we could create the PDC – the People's Democratic Congress… and at long last offer the British public a real voice.

———

Conclusion / Closing Thoughts

What really depresses me about our 21st century society is that all those who should be the pillars of our society, the most intelligent among us, who have been to the 'best schools and the most illustrious universities' - and who should be showing the way to those less fortunate than themselves - are systematically abusing that position of trust for their own benefit.

In fact, in the last ten years every major UK institution that the British public depends upon on to regulate their lives has let them down in one way or another;

- The **Politicians of both Houses** (Commons and Lords) let them down with their expenses scandal...but not only that; they constantly lie to the British public, forever making promises that they know they will never keep; they took the country to war against the people's wishes and - if Westminster computer records are to be believed - they regularly cheat on their spouses...all of which shows a complete lack of integrity and morality.

- The **Police** let them down with their lies about the Hillsborough tragedy and the phone hacking scandals...and furthermore they seem to be involved in some other rather questionable practices – Jean-Charles de Menezes, Mark Duggan, Pleb-gate etc. The police have also been caught leaking and selling stories to the press for example...and doctoring crime figures - while at the same time making outrageous compensation claims for themselves and trying constantly to trap the public with speed cameras – often unfairly - in order to supplement their budgets

- The **Banks** let them down with their financial meltdown and their seemingly-unstoppable reckless greed. In fact, the people we trust with our life-savings managed to bring down the world's economy while paying themselves multi-million pound bonuses...and on top of that, they have now been caught out again fiddling the Libor rates and laundering drug money after selling us PPI protection that we didn't need

- The **Justice system** has let them down by being too soft on criminals and releasing them back into the community to re-offend again and again

- The **Press** has let them down with their phone hacking scandals and their collusion with both the politicians and the police. Journalists are constantly trying to hack our computers and our phones seeking out our private information

- The **NHS** has let them down; people are dying unnecessarily due to a lack of care; Mid-Staffs hospital

- The **Social Services** have let them down; Baby Peter case...etc.

- The **Local Councils** which were set up to run local communities efficiently, spend most of their time snooping on private citizens trying to find reasons to fine them for just going about their daily lives, while at the same time, paying their chief-executives bloated salaries.

...and now we find out that the **Supermarket** food chain has been compromised – *horse-meat scandal* - by the greed of yet another group of people without scruples...

———

In fact, over the last decade or so, every area of our lives, every sector of our society has let us down...but these are not necessarily system, organisational or logistical failures; more often than not they are human failures...because if you break down any of these problems, at their core you will always find human beings;

- morally weak individuals with no conscience who have their priorities in the wrong order,
- people motivated simply by greed,
- people not applying the rules as they should be applied…or
- people not taking responsibility for the jobs they are being paid to do

So, who or what can we really trust?

Is there no-one of authority in this country that we can trust and rely on not to exploit us, abuse us or sell on our personal information?

Is there an institution out there that is not mired in scandal…or is every part of life just a scam; an opportunity for someone to fill their own pockets by emptying someone else's?

Is that really what life is all about?

———

Now, I am not naive; I am well aware that we live in a world of hatred and selfish greed and that this first draft of the PDC Manifesto is in no way complete or exhaustive.

Indeed, much of it may seem anachronistic to some - and a little abstract and over-simplified in places to others - but these simple ideas worked once to create the society we lived in up until recently; why shouldn't they work again?

Of course some of these ideas might already exist in one form or another; I do not pretend to have all the answers and I doubt that I have covered every issue…but I do believe that this manifesto contains enough ideas to set a tone.

It is not rocket science or revolution; it is just a question of respecting three simple rules to allow a better future for all;

1) a healthy respect for nature

2) the application of logic…and
3) the use of common sense

———

At the moment, we have a chronic lack of leaders in this country; a chronic lack of people with any kind of ethical spine or grasp on the concept of morality; we don't have any politicians with any real courage, backbone or convictions.

All three of the main parties just blow with the wind, desperate to hold onto their salaries as tight as they can, making sure that they keep their places on the gravy train, while hoping not to get caught for any of their misdemeanours, sexual, moral, financial, or fraudulent.

After a period of irresponsible and then hopelessly inept political one-upmanship, the whole belief system of the British public has been shattered and needs rebuilding on new foundations…but we need to address these problems rationally, with pragmatism respect and integrity, without letting our thinking be clouded by any rigid ideology or preconception.

As explained previously, every institution that should comprise a key pillar of our society has let us down and been shown to be 'not fit for purpose', so now is the time to re-build the people's confidence and the people's trust, by putting in place the right safe-guards to avoid this nightmarish situation ever happening again.

There are no guarantees of course, human beings being who they are with their greed and their selfishness but we must try in order to go forward…

- We need a new system, a system that is open, honest and accountable; a system that is transparent without compromising the integrity of government; there are far too many people out there whose only interest is making a profit out of playing the system

- We need a period of austerity and consolidation to re-balance our society so that we can move on to the next era of change with a solid foundation…but we should be careful not to develop an authoritarian regime – like New Labour - without checks and balances
- We need common sense and decency to prevail once again in all areas – especially in health and safety issues
- We need more structured schooling and more community spirit (Magnet centres / policing)
- We need a more targeted approach to universities for…
  o Nurses, doctors and midwives / dentists, hygienists, prosthodontists and dental lab technicians…and opticians… to reduce our dependence on foreign nationals…and to drive down exploitative costs
  o We also need a generation of new teachers and child-care professionals
- We need unity; a new momentum which draws on all those interested in re-launching the country's prosperity, irrespective of their previous allegiance
- We need to put an end to the politics of envy and greed…and most importantly…
- We need to inspire; we need to encourage and motivate our young to fulfil their potential…

People of Britain; IT IS TIME;
we need to lay the groundwork for our future **TODAY**.

Author's comment;

Always keep in mind the Thirty Year Rule;

o Remember what it was like thirty years ago
o Look at the thirty years since…and then
o Project thirty years into the future…if we do nothing to change things…

People say that the road to hell is paved with good intentions…but I believe that it is time to force the hand of democracy to show its cards;

- Let's get back to family values and upright morality – today's politicians are not interested in the squalid underbelly of our inner cities ravaged by drugs and violence but that is exactly where we should start the clear up; the political wheel turns and turns but essential change never seems to come
- Let us be about setting high standards for life, love, creativity and wisdom; setting high standards is what makes every day and every decade worth looking forward to. If our expectations in these areas are low, we are not likely to experience wellness
- Let's embrace the values which made this country great – democracy and freedom has been eroded; courtesy and respect have been lost. Let's get it back
- Let's get to know our neighbours again and recreate united communities
- Let's put an end to cronyism (the appointment of friends and acquaintances to positions without them having the necessary qualifications)
- Let's put an end to greed and materialism and create a new mature and emotionally literate society dedicated to the common good…and most importantly
- Let's put the pride back into Britain

The PDC would be the sensible party; the party which stands up for nature, logic and common sense…and its leadership message offering vision, structure and boundaries would be strong, clear and undiluted….

- Our goal would be to puncture the pompous
- to expose the hypocrites of all sorts to well-deserved ridicule…and
- to give a voice to the powerless

We would take democracy away from the self-serving political elite and give it back to the people, while at the same time;

- delivering justice,
- standing up for morality…and
- applauding integrity.

———

The PDC **Mission Statement** would be summed up very succinctly;

**Protect those who respect the law – and –
punish those that don't…**

o From the bullies in the schoolyard,
o to the thugs on the streets
o to the criminals that blight our daily lives (which includes greedy white-collar crime, organised crime, murderers, paedophiles, rapists and burglars)

…using the respect of nature, the application of logic and the practise of common sense as guiding principles

———

Our motto;

THE TRUTH AND HONESTY CANNOT BE WRONG

———

THE END

———

Addendum

Brief Synopsis of THE MANIFESTO

(First draft)

1) The first item on the agenda would be to separate **the State** and **the Church** as spirituality has no legitimate entitlement to be part of the democratic process. Only those democratically elected should sit in Parliament, therefore the PDC would remove all the bishops and any other religious representatives from the House of Lords unless they were re-nominated by the voters under the new rules. (See chapter on Westminster). No other religion is represented in the House and if equality is to be one of our guiding principles, this would be no more than logical reasoning.

2) We would then have to secure our borders and address the **Population** which has to be reduced in order to ease the strain both on natural resources and on civic services

3) The next priority would be to reform the **Justice System**, starting with the re-introduction of Capital Punishment (for murderers – irrespective of age, drug barons and traffickers, people traffickers and paedophiles where death of the victim is involved) The PDC would also introduce a simplified sentencing process (15, 10/12, 5 and 1 year penalties) and for those sentenced to less than 1 year; a reform-camp operation would be put in place staffed by ex-military personnel. There would be no deals and no early release clauses; you do the crime; you do the time

4) Our **Prisons** would be the next priority. They desperately need overhauling / renovating and while the newer more modern establishments are built to reflect the change in the justice

system, ships could be temporarily commandeered, fitted out and anchored offshore to house the over-flow of offenders until the new laws stem the tide.

5) The next task would be to get the **thugs** off the street. This would be done by bringing in a blanket ban on the use, the sale and the import of any type of firearms (except of course for the accredited authorities who would still need to combat organised crime) – and followed up with a targeted initiative against gangs and drug related offenders.

6) We would also need to change the **Law** in order to eradicate the ridiculous compensation culture that has beset our justice system. We need to stop money-grabbing, ambulance-chasing lawyers from clogging up the system and exploiting it for their own ends (with petty disputes and far-fetched human rights abuses) and as part of this reform we would also look into the pay structure of the legal system, re-visit the Legal-aid scheme, retire soft judges and disbar any lawyers accused of corruption

7) Next we would re-install the notion that an Englishman's home is his castle and side with home-owners when violence is used in disputes with intruders, burglars etc (at the same time, the police should only be given permission to enter forcefully when they are certain that a crime has been committed and when they have irrefutable proof that the offender is inside – government or council snoopers would not be allowed in and any local government officials using such tactics would be brought to book)

8) Then, we would look to negotiate a worldwide agreement that no matter where the offender comes from, crime committed in this country would be punished in this country to the fullest degree according to our laws. Of course we would expect other countries to do the same and we would warn our citizens that they should expect that same treatment when going abroad (in an effort to clean up our shameful image and reputation as immoral lager-louts throughout the world). Extradition treaties with every country would also need to be reviewed.

9) Next; the bigger picture – **Europe** - firstly we need to reclaim our sovereignty from the EU via a referendum. That is imperative if we are to take back control of our destiny.

10) The PDC would propose a few amendments to the **European Human Rights** act as part of its restructuring of justice plans. A British Human Rights Act tailored specifically to our needs would free our hands – which are currently tied in double bows – thereby allowing us the freedom to rule our own country as we see fit in certain circumstances and not as the grey suits in Brussels would have us do – law, immigration, borders etc

11) Our **military** has a great history but time has moved on and we need to down-size our forces by re-distributing them and integrating them into the new Border Police, the Prisons and the Reform Camps (while keeping our specialist units (SAS) and enough numbers to cover our NATO / UN obligations)

12) The next project; an overhaul of the **education** system. Back to basics forcing children to learn how to read and write properly, teaching them respect and social skills more in keeping with today's society.

13) The PDC would also prioritise a decentralisation of non-essential bureaucracy from Westminster to the various town-halls

14) **Opening hours** – we need a return to controlled opening hours in pubs and clubs together with the re-introduction of re-enforced off-licenses attached to pubs protected by CCTV (obligatory presentation of identity) and a ban on any other outlets, supermarkets and shops selling alcohol. The PDC might even consider banning alco-pops completely (after consultation) to remove the temptation. This measure is an attempt to eradicate the binge-drinking culture fostered by Tony Blair's shameless 24/7 drinking policy and in return for this, the brewing industry would be mandated to provide a regulated transport service between the hours of 23.00 and 00.30

15) We would then try to encourage the re-birth of the community spirit, in pubs and in the new **Magnet centres**

16) **Industry** – job creation, small businesses and larger businesses would all be encouraged and incentivised.

My 'Weary List'

which sums up my disillusion with the current state of British politics in 10 easy bullet-points

- I am tired of the general greed and self-interest that now courses through our society
- I am tired of the corrupt mentalities of politicians and high-ranking civil servants with their expenses scandals and their rewards for failure
- I am tired of the secrecy and the bullying that is going on in our institutions to cover up the failings of those in charge
- I am tired of people defrauding all our services – the benefits system, the NHS, the Legal aid system and those jumping the housing queue
- I am tired of the gagging orders being handed out – at great cost to the taxpayer – to protect the guilty and the incompetent
- I am tired of the EU dictating every aspect of our lives and meddling in our national affairs
- I am tired of the inherent generosity and kind-hearted nature of the British public being abused and exploited on a daily basis
- I am tired of the justice system not protecting the innocent from the onslaught of violence
- I am tired of the NHS being used as the world's free treatment centre forcing it to abandon its founding principles in order to cope with the excessive demand put on its resources...and
- I am tired of the constant threat of terrorism

...all of which currently symbolise our country

Note from the Author;

Thank-you for reading these pages but if you would like a more concise narrative of the state of society in the 21ˢᵗ century, just listen to the song 'Everybody knows' by Leonard Cohen; it pretty much sums up the folly of humanity and the mess we have made of it.

I would also like to add that this book is as truthful as any ordinary citizen can make it - using only information that is in the Public Domain. There is nothing scurrilous or spurious in its pages; just the truth...and if telling the truth is wrong - which is what I believe I have written in this book – then humanity is doomed.

However, for those who might feel uncomfortable or disquieted by anything I have written I have looked up the definition of the word **libel** as it appears in the OED. (Oxford English Dictionary) The OED defines libel as '**a published false statement** that is damaging to a person's reputation – a written defamation'. This tells me that the truth cannot be considered libellous.

In addition, I have also checked that there is nothing in the Data Protection Act to stop the naming of public officials who have failed in their duty to the public...so as to ward off any misguided indignation on that score.

...and finally, I have also kept a record of all my research, in double and triplicate form in order to avoid any misunderstandings; it is all referenced and everything mentioned in these pages can be easily verified should the need arise.

———

Author – Who am I?

I am nobody. I am not a politician or an economist. I am not a Westminster lackey or a disgruntled hack. I am not a financial analyst or a fiscal specialist...and I am certainly no miracle worker...but what I am is a pragmatist, a citizen of this country who is sick and tired of the way the professional politicians and our pseudo-leaders with their self-serving arrogance, their questionable morality and their slick tongues have ruined the country of my birth and its economy.

So, who I am is not important.

What is important…is the message, not the messenger delivering it.

Our politicians all pretend to be experts in the fields mentioned above...notably in economics and finance, but look where that has led us; to the brink of a triple-dip recession.

Experts...? What experts?

I repeat; I am not a politician but crucially some of our greatest leaders were not politicians either; Cromwell, Wellington and Churchill were all military men before turning to politics. None was spoon fed into the job like those of the current generation of Oxbridge educated INEPTs. (*Even Nelson Mandela, the world's most revered politician in recent memory was not a politician initially; he had trained to be a lawyer)...*but needless to say, despite their lack of political pedigree, Cromwell, Wellington and Churchill were real leaders; people who knew all about adversity...and it is someone of their ilk, their stature and their conviction that the British people now need to step forward, to take on the challenge of leading this once-great country back to prosperity before the INEPTs do any more irrevocable damage.

I might or might not be that person – but if there is somebody else out there willing to take up the mantle, please, please step forward now; your country needs you...

'Cometh the hour, cometh the man', so the old adage goes; lets hope that's true...

References

As I have already confirmed on Page 897 of this manuscript - under the heading 'Notes from the Author' - every comment made in these pages can be corroborated and backed up, using of the comprehensive research that I have carried out both before and during the writing of this book; research restricted only by the limits of what is in the public domain and available to any citizen of this country if they were so inclined.

For example;

Dennis MacShane – mentioned on page 878 – quit after fiddling expenses which was widely reported in the UK media, and notably on the MailOnline website in November 2013

Tessa Jowell – mentioned on page 880 – was implicated by association in the Daily Mail of February 19th 2009

Tom Watson – mentioned on page 880 - admitted in the Daily Mail of Wednesday January 8th 2014, 'that his party should never have licensed these machines', when talking about gambling machines

Tristram Hunt – mentioned on page 880 - admitted to 'dumbing down' education during the New Labour years in an article on the MailOnline website, dated 12th of January 2014

...and so on...and so on...

This is all information in the public domain. I have had absolutely no access to anything that might be considered 'confidential' by those in the upper echelons of power.

Lightning Source UK Ltd.
Milton Keynes UK
UKOW04f0044240215

246784UK00001B/82/P